C0-DVG-138

PSYCHOLOGY APPLIED

GEORGE W. CRANE, Ph. D., M. D.

Department of Psychology, Northwestern University; Consultant in Business and Industrial Psychology; Five Years Research Psychologist under auspices of the National Research Council of America, and the Carnegie Institution of Washington, D. C.

NORTHWESTERN UNIVERSITY PRESS
Chicago, Illinois
1938

FIRST PRINTING - - - - OCTOBER 12, 1932
SECOND PRINTING - - - JANUARY 12, 1933
THIRD PRINTING - - - - FEBRUARY 10, 1935
FOURTH PRINTING - - - JANUARY 12, 1937
FIFTH PRINTING - - - FEBRUARY 1, 1938

PRINTED IN THE UNITED STATES OF AMERICA

TO
MY FATHER AND MOTHER
APPLIED PSYCHOLOGISTS
PAR EXCELLENCE

PREFACE

Emerging from the pioneer research of Walter Dill Scott and the score of other eminent applied psychologists during the past third of a century, this textbook attempts to give a comprehensive survey of the applications of psychology in the field of human relations, thereby orienting the student.

It is intended as a basic textbook for use with students who have completed an elementary course in general psychology, or who possess its equivalent in mature reading and social experience. During the past ten years I have been modifying, supplementing, and rendering more applicable the views and data contained herein. Credit for many specific applications and my inclusion of certain entire chapters is due to the queries and demands of those practical minded men and women in my night classes at George Washington and Northwestern Universities, and to the business and professional men in my applied psychology courses at the Chicago Central College of Commerce of the Y.M.C.A.

The writer lays claim to no originality in treating several fundamental topics already excellently covered in other text books, relying rather on the students' use of these other volumes for any supplementary reading deemed necessary. For this reason such topics as the Influence of Drugs, Ventilation, Climate, and Illumination, have been condensed to give more space for chapters covering phases of applied psychology which, in the writer's experience with students, are more immediately practical, if not more important.

Of such nature are the five following chapters which have, curiously enough, been almost entirely ignored in present basic textbooks of applied psychology: Ch. VI. The Psychology of Improving Your Personality; Ch. X. The Psychology of Music and Morale; Ch. XI. The Psychology of the Public Platform; Ch. XII. The Psychology of Writing and of Art; Ch. XIII. Child Psychology. Applied Psychology certainly can lay claim to these fields as readily as to Advertising or Motion Study.

Professors Walter S. Hunter, Raymond Dodge, Robert H. Gault, Delton T. Howard, A. J. Snow and Lew Sarett are written into this book through the discriminating advice and inspiration which I received not only while in their classes but during the years since. For their particular criticism in regard to the manuscript I am especially indebted to Professors Gault, Howard, and Snow. To my brother, Dr. John B. Crane of Harvard, I am grateful for a careful reading of certain chapters from the viewpoint of an economist, and for their close scrutiny and criticism of the manuscript and proof I wish to express my gratitude to Robert M. Limpus, Roland E. Wolseley, Rowland H. Groff, and Dr. Marnè L. Groff. Credit for the drawings contained herein belongs to Craven Lee Miller.

For permission to reproduce material from other volumes I express my thanks to the authors, editors, and publishers designated wherever such material is employed. To members of the Office Managers' Association of Chicago, as well as of the International Display Advertising Men's Association, I am grateful for friendly cooperation in numerous investigations.

To President Walter Dill Scott, to Professor Frederic B. Crossley of our Law School, and to the Board of Governors of the Northwestern University Press I wish to make grateful acknowledgment for their assistance in expediting the publication of this textbook.

Finally, for her constructive criticisms of the manuscript, for her forbearance, encouragement, and clever application upon me of many of the laws of psychology contained within this book, I thank my wife.

GEORGE W. CRANE

CHICAGO, ILLINOIS

TABLE OF CONTENTS

A good example of the importance of human interest values in art. See page 435.

How Well Do You Know People?

Imagine yourself a publisher, selling books to the general public. Which one of each pair of book titles below would you select in order to sell the greater number of volumes? Place a check mark before one of each pair.

- ☐ Battles of a Seaman
- ☐ Privateersman

- ☐ Ten O'Clock
- ☐ What Art Should Mean to You

- ☐ The King Enjoys Himself
- ☐ The Lustful King Enjoys Himself

- ☐ Pen, Pencil and Poison
- ☐ The Story of a Notorious Criminal

- ☐ The Truth About Patent Medicine
- ☐ Patent Medicine and the Public Health

- ☐ The Art of Controversy
- ☐ How to Argue Logically

- ☐ The Art of Courtship
- ☐ The Art of Kissing

- ☐ An Introduction to Einstein
- ☐ Einstein's Theory of Relativity Explained

- ☐ Nietzsche: Who He Was and What He Stood For
- ☐ The Story of Nietzsche's Philosophy

- ☐ Quest for a Blonde Mistress
- ☐ Fleece of Gold

- ☐ Markheim's Murder
- ☐ Markheim

- ☐ How to Improve Your Conversation
- ☐ The Secret of Self-Improvement

- ☐ Eating for Health (Vitamins)
- ☐ Care of the Skin and Hair

- ☐ The Facts About Fascism
- ☐ The Truth About Mussolini

- ☐ The Mystery of the Iron Mask
- ☐ The Mystery of the Man in the Iron Mask

Since 1932 I have personally administered this test in their conventions or society meetings to over 5,000 editors, physicians, dentists, lawyers, engineers, advertisers, salesmen, merchants and parent-teachers. Others have given this test to over 50,000 adults. Scores of 13 to 15 are Very Superior; 10 to 12 are Superior; 7 to 9 are Average; while 1 to 6 are Below Average. The actual sales volumes are found in Chapter I.

Psychology Applied

CHAPTER I

METHODS OF MOTIVATING HUMAN BEINGS

The application of psychology consists chiefly of the manipulation of stimuli so that they will set off the desired habit patterns in the subjects under consideration. In some cases, of course, as in education, it becomes necessary to develop habitual responses which are not present originally. It is evident, therefore, that the applied psychologist must be familiar with the native habits or instincts possessed by mankind, as well as with the laws of habit formation and modification. He must also learn the varieties of stimuli which are capable of affecting the sense organs of the human being, and know the relative effectiveness of each.

His study will soon bring out the fact that human beings can be motivated and controlled by substitute or symbolic stimuli which, like the abbreviations in shorthand, represent other things, such as objects and actions. In this classification fall spoken and written words, pictures, graphs, figures, musical notes, money, and signs. The major portion of this book will consist of the development and utilization of symbolic stimuli by teacher, clergyman, salesman, employment manager, politician, writer, parent, physician, and lawyer. We shall begin with a consideration of those fundamental neural pathways which serve as the foundation for human motivation.

Bases of Motivation. There are two general bases of motivation, whose distinctions are of more academic than of practical significance inasmuch as it is almost impossible to separate their effect in the human adult.

(1) Instincts. These potent bases, frequently regarded as

early conditioned reflex chains, are determining factors in the behavior of both animals and man. They make their incidence from the fetal state until puberty, and actively influence behavior until the menopause, in the case of sex, and until death in respect to the others. Their number has been variously listed by numerous authors, almost all of whom have given too many. This error is easily appreciated when we recognize that a multitude of habits take root in these basic reflex chains, and become so intimately interwoven with them as to defy later dissociation. Here is our classification of instincts:

(a) *Self-preservation.* Under this category fall a group of motive bases, such as hunger, elimination, respiration, pugnacity, fear, desire to avoid physical pain and to escape curtailment of movement.

(b) *Love.* This term is employed in its broadest sense to include parental, filial, "sweetheart", and sexual attachment, the first three of which are probably admixtures of social conditioning with the more basic erotic reflexes.

(2) HABITS. These motive bases are legion, and serve as the differentiæ for human and infrahuman behavior. Animals below man share most of the instinctive behavior with him, but man alone is capable of that complex elaboration of habits which culminates in language and our social inheritances.

Although hunger is an instinctive motive base, it is habit superimposed upon the instinct which determines whether we shall dine upon Shredded Wheat or oatmeal; upon lamb or pork or beef. It is, moreover, this superstructure of habits that constitutes the immediate concern of those who are interested in motivating and controlling their fellows.

In the age of the Neanderthal, for example, the sex urge expressed itself directly and quickly. When a desirable stimulus—a young Neanderthal maiden—appeared within the vision of a mating-bent man, he could take her by sheer superior strength, speed, or size of club. Recalcitrant in-laws with crushed skulls may have marked the path to the cavernous domicile of the newlyweds.

Nowadays such behavior is taboo. When a young man wishes to possess a girl who has peculiarly stimulated his erotic mechanism, he may, as his past habits dictate, arrange for a formal introduction, or else begin after the fashion of informal modern youth. Thereafter follows a series of "dates" interspersed with candy, flowers, telephone conversations, *billets-doux,* and reciprocal presentation to the prospective in-laws. An engagement ring ensues, followed by increased and thrilling tactual stimulation; then marriage and a "one-room kitchenette and bath" or a cabin in the hills. The entire courtship, unlike the three-minute Neanderthal romance, may continue for years, depending chiefly on the man's skill in handling symbolic stimuli, both in the presence of the girl and also in the sanctum of his employer.

In summarizing the bases of motivation, therefore, we may state that instincts and habits are the neural foundations of human activity. The former are usually more potent than the latter, although habits may change the course of instinctive behavior. Because habits become so bound up with instincts, moreover, they form the immediate concern of those who wish to motivate their fellows. The next section will elaborate this point.

Coaxing vs. Clubbing. Fishermen realize that they cannot drive either bass or suckers to take hold of their hooks by use of threats or scorpions. They must entice the fish; they must pull them on from in front, instead of trying to drive them on from behind. And, of course, they must adjust their type of bait to the food habits of the species they seek. Furthermore, they realize that the food habits of the fish vary with their chemical condition so that what is effective in one month may not be so effective the next. In short, motivation involves a knowledge of the specific habits and instincts, plus a realization of the specific stimuli that will set off or ignite those habit patterns.

The same stimulus, therefore, will always and invariably produce the same response if the subject to whom it is presented is unchanged. The difficulty in human motivation is the fact that we cannot look at a person and from external appearance discover that today he has a toothache, or indigestion, or that he is raging with himself and the world at large because he lost a twenty-dollar bill, or because his stocks have dropped three points. As a result, we may never be able to attain perfection and an invariable infallibility in dealing with human beings. But a diligent and scientific study of mankind will enable us to be eminently successful, for it does not require every vote in the nation to put a president in the White House.

The art of coaxing people is worthy of study. True, the club may at times be effective, but even animal trainers today are finding that they obtain better results by using the fishball or lump of sugar, than by wielding the lash.

There is a marked psychological difference in the output under the two methods. When forced to labor, we do just as little as possible in order to get by; we are resentful meanwhile, and fatigue more quickly in consequence. When enticed to productivity, we work with more enthusiasm and pride in our products; we like our superiors or employers, and we feel less fatigue. Regarded purely from the economic angle, therefore, coaxing is far better than clubbing.

Goddard[1] has shown us an admirable example of this, when he describes how John, an adult in chronological age but with the mental attainments of a seven-year-old child, came down to the barns one morning and said he wasn't going to plow that day. The supervisor could have compelled him to harness his horses and get his plow in action, but he didn't. Instead, he

[1] Goddard, H. H., *Psychology of The Normal and Subnormal* (Dodd, Mead & Co., New York, 1919), p. 324.

expressed sympathy and concern over the condition of John's health. He urged John to go to the house and go to bed, so that he would get better more quickly, as they didn't have any one who could plow as straight a furrow as John, and they certainly couldn't get along without him. He was too good a man not to be missed.

John stayed around the barn, however, and a little later the supervisor again met him, and urged him to go to bed, for they wanted him back as soon as possible. They didn't wish to send another man out with John's team and plow, for the other man wouldn't do as good a job. Still John remained. When for a third time the supervisor urged him in like manner, John said he wasn't going to bed. He felt better, and was going to plow.

All day long John plowed, whistling at his job, and cutting every furrow just as neatly as he possibly could. There was no resentment in his mind; he didn't sulk and pout, and do a careless job. What produced the change in John? Not any tangible stimulus like ice cream or cake, or a shiny new rifle, or a suit of clothes, or a pocketknife. It was simply a few sentences uttered within his hearing. Those sentences had no market value in dollars and cents, nor could they be carried around like a pocketknife and shown to other workers. They were just little puffs of air that struck John's eardrums. However, they were very special puffs of air to which a definite meaning attached. They were symbolic stimuli. To John they meant that he was a leader, a desirable person who was valued highly by his "boss." They inflated his ego. John, a lowest grade of moron, could be affected by these symbolic stimuli so that he would stick to his plow all day. A dog or other infrahuman species cannot be motivated to ten hours of hard effort even with a thousand complimentary phrases.

The effectiveness of symbolic stimuli as bait was also presented in the famous story of Benjamin Franklin and the grindstone. They work equally well, however, with groups of persons, as advertisers and speakers can attest. In the public schools today we have stimulated the children to eat spinach and other forms of green vegetables by constructing charts with such terms as green beans, lettuce, cabbage, spinach, and others at the heads of columns. The children have the privilege of writing their names under each vegetable they ate the preceding day. And it is a distinct honor for a youngster to be able to see his name under several vegetable headings. They vie with one another to see who can have eaten the greatest number of vegetables. Social prestige is now involved.

Actually, under this system the children go home and ask their mothers to have spinach and other vegetables. In some cases I have known the youngsters even to do errands and housework in order to bribe their parents to increase the variety of vegetables on the menu, for possession of a blue or gold star next day puts them among the èlite.

One of the best examples of motivating a whole population is to be found in the popularization of the Irish potato. This beneficial tuber, when it had been introduced into England by Raleigh, encountered concerted opposition and prejudice. The laymen abused it in print, and the priests thundered at it from the pulpit. It was supposed to sterilize the soil in which it was planted, and cause all sorts of ailments.

But Thomas William Coke appreciated its potentialities as a means of staving off famine among the poorer classes, and determined to spread its cultivation. He began with his own neighbors and tenants, but they were indignant. For five years he couldn't induce them to grow potatoes, even though he resorted to mild attempts at coercion, and finally offered them land rent free. It wasn't until he himself had grown the large Ox Noble variety that he was able to get any farmers to concede that perhaps " 'twouldn't poison the pigs."

In marked contrast were the tactics employed by Parmentier of France. This young apothecary had encountered the potato during confinement as a prisoner of war. While his fellow prisoners were protesting at the outrage of having to dine on such "ungodly provender", he thoughtfully inquired about the methods of cultivating and cooking the new food.

Upon his return to France, he procured an experimental farm from the emperor, in which he planted potatoes. When it was time to dig them, at his own expense he hired a few soldiers to patrol all sides of his famous potato patch during the daytime. Meanwhile he conducted distinguished guests through the field, digging a few tubers here and there, which they peeled and devoured with evident gusto. At night, however, he withdrew his guards. A few mornings later one of the guards hastened to Parmentier with the sad news that thieves had broken into the potato patch at night, and had dug part of the crop.

Parmentier was overjoyed, much to the surprise of his informant, and exclaimed, "When the people will steal in order to procure my potatoes, their popularity is assured."

The psychological phases of coaxing, therefore, consist of placing stimuli before the subjects which will lead to pleasurable results. We have pointed out the superiority of coaxing to the more painful process of clubbing. The method is effective on animals, children, and large groups of adults. The art of coaxing individuals, of course, involves a more intelligent analysis of their bases of motivation than does the use of the whip, but it obtains far better results in most cases, and therefore is worthy of study by all those who wish to deal effectively with human beings in a business or social way. To be most successful, however, the one who wishes to employ this method must give heed to the importance of concrete stimuli, which we shall now discuss.

Specificity in Appeals. Appeals are simply stimuli to habit systems developed in the nervous tissue, and accordingly they operate as do all habit stimuli. One rule of habit is that the more specific the stimulus, the more immediate will be the response. The restaurant's slogan, "We serve good meals", is too general to cause an active flow of saliva with the attendant whetting of the appetite. We don't find sensory cells, such as taste buds, that are sensitive to "meals". But we do have taste buds that are sensitive to sweet, salt, sour and bitter. Therefore, sugar, strawberry shortcake, ice cream, or vinegar, lemons, persimmons, and quinine do have the power to set up salivary action.

We may grade stimuli with reference to their nearness to the sensory mechanism of the human body, into several degrees. Remaining in the gustatory realm, we may call sugar and sugar foods, such as candy and pastries, stimuli of the first degree. Stimuli of the second degree are those symbolic stimuli like the spoken or written words: sugar, cake, pie, candy. Stimuli of the third degree, therefore, consist of those generic spoken and written words, such as foods, meals, menus, diets.

In motivating people we shall find it an invariable axiom of psychology that *stimuli of the first degree are more effective than stimuli of the second degree, while stimuli of the second degree are more effective than those of the third degree.* It is apparent, of course, that we cannot carry sugar, or silks, automobiles, or pianos around with us constantly, so the science of human motivation resolves itself chiefly into using second and third degree stimuli. These are what we shall designate as symbolic stimuli.

Too many salesmen, speakers, teachers and leaders in general include an undue number of third degree stimuli in their dealings with others. And third degree stimuli seldom if ever elicit response for the very obvious reason that our habits are not developed in accordance with these vague, diffuse words and ideas. We don't ignite gasoline or wood with flame in general, but with specific sparks or matches. We don't grow enthusiastic over "service", "greater efficiency", "greater safety", etc. But we do throw off our lethargy when we find two deliveries henceforth instead of one; when we realize that tomorrow under this new filing system our clerk will file seventy three more vouchers than she could possibly file today; when we discover that tomorrow with the installation of one of these new electrical guards over each wall switch, not a workman in the factory can touch a live wire, as did Brown last week, with whose widow we just settled for $5,000.

Snow[1] gives the following excellent example of how even the mental appreciation of a saving of $190 on a piano was too vague a stimulus to produce action, until the salesman gave it more immediacy by translating dollars into social prestige and maternal duty:

A piano salesman had been working for a certain sale for two weeks. The prospect was a widow who was buying the piano for her daughter. She had intended to buy a higher-priced piano until this salesman came on the ground and showed her a saving of $190 in buying his piano.

Then she decided that she would rather have the higher-priced piano for her daughter—that the extra prestige in its name was worth $190—satisfaction and pride.

The salesman was up against it. His strong talk on the $190 saving that had started things his way was ineffective now. He sat down at the demonstrating piano and as he ran his fingers over the keys seized the opportunity to do a little hard thinking.

"My only argument is the same quality at $190 less price," he reflected. "But she doesn't care so much for $190 as for that high-sounding name on the other piano. That's vanity—and the only motive I have to play on is money."

Then an idea occurred.

If vanity was a motive in buying a piano, couldn't he . . .

Well, here is what he did:

"Of course, you know, Mrs. Houston," he said as he stopped playing and turned round on the bench, "how you enjoy a piano depends more on the one playing it than on the piano itself. By

[1] Snow, A. J., *Psychology in Business Relations* (McGraw-Hill Book Co., Inc., New York, 1930), p. 400.

the way, what instructor are you going to have for your daughter?"

"Miss Martin," the lady replied.

"Hum!" returned the salesman, "I would advise you to have Professor Habicht."

"Mercy!" she exclaimed. "He charges $5 for half-hour lessons! I cannot afford it."

"Miss Martin charges $2 a lesson, I believe?"

"Yes."

"Then," said the salesman, "the $190 you plan to spend by buying this other piano, is going to cost your daughter 60 *lessons* that she *might* have with Professor Habicht.

"Sixty lessons under Habicht is too big a thing to overlook, Mrs. Houston, when your daughter's musical ability is at stake."

He got the woman to thinking about what the $190 *would buy,* and finally sold the piano.

It is apparent that money may frequently be a third degree stimulus until the subject himself, or the salesman, translates it into a second degree stimulus, after which action is more likely to follow. This translation process is clearly portrayed in an unusual type of advertisement of tooth paste, shown in Exhibit 1. This type of advertisement has apparently been found quite successful, for in various forms it has been appearing regularly during the past year or two.

From the standpoint of psychology, therefore, specficity in appeals becomes imperative if old habit systems are to be re-aroused. One characteristic of habit is that the response is conditioned to a definite stimulus, and no other stimulus is effective unless it was also present in the learning situation and so became a conditioned or symbolic stimulus. We have advanced the three general types of stimuli as measured by their effectiveness upon the individual, showing that first degree stimuli are most satisfactory in their results but are often inconvenient to use. The problem confronting the applied psychologist, as a consequence, is chiefly that of selecting second degree stimuli in preference to the more vague third degree kind. This selective process is advisable regardless of which of the following motives is being employed.

With that $3 you save ON YOUR TOOTH PASTE

BUY 20 QUARTS OF MILK

The average person, using a tube of tooth paste a month, saves $3 a year by switching from a 50¢ dentifrice to Listerine Tooth Paste. There are hundreds of useful and pleasant things you could buy for that sum. Milk, bread, and eggs, are just the beginning of a list that would cover many pages.

or

BUY 6 DOZEN EGGS

or

BUY 30 LOAVES OF BREAD

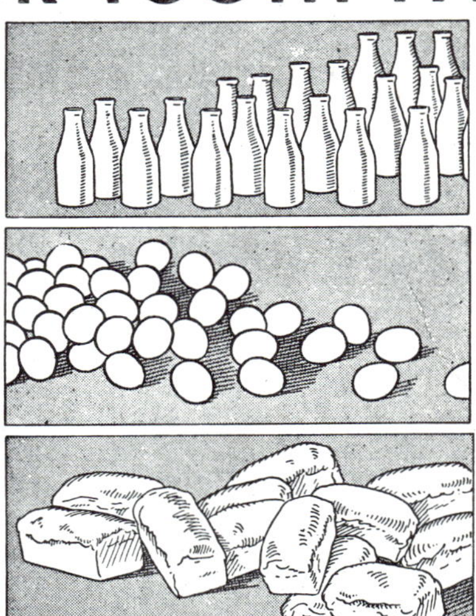

Acclaimed by millions, this tooth paste won on merit

Over four million persons have switched to Listerine Tooth Paste in nine years—and have kept right on using it. They are delighted with its better results.

Many of them were first attracted by its economy, half the usual price, 25¢ instead of 50¢.

But a mere saving of money could not possibly have held them. Especially the millions of women, whose first care is always to look their best. To them we had to offer a remarkable cleansing and polishing power. That is what you will find in Listerine Tooth Paste. It will give you new ideas about how white your teeth can be. And new pleasure in brushing them.

This unusual cleansing and polishing power is due chiefly to a *special polishing agent*. It cleans off tartar and tobacco-stains, dirt, decay, and discolorations—leaving teeth healthily white and flashing, as Nature meant them to be.

Yet, even though dirt cannot resist this polishing agent, it is too gentle ever to do your tooth enamel the slightest harm.

And after you finish brushing your teeth, you will be grateful, too, for the clean, fresh, tingling after-taste in your mouth—the effect you associate with Listerine itself.

We Save—*You* Benefit

We are able to give you a dentifrice of such extraordinary quality at half the common price—for two reasons. First, we have developed ultra-efficient and economical methods of manufacture and distribution. Second, quick and immense demand (over 4,000,000 users in 9 years) calls for production on a great, cost-cutting scale.

You want to improve your teeth and cut down your expenses. Try Listerine Tooth Paste today, and see how it will help you do these things. Lambert Pharmacal Co., St. Louis, Mo.

25¢

Ad No. 3460 R1*

EXHIBIT 1. An unusual example of the economy appeal in which the saving is translated into second degree stimuli. Courtesy of Lambert and Feasley.

The Relative Strength of Motives. Since instincts are such basic motive forces in human life, it is evident that any listing of the relative strength of motives will undoubtedly show a high ranking for such factors as we have placed under *self-preservation* and *love.* In the following table from Starch[1] are presented the general motive headings ranked in order of strength by 74 men and women, when given the instructions, "Ask yourself in connection with each one how important it is in determining your own actions from day to day. Write 10 after the very strongest motives, and a number between 0 and 10 after the others, according to their relative strength or importance."

Motives	Per Cent	Motives	Per Cent
Appetite-hunger	9.2	Respect for Deity	7.1
Love of offspring	9.1	Sympathy for others	7.0
Health	9.0	Protection of others	7.0
Sex attraction	8.9	Domesticity	7.0
Parental affection	8.9	Social Distinction	6.9
Ambition	8.6	Devotion to others	6.8
Pleasure	8.6	Hospitality	6.6
Bodily Comfort	8.4	Warmth	6.5
Possession	8.4	Imitation	6.5
Approval by others	8.0	Courtesy	6.5
Gregariousness	7.9	Play-sport	6.5
Taste	7.8	Managing others	6.4
Personal appearance	7.8	Coolness	6.2
Safety	7.8	Fear-caution	6.2
Cleanliness	7.7	Physical activity	6.0
Rest-sleep	7.7	Manipulation	6.0
Home comfort	7.5	Construction	6.0
Economy	7.5	Style	5.8
Curiosity	7.5	Humor	5.8
Efficiency	7.3	Amusement	5.8
Competition	7.3	Shyness	4.2
Cooperation	7.1	Teasing	2.6

EXHIBIT 2. Relative strength of motives as determined by introspection.

[1] Starch, Daniel, *Principles of Advertising* (A. W. Shaw Co., New York, 1923), pp. 272-273.

The disadvantages attaching to the method by which these data were obtained are twofold: (1) the subjects have difficulty interpreting several of the general terms into specific applications, and hence do not fully understand their full implications; (2) the subjects are not always competent judges of their own behavior. In other words, what they think they do and what they actually do are not always identical.

A better method, whenever it is feasible, is to place definite stimuli before the group, and then note to which they respond most readily and most often. An analysis of the returns from advertisements in which each of the above motives is in turn the chief appeal, would be more reliable. This sort of thing has been done by Haldeman-Julius[1] who sells the Little Blue Books solely through newspaper and magazine advertisements. These books are designated only by their titles, of which he now has 1260. The titles are subdivided under such headings as Humor, Love, Health, etc., but no title has any pictorial illustration to give it an advantage over any other title. Buyers send their orders direct, so there is no personality factor of a salesman intermediary to influence the readers. Exhibit 3 shows some of the most popular books.

In Exhibit 3 we see the preferences of approximately one million annual purchasers of the 5-cent Little Blue Books, which were advertised in media ranging from *Harper's* and *Review of Reviews* to *Liberty* and the *Chicago Tribune.* Because of the wide variety of advertising media, and the small cost of the books, these data are rather significant. It might be added that analysis of the sex of the purchasers indicates that 70 per cent are men and 30 per cent are women. This fact probably explains why some of the female sex books outsell those for men. The males are buying them, too. Sex analysis of the buyers is difficult, however, since many women, if order-

[1] Haldeman-Julius, E., *The First Hundred Million* (Simon & Schuster, New York, 1928).

Title of Book	Copies Sold Annually
Prostitution in the Modern World	129,500
What Married Women Should Know	112,000
What Married Men Should Know	97,500
Woman's Sexual Life	97,500
Man's Sexual Life	78,500
How to Improve Your Conversation	77,000
How to Improve Your Vocabulary	76,000
Toasts for All Occasions	55,000
How to Write Letters	53,500
Book of 500 Riddles	53,500
Care of the Skin and Hair	52,000
Best Jokes of 1926	50,500
Spanish Self-Taught	47,000
French Self-Taught	46,500
Hints on Public Speaking	46,500
What Do You Know	45,500
Facts About Fortune Telling	44,000
How to Psycho-Analyze Yourself	43,000
Facts About Venereal Disease	41,500
How to Fight Nervous Troubles	39,000
Facts to Know About Music	37,000
Eating for Health (Vitamins)	36,000
The Secret of Self-Improvement	36,000
Psychology for Beginners	35,000
100 Best Books to Read	32,000

EXHIBIT 3. Relative strength of motives as indicated by orders for Little Blue Books.

ing sex books, either have them sent in their husbands' names, or else sign only their initials.

When the twenty-five book titles are inspected closely they may be resolved into the following classification: (1) Sex; (2) Social Improvement; (3) Humor; (4) Personal Appearance; (5) Education; (6) Occultism; and (7) Health. It will be seen from a comparison with Exhibit 2 that the order of merit of these appeals does not coincide with those given by Starch's subjects. Health apparently loses rank whereas Humor markedly gains.

If we combine the results obtained by Starch with those of

Haldeman-Julius we find that motives follow closely the instincts which were cited earlier in the chapter. It is generally conceded that hunger precedes sex, with self-esteem or the desire for prestige and an inflated ego running a close third. The latter is probably an admixture of habits and instincts. The writer would be inclined to include pugnacity fourth, with its modern correlates, rivalry and competition. It is to this motive base that speakers and salesmen frequently appeal in short-circuiting reason with emotional stimuli. In the ensuing section we shall discuss the relative strength and quantity of motives as they affect the choice or decision of an individual.

Motivation and Will Power. The *Will* is not regarded as a mysterious force by which we can arbitrarily decide to go right instead of left, quite apart from all of our previous experiences. Such terms as "will" and "will power" belong in the category of third degree verbal stimuli and need to be simplified before they are understandable. They are no more esoteric than the tipping of a balance when five pounds are in one scale pan and six pounds in the other. The scales or balance does not "will" to go down on the side which is heavier.

In similar fashion human choice of action is determined in three ways: (1) by placing additional weights on the side where action is desired; (2) by removing weights from the other scale pan; (3) by a combination of the two preceding methods, whereby some weights are added to the positive side while others are removed from the negative. These weights, moreover, are motives, often dignified by being called reasons. "Selling points" are the weights placed on the side where action is desired and "objections" are the weights on the opposite scale pan.

A curious commentary on human behavior is the fact that the negative weights (objections) do not have to be removed invariably by destroying them through a logical process, although this plan is more effective for permanent satisfaction.

As long as the subject forgets the objections, that is, as long as his attention is completely absorbed by the "selling points", the negative weights do not exist for him at the moment.

In the majority of decisions the salesman (hereafter we shall use salesman as a generic term to cover everybody who motivates his fellows, whether it be minister, parent, teacher, or friend) works with both sides of the scales, placing positive weights on the one pan and definitely removing the opposing weights from the other by answering the objections in a satisfactory manner. But even here, he attempts to keep the attention of the subject focussed on the positive pan, carefully avoiding any negative suggestion which might arouse hostile "weights".

But an enthusiastic salesman with a sense of dramatic values and a rapid oral delivery, coupled with plenty of specific sensory words which he chooses for their speed in igniting basic habitual and instinctive nervous patterns, can take a group of otherwise intelligent citizens and lead them on a lynching party, or a snake-dance down the boulevard; can sell them a set of books they will never use thereafter, or some submerged real estate. After all, there is artistry in the technique of such a human motivator, even though we must frown upon unethical phases of his results. As a matter of fact, this type of salesmanship defeats its own end, for the customer feels tricked and disgusted, instead of satisfied with himself and his purchase.

For sheer speed of producing action, however, the above method is excellent. The dramatic presentation keeps the subject's curiosity whetted by suspense, and the rapid-fire delivery doesn't allow him opportunity for those mental flash-backs during which objections are likely to come into the forefront of his attention. Then, too, the inner or chemical environment of the subject sometimes makes him more susceptible to certain stimuli, just as roast beef is far stronger as a stimulus to a starving man than to one who has just gorged himself to satiety. He finds it more difficult, therefore, to think contrary ideas.

In "The Haunted Lady"[1] we find an exceptionally clear-cut example of a tremendous decision made by a very upright and intelligent young woman, whose entire previous and subsequent life was exactly opposed to her brief tragic step. Lack of will power, some would describe it, but we prefer the analogy of the scale pans with a temporary shifting in weights due partly to an unusual concatenation of sexual motivation. In Exhibit 4 we have attempted to show the motive forces for and against her step during the three stages: Before, During, and After. Later she excused herself for her behavior in the 9 P. M. period by saying that she must have been mad, that she had suffered a case of temporary insanity. Viewed in the light of her physiological environment at 4 A. M. and the normal stimuli then affecting her, it was impossible for her to understand why she had transgressed.

Her behavior resulted from the cumulative effect of a number of factors. Had any one of these factors been absent, she might have acted quite differently. If her son had cried out, if the moon had not been shining, if she had not read the lustful poetry, or if she had had a toothache, the scale pans might have remained in their normal position. In like manner, the behavior of every person depends upon four types of factors: (1) the inherited mechanisms, including quality of nervous tissue, sense organs, etc.; (2) his acquired experience, involving the sum of his habit patterns; (3) the physiological state of his body—his intra-cutaneous environment; and (4) the stimuli affecting his sense organs at the moment.

In illustrating these, we may state that we don't expect a hen to swim, nor a feeble-minded child to enter college. Inheritance is a partial determinant of development. But habit also

[1] Gallishaw, John, *The Only Two Ways to Write a Story* (G. P. Putnam's Sons, New York, 1928), pp. 345-362. Story by Adela Rogers St. John.

3 P. M.	
MOTIVES TO MORALITY *All positive*	MOTIVES TO IMMORALITY *All negative*
Husband present whom she really loves. Adored son also present. Married state emphasized by home surroundings. Religious and home training entirely moral.	
9 P. M.	
All negative	*All positive*
Husband gone on trip, and his memory not in focus of her immediate attention. Son asleep, and his memory not in focus of attention. Away from household stimuli; seated in garden. No church bells, thoughts of mother or other home training stimuli in her mind.	Romantic stimuli all about her: moon, roses, Spring. Physiological state probably attuned to Spring sexual acceleration. Just been reading wanton poetry urging many loves ere age kills passion. Frantic fear she's growing old and away from romance. Man appears who once kissed her before her marriage and set her pulse leaping. Thinks him a handsome god as moonlight glints his dark hair when he kisses her hand. His kiss enflames her more, and when he crushes her lips to his, all else is oblivion.
4 A. M.	
All positive	*All negative*
Husband gone, but his memory vivid in her attention. Son asleep, but in next room where she is aware of him. Back amid normal household environment and stimuli. Conscience vividly demonstrating her religious and moral upbringing.	

EXHIBIT 4. Example of the shift in motive forces causing a young woman to act in total disregard of all her previous habits. The boxed motives in the middle panel designate not objections overcome by reason, but simply supplanted in the focus of attention by other motives.

enters into behavior. A stimulus is not capable of igniting a given response until that response is built into the nervous system. References to Biblical and Shakespearean narratives and characters leave the average audience largely un-illuminated, although Lincoln constantly illustrated his speeches with such material. As regards the physiological condition, we have already described its effect on the immediately preceding pages. Its influence is probably more important than we have heretofore thought. The hyperthyroid's excitability and excessive irritability is the opposite of the cretin's sluggishness and dull mentality, largely because of excessive functioning of the thyroid gland in one case, and its hypo-function in the other. The seasonal mating of infrahuman animals, the salt hunger of cattle, and the nervousness and excitement of the smoker who finds himself without tobacco, are instances of organic changes in the intra-cutaneous environment that render them peculiarly susceptible to certain extra-cutaneous stimuli.

The preceding examples show that what is called the Will is simply the response to the sum of motives leading the individual to one kind of behavior in contrast to those influencing him in the other direction. This choice or decision depends upon the four factors previously cited, to wit, his inherited mechanisms, his acquired experience, his chemical environment, and the specific stimuli affecting his sense organs at the moment. It is valuable to remember, moreover, that inhibiting ideas can be dispelled either by answering them or by keeping the subject's attention so focussed upon the positive form of action that he forgets them. In the next section we shall continue our discussion of the conflicts involved in decision.

Conflicts Among Motives. Most of the decisions which we are forced to make in life are not between such simple extremes as good in contrast to bad, but between the good and that which is a bit better. There are, of course, numerous exceptions and plenty of unhealthy conflicts, which we shall mention in greater detail when we discuss psychiatry. To show the choice between two pleasures we need mention only the interesting experiment by Moss[1] in which he placed hungry white male rats in a central compartment, with a female in the oestrual period in one adjacent compartment, and food in another. From previous experience in the situation the rats had learned that if they chose the female, they could not get the food, and conversely. Five male rats were used, after a starvation period of seventy-two hours. Four of them chose the food, demonstrating to the extent of this one experiment, at least, the greater potency of food over a sex stimulus. Other experiments by Moss corroborated this finding.

A caution to bear in mind in such experiments is the physiological or intra-cutaneous environment of the subjects. Young and old rats are not as susceptible to sex stimuli as are rats in their prime. And some strains of rats are more highly sexed than are others. When one states that a certain motive produced a certain action in a certain subject, one must be sure to bear in mind the nature of the subject and generalize only for that type of subject under identical conditions. This, of course, Moss has done, but the layman frequently overlooks such very necessary precautions.

When a young person is deciding upon the college or university which he wishes to attend, he encounters a conflict of motives. And his decision, like that of the young woman's in Exhibit 4, will depend upon the number and weight of the arguments for one school in contradistinction to the other's. Decision is made on the basis of the motive pull exerted in one direction as opposed by that in the other. One must bear in mind the caution that one selling point for product "A" may outweigh ten selling points for product "B"; so it isn't number alone, but rather the weight or pull or the sum of the motive forces that determines the human as well as the scales response.

[1] Moss, Fred A., *Applications of Psychology* (Boston, 1929), pp. 12-13.

When Mark Antony was confronted with his great crisis of deciding between Cleopatra and the love and power which she could offer him, as opposed to Octavia and his imperial position in the world, he demonstrated behavior no different essentially from that of the youngster who has to give one of his two playthings to his little brother or sister.

The difference between logical decisions and impulsive decisions is simply the fact that in the former we carefully inspect the contents of both pans of the scales under little or no emotional excitement, whereas impulsive decisions are usually made under some emotional tension, and with little or no attention to the contents of one pan of the scales. Exhibit 4 is an instance of impulsive decision. In emotional turmoil we become restricted in our thinking; hence, the usual number of associated ideas do not come to our attention, and we don't have occasion to perceive the negative or opposing arguments that would otherwise likely be present.

Conflicts among motives, therefore, simply denote that the individual is attempting to determine which course of action will lead to the greatest pleasure. These conflicts may exist between two laudable and socially approved motives, or between a good and a socially decried motive. The bad motive, however, holds intrinsic pleasurable capacity or it would forthwith lose its power to cause a conflict. Moreover, an immediate pleasure may be contrasted with a remote one which is greater. The subnormal person and the animal usually select the immediate satisfaction. This tendency, therefore, is probably true of all persons, although the intelligent individual is more capable of selecting the deferred pleasure. Impulsive decisions are usually those made with reference to an immediate pleasurable stimulus in contrast to a greater but delayed reward.

The Motive Force of Symbolic Stimuli. When the child sees a candy bar for the first time it has no gustatory significance whatever, and gives rise only to an optical effect. After he eats the candy bar, and several subsequent ones, we find that the sight of the candy bar alone becomes sufficient to cause a flow of saliva—to make his mouth water. This process by which an originally inadequate stimulus, through repeated association with the natural or adequate stimulus, becomes capable of calling forth the response originally subject only to the adequate stimulus, is called *conditioning*. Thus, words become substitute or symbolic stimuli, replacing objects and actions. As shorthand symbols were devised as an economy in time and effort over use of the more cumbersome words, so words in turn are symbols by which we can more speedily and easily deal with objects and events in our environment. We have discussed the fact that words fall into the second and third degree classification of effective stimuli. But pictures, numbers, musical notes, in fact, anything used to denote something else, belong in the group of symbolic stimuli.

By means of words, therefore, we can symbolically dangle juicy beefsteaks, delicious peach shortcake, roses, automobiles, radios, silks and satins—indeed, any object we have in mind, before our subjects. We can make them thirsty. We can discuss savoury viands before a group that wasn't hungry until we began talking, and in a few minutes have them so restless from hunger sensations that they can scarcely sit still. We can discuss sleep, relaxation, perfect repose, pleasantly flaccid muscles, and deep restful slumber until we have the listeners in an artificial sleep, or a natural one.

Words can make the tears flow; they can wrench a staid personality from its moorings, incite it to lofty endeavor and noble deeds, or lead it to a lynching party and human ignominy. Words can make men lend a helping hand directly or through the medium of their contributed dollars, or can place bayonets in their grasp with which they viciously rip open the intestines of those same persons to whom they previously lent a friendly hand. Words, as in the mouth of an Iago, can destroy the sweetest faith of pure love, or they can build the highest type of human trust and confidence out of originally casual acquaintanceship. Words can sculpture a beautiful manhood or womanhood out of a helpless bit of animate human flesh, or they may render it bestial and cruel. They may build a small company into a billion dollar industry, or drive a great corporation into bankruptcy.

However, words are not effective stimuli unless in the personalities on whom they are employed, habit systems are already developed which may be ignited by such stimuli. Like pulling the trigger of the rifle, no energy discharge results unless a cartridge (habit) is present to be acted upon. This fact is illustrated in the quotation: "Give not that which is holy unto the dogs, neither cast ye your pearls before swine, lest they trample them under their feet, and turn again and rend you." Salesmen of every type must learn that a polysyllabic vocabulary is not effective on minds trained only to monosyllabic verbal stimuli. So, too, all of us who hope to deal successfully with our fellows must be adept in the employment of symbolic stimuli, since they are the most widely used motivating forces. "I am by calling a dealer in words," said Rudyard Kipling in a speech before the Royal College of Surgeons, "and words are, of course, the most powerful drug used by mankind."

"Give me the right word and the right accent, and I will move the world," says Joseph Conrad. This is not poetic hyperbole. The world moves as its human cogs. Note the following example of such specificity. A woman went into a shoe shop to buy a new pair of slippers. The salesman obligingly did everything he could to fit her, but in vain. At last he exclaimed, "Lady, I cannot fit you. One of your feet is larger than the other." The customer was incensed. She went to the young fellow's manager, who happened to have overheard his clerk's comment. He asked to see if he couldn't solve the difficulty. She sat down and the manager examined her feet. "Madame," he exclaimed seriously, "one of your feet is *smaller* than the other. What you need is a smaller size of shoe." He sent her away happy, and with a higher priced pair of slippers. The young clerk later said to his manager, "Why, I told her the same thing you did." But he was wrong. Words possess distinctive personalities, just as human beings do. Two words, like two brothers, may be so much alike that they belong to the same family—they may be synonyms—but like the brothers they are also very different in many characteristics.

Hotchkiss[1] has effectively brought out this distinction in the following: "We can speak of a *bunch* of flowers, but a bunch of girls is a *bevy*; a bevy of elephants is a *herd*; a herd of thieves is a *gang*; a gang of angels is a *host*; a host of wolves is a *pack*; a pack of geese is a *flock*; a flock of acrobats is a *troupe*; a troupe of bees is a *swarm*; a swarm of pigs is a *drove*; a drove of horsemen is a *troop*; a troop of fish is a *school*; a school of partridges is a *covey*; a covey of police is a *squad*; a squad of editors is a *staff*; a staff of salesmen is a *crew*."

The sixteen synonyms above do not exhaust those that we have in the English language for the idea of a group, but they clearly demonstrate that one word cannot be substituted for its twin without frequently giving rise to vague feelings of unpleasantness. Note the effect of "a gang of angels". A Spanish medical student recently told me of one of his experiences here in the United States. Having learned English only in the past four years, he was not fully cognizant of all its idiomatic usages. When the American college girl whom he was escorting to the annual ball entered the room where he was waiting, he noted her beautiful dress, and sought to compliment her. "What a lovely nightgown you have on," he said. "What?"

[1] Hotchkiss, G. B., *Advertising Copy* (Harper & Bros., New York, 1924), p. 228.

exclaimed the surprised girl. "I say, you are wearing a beautiful nightgown," he repeated, thinking she had not heard him aright the first time. In discussing this incident later he defended himself by saying, "How should I know that evening gown and nightgown weren't the same? My teacher told me I could use 'evening' and 'night' interchangeably."

Although a person with a protein hunger which specifically craves beefsteak, will dine upon pork or lamb or beans in the absence of his favorite, he will be much more satisfied by, and hence much more easily motivated by, the perfect stimulus of the moment. Fish, too, if sufficiently hungry, will bite on a variety of bait, but the alert fisherman endeavors to employ the most effective bait. In dealing with human beings, an incorrect or mediocre type of appeal may produce results of a sort but intelligent motivation demands a conscious effort to sift the best stimuli from the neutral and negative, realizing always that what is best at one moment may not be best at a later time, even with the same subjects.

The motive force of symbolic stimuli, therefore, depends upon the specific type of appeal employed, its relevancy to the immediate condition of the subject at that moment, and the neural patterns which are already developed in him. Polysyllables, as we have already mentioned, will not motivate people with no habits conditioned to polysyllables. Symbolic stimuli are the chief instruments of persuasion, but the applied psychologist must know of what his stimuli are symbolic as regards the group which he wishes to influence. Among other things this involves feeling tone.

Motivation and Feeling Tone. We have stated that words and other symbolic stimuli may possess personalities. There are caste systems among words in much the same fashion as among people. We actively or vaguely resent moving a term up or down from its accustomed level. These personality qualities attaching to symbolic stimuli are conditioned in much the fashion that salivary flow is conditioned to a visual stimulus, such as a gum wrapper. The word "skinny" in the phrase, "She was a skinny maiden", is definitely out of place, because "maiden" has a semi-poetic connotation, whereas "skinny" is suggestive of a vacant-lot baseball diamond, and freckled-faced boys, dirty and decidedly unfeminine. "She was a slender maiden", is all right. No verbal note is struck that is discordant with the motif of the sentence. Even, "He was a skinny kid," isn't bad, despite the slang, for "skinny" has a masculine connotation, as does "kid".

In earlier languages all nouns possessed gender—masculine, feminine, or neuter. Although we do not classify them in such fashion today, many words, including adjectives and nouns, have developed a feminine or masculine quality, partly from excessive use by one sex or the other. Which of the following words, for example, suggest masculine usage and which feminine: *gorgeous, bawl, cute, weep, cry, marvelous, cunning, kid, gosh, dainty?* It is partly on the basis of the choice of words employed by an author that the listener can usually determine whether it is a man or woman who is writing. But the setting or contextual environment of words also influences their feeling tone. Despite the fact that "skinny" and "slender" are approved English words, one of them has more desirable feeling tone than the other. In advertising copy as well as in ordinary speech, one should endeavor to avoid the terms with unfavorable connotation, inasmuch as they call attention away from the idea being advanced. In Exhibit 5 are listed two sets of verbal stimuli with obviously different feeling tone. Those words under the "Negative" heading are somewhat unfavorable in general usage, although there are many occasions when they fit the general mood of the moment, or of the verbal picture being created, better than do their more polished synonyms.

POSITIVE FEELING TONE	NEGATIVE FEELING TONE
Plump	Fat
Intestines	Guts
Aroma	Smell
Nude	Naked
Inexpensive	Cheap
Girl	Female
Decayed	Rotten
Intoxicated	Drunk
Child	Brat
Saliva	Spit

EXHIBIT 5. Paired synonyms illustrating pleasant versus unpleasant feeling tone.

Polysyllables are frequently found to possess more favorable feeling tone than monosyllables, probably owing in part to their less frequent association with the unpleasant situation, as well as their usage by a more educated class. Words apparently are known by the company they keep. If used excessively by vulgar people, the most desirable term may ultimately give rise to a feeling of coarseness. Some of these reasons just outlined explain our preferences for certain male and female Christian names. Our experience with people possessing these names emotionally colors our attitudes toward them. These experiences do not necessarily involve personal contact. We may encounter the name in fiction, belonging to hero or villain, or it may suggest French, German or Jewish backgrounds, and as we have been favorably or unfavorably conditioned to these nationalities, we may react accordingly. In Exhibit 6 are listed the preferences of two adult women from quite similar home environments as regards racial background, social and economic factors. In almost every instance, they later explained, their judgments were made from personal contacts with people of these names. The agreement between the two raters is probably rather close for this type of situation. It will be noted that both sets of names cover a fairly wide range of races or nationalities.

MALE NAMES	MRS. C.	MISS B.	FEMALE NAMES	MRS. C.	MISS B.
Peter	2	8	Rachel	1	1
John	1	1	Anna	9	4
Algernon	6	6	Belinda	5	6
Gilbert	3	4	Bertha	10	9
Herman	7	7	Geraldine	3	5
Patrick	4	10	Janet	2	3
Richard	5	2	Maud	7	7
Maurice	9	5	Minnie	6	10
Henry	8	3	Nora	8	8
Jacob	10	9	Priscilla	4	2

EXHIBIT 6. Expression of preferences for male and female names by two female raters.

From the psychological viewpoint, therefore, feeling tone denotes the unpleasant or the pleasant habits which have been conditioned to a given stimulus apart from its obvious and most apparent response. These affective habits are usually of an emotional type, and are not always predictable from *a priori* thinking. It is essential that stimuli possess pleasant connotations if they are to evoke approach and appropriative behavior. It is because of the avoidance reaction engendered by unpleasant feeling tone that advertisers in general refrain from using illustrations which produce horror, fear, or nausea. In motivating people by print, as we shall describe below, it is necessary not only to employ second degree stimuli which arouse basic neural patterns, but which are free from unpleasant emotional connotation.

Motivation by Print. Through the medium of the newspaper and magazine, the billboard and the book, symbolic stimuli can repeatedly exercise their effect upon human behavior.

Although we shall devote later chapters to this subject, it is appropriate here to cite some of the interesting data that Haldeman-Julius[1] presents regarding the sales volume of some of his Little Blue Books before and after he had changed their titles. Unless a book sold 10,000 copies annually, he had it

Old Title	Yearly Sale	New Title	Yearly Sale
The Tallow Ball (Maupassant)	15,000	A French Prostitute's Sacrifice	54,700
Privateersman	7,500	Battles of a Seaman	10,000
Fleece of Gold	6,000	The Quest for a Blonde Mistress	50,000
The Mystery of the Iron Mask	11,000	The Mystery of the Man in the Iron Mask	30,000
The King Enjoys Himself	8,000	The Lustful King Enjoys Himself	38,000
None Beneath the King	6,000	None Beneath the King Shall Enjoy This Woman	34,000
Ten O'Clock	2,000	What Art Should Mean to You	9,000
Markheim	Few	Markheim's Murder	7,000
Pen, Pencil and Poison	5,000	The Story of a Notorious Criminal	15,800
"Patent Medicine" and the Public Health	3,000	The Truth About "Patent Medicine"	10,000
Art of Controversy	Few	How to Argue Logically	30,000
Nietzche: Who He Was and What He Stood For	10,000	The Story of Nietzsche's Philosophy	45,000
An Introduction to Einstein	15,000	Einstein's Theory of Relativity Explained	42,000
The Truth About Mussolini	14,000	The Facts About Fascism	24,000
Poems of Evolution	2,000	When You Were a Tadpole and I Was a Fish	7,000

Exhibit 7. The influence of new titles on the next year's annual sale of copies of Little Blue Books.

[1] Haldeman-Julius, E., *op. cit.*

sent to the "hospital" where he doctored its name, hoping by a change of words to render it a stronger motive to buying. In Exhibit 7 are listed some of the volumes before and after hospitalization. These data furnish probably the best example of the influence of specific words and phrases as motive forces, that we have in the literature. According to Mr. Haldeman-Julius the magical words in titling, as shown by his records, are: *Truth, Life, Love, How to, Facts You Should Know.* A close inspection of Exhibit 7 will disclose the following important findings: (1) An intimation of sex greatly accelerates the pulling power of a title; (2) Vague titles (Markheim, Ten o'Clock) do not ignite habitual tendencies; so are less effective than specific titles; (3) A man's products or inventions apparently are more interesting than the man; (4) Titles intimating dramatic or narrative contents (The Truth About; The Story of) have more motive force than purely expositional titles; (5) Polysyllables don't pull as strongly as shorter words.

Specificity is the keynote underlying the improvement of all the above title changes, as a quick glance will show. Vague stimuli do not start the thought process in any definite direction. They are as static as a highway sign that reads "Ten Miles" but fails to indicate to or from where. The title "The Art of Kissing", sold 60,500 copies against 17,500 for "The Art of Courtship". Here is just another example of specificity in contradistinction to generality as a motive force. "Kissing" is much more definite to the reader than is "Courting". It is the difference between a second degree stimulus, such as lamb chops, and the third degree stimulus, food.

The emphasis heretofore in titling has been upon shortness. The fewer words employed, the better was supposed to be the title. The publisher just mentioned opposes this view, saying that there is no yardstick measurement for a good title. The majority of the titles in the previous exhibit demonstrate that increasing their length apparently had no adverse effect upon their appeal, provided the increased length gave more specificity. Publishers, advertisers and publicists in general may profitably keep this suggestion in mind. Too frequently in the past one has had to read a novel in order to understand the significance of the caption under which the volume was sold. Figurative and far-fetched titles may have poetic significance, but they don't seem to be very strong as motivating forces.

In the realm of the moving picture, this same condition still exists. At the time of this writing I have just recently seen an unusually good moving picture by the title, "Washington Masquerade". I doubt if ten per cent of the passers-by could divine the relevancy of that title to the type of drama depicted. Fortunately for the producers, Lionel Barrymore's name was also displayed in large letters, with much the effect of a reliable slogan on a new product, and the public patronized the theatre because of the actor's motive force. Here the actor sold the show. If there were patrons who did not react familiarly to the name Barrymore—and there are plenty of them, despite the wealth of publicity given to the histrionic art of that famous family—they would probably have thought the movie was a society picture somehow related to George Washington or his birthday.

Failure to use the motive force of a dynamic and dramatic title is not only poor business, but it places an undue load upon the actor's name that accompanies it. It is like putting out a number of entirely new commercial products with little or no advertising copy or cuts to illustrate the uses of the new goods, and then sticking an old, reliable slogan on the container or carton as the sole sales point. A slogan, an actor's name or a storage battery cannot constantly be drained of motive force, and still remain fully charged. There must be reciprocity between name and goods. The movie title should "pull" along with the actor's name for maximum effect.

Before leaving Exhibit 7 too far behind it might be interesting to call attention to the last title in the list. The change of name increased the sale 5,000 copies annually. But when the new caption was also taken out of the "Poetry" classification and placed under the heading, "Humor", the annual sale increased to 21,000 copies. A similar change was wrought in Shelley's "Defense of Poetry", which jumped from 1,500 copies when listed under the "Miscellaneous" heading, up to 6,000 copies when classified under "Cultural Helps".

The motivation of people by print, therefore, involves primarily the use of specificity in words, which usually means second degree stimuli. These words must fall in the categories of the fundamental motive bases if they are to be most effective on the mass of mankind. They must, moreover, be free from unpleasant emotional coloring, else they will not lead to approach behavior. In being specific, moreover, they will usually be more effective when not in the superlative degree, since superlatives tend to produce negative behavior or "sales resistance". The following section will dwell upon this phase of print stimuli.

The Motive Force of Sincerity. The familiar adage that truth is stranger than fiction might be paraphrased to read that truth seems to be a stronger motivating force than superlatives and exaggeration. This result occurs because truth or sincerity gives rise to a feeling of confidence and trust, where superlatives develop a feeling of skepticism. The use of the phrases, "Fire Sale" and "Bankruptcy Sale" show an attempt to draw customers by giving an ostensibly adequate reason for the intimated low prices. Because such slogans have been overworked, and because the public has learned that the prices were not always lowered, many individuals deliberately stay away from such business houses. A large store, such as Marshall Field's, which possesses a very high reputation for honesty in dealing with its patrons, doesn't need to use such blatant devices for assuring its customers that they will get their money's worth. The latter have already been educated to expect full value. In order to demonstrate the value of sincerity, we offer the following illustration.

HART, SCHAFFNER & MARX

Chicago, Feb. 28, 19__

Editor of *Printers' Ink*: We are sending you a copy of an advertisement which brought remarkable results for one of our customers, together with a little story on the accompanying sheet, which tells about it.

We know that you often make use of articles of this kind, and believe that this one will be of interest to your readers.

Hart, Schaffner & Marx.

Here's an advertisement that sold 100 suits in one day in a very small clothing store whose previous high record for a single day's business had been nineteen garments.

In addition it was used as an object lesson in honest advertising in the School of Commerce of Northwestern University, and proved so convincing that a number of students and even an instructor or two took advantage of the sale to replenish their wardrobes.

The store is located on a residence street in Evanston, Ill., nationally known as the "classic" or "highbrow" suburb of Chicago.

The clothes which it was desired to sell were the left-overs of several seasons, in colors, styles and materials which had not proved popular with discriminating buyers.

"You couldn't give those clothes away in Evanston," said the manager of the store. "Our trade is the most fastidious in the country."

You know every merchant, no matter where located, thinks he has a particular kind of trade, or some special situation which makes his problem different from all others.

The advertising department of Hart, Schaffner & Marx, however, thought that human nature in Evanston was very much the same as anywhere else, and persuaded the manager to run the advertisement.

It appeared Thursday and Friday afternoons.

There was a crowd in front of the store when it opened on Saturday.

When it closed that evening just two of the suits remained—one so small no one could get into it, and one which seemed to have been designed for a fat man in a circus.

At least 250 men had applied for the suits during the day, and as a number of the early comers bought more than one suit, the great majority necessarily was disappointed.

One result of the advertisement was that since it appeared sales of higher-priced clothes have been much larger than before.

(Below follows the advertisement)

$20

Beginning Saturday, February 19

We'll be frank about this.
These suits have been in stock for two or three seasons.
They are not in the very latest styles.
Some are in colors and patterns that have not proven most popular.
Some seem to be just as attractive as any we have, but for reasons we can't explain, haven't sold well. But—
Every one is all wool.
Every one is well tailored.
Every one is in perfect condition.
You see men—well dressed men, too—wearing suits just like them every day, suits they've had for a season or two.
Why not get one or two of these suits now when you can get them at one-third or one-fourth of the original price?
Sale opens Saturday morning, February 19.
It won't last long.[1]

The force of truth is felt frequently by the audience, which will render marked attention to an otherwise unpolished speaker who is so deeply and sincerely concerned with the project under discussion that the listeners are unable to do aught but heed his words. In fact, sincerity backed by a little emotional enthusiasm is one of the best attention-holders possessed by the public speakers. But we shall defer such topics as motivating children, juries, and audiences until later in this book.

It is sufficient in this chapter to emphasize the fact that there must be instinctive or habitual bases of a neurological nature on which the motive operates. We have conceived of motives as stimuli, or clusters of stimuli, that set off motor activity of some sort through the mediation of an inherited or acquired functional linkage of neurones. From this viewpoint the odor of a piece of cheese may be considered the motive for the random movements of the rat which ultimately lead to his suc-

[1] *Printers' Ink,* March 10, 1921, p. 33.

cessfully threading the maze. Here the motor response follows an external food stimulus. The same type of motor response, even in the absence of the cheese odor, will also follow irritation of sensory cells in the walls of the stomach, which is, incidentally, the usual maze learning stimulus. In the latter case, the stimulus is a specific internal sensory one. Frequently it is called hunger, but this word popularly seems to cover a portion of the motor response, so we have avoided using it. It is a common event for an intra-cutaneous sensory stimulus to be confused with its gross motor response, since the latter is more evident to the other senses.

The psychological explanation of the motive force of sincerity, therefore, concerns the fewer inhibitions which are aroused thereby. Trickery gives rise to unpleasant feelings, and is consequently repellent, as we have learned by experience. From our social environment we have acquired not only language but also the knowledge that unscrupulous persons employ it to our hurt. Because of our contacts with persuaders of all sorts, moreover, we have found that superlatives and a stretching of truth usually go hand in hand with such persons. We try to be on our guard, therefore, against anything which indicates that we may be caught in a trap, which means anything that is unreal or insincere. Sincerity, on the other hand, does not give rise to this "sales resistance" with its inhibitions; so we are motivated much more easily thereby.

REFERENCES

HALDEMAN-JULIUS, E., *The First Hundred Million* (New York, 1928).

HIGGINSON, GLENN D., *Psychology* (New York, 1936), chaps. II, III.

SNOW, A. J., "An Approach to the Psychology of Motives," *American Journal of Psychology*, vol. xxxvi, No. 5, January, 1926.

STARCH, STANTON, AND KOERTH, *Controlling Human Behavior* (New York, 1936).

THORNDIKE, E. L., *The Psychology of Wants, Interests and Attitudes* (New York, 1934).

VITELES, M. S., *Industrial Psychology* (New York, 1932), chap. xxv.

WEBB, E. T., AND MORGAN, J. J. B., *Strategy in Handling People* (Chicago, 1930).

WHITE, WENDELL, *The Psychology of Dealing With People* (New York, 1936).

YOUNG, P. T., *Motivation of Behavior* (New York, 1936).

CHAPTER II

THE PSYCHOLOGY OF LEARNING AND MEMORY

The basis for all learning consists of some animal tissue which is plastic enough to be affected by changes impressed upon it, and yet sufficiently retentive to keep a record of such influences. Simple animals like the amoeba, possessing no neurone cells or processes, and with no eyes, ears, or other sense organs, can nevertheless react to various stimuli in the environment. The amoeba possesses sensitivity, motility, and conductivity, despite its obvious lack of nervous tissue. Its responses to its surroundings are called *tropisms,* which Hunter[1] defines as "any unlearned form of response not under the control of a nervous system".

Lacking a nervous system, however, the amoeba can not store up the effects of its experiences in various situations, as can higher forms of animal life, and therefore profits little from experience in its watery habitat. The snail, on the contrary, has been conditioned to physical contact until it has formed a habit. If we take a snail and place food before it, we find that it makes expansive movements in the direction of the food. If, however, we now touch a definite spot on its body with the point of our pencil, the snail immediately retracts. Thereafter, if we simultaneously place the food before it and at the moment of expansive movement touch its body with our pencil point we find that eventually, instead of retracting to the pencil contact, it seems to expand and approach the food more readily. At length, we can omit the food altogether, after which stimulation with the pencil point alone will elicit the expansive or food getting behavior. The negative reaction to the pencil contact which originally was produced, has now been conditioned to a positive response. The snail has developed a

[1] Hunter, Walter S., *Human Behavior* (University of Chicago Press, Chicago, 1928), p. 50.

habit by contact with the special environmental situation which we have employed.

But the snail cannot learn a more complex type of habit, such as that of choosing between a right and left opening, one of which leads to the surface and air, while the other is closed below the surface of the water. The ant, however, can acquire more complex habits and learn to thread a maze. It is curious that the ant in learning a maze uses the sun, or the electric light—at least, some constant source of illumination—as a fixed point around which it orients itself. If, after the ant has learned the habit of successfully threading the maze, we were to turn the maze board around so that the light now is at the left where it previously was on the right side, the ant is as helpless as a tyro, and must begin all over again.

The so-called homing instinct of bees, as well as of pigeons, is now considered to be only a homing habit acquired by the individual after hatching. Bees have been taken out over arid wastes, and bodies of water, not so far but they could easily fly back again if they knew the way, and they have never returned. From much greater distances over fertile territory they have returned quickly. It seems that they must have developed a set of landmarks of some sort by starting out in ever increasing circles of flight over the fertile land. The same explanation is thought to clarify the homing of pigeons.

White rats and guinea pigs have been the popular types of animal employed in psychological laboratories for learning experiments involving the maze. Differences between rats have been noted which lead us to feel that, if we had mental tests for rats, we would probably find different levels of intelligence to parallel the human species. Some rats are morons, others normal, and once in a century we might even encounter an Aristotle.

It is interesting to observe a rat in process of learning the maze. He enters blind alleys as well as open ones. Eventually by a trial and error process he arrives at the reward box. With succeeding attempts on successive days he gradually eliminates some of his errors. The rat apparently learns the maze from the reward box backward toward the starting point. During the last quarter or third of his course he makes fewer errors and runs faster and more certainly. The human being learns the maze using both the end and the starting point as orientation centers, with the middle third of the maze being the most difficult region. After the rat has perfectly mastered the maze we may endeavor to find how adaptable or intelligent he is, by closing the main path and opening a detour through a previous blind alley.

Now when we place the rat at the starting point he races through the accustomed paths until he bumps against the partition which we have used to close the alley. If he is a moron rat, and the closure is in the section of the maze near the starting point, he goes back to the starting point and begins all over again, bumping into the partition as before. His behavior resembles that of the child reciting a piece of poetry who reaches a line where he is blocked by inability to remember the next word, and then returns to his starting point for a fresh attempt, apparently feeling that mental momentum will carry him through. An intelligent rat will choose the detour after a few more trials—indeed, some brilliant rats will learn on one attempt—but the moron rat continues to choose the old pathway and bump into the partition. It may require a score of trips to the starting point for fresh attacks before he seems to acknowledge defeat, and search for a new course.

The same perseverance in old habits, and refusal to attempt the formation of new and more adequate adjustments is true of human beings, too, and bears the name conservatism. Youth finds it easy to adopt new ideas and motor habits because it has few old ones at variance with the new. Age, however, finds it necessary to break established routine and habit in order to adopt the novel, and, disliking to expend effort and lower its prestige by acknowledging inadequate previous adjustments, it endeavors to retain the old by fiat. Observe the following reply written by the school board of Lancashire, Ohio, in 1828

A. D., to a group of citizens who had asked permission to hold a debate in the schoolhouse on the practicability of railroads:

> "You are welcome to use the schoolroom to debate all proper questions in, but such things as railroads and telegraphs are impossibilities and rank infidelity. There is nothing in the word of God about them. If God had designed that his intelligent creatures should travel at the frightful speed of 15 miles an hour by steam, he would have foretold it through his holy prophets. It is a device of Satan to lead immortal souls astray."

The Laws of Learning. In the region where the end-brush of one axone makes connection with the dendrites of the succeeding neurones is found that animal tissue which is both modifiable and retentive. These regions—called the synapses—number billions, and furnish the neurological bases for intelligence. To explain how they operate we can draw a crude analogy to the action of the rat in a new maze. Let us assume that the rat represents a nervous impulse; that each straight section of the maze constitutes an entire neurone with its processes, and that the point where an alley joins any other alley is the synapse. The rat is dropped into the maze from our hand. In much the same fashion a nervous impulse is dropped into the neural maze at a neural starting point, which is a rod or cone cell in the retina, or a Meissner tactile corpuscle of the palm, etc., by some physical or chemical force.

As the rat progresses along a straight stretch of unbranching pathway, so the neural impulse passes over a single neurone. When a fork in the path occurs (synapse), the rat and the nervous impulse may take either branch. Neither knows which is the correct turn. If the wrong fork is taken, the rat enters a blind alley and the nervous impulse innervates an ineffectual muscle or gland. Since the goal has not been reached, the rat may come back to the fork and take the other branch. The nervous impulse doesn't come back, but new impulses are constantly being set up at the starting point, because of the continued action of fire, or light, or sound on the sense organ. At last success crowns the efforts of both. The rat gets his cheese, and the nervous impulse innervates the muscles that lead to removal of the fire, dazzling light, biting cold, etc.

It is apparent that if only one fork (synapse) were involved, at the outset fifty per cent of the rats would be right by chance alone. The interposition of more forks (synapses) between starting point and finish prolongs the learning process.

If, in the above analogy, the rat is placed in the maze the second day, or if the stimulus sets up a nervous impulse at a later date, it may by chance alone omit some of the blind alleys previously traversed and enter some of the blind alleys previously ignored. But *always* the impulse and the rat traverse the correct pathway before they effect success. Thus the right course is chosen every day. If we assume that we have not precluded the factor of odor in the maze, we can readily see that more rat odor will soon attach to the correct pathways than to the less frequented wrong alleys, and each succeeding day will increase this effect. The nervous impulse, too, leaves an effect in the synapse which we call lessened resistance, and this enables each succeeding impulse to follow the correct pathways more readily. Since our rat, let us assume, is now following the paths where his odor is strongest, we can readily appreciate that anything which will increase the odor will make it easier for him to follow the right pathway. On a *priori* grounds, therefore, we can make the following logical predictions concerning habit formation: (1) The more times the rat traverses the correct pathway, the more odor will attach to it; (2) The longer the rat spends in the correct alleys, the greater will be the odor he leaves there; (3) The greater the lapse of time since he last tried the maze, the less will be his odor on the paths. Remembering that the rat's scent is homologous to the reduced resistance to the nervous impulse, we may now state the laws of learning.

(1) *Law of Frequency.* Of two neural pathways, the one which has functioned most often will, other things being equal, offer less resistance to the subsequent passage of a nervous im-

pulse. This law is embodied in the statement that practice makes perfect; that repetition leads to perfection.

(2) *Law of Duration.* Of two neural pathways, the one which has functioned longer will, other things being equal, offer less resistance to the subsequent passage of a nervous impulse.

(3) *Law of Recency.* Of two neural pathways, the one which has functioned last will, other things being equal, offer less resistance to the subsequent passage of a nervous impulse.

The three laws stated above give the specific functional reasons for synaptic modification. There are numerous other primary or secondary laws of habit which may readily be resolved into these more basic ones. The Law of Vividness holds that the more vivid of two experiences will be retained longer than the less vivid. The Law of Primacy affirms that the first experience of a type is likely to be remembered longer than subsequent ones. But Adrian's All-or-None Law precludes our having large impulses and small impulses running over a given neural arc; so vividness must be explained in terms of longer duration, greater repetition, or the formation of additional habits which may be conditioned simultaneously with the given neural arc. For any given elementary habit, therefore, Frequency, Duration, and Recency explain the functional effect on the synapse.

The Role of Intention and Attention in Learning. Not only must one attend to stimuli which are to be remembered, but one must have sufficient motivation to keep attending. One may look casually at a page of printed verses, reading them one hundred times, and yet not be able to recite them from memory. If one is given an equally difficult page and instructed to memorize all the material thereon, it may be possible to have all the verses committed to memory in thirty readings. The latter example represents the intention to remember. Wherein lies the difference? The one hundred exposures to the printed words cannot be said to have been ineffectual as visual stimuli, for you may have read the page aloud each time, thus tying the motor expression to the visual stimuli. In short, when you read a page thirty times with the intention to remember it, why can you recall far more than when you read the page one hundred times without intending to remember?

By recalling the three rules for learning, we gain some aid. Although optical reaction to the printed words has been tied to the oral expression through the same neural arc in each case, the greater frequency of one stimulus has been partly offset by the slower reading for reproduction in the case of the other. If, however, the thirty slow readings do not surpass the one hundred rapid readings in the time during which the neural arc was being exercised, we still have not entirely solved the problem.

As a matter of fact, in the second illustration above conditions were different in still another respect, namely, rote memory was modified in part by logical memory. Connections between words were noted which were ignored during the one hundred readings. Moreover, the reader kept trying to formulate succeeding words without looking at them on the printed page, and then, when he failed, corrected himself from the page. These additional motor responses were instigated by his realization of the need for later reproduction of the verses.

An interesting example of the above situation can be demonstrated for the reader's satisfaction by timing some one who has been requested to write the alphabet backwards, beginning "z y x . . . c b a". Then have the same individual write the alphabet in the normal order. It requires at least three times as long to write it in the inverted order as in the normal way. Although the average American has experienced "j" just as many times beside "i" as beside "k", he finds it much easier to write "i j k" than "k j i". We tend to think forward, not backward, a fact which advertisers can utilize to great profit. "When You Need a New Collar—Buy an Arrow" is much more effective than "Buy an Arrow—When You Need a New Collar", because the real life situation finds the man without a collar. "I Need a New Collar" is his thought. If he has been exposed to the former advertising slogan, his thoughts flow right along in a-b-c-d-e order, which means that he immediately recalls "Buy an Arrow". If the second slogan had been used in advertising, however, and the man had thought, "I Need a New Collar", the phrase "Buy an Arrow" would not have come to his mind so readily.

The importance of attention in learning is great. Although one can learn without attending to the maximum of one's ability, unless material is in the focus of attention while learning occurs, one cannot by a voluntary effort recall nor utilize the habits acquired. There are different degrees of attention, which we have attempted to show graphically in Exhibit 8. In the normal waking state there is always a focal point of maximum attention, but one is also aware in lesser and lesser degree of marginal stimuli. To be under voluntary control, however, stimuli must be brought into the focal circle of attention when memorized. For example, a man goes into a grocery to buy a can of beans. "What kind do you want?" asks the clerk. The customer doesn't know; in fact, he can't remember any branded lines. "What kind have you?" he counters. "Oh, we have Heinz, Van Camp's, Campbell's, Totem, and White House", is the reply. The purchaser instantly recognizes several brands, and selects the one whose advertising has probably fallen within his field of vision most often. Circle No. 2 probably illustrates the degree of attention which he has given to such advertisements.

In Exhibit 8 it is advisable to explain the meaning of Circles No. 3 and 4. Stimuli which lie in Circle No. 3 include those sounds, lights, and pressures to which we respond as in sleep, and of which we have but slight recollection thereafter. "Hunches" and woman's intuition may belong here. In Circle No. 4 fall the stimuli and habits which are entirely outside the subject's recall, such as the pupillary reflex conditioned to a bell, as in Cason's[1] experiments.

[1] Cason, H., "The Conditioned Pupillary Reaction," *Journal of Experimental Psychology*, vol. v (1922), pp. 108 *ff*.

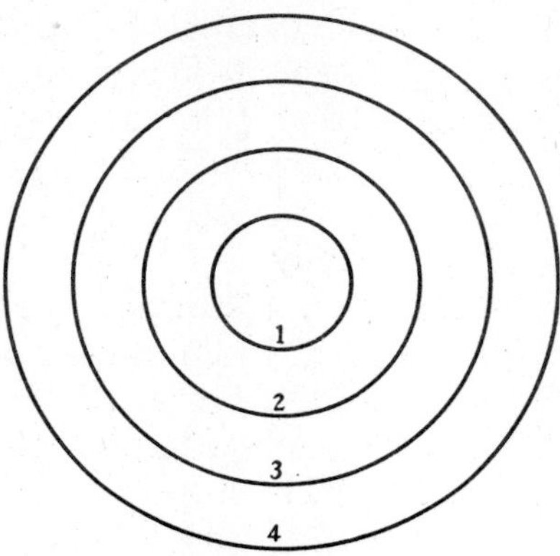

EXHIBIT 8. Showing degrees of attention. Stimuli in Circle No. 1 give rise to habits under the subject's voluntary control. Those in No. 2 are not under voluntary control, but are recognized when called up. In No. 3 the habits are vaguely conscious. In No. 4 both stimuli and habits are unknown to Subject.

Attention may be focussed now on one point, now on another. Thus, a stimulus in Circle No. 3 may usurp the focal point, in which case it then will lie in Circle No. 1. While reading a book we may suddenly become aware of a movement in the margin of our field of vision, and turn our head to see if it is a mouse. There are certain *Objective Determinants of Attention* which will force the subject to focus upon them. We shall present them in the following classification.

(1) *Change.* This usually involves movement, and is considered the most effective objective determinant. The flashing on and off of electrical advertising signs depends on this factor for part of its effectiveness. The gestures and changes in tone of the speaker, as well as the attention value of the directive motions of the orchestra leader are also effective for this reason.

(2) *Uniqueness or Novelty.* This factor probably obtains its effectiveness because of Change. The unique is different, which is the essence of change. However, the latter has a connotation of movement or spacial change, whereas novelty usu-

ally involves a qualitative change; so we shall make a separate heading for this factor.

(3) *Size.* Other things being equal, the larger of two objects will attract one's attention first. In advertising this is appreciated, and used as an argument in favor of the full page advertisement. The effectiveness of the quarter, half and whole page advertisements does not vary in the ratio: 1: 2: 4, however. As regards the total efficiency of such spaces, Strong[1] has determined that they approximate the ratios: 1.00: 1.41: 2.00. The efficiency of space increases approximately as the square root of the area, and not directly as the area. Efficiency of an advertisement, however, is not solely a function of the size. A full page advertisement, for example, eliminates the distracting effects of adjacent cuts and copy.

(4) *Intensity.* A thunderclap will usually break through the most concentrated attention. Richly saturated colors, and intense gustatory and olfactory stimuli are capable of capturing one's attention. The employment of color in advertising demonstrates in part the use of this method of forcing the reader to glance in the direction of a given advertisement.

(5) *Duration.* This factor in an intermittent form is called Repetition. Up to a certain point duration is effective as a means of compelling attention. Beyond that point adaptation sets in, and we become consciously oblivious to the stimulus. The loud tick-tock of a grandfather's clock is ignored by the dweller, at least until it stops. The cessations of sound may, from its fulfilling Rule (1) above, again command our attention.

(6) *Color.* Although part of the effectiveness of color may be explained under the heading Intensity, there is some evidence that hue alone, even when very unsaturated, is more compelling than black and white.

[1] Strong, E. K., "The Effect of Size of Advertisements and Frequency of Their Presentation", *Psychological Review,* vol. xxi (1914), p. 144.

The attention of pedestrian, audience, reader, and child is *caught* by one or more of the above objective determinants. But the next step is *holding* the attention, which involves an appreciation of the *Subjective Determinants of Attention,* which will be listed below.

(1) *Purpose or Attitude of the Moment.* The average man is not very observant of adult masculine attire until he heads for the city for the purchase of an overcoat, suit, hat, or shoes. Then he suddenly takes cognizance of his own sex, watching to see whether overcoats that others are wearing are double-breasted or belted, checkered or plain. Coats now fit in with his purpose or attitude of the moment, so they hold his interest. Having become overcoat conscious, he may even retain an active interest in men's coats for a few days following his purchase, but his interest soon begins to lapse. Herein he shows one of the sex differences distinguishing men from women. Women are usually alert to styles whether they are shopping bent or not.

(2) *Duty or Social Obligation.* This heading explains why men will study materials and labor attentively day in and day out at work which intrinsically is not interesting. The pay check at the end of the week is interesting, and the particular job in question is simply a means to an end. True, the work ultimately becomes habitual, in which case it does possess intrinsic interest, as shown in the next heading below. The difference between many a textbook and a novel is explicable on the basis of headings (2) and (4).

(3) *Earlier Education—Habits.* Individuals tend to see in life what they have been trained to see. The artist takes note of the pictures in the homes which he visits; the musician instantly observes the grand piano; the outdoor man sees the fishing tackle and guns in the host's den or study, and the grammarian notes the language employed by those around him. Trade journals are developed for those whose business and professional habits set them apart from others of mankind.

Speakers and advertisers must take these differences into consideration in order to hold the attention of their respective publics.

(4) *Instinctive Tendencies.* The reason one sex is interested in the other is obvious from this heading. Our movies are better attention holders than many political addresses and sermons, because they strike at fundamental motive bases, whereas politicians and clergymen don't always tie up their talks to fundamental urges. In a survey at New Haven some years ago, for example, six hundred copies of *True Story Magazine* were sold to the Yale students in contrast to one copy of *Century Magazine.* Moreover, material which holds the attention of people because of instinct is much less tiring in its effect than that which holds them through Duty or Social Obligation. Six or eight hours of study in one night is quite fatiguing, but college men and women will spend an equal amount of time together, often in active exercise, and not feel at all worn out, thus illustrating the psychical phase of fatigue. It is possible to employ instincts as an attention holding device by such apparently irrelevant material as coal. Here is a coal advertisement, for example, showing a cozy living room with an open fire before which two attractive youngsters are seated, while the caption and copy explain that there is no danger of these kiddies taking cold when XYZ coal is used in the furnace.

In concluding this topic we may state that Intention aids the learning process by causing the subject to keep the new material in the focal circle of his attention-field, thereby insuring a conscious control of and ability to reinstate the new habits acquired. It greatly reduces the number of repetitions necessary for successful reproduction. Besides Intention, of course, the subject's Attention is an invaluable ally in learning. We have distinguished between the six objective determinants of attention and the four subjective determinants. The former serve as attractors of attention while the latter hold it after it is once caught. In controlling human behavior, however. the applied psychologist must make sure that the objective determinants attract the subject to the desired form of behavior, not away from it. In the latter case they are distracters, and therefore produce inefficiency.

The Effect of Motivation on Learning. From the paragraphs immediately preceding, it is obvious that any device that will tie up closely with fundamental motive bases of human nature will hold the attention. And learning cannot progress very rapidly and successfully unless the subjects concentrate. Verbal coaxing and verbal clubbing are demonstrated on a group of 106 fourth and sixth grade pupils reported by Hurlock.[1] They were divided into four classifications for the purpose of the experiment, as shown in Exhibit 9. Problems in addition were given the children. After the first day's test, the members of the Control Group took the daily examination in a separate room so they would be entirely unaffected by the other procedures of the experiment. "Each day, before the test papers were given out, the names of the children of the Praised Group were called out by the experimenter, and the children were asked to rise, come to the front of the room and face the class. They were then praised for the excellence of their work of the preceding day, as shown both in the improvement made and the general superiority over the other members of the group. They were encouraged to do better, to try to avoid any careless mistakes, and to add as many problems as the time permitted. Following this, the members of the Reproved Group were called out and were severely reproved for poor work, careless mistakes, lack of improvement over the preceding day's work, and general inferiority to the other members of the class. The members of the Ignored Group heard the praise and reproof given to the two other groups, but they themselves received no recognition whatever." In Exhibit 10

[1] Hurlock, Elizabeth B., "An Evaluation of Certain Incentives Used in School Work," *Journal of Educational Psychology,* vol. xvi (1925), pp. 145-159.

	Averages				
Groups	First Day	Second Day	Third Day	Fourth Day	Fifth Day
Control	11.81	12.34	11.65	10.50	11.35
Praised	11.81	16.59	18.85	18.81	20.22
Reproved	11.85	16.59	14.30	13.26	14.19
Ignored	11.84	14.19	13.30	12.92	12.38

Exhibit 9. Showing total results in average scores for the various groups of school children, with 26, 27, 27 and 26 pupils of both sexes in the groups, respectively.

are plotted curves to illustrate the data in the preceding table. It will be apparent that the Praised Group did almost twice as well as the Control Group.

The effect of motivation on learning, therefore, is to increase the efficiency of the process. This result occurs because the attention of the subject is held more closely and continuously upon the task or problem at hand. Increasing the motivation means enhancing the strength of those subjective determinants of attention described in the preceding section. The value of different motives, and the significance of specificity in appeals were explained in Chapter I. A bonus in industrial plants, or praise and honors in school and social life are some of the chief methods employed in motivating persons to learning. Throughout the life of the individual, moreover, motivation will be effective in accelerating the learning process.

The Effect of Age on Learning. The ability to learn increases up till adulthood and then remains fairly constant until senescence sets in. The somewhat popular opinion that children learn more rapidly than adults is not correct. The ability to learn is both a function of innate intelligence and acquired knowledge or vocabulary. Since the neural connections do not reach their maximum efficiency until about the

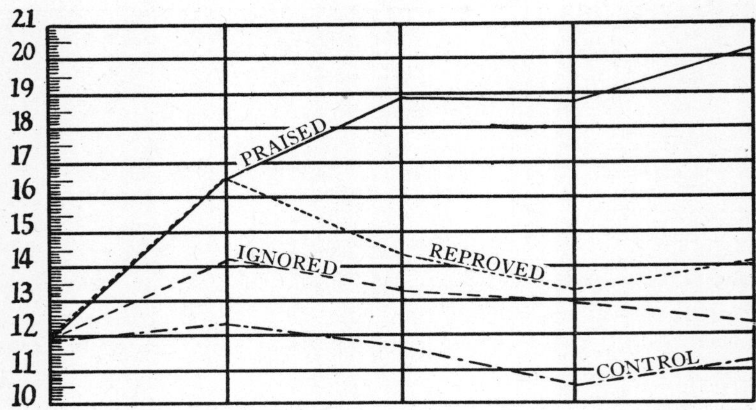

EXHIBIT 10. Graphic representation of the data in Exhibit 9.

age of sixteen years, the child is obviously handicapped in reasoning capacity when competing with adults.

The vocabulary factor is quite important in learning. Other things being equal, the man who possesses a vocabulary of 10,000 words is superior in learning capacity to the man who has only 7,500 words. Words are not only individual habits of vocal enunciation, but they also represent fineness of mental distinctions that have already been made concerning elements in the environment, and which can be used for future thinking. They are like various kinds of mental chisels with which one carves out knowledge concerning his milieu. The more such chisels he possesses, the more and finer discriminations he can make when confronted with a new situation.

To the savage a modern automobile is just a large moving object—more elephantine than anything else he can think of. To the modern man it consists of wheels, spokes, hub caps, radiator, motometer, headlights, tires, steering wheel, and a hundred or more other things. Moreover, the modern man sees many of these things, while the savage misses them, especially if the exposure to the machine is brief.

Poffenberger[1] gives the average vocabulary of persons of different ages as follows:

Superior adult	13,500 words
Average adult	11,000 words
12 years	7,200 words
10 years	5,400 words
8 years	3,600 words

In another sense, words may be likened to fishhooks. The more hooks on a line, the more likelihood of catching fish. So, too, the more intellectual hooks that one has when dipping into a new subject, the more likelihood of pulling the known out of the unknown, thereby leaving the strange for special concentration and study.

It is true, as we have mentioned before, that age tends to become fossilized, whereas youth, with its abundant enthusiasms and energy and curiosity may be motivated more strongly to learning. But if we grant equal motivation and energy, the workman with the largest equipment of tools should turn out the best product. An average adult with 11,000 words has at least double the epuipment of the ten-year-old child. The drawback to age is the fact that it doesn't possess the exuberant energy of youth, and in hoarding its strength prefers to stick to the already learned. Men of fifty and sixty years of age can begin a new trade if they wish to do so. Their age certainly should not deter them from mentally coping with the new situations.

In summing up the influence of age upon learning, we may state that the capacity to acquire new habits seems to increase until adulthood is reached. Because of the lower energy supply and probably a lesser motivation of middle-aged persons, however, they are less inclined to change from the *status quo*, and hence are deemed much more conservative than their children. After adulthood is reached, the rate of learning

[1] Poffenberger, A. T., *Applied Psychology* (D. Appleton & Co., New York, 1927), p. 430.

depends largely upon motivation and previous experiences or vocabulary, since the nervous system reaches its maturity during the middle teens. In the period of senescence the learning capacity wanes, probably through lack of motivation because of physiological changes in the subject's intra-cutaneous environment.

The Most Economical Methods of Learning. Many students spend literally hours on assignments that could be learned in thirty minutes by others of no greater intelligence, but possessed of superior methods of study. One of the first things to be guarded against is distraction of attention, either through daydreaming of more interesting topics, or because of noisy and fatiguing environments. The objective determinants of attention are distracters as well as attractors, depending on whether they pull one away from his task or to it.

Distraction increases fatigue even though in some experiments[1] it has been found that output does not decrease. The worker in those cases seems to muster more effort so that he not only overcomes the disturbing tendencies, but may even have a surplus. This condition, however, is detrimental to efficiency. Where concentration of effort and attention is desired, distracting forces should be eliminated in so far as possible. One way to keep a dog from chasing cats is to keep the cats away from him. In the student's room, therefore, a pile of love letters on the table, several issues of popular magazines, a phonograph or a radio, or a plate of cookies or apples certainly do not accelerate his studying. As one of our famous fiction writers recently said, "I waste more time sharpening pencils, oiling my typewriter, getting out fresh carbon sheets and doing everything else that I can think of before sitting down to creative effort, than I spend in original thinking." The same individual said he finally got around the difficulty by having his wife do every one of those tasks in ad-

[1] Morgan, J. J. B., "The Overcoming of Distraction and Other Resistances," *Archives of Psychology*, No. 35 (1916).

vance of his entry into his study, so that he would then have no possible excuse to dally along and procrastinate.

Irregular disturbances, such as noises, are more detrimental to efficiency than are regular ones, because the sudden sounds tend to set off a fear reaction, while the regular hum or drone leads to negative adaptation on the part of the listeners. When the Air Personnel force of the Army was small, all typewriters had to be stopped whenever long-distance telephone calls came in. But the office force grew much larger with increased pressure of work so that, as Watson describes it, "it was no uncommon sight to see a man answering a long-distance telephone call with fifteen or twenty typewriters going in his immediate neighborhood and a hundred or more going in the one large room."[1]

After eliminating distraction, the matter of motivation should be kept vividly before the workers or students. In addition to the examples already cited, the use of graphs of daily output are quite effective, for they stimulate the competitive motive base in human beings. Thereafter the following methods should be applied.

(1) *Distribute the Trials.* The more the trials are distributed in point of time, up to certain limits, the faster will be the learning as measured in number of trials. Of course, if one has only half a day in which to learn to drive a machine, or master a speech, it becomes necessary to bunch the repetitions. The less time available for learning, the more trials ncessary for perfection.

(2) *The Whole vs. the Part Method.* Experimental data show that the whole method of memorizing is usually superior to the part. Instead of stopping with smaller units, such as stanzas and paragraphs, the entire piece should be read through from start to finish. There are several advantages

[1] Watson, John B., *Psychology* (J. B. Lippincott Co., Chicago, 1924), p. 400.

attaching to the whole method. (a) Attention is uniformly distributed throughout. In the customary method of learning, the first stanza is memorized; then it is repeated with the second, etc. In this manner, the first stanza obtains much more emphasis, which partly explains why we remember first stanzas of poems we learned in grammar school, but seldom remember the last ones. (b) Many faulty habits are eliminated. In the part method the learner keeps returning from the last line of the first stanza to the first line again, with the result that the last line becomes tied up with the first by such associations. This may block the later association of the last line of this stanza with the first line of the second stanza.

When the material is so long that fatigue sets in before the end is reached, or when the process of learning doesn't seem to be moving forward advantageously, it is advisable to break the material into smaller units. By the whole method, of course, it seems longer for the student to master sentences and phrases, because of his distributed effort, but when he is able to reproduce the material, he can usually reproduce all of it.

(3) *Learn One Thing at a Time.* For the quick development of any given habit, it is well to concentrate on one habit at a time. The experimental work of Ulrich shows that animals learning three problems simultaneously require more trials for each problem than when they learn the problems separately. If we can use this analogy as typical of human learning it justifies the single-track mind. Monotony, of course, may tend to appear more quickly thereby, so the teacher must keep the motivation strong.

(4) *Active vs. Passive Learning.* Active learning shortens the learning time, and renders more serviceable the material acquired. In our previous example of the thirty in contrast to the one hundred readings of a page of verses, we found that Intention to memorize greatly speeded up the learning process. The one hundred readings may have affected the

nervous arcs so that in an unguarded moment the reader might have recited the entire page of verses subconsciously, but he could never voluntarily and consciously recite them. Persons may see repeated demonstrations until they are positive they know all about the act in question, only to find themselves perplexed later on when they actively attempt the supposedly learned form of behavior. In our dental, medical, and law schools we employ the case method of instruction to prevent such a catastrophe. The tutorial system also makes use of this plan, as do examinations in courses, whether written or oral.

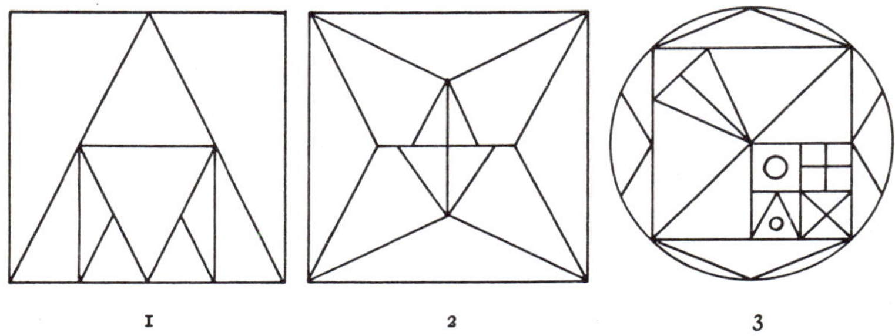

Exhibit 11. Showing three drawings used in learning experiments described in the text.

By the drawings[1] shown in Exhibit 11 the writer has annually demonstrated to classes in psychology the effectiveness of frequent attempts at reproduction during the exposure period. The third drawing is obviously the most difficult. When it is presented to the students there is usually a groan forthcoming, but half of those same students can reproduce the drawing perfectly from memory after 20 seconds exposure to it, provided the exposure time is broken into 5-second intervals, with an attempted reproduction immediately following each exposure. The students discard each attempted drawing when making a successive attempt, that

[1] The writer is indebted to Rex Collier for these drawings.

is, they don't simply fill in omitted parts of their first drawing until they have it correct. Each attempted reproduction is made on a fresh sheet of paper.

Half of the students are sent from the classroom, while the remaining half engage in the experiment. The writer then begins the 5-second exposures, and continues until at least fifty per cent of the subjects have a perfect reproduction. Then the group of students previously sent from the room is recalled and given a single exposure totaling the time taken by the first group in 5-second doses. A comparison of the two halves of one of my classes follows:

No. Students	No. Trials	Duration of Trial	Pct. Correct
48	4	5 seconds	50
48	1	20 seconds	0

Several advantages result from an active attempt at learning. (a) The subjects do not waste time studying already assimilated portions of the lesson or task, but keep the focal point of their attention always on the unknown or unassimilated. This obviously results in great economy in time. (b) By employing motor activity in response to the stimulus, they render more permanent the effects which they do assimilate. Two of my students a full twelve months after the experiment just mentioned, reproduced from memory the third drawing in Exhibit 11, with very little hesitation. (c) Rivalry usually develops and heightens the interest or motivating force of the strange task. This rivalry may be employed even when one is working alone, for one is competing with one's earlier records or the clock, and sees the progress made between each successive attempt at reproduction.

For at least fifty per cent of the university students to be correct in their reproduction of the drawings in Exhibit 11, requires two 5-second exposures for Drawing No. 1; three 5-second exposures for Drawing No. 2; and between four and five 5-second exposures for Drawing No. 3.

In concluding our discussion of the most economical methods of learning, it would be well to state that distractions of all sorts are generally productive of inefficiency, even though the actual output may not always be decreased. After the learner is in the most favorable environment possible it behooves him to distribute the trials unless time is at a premium, to adopt the whole method instead of the part, subject to the qualifications previously mentioned, to concentrate on one thing at a time, and especially to adopt the active method. Overlearning and frequent repetitions after the material is fully memorized also lead to greater retention.

Subconscious or Marginal Learning. It is difficult to estimate how important a part is played in our behavior by the habits which have been acquired in the second, third, and fourth Circles of Attention, as shown in Exhibit 8. The tolling of church bells, heard by the business man while he is shaving in the morning, may not have consciously been noted by him, yet the sound may set off an emotional habit that was occasioned years earlier when a similar tolling of bells became connected with the death of his mother. This emotional habit may produce a feeling of melancholy in the business man, without his ever realizing why he feels sad, and the resultant mood may lead to his decision to run down to visit his native village.

In such fashion many stimuli in the margin of our present attention-field may set off habits, the products of which are powerful enough to break into the center of our attention-field. The linkage of reflex arcs in the child's food-taking behavior occurs in much this manner, as can be witnessed in Exhibit 12. Here the reflexive stimulation by contact against the infant's cheek produces the quick turning of the youngster's head. The result of this behavior happens to be that the nipple is in physical contact with the lips of the child. This physical fact in

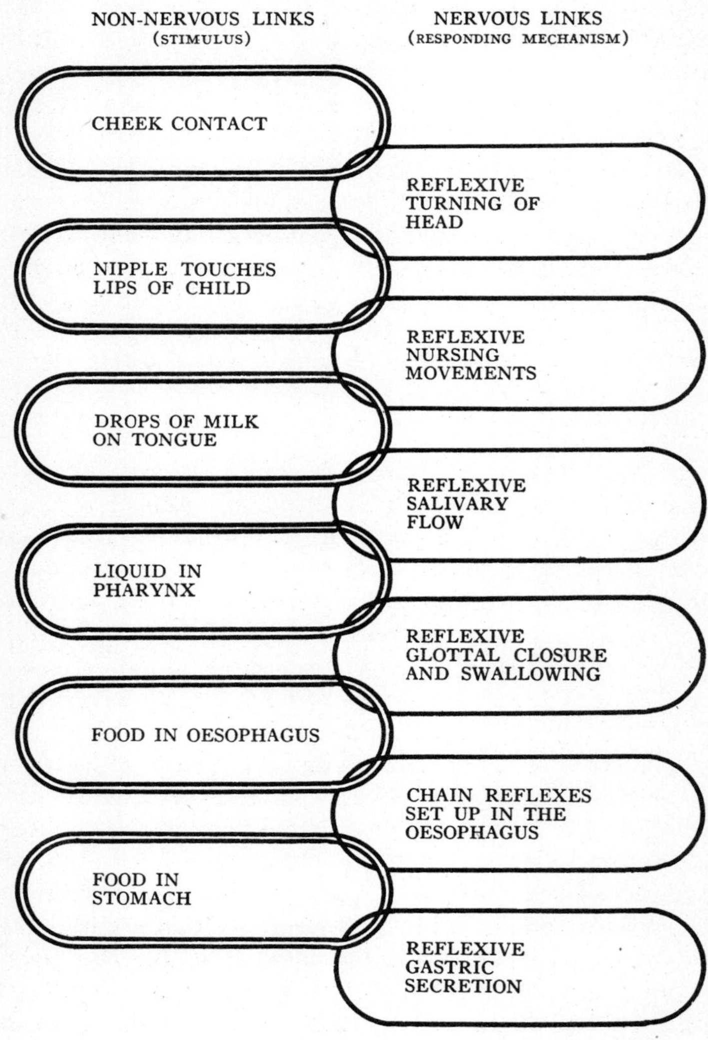

EXHIBIT 12. Showing how reflexes are linked through their individual effects, the chain being called an instinct.

turn becomes the stimulus for a second reflexive form of behavior which involves his pursing his lips about the nipple and producing a partial vacuum in his mouth. The result of the vacuum is a flow of milk upon the infant's tongue. The physical presence of this foreign substance incites another reflexive arc that causes saliva to flow into the buccal cavity. Liquid, acted upon by the force of gravity, rolls down into the pharyngeal region, where it stimulates the reflexive closure of the glottis and initial swallowing action. Skipping the chain reflexes in the oesophagus which serially operate, we find the food squeezed into the stomach, where its contact incites gastric flow, etc. In this series of events, we note that the reflex arcs are not natively tied up, one to another. If they were, the simple stimulation of the infant's cheek by a pencil point which was quickly jerked away would cause the entire sequence of neural reflexes to occur. But such stimulation would not result in the hook-up shown above. Most of the reflexes bound up in instinctive action, therefore, are simply so placed, anatomically, that the product of Number 1 becomes the stimulus of Number 2.

In one of the short short stories a few years ago the hero, a young newspaper reporter, found that as he wrote at the typewriter in his study at home, he kept growing very thirsty. The desire for liquid refreshment became so strong that he had to stop writing, go to the refrigerator for ice cubes, and fix himself a glass of ice water. Within twenty minutes his thirst again broke through the attention he was concentrating upon his writing, and he was compelled to get another glass of ice water. This happened at fifteen or twenty minute intervals for an hour. He knew there was no real need for so much liquid intake, but he couldn't prevent his apparently insatiable thirst. Then he noted, across the little court and suspended in an open window, a pendant wind chime whose pieces of glass were emitting a tinkling sound resembling ice in a glass. This auditory stimulus, though in the margin of his attention-field, had been sufficient to set up an organic thirst reaction of sufficient strength to usurp the focus of his conscious attention.

To the effect of such marginal stimuli, too, belong the vague feelings of liking or dislike which we have discussed in Chapter I under the heading of feeling tone. Likewise our fondness for one type of food and nausea at the thought of another have frequently been formed without our being aware of the reasons therefor. To the four primitive gustatory stimuli have been conditioned the great variety of food likes demonstrated by the viands described in cook books and restaurant menus. Hollingworth gives the following table of likes and dislikes of infants, based on the findings of Peterson and Rainey.[1] The fondness for beefsteak, in the light of these early sensory re-

Reaction of Infant	Number Showing Such Responses to Sweet	Salt	Bitter	Sour
Contented sucking	747	503	31	136
Discomfort reaction	37	295	780	659

Exhibit 13. Gustatory reactions of infants during the first week after birth.

sponses to the taste, can be explained only on the basis of its saline quality. But we adults like beefsteak for more reasons than that it is salty. Its odor, feel upon the tongue, and temperature are simultaneous reactions that have been acquired unwittingly, and conditioned to our general pleasant emotional state when with our parents at the table. Cod liver oil is used as a reward with a set of twin girls of my acquaintance, while the same substance is taken under force by many youngsters. Why a food tastes good or bad depends as much upon the marginal stimuli playing upon the individual at the time of first

[1] Peterson and Rainey, "The Beginnings of Mind in the New Born", *Bulletin of the Lying-In Hospital* (New York, 1910).

encountering the food as upon its chemical reactions of sweet, sour, salt, or bitter. Tobacco, beer, and grapefruit have probably unpleasant native tastes, but they soon become conditioned to a pleasurable response.

From the standpoint of psychology, therefore, subconscious or marginal learning has today come to be regarded as of even more significance than was frequently thought. The psychoanalysts work with the habits which have been acquired unwittingly by their patients, and the advertisers depend for much of their success upon the subconscious or marginal learning of their public. The emotional coloring which attaches to many of our memories results from marginal memories or habits. Indeed, many of the likes and dislikes which we have are a consequence of marginal learning. A peculiar characteristic of marginal learning is that such memories are not under the conscious control of the possessor. Emotional memories are chiefly of this sort. The conscious utilization of marginal stimuli in child training is not even yet developed to the degree to which it should be.

The Facts About Memory Improvement. Probably ninety per cent of students and the general public feel that their memory is poor. They base their attitude on the fact that they don't remember all the experiences which they have encountered in life. As a matter of fact, it is probably fortunate that most of the stimuli which affect us do not leave permanent functional memories. We need a certain amount of perspective for distinguishing the important from the trivial, and we gain this by forgetting the unimportant.

Memory is looked upon as the physiological retention in the synapses of changes once made therein. As such, therefore, there is no way of improving memory, unless possibly through a general improvement of health. If impressions have been made, they will remain. The time when stronger impressions can be made is chiefly at the moment of exposure to the stimulus. Memory improvement, therefore, really amounts to improving our methods of learning. After the photographic film has been once exposed to light, it is too late to try to increase the clarity of the impression thereon. That should have occurred at the moment of exposure. If the image is too faint, the time of exposure should have been increased or the larger shutter opening should have been used, or both. In a similar fashion, we can increase the distinctness of the neural impression by more time spent considering the things to be remembered, or by enlarging the associations with which we connect them. If we meet Mr. Brown at a dinner, and are introduced by some one who doesn't enunciate the name distinctly to us, and if we are concerned with making the proper acknowledgement *a la* Emily Post so that we are only partly attentive to the stranger, it is no wonder we cannot recall his name two hours later, especially if we have given no thought to it in the interim. We simply used a 1/50 second exposure time and a tiny shutter opening, when the situation demanded a time exposure and a twilight shutter.

The motivation is the first step in remembering names or other items. Any intelligent man or woman could probably remember every stranger he had ever met, if he were paid $1,000 per name remembered. There is nothing esoteric about memory improvement. In the case of Mr. Brown, above, we need to get the correct stimulus to begin with. This demands actually hearing the name aright. Next comes the active use of, or response to, the name, such as, "I'm glad to meet you, Mr. Brown". Names which are spoken are much more easily remembered. The reason so many fail to recall names is because they respond to an introduction with only "How do you do", and are so self-conscious or introvertive that they are paying most of their attention to the good appearance they hope they are making, instead of to the individuals they meet. By thinking about the name, visualizing it spelled, and preferably writing it down, we help increase the effect on our synapses. Through such procedures and arbitrary associations we fulfill the two laws of learning, frequency and duration, and retain the name longer.

Unlike the camera analogy, however, human beings can keep the synapses active after the actual stimulus has disappeared, and hence can "set" the effect more surely. It was of such a situation that William James wrote when he said that "we learn to swim during the winter, and to skate during the summer".

The laws describing the four methods by which ideas and events are recalled in memory are given below. The first two relate to the temporal factor involved at the time of learning, while the last two pertain to qualities possessed by the objects themselves.

(1) *The Law of Contiguity.* If two things are experienced together in point of time frequently enough, the presence of one will lead to recall of the other. It is this law which explains the majority of memories, as can be noted from an inspection of Exhibit 14. The various conditioned habits also belong here.

(2) *The Law of Succession.* If two things are frequently experienced in immediate succession in point of time, the presence of the first one alone will tend to produce recall of the second. This law is not so easily demonstrable as the first, but it explains why one cannot recollect the third word in the first line of the poem regarding Mary and the Lamb until one has uttered or thought the first and second words.

(3) *The Law of Similarity.* If two things are similar, that is, have elements in common, the presence of one is likely to lead to recall of the other. Synonyms are of this type. In Exhibit 14 are several responses that fall under this heading.

(4) *The Law of Contrast.* The extremes or opposites tend to be associated in memory so that the presence of one leads to recall of the other. This really might be considered negative similarity, and is evident in six or seven of the most frequent associations in Exhibit 14.

Stimuli	Responses							
	Most Frequent		Second		Third		Fourth	
1. Table	chair	(267)	wood	(76)	furniture	(75)	eat	(63)
2. Dark	light	(427)	night	(221)	black	(76)	color	(28)
3. Music	piano	(180)	sound	(95)	song	(68)	singing	(48)
4. Sickness	health	(142)	death	(115)	illness	(71)	doctor	(62)
5. Man	woman	(394)	male	(99)	boy	(44)	strength	(32)
6. Deep	shallow	(180)	water	(134)	ocean	(93)	sea	(90)
7. Soft	hard	(365)	pillow	(53)	easy	(34)	cotton	(28)
8. Eating	food	(170)	drinking	(166)	bread	(46)	hungry	(44)
9. Mountain	high	(246)	hill	(184)	valley	(90)	height	(73)
10. House	home	(103)	building	(78)	barn	(74)	dwelling	(68)
11. Black	white	(339)	dark	(172)	color	(129)	night	(51)
12. Mutton	meat	(257)	sheep	(204)	lamb	(121)	beef	(97)
13. Comfort	ease	(165)	pleasure	(77)	home	(63)	easy	(61)
14. Hand	foot	(204)	fingers	(83)	arm	(63)	work	(49)
15. Butterfly	insect	(261)	bird	(64)	fly	(44)	pretty	(39)
16. Chair	table	(191)	seat	(127)	sit	(107)	furniture	(83)
17. Whistle	noise	(173)	sound	(103)	blow	(95)	sing	(75)
18. Wish	desire	(197)	want	(66)	hope	(51)	thought	(47)
19. River	water	(393)	stream	(117)	lake	(65)	deep	(35)
20. Beautiful	pretty	(113)	nice	(73)	ugly	(66)	lovely	(64)
21. Citizen	man	(278)	person	(64)	people	(41)	American	(35)
22. Spider	insect	(276)	web	(188)	fly	(136)	bug	(58)
23. Sleep	rest	(300)	awake	(94)	bed	(75)	wake	(60)
24. Trouble	sorrow	(202)	worry	(65)	sickness	(47)	care	(27)
25. Cabbage	vegetable	(394)	plant	(48)	green	(44)	garden	(43)

Exhibit 14. The four most frequent responses from 1,000 individuals to a number of common words. (Kent and Rosanoff).

Because of the different associates attaching to a list of common words, Kent and Rosanoff[1] hoped to be able to detect symptoms of mental derangement. They constructed a list of 100 common words; then gave these to 1,000 individuals from

[1] Kent, Grace H., and Rosanoff, A. J., "A Study of Association in Insanity," *American Journal of Insanity*, vol. lxvii (1910), pp. 37-96.

a wide range of intellectual, educational and business groups. In Exhibit 14 we have included twenty-five of the original stimuli, followed by the four most frequent responses. The figures in parentheses indicate the number of persons giving the response. Although these experimenters didn't find the lists to be of much practical benefit for their purposes, they do show the uniformity of response of this fairly typical group of normal men and women.

Our discussion of the facts about memory improvement, therefore, has shown that it really amounts to improvement in the learning process. The three laws of learning, coupled with motivation, attention, and the intention to remember, are the chief instruments through which an individual increases the memories available for pleasure and profit. After an impression has been made upon the synapses, this impression tends to remain. A part of memory improvement is concerned with making vivid impressions on the nervous system. Another phase of the process, however, involves the linkage of one idea with numerous associated memories so that it becomes more available to its owner. We have mentioned the four laws of association which describe the manner in which such linkages occur.

The Various Degrees of Memory. The degrees of memory correspond roughly to the regions in our attention-field where the stimuli affect us. Thus, stimuli which were in the focus of our attention-field give rise to habits that we are aware of having formed, and which we can voluntarily reinstate. We may call this *first degree memory.* The secret of improving one's memory lies primarily in getting the items to be retained into the focus of our attention-field, so that we shall have active functional memories of them which we can utilize whenever we desire.

Second degree memory is illustrated by the example previously mentioned of the man in the grocery store asking for a can of beans. Multiple choice examinations have been devised to tap this second degree memory of the student. This is called the "Age of Stimulus" method by Hunter and others, measuring a less active kind of memory from the standpoint of the subject's voluntary control.

Third degree memory is a stage farther removed. Here we not only cannot voluntarily recall, but when the stimuli are presented to us, we are not conscious of having experienced them before. We may say they are new to us, yet our behavior may not bear out our words. Often, however, we have a vague sense of familiarity with the stimulus but don't know how we obtained it. It is a hunch, or intuition. Scott[1] explains the genesis of such vague memories regarding advertising thus:

> The passengers on street railways have but little to distract their attention. They go over the same road so frequently that the streets passed through cease to be interesting. Since newspapers and magazines cannot be easily read, the cards have but few rivals for attention. Even those who have but little interest in the advertisements find that they glance at the cards frequently and that the eyes rest on a single card for a considerable length of time. . . . The goods which through their advertisements have occupied our minds for long periods of time assume in our minds an importance which is often far in excess of anything which would have been anticipated by one who is not familiar with the peculiar power here described. In estimating the relative values of two competing lines of goods, I assume that my judgment is based on the goods themselves as they are presented to my reason. I am not aware of the fact that I am prejudiced in favor of the goods that have occupied my mind the longest periods of time.

Fourth degree memory is of lesser concern to us in a practical way because of its further removal from our active control. The conditioned reflexive contraction of the pupil of the eye to the sound of a bell is an instance in point. It is possible that our sense of time belongs in this category. Probably many segmental forms of behavior involving reflexes connected with

[1] Scott, Walter Dill, *Psychology of Advertising* (Small, Maynard Co., Boston, 1908), p. 224.

the emotions are in this class. Here we haven't even hunches or intuition, but the products of these reflexes may, like the glass wind chime's effect on the reporter, break into a more active attention-field, and affect our behavior. The psychoanalysts do their work with third degree and possibly fourth degree memories.

A psychological summary of the degrees of memory shows that they parallel closely the degrees of attention which we described hitherto. First degree memories are capable of voluntary reinstatement by their owner, while second degree memories are illustrated in multiple choice examinations. Third and fourth degree memories are far removed from the subject's attention-field, but may indirectly exert some control of his behavior. We have already explained the importance of these various degrees of memory from the advertising man's and the psychoanalyst's standpoint, and of the need for their utilization by the child psychologist and teacher. The cortical process which we call thinking is concerned primarily with first degree memories, as the following section will further demonstrate.

The Relationship of Thinking to Habit. Since words are abbreviations for actions and objects it is fairly clear that our thinking, which depends primarily on our established habits, must be concerned quite generally with words and other forms of symbolic stimuli. And as we try first one act or object, then another, in real life situations, so in mentally attempting to solve a new problem it is apparent that we go through a trial and error process with words. An excellent illustration of this is given by Watson[1] who compares the situation throughout to the trial and error physical movements of the rats in the maze.

A colleague of mine came on a visit to stay in an apartment in which I had rooms. In a passage leading from the shower bath was

[1] Watson, J. B., *Psychology* (J. B. Lippincott Co., Chicago, 1924), pp. 349-350.

a peculiar piece of apparatus standing near a sink. The essential features were a curved shallow nickel pan about twelve inches wide by twenty inches long; at one end the pan had been bent in the form of a half circle, while at the other end the side pieces did not extend for the full width. The pan was mounted on a stand adjustable in height. Furthermore the pan itself was attached to the stand by a ball and socket joint. My friend had never seen anything like it and asked me what in the world it was. I told him I was writing a paper on thinking and pleaded with him to think his problem out aloud. He entered into the experiment in the proper spirit. I shall not record all of his false starts and returns but I will sketch a few of them. "The thing looks a little like an invalid's table, but it is not heavy, the pan is curved, it has side pieces and is attached with a ball and socket joint. It would never hold a tray full of dishes (*cul de sac*). The thing (return to starting point) looks like some of the failures of an inventor. I wonder if the landlord is an inventor. No, you told me he was a porter in one of the big banks down town. The fellow is as big as a house and looks more like a prize-fighter than a mechanician; those paws of his would never do the work demanded of an inventor" (blank wall again). This was as far as we got on the first day. On the second morning we got no nearer the solution. On the second night we talked over the way the porter and his wife lived, and the subject wondered how a man earning not more than $150 per month could live as the landlord did. I told him that the wife was a hair-dresser and earned about eight dollars per day herself. Then I asked him if he did not see the sign "Hair-Dresser" on the door as we entered. The next morning after coming from his bath he said, "I saw that infernal thing again" (original starting point). "It must be something to use in washing or weighing the baby—but they had no baby (*cul de sac* again). The thing is curved at one end so that it would just fit the neck. The woman you say is a hair-dresser and the pan goes against the neck and the hair is spread out over it." This was the correct conclusion. Upon reaching it there was a smile, a sigh and an immediate turn to something else (the equivalent of obtaining food after search).

Not only does thinking involve previous experiences or habits of the individual, but the act of thinking can become habitual. The logical manner in which debaters, lawyers, and professional reasoners attack new problems is a result of practice. Fallacious reasoning is avoided with the skill and dexterity of the fencer. The reverse of this mental agility is expressed in the statement that there can be feeble-mindedness by deprivation. This situation refers to the dulling of the curiosity by a monotonous and unstimulating milieu, so that by adulthood the individual is "set" in habits of sluggish response, even though he is surrounded thereafter by choicest gems of music, literature, and art.

William James was once asked why his family had been so brilliant, and replied that it was largely due to the free discussion in the home while he was a child. He said that his parents encouraged debate, even at the table, and the children "whetted our wits on each other's". Children can be encouraged to original thinking in many ways. Many a child in a poor home where there was no abundance of toys has utilized sticks and paper, and by use of imagination has created a wealth of playthings. True, a stick may have to represent a horse, or a walnut may stand for a pig, but this very act of symbolizing other objects with substitutes involves an additional thought process, so keeps his cortex from fossilizing. Since no one of us ever uses anywhere near his maximum mental capacity, we need have little fear of burning out a synapse.

Three types of thinking are generally differentiated. (a) Reverie. In reverie our thoughts follow spontaneously wherever fancy leads us, and we feel no sense of effort or strain. This category incudes daydreaming. It is a case of free association. Animals also probably engage in this type of thinking. I have come in from the hay fields with my dog, which had been chasing rabbits all afternoon, and have observed this dog in his sleep, where he lay stretched out upon the ground, begin to grow tense, growl faintly and frequently, until he finally engaged in overt barking which became more and more excited until with a triumphant yelp he ceased, licked his chops in a relaxed and contented manner, and then subsided. During this entire process he never once opened his eyes. If he wasn't going through a canine dream, then it will be difficult ever to determine such a thing in an infrahuman animal. Dewey suggests that reverie makes up the greater part of mental life.

(b) Routine Thinking. This is a middle stage between reverie and reasoning. It is demonstrated by the business man and the housewife, the scientist and the child who are concerned with meeting the demands of their positions which involve habitual responses. Many a business executive who attains his success through original thinking finally gets much of his day's work reduced to a routine level where he can simply note that the objections raised in this morning's letters are already answered in Form Letters No. 3, No. 9, or No. 27. We are all guilty of this "coasting" after we have attained a certain intellectual speed.

It is demonstrated every semester in my classes heavily patronized by business and professional men. They often say that they feel mentally rusty; that it takes them almost a whole semester to get back into the swing of effective study. Such statements indicate that they have been slipping into a rut of routine thinking. The school child probably uses his brain for reasoning activity far more than the average business and professional man, for the child is confronted with entirely new problems daily, whereas the rest of us have reached the "catalogue" state in which our already developed habits take care of almost every situation that arises, and we simply need to do the cataloguing in the morning, and our secretaries take care of the rest of the work.

(c) Reasoning. This noble function of the human cortex is seldom if ever called into action except in times of maladjustment. As long as there is smooth sailing we avoid expending the additional effort called forth by original thinking. It is the hungry rat which keeps running throughout the maze until he finds the reward box and food. A rat which has been fed prior to entrance into the maze will wander around casually a little while; then lie down and go to sleep.

The contented young man likewise enjoys life with seldom a need for more than routine thinking until a wife or youngster forces him into a new situation that cannot be fully met with existing habits. Then the man buckles down to his job, perhaps takes courses in the university at night, and, much like the maladjusted rat, keeps striving until he pulls himself a few degrees higher in the financial world, when he again begins coasting. The recent economic depression in America has probably brought into activity more idle and rusty neurones than any event since the preceding one. And some men, like the obstinate rat who encountered the closure of his accustomed pathway in the maze, will keep on with the old methods and ideas, and wonder why they don't break through the red side of the ledger on to the paying side once more, while other men will quickly adjust and be in the van of business success on the economic rebound.

Reasoning is hard work, which explains why we prefer the *status quo* as soon as we are successfully adjusted to it. But there is a certain exhilaration that results from stiff mental work which can scarcely be matched in any other manner. And the more frequently we experience such a thrill of accomplishment in this fashion, the more inclined we become to the methods of creative thinking. A chronic debater actually gets homesick for a good difference of opinion, and jumps at the intimation of a test of wits as a hungry dog dives for a bone. It is this type of whetting the wits which William James had in mind.

In concluding our treatment of the relationship of thinking to habit it would be well to mention that the bulk of our thinking involves language, which in turn is composed of thousands of discrete word habits. Watson's comparison of the act of reasoning to a trial and error process involving words is especially illuminating in this regard. The three types of thinking have also been discussed, namely, reverie, routine, and reasoning. We have brought out the fact that maladjustment is the usual stimulus for reasoning, and that creative thinking may even be considered a habit in itself. The formal technique of the latter we have left for the student to acquire from a textbook of logic.

Emotional Habits. There are individuals who seem to pride themselves on the possession of a temperamental disposition. Such a disposition usually means that the parents of said individuals refrained from using the hairbrush on too many occasions. The temperamental person is usually one who has a "spoiled" child disposition. Like the child who is cruel, however, he can be changed into a sympathetic and extroverted youngster by training. The following paragraphs show the beginning of such a procedure with a four-year-old boy who had been surrounded by adults and inanimate toys all his life.[1]

> . . . Four years of habitually thinking about his own desires cannot be overthrown in a night. Indeed, on the morning of the kitten's arrival Paul presents a pathetic spectacle as he vainly strives to play with Fluff.
>
> He doesn't know how to play with a weaker living thing. At first he seizes the kitten as if it were his football and tosses it high in the air above his head. The kitten falls to the floor, bruising its mouth until the blood flows.
>
> Paul has not meant to be cruel. He simply does not know that a living playmate must not be treated like a ball.
>
> "Paul, dear, you have hurt Fluff," his mother protests. "How would you like to have a big man throw you up in the air and let you fall upon the sidewalk so hard you hurt your mouth?"
>
> "He would be a bad man," Paul immediately replies. "I would not like him".
>
> "Then you know how Fluff feels," his mother continues. "The poor little kitten has been taken away from its mother and its brothers and sisters. It has come to live with you. It likes you. But

[1] Crane, George W., "Kiddies and Kittens Make Perfect Pals," *Forecast,* vol. xxxvi, No. 3 (1928), pp. 149 *ff.*

then you throw it in the air and hurt it. Do you think it will like you, if you do that again?"

Paul shakes his head soberly. This is a new thought to him. He must keep it in mind in the future. A kitten is like himself. It gets hurt when it falls. A ball is not like himself. It doesn't get hurt when it falls.

Although Paul was a brilliant child with an I. Q. of 145, he needed to be extroverted and to have analogies drawn between himself and the kitten. Fortunately, his mother kept at the job day after day until in a few weeks Paul was growing considerate of the feelings of his playmate. He had become able to identify himself with it, and to suffer pain vicariously when it was hurt. Many thoughtlessly cruel and unfeeling adults would be more considerate if they could have gone through such experiences as Paul had. Brutal tendencies can usually be eliminated without great difficulty if they are caught early in the life of the child, for the initial brutalities are quite often thoughtless actions. Thus tenderness can be inculcated and developed through training. In Chapter XIII we shall expand this subject when we consider the means of lessening the youngster's future divorce hazard.

A mother came to see Dr. H. D. Williams of our staff with the complaint that her twelve-year-old son would go into tantrums when he didn't get what he wanted, and lie on the floor, scream, kick, scratch, and in general make himself unbearable. She wanted to know how to eradicate this behavior, for she had found nothing effective hitherto. In her son we see a temperamental adult in the making.

"Well," Dr. Williams answered slowly, "I'll give you a plan which will work, I believe, if you are willing to try it, and probably work rather quickly. Just get a large pail, let the water run from a faucet until it is icy cold, fill the pail, and throw it on him." The mother consented to try the plan. The next day her son went into his usual tantrum. She followed Dr. Williams' advice to the letter, filling a large pail and approaching her boy. "Get up!" she ordered as severely as mothers can order. No action. Douse! The boy yelled, but it was an entirely different sort of yell from his tantrum cries.

The shocking change in his mother's behavior was probably as great a jolt to him as was the contact of three gallons of cold water. But the following afternoon he again went into a tantrum. Slowly, obviously, his mother procured the pail, walked into the bathroom and filled it, and returned to the living room. But her young heir was gone. Some sentimentalists may aver that the mother's behavior was brutal, but it frequently requires a revolutionary act to convince a youngster of the change in disposition of a parent on whom he has been imposing chronically. Three gallons of water is a cheap price to pay, however, for the development of a wholesome disposition in place of a temperamental one.

Self-confidence is a vastly important behavior trait which can also be developed, for confidence is a habit. The child who is given tasks beyond his ability, or who is not motivated to their performance, ends the day with failure behind him. On the morrow, when he attacks a new problem he may be influenced by his previous lack of success, and again stop short of victory or completion. If this sequence of events continues over a period of a few weeks or months, the child has a defeatism complex, and enters upon new jobs with an inferiority complex. On the contrary, the child who is given tasks which he can finish without unduly taxing his strength, and who is motivated adequately by praise, begins the new day with the exhilarated feeling of accomplishment well done, and this attitude soon becomes a habit. In adult life, therefore, when a new job comes up he attacks it without even thinking that he may not be successful. Why shouldn't he be able to do the task, he reasons, for he's done everything else he has ever tried. Shannon Fife's[1] story is especially appropriate in this connection.

[1] Fife, Shannon, "Half-Way", *Liberty* (Feb. 21, 1931), p. 59. Courtesy of *Liberty*.

HALF-WAY

When Hurley's wife telephoned me that he was desperately ill with pneumonia I was preparing to sail for Europe within the hour, but I dropped everything to hasten to his bedside. I had been Hurley's roommate at college and best man at his wedding, and although I had not seen him for several years the warmth of our friendship persisted.

As I taxied posthaste to the hospital I carried with me the mental picture of the same unchanging Hurley I had always known—an undersized, mild-mannered type of man, hesitant and undecided as to character, now nearing forty, and apparently reconciled to remain forever a plodding clerk.

But the moment I glimpsed him I was conscious of a startling change. Hurley had been somehow transformed into an entirely different type of person, and solely through the alchemy of a smile.

It was not the resigned smile of one reconciled to death. It was a smile of victory, of proud achievement, of triumphant success—things never even remotely associated with Hurley.

"I've won," he breathed. "I've won at last. Thank God I'm a success."

Through the delirium of intermittent unconsciousness Hurley's declaration of victory and success was repeated again and again.

The nurse, sharing my startled wonderment, whisperingly confided the details. At the time of the attending physician's diagnosis they had thought Hurley asleep, only to discover that he had overheard the tragically brief remark of the physician—a few ominous words virtually sealing Hurley's doom. And it was upon hearing these words that Hurley had first smiled his smile of success.

To add to our bewilderment we knew that Hurley wanted to live. Among many other reasons was the bond between him and his wife, a colorless, repressed little woman who moved meekly in an aura of self-obliteration, and who seemed a perfect complement to Hurley's mild negations of character. Between them was a deep love, a piteous, clinging-together type of devotion which had always been woven through the drab texture of their lives.

She was sitting there at his bedside, tremulously whispering words of endearment and encouragement to him. The pressing proximity of my sailing hour drew me reluctantly from the room. As I paused at the door for a last lingering look at my friend, there came once more Hurley's exultant tocsin:

"I've won; I'm a success."

And accompanying the words was the illuminating glory of his triumphant smile—a smile born in the same moment that he had heard the sentence of death passed upon him.

I was well out at sea when the agony of my suspenseful waiting was finally relieved by the arrival of a radiogram. I opened it tremblingly. Hurley had passed the crisis and would live! . . . .

Business kept me in Europe for more than a year. Almost immediately upon my return home a telephone message from Hurley took me to his office. If I had been amazed at the metamorphosis of the man at the hospital, I was dumbfounded now. Hurley, radiant with success, was established in a splendidly appointed office, the enthusiastic head of a flourishing brokerage business.

He immediately sensed my profound bewilderment, chuckled delightedly, settled back in his chair, and told me his story—the story of "Half-Way" Hurley.

He began with his entrance into matrimony, only half-way prepared for its responsibilities. He dwelt at length upon his half-way success as an accountant; of half-way health; of the half-paid mortgage upon his home, a home which was bereft of children because Hurley felt himself only half-way fitted for the exactions of parenthood.

"And so I drifted on and on," he explained, "always at the half-way mark in everything, until my inner mind was dominated by the psychology of defeatism, and my subconscious self labeled me 'Half-Way' Hurley.

"Finally I began to grow ashamed of myself. I thought of my wife. I began to want success. Desperately I began to plan success. I knew that I was a victim of psychology, and I knew that the laws of psychology work both ways. I reasoned that if there could be one thing in my life not done half-way that thing would serve as a psychological symbol of success.

"On the spur of the moment I selected my half-completed garden as that symbol. I worked furiously, trying to rush it to a completed condition. I badly overtaxed my strength and in a moment of lowered resistance contracted my pneumonia. I was carried to the hospital bitter with the realization that I was still 'Half-Way' Hurley—that I still lacked my symbol of success. Man, how I wanted that symbol of one thing well done. How I needed it!

"And then, suddenly, the physician who examined me gave that symbol with words never intended for my ears—words which virtually portended my death but which, ironically and whimsically enough, were to me the elixir of life; words which gave birth to my smile of achievement; words which made me resolve not only to live, but to push everything in my future life to completion and success. They were the words spoken by the doctor to the nurse when he said: 'There's nothing half-way about this case; he has DOUBLE pneumonia.'

"And there was my symbol. At last I had stopped doing things by halves."

In the silence that followed, Hurley's telephone rang and I heard him conversing with his wife. And in those few sentences was tenderly crystallized all of the love one human can bear for another.

"This time it's my wife who is in the hospital," Hurley said as he hung up. "I've got to hustle over there at once and you must come along. You see, that's the real reason I've sent for you. There's to be an addition to the family and you're to be godfather."

Enthusiastically I shouted my congratulations, and asked: "What is it—a girl or a boy?"

Hurley threw back his head with a long joyous laugh—a laugh vibrant with the pride and strength and power that comes with assured success.

"There's nothing half-way about that, either," he exulted. "It's both!"

The emotional habits which attach to music and art we shall consider in a later chapter. Suffice it to conclude by repeating that Confidence or Defeatism, Tenderness or Brutality, Culture or Ignorance, Tact or Boorishness, Courage or Cowardice, these attributes of human behavior are wholly or in part dependent upon the emotional conditioning the individual has received. His native intelligence, of course, is a factor to be considered, especially when we regard the degree to which conditioning will carry him. A person of normal mental alertness can obviously surpass a moron in cultural attainments, if given the same training, but it must also be borne in mind that a normal person exposed to boorish surroundings may be far less cultured than a high grade moron in an ideal environment of music and books, correct language and social etiquette. A high grade moron may possess the mental alertness of a twelve-year-old boy or girl, and at twelve the normal child can be speaking perfect English, can be familiar with good music and art, and can deport himself admirably in social situations, if he has been correctly trained.

REFERENCES

ADAMS, D. K., AND McCULLOCK, T. L., "On the Structure of Acts," *J. Gen. Psychol.*, 1934, vol. 10, pp. 450-455.

BLANCHARD, PHYLLIS, *The Child and Society* (New York, 1928), chaps. i, xiii.

CARR, HARVEY A., *Psychology* (New York, 1925), chaps. v, x, xi.

GAULT, R. H., AND HOWARD, D. T., *Outline of General Psychology* (New York, 1925), chaps. iv, vi, viii, xii.

GILLILAND, A. R., MORGAN, J. J. B., STEVENS, S. N., *General Psychology for Professional Students* (Chicago, 1935), chaps. iii, vii, viii.

GRIFFITH, C. R., *Introduction to Applied Psychology* (New York, 1934).

GRIFFITHS, J. H., *The Psychology of Human Behavior* (New York, 1935), Part II.

HOLMES, S. J., *The Evolution of Animal Intelligence* (New York, 1911), chaps. ii, v, x, xi, xii.

HUNTER, WALTER S., *Human Behavior* (Chicago, 1928), chaps. vi, vii, viii.

HUNTER, W. S., "Conditioning and Extinction in the Rat," *Brit. J. Psychol.*, 1935, vol. 26, 135-148.

HUSBAND, R. W., *Applied Psychology* (New York, 1934), chap. xxv.

JAMES, WILLIAM, *Psychology, Briefer Course* (New York, 1920), chaps. x, xviii.

MAIER, N. R. F., & SCHNEIRLA, T. C., *Principles of Animal Psychology* (New York, 1935), Part III.

MOSS, FRED A., *Applications of Psychology* (Boston, 1929), chaps. viii, ix.

MURCHISON, C. (Editor), *A Handbook of General Experimental Psychology* (Worcester, Mass., 1934).

PILLSBURY, W. B., *The Essentials of Psychology* (New York, 1930), chaps. iv, v, vi, ix, x.

POFFENBERGER, A. T., *Applied Psychology* (New York, 1927), chap. iv.

TAYLOR, W. S., *Readings in Abnormal Psychology and Mental Hygiene* (New York, 1926), chap. v.

WARREN, H. C., AND CARMICHAEL, L., *Elements of Human Psychology* (Boston, 1930), chaps. iii, viii, ix.

WATSON, JOHN B., *Psychology* (Chicago, 1924), chaps. viii, ix.

WOODWORTH, R. S., *Psychology* (New York, 1921), chaps. xi, xiii, xiv, xvi.

YOUNG, KIMBALL, *Source Book for Social Psychology* (New York, 1927), chaps. ix, x.

CHAPTER III

INCREASING HUMAN EFFICIENCY

The matter of increasing human efficiency has been of notable importance in the industrial and commercial field where the vital ratio between output and overhead charges is a subject of constant concern. But there are other aspects of the question of broader social significance, which, though we cannot go into them here, are of recognized importance. The leisure time of the mass of our people is becoming greater. What methods of improving their capacity either to enjoy this extra time, or to employ it for personal, financial, or educational advancement are available? Are we utilizing the most efficient technique in our school system, not alone in regard to methods of presenting material to the young minds, but also as regards the choice of curricula? It is obvious that such phases of the question necessitate a careful study of the basic philosophy of society. It is not our purpose to develop this theme further, though we acknowledge the essential value of such orientation.

Efficiency Engineering. This topic covers those aspects of applied psychology in the industrial field wherein men and women are primarily endeavoring to speed up production by elimination of superfluous moves of the worker. This may involve the designing of new machinery, or a re-education process concerning the function at hand. In his analysis of the standard typewriter keyboard, Hoke[1] gives us an excellent example of what efficiency engineering can do. His proposed new keyboard is contained in Exhibit 15, and illustrates a change of the tools employed instead of a change in habits of the individual. Although the ratio of ability of the right hand to the

[1] Hoke, Roy E., "The Improvement of Speed and Accuracy in Typewriting," *Johns Hopkins University Studies in Education*, No. 7 (1922), p. 35.

	LEFT HAND				RIGHT HAND			
	FINGERS				FINGERS			
	4	3	2	1	1	2	3	4
	Y	D	M	CW	QF	V	L	K
	R	N	T	HU	S I	E	O	A
	B	P	G	J X	Z ?/	⁝	:	;
Load on above keyboard	858	888	982	1031	1098	1093	996	971
Ideal load	855	900	975	1028	1097	1097	991	968
Load on present keyboard	803	658	1492	1535	1490	640	996	296

EXHIBIT 15. Proposed new typewriter keyboard adjusting the loads on the various fingers more nearly to their capacity. (By Roy E. Hoke).

left is found to be as 100 : 88.87, Hoke finds the left hand carrying 47.7 per cent more load than the right, according to the present typewriter keyboard.

The Gilbreths have also done much outstanding work in this field of applied psychology. In the bricklaying trade, for example, every movement involved in picking up, mortaring, and laying the brick was carefully analyzed. By changes in the placement of materials, and in the routing of work, useless moves were eliminated until the number involved for laying each brick dropped from 18 to 4, with a resulting increase in hourly output per man from 120 to 350 bricks.

The use of the motion picture machine has been decidedly

helpful in many cases. By photographing all the processes or steps in the performance of a given task, and then carefully analyzing the films for unnecessary moves and opportunities for short cuts in the routing of work, the experimenters have effected marked economies. Even in the realm of sport this method has been employed as a means of finding ways of speeding up the runner or of reducing the "slice" of the golfer.

The matters of individual differences in working time or speed of performance have also been studied. In general, the movements of the smaller individual are faster than those of the larger. In work involving shoveling, for example, it was found that a decided increase in output resulted from adjusting the length of handle and size of the blade to the size and strength of the man. Although the smaller individuals took less per shovelful, they more than made up for this difference by their faster rate of shoveling. Not only did output increase, but the men felt less effort expended.

Wyatt[1] reports a somewhat similar type of study undertaken by the Industrial Fatigue Research Board in England, in which the speed of the factory machine was adjusted to the reaction time of the individual worker. The investigators found that in general the machines were running too slowly for the optimum working rate of the employes. When they increased the rate, they found it possible to increase output by 18 per cent. Some employees were able to work as much as 50 per cent faster than others. In all such types of experiment, of course, it is necessary to make sure that the increased output is not made at the expense of the worker's health. The improvement must result by decreasing present inconveniences and useless expenditure of energy, not from simply increasing the worker's performance by undue motivation.

The principles involving improvement of production by mechanical adjustment of worker to machine in a more efficient

[1] Wyatt, S., "Machine Speeds and Output," *Journal of the National Institute of Industrial Psychology,* London (October, 1927).

manner may be designated under the three major headings, Individualization, Standardization, and Specialization. As we suggested at the beginning of the chapter, although industry has held the focus of attention in regard to efficiency engineering, we can profitably bring some of these same research methods into many other phases of human endeavor. Gilbreth[1] estimates that a system of simplified spelling would save in the neighborhood of two years time for the child in his school career. In many other respects his time could also be conserved. "Counting the English units bearing the same names as our own, we have in use 4 different sizes of pints, quarts, and gallons; 3 different sizes of gills; many sizes of barrels; and untold numbers of different sizes of bushels of things in different states, such as apples, potatoes and the like; 3 kinds of ounces, drams, and pounds; 3 different sizes of hundredweight, 4 different tons, and 2 or 3 kinds of miles." The metric system, which could be learned by a child in half an hour, would greatly simplify measurements of all sorts, and relieve Uncle Sam of an estimated 300 millions of dollars annually spent unnecessarily in teaching the cumbersome system of weights and measures now in vogue.

In the realm of printed matter, for example, we could greatly improve our reading rate if some of the vowels were changed. In fine type it is difficult to distinguish such words as "minimum", "resonance", etc., because the letters "e", "a", "r", "s" or the letters "m" and "n" have the same general dimensions, and hence require closer discernment that "l" and "s". Moreover, words in which letters are of one height, as the two given above, or words printed all in upper case are much more difficult to read than those giving a more irregular word pattern. Eliminating the internal curves of the letters making up a word, and considering only the external outlines,

1 Gilbreth, F. B., "Wealth from Standardization: A Typical Example in Simplified Spelling," *Bulletin of the Society of Industrial Engineers,* vol. v (1923), pp. 3. *ff.*

which are incidentally quite significant reading cues, we can represent the peripheral contours of easily distinguished words in Exhibit 16.

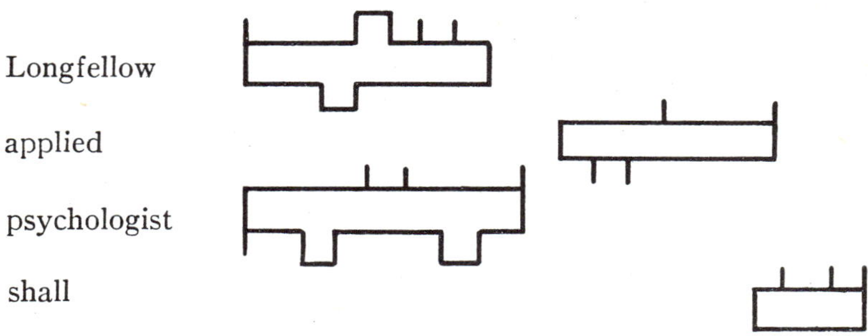

EXHIBIT 16. Illustration of the peripheral visual patterns of easily discriminated words.

If some of the confusing vowels and consonants which are of lower case could be changed, our reading time and inaccuracy would be reduced. There is no reason why a small triangle couldn't be used in printing instead of the letter "e", thus removing one of the chief sources of visual strain and confusion. At the University of Chicago, for example, Professor William S. Gray tested the reading speed of 664 freshmen, finding that the slowest readers covered less than two words per second, while the fastest averaged slightly over seven. This means a difference in reading materials covered that runs from 18 pages to 63 pages per hour. The fastest reader would cover a full page of print in this textbook in one minute while the slowest college reader would require 3.5 minutes. Improving the legibility of our print alphabet would undoubtedly increase the reading rate of all groups, and quite likely would lessen the gap between the extremes, since eyestrain and lack of adequate reading habits explain much of the discrepancy between rapid and slow readers in this intelligent group.

In general, therefore, anything which will eliminate a human adjustment will correspondingly reduce the time required for the performance of a given task. This holds for the housewife, the stenographer, the schoolboy, factory worker, or executive. In setting the piecework rates in factories it has been found wise to compute the number of essential moves necessary in the completion of the task; then use the normal reaction times for the muscular components of the act, thereby finding the maximum piecework items possible of production by the normal worker. With this as a standard the wage per piece is computed, so that the average worker, moving without a single useless act and not affected by fatigue might make let us say, $1.20 per hour. Allowing for fatigue, however, the fast worker may seldom average over $1.00 per hour, while the slower men and women scale down accordingly. To illustrate how the method operates, let us consider the writer's signature given below. The average time required for changing

George W. Crane

the direction of the wrist movement is placed at approximately 0.00175 minutes. To find out how many signatures I can make per minute exactly like the one above, it is necessary to count the number of changes in direction of the wrist activity during the writing process, keeping in mind dots and movements down to the line below when beginning subsequent signatures. Assuming sixty such wrist changes at 0.00175 minutes per change, we find that it takes me 0.105 minutes to make my signature once. Dividing one minute by 0.105, we find that I can repeat the signature above only 9.5 times per minute. Actually, when time is called, I have nine full signatures completed, and am just writing the capital "C" on my tenth. I note, however, that

I have slurred my writing slightly in speeding; so that I have eliminated a few wrist movements originally employed in the signature above.

If I were being hired to write my signature, therefore, the basis of the piecework rate would be made on 9.5 signatures per minute. Fatigue would soon affect me, thereby reducing my output, and causing me to fall below the maximum wage.

A conclusion of this section devoted to efficiency engineering should emphasize the fact that efficiency is increased with the elimination of extra movements or thought processes entailed by the given task. The adjustment of the machine to the man, or a new course of instruction may be necessary in this process. Individualization, standardization, and specialization are the three principal ways of improving production by the adjustment of the worker to the machine. The importance of morale is significant, but will be deferred till a later point in the book.

The Effect of Drugs and Stimulants on Efficiency. Drugs of some sort have been a portion of man's chemical environment as long as history records. Alcoholic beverages may have been first, followed by narcotics; then, later, tea, coffee, and tobacco. We shall discuss them in the general chronological order of their use by mankind.

(1) *Alcohol.* Dodge and Benedict[1] have made one of the most exhaustive and controlled experiments of the influence of alcohol on the behavior reactions of man that we have on record. Contrary to the popular opinion, they found alcohol to be a depressant in all respects except the pulse, and even here there was no absolute increase. The pulse simply did not decrease gradually in the course of moderate physical and mental labor, as is true of the non-alcoholized subject. There was an increase in the latent time of the knee jerk and other re-

[1] Dodge, R., and Benedict, F. C., *Psychological Effects of Alcohol,* (Carnegie Institution of Washington, D. C., 1915).

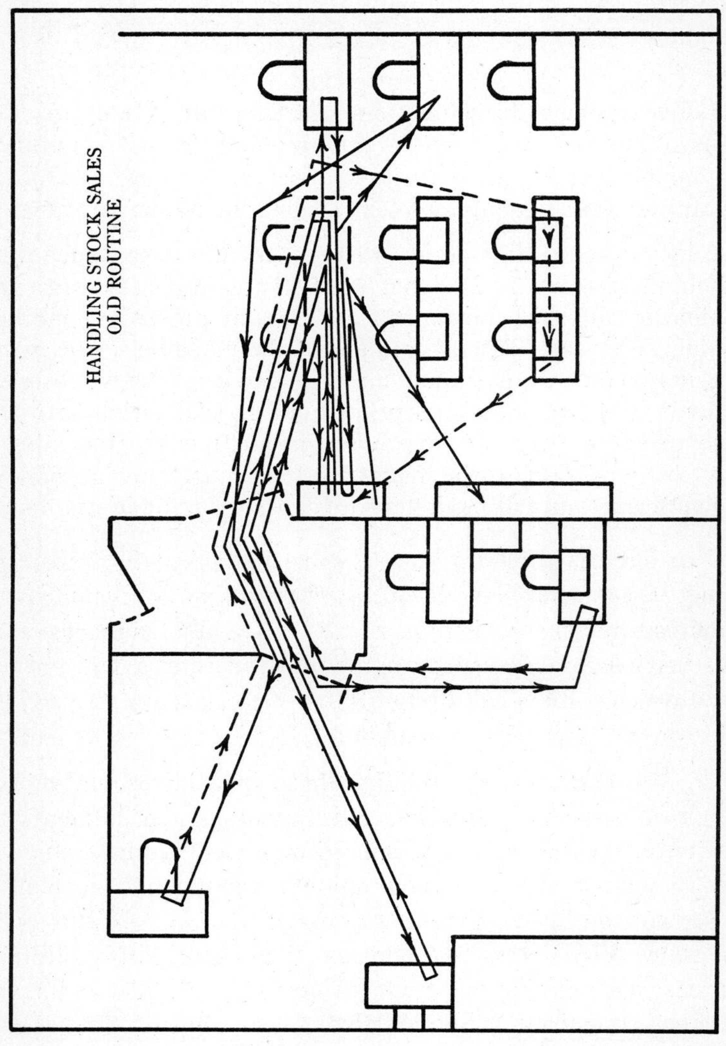

Exhibit 17. An inefficient routing of work which has been much simplified in the next chart. (Courtesy of William J. Gyles).

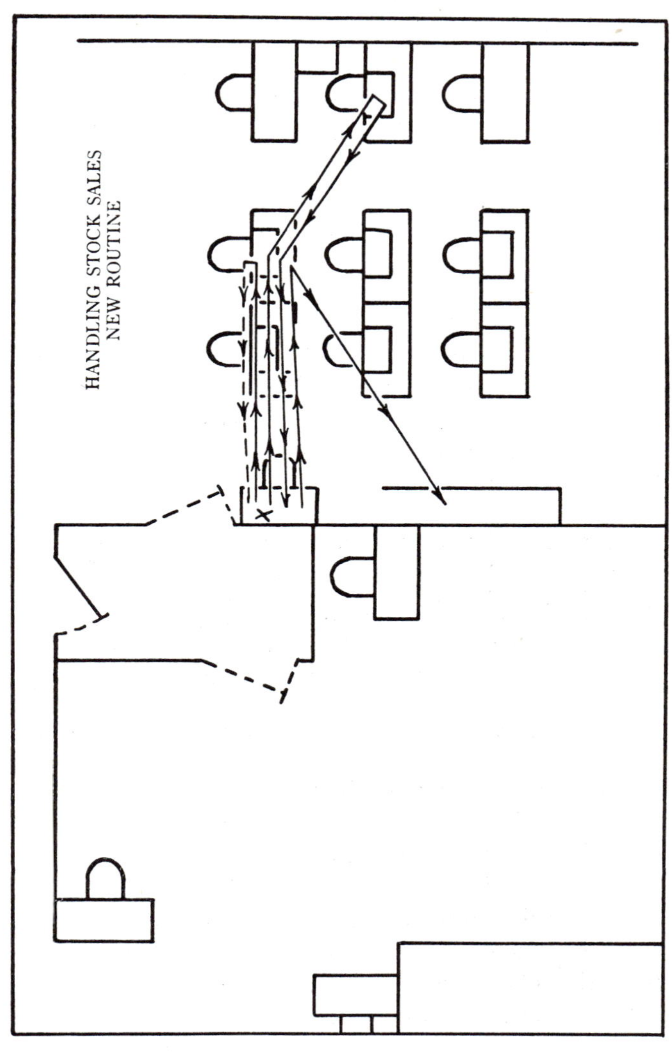
HANDLING STOCK SALES
NEW ROUTINE

flexes. The change, converted into per cent, is tabulated in the accompanying table from Poffenberger.[1]

	Per Cent
Increase of latent time of the knee jerk	10
Decrease in thickening of the quadriceps muscle	46
Protective eyelid reflex, latent time increased	7
Extent of eyelid movement decreased	19
Eye reactions, latent time increased	5
Speed of eye movements decreased	11
Sensitivity to electric stimulation decreased	14
Speed of finger movements (tapping) decreased	9

EXHIBIT 18. The effect of alcohol on simple motor activities.

One of the observations true of alcohol as well as of most other drugs is the fact that individuals vary greatly in their responses to such stimuli. The words of Cushny[2] probably delineate the common varieties of response that have been observed by the reader:

> One person is rendered sentimental, another bellicose, while in a third there may be no appearance of excitement, the first distinct symptom being profound slumber. When drinking is indulged in in company, the excitement stage is a very common phenomenon, but if alcohol is taken without the exhilarating accompaniments of bright lights and exciting companionship, it is much less frequently seen, and the question has therefore arisen how far the environment produces the excitement in alcoholic intoxication.

The reasons for the use of alcohol are quite numerous. One takes it because he has had it in his home constantly, and it has been a habit since childhood. Another indulges because he wants to escape from a painful, humiliating, or monotonous environment, and, lacking a rich imagination by which he could have fled the present, he deadens himself to reality. The dope fiend is of this class, too. A third, who is rather timorous and shy, takes it so that he can escape these inhibitions and appear

[1] Poffenberger, A. T., *op. cit.*, p. 243.

[2] Cushny, A. R., *Pharmacology, 9th Edition* (Lea and Febiger Co., Philadelphia, 1928), p. 186.

nonchalant as he makes his public speech, sales talk, or other normal appearance. A fourth indulges to set an example for his customer or companion so that the latter will be more amenable to his business or erotic desires.

Chronic alcoholics demonstrate a peculiar form of behavior known as delirium tremens, in which there are fantastic visual and tactual hallucinations. At the height of his excitement, the patient may imagine himself covered with insects or snakes, and he is constantly endeavoring to brush them off. If an interne attempts to take a blood sample, the patient shrieks, belabors the doctor, and calls him a vampire who is draining his blood vessels dry.

Because there are more feeble-minded among the alcoholics than in the general population, the opinion has grown that alcohol is conducive to feeble-mindedness. Although there is general agreement among investigators that alcohol reduces mental efficiency in the individual consuming it, we have no data to prove that it affects the germinal cells, and becomes transmissible in its effects. Perhaps a more logical explanation of the prevalence of feeble-mindedness in the alcohol group is the fact that those of subnormal mentality are more inclined to alcoholic indulgence and excess.

(2) *Opium.* This drug has a soporific effect which lasts during the early stages for the duration of the night. Vivid dreams and hallucinations are the rule, during which the patient usually revels in imaginary situations of great pleasure and beauty. Following this dream stage, the subject drops into a deep, dreamless slumber. Because of the pleasant revels through which the patient has passed, the waking world appears more drab by contrast, and it isn't long until he craves the excitement of his former dream state. Like the alcoholic, the addict is probably inclined to inferiority complexes which prevent his realizing his joys in real life; so he is psychologically disposed to a resumption of his tryst with his gorgeous-

hued Morpheus. Ultimately, the addict becomes reduced to a chaotic condition mentally, physically, and morally. He takes little nourishment and finally dies of malnutrition. Morphine differs from cocaine in that the latter is a stimulant, deferring the onset of fatigue, but a depression ultimately follows. The cocaine habit leads to even greater moral degradation, and the chance of breaking the habit is even less than the morphine habit.

(3) *Caffeine.* This is the active principle of tea and coffee. In the average cup of coffee with milk there are about 2.5 grains of this drug, and a cup of black tea contains about 1.5 grains. Because of the fact that persons develop headaches when deprived of their accustomed caffeine beverages, the drug is considered to be in the class of mild habit forming substances. The results of Rivers'[1] careful experiments in which he excluded the influence of suggestion, show a small stimulation value for caffeine, producing an increase in muscular work.

There is no question but that caffeine excites the subject who has not developed a tolerance for it. It seems to enhance the nervous condition of such an individual, rendering him sleepless. There seem to be no deleterious effects, however, if an individual does not imbibe directly before retiring. Its chief drawback is the fact that it robs individuals of a few hours of necessary slumber if taken late at night. The effect is subject considerably to the degree of tolerance of the individual in question.

(4) *Tobacco.* This substance with its effect on mental actions has been argued pro and con. Investigators have cited the fact that the non-smokers make the highest scholastic grades. Although the effect of tobacco may be a causative factor in these cases, there is also the possibility that the smoker is inclined to be more sociable than the non-smoker, and this

[1] Rivers, W. H. R., "The Influence of Alcohol and Other Drugs on Fatigue" (Arnold, London, 1908).

greater fraternal tendency may be the more basic explanation for the difference in school attainment of the two.

Probably the most thoroughly controlled investigation of the effects of tobacco smoking was made by Hull.[1] His conclusions follow:

> In a final review of the various effects of tobacco enumerated above, it will be noted that only three of the twelve forms of behavior investigated reveal an unmistakable influence of smoking. Two of these (pulse and tremor) are essentially physiological. The interest of the present investigation, on the other hand, is primarily in the more strictly psychological processes. Of these, only one (Addition) shows an unmistakable effect. Several others show effects with a fair degree of reliability, however, and are entitled to consideration. Probably the two most significant tests of this intellectual group as revealing the influence of smoking on mental efficiency, are Complex Mental Addition and Rote Learning. The first, together with Reaction Time, may be presumed to give some indication of the effects of smoking upon ordinary routine thinking, which is essentially the functioning of old associative bonds. The evidence in this case is favorable to tobacco where the subject is accustomed to its use. Rote Learning, on the other hand, possibly supported by Memory Span, presumably indicates the effect that tobacco is likely to have where new associative bonds are in the process of formation, as in most school learning. The results in this case, while not so reliable, are unfavorable to tobacco. It must be remembered, of course, that the above formulations apply with strictness only to the first hour and a half after the termination of smoking. Generalizations from them must be made with extreme caution.

In summarizing the effects of drugs and stimulants on human efficiency, we can state that the general tendency of those herein described is unfavorable, although there are many, including caffeine and various medicines not treated in this chapter, which may be beneficial. Moreover, a number of drugs which have marked medicinal value or act as aids in relieving pain, may be detrimental if applied in large quantities or habitually taken. Tolerance to a drug is also of considerable im-

[1] Hull, C. L., "The Influence of Tobacco Smoking on Mental and Motor-Efficiency", *Psychological Monographs*, vol. xxxiii (1924), No. 150.

portance in measuring its influence upon human efficiency. Narcotics are generally harmful, especially because of their habit-forming nature. Alcohol is less detrimental, while tobacco is probably the least injurious of the three.

The Effect of Climate and Ventilation on Efficiency. A study of the historical records of races whose habitats range from the tropics to the polar regions indicates that a moderate temperature environment and rainfall have been most conducive to progress. Physical and physiological causes underly this result. In the first place, the tropical heat is so great that physical exertion must be held to a minimum in order to keep the normal blood temperature at 98.6° Fahrenheit. Muscular exercise produces heat, and a body surrounded by external heat cannot endure too much internal combustion without showing pathological effects. Sluggishness is nature's way of protecting her children in such a situation.

The physical environment in the tropics has also conspired against civilization's advance. Because food was so easily procurable, the inhabitants found little necessity to labor and devise means of insuring a steady diet year in and year out. Clothing problems consisted chiefly in protection from insects instead of cold. In our chapter on learning we mentioned that maladjustment leads to the acquisition of new habits and progress mentally. The tropical native was fairly well adjusted from birth till death, so he lacked the goads that drove his northern neighbors.

In the polar regions, on the contrary, men were so much concerned with the struggle for physical existence that they had little time free to think of anything else. They were frequently maladjusted, but the range of situations to which they were maladjusted was very limited. They procured food from roving animals or the sea. If the animals were present, their crude weapons were adequate to procure a supply of provision. If the animals weren't present, to their primitive mental condition the situation was incapable of solution. Even a highly civilized chemist would be relatively helpless in the same circumstances. One cannot make proteins out of ice and snow.

In the temperate zones we find a climate that shows a change of seasons which are mentally stimulating, and a variety of temperatures which present varying problems to the inhabitants. Nature is therefore much more stimulating. Maladjustments are numerous but not insoluble. Aggressiveness and productivity are at the maximum in those races whose habitats show average temperatures ranging from 50° to 70° F. Changing emotional states also seem to be engendered by the seasons, as is evident from their standardized portrayal in pantomine. Spring is, moreover, the time of mating among animals, and apparently influences the thoughts of men in a similar fashion, since June is the favorite marriage month.

Ventilation seldom presents important considerations for the average individual since homes, apartments, offices, and factories have now been regulated to give a standard air content per occupant, and an appreciation of ventilation technique has become commonplace. In the description of the tragic drama enacted in the Black Hole[1] of Calcutta, however, we see clearly the necessity for an adequate ventilating system. Had these men been incarcerated at a temperature of 32° F. most of them would probably have been alive the next morning, for the two windows, even though small, would probably have supplied enough oxygen. Need of coolness, which is one of the great benefits of the moving air in well ventilated buildings, was the basic cause of a large percentage of the deaths described below.

One of the hottest of the hot nights of British India, a little more than one hundred and fifty years ago, Siraj-Uddaula, a youthful merciless ruler of Bengal, caused to be confined within a small cell in Fort William one hundred and forty-six Englishmen whom he had that day captured in a siege of the city of Calcutta. The room was large enough to house comfortably but two persons. Its heavy door

[1] Lee, F. S., "Fresh Air," *Popular Science Monthly*, vol. LXXXIV (1914), pp. 313 *ff*.

> was bolted; its walls were pierced by two windows barred with iron, through which little air could enter. The night slowly passed away, and with the advent of the morning death had come to all but a score of the luckless company. A survivor has left an account of the horrible happenings within the dungeon, of terrible strugglings of a steaming mass of sentient human bodies for the insufficient air. Within a few minutes after entrance every man was bathed in a wet perspiration and was searching for ways to escape from the stifling heat. Clothing was soon stripped off. Breathing became difficult. There were vain onslaughts on the windows; there were vain efforts to force the door. Thirst grew intolerable, and there were ravings for the water which the guards passed in between the bars, not from feelings of mercy but only to witness in ghoulish glee the added struggles for impossible relief. Ungovernable confusion and turmoil and riot soon reigned. Men became delirious . . . All efforts for relief were vain until at last bodily and mental agony was followed by stupor.

As soon as the moisture in the atmosphere becomes so great that evaporation from the skin and lungs is reduced, we begin to grow uncomfortable. The body has difficulty keeping its temperature from rising above the normal 98.6° F. This situation explains our discomfort on humid, sultry days when the perspiration remains on the skin without quickly evaporating. The reverse of this situation may also be true. A story has come down to us that at a certain festivity in Europe a young boy was entirely covered with gold leaf. Inside of fifteen minutes he was dead. His temperature probably dropped rapidly through increased heat radiation from his skin.

In summarizing the effects of climate and ventilation on efficiency, the keynote to our discussion lies in the fact that for human beings the healthful bodily temperature averages 98.6° Fahrenheit. Climates which make it difficult for the human being to keep his temperature at that point are detrimental to his mental progress. Hot temperatures produce partial inertia of body and mind as a safeguard against too much internal combustion, while frigid climates consume most of the person's available energy in preventing the bodily temperature from becoming lowered. The chief value of well ventilated buildings, moreover, lies in the better circulation of air with the resulting increased evaporation from the skin of the occupants. The oxygen and carbon dioxide contents of the room seldom vary enough to be a significant problem.

The Effect of Illumination and Posture on Efficiency. The most efficient lighting system is the indirect. There are several adequate reasons therefor. In the first place, indirect lighting gives a more uniform distribution over the room, pages, or work immediately before the subject. As a result, there is less tendency for the eyes to turn toward the contrast points. The native inclination of the eye to focus upon sources of light, is a second reason why direct lighting is objectionable. If one is reading, sewing or working at his desk or bench, and a low hanging light, or bridge lamp is anywhere in the field of vision, the eyes tend to turn toward the light. In order to offset this inclination, the reader must expend more energy through the contrary muscles of the eyeball. Obviously inefficiency results with additional eyestrain. Astigmatism demonstrates much the same strain upon the muscles of the eyeball that we find operative in a field unevenly illuminated, for the lens has lost its uniform curvature. Some images upon the retina are clear, while others are blurred. The eye keeps adjusting in an effort to produce uniform clarity in the fovea, and eyestrain ensues.

Habit also explains some of the inefficiency in direct lighting. We are accustomed to seeing objects in contradistinction to space, so the eye tends to focus upon the tree or house or man, instead of upon the horizon behind. Black print on white paper is superior to white print on black backgrounds, for in the latter instance we tend to regard the white spaces as the customary light horizon showing through; so we try to focus upon the black regions, as in Exhibit 19.

The great number of shadows in the field of vision under

EXHIBIT 19. Showing the difference between black and white print on the opposite background.

direct lighting, therefore, tend to operate as objects and offer counter attraction to the stimulus of the page or task at hand. Eye shades are accordingly helpful when working under direct lighting, but the under side should be covered with a light strip of paper so that the contrast between it and the environment is not so great as to call attention to the shade itself. A dark eye shade offers constant stimulation to the eye to turn and focus upon it. Individuals who wear glasses should also be careful to avoid lights and windows which reflect against the inner side of the lenses of their spectacles. This is a source of distraction seldom considered, but it can greatly increase visual fatigue.

The different fatigue effects of various colored lights is expressed in the following Exhibit 20, taken from Ferree and Rand's[1] experiments. It demonstrates the fact that the red end of the spectrum seems more efficient regarding acuity than the green, with blue running close to green, but slightly lower.

In measuring the fatigue effects of motion pictures, the

[1] Ferree, C. E. and Rand, G., "Some Experiments on the Eye with Different Illuminants, Part II," *Transactions of the Illuminating Engineering Society* (April 30, 1919), No. 3.

	PER CENT LOSS OF EFFICIENCY	FEELINGS OF DISCOMFORT APPEARED AFTER SECONDS
Unsaturated yellow	5.43	116
Reddish yellow—more saturated	7.57	94
Unsaturated yellow, with trace of red	8.29	90
Orange-yellow	8.39	90
Unsaturated yellow, with trace of green	8.48	90
Unsaturated yellow, with more green	24.00	48
Unsaturated yellowish-green	25.51	34
Unsaturated yellowish-green, with more green	33.14	25
Greenish	39.14	21
Bluish-green	54.86	14

EXHIBIT 20. Efficiency of colored lights.

same investigators, using relative scores in accurate visual perception on tests made immediately prior to, and immediately following the moving picture situation, found that there was a considerable loss of efficiency, but the loss seems to be about the same as that suffered by one who reads clear print for an equal length of time under ordinary artificial illumination. They found, moreover, that the distance from the screen had some influence on the degree of the fatigue. When the subject sat a distance of 25 feet from the screen his loss of visual efficiency was 50 per cent; at a distance of 48 feet it was approximately 40 per cent, and at a distance of 71 feet it was about 30 per cent.

The intensity of light is of less significance than its uniformity over the visual field, for the eye can make remarkable adjustments to brilliant or to faint illumination. Coming from sunlight into an artificially lighted room, the individual shifts from an intensity of approximately 10,000-foot candles of light to about 5-foot candles. Shiny objects, therefore, such as the keys of a typewriter and polished metal work on various objects in the room, reduce visual efficiency. It would be an economical move in this regard if our books were all printed on pulp or non-glossy paper and if dull finishes were given to woodwork and metal ornaments.

The matter of posture is one of the factors by which Gilbreth[1] introduced efficiency into many of the factories which he investigated. The secret of postural change simply involves reducing the number of muscles or the number of moves involved in work. In one case, for instance, a 50 per cent increase in output was effected with girls who were sorting and filing cards, by a slight change in the height and slope of their work table. The larger the muscle employed or the more muscles utilized in an act, the greater will be the fatigue resulting from the performance of a given task. If an individual who works standing must bend over frequently, it is evident that the fatigue will be much greater than if his work is raised so that all his adjustments can be carried on without bending at the waist.

Another important consideration appropriate here is the fact that frequent periods of relaxation should be introduced. These may be brought about by occasional recesses in which the worker or student changes posture, thus relieving the strain on the set of working muscles. In the crawl stroke it is essential that the swimmer relax his arm as much as possible as he brings it over head for the down thrust, otherwise he fatigues much more quickly. Nervousness and excitement are fatiguing because the tonicity of the muscles is increased, thus producing a more rapid development of fatigue products. The worker who is contented doesn't consume as much energy as the fearful or discontented employee, and therefore he doesn't fatigue as quickly.

The effects of illumination and posture on efficiency, therefore, are explicable on the basis of the additional movements which are eliminated when the lighting is made uniform and

[1] Gilbreth, F. B., *Fatigue Study* (New York, 1916).

indirect, and when the work bench is raised or lowered to meet the individual needs of the employees. Shadows and dark objects in the field of vision tempt the eyes to turn toward them. In order to avoid doing so, the worker must expend more energy on the opposing muscles of the eyes. The value of frequent changes of posture to avoid undue fatigue of any one set of muscles has long been appreciated in the public schools as well as in the industrial world. In recent years the understanding that a change in posture might lessen the number or size of the muscles necessary to the performance of an act has led to marked improvement in efficiency.

The Effect of Diet on Efficiency. Physiologically we are really living on the river banks of our blood vessels. The cargos which float past the colonies of cells may produce health or death. Except for the air intake by way of the lungs, we are dependent on the food intake of the mouth for our imports, and these imports are essential for existence. We know that certain drugs will quickly alter our behavior, as opium, alcohol, anaesthetics, strychnine, and bichloride of mercury. And we know that other drugs (foods) produce strength and alertness. But it has been only recently that we have appreciated the significance of such things as vitamins. Even now we don't know the chemical formulae for all the vitamins, nor just why they affect the human organism as they do, but we have gradually narrowed the field until we have cornered them in their "dens" and know they hide in lettuce, butter, cod liver oil, and many other foods.

In the Philippine Islands and adjacent countries the most energetic and alert natives often slip into a depressed and languid mental condition which leads to paralysis and death. The sailors in the Japanese Navy used to succumb in great numbers to this strange malady. It is known as beriberi, and apparently results simply from the fact that the victims have lived on an unbalanced diet of polished rice. We now know that the husk of the rice grain contains chemicals which will prevent this nervous disease.

Since the presence or absence of minute quantities of certain powerful chemicals will produce life or death, it is not surprising, therefore, that the presence or absence of certain unknown chemicals over long periods of time, as in our food, should exercise alterative effects on our behavior. Perhaps glandular deficiencies in our bodies are owing partly to improper diet over long periods of time. This field of research is one of the most promising which has ever been opened to the physician and the psychologist. In diabetes, for example, we know that clusters of cells in the human pancreas called islands of Langerhans seem to have gone on strike. We can examine these colonies of cells on a histological slide, and we can by insulin apparently inject into the blood stream of the patient the same chemical produced by the Langerhans cells. But we cannot prevail on the million[1] or more colonies of cells to call off their strike. As long as the patient lives we have to inject the substance which these idle cells should be producing. In short, we don't act upon the islands of Langerhans with insulin and set them into functional activity once more, but we give the system the product of those cells. Why the cells went on strike in the first place we do not know. One of these days we may be able to administer a drug which will make them start activity again. It is conceivable that a dietary lack of some particular chemical may have aided in their stopping work.

From the psychological viewpoint, therefore, the diet to which an individual has been accustomed for long periods of years may hold the key to a part of the premature aging which we note in some men and women. The action of the ductless glands is still one of the new fields for medical and psychological study. The interrelationship of internal secretion and the action of external chemicals in the food which we eat may be found to have an important bearing upon much of the beha-

[1] Maximow, A. A., *Textbook of Histology* (Philadelphia, 1930), p. 559.

vior of an individual. Beriberi, rickets, scurvy, and numerous other ailments which reduce the efficiency of the individual are already known to be the result of dietary deficiencies in respect to some necessary food chemical.

The Effect of Noise and Distraction on Efficiency. The introduction of noise while subjects are working produces at first a slowing down of output. If the noise is continuous and not too intense, there follows an apparent increase in the speed of output of the workers. The explanation for the change is supposed to lie in the fact that the worker actively attempts to focus his attention more closely on the work in order to disregard the disturbance, and so he keeps up his accustomed output, but at a greater expense of effort.

The general effect of distractions of all sorts is to introduce additional muscular activity for the continued performance of the given task. Accordingly, distraction is a source of inefficiency. We have pointed out the visual distractions and their reasons for being detrimental to human productivity, as well as such psychological distractions as fear, whether it be of a dangerous machine, loss of a job, or the leaving of dependents unprotected by insurance.

The influence of distraction is, of course, more apparent in tasks which have not been reduced to routine performance. When workers are attacking problems involving a certain number of new adjustments, the presence of disturbing stimuli is more inimical to output than in the habitual manual processes. Every motorist, for instance, has felt the difference in tenseness of musculature when driving an automobile through the city, and when speeding along the country highways. Even when driving in the city, one can carry on a conversation until a traffic jam occurs or a difficult street crossing is passed. Who has not then found that he could not speak and drive simultaneously in a critical situation and so has left a sentence hanging in the middle, only to complete it a block farther down the boulevard?

Let us arbitrarily represent the total attention of an individual as 100 per cent. Distractions, as the feel of one's clothing and shoes, the temperature and vague auditory, olfactory, and other stimuli, pull some of this maximum attention total away so that we can probably muster no more than 70 per cent of our potential attention in our normal waking state, although under hypnosis we can materially increase this percentage. If it requires a minimum of 40 per cent for casual conversation and 30 per cent for driving our automobile, we can simultaneously do both. But when a critical spot appears in the driving situation, demanding perhaps 50 per cent of our controllable attention, the remaining 20 per cent is insufficient for conversation; hence, we stop that activity for the moment, and resume it only when a simpler driving condition frees at least 20 per cent of our attention for a return to speech.

Monotony is another of the important factors reducing efficiency. To be happy in a job the worker must meet enough demands on his intelligence to keep the bulk of his attention occupied. As soon as his task becomes so routine that he has considerable attention free, he begins to grow bored. The task is monotonous, irksome. He dislikes it, and dislike is similar to fear in its influence upon fatigue. In his imagination he may be able to avoid the monotony by spending time in daydreams of a pleasanter world. Some of our large factories have introduced phonograph music as a means of preventing the onset of monotony in mechanical jobs. But, lacking such escapes from the boredom of the routine task, the worker finds himself confronted day after day with the same old thing. His work has lost novelty and interest. He has to force himself to attend to those aspects of it which do demand more than habitual attention, and this forcing is comparable to the behavior of the person who forces himself to a task when noise or visual objects are constantly tempting him away.

In summarizing the effects of noise and distraction on efficiency, we can repeat that noise reduces efficiency as measured in the energy consumption of the worker even though it may occasionally show no detrimental effect upon output. Intermittent noises, however, are much more disastrous than fairly regular ones, since the worker becomes somewhat adapted to the latter. Distractions of any sort cause the ulitization of more muscles or more energy than would otherwise be necessary; hence, they produce inefficiency as judged by the energy consumption of the worker.

The Effect of Sleep on Efficiency. The individual who has lived to the age of sixty years has spent twenty years in sleep. The temporal importance of sleep is, accordingly, quite large. Sleep has also definite physiological significance, for it is during this state that the effects of fatigue are eliminated. Our body goes on a semi-vacation for eight hours each day. We refrain from active mental and physical endeavor. Whether or not we demand eight or nine hours of sleep depends both on the amount of energy we have expended the previous day, as well as upon habit. Some individuals, like Edison and Napoleon, seem to be able to get along on half the sleep which others require. It is possible that excessive visual work with its strain upon the visual apparatus may be a factor in determining the length of sleep required. Mosso found that overfatiguing a muscle resulted in a disproportionate amount of time necessary for recovery.

Likewise, persons of a nervous disposition consume more energy than the more phlegmatic persons, and hence we see a possible logical reason for a difference in sleeping time demanded by the two. In physical exercise, moreover, persons seem to be able to get along with less sleep than under severe mental strain.

In 1925, Moss and seven associates went without sleep for a period of sixty hours, taking various mental and physical tests during the interim. Analyses of the blood and urine of the subjects then gave indications of the same conditions as are present in a mild infection, but the conditions returned to normal after a single night's sleep. The blood pressure and strength both decreased during the period of the test, and the visual and auditory apparatus reacted less sensitively. On mental tests these subjects did as well after as before the experience. The power of sustained attention after sleepless periods of long duration seems to be affected somewhat adversely, even though tasks of short duration can be effectively accomplished.

That sleep is a chemical phenomenon seems fairly well established. The blood of a fatigued dog has been transfused into the veins of a fresh animal, and shortly thereafter all the signs of fatigue have been observed in the fresh animal. The toxins of our waking metabolism are eliminated in the sleeping process. The depth of sleep is represented in Exhibit 21 taken from Kohlschutter who used the sound made by a falling ball dropped from different heights as an index of the soundness of slumber. According to his results, sleep is most profound at the end of the first hour, and by the conclusion of the third hour the sleeper can be awakened by a very light sound. If there is any relationship between the depth of sleep and the degree of detoxication going on, we might infer that three hours of sleep would be sufficient, or at least that it would be wiser to split up a six hours' slumber into two naps of three hours apiece.

The psychological onset of sleep must not be ignored. Traveling salesmen frequently kill time while riding between stops by sleeping. Incidentally, this is one of the theories for the onset of slumber. The caveman couldn't see after night, so, like the hen, he ceased activity, and found it pleasanter to endure the monotonous night in an unconscious condition. Students frequently find themselves intolerably drowsy when confronted by a difficult and uninteresting lesson, but their fatigue seems to vanish quite often when some one suggests a movie. In a similar manner the householder finds that he re-

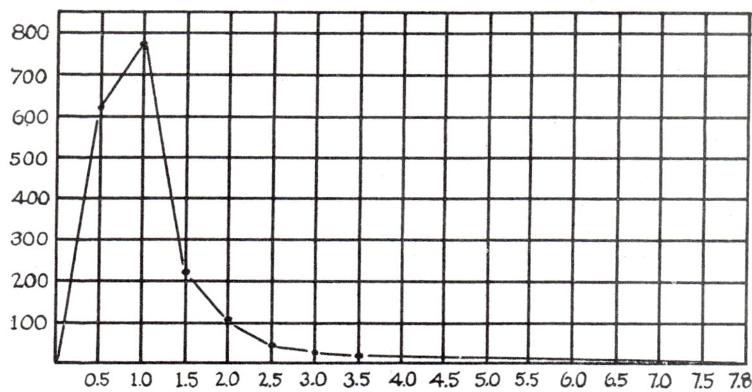

EXHIBIT 21. Curve showing depth of sleep as measured by the intensity of sound necessary to waken the sleeper. (After Kohlschutter).

sists the waking stimulus of his wife's insistent calls much more strongly when they mean that a rug is to be beaten, or the car washed. Sleep is readily conditioned by darkness. Even in the middle of the morning when they should be quite refreshed, medical students will fall sound asleep during a lantern slide lecture, despite an interesting presentation of the subject matter by the lecturer of the day. The darkness has conditioned a sleep response in much the fashion of the tinkling wind chime's sound and the thirst response. Similarly, the presence of a bed or couch in the study room is a constant sleep suggestion, and renders study much more difficult.

The general effect of sleep upon efficiency, therefore, is beneficial, for it is during slumber that the detoxication process goes on most advantageously. Sleep is a chemical phenomenon, although it can be conditioned by darkness, boredom, monotony, and the hypnotist. Its greatest depth at the end of the first hour with a very light sleep after the third hour, coupled with Edison's apparent ability to get along successfully on three to five hours of sleep per night, give rise to the thought that we might be able to reduce our sleeping time by several hours.

The Influence of Age on Efficiency. There are five age distinctions commonly recognized in science today, on the basis of which human beings can be classified. We shall list them in the following order:

(1) *Chronological Age.* This is the age determined by an individual's birth certificate, and has been the most frequent basis for age classification purposes. Our laws state that citizens must attain the age of 21 years before they are eligible to vote; they must start to school at 6 and may leave it at 16; under 5 they ride free on public carriers, and at half rates from then till 12; at 25 they may become United States Representatives; at 30 Senators, and at 35 they are eligible to reside in the White House.

(2) *Physical Age.* This is best represented in the case of girls and boys before puberty. At the age of ten years, for example, girls are physically more mature than boys, as measured by bone development, a fact which probably explains why boys' medians on intelligence tests lag behind those of girls until the middle of puberty. Even in the case of individuals of the same sex, however, all sorts of variations may occur. One man at the age of 60 is no older physically than another at the age of 40. Indeed, this variation is also found in the age of onset of puberty, which some girls reach at 10 while others do not enter until 16.

(3) *Mental Age.* This is becoming increasingly important in modern times as a means of classification of school children. It is ascertained by comparing the intellectual capacity of an individual with that possessed by average children of different chronological ages. Thus, a child aged 6 might have the mental age of normal children aged 9. This would clearly make the youngster very superior. On the other hand, at the age of 6 he might possess the mental age of normal children of 3, in

which case he would be a low grade moron. The mental age of an individual tells us little, however, until we know his chronological age, for we might have a grown man with a mental age of 8, or a grammar school boy with a mental age of 18. To express the ratio between mental age and chronological age Terman prefers the Intelligence Quotient. The I. Q. equals the mental age divided by the chronological age. For adults the chronological age is taken as 16. In the first example of the child aged 6 with a mental age of 9, the I. Q. would be 1.50; while in the second example he would have an I. Q. of 0.50. Intelligence Quotients are commonly employed without using the decimal point, the two above being stated simply as 150 and 50, respectively. There is no reason why we shouldn't also devise a Physical Quotient (P. Q.) for boys and girls, as well as men and women. It would be of more scientific value than the chronological age, and should be employed in numerous situations. The physical age would be a more accurate denominator in computing the I. Q. than is the present chronological age.

(4) *Educational Age.* This refers to the schooling level attained by the child, and is roughly employed by saying that an individual is a grammar school, high school or college graduate. If poverty and lack of educational opportunities were not involved, children of high I. Q. would of course possess the high educational attainments, but frequently men and women of brilliant intellects are met who have had little contact with the school system. A man might have a high mental age with a low educational age, but the converse is not possible.

(5) *Emotional Age.* Some of the brilliant young criminals of the past decade demonstrate cases of emotional retardation co-existent with high mental age. The emotions are closely bound up with the glandular development and functioning of the body, although training and experience also are factors. Some women at the age of 25, for example, have undergone

the gamut of passions, having experienced love and marriage twice or even thrice, with children by two or three husbands, with deaths of offspring and loved ones, or with divorce, ostracism and shame. Others reach old age with only a puppy love affair to upset the smooth course of their emotional lives, and with no social or family crises to mar the even tenor of their careers.

Prior to puberty children go through a "gang" stage in their development, when they are concerned primarily with their own sex. As they slip into puberty one after another of the gang members deserts the ranks for the greater attraction of some one of the opposite sex, until only a few of the die-hards remain to console each other for the dereliction of the majority from those sacred tenets signed in blood. This period is critical in the emotional development of the individual. If he leaves the attractions of his own sex for those of the opposite sex, his homosexual tendencies become submerged in heterosexual attachments.

The home, school, and social environments tend to prepare the child for this transition, for all around him he sees the father and mother and husband and wife matings. He expects ultimately to have a wife, or the little girl takes it as a matter of course that she will have a husband. With this heterosexual conditioning antedating puberty by a dozen years, it is quite natural to expect the majority of youngsters to encounter no stoppage in their emotional growth.

But some become unduly attached to their own sex, especially if surrounded by their own kind exclusively during the early pubertal years. Schoolgirl "crushes" are frequent, and represent simply the maturation of the sexual instinct. Some of these crushes, however, continue into adult life. The subjects are checked in their normal emotional development, and retain a more puerile emotional state throughout adulthood.

Others seem to be endowed with hypofunctioning glands, and never feel the wealth of emotional experiences which their more normal associates undergo. They may be emotionally passive and cold. On the other hand, hyperactivity of certain glands, such as the thyroid, leads to excessive excitability and emotionalism. The intimate relationship between the glands and personality is given rather optimistically by Berman[1]. Eventually we may be able to rate a child in grammar school in this regard, giving him an age "profile". At present our research in the field of emotions is still in its infancy.

The effect of age upon efficiency may be summarized by saying that the synapses are capable of being modified at least until definite senescence begins. With advancing years, however, the energy and emotionality of youth slip away, two factors which are extremely important for learning. Kenagy and Yoakum examined a group of superior salesmen, whose average age was 39. Almost 80 per cent of them fell between the ages of 30 to 50. In respect to mental ailments we know that dementia praecox and manic depressive psychoses usually make their incidence before the age of 35; the bulk of the cases of paresis fall between 35 and 55; while senile dementia seldom is noted prior to the three score mark.

The Relationship of Fatigue and Output. The chemical cause of fatigue is accumulation in the blood of carbon dioxide. This is a product of muscular activity and is exhaled in the lungs. When it is produced faster than it is eliminated it tends to clog the chemical activities of muscle cells; hence we feel tired. But the individual's own judgment of his fatigued condition is not always reliable. Often a person feels tired without having done enough work to warrant any such statement, and again he may say he isn't a bit tired after he has been working steadily for two or three hours. His incentives may markedly alter his sense of fatigue.

Because of the apparent variability of the thing we call fatigue, some have advised omitting the word from our scientific

[1] Berman, L., *The Glands Regulating Personality* (New York, 1921).

terminology, and attempting to obtain a physical or physiological standard by which to measure the actual bodily state after the duration of the working condition. The respiration calorimeter[1] is a device by which the oxygen intake and carbon dioxide outgo are measured and the heat production resulting from muscular activity is determined. By such a device it is possible to determine the energy required for definite units of work, both physical and mental.

Because of the fact that there does not result a perfect correlation between output and expressed fatigue, we cannot use the introspective report of the worker as an absolute index of his real fatigued condition. He confuses interest with physical incapacity for work. He says, "I am tired of this job", meaning that he is bored by it, or dislikes it. Again, he says, "I am tired", and means that he is unable to work at par, at least without undue strain and abnormal incentives.

The "warming up" effect is also noted in mental and physical work. At the outset one feels quickly tired, then a "second wind" seems to arrive and one continues at a comfortable pace for a long period. This second wind has a physiological foundation, and is apparent in the output of factory workers. The typical production curve shows a low output during the first hour, with the maximum reached three or four hours after the beginning of work, and a lower output at the end of the day. Part of this reduced productivity at the two extremes of the working day is due to slowness in getting started, and premature quitting to get washed and ready to leave when the whistle blows. That workers will do as much or more work in eight hours as in the ten hour day is a matter of common knowledge. We tend to strike a congenial pace, which we make faster if we know the course is shorter. The fatigue effects of too long a working day, moreover, may carry over to the next so that the worker becomes progressively more tired.

[1] Bodansky, Meyer, *Introduction to Physiological Chemistry* (New York, 1930), chap. xvi.

In one of the war industries of England, Vernon[1] reports the output in a moderately heavy lathe operation for a period of 93 consecutive weeks. During this period there was no change whatever in the test situation save in the hours of work. After the change from 66.0 to 54.4 actual working hours there was no resultant change in production for a period of about a month. Then a rise in output from the previous figure of 108 kept up for two months until it reached 131. When the actual working time was cut down again to 47.5 hours, there was another period of no effect, followed by a second rise for a period of three months to a new level of output at 169. These data suggest the fact that it is wise in making changes in working schedules to give the new regime at least a three months' trial.

The effect of short rest periods inserted into the working day at frequent intervals has been found decidedly beneficial. The particular number and frequency vary for different occupations and should be determined by watching the production records. As long as the output keeps rising, more rest periods can be introduced. A limit will of course be reached at which the worker will not be able to profit by the warming up phenomenon before he is called off the job for another rest. This of course represents the point of diminishing returns.

In studying the working time of laborers for the Bethlehem Steel Company, Taylor[2] found it advisable to make certain changes. Prior to his changes he found that the average workman loaded 12.5 tons of pig iron daily. The usual procedure was for the men to pick up a pig of 92 pounds weight, carry it up an inclined plank, and deposit it in a railway car. Taylor had work periods interspersed with rest periods which were accurately timed by the foreman. The men all ceased work on signal, and resumed at the foreman's drection. Under this

[1] Vernon, H. M., "The Speed of Adaptation of Output to Altered Hours of Work" (Industrial Fatigue Research Board, London, 1920), No. 6.

[2] Taylor, F. W., *Principles of Scientific Management* (New York, 1915).

plan the men's output increased to 47.5 tons per day, while the men were under load only 42 per cent of the time.

From the standpoint of the psychologist, therefore, fatigue may be psychical or physical. In the former case the worker is tired without a corresponding increase in the toxins in his blood stream. His fatigue is, therefore, not real and may give way quickly to some one's invitation to go to a movie. Another striking phenomenon of fatigue is the apparent fact that it becomes cumulative. The converse of this idea, namely, that energy is also cumulative, was demonstrated in our citation from Vernon, who holds that it may require three months before a group of overworked employees react with increased output to a shortened working week. Short rest periods inserted frequently into the day's schedule are usually conducive to greater production with no apparent increase in the fatigue of the employees.

The Effect of Psychological Factors on Output. We have discussed in previous chapters some of the things that can be utilized here. The motivation by various incentives other than wages or salary is of considerable importance. Honors, promotions in rank, even with little or no money increase, are potent forces in affecting efficiency. After all a satisfied worker, like a satisfied customer, is the ultimate source of financial profit to the factory or mercantile house.

The personnel office by co-operating with the foremen and department heads can render a distinct service by avoiding placing a square peg in a round hole. We shall go into this phase of efficiency improvement at more length in Chapter IX. This task involves the recognition of intelligence levels and job specification. The man of low I. Q. can fulfill many factory functions more successfully than his more intelligent mate, for he will be more contented in them. And the worker's contentment in his niche is one of the aims of personnel administration.

This aspect of industrial improvement is becoming more apparent today than ever before. Psychology formerly was called upon chiefly as an instrument for accelerating production without increasing the overhead. The worker was looked upon too often as simply a cog in the machine. The mechanical aspects of production have now reached a high level of development. The efficiency engineer, although an excellent adjunct of the modern factory, is now sharing honors with the personnel manager. This is as it should be. The two render reciprocal services, and accomplish most by co-operation. All too often in the past the efficient methods of the applied psychologist have been met with resistance by the working man and the trades union. The attitudes of the latter have been that the management was trying to get more work out of the employees at the same wage as before.

The effect of psychological factors on output has become, therefore, an important consideration of the personnel department. A contented worker is usually a fairly efficient worker. Alteration of the machines to fit the needs of the workmen, and attention to lighting, ventilation, and other methods of reducing inefficiency may make the employee's task less fatiguing, but unless his mental attitude is wholesome, these very assets may become liabilities, for the employee will grumble at every innovation, regarding it as another indication of the employer's attempt to get more work out of him. Efficiency engineering, therefore, involves the salesmanship of new ideas and methods to the workers along with the evolution of these same improvements. Some of these psychological factors we shall discuss in later chapters under personnel administration and the development of morale.

REFERENCES

BERMAN, LOUIS, *The Glands Regulating Personality* (New York, 1921).

BILLS, A. G., "Fatigue, Oscillation, and Blocks," *J. Exp. Psychol.*, 1935, vol. 18, 562-573.

BODANSKY, MEYER, *Introduction to Physiological Chemistry* (New York, 1930), chap. xvi.

DAVIDSON, H. P., "A Study of the Confusing Letters, B, D, P, and Q," *J. Genet. Psychol.*, 1935, vol. 47, pp. 458-468.

Dodge, R., and Benedict, F. C., *Psychological Effects of Alcohol* (Carnegie Institution of Washington, D. C., 1915).

Ferree, C. E., and Rand, G., "Some Experiments on the Eye with Different Illuminants, Part II," *Transactions of the Illuminating Engineering Society* (April 30, 1919), No. 3.

Ferree, C. E., & Rand, G., "Care Needed in Lighting," *Person. J.*, 1936, vol. 14, 323-326.

Gilbert, J. G., "Mental Efficiency in Senescence," *Arch. Psychol.*, (New York, 1935), No. 188, p. 60.

Gilbreth, F. B., *Fatigue Study* (New York, 1916).

Heinrich, H. W., *Industrial Accident Prevention* (New York, 1934).

Hoke, Roy E., "The Improvement of Speed and Accuracy in Typewriting," *Johns Hopkins University Studies in Education*, No. 7 (1922).

Hull, C. L., "The Influence of Tobacco Smoking on Mental and Motor Efficiency", *Psychological Monographs*, vol. xxxiii (1924), No. 150.

Husband, R. W., *Applied Psychology* (New York, 1934), chaps. xiii, xiv, xxvi.

Husband, R. W., "The Comparative Value of Continuous Versus Interrupted Sleep," *J. Exp. Psychol.*, 1935, vol. 18, 792-796.

Katz, S. E., and Landis, C., "Psychologic and Physiologic Phenomena During a Prolonged Vigil," *Arch. Neurol. Psychiat.* (Chicago, 1935), vol. 34, pp. 307-317.

Laird, Donald A., *Psychology of Selecting Men* (New York, 1927), chap. xviii.

Link, Henry C., *Employment Psychology* (New York, 1928).

Marks, E. S., "Individual Differences in Work Curves," *Arch. Psychol.*, (New York, 1935), No. 186, pp. 60.

Mateer, F., *Glands and Efficient Behavior* (New York, 1935).

Moore, H., "Diagnosing and Caring for the Reading Difficulties of College Freshmen," *J. Psychol*, 1936, vol. 1, pp. 139-143.

Poffenberger, A. T., *Applied Psychology* (New York, 1927).

Scott, W. D., and Clothier, R. C., *Personnel Management* (Chicago, 1923).

Shen, N., "Simultaneous Lifting of Equally Heavy Weights by Both Right and Left Hands," *J. Exp. Psychol.*, 1935, vol. 18, pp. 792-796.

Stanton, F. N., and Burtt, H. E., "The Influence of Surface and Tint of Paper on the Speed of the Reading," *J. Appl. Psychol.*, 1935, vol. 19, 683-693.

Taylor, F. W., *Principles of Scientific Management* (New York, 1915).

Viteles, M. S., *Industrial Psychology* (New York, 1932).

Wechsler, D., *The Range of Human Capacities* (Baltimore, 1935).

CHAPTER IV

INDIVIDUAL AND SEX DIFFERENCES

Although the members of the human race are so similar that we would never mistake one of them for even the nearest related form of the apes, each member of mankind is likewise distinct from all others. Thus we have difference in similarity. In any given trait, however, we fall within a rather narrow range from the median score. For example, the height of men falls at about 67 inches, plus or minus 7. This means that the bulk of all mankind lie within 7 inches of the middle score. Appreciating such narrow limits of physical variability, the clothing stores and manufacturers can afford to make up millions of suits, dresses, coats, hats and shoes without taking our individual measurements, for they know the proportions of the average American man and woman, and how far the majority deviate therefrom.

The purpose of this chapter is to consider those differences which separate two individuals from each other. We shall, of course, attempt to restrict our examination to matters of practical importance in our business, social, and educational life. One of the most fascinating as well as obvious differences in the human species is that of sex, which we shall consider first. Because of the greater intelligence of *Homo sapiens,* these differences are much more complex than the sex distinctions of any other form of animal life.

Factors Influencing the Determination of Sex. From the beginning of time man has speculated as to the reasons underlying the birth of male and female offspring. Many of them have been quite humorous as viewed in the light of our present superior knowledge of embryology. The physical and sexual vitality of mother and father, their difference in age, the positions occupied during the act of mating, and various magical potions have been used as indices of sex determination at different periods in the past, and even continue into the present generation. The modern scientific view is based on the type of sex chromosomes found in the fertilized ovum. When the secondary spermatocyte cell is formed the usual number of 48 chromosomes is reduced to 24, which is the number found in the spermatozoön. The spermatozoa are of two types, one of which holds 23 ordinary chromosomes plus an "X" sex chromosome (23+X), while the other contains 23 plus a "Y" (23+Y). Every female ovum at the time of fertilization contains 23 ordinary chromosomes plus an "X" sex chromosome (23+X). If the (23+X) spermatozoön unites with the ovum, we have a fertilized egg cell with 46 plus 2 X chromosomes (46+2 X), and this develops into a female. If the other type of spermatozoön reaches the ovum first and fertilizes it, we have a male resulting (46+X+Y). Because the "Y" spermatozoön is thought to be slightly smaller, and therefore more motile, we find a possible explanation for the greater predominance of males over females at birth (106:100).

The above explanation, therefore, would seem to exclude all such factors as the influence of the environment, the time of coitus, and the relative vigor of the two parents. But in lower forms of animal life we find that diet and temperature apparently contribute to sex determination. Feeding Rotifera, minute many-celled aquatic animals, solely upon chlorophyll protozoa results in female offspring only, while a diet devoid of chlorophyll protozoa results in male progeny exclusively. Fatherless female frogs may be produced by mechanical stimulation of the unfertilized eggs. In water of normal temperature, moreover, Witchi has found that fertilized frog eggs hatch into approximately an equal number of male and female offspring, but if the water is kept at 90° F. all the eggs result in males. Of pigeon eggs laid in winter the ratio of males to females in the hatched offspring is 153:100 whereas the summer eggs hatch into males and females in the ratio of 70:100.

Siegel used data procured during the recent World War regarding the time husbands returned home on short furloughs as it related to the onset of menses in their wives and the resulting sex of the children produced. One of his tables of 115 cases, as reported by DeLee[1], is given below. Although the number of cases is too few for generalization it seems to indicate that conceptions occurring from two days prior until nine

PERIOD DURING WHICH CONCEPTION OCCURRED	BOYS BORN	GIRLS BORN
27th day to onset of menses	4	0
1st day of menses to 9th	48	8
10th to the 14th day	10	14
15th to the 23rd day	5	26
24th to the 26th day	0	0

EXHIBIT 22. Showing date of conception as related to menses, with the resultant sex of offspring.

days following the onset of menstruation give rise to a preponderance of males, while the period from the fifteenth day after the onset of the menses to the twenty-third day shows a decided majority of females. The first period is that of the overripe ovum, which Siegel finds gives rise to 86 per cent boys; while the second period is that of the young ovum, which he states shows 84 per cent girls. The human ovum ruptures from the ovary on the twelfth or thirteenth day after the onset of the menses.

From his study of 10,500,000 human births Düsing found that more boys were conceived in winter than in summer,

[1] DeLee, Joseph B., *Principles and Practice of Obstetrics* (W. B. Saunders Co., Philadelphia, 1928), p. 69.

while Ploss discovered that women in high altitudes give birth to more sons than those on the plains. If the chromosome theory is correct, as the present consensus would indicate, then such temporal and environmental factors would seem to alter the reactive behavior of the ovum. An overripe ovum would appear to be more accessible to fertilization by the "Y" spermatozoön, making its chemical composition the ultimate determinant of sex.

Physical Differences Between the Sexes. Aside from the primary sexual characteristics involving the genitalia and their function, we find a number of secondary sexual factors that separate male from female. Men are heavier than women; they are taller than women; their hearts beat slower than women's; they have less fat than women; they are stronger than women not alone in proportion to their greater size but absolutely; their legs are longer; their voices are pitched lower; they have a wider distribution of hair; the development of the breasts is vestigial in men but full in women; and the erogenous areas vary in location, speed and concentration of excitability.

Many, if not all, of the behavior differences of males and females are traceable directly to these physical differences. The greater strength of males explains most of the recreational and vocational differences between the sexes. Apart from early training effects, we would probably find such differences arising again in the race if we were to segregate a group of infants from all adult influences, and let them spontaneously evolve their new civilization. Because the girls as a class would fatigue sooner and be less competent in rough activities, a cleavage would soon appear, and the weaker half of the population would begin to develop games and tasks not only more commensurate with their strength, but also enabling them to compete in a more restricted group where chances of victory would be greatly enhanced. After pregnancy and childbirth, of course, the physical cleavage would be more accentuated, the women being tied to the home site by greater inertia resulting from additional weight, as well as the emotional habits conditioned to the babies.

The lesser strength of women and girls partly explains why they are more suggestible, and also more socially minded. Having been forced to rely on wit rather than brawn to gain their ends in the contacts with their brothers and schoolboy neighbors, they tend to excel in language functions, as we shall discuss later in the chapter. Because they have repeatedly been defeated by boyhood playmates in physical contests, in womanhood they are physically less aggressive, for aggressiveness and confidence are to a considerable extent the result of habitual adaptations to situations that ended in success. Their general superiority in classroom work may, therefore, be an evidence of compensation.

Because they have formed habits of acknowledging masculine physical supremacy, even despite their later educational superiority, the more basic reactions dominate them; so they take orders from men with little resentment or resistance. Women as a class much prefer masculine employers to feminine, while men do not relish working under even intellectually superior women. The immediacy of muscle outweighs the less evident and tangible mental strength, which partly explains the sexual attractiveness of the athlete in contrast to the Phi Beta Kappa man.

One of the basic causes of behavior differences between men and women is the fact that, although both boys and girls are inferior to adults in physical strength, the boys may finally excel their mothers and equal or excel their fathers, while the daughters never can hope to excel more than their mothers. This "coming of age" situation brings the boy into a state where physically he feels the equal of anybody, and superior to half the population, whereas his sister reaches womanhood with the feeling of equality to half the population and inferiority to the masculine other half. In short, she never reaches the state of psychical adulthood attained by her brother. Throughout adulthood, therefore, she retains half of the physical inferiority outlook possessed by the child, while the man throws off almost all of his. Women have more in common with children, therefore, then do men, which partly explains why mothers seem to be more accurate interpreters than fathers of both their sons' and daughters' wishes and actions.

The differences in specific gravity of the male and female body explain why women float on water more readily than men, as well as why they do not mind cold water as do men. The fat renders them relatively lighter and warmer. The lesser clothing demanded by girls is probably founded on this basic physiological difference, despite the contradictory dictates of fashion.

Such physical differences as mentioned above apparently hold true of men and women, whether of civilized or more savage races. In his studies of Indians, for example, Hrdlicka found that the average Indian woman is only two-thirds as strong as the average Indian man despite her much greater participation in hard manual labor. Indian women are just as much shorter than Indian men as white women are shorter than white men. And the Indian man's heart beats as much slower than the Indian woman's, as the white man's heart beats slower than the white woman's. The difference in muscular strength that is true of men and women has been found to have the ratio 29:18, when weight has been the same. This means that a woman weighing 125 pounds is only 62 per cent as strong as a man of the same weight.

The difference in length of legs explains in part the preference of a woman for high heels. By elevating herself through addition of two or three inches to her pedal extremities, she not only slenderizes her ankles and gains a more shapely calf, but she attains more masculine bodily proportions and appears more slender in figure. She also looks out upon the world from an elevation of an additional inch or two. The latter effect enables her to feel more grown up; so it materially adds to her poise and self-assurance. We shall defer until later in this chapter a discussion of the effects of erogenous differences between male and female.

As regards the menstrual function and its effect upon female efficiency, we find that women take as much as three times the number of days sick leave as men in one of our governmental departments where a thorough study of the subject has been made. In almost every industrial and commercial organization where the subject has been investigated, women have far exceeded men as regards rest periods and absences on account of illness. These factors are not alone indicative of the menstrual influence, for women are usually in positions of less importance, and hence can be absent with less detriment to production. Moreover, many employed women are not free from labor when the office or factory closes, but return home to housework, cooking, etc., tasks which demand strength and often incite worry. As a general rule, the attitude toward the menstrual period has changed with the franker and more athletic views of the modern world. In Tennyson's day feminine fainting and indisposition of women for several days each month were expected of them. The psychological factors were prominent in producing her incapacity. At present a different mental attitude is also lessening the influence of menstruation on her efficiency.

In considering the physical differences between the sexes, therefore, we have brought out the importance of such things as height and weight as they affect the mental attitude of the respective sexes. The greater strength of the male explains much of the social order of all races and ages of mankind. The difference between the coming of age of the male and of the female as it affects their outlook upon their fellowmen has been emphasized. Because of this strength difference females tend to be more alert in detecting the psychological states of those around them, whereas the males are less attentive to people.

The Relationship Between Glands and Genius. In the interesting experiments of Steinach we find that the grafting of an ovary in a previously castrated male guinea pig led to the development of female secondary sexual characteristics. The mammary glands became functional, the pig nursed young, and performed in the presence of male pigs after the fashion of females. The converse of this experiment was carried out. Testes were grafted in females whose ovaries had previously been excised, and the females developed masculine behavior, courting normal females and fighting with males as pugnaciously as congenital males. Apparently, shifting the sex glands about will almost completely change the behavior, and probably the instincts, of animals. As regards instincts Thorndike believes that men and women differ in two basic ways. Men are more pugnacious than women, while women are more protective and loving in regard to their offspring. Whether or not these differences are instinctive, we know they exist in the adult, and are correlates of sexual glands. These glands, through the network of neurones of which they are a part, give rise to the motive bases on which the home and business are built up.

The difference in cultural attainments of two brothers in whom we shall grant equal innate intellectual capacities and equal opportunity to partake of educational advantages, might be explained on the basis of different glandular influences. The more sexually inclined boy would probably develop social interests, spending recreational time in dancing, parties, and heterosexual activities. Becoming adept in such matters, he might go into some phase of business in which he could capitalize upon his knowledge of human nature. We might find him in salesmanship, fiction writing, or the like. He might have made his college letter in sport, and have graduated with a "C" rating.

His more sexually frigid brother, on the contrary, might become a famous scientist, leaving a formula or invention behind him to keep his memory fresh in the archives of fame. Lacking the richly developed motive bases which would make him more receptive to sex stimuli in the form of pretty college girls, he would not find it so difficult to sit alone in his study room night after night. There would be less distraction that he must overcome. And lacking the distraction of athletic endeavor and competitive sports, his attention could steer a more placid course. His honors would be intellectual ones, and he would be content therewith. Because of his greater time spent in scholastic thought, he would progress much farther than his brother in such lines, graduating with a Phi Beta Kappa key, and a traveling fellowship. In this connection Pitkin[1] says:

> "Not by chance has it happened that many eminent men have been sexual inferiors, sexual defectives, poor family men, recluses, ascetics and even rabidly anti-social. The explanation is so simple that it has escaped some otherwise acute observers, who have gone the lengths of Freud and Adler in their search for causes. Far deeper than all compensative urges and transfers, which unquestionably come into play here and there, we find a *constitutional narrowing of competitive interests.*
>
> "A man of weak sexuality is in luck from the point of view demanded by achievement. For he is not distracted by blonde winks and brunette giggles. For him none of the struggles of good St. Anthony."

It is doubtful, however, if too weak sexual glands can be looked upon so generally as sources of motivation to high attainment. The driving energy of the sexually mature individual is evidently a powerful force for intellectual productivity if it can be harnessed aright. Sublimation of such in-

[1] Pitkin, Walter B., *The Psychology of Achievement* (New York, 1930), p. 262.

clinations probably explains a large part of the literature, art and poetry which stands in the pre-eminent class today. The ascetics and priests of the middle ages who translated their sex energy into literary and scientific products might never have attained as high a pinnacle of excellence if they had been bereft of this powerful driving force. Castrated animals and men seem to lack the alertness and energy of the normal creatures. They grow fat, contented, and less responsive to many stimuli in their environment. If sex is so potent a source of motivation that it runs a close second to hunger, then we may reason quite logically that the stronger the sexual inclinations, the greater the possibility of tremendous intellectual attainment when they are harnessed in the interest of science and the arts. The sex glands are, therefore, bases for production as well as reproduction.

Sex Differences in Sensory Preferences. In acuteness of sensory discrimination there seem to be no valid sex differences. Women are the equal of men in regard to auditory and visual sensitivity. In reaction time they may even slightly excel men, a fact that is probably explicable on the basis of the male's greater size and weight. The passage of a nervous impulse requires time, so the longer the neural arc, the slower is the response. The eye-brain-finger pathway is shorter in the female than in the male. Moreover, the greater the weight of an organ, the greater is the inertia which it offers.

In the realm of color vision, we find a curious sex difference evident. The male is more susceptible to color blindness than is the female. This defect seems to be sex-linked, being carried by the female, and becoming apparent in her son. The incidence of this defect has been estimated as 2 to 4 per cent of males and 0.01 to 1 per cent of females.[1]

The preferences existing for colors and odors have been measured in several surveys and experiments. The following

[1] Howell, W. H., *A Textbook of Physiology* (Philadelphia, 1930), p. 356.

table from Wissler[1] shows the visual likes and dislikes of the men and women in his investigation. The male preference for blue, and the female preference for red bear out the findings of Jastrow's extensive survey. These likes and dislikes probably are not so much due to intrinsic qualities of the different hues, as to childhood experience with them.

	FRESHMEN		WOMEN	
	LIKE	DISLIKE	LIKE	DISLIKE
Red	22	7	42	8
Orange	5	25	8	31
Yellow	2	32	5	8
Green	7	15	9	21
Blue	42	12	9	23
Violet	19	8	19	9
White	3	1	8	0

EXHIBIT 23. The color preferences of men and women students.

When my elder son was one year old, for example, I set six colored discs against the baseboard of my study. These were red, orange, yellow, green, peacock blue, and blue—the colored discs used with the rotary color mixer for classes in general psychology. Then I placed the boy on the floor on the opposite side of the room. Immediately he began crawling toward the orange disc until he seized it, whereupon I took it away from him, escorted him out of the room, mixed the color discs so orange was at the other end of the row, and repeated the experiment. The child crawled again straight for the orange circle of cardboard. A third time I repeated the procedure, but placed the orange disc in the middle of the series. He chose it for the third successive time, but refused to continue for the fourth trial. Why did he like the orange better than the other

[1] Wissler, Clark, "The Correlation of Mental and Physical Tests" *Psychological Review Monographs*, vol. iii (1901), No. 6, p. 17.

colored discs? Probably not because orange was intrinsically more pleasant to him, but because orange looked like the fruit with whose juice he was familiar. He had, moreover, played with an orange on the tray of his high chair on one or two occasions. Familiarity probably bred pleasure, as it usually does. This fact may be the explanation of most of the color preferences cited.

In their comprehensive survey of the color preferences of males and females from kindergarten through college, Katz and Breed[1] found blue to be the constant choice of the males, and the usual choice of the females. In Exhibit 24 appear the

	COLOR PREFERENCE OF MALE SUBJECTS						COLOR PREFERENCE OF FEMALE SUBJECTS					
GRADE	R	O	Y	G	B	V	R	O	Y	G	B	V
Kdg.	3.5	5	2	3.5	1	6	5	3.5	1	6	2	3.5
1	3	4	5.5	2	1	5.5	3	6	4	2	1	5
2	4	6	5	3	1	2	3	5.5	4	2	1	5.5
3	2	4	5	3	1	6	3	4.5	6	2	1	4.5
4	2	4	6	3	1	5	2	6	5	3	1	4
5	2	3.5	6	3.5	1	5	4	6	5	2	1	3
6	2	5.5	5.5	3	1	4	3	6	5	2	1	4
7	3	5	6	2	1	4	3	5	6	2	1	4
8	3	6	4.5	2	1	4.5	3	5	5	2	1	5
9	2.5	5.5	4	2.5	1	5.5	2	6	3.5	3.5	1	5
10	2	5.5	5.5	4	1	3	5	5	3	1	2	5
11	3	4	5.5	2	1	5.5	3.5	5	2	1	3.5	6
12	2.5	5.5	5.5	2.5	1	4	4.5	6	3	2	1	4.5
College ..	3.5	5	6	2	1	3.5	4	6	5	1	3	2

EXHIBIT 24. Color preferences of males and females from kindergarten through college.

data for both sexes. The number of male subjects tested at each grade level ranged from 28 to 109, while with the females it stretched from 10 to 105. The median number in each case lay at around 60. They found that red was a greater favorite

[1] Katz, S. E., and Breed, F. S., "The Color Preferences of Children," *Journal of Applied Psychology*, vol. vi (1922), pp. 255-266.

of the poor than of the children from well-to-do neighborhoods during their early years, and that the reverse was true of green. These differences due to social status tended to disappear as the children had longer contact with the school system.

This general markedly pleasant effect of some colors on people is obviously a phenomenon which should be given careful consideration by advertising men and others who are interested in using various color effects in their work.

As regards preferences for different odors we can cite the following table from Poffenberger[1] showing the age and sex choices between six varieties of olfactory stimuli. In this table the 3,000 subjects voted simply for the most pleasant odor, according to their own experience. Rose and Violet seem to be the least popular, while Lilac and French Bouquet are considered most pleasant.

	YOUNG				MIDDLE AGE				OLD			
	MALE		FEMALE		MALE		FEMALE		MALE		FEMALE	
	Number of Votes	Order	Number of Votes	Order	Number of Votes	Order	Number of Votes	Order	Number of Votes	Order	Number of Votes	Order
Rose	25	5	109	6	32	4.5	79	6	1	6	11	5
Violet ...	12	6	207	5	31	6	129	4.5	5	4	13	4
Lilac	48	1	229	3	51	2.5	441	1	5	4	70	1
Jasmine .	29	3.5	261	1	51	2.5	129	4.5	5	4	10	6
French Bouquet .	31	2	213	4	59	1	162	3	7	1	21	2
Oriental Bouquet .	29	3.5	237	2	32	4.5	186	2	6	2	19	3

EXHIBIT 25. Age and sex preferences for various odors.

1 Poffenberger, A. T., *Psychology in Advertising* (A. W. Shaw Co., New York, 1932), p. 591.

In concluding our discussion of sex differences in sensory preferences we may say, first of all, that males and females seem to be about the same in acuity of sensory discrimination except for the slightly greater percentage of men who are color blind. As for the preferences of the two sexes regarding color those investigators who carried on their research thirty and forty years ago found that women definitely preferred red, whereas men were most fond of blue. In more recent studies, however, men and women both showed greatest preference for blue. As regards olfactory preferences, we shall refer the reader to the table from Poffenberger.

Sex Differences in Buying. The advent of modern transportational facilities has played a part in the increasing participation of women in retail buying. When it was more difficult to get into town, the housewife left the task of purchasing to her husband. Now she not only does her own buying, but has usurped many of his former prerogatives, probably much to the mutual pleasure of both sexes.

Another reason for the increasing female participation in retail buying has been the rising economic independence of women. With their own pay checks they feel entitled to do their own shopping. The old paternalistic home where father carried all the money and wife and daughters depended on his largess and good humor for doles is fortunately disappearing.

There is, however, a difference not only in the relative degree of participation by women in purchasing and in the range of articles that she now buys, but also in the behavior of the two sexes in their methods of buying. Women are more attentive to fashions. They will keep alert to any innovation, even though they have no money to buy at present. And they are more exacting in their demands upon the clerks. Instead of looking at two or three articles, they wish a thorough inspection of all the stock. Very few men will go into a shop just for the sake of looking around. When they enter they are purchasing bent. Women, however, will more frequently stroll through a store just to look around. As the chief buyers of the American home, it is wise that they do this, for it gives them a current knowledge of prices and qualities.

In their purchasing women resemble the professional buyers of mercantile firms more than men resemble them even though the latter are usually male. The reason lies in the fact that the wife always is buying with the husband's opinions in mind. Even though he gives her free rein, she still is not freed from his ever-present shadow when she goes shopping. She feels herself custodian of the family funds, and therefore must be sure that she gets a bargain. In her sense of responsibility to another for the wise disbursement of the pay check, she resembles the professional buyer.

In order to assure herself of adequate quality for the price she pays, she alertly scans the newspaper and magazine advertisements, which are usually written for her, anyway. She is also familiar with cloth, and means of detecting pure fabrics from imitations. Men as a rule don't know the difference between voile and crêpe de chine. On Test 8 of Army Alpha they repeatedly call "denim" a dance, and écru and beige are just names, nothing more. After men are married a few years they forget even what size of shirt they wear, and sometimes let their wives buy their shoes for them.

In discussing the woman buyer above we have had in mind the typical American housewife. It is true that a certain small and wealthy class of women buy with little heed to prices, letting father or husband take care of the bills when they arrive, but this group is small. Its purchases are frequently of a costly sort, but the total volume of business is relatively slight compared to that of the average American housewife.

In their attention to little things women also differ from men. Whether this tendency of woman to pay attention to details is instilled through habit or is a part of her original nature is immaterial, for she surpasses man in this respect. Lace and curtains, doilies and the like are really feminine items, despite the era of masculine frills in Elizabethan England. Although men appreciate the feminine environment that surrounds them, they would seldom voluntarily attempt to duplicate it if left to themselves. When left alone by their wives, they dine in the kitchen. Then they exercise unusual effort trying to figure how to eliminate an extra dish or piece of silverware, finally reducing things to a minimum. As a last resort they may even dine from the drain board of the sink, and use their fingers to avoid washing dishes.

The woman, on the other hand, likes salads. She will spend time garnishing her foods for the visual effect, and decorate her grapefruit by scalloping its edges. She has an eye for the artistic, even in culinary matters. In his physiological research Ivy has shown that there is a definite cephalic or psychological phase to the process of digestion, thus justifying all these efforts to make more appetizing the viands placed before her family. With her greater attention to such niceties of method and apparel goes her corresponding greater attention to matters of deportment and etiquette. She is more interested in persons than is the male, and desires change in her environment and clothes far more frequently.

In making a final survey of the sex differences in buying, we may state that women do the majority of the retail buying of household goods, their own and their children's clothing, and have even assumed much of their husbands' purchasing. The advertisers realize this fact and construct most of their advertising for the women. Women are also the major purchasers of magazines of a general nature. They are more difficult to please than are men, and resemble the professional buyer in that they are after bargains for they feel themselves more or less responsible to their husbands for the wise disbursement of the family funds. Buying becomes both a business and a pleasure for them, so they are ever on the alert for new styles and sales even though at the time they are not strictly shopping bent. In this regard, too, they resemble the professional buyer, for he interviews salesmen often for no other reason than to keep abreast of styles and prices.

Sex Differences in Mating. The coyness of the female is an axiom of social psychology. In human and infrahuman species she must be courted, and retreats as long as pursuit is forthcoming from the more aggressive male. In the absence of such pursuit, however, she may reverse the process, as Moss[1] found true of white rats in his clever experimentation. In one of two compartments in his experiment box he placed a female in the oestrual condition. Between her and the other compartment was an electrode giving a 28 volt electrical shock. One male after another was placed in the first compartment. If it deemed its sexual gratification by the female more desirable than the pain suffered in taking the 28 volts, then it went across; otherwise it remained in the compartment where it was originally placed. Of five male rats tested, only two went across in the hour they were allowed in the test situation. The reverse of the experiment was then undertaken. The males were confined in the compartment whose door opened inward, while the females were placed across the electrode, and allowed to come to the males if they were willing to take the shock to do so. In the hour's test three females crossed over to gain access to the males.

The proverbial shyness of the girl is probably ascribable in part to the more scattered erogenous regions in her body with a resulting diffuse erotic sensation. The male is not only more localized in his sex zones, but demonstrates a correspondingly quicker and more intense excitement. It isn't until after prolonged experience that the female's neural eroticism is trained to a unified muscular response. Because of this diffusion of sensitive zones, therefore, the female enjoys the courting stage more than her mate, for it offers a heightening to her slower

[1] Moss, F. A., "A Study of Animal Drives," *Journal of Experimental Psychology*, vol. vii, No. 3 (June, 1924), p. 98.

sexual passion comparable to the psychical phase in the digestion process. The direct physical union of the two sexes is but partially satisfactory to the female unless this imaginative, psychical phase of love is indulged in. The usual masculine tendency in both food and sex indulgence, however, is for directness of satisfaction.

In devious ways the sexual urge expresses itself. It may be given indirect outlet through dancing, skating, romantic moving pictures, love stories, pornographic pictures and the burlesque show, or it may seek the more refined outlets of music, poetry, and art. Horseback riding is a source of erotic stimulation for the equestrienne. A curious thing about this basic motive force is the fact that individuals may seldom realize the devious workings of their sex expression. Very often the sex urge is at the bottom of a series of rationalized arguments which easily obscure it from the unskilled analyst.

The following data from one of the writer's classes in social psychology suggest a sex difference in the preference for a male or female stepchild. The question was put as follows: "If you were to marry a widow (widower) with a young child, would you prefer the youngster to be a boy or a girl?" The following apportionment of replies shows considerable uniformity among each sex voting.

	PREFER STEPSON	PREFER STEPDAUGHTER
College Men (24)	6 (25 %)	18 (75 %)
College Women (28)	20 (71.5%)	8 (28.5%)

EXHIBIT 26. Male and female preferences regarding sex of a stepchild.

Five of the women in explaining their choices admitted they wouldn't want a stepdaughter because the child would probably remind the husband of his former wife, and they were jealous enough not to wish that. Four of the men expressed similar reasons. The others gave thirteen different reasons, yet arrived at uniformity of choice in three-fourths of the cases. Obviously, the more basic explanation is that given by the five women and the four men. The others may not have consciously faced the basic sex reason for their choices, but that reason was probably operative underneath their rationalized explanation to the extent that it controlled their decision.

The psychological phases of mating and sex behavior, therefore, reveal that males are more blunt, more easily aroused in passion, and more aggressive throughout the courtship. In the exceptions to the above statement, the female may, however, become the pursuer, as Moss has shown in his experiments with rats. The female, moreover, seems to show her characteristic interest in details by placing a premium upon the possession of rings, billets-doux, gifts, love tokens and gentle caresses. She is much more prone to keep diaries. In the limited data shown in Exhibit 26, she also seems to prefer a stepson to a stepdaughter, which is the opposite choice of the male.

The Basis of Woman's Intuition. The basis of woman's intuition is ascribable to the same environmental factors which make the younger children more intuitive than the oldest, namely, the need of utilizing wits to match superior muscular development. The physically weaker person, of necessity, must begin to watch the reactions of his fellows and learn to interpret their shades of facial expression and vocal intonation, so that he may thereby judge when to act with impunity and when to refrain.

In a survey of salesmen the writer has found that oldest and only children fall below their percentage of occurrence in the general population. Some selective factor, therefore, has operated to favor the younger sons as salesmen. That factor appears to be the greater social knowledge of the younger son, who has acquired it through adjusting his actions to the mood of his older brother, as that was written in the latter's tones and looks. A salesman must be closely attuned to the emotional and mental turmoil going on within his client or customer, and a background of thirty years of human scrutiny gives the younger brother an opportunity to diagnose symptoms mechanically.

The oldest child and only child are more accustomed to getting what they want by brute force. Why should they attempt conciliatory measures when the latter are unnecessary? As a result, we find that oldest and only children are frequently more introvertive than their younger brothers. They find it more difficult to adjust, and placate. Therefore, they tend to grow angry when selling if their customers fail to respond readily.

Like younger sons, girls grow up with the physical inferiority to their brothers. They learn to gain their ends by strategy. This is decidedly superior mental training to that of brutishness. Darwin's theory that man evolved his superior intelligence because of his physical inferiority to other animals about him is a case in point. On Moss' Social Intelligence Test women excelled men in their ability to detect the emotion of an individual from his photograph. They also were better than men in judging the mental state of a speaker from his printed words. In observations of human behavior and knowledge of the correct procedure in social situations involving tact they likewise showed their superiority. Ability in all of these items is based on a lengthy training in adjusting to a human environment.

Sherlock Holmes observed clues in every murder mystery that were unseen by other lesser detectives, even though they were a part of each tragic situation. It is adeptness in seeing these clues of emotional and mental states possessed by people, that goes under the name of intuition. After years of such tutelage, women and many men quickly learn to feel the hostility or friendliness, jealousy or dislike of those with whom they mingle. They may not be able to describe accurately the reasons for their feelings, relying on the feminine "just because", or the masculine "hunch", but there are reasons. Oftentimes they may have been conditioned to such feelings without being conscious of the stimuli in the initial learning situation.

Another characteristic of younger brothers and of women is the fact that they usually take criticism or rebuff with less hurt or discouragement than oldest and only children. Having been accustomed so long to reproof and reprimand in the childhood situation, they have become somewhat inured to it. Oldest children may whip themselves along in sales work, but rebuffs cut more deeply than in the case of their younger siblings.

In concluding this section concerning woman's intuition, we can state that women have acquired their intuition by closer study of their human milieu. It has been to their advantage to detect the slight changes in tone and expression of their male companions since their lesser physical strength has forced them to a greater reliance upon tact and cajolery. Moreover, the social restrictions which do not permit women to select their male friends with the ease and directness with which men choose their sweethearts has compelled them to become skilled in stratagems and finesse. After years of such social schooling, they find it possible to form opinions without being able to state the reasons therefor. It is this susceptibility to many slight stimuli in the total situation which we designate as woman's intuition.

Introverts vs. Extroverts. The above discussion leads us directly into a consideration of extroversion and introversion. These two types of personality are represented fairly well in Theodore Roosevelt, Sr., and Woodrow Wilson. People in any trait, as we pointed out at the opening of this chapter, tend to fall closely around the mid-point; so the mass of people are neither introvertive nor extrovertive, but both. The central category we call the ambivert group, which is where most of us will be found. In the following classification of traits taken from Laird[1] the reader may check with a plus mark the items that fit him, and with a minus sign those which distinctly do not apply, reserving a zero for cases of doubt or neutrality. Then let sister, wife, or brother check him, too, and note how close agreement exists between the self-rating and that of an intimate acquaintance. It was Dr. Carl Jung of Zurich, Switzerland, who began classifying patients as introverts and extroverts. The extroverts express their emo-

HOW TO TELL AN INTROVERT OR EXTROVERT

Personality signs revealed in actions:

1. The introvert blushes easily; the extrovert rarely blushes.
2. The extrovert laughs more readily than the introvert.
3. The introvert is usually outspoken; the extrovert is usually careful not to hurt the feelings of others.
4. The extrovert is a fluent talker; the introvert can prepare a report in writing easier than he can tell it in conversation.
5. The extrovert loans money and possessions more readily than the introvert.
6. The extrovert moves faster than the introvert in the routine actions of the day, such as walking, dressing, talking, etc.
7. The extrovert does not take particular care of his personal property, such as watches, clothes, etc.; the introvert is found continually oiling, polishing, and tinkering.
8. Introverts are usually reluctant about making friends with the opposite sex, while extroverts are attracted by them.
9. Introverts are easily embarrassed by having to be in front of a crowd.
10. The extrovert is a more natural public speaker.
11. The introvert likes to argue.
12. The introvert is slow about making friends.
13. The introvert rewrites his letters, inserts interlineations, adds a postcript, and corrects every mistake of the typist.

[1] Laird Donald A., *The Psychology of Selecting Men* (McGraw-Hill Book Co., New York, 1927), pp. 304-305.

Personality signs revealed in thinking and attitudes are:

1. The introvert worries; the extrovert has scarcely a care in the world.
2. The feelings of the introvert are easily hurt; the extrovert is not bothered by what is said about him.
3. The introvert deliberates in great detail about everything—what to wear, where to eat, etc., and usually tells one why he decided to do what he did.
4. The introvert rebels when ordered to do a thing; the extrovert accepts directions as a matter of course.
5. The introvert is urged to his best efforts by praise; the extrovert is not affected by praise.
6. The introvert is suspicious of the motives of others.
7. The introvert is usually radical in religion and politics; the extrovert—if he entertains any opinions—is usually conservative.
8. The introvert would rather struggle alone to solve a problem than ask for help.
9. The introvert would rather work alone in a room than with others.
10. Extroverts follow athletics; introverts, books and "high brow" magazines.
11. The introvert is a poor loser.
12. The introvert daydreams a great deal.
13. The introvert prefers fine, delicate work (die making, accounting), while the extrovert prefers work in which details do not bother.
14. The introvert is inclined to be moody at times.
15. The introvert is very conscientious.

(See page 591 for an Introvert-Extrovert test)

tions in motor performance and contacts with others, whereas the introverts are more self-centered and shy. Extroverts might be thought of as men of action while introverts would be the thinkers and scholars. Daydreaming is a case of introversion; an instance where the emotional expression is inward.

Salesmen and younger children tend to be more extrovertive than those persons, such as scientists and engineers, who work with tools and abstract symbols. This is well demonstrated in the following case of one of the writer's students who had been an engineer for a number of years; then changed into sales work. He says of himself:

> I never realized the change in my personality after getting into sales work until the other night when I attended the opera. Arriving early, I engaged the person who sat on my right in conversation, and had an interesting chat with him before the music started. I never did such a thing in my life previously, always remaining quiet until some one else asked a question of me. It was rather surprising when I analyzed my behavior afterwards for me to recall that I had obtained the man's name, the number of his children, where they attended school, and where he lived. I knew his profession and hobbies, and his church affiliation.

The student was a salesman of an encyclopedia, which accounts for his interest in children and their place of schooling, since this encyclopedia company uses the school children as a means of initial contact for their salesmen. The student had taken the company's course in salesmanship and had been in the field only six weeks; yet his introvertive behavior had begun to undergo a marked change. As we shall observe in more detail in a subsequent chapter, we can alter the personalities of children and adults by a conscious technique. The nursery school, for example, is of great value in extroverting children.

In his tests of the socially and mechanically minded persons Freyd[1] presents a number of distinctions which we have embodied in Exhibit 27. In this classification he refers, as we have done throughout this book unless otherwise stated, to central tendencies of the majority, allowing of course for the exceptions to the rule. Moss developed his Social Intelligence Test in the hope of differentiating the salesman type from the more introvertive mechanically minded. No attempt is made here to say that salesmen enjoy life more than mechanically minded individuals, or that they contribute less to cultural and mechanical evolution. Such a debate is not within the scope of this textbook.

[1] Freyd, Max, "The Personalities of the Socially and Mechanically Minded," *Psychological Review Monographs*, vol. xxxiii, No. 151 (1924).

CHARACTERISTICS OF SALESMEN	CHARACTERISTICS OF THE MECHANICALLY MINDED
Credulous	Assured in beliefs and attitudes
Objective or universal in their verbal association	Subjective in verbal associations
Careless of details	Careful of details
Impulsive	Inhibited and cautious
Deficient in fine motor co-ordination	Able to make fine motor co-ordinations
Not self-conscious	Self-conscious
Not conceited	Conceited
Adaptable	Not adaptable
Persevering	Not persevering
Excitable	Calm and reserved
Self-confident	Lacking in confidence in their abilities
Open-hearted and talkative	Reticent
Quick to make friends	Slow to make friends
Present-minded	Absent-minded
Good-natured	Glum
Neat in dress	Careless in dress

EXHIBIT 27. Freyd's personality differences between salesmen and the mechanically minded.

From the standpoint of psychology, therefore, introversion and extroversion are two categories probably covering the extremes of such human traits, the majority of people falling in the ambivert group. The introvert tends to be more egocentric than the extrovert. He and his possessions are very closely linked up. The hermit and the miser are two cases of extreme introverts. Children who are alone, lacking the extrovertive influences of living playmates, whether human or animal, are likely to become self-centered and individualistic. Introversion and extroversion are therefore chiefly the products of environments which predispose to one or the other types of personality. A child with an inferiority complex, however, may become more and more introvertive as his social contacts widen, especially if some organic inferiority or physical stigmata is the cause of his complex. Cripples, therefore, tend toward introversion. The salesman is a good example of the extrovert.

Individual Differences in Perception. One of the basic causes of arguments is explained as resulting from differences of perception, which depends on the past habits of the individual. We have shown previously that words possess feeling tones, or personalities. But words and other stimuli may not give rise to the same effects in two persons. People will even argue violently over the same printed phrase or sentence, yet never lock horns because they are talking about different things and don't know it. The story of the blind men of Hindustan is quite relevant here. One fell against the elephant's side only; the second seized just his tusk; the third his knee; the fourth his ear; the fifth his trunk; and the sixth his tail. Thereafter they argued violently as to the creature bearing the name "elephant", maintaining hotly and in turn that an elephant was a *wall,* a *spear,* a *tree,* a *fan,* a *snake,* and a *rope.* Unanimity of opinion cannot result unless all the stimuli presented to various subjects give rise to similar associations and responses. The college debater's first task is a definition of the question, translating it into terms of common acceptance to the affirmative and negative sides.

But even then debate results because the various subjects have different experiences in relation to the words. Theoretically there should never be any possibility of debate when reason is employed. If all of our experiences had the objectivity of figures, as in 25 x 35, we could never develop a difference of opinion over such results as 875. Debates of all sorts, therefore, simply indicate different perceptions, and these in turn denote different learning situations on the part of the combatants.

Fortunately, the majority of men and women in the same nation, state, and city have fairly uniform experiences so that they can get along with a reasonable degree of friendliness and cooperation. But all differences of experience, resulting from defective sense organs, subnormal intelligence, differences in race and custom and creed, militate against a sense of social unity, complicating therefore such matters as government, employment management, and world peace.

The whole matter of mental testing is also complicated because of different perceptions. Even with non-language tests, such as Army Beta, where words do not enter in, it is conceivable that a Hottentot might have less experience with reference to geometrical forms than an American child who had played with toys and blocks of every conceivable type. And this same factor enters, even though slightly, in our mental test results for American girls and boys. The fact that one sex apparently excels in one mental operation while the other is superior in another is probably reducible to different motivation and training in the respective fields. We have already pointed out what appears to us an adequate explanation for feminine superiority in those phases of Moss' Social Intelligence Test that have to do with observation of human behavior.

In his extensive investigation Terman[1] found no significant sex differences in intelligence, the average intelligence of women and girls being as high as that of men and boys. When the I.Q's. of boys and girls were separately treated, he discovered a small but fairly constant superiority of the girls up to the age of 13, but at 14 the curve for girls dropped below that for boys. The superiority up to that year, moreover, was only 2 or 3 points in terms of I.Q. We have advanced a probable explanation for this superiority under our discussion of physical age differences.

In only a few tests were sex differences marked. Terman describes these as follows: "The boys were decidedly better in arithmetical reasoning, giving differences between a president and a king, solving the form board, making change, reversing hands of clock, finding similarities, and solving the 'induction

[1] Terman, Lewis M., *The Measurement of Intelligence* (Houghton Mifflin Co., Boston, Mass., 1916).

test'. The girls were superior in drawing designs from memory, answering the 'comprehension questions', repeating digits and sentences, tying a bow-knot, and finding rhymes."

The reasons why gossip and rumor become so distorted are also based (to a considerable degree) on errors of interpretation. In his description of the growth and elaboration of the rumor that Belgian and French priests were committing all sorts of atrocities against German soldiers van Langenhove[1] shows this fact very clearly. In a simple form we may similarly note the changes in reports by students of the same print situation, by regarding the following horrifying description. The first student read the original version, then wrote immediately thereafter his account of what he had read. The second student in the series read the report of the first student, then wrote his remembered version of it, which in turn became the reading copy for the third. This procedure was carried out through a series of three or four students. The third or fourth versions from several classes in which the experiment was tried follow the original as described below.

(Original)

Alone, crushed beneath the fallen trunk of a cypress which had crashed during a thunderstorm, Janet Gordon lay gasping painfully for breath. There was no other human being within three miles, and the pain in her chest prevented her calling aloud.

Night fell, and with it a swarm of biting gnats and mosquitoes feasted upon her defenseless head and face. One arm was broken above the elbow; the other pinioned beneath her; so she could only turn her head from side to side in a vain attempt to frighten away the insects.

Three days later the hungry vultures descended upon the fallen tree and gradually drew closer. Finally one alighted on her chest and glared down into her staring eyes. It darted its head at her—she blinked feebly—and the vulture's beak punctured her left eyeball, tearing part of the eyelid away. . . . Her skeleton was bleached when a trapper came upon the scene a month later.

[1] van Langenhove, *The Growth of a Legend* (New York, 1916).

(Third version in Section A)

Alone with a fallen cypress across her chest pinioning her down Dorothy Gordon lay helpless. She could not call for help.

After 3 hours insects began to bite her and she could not ward them off because 1 arm was pinioned under the tree while the other was broken at the elbow.

After 3 days vultures circled over her and one became bold enough to perch on her body and look into her open eyes.

After 3 months her bones were all bleached.

(Third version in Section B)

A girl went into the forest and got her arm pinned under a tree. During the night she was bitten by rats and mosquitoes. Then a vulture came and ate her eyes. A month later her skeleton was found.

(Fourth version in Section C)

Alone, crushed under a cypress tree lay Janet Gordon. She was very weak. There was not a human being within three miles. Her chest was hurting her so she could not call out.

Gnats and flies were bothering her but she could not shake them off. Her head was hurting. A vulture came along but she could not open her eyes. He picked at her eyeball and took away her eyelid.

Three days later a trapper found her bleached skull and skeleton.

Under conscious endeavor to reproduce verbatim what had been read, the students in the series described above were yet guilty of numerous omissions and inclusions. If an individual of superior intelligence makes so many errors in transmitting information, it is apparent why the laymen in emotional situations may ignore some stimuli and add others not present. The writer in several experiments based on the procedure just described, but using material that did not set off strong emotional reactions, has found that many errors arise because subjects

(1) See the things which fit into their habitual backgrounds, ignoring others.

(2) Translate specific stimuli, such as "river", into more generic categories, like "water", and then at the time of repro-

duction of the material again translate the generic terms like "water" into a specific word. The latter word may be "lake" instead of the original "river", depending upon the habitual reactions of the subject. Here in Chicago, for example, students quite frequently change "river" in the original passage to "lake" in their reproduced version. And citation of cities in the original, such as Pittsburg and Philadelphia, as in the passage quoted below, become simply Pennsylvania in the reproduced version. This common memory process of placing an individual element upon its generic category not only leads to speed of logical learning, but also results in errors of fact.

(3) Shorten their reproduced version by forgetting.

(Original passage read aloud to class)

Jim Laughton, despite his six years experience as an aviator, was lost in a fog between Philadelphia and Pittsburg. Fearing a crash against the granite peaks of the Alleghenies, he pulled the stick and zoomed to an altitude of ten-thousand feet. It had been raining, so the rapid ascent froze ice on the yellow wings of his biplane. While he was attempting to level off, the Liberty motor spluttered and died.

Jim's heart sank. Below him lay an invisible landscape full of forests and rivers. He raised his goggles and looked down, but could see only a faint glow to the west. Then he threw his left leg over the fuselage and jumped. While his plane clattered earthward Jim pulled the cord that loosened the silken parachute. He landed in the top of a birch tree with only a scratch across his right cheek.

(Usual type of response written one hour later)

An aviator was lost above the mountains in Pennsylvania. A cold rain was falling and he couldn't see anything below him. He pulled the stick and rose to an altitude of 10,000 feet. Then the Liberty motor died.

He threw his leg over the side and jumped out of the plane. He pulled the cord of his silk parachute and landed in a tree with only a few scratches.

From the foregoing cases, therefore, we see that individual differences in perception are not only the causes of most arguments, but they thwart such forces in society as attempt to heighten the sense of social unity existing between people. They also explain much of the rumor and distorted gossip which one hears, and account for many of the omissions from memory of events which one witnesses. Defective sense organs and subnormal intelligence are causative factors in producing differences in perception, but even among brilliant individuals almost the same degree of difference will be found. Schools and churches are partly effective because they standardize the perceptions of the majority of the people on a number of subjects, such as patriotism and religion. The essence of differences in perception between people goes back to differences in the original learning situations as involves their intelligence, the functional state of their sense organs, the stimuli acting upon them at the time, and their interests and motivation.

The Influence of Inheritance on Behavior. The conflicting views regarding the relative influence upon the human adult of heredity versus environment have shifted from one extreme to another. It is true that an insufficient inheritance of neural equipment may prevent a child from becoming a college graduate despite the most cultural environment, and yet the nervous tissue alone is not an indication of a high I.Q., for there is the possibility of functional feeble-mindedness by deprivation of stimulating environments, as we have already discussed. As the biceps muscle depends not only on inheritance but also on the specific exercise of that particular arm, so also the quality which we call intelligence appears to be dependent on both heredity and environment.

Some psychologists, such as Watson, emphasize environment almost exclusively, claiming they can make a child into a chemist, musician, lawyer, orator, or salesman simply by complete control of the stimuli playing upon the youngster. Complete control of the stimuli is obviously impossible, but the writer doubts the result even if it were possible to manipulate the environment perfectly, unless the child possessed a normal inherited capacity. With only 100 for his I.Q., however, the child could probably be made into a genius of any sort desired, with perfect control of his milieu, since we avail ourselves of much less than our capacities. A normal boy could therefore be drilled to such an extent that he would probably far excel in ultimate attainment the child with an I.Q. of 150, assuming that the latter had not been subjected to such an ideal training system. A normal mentality with a tremendous perseverance in learning will usually far outshine the sporadic efforts of brilliance.

As regards heredity and its influence upon mankind we know that obesity and slimness of figure run in families. Longevity is another factor which appears in some families and not in others. Deafness, feeble-mindedness, color blindness, eye color, tendency to multiple pregnancy, tendency to have extra digits, such as a sixth finger or toe, and even nervous instability apparently follow hereditary paths.

Many of the defects apparent in children and ascribed to heredity, however, are more likely a result of physical or chemical factors operating on the embryo while it is in the uterus. There is a definite temporal sequence in the development of the various anatomical structures in the body. If anything interferes with the embryo at the time the limb buds are to appear, they may be stunted so that they do not form perfectly or at all. There are anomalous infants born without feet or a leg, or with hands growing directly from the shoulders, no arm intervening.

The effect of the maternal environment on mammalian offspring may lead to infection of the child by a disease that the mother has while pregnant. A syphilitic mother may infect her baby before its birth. An infected mother may also give it scarlet fever or measles. The distinction between inherited and acquired factors must be kept in mind. Although the baby is born with syphilis he does not inherit this disease. He has simply caught it from his mother by proximity to her while she had it. There is no nervous connection between a pregnant mother and her child, nor do they have the same blood supply. The child has its own heart and blood system, and its own nervous mechanism. It is just about as distinct from its mother before its birth as it is after its birth while it is nursing. She is simply its food and oxygen supply. As the villi in the intestine dip into the flow of liquid food passing along them, so the villi of the placenta dip into blood sinuses of the maternal uterine wall and filter out the food required by the child. In contrast to such relationship of child to mother we have the chicken developing in the egg entirely free from contact with its mother, as in an incubator. If hen or rooster parent possessed a disease which we found appearing in the chick that had been hatched by an incubator, then we could probably say the disease was inherited.

Children of the same parents would, of course, be expected to resemble one another more closely than other children of the neighborhood. Sometimes these family physical resemblances are very marked, even in children who are not identical twins. Twins that arise from the same ovum are called identical. They always have the same sex and the same parents and share alike the chromosomal factors of both parents. Apparently they develop similar mental diseases, for we have cases of such twins, separated in childhood, who later in adult life and in different parts of the country developed the same form of insanity.

Fraternal twins, however, may be of the same or of opposite sexes. They may even have different fathers, as is true of puppies born to the same mother in the same litter. Fraternal twins have no particular reason for being any more alike than brothers and sisters born to the same mother at intervals of several years, for they develop from different ova that have been fertilized within a few weeks of each other and occupy the same uterus. They may not look at all alike, and in their intellectual attainments resemble each other only as non-twin children of the family do.

Since feeble-mindedness is heritable we may also expect a rich neural capacity to show itself in succeeding generations. Children of superior parents tend to approach the parents in the traits they possess. The aim of eugenics is to encourage the mating of superior parents for the sake of breeding a higher type of mankind. The matter of inbreeding is of interest in this connection. Although the Mosaic Law inveighed against incestuous mating, and our present statutes in most states designate that first cousins (sometimes second cousins, too) shall not wed, there is no physical nor mental deficiency resulting from such unions if both parents are of sound stock. Because many of the bodily and mental defects are recessive traits, however, an apparently normal parent may be the carrier of feeble-mindedness or deafness, and when mated to a similar person, as his cousin, may find himself with subnormal or defective children. Dunlap has recommended inbreeding, however, for the very purpose of quickly bringing out these defectives so that they can be institutionalized, and the race freed shortly from the latent defective strains.

The writer has been told of a certain family in which deafness had appeared, wherein cousins married cousins until the deafness was so accentuated that now it is almost impossible for a normal hearing infant to be born. Over a score of members of the family have attended Gallaudet College for the Deaf at Washington, D. C. It was against this result that Alexander Graham Bell tried to encourage the mating of deaf and hearing individuals so that a deaf species of the human race could not be evolved. The unfortunate situation today is that the deaf are isolated from hearing people, marry their own kind as a consequence and tend to add more deaf children in succeeding generations.

In concluding this section we ought to mention another rather obvious difference between people, namely, handedness.

Approximately 95 per cent of men and women are right-handed. Hitherto this difference has been ascribed to heredity. It is possible that the relative freedom of its two arms during the last two months of pregnancy may have a bearing on this matter which will indicate that the child's right-handedness is acquired while carried in the uterus. In his research upon this topic, however, Joteyko finds that exercise of the left hand and arm has a greater effect on heart action than does exercise of the right side, and that this result holds true for both left-handed and right-handed persons. In this event, right-handedness may be simply a result of natural efficiency.

In summarizing this important topic of the influence of inheritance on behavior, we may cite such valuable heritages as vitality or a tendency to longevity and resistance to disease, a rich neural equipment, physical beauty and muscular development, height and complexion as some of the factors that descend by way of the germ plasm. On the other hand, feeblemindedness and a susceptibility to nervous instability and disease may descend upon children, along with certain stigmata such as deafness, color blindness, etc. In either kind of heredity, however, the action of the environment may greatly influence the heritage from the past. Vaccination, a well balanced diet, and an adherence to the rules of health can greatly offset the possible tendency to disease.

A rich cultural environment can stimulate both types of neural mechanism to much greater attainment and development than would likely result under a monotonous milieu. Aside from the practice of eugenics, the average person had better concentrate upon the manufacture of a favorable environment for he will thereby influence himself and his progeny to higher attainment. The average person cannot greatly alter the physical and mental inheritance of his children but he can elevate the cultural surroundings of his youngsters from a vulgar and monotonous life to a beautiful home in which music and art and literature vie with morality and love in their uplifting influence upon the youngsters' personalities. As regards the milieu, therefore, one can theoretically make it whatever he wishes.

REFERENCES

Ellis, Robert S., *The Psychology of Individual Differences* (New York, 1928). chap. x.

Finch, F. H., "Sex Differences in Mental Growth," *J. Educ. Psychol.*, 1935, vol. 26, 623-628.

Flory, C. D., "Sex Differences in Skeletal Development," *Child Develpm.*, 1935, vol. 6, pp. 205-212.

Garth, T. R., and Porter, E. P., "The Color Preferences of 1032 Young Children," *Amer. J. Psychol.*, 1934, vol. 46, pp. 448-451.

Gault, Robert H., *Social Psychology* (New York, 1923), chap. iv.

Gault, R. H., and Howard, D. T., *Outline of General Psychology* (New York, 1925), chap. vii.

Griffith, C. R., *Introduction to Applied Psychology* (New York, 1934).

Griffitts, Charles H., *Fundamentals of Vocational Psychology,* (New York, 1924), chap. i.

Hunter, Walter S., *Human Behavior* (Chicago, 1928), chap. ii.

Husband, R. W., "Sex Differences in Dream Contents," *J. Abnorm. Soc. Psychol.*, 1936, vol. 30, pp. 513-521.

Laird, Donald A., *Psychology of Selecting Men* (New York, 1927), chap. xvii.

Leuba, James H., "The Weaker Sex," *Atlantic Monthly* (April, 1926), pp. 454-460.

Link, H. C., *The Return to Religion* (New York, 1936).

Malchow, C. W., *The Sexual Life* (St. Louis. 1923), chaps. iii, iv.

McGraw, Myrtle B., *Growth—A Study of Johnny and Jimmy* (New York, 1935).

Moss, Fred A., *Applications of Psychology* (Boston, 1929), chaps. vii, x.

Peterson, G. M., "Mechanism of Handedness in the Rat," *Comp. Psychol. Monog.*, 1934, vol. 9, No. 6.

Poffenberger, A. T., *Applied Psychology* (New York, 1927), chaps. ii, iii.

Popenoe, P., "The Fertility of Divorcees," *J. Hered.*, 1936, vol. 27, pp. 166-168.

Schmalhausen, S. D., *Our Changing Human Nature* (New York, 1929), chap. i

Shen, N. C., "A Note on the Color Preference of Chinese Students," *J. Soc. Psychol.*, 1936, vol. 7, pp. 68-81.

Snow, A. J., *Psychology in Business Relations* (New York, 1930), chap. iv.

Starch, Daniel, *Principles of Advertising* (Chicago, 1923), chap. xvi.

Strong, E. K., Jr., "Interests of Men and Women," *J. Soc. Psychol.*, 1936, vol. 7, pp. 49-67.

Terman, Lewis M., *The Measurement of Intelligence* (Boston, 1916).

Woodworth, Robert S., *Psychology* (New York, 1921), chap. v.

Young, Kimball, *Source Book for Social Psychology* (New York, 1927), chap. vi.

CHAPTER V

THE EFFECT OF SUGGESTION ON BEHAVIOR

Before we consider the effects of suggestion on human behavior it would be well to lay down a rigid definition of the term, for it has been employed quite differently by several writers. The popular use of the word in the sentence, "I made a suggestion that the society table the motion", is not the one we shall employ throughout this chapter. Furthermore, we do not use the word to designate *any* stimulus that sets off a determining tendency, as Titchener employs the term, nor as a state of susceptibility to excitation by a stimulus, as Bunnerman uses it, but rather, like Gault, as a stimulus that indirectly operates (usually in the marginal fields of attention) to set off a habitual response.

The tinkling sound made by the pendant wind chime described in Chapter II fell upon the ears of the reporter engrossed in writing his story for the day, and set off an organic thirst response. It was, therefore, a suggestion. One of my students reports that as a joke on his guests he frequently offers them a coat hanger, book, or his wife's purse just as they are standing at the door putting on their wraps, and busily engaged in goodbyes. They accept whatever he hands to them, mechanically reacting to the stimulus while their major attention is devoted to their conversation. As they leave the room, this student then calls them back and asks what they mean by carrying off his books, purse, etc. The discomfiture of the guests is an occasion for laughter. In both of these examples the stimulus was applied marginally to habit systems already established in the individuals reacting.

The other kind of suggestion is that classic instance of the dilemma, "Have you stopped beating your wife?" Here an apparently innocuous visual or auditory stimulus sets up an additional thought process over and beyond the immediately obvious. This type of suggestion is often employed in advertising, as shown in the car advertisement, "136 Doctors are Members of Postl's Health Club". It is employed effectively with children who won't eat their spinach, by the father who shows his biceps to his young sons and then eagerly exclaims, "Yum, give me some more of that spinach, please, Mother!" In the famous Cream of Wheat advertisement the happy child sets up the thought in the spectator's mind, "Cream of Wheat must be good." The advertisement itself does not make that statement, yet the observer goes through that thought process by means of an indirect stimulation of the neural pattern.

Bases for Suggestibility. The instinctive and habitual neural patterns that are developed in the individual are the real bases for suggestibility. A person cannot be stimulated to a reaction which he has never previously made, without his full attention being called to the process. Only mechanical or habitual action is capable of being called out without his directing the focus of his attention to it.

Suggestions, therefore, split off segmental portions of the total experience of the individual, and cause them to function more or less independently. There is a mild form of dissociation of the personality whenever suggestions operate. Dual personalities offer extreme cases of this splitting off of the habits of a subject by the presence of suggestion. When Irene, the girl cited by Janet who nursed her mother through a lengthy illness culminating in death, was working about the house thereafter, perhaps at her sewing, some stimulus, such as a pillow made by the mother, or a book or chair always the favorite of the departed parent, would excite her retinae and set up neural processes which re-aroused mother memories so vividly as to throw Irene into somnambulistic trances.

To any one else except Irene, of course, those pillows would not have been the cause of parental memories, nor adequate to excite the emotion of grief. Irene had to possess neural patterns in connection with the pillows etc. before they could be effective as suggestions. In a similar vein, the pecking action of a hen taking food is not an effective stimulus for corresponding behavior on the part of an ape because the latter has no habits of such a nature nor is he conditioned to her kind of food. Yet a hungry hen's pecking will cause a surfeited hen to resume eating, as Bayer[1] has shown.

The first hen was permitted to peck at a large heap of grain until she stood motionless before the food. Then Bayer introduced a second hen which was quite hungry. As the latter began pecking vigorously the first hen resumed her eating and kept on until she had consumed 60 per cent additional. She will eat still more if three hungry hens are pecking before her, showing the suggestive influences of the extra stimuli. In the converse of the above experiment Bayer began with three hens which had eaten until they were full. When he introduced a fourth hungry hen, the other three were little affected by her pecking, only occasionally striking at a grain of food. Each surfeited hen was surrounded by two non-eating hens and one eating hen. Apparently her behavior was controlled by the greater mass of suggestion operating upon her. Since the child with insufficient appetite is usually the child lacking siblings, his food habits can probably be stimulated successfully by letting him dine with other youngsters.

Bayer conducted additional experiments with hens that show the influence of suggestion. When he placed a hen which had fasted for twenty-four hours before a pile of wheat weighing 100 grams, he found that the hen would eat until she had consumed on the average 50 grams, leaving the remaining 50 grams undisturbed. If he placed a larger pile of wheat before the hungry hen, then she wouldn't stop eating at the 50 gram point but would consume 33 to 50 grams additional. Assum-

[1] Bayer, E., "Beiträge zur Zweikomponententheorie des Hungers," *Zeitschrift für Psychologie,* vol. cxii (1929), pp. 1-54.

ing that similar suggestive influences hold true with men and women, we can better understand why people eat more when seated at a heavily loaded banquet board, with opportunity to help themselves as long as they wish. To avoid overweight, therefore, it would seem wise to keep all food off the table except the portions on the diners' plates.

A third type of experiment consisted of leaving a hungry hen before a pile of grain until she was satisfied, as judged by her motionless behavior in front of the remaining grain. Then Bayer carefully removed the food, sweeping out every grain. Immediately he replaced it. As a result, the hen invariably began eating again. When she stopped, he went through the same procedure once more, and the hen resumed pecking as soon as the food was returned. In this manner he found that many hens would consume as much as 67 per cent more food than before. The practical significance of this experiment may lead to quicker fattening of hogs and poultry through similar methods.

In summarizing our discussion of the bases of suggestibility, therefore, we may state that they coincide with the instinctive and habitual neural patterns possessed by an individual. The stimulus which is meaningless to the subject or for which he has no habits developed can not cause him to respond. Moreover, he may be acted upon by antagonistic stimuli, as in the case of Bayer's surfeited hen surrounded by two others like herself and one hungry hen, in which case the stronger suggestion determines the resulting behavior.

Suggestion vs. the Direct Stimulus. The advantage of suggestion over the direct stimulus is that action can be produced more easily. "Sales resistance" and inhibiting ideas are not so likely to be set off. The subject reacts to the suggestion in a childlike, uncritical manner. A suggestion operates like a surprise attack in a military campaign in the sense that the subject reacting is unable to marshall his thoughts to meet the issue rationally. When suggestions are employed, the subject performs as mechanically as a marionette. At the moment of reaction he has no more conscious control over the suggestion-response behavior than Irene possessed over her somnambulistic trance.

Whenever a stimulus is applied to an organism that has become habituated to it, the accustomed reaction will follow unless it is impeded by conflicting ideas or physical circumstances. The function of suggestion, therefore, is to escape the arousal of the rival ideas. In so doing, it not only leads to a quick response, but the subject, if he becomes aware of the response, feels that it is a spontaneous act of his own volition, especially as he was unaware of the external influence playing upon him. Shakespeare gives us an excellent case in which Iago indirectly produced jealousy and hatred in Othello by suggestion. A direct attack by Iago upon Cassio would probably have resulted in Othello's defense of the latter. To damn a man by innuendo avoids antagonizing his friends, yet leads to their detecting real or imagined faults in him, and they think they have done so of their own accord. The following passage is a classic example of the employment of suggestion in the interest of villainy:

IAGO: My noble Lord,—
OTHELLO: What dost thou say, Iago?
IAGO: Did Michael Cassio, when you woo'd my lady, know of your love?
OTHELLO: He did, from first to last: why dost thou ask?
IAGO: But for a satisfaction of my thought;
No further harm.
OTHELLO: Why of thy thought, Iago?
IAGO: I did not think he had been acquainted with her.
OTHELLO: O, yes, and went between us very oft.
IAGO: Indeed!
OTHELLO: Indeed! Ay, indeed; discern'st thou aught in that? Is he not honest?
IAGO: Honest, my lord?

OTHELLO: Honest, ay, honest.
IAGO: My Lord, for aught I know.
OTHELLO: What dost thou think?
IAGO: Think, my lord?
OTHELLO: Think, my lord!
By heaven, he echoes me
As if there were some monster in his thought
Too hideous to be shown. Thou dost mean something;
I hear thee say but now, thou likes not that
When Cassio left my wife. What didst not like?
And when I told thee how he was in my counsel
In my whole course of wooing, thou criedst, "Indeed!"
And didst contract and purse thy brows together,
As if thou hadst shut up in thy brain
Some horrible conceit: If thou dost love me,
Show me thy thought.

IAGO: My lord, you know I love you.
OTHELLO: I think thou dost.
And for I know thou'rt full of love and honest
And weigh'st thy words before thou givest them breath,
Therefore these stops of thine fright me the more:
For such things in a false disloyal knave
Are tricks of custom; but in a man that's just
They're close dilations working from the heart
That passion cannot rule.

IAGO: For Michael Cassio
I dare be sworn I think that he is honest.
OTHELLO: I think so too.
IAGO: Men should be what they seem;
Or those that be not, would they might seem none!
OTHELLO: Certain; men should be what they seem.
IAGO: Why then I think Cassio's an honest man.
OTHELLO: Nay, yet there's more in this;
I prithee, speak to me as to thy thinkings,
As thou dost ruminate, and give thy worst of thoughts,
The words of words.

From the psychological standpoint, therefore, suggestion is superior to the direct stimulus in that it avoids the arousal of contrary ideas. When the suggested action takes place, its sponsor believes the action has been originated by himself, and is therefore much less critical of his behavior. As a consequence, he responds more easily and is more satisfied with his performance. The skilful employment of suggestion, of course, necessitates more thinking and planning than does the use of direct statements, which probably explains why it is not so frequently practiced as the latter.

Positive and Negative Suggestion. Probably the clearest delineation of positive and negative suggestion can be obtained by recalling the instance of the snail cited at the beginning of Chapter II. We noted that a bit of lettuce in front of it caused the snail to expand, to approach the stimulus, whereas at the outset the physical contact of our pencil point caused it to retract. If we assume the snail has its major attention upon some political or economic problem of the day, and then we apply the lettuce leaf, we are using a positive suggestion. The snail will advance. If we employ the pencil point, the snail retracts, and we have employed a negative suggestion.

Although stimuli which occupy our major attention are more likely to set up conflicting reactions, the marginally applied suggestions may also do the same. It is possible to have several suggestions of a rival nature operating upon sense organs of the individual simultaneously. This has been appreciated in the field of advertising, the major effect of which is in the nature of suggestion. We gaze upon cuts and copy while engaged in conversation, consciously unaware of the pictures and words which we are mechanically scanning. If we read, "Eat Red Wing Apples and Avoid the Worms," it is obvious that we have applied both a positive and a negative suggestion at the same time. The case is similar to that of the snail when we first offered him the lettuce and touched him with the pencil.

If our retraction or worm-avoidance behavior is stronger

than our desire to eat apples, we react negatively to such advertising. If the two are equal, then indecision results. The recent advertising campaign with the slogan, "Reach for a Lucky instead of a Sweet," is a case in point. Because of the danger in suggesting antagonistic responses to the individual the usual statement in previous advertisements, "Beware of Substitutes," is being rapidly omitted. To be most effective, advertisements must concentrate on a unified impression that is positive in its suggestive influence.

There are certain exceptions which appear to stand out. Not long ago the Philco advertisement depicted a driver in a predicament because of a stalled engine. The motorist exclaimed that he would never again be caught without a Philco battery. Then there was the Listerine campaign with the ugly thought of "halitosis". And Fleischmann's Yeast campaign depicting viscera and explaining that we needed vitalizing through better elimination. In the summer of 1932 came the astounding Razor Company's pronouncement all over the country, "We Made a Mistake." Throughout the copy we learned that as users of these razor blades we had been given inferior steel blades, but it would not happen again.

The superficial success of such advertising as the above examples may be explained on the basis of the following facts: (1) As long as enough money is spent, even on psychologically imperfect advertising, of course the volume of sales will increase. If a company spends $1,000,000 this year against $250,000 last year, we should expect an increase in its sales, but whether that increase is as large as it would be with positive suggestion advertisements is a different matter. (2) As long as the advertising commands the major attention or consciousness of the readers it is possible to use "reason why" copy, and educate the readers to the significance of the negative contents of the copy and cuts. But, also, it requires unlimited financial resources and ever changing advertisements to keep the focal circle of the average reader's attention. It cannot be done economically. The chief value of advertising is its marginal or subconscious stimulation of the readers.

"Reason why" copy is not very effective when acting upon us in the marginal rings of our attention, for reasoning involves many generic words and a greater percentage of our attention than is found out there. Consequently, after once having seen such an advertisement we lose interest in it, which means it operates thereafter in the margin of our attention. We do not heed the finer type of explanatory copy, but daily react to the slogan in bold black headlines, "We Made a Mistake," In the preceding chapter we cited similar examples of how people recall the general items and forget the details. The slogan just quoted, therefore, is inferior to "Eat Red Wing Apples and Avoid Worms," for the latter is only 50 per cent negative when operating as a suggestion.

(3) A third reason for the success of such negative advertising as the Listerine and Yeast variety is the fact that a large number of people are already afflicted with ills or think they are. They are consequently alert for relief and not only do not retract or wince at the sight of such illustrations and slogans, but actually are drawn to them instead. Once a person has lost his health or his position, he no longer feels the scorn or disgust for infection and failure, especially as it is depicted in the advertisements, but goes through a process of immediate identification, and avidly scans the copy for information as to his own cure. For this type of individual, and the success of patent medicines proves there are millions of such, the picture of a sick man, especially when the "Before and After" illustrations are employed, may even be an asset. It holds his attention because it fits in with his chronic attitude of the moment—freedom from his defect.

In repeating our stress upon positive suggestion, it is well to recall what happens during forgetting. The generic headings, such as slogans and cuts, are retained, while the minor items usually appearing in small type, drop out. In the case of the Razor Company's slogan mentioned previously, the company undoubtedly felt that the novelty of their admission would stimulate belief in the Razor Company itself, relying on the attitude that confidence is often increased in the salesman who acknowledges an occasional defect. But many, if not the majority, of this razor's users hadn't even noted any inferiority of the blades. An unnoticed defect was now carefully pointed out by the company itself, with the additional unpalatable thought that they had been selling an inferior blade to us for some time. Since no refunds were announced, the normal man felt the displeasure that results from being tricked, and no promise about future good behavior can completely erase the ego deflation of being made the "goat". This unpleasant emotional conditioning is dangerous.

Even the previous non-user of this company's blades will retain ultimately the recollection that this company made an error, which becomes shortened in memory until finally all he recalls is "Blank Razors—Defective". It seems strange that there is lack of appreciation of the fact that ingenuity can always produce an advertisment or cut which is just as good at attracting attention, just as good at holding attention, just as good at impressing the memory, and certainly far more desirable in feeling tone and positive suggestion, than any negative advertisement yet produced.

About ten years ago the advertisement reproduced on the next page was sent to Professor A. J. Snow for criticism. He used it with his classes and the writer employed it in his own sections of psychology to determine the student reaction. Because of the unpleasant feeling tone noted by many of the feminine students in particular, Professor Snow voted against it, despite his realization of its uniqueness and attention attracting value. In the autumn numbers of *Advertising and Selling* for 1930, the wisdom of this advertisement was still being debated. It is said, however, to have been the most successful of any used by that company.

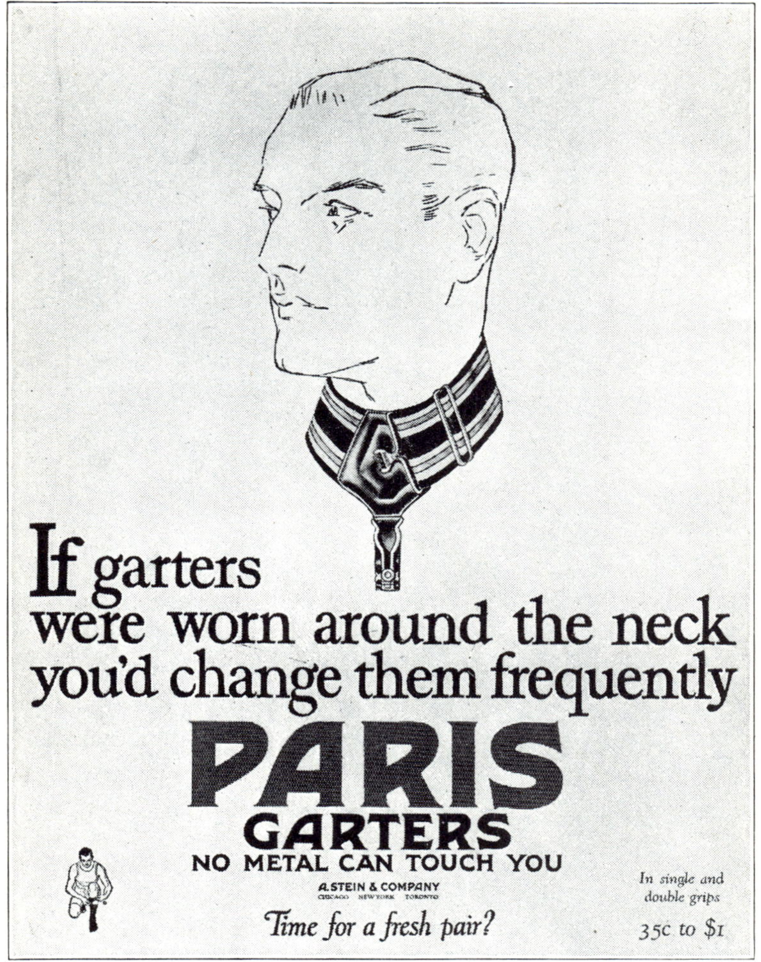

EXHIBIT 28. One of the most debated advertisements ever run, coupling an excellent attention attracting cut with a possible unpleasant feeling tone. (Courtesy of A. Stein & Company).

(MERCIREX)

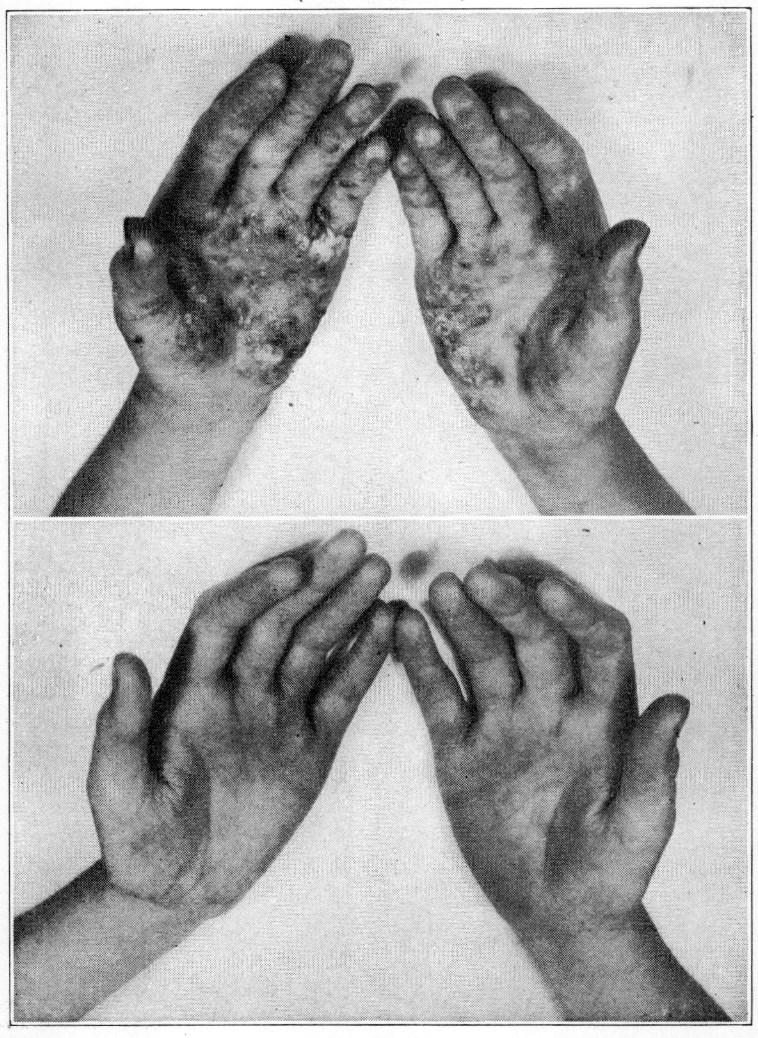

EXHIBIT 29. A good example of suggestion in advertising with the unpleasant feeling tone neutralized by the pleasant illustration. (Courtesy of The Mercirex Company).

As we shall consider more fully later, the behavior of the salesman, speaker, and leader may be either negative or positive in its results. In the example of Bayer's surfeited hen we saw that the pecking of another hungry hen incited her to action, but the restraint of two other satiated hens offset the positive suggestion of the single hungry creature. A former student of mine who was professional buyer for a Chicago organization told me about an incident which bears upon this point. A salesman of check writing machines interviewed this buyer. He presented his sales talk, and saw that the buyer was in a receptive frame of mind. "How many do you want?" asked the salesman. "Thirty-five," responded the buyer.

At this point the salesman, who apparently was expecting an order for one or two machines, became so excited that he could hardly fill in the order blank, whereupon the buyer said, "But I want to think it over, so I shan't be in the market today." Later he bought of another salesman who gave no better sales presentation, but who never batted an eyelash when he found out the size of the order. The buyer, in commenting upon the first salesman said, "You know, I began to feel that he wasn't used to selling large orders, so probably his machine wasn't any good."

The psychological phases of positive versus negative suggestions, therefore, point to the greater desirability of the former. Because suggestions are indirect and consequently in the marginal circles of the attention-field, the subject on whom they are operating cannot reason with them. They produce apparently spontaneous action. If they are negative, the resulting behavior is of the avoidance or retractive sort. Since the "reason why" copy of the advertisement cannot be understood in the marginal circles of the attention-field, the subject responds only to the stimuli of the headlines, cuts, and pictures, for these can set off habit patterns from the margins of the attention-field.

Specificity in Suggestion. In our discussion of methods of motivating human beings we distinguished between the three degrees of effective stimuli, the first being the actual objects themselves; the second, specific words denoting individual objects; and the least effective being generic and non-sensory terms. Because a suggestion leads to igniting habit systems already possessed by the subject, it is apparent that the more specific the suggestion, the more readily it will set off or ignite habitual behavior.

In the old days of wall telephones, hotels found it necessary to place a memorandum pad beside the telephone in order to protect the walls, for salesmen and even fastidious ladies would soon be scribbling on the wall, making geometric patterns and hieroglyphics while they conversed. The presence of a pencil on the desk in front of the average person who is engaged in talking, either over the telephone or directly to his interviewer, is an almost irresistible suggestion to the accustomed action of writing. It is, moreover, almost impossible for boys, and even for their fathers, to walk along a stream where there are round, smooth pebbles and not pick up a handful to throw.

In the manufacture of ammonia by Germany during the World War the Haber process was adopted, which entailed the use of enormous pressures. It is reported that the employees refused to endanger their lives further by working in such an environment, particularly as many fellow employees had been killed in several previous explosions. To placate them, the management called a halt in production, and issued the statement that a new method entailing less pressure was going to be installed in the plant, and set its engineers to work for a few days. When the employees were finally recalled, they felt much reassured. Pressure dials that formerly had read, say "5000 pounds per square inch", now were only "50 pounds per square inch". But the security felt by the workers was obtained simply through the installation of new pressure gauges from which two zeros had been removed, even though a pressure of 50 pounds was sufficient to cause a fatal explosion. The absence of those two ciphers was far more effective than hours of haranguing would have been.

The story is told of a gardner who found that his neighbor's hens kept digging up his seeds and ruining his tomatoes. Protest after protest that he made to their owner was of no avail. One night the gardener placed a dozen eggs at strategic points around his garden. Next morning he nonchalantly went out with a basket, and while his neighbor's wife looked out of her window at him he gathered the eggs. His neighbor penned the chickens within his own lot before another day had passed.

It is imperative, therefore, that specificity be employed in suggestions because habits are originally formed by definite stimuli, and must be set off by the same kind of object or quality. Abstractions and generalities may be used when the focus of attention is being monopolized, but in the marginal circles of the attention-field such stimuli are relatively ineffective. As a general rule we may say that the less attention being given to a stimulus, the more specific it must be in order to produce a reaction.

Sex Differences in Suggestibility. Since women have been more accustomed to taking orders from men than have men, it follows that we should expect females to obey more mechanically than do males. They should not be so likely to consider masculine commands critically but should submit from habituation. Although we have no tests which adequately measure suggestibility of men and women as Army Alpha, for instance, will measure their intellectual abilities, empirical data would seem to indicate a slight sex difference. It must be kept in mind that by our definition of suggestion, however, the reason women may be more suggestible than men in the social environment is the fact that masculine commands are not confronted so consciously as is true of men who hear the same orders given. The male tends to make an issue out of his submission, which thereby keeps his action in the focal circle of his attention-field. The woman, by her lack of conscious attention to the orders given, is reacting to marginal stimuli.

The relationship between suggestibility and intelligence is a peculiar one. On the basis of the greater number of habits possessed by the more intelligent individual, we should say that he could be stimulated by a wider range of suggestions. The familiar stories about absent-minded professors are almost always clear examples of responses to suggestion by men whose attention-field is preoccupied with direct stimuli. On the other hand, the more intelligent person has profited from his many ludicrous automatic acts so that he is somewhat on his guard thereafter. He has developed a "suggestion resistance" comparable to "sales resistance", and this is possible through a shifting attention and critical inspection of himself. He doesn't let himself be carried away with emotional enthusiasm as does the novice, because he is more experienced in such situations, and remains on his guard.

The apparently greater suggestibility of children is not explicable on the basis of the number of habits that can be set off by marginal stimuli or indirectly aroused by focal stimuli, for the child is obviously inferior to the adult in total number of habits. The child, however, has not learned to be so self critical as the adult. He is less wary of life, and is more inclined to do a thing without realizing what he does as he does it.

In concluding our discussion of sex differences in suggestibility, we may state that women are probably more suggestible than men because they have been more accustomed to taking orders from a source of greater physical prestige, and therefore the act of submission is more mechanical. This difference is consequently traceable to the physical differences between the sexes. Children are more suggestible than adults for the same reason.

How the Subconscious Affects Our Purchases. In discussing the subconscious throughout this book we employ the term synonymously with the marginal fields of attention illustrated in Exhibit 8. Those stimuli that lie in the outer circles are subconscious or marginal. We have called them suggestions in this chapter. And those habits ignited by such stimuli constitute the subconscious or marginal behavior of the individual. We have already intimated that the chief value of advertising is produced through its effects upon the marginal fields of attention.

Manufacturers and retailers also produce buying activity by playing upon us through these marginal zones. We know that certain anatomical aspects of the eye make it more of a strain for us to look up and down than to swing our gaze horizontally. The psychological effect of this condition makes us overestimate vertical distances. In a similar manner we think that filled space is greater than empty space, as Exhibit 30 demonstrates. A number of such illusions are employed by merchants and advertisers for the purpose of increasing sales. In having his subjects rank a number of cans in order of apparent size, Starch[1] found that cans of the same cubical contents were considered of different sizes by observers. One can was uniformly voted to be more than one-quarter larger than another of the identical cubical capacity. The significance of this fact is of monetary value to concerns merchandising their products in such containers.

On many cartons and cans, moreover, contents are designated in ounces instead of pounds, especially if the net weight is exactly one pound. The statement, "Net contents 16 ounces," is often likely to create the attitude that the weight is greater than if the statement read, "Net contents one pound." This results in part from an uncritical reaction to the number "16" and the number "1". Moreover, many in-

[1] Starch, Daniel, *op. cit.*, pp. 724-726.

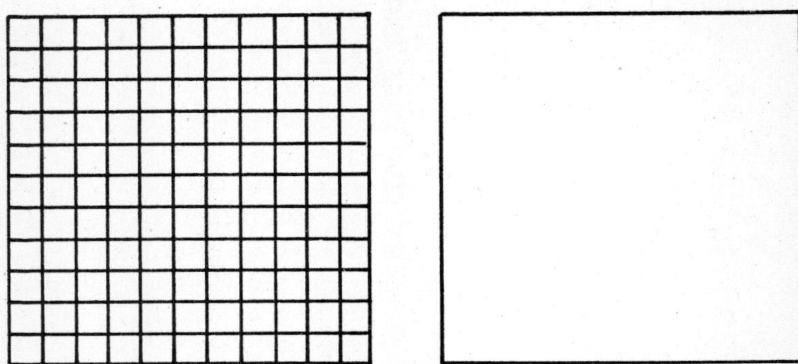

EXHIBIT 30. Showing the apparent difference in size of equal areas when one is filled space and the other empty.

dividuals may think the pound contains only 12 ounces, and hence feel they are getting 4 ounces more.

One of the writer's former students who was a radio retailer described how he used to convince his customers of the musical excellence of a radio. He would tell them in advance that good reproduction of tone on the part of a radio should enable the listener to visualize the movements of the musicians at the studio, or the throat and lip movements of the singer. Then he would have his customers sit down and close their eyes, while he tuned in. As the music issued from the radio he let them concentrate upon what they thought was occurring at the other end of the line, thus capitalizing upon their visual memories as an aid in increasing their enjoyment of an otherwise purely auditory concert. Their greater enjoyment was therefore assumed to be wholly a product of the tonal qualities of the instrument in question.

The same retailer used to enlist the co-operation of his Italian customers who wanted phonographs by always having a Caruso record in the demonstrating machine. The customer soon began to hum or sing along with Caruso, thereby rearousing memories of home and love and youth. The pleasant emotional state of the customer was skilfully ascribed to the excellence of reproduction of tones by the given phonograph.

Since the great majority of our opinions and decisions are really based upon marginal stimuli, and only break into the focus of our attention-field after the manner outlined in our discussion of the thirst reaction of the young reporter, we shall study more specifically these influences under the next four sectional headings of this chapter.

Suggestive Advertising. All advertising soon slips out of the focus of our attention, in which case its influence upon us is by way of suggestion. But there are also certain types of advertising that are definitely classed as suggestive, for their effect is indirect even when they are viewed consciously. During the past decade, for example, the American public has witnessed an era of testimonial advertising. Football heroes and other athletes of all sorts have endorsed everything from correspondence short story courses to cigarettes, and even staid old American families of blue blood stock have been subscribing to the merits of cold creams, beauty lotions and tooth paste. Moving picture actors and actresses get almost as much publicity through their photographic appearance on cartons and cigarette billboards as from their histrionic endeavors on the silver screen.

The purpose behind this sort of advertising is not only to attract attention to the product, but to suggest that the reader will also become athletic or beautiful by using the cigarettes and cold cream. In the late summer of 1932 the breakfast foods began to enlist moving picture stars in their advertising campaigns, hoping thereby to increase the pulling power of their advertisements.

But the response in other fields has also been increased by adjusting the coupon to the type of product being merchandised. In this connection Simons[1] finds that triangular cou-

[1] Simons, Eric N., "To Increase the Pulling Power of Advertisements," *Printers' Ink* (Dec. 15, 1921), pp. 109 *ff*.

pons are better when the request is for catalogues or literature, whereas a rectangular coupon is superior when free samples, goods on approval, or a trial order are being sought. When the coupon is being directed to one of the executives of a firm it is wiser to call it a "Request Form". Pointers or arrows in the body of the advertisement which are directed toward the coupon also increase the pulling power of the latter. The drawing of a man at his desk pointing to the coupon, and that of a hand holding a fountain pen with its point projecting into the coupon as if beginning to fill it out also increased the applications received.

The effectiveness of color as an attention attractor is self-evident, but that is not its only virtue in the advertisement. Color conveys an impression of richness and good quality which is impossible to portray in black and white. Unless a concern is very careful in the use of color, however, its patrons may obtain a feeling of disappointment when the dress or bedroom suite arrives. The buyers reacted not alone to the purchased article when they saw it pictured in the advertisement, but they indirectly absorbed some of the suggestions of style and trimness of the girlish figures attired in the frock in question, or of the other room furnishings in which the bedroom suite was situated. As a result, if the housewife does not have the graceful figure of the model, or if her bedroom is not the duplicate of the one seen in the advertisement, she may experience disappointment, and project her displeasure upon the concern whose product she has purchased. Even in direct retail selling the same displeasure frequently follows the purchaser's return home. While in the shop she reacted to the richness of the surroundings. Her more drab home environment doesn't contribute the pleasurable sensations which she experienced in the buying situation, and she cannot understand the apparent change in her attitude toward the hat. Like the radio and phonograph customers described above, she had unwittingly transferred many additional sensory experiences to the hat which the hat did not possess. Her brutally frank husband or relatives may also present comments concerning her appearance which are very different from those of the saleslady.

As regards the types of products that can be presented successfully through suggestive advertising, Hollingworth[1] gives the following list:

1. For all *personal* articles, the use of which is *intimate* and *private,* as toilet articles, gifts, stationery, and so forth.

2. For articles of *luxury, display,* and *adornment,* as jewelry, fancy dress goods, feathers and plumes, flowers and so on.

3. For articles enjoyed *in themselves* or *for their own sake,* rather than for remote service which they may render, as drinks, musical instruments, sweetmeats, toys.

4. For articles calculated to promote the *bodily safety* of the individual or of those dependent on him, as disinfectants, safety devices, insurance, weapons of defence.

5. For *all food products.*

6. For all clothing which tends to be ornamental rather than utilitarian in character, as ties, collars, laces, canes.

As a matter of fact, almost any product can be presented at times through the medium of suggestive advertising. Note the following statistical advertisement of Packard automobiles. It ran in Chicago where the suburban towns and cities mentioned are well known as being decidedly above the average in wealth and culture. The region is a continuation of Chicago's "Gold Coast". As a result, the readers not only saw the actual percentage of Packards in use, but they indirectly reacted to the fact that this automobile was popular with the wealthy residents.

From the psychological viewpoint, therefore, almost all ad-

[1] Hollingworth, H. L., *Advertising and Selling* (D. Appleton & Co., New York, 1920), p. 245.

TOWN	PACKARDS*	NATIVE WHITE FAMILIES**	RATIO
Highland Park	174	1337	1 to 7.6
Glencoe	153	875	1 to 5.7
Winnetka	338	1389	1 to 4.1
Kenilworth	91	206	1 to 2.2
Wilmette	205	1799	1 to 8.7
Evanston	1103	7300	1 to 6.6
Entire North Shore	2064	12906	1 to 6.25

*Actual count from vehicle registrations.
**Good Housekeeping (Magazine) calculation based on census figures as of 1925.

vertising sooner or later becomes suggestive in its influence, for the reader soon tires of the given advertisement and lets his conscious attention dwell upon something else even though his eyes still rest upon the cuts and headlines before him. At this moment, accordingly, the advertisement acts as suggestion unless it is strictly a copy advertisement with reason why matter throughout. Much of the advertising which falls within the visual field of the reader, however, is suggestive from the very first glance, and constitutes what is technically termed suggestive advertising. Such advertising is especially valuable for all merchandise which appeals strongly to the senses.

The Origin of Fashions. The difference between the source of clothing styles of men and women is very distinct and interesting. Women like to have clothing that is Parisian. To advertise a frock as the most popular among Berlin women, or among the feminine population of London, Brussels, or Rome would lead to little effect in America today. But to offer the latest style creation of a Parisian modiste immediately stimulates buying. There are a number of reasons which explain this trait of American women, but probably the most basic one can be illustrated by answering the following question. If the average American girl were to pick out a nurse for her convalescent sweetheart, assuming that all of the following girls spoke English and were equally pretty, would she choose a German girl, a French girl, an English girl, or an Italian girl? The answers of 45 college girls are listed below.

NO. OF	PER CENT CHOOSING			
SUBJECTS	GERMAN	FRENCH	ENGLISH	ITALIAN
45	44.4	8.8	33.3	13.3

EXHIBIT 31. Showing racial preferences expressed by college girls in choosing nurses for their sweethearts.

It is of interest that two of the four girls who chose the French nurse gave as their reason that they wanted to "test" their sweethearts. If the men could resist the French girl, then they would certainly be true to their wives after marriage. It is partly because of these reactions listed above that the French clothing is popular among our women. The most dangerous woman as regards influencing men is the one whose methods, including clothes, are most likely to be envied and imitated. The testimonial advertising previously mentioned often depends on a similar appeal.

As regards men's clothing styles, however, a Parisian trademark would often be a detriment instead of an asset. The foreign source of male fashions in clothes is London. But not all of the London styles are adopted over here. One of the leading authorities in men's fashions in this country, John Starbuck, says that the three most important sources of style influence in America are (1) Yale and Princeton, (2) Wall Street, and (3) Broadway. At these three centers the London styles that will ultimately become popular in this country are first adopted.

Previous to the arrival of the Prince of Wales in America in

1924, manufacturers had estimated the 1924 demand for double-breasted suits at 3 per cent of their total output. Sumner[1] describes the effect of the fact that the Prince wore two double-breasted suits rather frequently. Within two years following his visit the proportion of double-breasted suits had risen in America to 45 per cent.

The shirt manufacturers had produced their 1924 lines with scarcely a shirt like the soft blue kind with collars attached which the Prince frequently wore. The demand for this type of shirt became so great that an entire new production schedule had to be introduced at midseason, and some manufacturers suffered considerable losses in getting rid of their overstocks of white shirts.

The summer styles of men are definitely forecast in the apparel worn during January and February at Palm Beach. A number of "style detectives" follow the men around and tabulate the golf, bathing and dinner costumes, rushing off their results to New York immediately. The next summer these styles are prevalent in men's wearing apparel. If the men don't react to them at once, their wives and sweethearts soon make them conscious of the changes.

In considering the importance of the three American sources of style, we can see why these groups influence others. In the first place, styles and fashions run downhill from the financially and socially élite. The financiers and business men of America have their eyes focussed on the New York stock market and Wall Street. The incoming buyers and salesmen patronize the theaters, and night clubs, while the wealthy Princeton group of students just outside of New York City have social prestige, plus great popularity among the many women's colleges nearby.

With regard to Princeton students we may mention that they

[1] Sumner, G. Lynn, "The College Man—Style Mentor," *Advertising & Selling* (June 26, 1929), pp. 17, *ff*.

were the first to go hatless, and to discard the garter. In 1925 they set the derby hat fashion among college men. In 1926 they adopted the suspenders, and Yale followed suit. By December, 1926, the suspenders had arrived on the campus at the University of Southern California. In January, 1927, they appeared at the University of Illinois. By June, 1927, three out of five Harvard men were wearing them, and by autumn of that year the college men all over the middle west were victims to the craze.

In general, therefore, the desire to be in fashion results from an unwillingness to be socially ostracized through too great an individual attire, especially among males. The men seek uniformity and a common denominator of dress; the women seek individuality within certain very narrow limits. The greater diversity of feminine dress is largely reducible to color and more frequent seasonal changes, for women will not attempt to alter such matters as skirt length or neck and sleeve dictates of the current styles. Their individuality of dress is obtained within the sharp delineations of fashion.

Basic determinants of fashion itself have in part been dwelt upon hitherto. The child imitates its parent—a superior individual—and mankind has followed the same general principle in its clothing. Whim, caprice, professional jealousies, and a desire to make more profit are the chief factors that cause the modistes to evolve a new type of garment. They know that the established pacemakers of both sexes will be always on the alert to maintain their reputation for style leadership. When a few princesses and actresses have appeared in the new frocks, the rest of the popularization process is similar to that of the book salesman who begins with the bankers, teachers, society leaders, and ministers and works down.

Probably no more clear-cut instance of the conscious acceptance of fashions is available than that of the young immigrant. In order to avoid being conspicuous, he quickly dons the conventional clothing of the new country, and, more slowly, its manners and customs. He attains a sense of greater social unity thereby. Back in the tenements where he lives his social prestige is likewise enhanced. His models, however, are frequently changed from touts to pugilists to aldermen as his knowledge of social distinctions develops.

In considering the origin of fashions, therefore, we must distinguish between their actual creators in the fashion marts of the world, and their popularizers, those social pacemakers who are aped by the majority of mankind. The designers and modistes of Paris, London, New York, etc., do the actual evolving of new patterns. These are then presented to the public by means of a few men and women who hold a place of preeminence in social and financial circles, for fashions are adopted in part as a means of elevating one's prestige and therefore must pass from the higher social strata to the lower. This fact is fairly well demonstrated here in the United States by viewing the three first acceptance groups for men's styles: Yale and Princeton, Wall Street, and Broadway.

The Place of Suggestion in the Sale. The more that suggestions can be employed in selling, the less likelihood there will be of objections from the customer or client. We have discussed the relative merits of positive and negative suggestions. "Take a Kodak with You" is not a suggestion as long as it is consciously reacted to, but as soon as it affects the eye or ear subconsciously it is an effective positive suggestion. The salesman, however, has more difficulty than the advertiser in employing marginal stimuli in his sale, for he cannot keep reiterating his commands until they are relegated to the fringe of attention. But the other type of suggestion—the stimulus that indirectly sets off habitual behavior from the focal region of attention—he can employ to his profit throughout the sale.

We are not decrying his use of marginal stimuli whenever he can. On the contrary, he should employ them wherever possible. We have simply indicated that he cannot use them as frequently as the direct stimulus with the indirect result. When he says, "The wives of 351 doctors are using this vacuum cleaner," he gives a direct statement which indirectly leads to the thought, "Doctor's wives would certainly want to use the vacuum that kept the floors most free from dirt and infection." The customer is led to the thought, "This vacuum cleaner picks up more dirt than others do." The salesman didn't make this statement. Therefore, the customer's tendency to doubt such an assertion is avoided, since it arises in her own mind. Thoughts that come out of our own heads we tend to believe. At least, we don't salt them so heavily.

Whenever the salesman can get his customer to evolve the selling points for his product, he profits thereby. He needs to utilize this devious method of presenting his ideas, for he encounters what is commonly spoken of as "sales resistance". This phrase is one of those generic, third degree stimuli that lead nowhere until they are torn down into their constituents. Sales resistance simply covers the fact that the buyer has no money to spend; that the buyer spent unwisely last time and is vividly recalling that chagrin; that the buyer's husband will scold if she purchases this article; that she has a similar article on hand now; that she can get a cheaper product than you offer; that she would rather have a new coat for the $75 and use a broom than have the vacuum cleaner and last year's coat; that she has an aversion to men with your type of ears or nose; that she resents your high pressure, masculine dominance; that the baby is crying for its bottle, and she hasn't heard half of your sales talk. These are only a few of the main reasons why the buyer doesn't respond. We have used the woman buyer instead of the professional male buyer in this discussion because the reasons for sales resistance are almost identical and more of the readers can identify themselves with her situation.

The suggestive value of questions should be noted here.

They are, by the way, similar in function to the fever thermometer in that they offer an outsider a means of taking a record of the customer's internal state. With some clients who refrain from speaking voluntarily and who present a stoical face, the salesman has difficulty in knowing where he stands. By means of the question he takes a reading. But there is a technique in its use which must be adhered to constantly. Since the salesman should control the interview, he must not let the conversation get away from him. In putting his queries, therefore, he should have them phrased so that the customer cannot readily respond other than in the method the salesman desires. He should employ what the lawyer calls "leading" questions. If he asks his customer, "Do you think this vacuum cleaner has a strong suction?" he leaves her with perfect freedom to answer yes or no. It is a 50:50 type of question. But because she is careful to avoid committing herself, she may either say, "I guess it has," or else "Well, it seems that Mrs. Brown's is stronger than this." By the proper intonation, however, he can make a leading question out of the 50:50 variety.

Much better than the previous query is one like, "This vacuum has a strong suction, hasn't it?" Or he may put it, "Doesn't this have a powerful suction?" Such a query we call a 60:40 type. The salesman has already steered his customer into the desired response, and a negative reply on her part demands an open revolt. Her accustomed habits of politeness force her to answer in the affirmative, or at worst, remain quiet. Her yea:nay reaction has, we shall assume, the ratio 60:40. And as long as a customer doesn't say no, the salesman can continue with the interview.

If a salesman, or a lawyer, were to put the query, "Did you see a red barn?" it would not be a leading question. But note the degrees of suggestion demonstrated by the following: "Did you see the red barn?" "Didn't you see a red barn?" "Didn't you see the red barn?" It wouldn't be long, therefore, until children would be remembering the red barn, and adults would also begin to recall it. We tend to see what we want, or are expected, to see. Since we have all observed red barns, it is no insurmountable task for our imagination to shift a red barn wherever we think it should be located.

The salesman must be on guard, therefore, when describing absent objects in order to avoid letting the subject's fancy run riot. The student has probably experienced the situation when he has gone on a so-called "blind" date. His friends have told him the girl was pretty. Lacking her physical presence to check the flights of his imagination, he translates pretty into what he considers it—probably an unusually beautiful creature. The contrast between his imagined picture of her and the real girl may be marked, despite the fact that she may be a normally attractive college girl.

In using adjectives describing merchandise the same danger is run. Although the active employment of the customer's imagination may help sell the product, a good sale involves not just the name on the dotted line, but a satisfied customer. For

GENERALITY	SPECIFICITY
Our candies are made of the best and purest ingredients selected with utmost care and combined with superlative skill.	A lemon fondant made from real fruit, freshly grated; vanilla caramel produced from pure country butter and cream; these rolled together and then covered with Norris chocolate.

EXHIBIT 32. Showing the superiority of second degree stimuli over generalities. (Hotchkiss).

this reason specificity is better than generality as the examples from Hotchkiss[1] plainly indicate. Superlatives, when they do

[1] Hotchkiss, G. B., *op. cit.*, p. 227.

lead to trains of thought, may cause too much individual interpretation on the part of the subject, and they do not suggest specific responses, either in selling or advertising. Hence, as suggestions they are ineffective.

Suggestion also is operative when "odd" prices are employed. The sales value of "odd" prices is largely owing to suggestions of bargains. As Snow[1] points out, storekeepers have been unable to sell certain merchandise at $1.50 when a change of the price tag to $1.69 caused the article to move rapidly. The latter price indirectly aroused the idea, "This is a $1.75 article," or even, "This is a $2.00 value." The figure $1.95 is really much cheaper than $2.00 in its suggestive value than the five cents would indicate. We tend to react principally to the number on the left of the decimal point. A label of $1.95 not only suggests a bargain price on a more costly article, but it suggests a much greater bargain than it really is. There is also the suggestion, as in mail order firms, that the odd figures denote close estimating and low profit for the company, thereby indicating higher value and quality for the customer.

The suggestive value of names is also important in selling. Perfumes bearing French labels can be sold much more readily than those with English names. There are cases on record where changing the English name to French and raising the price materially, have greatly speeded up the sale of the product. The French label intimates that the perfume is imported, and the word "imported" also suggests superior quality and price. A good case of negative suggestion in a name is that of "Barkeeper's Friend", a variety of polish or powder which I have seen advertised in the middle west, with the appeal directed to mothers. The name "Ivory", on the contrary, suggests richness, importation. "Camay", even without our advertising knowledge of the word, suggests a different thought than "Lifebuoy".

[1] Snow, A. J., *op. cit.*, p. 106.

To show how a retailer can offset the effect of advertising, and change the opinion of a customer by use of suggestion I shall cite the following sale, as recounted to me two years ago by the radio dealer mentioned earlier in the chapter.

A man came into my radio shop the other evening and asked to look at the various instruments. He said he wanted a Philco, and seemed determined that no other radio would do. I told him that I didn't have a Philco (I don't handle that line) but I would be glad to get it for him. I asked him if he had any particular model in mind.

"No-o-o," he replied.

I realized then that the fellow wasn't sold on anything but the Philco name, so decided to break his fondness for that type of radio, and try to sell him one of my own. I asked him if he wouldn't care to look around at the various models in the display room, and see which he liked, meanwhile leading him to one of my most expensive brands.

After we had inspected it closely and I had pointed out some of the points of importance in examining radios, I told him that this machine we were looking at was, of course, more expensive than the Philco. I knew this would cause him to have a let-down regarding the prestige of the Philco in his mind. He would now realize that there were other radios of excellence on the market. This was all I wanted to do up to that point, namely, simply get him open-minded regarding radios.

Then I let him look inside a number of machines, meanwhile finding out what price he could afford to pay. I described the various tubes, telling him that Philco had a good tube, all right, but it had been perfected in 1926. The majority of modern radios, like these models I was showing him, were all equipped with the new tube just patented this year. Of course, my emphasis on *modern* and *latest style* made him feel that Philco was an old model.

Finally, I asked him to try the real test of a radio, namely, the sound test in which he attempted to visualize the singer's lips while his eyes were closed and he was listening to the music.

When he left the shop I had sold him a Fada radio.

In demonstrating his goods the salesman may also be able to employ marginal stimuli by letting the housewife participate in the demonstration. While discussing the vacuum cleaner mentioned above he may incline the handle toward her as he stoops to insert the plug into the wall socket. The suggestion of taking hold of the handle usually is sufficient to cause the housewife to grasp it. The salesman now has his customer helping him sell her, for the pleasurable tactual and kinesthetic sensations as she later moves the shiny new machine over her rugs give rise to a desire for possession. The salesman studiously avoids taking the machine from her hand. "Just notice how easy it is for you to turn it on," he begins. "See that little lever where the handle joins the motor. You don't have to stoop, for you can just touch it with the toe of your slipper. Yes, just push it a bit harder."

In the realm of foodstuffs the offering of samples is suggestive salesmanship, for the gustatory delight resulting begins to set up appropriative reactions, and the customer wants a continuation of the pleasing stimuli. The taste qualities are operating while her attention may be focussed on the salesman's words. For a further explanation of the influence of suggestion in the sale the reader is referred to Chapter VII.

Viewed psychologically, therefore, the place of suggestion in the sale is everywhere, for the more it is employed the less likelihood of antagonizing the customer. There is no special point at which the salesman must use suggestion and then refrain from so doing elsewhere. The value of the leading question or the 60:40 query, moreover, is considerable, and demonstrates one form of suggestion. "Odd" prices, foreign trade names, samples, the minor close, and the incorporation of the customer in the demonstration—these are just a few of the other obvious ways in which suggestion operates to the advantage of the salesman. Even in his personality and method of introduction the salesman may create confidence and prestige, which thereby render his customer more liable to his suggestive salesmanship.

Securing Conviction by Suggestion. We have already mentioned that people are much less critical of ideas which apparently are a creation of their own thinking, than of ideas advanced by outsiders. Belief in a thing results from our having no contrary experiences or habits that oppose it. If an outsider presents the idea, from past experiences with salesmen and other persuaders we find ourselves cautious, doubtful. If it is evolved within us, we don't have that chronic distrust, for why should we trick ourselves?

In the sale of an automobile tire, for instance, the statement may be made that the United States mail trucks all use it. This in itself is no selling point. We must first have familiarity with the United States; we must recall that there are thousands of mail trucks, since this is a large country; we must also remember that large businesses attempt the strictest economies; therefore, the government has probably found this tire the most durable and cheap. Until we have reached this resultant thought, the initial statement means nothing. If a magazine, such as *The Literary Digest,* advertises that "29,374 Bankers Read *The Literary Digest*" we are unaffected until subconsciously we go through a translation process somewhat as follows: "Important men read this magazine—men who must keep posted on latest developments nationally and internationally. *The Literary Digest* must offer a quick means to keep abreast of world affairs." The testimonial advertising involves similar marginal thinking if it is to contribute anything beyond the attention attracting value of pretty girls and women.

In the statement concerning the number of bankers reading the magazine mentioned, the reader will quickly perceive the greater convincing power of "29,374 Bankers" over "30,000 Bankers". A little introspection will reveal the fact that the former suggests an actual count that can be authenticated, if challenged, whereas the larger figure intimates a hasty generality that might be considerably over the true statement. The first connotes science and accuracy, the second denotes salesmanship and a stretching of truth for effect.

In dealing with people it will be found desirable to spend considerable time developing ways of stating selling points for a product, a personality, an idea, or a service which will avoid arousing the inhibitions attaching to direct commands. To say, "You ought to read *The Literary Digest.* It gives you the most condensed and comprehensive survey of World News," may lead to a slangy and resentful, "Oh, yeah?"

In salesmanship, speaking, or advertising one must be careful to avoid such terms as "You ought . . . ", "You owe it to . . . ", "Common sense demands that you . . . ", "You need . . . ", "You should . . . ", or "You must . . . ". Such phrases suggest that the speaker has done your thinking for you, that he is superior to you and has found you in error. These ideas tend to arouse dislike, even open hostility on the part of the customer or audience, because the "negative protest" discussed in Chapter XIII is immediately brought into action. Americans in particular resent commands. The best logic possible may be unavailing on a person rendered bullheaded by such negative suggestions as these just described.

In persuading a person that a certain joke is funny, it is obviously ineffective to keep affirming its humor, to keep telling him that he will split his sides laughing when he hears it, that he will think it the most witty thing he has ever listened to. Why not tell him the joke itself and let him decide? Yet the number of speakers and salesmen is legion who spend good selling time telling their listeners that they will profit from the article in question, that they will save money, that they would not get along without it after they try it, that they need it in their business, etc., when they should be citing specific data, and avoiding the negative suggestions incurred by such authoritative statements about their customers' thought processes and reactions.

REFERENCES

ALLPORT, F. H., *Social Psychology* (Boston, 1924), chaps. xi and xii.
BROWN, W., *Individual and Sex Differences in Suggestibility,* University of California Publications in Psychology, vol. ii (1916), No. 6.
GAULT, ROBERT H., *Social Psychology* (New York, 1923), chap. vi.
HART, BERNARD, *Psychology of Insanity* (Cambridge, 1921), chap. iv.
HOLLINGWORTH, H. L., *Advertising and Selling* (New York, 1920), chap. xii.
HUMPHREY, G., "The Conditioned Reflex and the Elementary Social Reaction," *Journal of Abnormal and Social Psychology,* vol. xvii (1922), pp. 113, *ff.*
HULL, CLARK L., *Hypnosis and Suggestibility* (New York, 1933).
JASTROW, J., *Fact and Fable in Psychology* (New York, 1900).
KITSON, H. D., *The Mind of the Buyer* (New York, 1924), chap. xii.
MYERS, G. C., "Control of Conduct by Suggestion: An Experiment in Americanization," *Journal of Applied Psychology,* vol. v (1921), pp. 26 *ff.*
OTIS, M., "A Study of Suggestibility of Children," *Archives of Psychology,* No. 70 (1924).
POFFENBERGER, A. T., *Psychology of Advertising* (New York, 1932), chap. xii.
ROSS, E. A., *Social Psychology* (New York, 1908), chaps. ii, vi.
SCOTT, W. D., *Influencing Men in Business* (New York, 1923), chaps. vi, viii.
SIDIS, B., *The Psychology of Suggestion* (New York, 1920).
STARCH, D., *Principles of Advertising* (New York, 1925), chap. xviii.
STRONG, E. K., *The Psychology of Advertising and Selling* (New York, 1925), chap. xiii.
TAYLOR, W. S., *Readings in Abnormal Psychology and Mental Hygiene* (New York, 1926), chap. xviii.
TRAVIS, L. E., "Suggestibility and Negativism as Measured by Auditory Threshold During Reverie," *Journal of Abnormal Psychology,* vol. xviii (1924), pp. 364 *ff.*
VAUGHN, W. F., "An Experimental Class Demonstration of Suggestibility," *J. Abnorm. Soc. Psychol.,* 1935, vol. 30, pp. 92-94.
YOUNG, K., Source Book for Social Psychology (New York, 1927), chap. xi.

CHAPTER VI

THE PSYCHOLOGY OF IMPROVING YOUR PERSONALITY

The art of winning people's respect and admiration, and of gaining their friendship is one which should be understood by every individual who expects to live in a social environment. Indeed, everybody vaguely or consciously aspires to develop a personality which will be most attractive, and there is hardly a person who is not engaged in the process of "selling" his personality to his "public". Refusal to acknowledge the fact neither alters this fundamental truth, nor does it enable the individual to eliminate the flaws which appear in the sales method which he now subconsciously follows. The improvement of one's personality consists, therefore, not only in the development of virtues, but in the presentation of these talents to one's associates in a manner which will make the latter feel happier and prouder of themselves.

The employment of psychological principles in sales work has hitherto been almost wholly focussed upon the merchandise or ideas of the salesman. It is time we realized that one of the most important products which any boy or girl, man or woman has to offer the public is his or her personality. For example, here is a girl with mental talents and physical beauty who is blunt, boorish, and such an egotistical self-advertiser that people dislike her. Across the street is a girl with equal mental and physical charms, but people all love her. Boys are constantly calling for her. She isn't thought of at all as a self-advertiser, yet that is exactly how she has attained her social eminence. The difference lies in the fact that the second girl used suggestion and let her friends evolve her charms from their own thinking, whereas the first girl told them bluntly that she had travelled abroad, was a college graduate with honors, owned a costly roadster, was related to the governor, and belonged to the D. A. R. The popular girl was also known as possessing all these distinctions, but she had never told anybody—at least, no one ever remembered that she had.

The Importance of Personality Development. Every person surely has some virtues and good points. In our discussion throughout this chapter, therefore, we are only endeavoring to show how these good points can be utilized to best advantage. We do not advocate attempting to make an English sparrow into a canary, but we believe honest salesmanship of a legitimate product should have every encouragement that psychology can offer. In the quotation from President Glenn Frank we see the importance of learning this art.

THE ART OF SELLING YOURSELF

By Glenn Frank

It doesn't pay to take the old adages too seriously.

I am sure that no end of harm has been done by the time-honored theory that if you build a better mouse trap than any one else you can bury yourself in the woods and rest assured that the world will beat a path to your door and demand your superior product.

This is a very busy world we are living in. Even excellence must fight for attention. The world is sure to be waylaid by a good salesman long before it reaches your cabin in the woods. The regrettable truth is that you dare not do good work and let it go at that. Miracles do not happen even for the right. You must know how to sell as well as how to create.

I suspect that the most important man in the world is the good salesman. I do not mean simply the clerk or the commercial traveler, but the man whose whole life and work are guided by the principles of good salesmanship.

The art of civilization is largely the art of salesmanship. Nothing of permanent value has come down to us from the past save by the grace of good salesmanship on the part of somebody.

We would have no great literature to feed our spirits but for the fact that through the ages the great writers have been good salesmen. The great writers have not spent their time hawking their own wares and advertising themselves, but in the way they have thought and written they have, consciously or unconsciously, observed the few fundamental laws of salesmanship. The art of literature is the art of capturing the reader's attention and then charming his senses or convincing his mind. And that is salesmanship.

Long ago, in ancient Greece, Plato thought out most of the things that are today being hailed as progressive ideas about politics and education. But we moderns would know nothing of Plato but for the fact that, in the way he thought and wrote, Plato was a good salesman. And Socrates can still give pointers to ad writers.

The greatest statesmen have always been good salesmen. For every hour a President spends inside his study "thinking it over," he must spend two hours outside his study "putting it over." A time comes when peddler and President stand on the same footing. Both must be good salesmen.

And it may be said without irreverence that the triumph of Christianity has been, in a very real sense, a triumph of salesmanship. The Nazarene had no regiments of soldiers behind him; he employed no press agent; he controlled no syndicate of newspapers; the hillsides of Palestine were not dotted with billboards plastered with his pronouncements. By the sheer force of knowing how to teach, which is just one way of saying salesmanship, he captured and has held the attention of the planet.

The salesman is not the high priest of a sordid commercialism; the salesman is the spark plug of civilization.

We must see to it that we make ourselves and our work worth something to the world, but we must also see to it that the world's attention is called to the fact. Bullion is valuable, but it does not become currency until it is coined and stamped at the mint. Intelligent attention to the principles of salesmanship is the thing that coins the bullion of sound character and good work into the currency of success.

We must master the twin arts of creating and salesmanship.[1]

Young people in America vaguely realize that all is not well as regards their personalities. This fact is evident from the advertisements purporting to make the reader into an orator, a saxophone player, a magician, a pianist or violinist, an artist, a singer, or an elocutionist in the space of six or eight weeks

[1] Copyright, 1925, by The McClure Newspaper Syndicate. Used by permission.

through the medium of correspondence courses. That such advertising can continue denotes that American youths are taking the courses. That American youths are taking the courses indicates they are not fully satisfied with their present social and economic status, but aspire to improve their positions. The development of magnetic personalities and popularity is of constant interest, at least to young people.

Even many of our social attitudes are a result of successful personality salesmanship by one individual or race, or a lack of it by another. Although the Negro has far excelled the attainments of the American Indian, the latter enjoys more prestige among the majority of citizens. The reason is probably the fact that the Indian, as portrayed by Cooper and Longfellow, is idealized, while the Negro's slave background hampers his social advancement. Nevertheless, after four hundred years of contact with white civilization the red savage has been able to make almost no adjustment, nor leave important art, literature, or music as a monument to his race, while the black savage in seventy years has gained wealth, education, churches, and seats in the United States House of Representatives.

An individual, moreover, not only creates positive or negative feeling tone for himself, but also for the race or nation to which he belongs. In the following table from Bogardus[1] are seen the races toward which the greatest antipathy was felt by a group of student raters. The larger the score, the greater the aversion felt for that race. In many instances, of course, these raters had had few if any personal contacts with members of some of the races, but from their vicarious contacts by way of newspapers and novels, they had developed positive or negative attitudes. Propaganda, incidentally, is the basis for many of the dislikes of American citizens for one race or another.

[1] Bogardus, E. S., "Social Distance and Its Origins," *Journal of Applied Sociology,* vol. ix (1925), pp. 216 *ff.*

Turk	119	Hungarian	11	Portuguese	3
Negro	79	Servian	3	English	2
Mulatto	75	Russian	8	French	2
Japanese	61	Czecho-Slovak	8	Roumanian	2
Hindu	44	Syrian	6	Spanish	2
Jew—German	42	Bulgarian	6	Swedish	2
Mexican	41	Filipino	5	Canadian	0
Jew—Russian	41	Italian	5	Dane	0
German	38	Bohemian	4	Dutch	0
Chinese	30	Finn	4	French-Canadian	0
Greek	19	Polish	3	Norwegian	0
Armenian	17	Irish	3	Scotch	0

Exhibit 33. Races against which the greatest antipathy was felt. (Bogardus).

For all those individuals who have a reasonable number of human contacts, therefore, it is necessary that tact and the art of displaying mental and physical charms be fully developed. True, some taciturn or surly individuals carry their graciousness and social charm largely in their wives' names, but this places an undue responsibility on the wives. Occasionally the reverse is the case, and we find the glum, unsociable wife with a popular husband.

Since the improvement of personality, therefore, involves not only the cultivation of talents but their presentation to one's associates, it behooves everybody to keep this two-fold process well in mind. A genius may not have an attractive personality, nor does it necessarily follow that a person who is skilled in music, art, and the sciences will be popular. On the other hand, one should endeavor to nourish one's talents so that they will furnish something worth offering to one's companions, for successful salesmanship really involves the correct presentation of a desirable and satisfactory product.

The Universality of Self-Salesmanship. In the summer of 1932, Camay soap advertisements carried the heading, "You're in a BEAUTY CONTEST every minute of your life!" Not only is this statement true, but we are in perennial personality contests. When we least expect it, our associates are mentally noting faults that we possess. We do not realize the fact until later, as in a quarrel. Then watch the parade of flaws! These may be resurrected from years back. As errors are tabulated subconsciously and consciously by our fellows, so too are the virtues and graces which we possess. On a certain date some one asks us if John is neat in his attire, for he is applying for a position as floorwalker in a department store. We don't have John before us at the time we write our letter, so we go back in memory and try to resurrect some incidents which bear upon his personal neatness. Much to our surprise, for we had hardly been aware of noting these items, we recall that John wore a faded tie with soup stains on it. We recall that the cravat was loosely knotted so that it seldom fitted snugly against his throat. More memories begin to freshen, and we recall that John never was particularly careful about keeping his trousers pressed, for our picture of him is with baggy knees. And, finally, we remember the time he appeared at work with his Sunday suit but with unshined shoes which contrasted sufficiently with his neater clothing to call our attention to them.

We frequently find that our likes and aversions are founded on the basis of a few outstanding items. We dislike a certain person from childhood. Critical analysis reveals that the man threw a stone and injured our pet dog when we were just out of kindergarten. We like some one else who may never have contributed anything but friendly smiles from day to day.

Not only may we react to people with likes or dislikes, but we may be forming opinions concerning their uncouthness at the same time that we are growing fond of them. In politics it occasionally happens that a man's friends refuse to vote for him when he begins to run for an office which they feel is too high for his social standing. The writer heard a man say in a recent presidential campaign that he had always voted for one of the candidates for governor, but he wouldn't vote for him for President because he didn't possess quite the dignity and prestige that went with the higher office. When politicians want to show their fondness for the farmer they frequently permit themselves to be photographed pitching hay or running a tractor, but they are wearing white shirts with collars and ties, even though they may also be protected by overalls. The white collar shows that they really aren't farmers even though they can function as such. It is a necessary distinction. Farmers seldom send farmers to Congress, despite our class distinctions and grumbling against the rich. We may be socialists in our attitude regarding wealth and big business, but we want to be represented at Washington by men who can wear a silk hat and use a gold headed cane as if they knew how.

It is well to keep in mind, therefore, that we are really walking department stores of human characteristics and the feeling tone we develop for one trait may not be typical of the entire stock which we carry. If we become too democratic in our behavior, we lessen the dignity that we may have wished to establish. The genial secretary of a social organization frequently remains the secretary, despite the fact that all of his fellows like him very much. The overly athletic individual who is selling the public on her possession of health and vitality may also be losing the charm of the girl who depends upon the strong right arm of her escort and thereby inflates his masculine ego.

One of the writer's classmates, who has gone into executive work and holds the position of dean in an American university, is possessed of a blonde, boyish complexion and general appearance. Obviously it militates against his success as a leader. To offset this influence he consciously adopted a pipe, that badge of masculinity that ranks next to the beard so generally started by medical students of the '90's when they approached graduation. Pipes, profanity, and hirsute facial ornaments should probably be called the masculine secondary sexual characteristics of this generation. One of our pre-eminent political leaders adopted them, probably consciously, for much the same reason as that of the dean just cited.

To illustrate not only the fact that men in established positions of prestige and wealth do not cease their self-selling but that they have it reduced to a habit, the writer wishes to make the following quotation. The scene was at a banquet of a Chicago executives' organization which the writer was to address immediately after the meal on the topic which titles this chapter. The president of the organization sat on the writer's left, while a dignified director of the national organization who happened to be in the city, was seated on his right. We shall designate him as Mr. X.

The discussion which ensued took place during the 45 minutes of eating. The writer jotted it down from memory as soon as he returned home that evening. Intermittent questions which he had forgotten cause the apparent unrelated nature of many of the paragraphs. When the reader finishes the dialogue, he should try to tabulate the number of selling points which Mr. X. displayed in this short time. They are numerous and interesting.

"Yes, Dr. Crane, I know your president very well. You might be interested to know that he began his initial work in the applied field with our company about twenty years ago. He was a good man. I'm sorry I'm so busy these days that I don't get to see him any more."

"Mr. X, from your extensive travelling what impression have you obtained of present business conditions?" I inquired.

"No improvement whatever. In fact, I notice a slight decline in progress. We'll never be able to get out of our financial depression until we rescind the war debts. Conditions are bad here and abroad. I am in constant correspondence with continental European countries. Hardly a week passes that I don't receive a letter from Germany and England. The first nineteen years of my life were spent abroad, so you can appreciate undoubtedly that I am better able to understand the European attitude than the average American. I look to see England recover first, followed thereafter by Germany. Indeed, Germany is likely to surpass America as soon as she gets on her feet.

"I was much interested in what my friend, Prime Minister Baldwin, said to me at luncheon one day while I was in London. He turned to me and stated that England's unemployed group is identical with the number of people who have refrained from emigrating to the colonies. A quarter of a million each year used to leave England for Australia, Canada and South Africa. Since the war, this emigration has ceased.

"What we need in this country is a new conception of Business Management. The only place in the world where that is being preached is in Germany. There a young professor, Dr. F——, has been issuing a series of monographs on modern leadership which are the best in any language, and I have studied the field pretty thoroughly. As a matter of fact, I have translated one or two of these monographs so that those who could not read German might have access to them."

"I'll wager you have a weakness for books," I said.

"Oh yes, I have quite an extensive library. I wouldn't take $50,000 for my collection, and there are over two hundred etchings in my apartment that I have been gathering during the past ten years. Some of my journal files are perhaps the only complete ones in existence. The *Tailor's Journal,* for instance, asked if I would permit them to photostat some of the early numbers of their magazine, since they didn't have a complete file of their own."

"What do you think of the political situation?" I interrupted.

"Well, I'd personally like to see Al Smith in the White House. I don't drink but I'd like to cast my vote for him as a protest against intolerance. At my club in New York the other day I was talking to some of my friends on this very score. Two of them who are leading bankers in New York said they were afraid he could never be elected. I told them it was just because of people who thought he couldn't be elected that he was not now in office."

"How about Ritchie?" the president of the Chicago Club asked.

"Governor Ritchie would make a fine candidate. Surely, I know him quite well. It was only a few weeks ago that we attended a banquet together. As I was the principal speaker of the evening I turned to him before my talk and said, 'Governor, what I'm going to say is probably not news to you, so I shall not feel offended if you wish to leave early.' But he refused and remained there for three hours. At the conclusion of my address he congratulated me heartily, and in a very nice fashion.

"Yes, I was pleased to see that Hoover had enough good judgment to appoint Cardozo to the Supreme Court. Cardozo is a friend of mine. He has a brilliant mind. A graduate of my alma mater, you know."

"Mr. X, are you as methodical in your private life as in your business affairs?" asked the president.

"If you could just visit my apartment you could see for yourself. We have a suite in the hotel, for my wife is one of the responsible members of the firm, so we must be close to the office. I have set aside one room in the suite for my study, and I don't leave a thing out of place. Why, man, while out on the road, I've frequently called the office in New York and told one of my men to get the pass key to the apartment from my wife, go up to my study, look on the second shelf from the bottom in the bookcase at the left of my desk, and there, about the fifth book in, he would find such and such a volume. I seldom miss hitting the exact spot by more than one or two books.

"Yes, I give a course at ——— University. But I would not consent to offering the course until the president promised that I could shift the teaching to some of my assistants in my absence. I told him that it was a physical impossibility for me to be present in New York for thirty Monday evenings. It just couldn't be done. So the course is listed as being given by Mr. X and Associates.

"Last fall I vowed that I wouldn't give any speeches this year, but do you know, to date, I have made 51 addresses that I just couldn't get out of. And that isn't all, unfortunately. I'm to make the chief address at the national convention at S——— next month. I couldn't avoid that, for this address is to furnish direction for the whole convention.

"Then I should like to get away for a little rest and take in the international convention at Amsterdam this summer. However, I may skip that and go to Geneva instead, for I don't want to disappoint my old friend, Dr. F———, who is the chairman. But that would take about five weeks—one going, one coming, and give me only three weeks abroad.

"Really, what I feel conscience-stricken about, however, is the fact that I've promised my publishers three books, and I ought to get them out of the way. Ordway Tead met me on the street in New York just last week, and implored me to give him just an outline of my book in business management so that he could announce it in his fall catalogue, but I told him nothing doing. I knew if it were announced, there'd be nothing for me to do but to get to work on the book, for I couldn't disappoint the public in that way.

"You know, I've spent $26,000 to date just gathering data for one of my books. It's to be a doctoral dissertation at ——— University, which I had hoped to get out by 1930, but it can't see the printers before 1933. I made one oversight that cost me $6,000 and delayed the book at least a year."

"Too bad, but we all do that at times," I consoled him.

"This wasn't a careless one, however. In fact, it was because of my extensive study in the field that I was tricked. I became a victim of my own vast experience. One of my assistants, Dr. Y———, asked me if annuities entered the insurance field by 1907. I told him no. Then he asked me if they had begun to appear by 1914, or 1921. I told him not much before 1922 or 1923. Annuities are an English custom. He wanted to know if he should examine the data—I've been analyzing management in 14 of our largest insurance companies, you know—but I told him not to bother with 1907. There's where I made my error! I was too sure of myself. With all my experience in the insurance field, as you, of course, can imagine, Mr. ———, (addressing the president on my left) I didn't think I need consider 1907. But my correlations wouldn't come out; so finally I examined the data myself, and then found my error. But it cost me $6,000."

"Say, I just had a letter from Z——— yesterday," said the president.

"He's editor of ——————— Magazine, Dr. Crane," Mr. X addressed me. "Z——— is a good fellow. You might be interested to know that he takes night classes at ——— University. He drops in for advice about once a month, and last week he called on me about his program for next fall for he knew I could steer him into the best courses. I know the men teaching the classes, and the personal factor is a large one, you know."

It is obvious, therefore, that self-salesmanship is not confined to young people who are desirous of making a name for themselves in the world, but pervades all ranks and social strata. This fact is so evident to the reader that he may wonder why it has been granted space in this chapter. Curiously enough, many people frown upon even the thought of a conscious technique in dealing with people and effectively and tactfully advertising themselves. Unfortunately, however, many of these same individuals are constantly trying to "sell" themselves but, having refused to focus upon their methods, are doing such a poor job that they antagonize instead of attract.

It requires great care and forethought in order to demonstrate finesse in this delicate procedure.

Tactful vs. Blunt Selling Points. We have previously commented on the advantages of suggestion in salesmanship. Direct statements of fact concerning one's products may, however, have a certain amount of influence, but they are much less effective when made about one's personal talents and abilities. A person may say, "This automobile is the most economical to operate of any on the market." The listener will probably discount such a statement considerably, but not nearly so much so as its homologue, "I am the greatest economist in the world today."

It becomes imperative, therefore, that we become adept in the use of suggestive salesmanship when we are attempting to merchandise our own personalities. The individual who attains skill in this respect can present all of his good points without danger of incurring the ill will or resentment of his associates. Like the magician, such a person keeps his public attending to the obvious while he subtly produces the changes necessary for the accomplishment of his purpose. And his public, like the magician's, obtains the effect, but has little if any knowledge of how it was produced.

"Don't you think it was sweet of Jane to give me this cute little hand painted box for my recipes?" Bill's girl innocently inquires.

The next morning at breakfast Bill's father tells him he ought to cease running around with frivolous girls and pick out one who can cook and sew and run a house.

"Say, my girl can cook fine," Bill defends, not even realizing that his sweetheart with her verbal legerdemain deftly slipped this selling point into his memory while she had him focussing upon the hand painted recipe box.

The man or woman who can continue the method of Bill's girl friend will find it possible to present the facts concerning his or her health, family tree, education, cultural attitudes, generosity, morality, love of offspring, popularity with the opposite sex, and a host of other sales points which materially strengthen one's prestige. It is on this score that my students frequently complain that psychology takes all the joy out of conversation, making them self-conscious and analytical. "I certainly wouldn't want to think that my boy friend had deliberately planned what he was going to say to me," one girl protests. "It would take all the spontaneity out of conversation."

Perhaps to a similar degree one wouldn't want to think that Stevenson wrote and rewrote his *Treasure Island* seven times before it had that simplicity and spontaneity which make it so refreshing, or that genius has aptly been defined as the exceptional capacity for taking pains. The salesman who presents the most interesting and apparently spontaneous sales demonstration, and the surgeon who shows the greatest simplicity and skill in his operative technique certainly do not rely on the inspiration of the moment. From his experience as a sales manager, the writer can truthfully state that the large commission checks go to those individuals who have most carefully planned their interviews and have previously memorized not only the outstanding selling points of their products, but have also phrased them in the most graceful and effective manner.

When one has analyzed himself for selling points and has not only formulated those advantages in the best fashion, but has memorized them, he will soon find that he can mechanically deliver them at the right time and place. Only the tyro makes himself and his public feel a lack of spontaneity in the process. In regard to memorizing a sales talk, the writer does not mean to infer that the entire speech should always be given in "1-2-3" order, with utter disregard for the exigencies of the moment. But he does insist that the "1" and the "2" and the "3" be fully memorized. They may be rearranged in the actual interview, and some may be omitted—in short, the serial order of presentation may be left to inspiration of the moment—but the phrasing of the units of the complete speech must be previously learned. When one is dealing with suggestions a single word omitted from a sentence may defeat the psychological purpose behind the statement. Precision in words must be just as great as precision in the use of a scalpel if perfection is to be attained.

The wife of one of America's foremost after-dinner humorists remarked that much of her husband's reputation for spontaneity in his sallies depended upon her. She steered the conversation so that at the proper time she could make a comment which served as the cue for him to begin, "That reminds me . . . " Most of us cannot depend on wives or husbands in such manner, but must direct the conversation tactfully so that we produce our own cues. In the student's paper[1] reproduced below the italicized words indicate a conversational cue or "detour" which enables the speaker to introduce sales points (5), (6), (7), and (8). The student has annotated his assignment.

(It's Friday night. They're at the dance. She is selling him now, doing most of the talking, but some of it is wasted as he is very busy taking note of how many fellows are envious of his choice of partner.)

You think I dance well? That's very chivalrous of you indeed, but of course I should be able to dance a little as I took esthetic dancing at college (1), and had the honor of leading the ballet in our spring festival (2). And I nearly died of surprise, because the ballet lead is supposed to go to the most attractive girl in the class by popular vote (3), and fancy them giving it to poor little me.

Oh, my gown? I'm glad you like it because I worked awfully hard over it. Why yes, I make my own things (4) and get a big kick out of it. *You know I made both of my costumes for that play last spring* and made up the girls in the cast besides. Why no, I had very little make-up on myself, sometimes I wish my complexion wasn't so shockingly vivid (5).

Oh, you didn't see the play then. And all the time I thought you had. Well, I took a boy's part, you know. All the slender girls had to take boy's parts (6), and besides you know I sing

[1] **Paper written by L. J. Lutz.**

contralto, so I had to be a boy (7). And you should have seen me in that riding scene with those awful old cavalry boots. Why we searched the town over, and couldn't find a pair of riding boots half small enough (8). I wear a four quadruple A, you see.

Why surely I'm going back to school. I didn't do much last semester though, just about lived in the music room at the piano and at the gym in the tank. Why yes, I adore swimming (9), but I do need a little more tutoring until I get sufficient confidence in myself. You say you will teach me? How perfectly thrilling! (10).

1. Selling prospect on her dancing ability and college training.
2. Is a leader in her set too.
3. Perhaps he hasn't noticed how attractive and popular she is with both sexes.
4. Reaching deep down with that old domestic appeal. They *all* say they can sew.
5. If her complexion is vivid, then it's different. Do not all men want their ideal just a little different?
6. A most tactful way to sell the figure.
7. A contralto voice. Again different, rich, mellow, crooning. (Good accompaniment for a "uke" on a moonlight night.)
8. Tiny feet. The badge of aristocracy since the beginning of time.
9. Enjoys outdoor sports too—healthy.
10. The blow that slays them. Appealing through her charming feminine weakness to his rugged strength. (She could probably swim circles around him with one arm while reading her current copy of *College Humor*.)

Several of the girl's comments cited above are evidences of direct self-selling instead of the more tactful suggestive method, but it is better to make direct statements than to go around tongue-tied, especially if the physical attractiveness of the speaker is sufficient to offset the resentment aroused by her words. The unpleasant reaction to direct or blunt sales statements can be materially reduced by the way in which the speaker acts at the moment. A deprecating laugh, or thumbs stuck in the armholes of one's vest while one purposely struts around as he enunciates his own honors, may lessen the resistance of his public or make them laugh. If you can make your public laugh at your antics, or if you can keep their attention focussed upon your actions, the import of your words may slip into their memories indirectly; hence, as suggestions.

Bluntly stated selling points are familiar to most readers, so we shall not devote space to a list of them. And in presenting statements which demonstrate finesse and tact, we assume temperance in their use. The woman who is chronically criticizing the orchestra, or the food, or the decorations, or the service may intimate that she has been accustomed to better, but too many intimations of the same nature begin to grow obvious. Behavior of this sort is a frequent attribute of the newly rich. Dave, a high school athlete, always "popped the question" to whichever girl he happened to be with, but it ran, "Do you like football?" That was his sole cue for launching upon a sales' monologue with his own prowess on the gridiron as the central idea. In the ensuing statements gleaned from students' papers, are a heterogeneous group of suggestive sales points. Some are not as good as others, but they all give rise to additional thoughts in the minds of the readers.

One of the biggest "kicks" I have is getting down on the floor with my nieces and nephews and playing with the toys and electrical contrivances. (Likes children—a good father type.)

I have more fun listening to the good-natured debates of Mother and Dad over the respective merits of the Virginia Penfields and the New England Brewsters. (Comes of excellent family inheritance on both sides.)

They say the good die young. If that's the case, my family is full of black sheep. (Longevity indicates health—good stock.)

I never appreciated morality until the war when I was thrown in contact with men without any whatever. (Comes from good home environment, and also served his country.)

Bill's car has the most peculiar dashboard. (I've had a date with Bill, the village hero.)

The last Derby wasn't nearly the spectacle the Preakness was. (I've attended both, so am wealthy, interested in sports, etc.)

Homecoming games always have a rejuvenating effect on me. The old spirit never seems to die out. (I'm a college person.)

One hears so much about the aged-in-the-wood variety of beauty, but believe me it's mighty good to see the Statue of Liberty after months spent in musty cities abroad. (I've travelled in Europe.)

Imagine *me* as Queen of the May with one of those ridiculous wreaths on my head! (I am the most popular girl in the crowd.)

I didn't like to think of her going that far on the street car, so I arranged a ride for her with one of the boys who goes her way. (I am considerate and generous.)

I thought the "Cuban Love Song" was an excellent picture, for it shows Cuba as it really is. (I have travelled in Cuba and know it very well.)

Our annual convention is to be in San Francisco this year. It's a nice town, but I was hoping they'd have it in New York, for there's always so much more doing there. (I'm a connoisseur of American cities and a regular delegate to the convention.)

I don't think so much of him as a critic. Personally, I see nothing in contemporary authors to compare with the power and beauty of 18th and 19th century literature. (I'm well read both in current and past literature.)

As variants of the above procedure some people find it advantageous to put such queries as, "What did you get in the exam?" The reversal of this question is expected, at which time the first speaker can say that he made an "A". Again, we hear a comment like this, "I just hate this dress. It makes me look so fat!" The girl speaking has a graceful figure, and by bringing out the contrasting thought of stoutness obtains even greater slenderness in the eyes of her listeners.

Hepner[1] devotes a few pages to this matter of self-selling when he points out that the office worker can capture the attention of his superior by constructing charts of his own output, depicting the relationship of his task or department to that of the office as a whole. Ostensibly these graphs and curves are simply for the worker's own interest. If displayed properly, and clearly labelled, they not only call attention to the employee, but they intimate a scientific type of mind, all of

[1] Hepner, H. W., *Psychology in Modern Business* (Prentice Hall, Inc., New York, 1931), chap. xii.

which are not inimical to his advancement. Some workers type a list of items to be developed and fulfilled during the current month, and post it in their office. As the work is finished they scratch off the items in red pencil.

In the preceding pages, therefore, we have gone into detail regarding the blunt versus the tactful methods of presenting our virtues and talents, showing how indispensable is the use of suggestion in this dangerous but very important field of personal salesmanship. As in the merchandising of a commercial product the salesman must first analyze his goods for their sales points and then phrase these in the most advantageous fashion, so also the one who wishes to present his personality most favorably should follow a similar technique.

The Two Essential Steps in Becoming Popular. In the preceding section we have presented part of the first phase of gaining friends, which is that of showing our merits, virtues, and capacities, for as a general rule, people like to number as friends those individuals who are important.

But only half the problem is solved when we have presented our personalities in the most favorable light, for the most excellent product cannot be merchandised successfully unless it fulfills some need or function of the public. Our personalities, therefore, must meet the public's universal desire for self-esteem. People all like to feel educated, beautiful, graceful, powerful, proud of themselves. The more their ego is inflated, the more pleased they are. And the important psychological law involved in making friends is the same which explains our likes for food. Spinach, if presented to children in a pleasurable emotional state, begins to take on part of that pleasant atmosphere, and soon is liked by the child. In the same manner, when we meet strangers and leave them feeling proud of themselves, they are in a pleasurable emotional state, which in turn attaches to us as an important part of the environment. They like us.

The secret of friendship and popularity is simply this:

Whenever you leave a person feeling more satisfied with himself as a result of his contact with you, he will like you. And love is only a heightened type of liking with an erogenous coloring. Introverts are not as popular as extroverts because they don't pay heed to the ego demands of their associates. And friends will not long remain friends if they don't keep accounts fairly even between themselves and those of their intimates. This fact is subconsciously realized by almost everybody, as demonstrated by the common statements, "We ought to entertain the Browns. They had us over for dinner last;" or, "We ought to send the Jacksons a greeting. They sent us one last year."

Complimentary remarks made to us and about us are valued, regardless of their source. A bootblack may tell his college girl customer that she is the prettiest girl he ever saw, and it certainly will not make her patronize his rival thereafter. But if Ronald Coleman or Robert Montgomery told her the same thing, it would have even greater effect. Thus, the weight given to our compliments depends in part upon the prestige that we ourselves enjoy. The two steps in becoming popular, therefore, consist of (1) Gaining all the prestige we can legitimately obtain in the eyes of our associates, and (2) Using this prestige to add weight to the tactfully phrased compliments we pay our associates.

A little self analysis will reveal that most of us attempt the first step, although seldom with the conscious technique described in this chapter, but too frequently forget the second step. Of the two, the latter is probably the more essential. Note the difference in the popularity which Janet gains by employing the second of the two speeches given below.

"You like my coat? Thanks, I got it at Saks and paid enough for it so it ought to be good. Yes, Jack took me to the Edgewater Beach for dinner last night. We had the best food. Jack knows Paul Whiteman, and introduced him to me. Paul played a special number just for me. Jack's taking me to dinner at the Medinah tonight, and we're going to a show afterwards."

"Do you really like it? I'm so glad, for you certainly know how to judge materials. Do you think it will wear well? I paid more for it than I should, but I remembered that your clothes always wear so much better than the cheaper things. Jack took me to the Edgewater Beach for dinner last night. It was a treat for me, but I suppose you've been there lots of times. I got to meet Paul Whiteman. Jack knows him, and introduced us. Paul even played a special number just for me! Wasn't that sweet of him? By the way, Jack's taking me to the Medinah for dinner tonight, and to a show afterwards. I'm to pick out where I want to go. You know about all the theaters, so tell me something you think I'd enjoy."

In addition to increasing the friendship of her office associate, Janet has probably created for herself in the reader's mind a much more attractive personality by her second speech than she had in the first. It is true that she employed a few more words, but as Haldeman-Julius demonstrated in lengthening his titles, she increased the good will and appeal of her personality thereby. In the following paragraphs we shall discuss more specifically these two steps in gaining popularity. The methods of fulfilling the initial step will be treated first.

(1) The physical appearance, like the show window in the shop, makes the initial impression upon our public. In our height, weight, complexion and attire we create a definite feeling tone. Some of these features are not modifiable, but many of them we can definitely improve. Aside from such well advertised flaws as halitosis, body odor, greasy skin, oily hair, twisted seams in hose, run down heels, soupy vests, frayed collars, and baggy trousers there are a number of other minor items which may detract from an otherwise admirable appearance. We have become surfeited with tooth paste advertising. But the teeth are subconsciously taken as indices of health and vitality. Decayed teeth connote an unhealthy physical condition. Dirty teeth suggest that the person may also be letting moss grow in the family bath tub. White teeth suggest

purity, as restaurants, hospitals, and soda fountains appreciate by their emphasis upon this color. Morality is denoted subconsciously by white teeth, while villains are not thought of as being good advertisements for Pepsodent.

Even international affairs have been complicated by dirty teeth, as the experience of the former king of Spain attests. When King Alfonso went to England in quest of a pretty princess who would share his throne with him, he met Princess Patricia of Connaught, niece of Edward VII. The Spanish monarch fell in love with her and, as Princess Radziwill[1] comments,

> " . . . one evening after dinner, bluntly asked her to become his wife.
>
> "To everybody's surprise Patricia refused him!
>
> "The scandal, although suppressed, was the only subject of conversation in European courts and salons for weeks. The princess was severely criticized for her indifference to such a great offer of marriage. King Edward himself expressed in no veiled terms his disgust at her behavior—which was upsetting his political apple cart. But Patricia was obdurate. When she was asked to give her reasons for declining the Spanish throne, she replied that the king of Spain did not brush his teeth as well and as often as he should."

The king is probably not the only man who has failed to win his sweetheart for such a reason. In addition to teeth, however, we may cite the finger nails as important adjuncts of an attractive physical appearance. Black nails do more than connote mourning. The tendency of women, moreover, to redden their nails gives rise to a fundamental feeling tone connected with blood, despite whatever harmony of color scheme they may attain. See "Test for Sweethearts," page 594.

The clothing of individuals is also effective not only as regards its neatness and cleanliness, but in its pattern and color as well. Dark hues make one look less corpulent. Checkered and flowered fabrics make one look larger, for the reason un-

[1] Radziwill, Catherine, "The Woman Who Lost Her Throne," *Midweek, Chicago Daily News* (May 27, 1931), p. 4.

derlying the illusion depicted in Exhibit 30. Dark colors make one look older. A double-breasted coat makes a heavy man look thinner, and a single-breasted coat makes a slender man appear more stalwart. The reasons underlying such phenomena are contained in the discussion of illusions in any good textbook of general psychology.

(2) The honors, creations, and other assets which we possess should be thoroughly studied, just as the salesman studies the good points of his merchandise, so that we may formulate our selling talk. We have discussed in the preceding section the superiority of tactful vs. blunt sales arguments. The use of suggestion is even more imperative in personality merchandising than in that of goods. Not all of our virtues, however, require verbal treatment. Sometimes our polite and considerate actions will convey the ideas as well as language.

After we have adequately established our prestige in the manner just described, we must extrovert ourselves, like Janet, so that we can make sure that those around us feel complimented. We don't have to be blunt in telling people they are pretty, or cultured, or good cooks. The same suggestive method which we employed in building up our own prestige can also be utilized in this regard. Indeed, our compliments are more likely taken at par value when indirectly offered than when made too bluntly. But even blunt compliments have value, so we should never remain silent when speech will make our hosts and hostesses happy.

Curiously enough, even when we realize that our friends are deliberately complimenting us, we still rather like it. In the process of inflating the ego of those around us the following methods will be found of value.

(1) Ask the persons for information, advice, or direction. Janet's second speech, as given above, illustrates this point. A question is a subtle form of compliment that even the most skillful psychologists frequently fail to detect. The reason why questions are of value in this connection is the fact that

the questioner indirectly acknowledges the superiority of the questioned by coming to him for assistance. Scoldings and criticisms can often be avoided if the clever student can slip in his question before the other party can get launched into the tirade. By habit we tend to respond whenever questioned. A policeman will answer a question, much as will a child, so that the erring driver may often undermine the officer's ire by letting him dissipate his emotion through the motor activity of a number of responses to questioning.

(2) Impute knowledge and experience to your associates whether or not you know they possess it. Janet illustrated this method, too, when she said, "It was a treat for me, but I suppose you've been there lots of times." A book salesman may say, "You, of course, remember that old adage etc." The customer feels much like the penniless actor who was approached by a pedestrian who wished a $20 bill changed, and to whom the actor replied, "I can't change it but thanks for the compliment." The public speaker frequently employs this method, as we shall develop at greater length later.

(3) Be sure to intimate that the other person has or had "it". One of the best methods of making your associates feel good is to allude to their "past", if male, or to the string of broken hearts they left when they married, if female. Most men expand and mentally preen themselves if called a Don Juan or Romeo, and seldom will a woman resent the title of Cleopatra. The surest way to incur lasting enmity is to lower a person's sex vanity. Women of sixty are just about as vulnerable to sex compliments as are those of twenty. If the compliment cannot be made of them in the present, at least it can be used with reference to their youth.

(4) Compliment the products or children of your associates, or their dogs, cats, and canaries. This is a subtle form of inflating the ego. Alexander Pope once said that the best way to compliment a man was to comment favorably on the thing in which he wanted to be proficient rather than the thing in

which he was adept. For example, the salesman who always aspired to be a writer would probably be more flattered by comments on his literary skill than upon his salesmanship. The books, clothes or ideas of people belong in this same category of objects or possessions in which the owner takes pride.

(5) Finally, make direct compliments. These are not so effective as a general rule, however, because they arouse the suspicion that you may be flattering, not sincerely praising the person.

The two essential steps in becoming popular, therefore, consist of gaining all the prestige which can legitimately be procured, and then employing this prestige to give more weight to the tactfully phrased compliments which are paid to one's associates. This simple two-stage process becomes an open sesame for the skilful person, but too many individuals don't meet success because they forget the important second step. Moreover, many fail in the first half of the problem by not using suggestion and finesse. We have recounted the two general devices for accomplishing the first step and the five ways for complimenting one's associates.

Dangers to Avoid in Self Salesmanship. We should never utilize our associates as a means of elevating our prestige at their expense. The Biblical statement, "A prophet is not without honor save in his own country and in his own house," is based on an appreciation of the thing we are decrying. The reason a man's intimate friends are so ready to use his Christian name freely after he becomes famous is evident to the careful analyst. They simply try to pull themselves up by the act of familiarity or criticism, the assumption being that the one who criticizes is of necessity superior to the one criticized. The trait is very widespread. Moreover, whenever a member of an organization, a political party, or even a department in a university becomes nationally known, many of his colleagues and former associates subtly undergo a change regarding him. Their friendship becomes less sincere, and they may ultimately begin to damn him by innuendo if not more bluntly.

When tenement women and children are taken to the circus through the generosity of settlement workers and other charitable agencies, we frequently hear them say that it is "a bum circus" or that they've had "rotten seats". When sent to neighboring farms for a week's respite from the city heat, some will complain at the station because they cannot have redcaps to carry their luggage onto the train for them. At the farms where they are guests of kindly farmers, they ask if there isn't cheese for the pie, for "We never have pie without cheese at home." The farmers have frequently asked that they be taken back, saying, "They're used to better fare than we are."

These tenement folks probably do not intend to be rude. They are simply so concerned with inflating their own egos that they minimize their associates in the process, thereby angering the latter. They criticized the circus to suggest that they were accustomed to better seats and better entertainment.

Everybody at some time or other has probably felt the resentment of having a partial stranger familiarly employ his name. Why is it that the president of our company may call us by our Christian name without irritating us, when the same action on the part of the office boy leads to intense resentment? The answer is simple. In the first case our ego is inflated by the fact that the higher officer intimates our equality by his familiar use of our name. In the latter case our ego is deflated by the fact that the office boy intimates equality with us by his familiar use of our name. In the former case we rise in prestige, while we sink in the latter instance.

Another important tning for salesmen as well as for the average person to bear in mind is this: when we are on the defensive, we feel uncomfortable. This fact explains our discomfort if salesmen call upon us. Moreover, when we recommended as a method of complimenting people that we impute knowledge and ability to them, we meant that they were not to be quizzed upon such matters, nor were we to suggest that such questioning would follow. The students well remember the nervous strain they feel when unprepared but expecting to be called upon before the class period is over.

In summing up the dangers to avoid in self-salesmanship, we should state that they arise primarily because the individual is so intent upon trying to inflate his own ego and self-esteem that he attempts to utilize his associates in the process. It is obvious that this procedure deflates the ego of each one around him, and therefore is decidedly inimical to the development of friendly relations between the self-salesman and his public. As simple as this error is, we find it illustrated among college graduates as well as among the less educated.

Why the Novice Fails in Selling Himself. The chief fault of the person who is inapt at selling himself skilfully is the fact that he fails to realize the two-fold nature of the process. He stops when he has shown off his virtues. The end of the first step is a dangerous place for him to mark time for the evident reason that we rather dislike finding our associates rising in esteem and popularity unless we partake somehow of that same elevation. If the novice will discreetly keep his associates placated by asking their opinions and complimenting their performances, he will retain their favor while he rises in general prestige.

One of the writer's girl students obtained a temporary position in an office during the absence of the stenographer. This girl was attractive in physical appearance, possessed ability and education, but was disliked by the ringleader of the office force—the stenographer—as soon as the latter returned from her vacation. The stenographer openly showed her animosity by telling the other girls in the office that the stranger would probably be let out by the ensuing Saturday. On the contrary, the new girl rapidly rose until she became secretary to the advertising manager. The stenographer continually made things unpleasant for her, however, until the new girl finally came to me for advice. Her situation, she said, was intolerable unless she could gain fairly friendly relationships with the group with whom she associated.

Since this girl could not ask advice of the ringleader without lowering her prestige in business matters, for the ringleader might then tell the advertising manager that she was really doing all the work of the new girl, there was only one short cut by which to win over the ringleader. That lay in playing to her desire to appear popular with the male sex. The ringleader prided herself on her wild parties, and general knowledge of places of amusement in the city. Here was a field in which the new girl, although more attractive than the ringleader, could nevertheless consciously humble herself to the extent of asking advice regarding places to go, shows to see, etc.

In sexual competition it is particularly difficult for a girl to take a secondary role to a rival whom she feels superior to, but the individual who can intelligently do this will often win her rival's friendship. Meanwhile she doesn't lessen her attractiveness with her own masculine friends, for they don't know anything about her office conduct, and probably wouldn't be influenced adversely by it if they did. When the new girl began to go to the ringleader for social advice, the latter underwent a change of feeling toward her. It wasn't long until she began to incorporate the stranger in her circle of friends, and eventually she became an active defender of the new girl.

Whenever people invest either money or advice in a project or person they begin to take an interest in the latter. It is frequently an advantage to allow others to do you favors because of this psychological effect. The young person, however, usually resents being under obligations to anybody, so he deliberately defeats his own ultimate good. Many an aged parent, uncle, aunt, or grandparent could be wrapped around the little fingers of the younger generation if the latter would only assume an interest in the advice coming from the older generation, and even actively court it. Many a husband, too, could hold his wife's devotion more securely if he permitted her to feel that she was important to him and his business because of her counsel and criticism. The male, however, resents what he considers lowering his dignity, especially when it involves even intimating the female's superiority, so he loses this powerful means of really becoming a surer master in his own home. This is the situation which truly involves stooping to conquer. Women, on the contrary, have no such aversion, so they frequently utilize this excellent device.

The novice fails to sell himself, therefore, either because he is not familiar with the proper technique of being his own publicity agent or because he is unwilling to undergo the process of apparently deflating his own ego in order to inflate that of his neighbor. The negative protest of young people makes them refuse to humble themselves, even when they could easily stoop to conquer if they would.

The Tactful Winning of Young People. There is one central idea which young people constantly have in mind, and that is their independence of their parents and adults in general. Age and maturity spell this freedom, while any symbol which connotes youth or childhood is a reminder of the hated serfdom out of which they have been scrambling. From his experience with Little Blue Books Haldeman-Julius says that his Juvenile Books classification proved quite unsatisfactory, and that young people don't even like to be referred to as "Young People".

Recalling Pope's advice to compliment a person on that quality in which he strives to be outstanding, we find that a safe and certain method of eliciting favorable reactions from young people is to intimate that they are grown. In the following student reports we shall observe that this principle is generally involved.

You are a senior this year? Oh, your second year. Well nobody would ever know it from the looks of you. (I look grown.)

I'm certainly glad I found a girl I don't have to be afraid to leave Jackie with. (I can be trusted—like an adult.)

Pardon me, sir (he's seventeen), but have you got a match on you? (The boy will probably carry matches the rest of his life!)

(Girl seventeen to boy of equal age, as she rubs his cheek) I don't believe you shaved tonight. You ought to be ashamed! (Does anybody think he is?)

Do you know, Mary, to hear you discussing these important matters, I'd be sure you were twenty, at least.

Boy, what big leg muscles you have! Does that come from track or basketball? (I'm strong—strength is a symbol of adulthood.)

(Older sister's beau to her younger brother) I wish I could make a radio like yours. If you could spare the time some day I wish you'd show me something about them. (I'm asked for advice by an older man—intimation being that I am his equal or superior.)

(Mary is eighteen) Gracious, Mary, you're quite an authority on Sir Walter Scott, aren't you? (Authority has always meant adulthood to the young person.)

Most women are poor drivers but here is one girl who can run rings around any man. (I'm classed better than *women,* and even superior to *men*—certainly I am grown.)

Really, it certainly is refreshing to find a girl who knows something to talk about other than the movies. (I'm more experienced than the usual girl—experience connotes age.)

One of the writer's men students remarked that he once had a date with a girl who knew and talked of nothing but movies, until he became almost nauseated. Finally he happened to learn that she could whistle, so he suggested one tune after another, praising her after each one. She reacted like Franklin to the flattery of the man with the ax, and whistled for an hour till he could discreetly make his exit.

The following student's paper[1] belongs in this section, but

[1] Paper written by Anne Filwett.

pertains to young men and women of marriageable age. We shall present it in entirety. If the girl's comments seem too obvious at times, we must bear in mind the fact that a physically attractive young woman can be much more blunt than this one, and yet have her statements discounted but slightly by the male with whom she is talking.

SCENE I. *At the Dance*—With adoring eyes directed on her subject—

She Merely Said This: "This is a new step for me but I find it so easy to follow you, Jack. I guess you *do* dance a lot, don't you? You say you don't?"

He Felt Thus—"Just a born dancer!"

SCENE II. *At the Wheel*—A calm glance at the speedometer and she settles back comfortably with a sigh—and

She Merely Said This—"Seventy miles, Jim, and I'm not a bit scared—but I'd never let my brother Ed risk my life like this!"

He Felt Thus—"She trusts my driving ability. Just a Speed Demon but a reliable one."

SCENE III. *At the Library*—Fingering the book her intelligent looking boy friend offers her—she hands it back with a sigh, but—

She Merely Said This—" 'Stoo deep for me, Bill. I wish I could interest myself in the worth-while literature that you do. You do like the deepest books!"

He Felt Thus—"Just a deep sea diver delving into the sea of knowledge. Crave only the best that's written! No depraved tastes here."

SCENE IV. *At Christmas*—Regarding *his* gift with *strong approval* and that Xmas Smile—

She Merely Said—"Someone must have told you that I needed a purse! I'll bet you asked mother! You didn't? Even my brother Ed never hits it right. I guess just a *few* men are inspired."

He Felt Thus—"Just blessed with that sense of observation with a feeling of the appropriate thrown in."

SCENE V. *On the Telephone*—Lowering her voice to a very pathetic and appealing tone—

She Merely Said—"Tonight? Yes I'd love to see you tonight, Frank. I've so much on my mind. I can't tell the family anything because they just laugh at me. It's so nice to have someone who understands and takes me seriously."

He Felt Thus—"So Understanding! Women know I have the type of shoulder they can cry on. Always in demand."

SCENE VI. *At the Party*—In quite an awed voice—

She Merely Said—"And you never told me before that you had a book published! If that were Ed he'd have broadcast it all over.

He Felt Thus—"Just the 'umble type.' Brains haven't gone to *my* head."

SCENE VII. *At the Piano*—Gazing enraptured at his rhythmic fingers traversing the keys—

She Merely Said—"Do you think I could ever learn to play like that? My brother said I'm not sociable just sitting here but I'd so much rather listen than dance."

He Felt Thus—"Paderewski's only rival! A musical magnet."

SCENE VIII. *Just Outside the Parental Door*—With a little laugh—

She Merely Said—"Three o'clock, Ray? Mother angry? She never scolds when she knows I'm with you. Makes me laugh."

He Felt Thus—"Friend of American Mothers. Type to be trusted."

SCENE IX. *At Sambo's Inn*—In that surprised voice—

She Merely Said—"Do you know *everyone,* Tom? Isn't there someone who won't come over and slap you on the back? How does it feel to be so well acquainted?"

He Felt Thus—"What a popular young man I turned out to be. Just over-run with friends. No end to my followers."

SCENE X. *Any Place*—Head on a 33⅓ degree angle and knowing smile—

She Merely Said—"Bobby picked out a Hart, Schaffner and Marx ad the other day and said that he looked like you. They do have such fascinating ads, don't they? If I were a man I'd want to look just like that."

He Felt Thus—"I'm a living model showing just what the well dressed man should wear. And how it wilts the feminine hearts and blows them in my direction."

The tactful winning of young people, therefore, consists principally in complimenting them upon the traits in which they aspire to excel. Since from childhood onward they have been desirous of freedom and adult privileges, it is obvious that they like to be considered grown, strong, competent, experienced, etc. Since they have been worshippers of muscular strength and sophistication for so many years, they are more influenced by persons who also possess such qualifications.

The Tactful Winning of Middle-Aged People. The usual rules for compliments hold in this age group. One must keep in mind, moreover, that such persons have now reached the stage in their mental development when they no longer resent being thought youthful. Indeed, they react very favorably to indirect and even direct comments upon their vitality, lack of gray hair and wrinkles, springy step, and schoolgirl complexions. Because they have been in business and their own homes long enough to have products of such environments, as executive positions, automobiles, pretty dwellings, and children, the intelligent observer will find a host of things by praising which he indirectly compliments their owners and creators.

The difference between such tactful compliments and those employed with young people will be apparent from an inspection of the following student reports.

Your children have such good manners, Mrs. Fox. I wish mine were half as polite. (I understand child psychology — a good mother.)

One has only to look at your wife's happy face to know what kind of a husband you are. (I am a gentleman and perfect lover.)

I sometimes wonder how you manage to stand up under the tremendous strain, with your business and practically all the work to do at the lodge. I'm afraid I'd be all worn out in two weeks if I were as active as you. (I'm virile, masculine and healthy—meaning youth.)

Really, Mrs. Brown, teaching would be a pleasure if all the boys were as alert and well trained as your Richard. (I'm a good mother.)

What kind of cold cream do you use? I've tried several kinds, but my skin never has that lively glow which is so important if one is to keep youthful looking. (I look youthful—a schoolgirl complexion.)

Don't forget to come to the country club dance on Friday night, Mrs. Miller—all the younger set will be there. (I'm still youthful enough to be included in the "younger" set.)

You and Jack certainly do look alike. I was walking in back of the two of you tonight, and I could hardly tell which was Jack. (This compliment may be taken by both father and son if the boy is not over twenty-five. It admirably illustrates the difference in attitude of father and son regarding the matter of age.)

I hope I'm not keeping you from dancing with the other girls. They've been casting pointed glances at you ever since you started talking to me. Girls do go for distinguished looking men, you know. They have so much more poise than the boys in our set. (A father-in-law cannot long maintain his objections to his son's wife, if she follows the procedure of this young diplomat, regardless of her frivolities.)

The tactful winning of middle-aged people, therefore, follows the same fundamental technique as that which we described for winning young people. They have enjoyed adulthood long enough, however, to be looking back to youth with fond memories. They want to retain as many symbols of youth as possible, included among which are, of course, health, vigor, no wrinkles, no gray hair, and sex appeal. Because they have products of their years in business or in the home, they may also be complimented on these.

The Tactful Winning of Elderly People. This group possesses many of the characteristics of the middle-aged men and women as regards the things on which they pride themselves. They still like to be considered healthy and spry, although they have relinquished the active attempt to be incorporated in younger groups. They admit they are aged, but they wish to show how little time has affected them. They have children and grandchildren concerning whom they take pride, but they are more susceptible to direct compliments about their immediate deeds and products. They are slipping into the attitudes of children in this regard. A bit of praise for their knitting or gardening seems to carry more weight than a compliment on their children. This fact probably results from the tendency of younger people to shelve their grandparents or elderly parents by taking over control of the business or household and even apportioning the furniture and heirlooms. To the man and woman past seventy, physical comforts, cushions, and easy chairs play a more significant role than in the lives of younger persons. They are also especially complimented through the question, as some of the examples below will demonstrate.

(To the man of 65 who has a wife of 55) Did you and your wife marry as a result of a school days' romance? (It would be wise to put such a question in the absence of the wife, of course!)

(To her future grandmother) Jack says he wants me to come over here and take some cooking lessons from you before we get married. (Does anybody think the grandmother will oppose this match thereafter?)

I wanted to ask your advice about buying some stock.

You can't fool me, Grandmother. I'll bet you were the life of the party before you married Grandfather.

Grandfather, tell me some of your experiences during the war?

Grandmother, you are an artist, the way you can make such beautiful rag rugs.

In the tactful winning of elderly people, therefore, one should keep in mind that the technique employed with middle-aged persons is usually effective here. However, elderly people are not so concerned with being considered youthful as they are with being younger looking than some other elderly person. The rivalry factor is now quite apparent. Because they have had some of their independence taken away from them by their children, they are interested, therefore, in being considered competent to run their homes and their businesses, and react in many ways like young people. In fact, youth looks forward to independence while age looks backward toward independence, so the same type of compliment will work with both groups.

Developing Your Social Intelligence. In this and preceding chapters we have mentioned the principal features to be considered by the person who wishes to be adept in social situations. The nursery school and the presence of playmates and siblings are quite important as early means of extroverting people. Even a few months of salesmanship is a great help, as we illustrated in the case of the young engineer cited in Chapter IV. Social intelligence can be consciously cultivated. It is not an innate characteristic of a person. To a certain extent, of course, it depends on the possession of mental alertness or abstract intelligence, for the imbecile cannot hope to become socially intelligent, but even a genius in terms of I. Q. is not socially alert unless he has been so trained by his environment. We have many brilliant men and women who are as tactless and boorish as any subnormals. In the conscious technique of acquiring social intelligence or developing it in children the following items should be considered.

(1) Recreational Habits. Learn to play the games that are conventional. Attain some knowledge and skill concerning tennis, baseball, golf, bridge, dancing, swimming and the like. Be aware of current actors and actresses, and the plays in which they appeared. Know some of the popular authors and the present best sellers in fiction. Keep up with popular music and styles. In this manner you not only direct your attention outward, but also gain a feeling of social unity with your group, and feel little shyness or hesitancy regarding the amusement plans of your social set.

(2) Etiquette. Be conversant with customary usage of language and deportment in such situations as a ballroom, a restaurant, a pullman car, or a church. Underline in red such important events as birthdays, anniversaries, and sailing dates, remembering that candy, flowers, and even a simple greeting card mean much. Quoting a few relevant lines of verse or an appropriate phrase from a popular song certainly

doesn't do any harm, especially when such quotations are complimentary to the recipient. Emily Post and Dorothy Dix can usually offer material aid in this connection.

(3) Methods of Motivating Human Beings. We have discussed this subject in Chapter I, and in the latter half of the present chapter. The art of complimenting people involves an understanding of their age and accomplishments, plus a tactful phrasing of the commendatory remarks, all of which involves extroversion of our attention. Instead of being wholly preoccupied with our own hobbies and interests, we become aware of those of our associates. It is possible to form the habit of making other people happy. The stumbling block over which most people fall is their failure to perform the second step in the two-stage process of becoming popular. They are so concerned with making a good impression that they forget the basic purpose for which that good impression is desired, namely, the weight it gives to their compliments of other individuals around them.

In conclusion, therefore, we may state that the development of social intelligence is practically synonymous with the process of extroverting an individual. It involves attention to the social habits of people and an understanding of some of the basic principles of human motivation and control. Like any other profession, the art of social diplomacy can be acquired by any intelligent person who is willing to study it diligently. It can also be taught to one's children. Because almost every business deals with people in some regard, the possession of social intelligence becomes a financial as well as social asset to the man and woman in the workaday world. See my "Formula For Being An Interesting Conversationalist" on page 594.

REFERENCES

CRANE, G. W., *Secrets of an Attractive Personality* (Chicago, The Formfit Company, 1934), pp. 68.

HIGGINSON, G. D., *Psychology* (New York, 1936), chap. 19.

ROBACK, A. A., *Improving Your Personality* (Cambridge: Sci-Art, 1935), pp. 40.

WHITE, WENDELL, *The Psychology of Dealing With People* (New York, 1936).

CHAPTER VII

THE PSYCHOLOGY OF SELLING YOUR PRODUCT

In discussing personality development we have already treated one phase of salesmanship. The public speaker also utilizes many of the principles offered in this chapter when he convinces his hearers of the merits of his cause. The teacher should really be interested in doing the same thing, although too often the material is "dished out" to the students with little regard for the state of their intellectual appetites, or their skill in assimilating the new facts.

In the realm of business, the salesman sells products, ideas, and services. Tangible objects, of course, are easier to merchandise than are the more ephemeral ideas and services, because they have immediate sensory qualities. The customers can feel silks, or taste foods, or ride in automobiles. Insurance policies and efficiency systems cannot be experienced so directly by the sense organs; hence, they are sold with greater difficulty. Moreover, the more remote the profits in point of time, the more difficult is the sale. Animals and children, for instance, want things *now*. Even in college the students will usually prefer a half day's holiday today to a full day off next week. Future rewards, like third degree stimuli, are too vague to surpass first and second degree stimuli.

In devoting only one chapter to the psychology of salesmanship, it will be obvious that we can delineate only the important aid which psychology offers, and let supplementary volumes on the subject fill out the remainder.

The Function of Enthusiasm in Salesmanship. The majority of sales managers realize the importance of "pep" meetings. A successful salesman must be full of vigor. He cannot drag along in his walking or thinking like a foot soldier on his twentieth mile, for it is almost impossible to arouse action in a customer unless the salesman is full of enthusiasm. Lacking this quality, the salesman is likely to be convinced by his customer instead of convincing the latter. The excessive vitality demonstrated by the orchestra leader, for example, is an attempt to overcome the inertia of the audience so that they will participate in applause, laughter, or singing.

Salesmanship is one of the most difficult tasks on earth. It drains one's physical vitality and subjects one's enthusiasm to repeated deflation, for the best salesman usually meets more rebuffs than he does successes. The principal function of the sales manager is to offset the effect of the failures encountered by his men. He accomplishes this result in numerous ways, one of which is by keeping in daily contact with his road salesmen so that they obtain a morning letter of encouragement. In this letter he may cite new selling points, or enclose a record of all the salesmen so that each one is aware of what the others are doing.

Lacking this letter the salesman who has encountered rebuffs for several days, is likely to lay the blame for his failure on lack of money by his customers or the depression. When he receives records of the other men on the force, however, and finds they are selling regularly, he is more inclined to buckle down to greater effort. As a further means of increasing his enthusiasm, teams are devised so that one group of salesmen is pitted against another. Prizes may be awarded to the winning captains, who are the high point winners of the week or month.

If the salesmen are working within an hour's ride of a central office, they usually meet each morning or at least once a week for "pep" sessions. The leading salesmen give talks on how they attained their successes. The sales manager demonstrates new uses of the product or calls to his assistance one of the chemists or engineers to explain interesting processes or stages in its manufacture. The old time sales manager, like the old football coach, used to engage in fist shaking and profanity as the chief means of stimulating his men to greater accomplishment. The new type of sales manager, although adept in the use of speech which incites his men to action and builds up their confidence and enthusiasm, nevertheless is a closer student of psychology, and adapts his methods to the individual personalities of those under him. If praise stimulates Brown while rêprimand incites Smith, he modifies his speech and letters to meet the differences in his crew.

Sometimes only a few degrees difference in a man's confidence and enthusiasm will change defeat into victory, for the customer subtly feels the mental state of the salesman. Just as enthusiasm is infectious, so doubt and uncertainty likewise are perceived by the potential clients with a resulting lack of decision on their part. As in the realm of mental disease, the attitude of the salesman may be the basis of success or failure. A conquering mood on his part is more likely to lead to conquest. Every professional salesman knows that the days on which he starts out with an early sale to his credit are the days when he should work doubly hard, for the effect upon his confidence of this initial victory may bring several more sales into his order book before nightfall. These are the times when a salesman feels invincible. On the other hand, the sales manager often encounters his men when they are like Half-Way Hurley, described in Chapter II, and must be stimulated by some such device as the following:

In 1928, Mr. Lee[1] decided that his salesmen could increase their orders for Protectographs from the 8 or 10 weekly average up to 12 or 15. Having been a salesman himself, he challenged his force, and set the week of May 7th for the test. All challengers gave a list of their prospects, who were sent direct-mail advertising in advance. On Monday the contest began. No order of more than two to a customer could apply,

[1] Lee, George W., "Our Weekly Sales Record Was Broken *Four* Times in 1928," *Printers' Ink* (Dec. 27, 1928), pp. 25 *ff*.

and all orders had to be signed that week—no hold-overs and no deferred deliveries. Mr. Lee had the agreeable surprise of selling 22 Protectographs, a record which was tied by one of his salesmen.

He thereupon made a standing offer of $100 to anybody who would exceed this mark. Shortly thereafter Mr. Johnson offered himself as a candidate, and brought in 27 orders during the week of his test. Mr. Poff raised the mark to 29 not long thereafter, to be followed during the busy week of December 15 by Du Rocher's 31. High marks like these would have been deemed impossible by the salesmen until the initial contest showed that over twenty machines could be sold in a week. This fact simply gave them confidence or belief that it could be done, a conviction that even led to the astounding peak of 31 orders in six days, a previous month's business.

A salesman's enthusiasm, moreover, must be kept at a high level and maintained there even during unsuccessful interviews, for often it is almost impossible to gain an order on the first contact. It may require several visits on the salesman's part before he has created enough confidence in himself and has sufficiently impressed the conservative dealer with the desirability of his goods to produce favorable action. A survey by 1000 retailers who kept accurate check for six months to learn how many calls salesmen made on them before giving up the job as hopeless led to the following results[1]:

48.2 per cent made 1 call and quit.
24.4 per cent made 2 calls and quit.
14.7 per cent made 3 calls and quit.
12.7 per cent made 4 calls and quit.

Only one salesman out of every eight made as many as four calls on a new dealer, yet these same 1000 retailers discovered that the great bulk of all their buying was not made until after the third call. In short, only those men who called four or five times stood much chance of getting orders.

[1] *Advertising and Selling Magazine* (Jan. 30, 1924), p. 21.

"Nothing succeeds like success," runs an old saying which is certainly borne out in the realm of salesmanship. The salesman knows, as does his manager, that as soon as his enthusiasm wanes, his sales fall off. The records of his co-workers aid in maintaining his morale, as do inspirational speeches by his manager. Increasing his motivation, as by offers of prizes, bonuses, or positions on paper ball teams and the like have marked value. Sometimes his need of additional money, or jealousy of seeing his record topped by a rival will spur him on to greater productivity.

One of the indispensable qualities of a salesman is a constant realization of the fact that he will sell a certain percentage of his customers if he just keeps driving vigorously ahead. Unfortunately, it may be that in some cases the last day or two of the week are the only ones that result in business. For days in succession he meets deferments and rebuffs. But a knowledge of his basic percentage rate will be invaluable as a spur to his enthusiasm, and carry him through the dreary period of no sales.

A fortunate thing in the salesman's favor is the fact that he can always count on a certain number of sales for any legitimate product, if he just makes his calls. There are always some customers just ready to order his goods, and who don't need a sales talk to persuade them. Then, too, his personality will have a greater appeal to some customers than to others, for he will remind them of a relative or friend. Maybe they do not consciously realize why, but they will feel drawn to him. Unfortunately for the salesman, of course, this number is usually too few to insure him a comfortable salary without more active effort on his part.

In discussing enthusiasm one must not confuse it with so-called "high pressure" salesmanship. Although the latter involves enthusiasm, it frequently connotes an unpleasant disregard for the actual needs of the customer and a sheer physical and mental dominance by the salesman. In a certain number of persons, it is true, the salesman encounters a vacillating type of personality so that he may at times have to make up the customers' minds for them, but when he deliberately utilizes his greater skill to intimidate his clients, he is employing a figurative club. Such a method cannot lay claim to being a high grade of salesmanship. It belongs in the category of the procedure formerly in vogue whereby the salesman took his client to a risquè show and afterwards plied him with liquor until the stupefied customer allowed his hand to be steered along the dotted line.

The function of enthusiasm in salesmanship, therefore, is twofold. First, it incites the salesman himself to greater effort, and second, it infects the prospects so that they feel more interested in the merchandise and confident of its worth. The principal function of the sales manager is to keep up the enthusiasm of his men. We have recounted a few of the methods by which he accomplishes this end. Depending, of course, upon the type of merchandise and the amount of time which he can devote to the sale, the salesman should be impressed with the importance of following up one interview with later calls.

Fitting Your Product to Your Public. This problem entails some sales' prospecting, as well as a close scrutiny of the goods to be sold. It is a waste of time and energy for the salesman to call upon people who are only remotely interested in the type of article which he has to sell when he might be interviewing another class of purchaser in which he would find a ready market. If the article offers the salesman only a slight commission, he cannot devote the time for an excessively careful weeding out of prospects. On the other hand, if he is selling Packard automobiles or bonds he must select his clientele beforehand. Salesmanship is somewhat like fishing, for one must adapt the "bait" to the species for which one is angling. Because there are so many rival baits, one cannot expect his commissions to be large unless he first studies the habits of the species (clientele) with which he expects to deal.

Even in house-to-house canvassing, however, certain rough distinctions can be made. Homes in which there are maids offer a much greater resistance than those where the housewife herself appears at the door, and speaking through a tube in apartment buildings is enough to test the ingenuity of any salesman.

In his analysis of the problem undertaken in this section, Starch[1] offers six criteria of the consumer which are important to the salesman as well as to the advertiser.

(1) Who are the users and buyers of the article in question? Since the user is not always the buyer, it becomes important to make this distinction. Mothers are the chief buyers of their childrens' and even their husbands' clothing.

(2) Where do they live? Although this seems such a simple query as to be self-evident, it is surprising how many merchants and manufacturers are not clear as to the actual source of their purchasers. They may know, to be sure, that they live in the city or state, but it often requires an advertising firm to tell them which quarter of the city or state. The writer knows of a manufacturer, for example, with his salesmen on the road, sometimes 1000 miles away from the home plant, who made this same error. The distant salesmen lacked the advertising of the men closer home, and also missed many of the "pep" meetings. A survey of the city in which the company was situated revealed that the distant salesmen could profitably be called home and set to work within a radius of fifty miles of the manufacturing plant. Not only were their travelling expenses saved by the company, but the men were stimulated to greater enthusiasm by the frequent home contacts. Moreover, the salvaged expenses were available for more intensive local advertising purposes.

(3) How many potential buyers and users are there? In cities with large labor populations, as mining towns, one could

1 Starch, Daniel, *op. cit.*, chap. v.

not expect as wide a range of prospects for expensive automobiles or opera tickets as in a wealthy university town.

(4) How much of the goods can the buyers and users consume? This problem is of especial concern to the manufacturer and retailer, but it is also important to the salesman.

(5) How do the actual or possible users now satisfy the want which the new product is intended for? This question involves an understanding of the rival or competing goods in the field.

(6) What are the preferences with reference to the satisfaction of the need which the new commodity is to fulfill? In other words, do the people prefer one-pound or two-pound cans? Do they choose branded goods in cartons or buy them in the bulk? Which colors and styles do they like?

The last question above covers the psychological aspects of the consumer and is really the crux of the marketing problem. It offers the greatest trouble to the merchandiser and advertiser. In contrast to it the first five questions present no grave concern for they can be answered with less difficulty. One of our large mail order houses, for instance, decided to establish branch stores at numerous points throughout the country. These were located in cities and towns that usually did not exceed 25,000 to 40,000 population. A rival firm also began developing branch retail outlets, but placed its stores in larger cities. The first company has had to close most of its retail stores, whereas its rival has not been adversely affected. The second firm realized that mail order goods can be sold cheaper than when merchandised through retail outlets, and the farmer trade is interested in price. Accordingly, when it opened its retail branches, it located them in the cities, and actively began competing for new trade. The first company simply shifted much of its rural business into the county seat branches, and neglected its mail order trade. As a consequence, its customers drove to town and bought at the store, or may have continued ordering by mail from the competing firm.

The J. C. Penney Company appreciated this same desire for economy on the part of the working man when it featured overalls at $1.25 while standard overalls were selling at $2.25. It knew, of course, that overall wearers recognized differences in quality and would be willing to pay more for a better garment, *but not* 80 *per cent more*. It used the overalls as a "leader", much as sugar and nails are often employed by grocery and hardware dealers. Once the customer was in the store, he usually bought other articles, the prices of which were no lower than that of competitors. But the customer felt that he was getting bargain prices on the other articles since he used the staple as an index for comparison.

To combat Penney's method, the Oshkosh Overall Company tried to get independent merchants to buy its goods, and sell without a profit, in fact with a slight loss when overhead costs were figured in. But, as Wittmack[1] comments, the independent dealer replied, "Why should we work for you free? You get your price on overalls, and we stand the loss." The Oshkosh Company wanted to sell to the retailer at $1.70 and have him offer Oshkosh Overalls at $1.75 to $1.95.

In the process of fitting its product to the consumer the Gillette Company found that 25 per cent of its 250,000 dealers were doing 70 per cent of the selling. It found it advisable, therefore, to concentrate on these 25 per cent, making special boxes for chain drug stores, and different containers for the cigar stores. A special contest was conducted in a mid-western city with four prizes offered to the employees of a certain chain who sold the most razors in a given period of time. The Gillette Company was surprised to learn that first prize went to a cashier in one of the stores, while second prize was won by a soda fountain clerk, neither of whom had ever sold a razor in his life before. The contest brought out the

1 Wittmack, C. E., "We Tell Our Dealers: Sell Our Goods at No Profit," *Printers' Ink* (Dec. 27, 1928), p. 6.

value of the cashier's desk and the marble bar as sales positions.

The psychological phases of fitting your product to your public, therefore, consist primarily of determining the preferences with reference to the satisfaction of the need which the new product is to fulfill. The other five criteria are chiefly statistical problems. We have also cited under this heading the need for a study of the methods of merchandising the product, involving an appreciation of the most efficient retail outlets as well as a knowledge of the habits of the consumer. In the following section we shall dwell upon the problems entailed by the salesman-consumer situation where they are face to face.

The Steps in the Sale. Any attempt to divide the sale situation into steps or stages must be an arbitrary process, at least if regarded from the temporal aspect. The sale may last for a few moments or it may be a product of a year of thought and planning. Snow[1] has pointed out the fact that a purchase may often be made "mentally" a number of times before the actual transfer of the article for cash takes place. In this mental prepurchasing the customer tends to think in terms of brand names and known articles, thereby indelibly impressing them in his mind. In our discussion of the sale we shall consider the following steps, beginning with the actual salesman-customer contact:

(1) Focus the customer's attention on the product. Although there are many cases where it is well to spend some time chatting about inconsequential matters and creating in the client a feeling of confidence, the writer has always found it advisable in dealing with busy men to offer the strongest appeal as quickly as possible. Then, when a motive base is aroused, the salesman can go through a verbal flash-back in which he more leisurely develops the customer's confidence in

[1] Snow, A. J., *op. cit.*, p. 123.

him. There are many products for which there are no striking appeals, in which case the personality of the salesman is a deciding factor in the resulting action. In such an event, the more roundabout opening is valuable. Whether one opens with the incisive appeal followed by the flash-back, or with the circuitous approach, one should spend no unnecessary time in getting the favorable aspects of the merchandise before the customer.

(2) Arouse desire. This step involves showing the many ways in which the product will benefit the customer. In addressing a convention of salesmen some years ago Simmons urged the men to "Sell them the holes and they'll buy the augers in order to make the holes." No more pithy summary of successful salesmanship was ever made. The stress should always be placed on the *functions* of a product which enhance the pleasure or ego of the customer. An automobile's pick-up is slightly interesting unless the salesman shows you that by means of it you can beat the other cars away from a stop light, thereby intimating to your sweetheart that you are always in the lead. Its speed is a vague selling point until translated into specific situations where you can whirl past your rival on the highway, or get out of a dangerous situation more readily. The car itself is desirable not because it is a shiny four-wheel vehicle, but because it enables you to take the children into the country, or to drive to your golf club and enjoy nine holes before dark which would be impossible without the car, or to indicate your business success and financial standing to the neighbors.

Railroad advertising has aptly demonstrated this principle in recent years. To look at their posters, one would think California or Florida or Canada or Yellowstone National Park were really the sponsors of the advertisements. They show us the pleasures of wintering in Florida, then state that they can take us there most quickly and economically. This accords with the fact that the more habit patterns of a pleasing sort which can be aroused by the salesman during the interview, the greater will be the desire for the article. It is imperative for the salesman to translate his product into its pleasing functions as regards the customer, since few articles are of interest to people in their own right, for most persons are not in the category of Silas Marner. Robinson Crusoe, for example, was astounded to find that even gold had no interest for him while he was marooned. *The value of any article depends not on the article but on the customer who regards it.* The task of the salesman, therefore, is to change the customer's attitude by successively employing his product to set off additional habit systems.

(3) Produce action. This problem is really answered almost entirely when desire is aroused, for action is the normal result of desire. In Chapter I we discussed the subject of choice or "will", showing that it is synonymous with desire, using the analogy of the scales. We pointed out that the negative weight or objections could be removed by logic, or by heaping positive weights so rapidly on the other scale pan that the customer forgot the negative ones. In the latter case desire spelled action. In the former case where the customer has time to break away from the salesman's line of thought occasionally, objections may arise. From habit, one has learned that there are many articles of the same general class, so that one should compare prices. In this type of sales situation the customer must be convinced of the superiority of the given article over all competing brands. Writers have frequently made a separate step in the sales process which they have called "Producing Conviction". The present writer looks upon this heading as comparable to the rebuttal of the college debater. If a salesman has perfectly performed his task, no formal rebuttal is necessary.

Action usually denotes signing an order blank, making out a check, or reaching into one's pocket for money. At this time the salesman usually loses some of his dominance of the customer's attention, and the latter is at liberty to do voluntary thinking. Doubts appear, and the enthusiasm of the customer frequently cools. In other words, the unanswered negative weights are suddenly called to mind, tending to restore the scales to equilibrium.

In the three steps just recounted we have outlined the essential phases of the actual sales situation. The pre-approach with its problems of fitting the product to the customer is of tremendous significance in guaranteeing a higher percentage of sales, and the matter of consumer satisfaction is also worthy of comment at this point. Even though the customer signs the order blank or pays for the goods without the necessity of a demonstration the salesman should never let him go away with his purchase without trying to present some of the functions of the product. If he does, a friend of the buyer may later say, "What on earth made you buy that kind of an automobile? You ought to have purchased a *good* car like mine." The customer finds himself at a loss to answer his friend's objections, so the friend may ultimately persuade him of the folly of his choice. When the customer meets the salesman thereafter he will think, if not actually say, "You certainly sold me a 'lemon'." On the other hand, by placing good sales points before the customer, who may not need them himself, the salesman makes another salesman out of his client. The latter may as a consequence direct additional business to the man who sold him the car.

In summarizing the psychological steps in the sale, therefore, we may state that they involve focussing the customer's attention upon the most significant aspects of the goods, arousing desire, and producing action. The salesman should never forget that the value of his merchandise depends on the attitude of his client. It becomes imperative, therefore, that he stress the functional relationship of the goods to an increase in the satisfaction of the buyer. This task involves, of course, a recognition of the customer's fundamental motive bases.

The Two Danger Zones in the Sale. Where the majority of salesmen are most guilty of error is in the opening ten sentences and in the few sentences involving the closing. In the body of the sales demonstration the exigencies of the moment can usually be met by the salesman. He doesn't need a stereotyped formula to rely upon. But in his remarks immediately following his salutation and those in which he asks for the customer's signature or cash, he needs special preparation and a memorized formula.

(1) The Opening. When the salesman first encounters his customer he needs his attention free to observe the latter's reactions. If he is mentally struggling for the right thing to say, his attention is preoccupied, and his customer can calmly survey him, having instantly gained the advantage of dominating the situation. The salesman slips into the defensive role, and his client is likely to terminate the interview quickly, or control it by his questioning.

In order to avoid this disaster, the salesman must have his initial sentences so memorized that he is free from embarrassment and can look ahead. He can, therefore, retain the offensive role throughout the interview. Take the following situation, which is one of the most critical ever confronted by the salesman. An insurance salesman has called to see a busy executive. The latter steps to the swinging gate separating the outer waiting room from the inner office. Two other salesmen are seated near by and the secretary or information girl is within hearing. The executive asks, politely but with apparent desire to get back into his office alone, "What is it you want to see me about?"

Obviously, the salesman cannot begin, "Isn't it a pleasant day, Mr. Brown? Do you play golf?" If he did the smiles of the audience would probably unnerve him, and check his speech in flushed confusion. In order to veer away from a revelation of his real purpose, he may say, "I want to discuss a little matter of private business with you," meanwhile moving as if to enter. If his suggestion of entering does not produce a favorable response from the unyielding executive, he probably receives a further question, "Well, I'm rather busy today, so if you'll tell me what it is about . . .?"

The average salesman is at a loss in this type of situation. He must now make his purpose known, since he has already indicated by his reticence, that he probably has something to sell. He feels somewhat embarrassed, of course, because other salesmen are looking on. He may bluntly say, "I wanted to see you about an accident insurance policy for your children." The reader knows the usual response.

Suppose, however, that the salesman had confidently walked over to the executive, and with no sign of embarrassment or confusion had cordially said, "Good morning, Mr. Brown. Since I was in your building I thought I'd drop in to get your advice about Betty." Here he ever so slightly turns his head to note the eavesdropping salesmen, and suggests entering by a slight forward movement of his hands to the swinging gate. Mr. Brown will usually invite him inside, for the cordial attitude of the young fellow and confident air vaguely suggest that Mr. Brown has met him before, and the mention of his college daughter by her first name increases the impression that this fellow may be a friend of hers.

If Mr. Brown is still resistant, which is rather unlikely, and asks, "What do you want to know about her?" he immediately lays himself open to having private affairs discussed before strangers. The salesman has him pretty well cornered, and the subtle compliment contained in the request for advice also conveys the intimation that Betty may be in trouble, or is contemplating marriage, or is looking for a position. Should an obdurate father put such a second question, however, the salesman can come back with, "I don't know if you are aware of it, Mr. Brown (voice now is slightly lowered), but Betty is in danger of a serious lawsuit."

From the psychological standpoint, the opening statements

of this salesman will very likely get him into Mr. Brown's office, although they may also lead to some resentment on the part of Mr. Brown unless the salesman is very competent. If the salesman intimates by word or action that he thinks he has outwitted Mr. Brown, he will quickly be escorted out of the office, but if he presents his facts in a sincere manner, showing that carefree Betty is likely to injure some one with her automobile and thereby jeopardize her freedom and her father's business, the salesman's previous remarks are made more relevant. In any case, he has passed the almost insurmountable barrier of the swinging gate, without which action his prospective sale is foredoomed to failure.

In our discussion of personality development we have already stressed the personal equation. Although it contributed part of this nonchalance and assurance of the second salesman, his confidence was partly owing to his knowledge of his opening. Regardless of whether he has to meet the secretary first or half a dozen intermediaries, he has an introduction that fits them all, and they will quickly send him to the inner office. Since he has no need for worry about the excellence of his lead-off sentences, he can calmly note the factors in the environment, including his customer, which can be utilized in his campaign. He is master of the human beings around him because he has verbally manipulated his sentences beforehand until he has a perfect arrangement. Knowing this fact, he is confident, and his confidence impresses his customers.

(2) The Close. The writer told one of his classes in applied psychology to write down ten sentences covering the actual asking for money, or the name on the dotted line, in a hypothetical sale of a vacuum cleaner to a housewife. The students could employ any type of closing they desired. Of 55 men and women who handed in the assignment *only five* actually closed the sale. And one of these ended with the nonplussed query, "Well, what do you say? Take it or leave it!" The writer offers these figures simply to show that the

salesmen themselves may tend to react like these students, and avoid the closing. As a matter of fact they often begin a recapitulation of selling points and mark time in the vicinity of the dreaded dotted line, but fail to finish their task, or else delay so long that the customer's interest has waned.

The salesman should fear the closing no more than the insurance salesman previously mentioned showed fear of his opening. In fact, the salesman should relish approaching the dotted line stage, since that means he is entering upon a mechanically perfect formula which frees his attention for keener observance of his customer. The man who shows the confidence and tact of this insurance salesman seldom excites his customer during the critical period of the close. The embarrassed and uncertain speech of the tyro salesman, however, produces uncertainty in the client.

The usual type of closing is that which involves the minor decision. The salesman tacitly assumes the sale is made, and inquires, "Would you prefer this order to be shipped by freight or express," Or else, "Would you want this vacuum cleaner in time for Saturday's cleaning, or shall we deliver it on Monday?" To illustrate the delicate approach to the crux of the sale note the importance of the word "just". It appears in almost every closing. "If you'll just sign here, we'll have this machine delivered tomorrow." That single word eliminates much of the bluntness that might otherwise attach to the closing. The salesman must avoid intimating that the customer's word is not as good as his bond. He should never say, "You have to sign this contract before the company will send you the goods." Instead, he should smilingly comment, "If you'll just O.K. this along here, we'll have the goods sent out immediately."

In concluding our discussion of the two danger zones in the sale, therefore, we can repeat that they consist of the opening few sentences and the closing. Amateur salesmen err at those two points more frequently than anywhere else in the sale situation. With an opening whose units are memorized so that the salesman can devote the major portion of his attention to the reactions of his client, the salesman retains his dominance of the situation and creates confidence. In a similar fashion his assurance at the closing prevents the arousal of negative ideas or objections in the mind of his customer.

Hitting the Bull's-eye with Your Appeals. In our consideration of the methods of motivating human beings we stated that stimuli must set off habits and instincts in order to be effective. In salesmanship the chief task consists in translating or showing the numerous facets of an article so that it will arouse more habit systems. But we have also previously commented on the fact that motives have both number and weight. One may be as important as several others. The good salesman appreciates this fact, and at the outset endeavors to show those aspects of his merchandise which arouse the most basic neural patterns.

In a selling talk prepared for use by salesmen of a city light and power company, the following sales arguments are presented in their apparent order of merit. The article being merchandised is an electric, wet-proof heating pad. We shall list only the first few arguments.

1. This new wet-proof heating pad is a new invention.
2. Here's the switch that controls the heat.
3. This pad has an all-over heating unit.
4. The cord is all silk and has 68 strands of small copper wire each as fine as the hair on your head.
5. The cover is eiderdown.
6. The cover can be taken off.
7. BUT THE BIGGEST THING ABOUT THIS PAD IS THAT IT IS GUARANTEED TO BE WET-PROOF.
8. On account of the pad being wet-proof you can use it for keeping wet packs hot.

An inspection of these eight arguments as given in chronological order in the sales talk shows that the only one that hits the bull's-eye is number eight. All the other sales arguments are trivial matters. It doesn't make any difference to a housewife if the cord has 68 or 68000 fine copper wires in it as long as she has thus far seen no basic use for it. Every housewife, however, can appreciate having a constant heat available for headaches, rheumatism, baby's colic, etc. Even the seventh argument which apparently was deemed sufficiently valuable to warrant capitalization has no significance until the eighth is given, and we realize that the pad fits inside a wet towel, keeping the towel warm. This sales talk certainly is a good case of putting the cart before the horse. The average housewife probably would have the door shut long before Number Eight was reached.

Perspective, or the ability to distinguish fundamentals from trivialities, is one of the keynotes of successful salesmanship. Without it one may not even hit the target, let alone the center of it. We have shown in the preceding section how the insurance salesman employed his knowledge of human nature for his own profit. Others make successful entries by striking directly at the center of the situation. Here is a salesman who wishes to see the professional buyer of a large department store. The secretary insists on a card. Instead, the salesman writes on a slip of paper the following: "After the Toonerville Emporium placed one of our electric dishwashers on display, they sold 13 of the machines during the first six days and cleared $217.50 on them. Wouldn't you like to hear me explain the method they employed?" In using the example of another store, it is advisable to cite a firm from a neighboring city.

One of my former students tells me that he has found it desirable to omit carrying his brief case when he calls upon the trade, and wrap his samples in a large package, which he carries into the store when he sees the tradesman has a customer, and, laying it on the counter, says, "Go right ahead. I'm in no hurry." The shopkeeper's curiosity is stimulated. He wonders what is inside the large bundle, and is willing to talk to the salesman until it is opened, whereupon he sees the line of samples carried, and is likely to order.

In salesmanship it is also well to keep in mind the fact that we are composed of a mass of neural networks which represent our habits. Some of these habits are at variance with others. In the following paper one of the writer's former students has delineated a few of the various attitudes which she has when in one situation, then another. Since she is both motorist and pedestrian at different times, her thinking is colored principally by the role she plays at the given moment.

PROBLEM—List the groups to which you belong. How do your habits and attitudes vary according to which you are with?

FEMALE—Feel on defensive when insinuations are made that women are not as smart as men, are not able to do certain things as well as a man, etc.

(Sub-groups, I suppose they would be called.)

Brunette—Resent the well known saying, "Gentlemen prefer blondes" or other remarks to the effect that brunettes are not attractive, smart, good natured, etc. Feel pretty good when something nice or complimentary is said about a brunette.

Slender—Feel that slenderness is much to be preferred to fleshiness, have feeling would never want to be "fat", feel sorry for those who cannot eat what and as much as they want to for fear of hurting their figures, etc.

AMERICAN—Feel that United States is by far the best country to live in and that most everything we do or possess is better than any other country.

SINGLE—Have a rather pleasant reaction, for instance, when I can get a new fur coat because I have only myself to think of. On other hand, rather envy a married friend when seeing her with her baby.

FAMILY—Am inclined to "let go" of my feelings more when in the family group. Also consider them when wondering what to do on various occasions.

STUDENT—Feel a loyalty to my University, want it to be the best in the country, want it to win its football games, etc. Even when seeing a football game between two other universities, would rather see one of our "enemies" get beaten because I have developed that feeling from playing against them in our own games. Also wonder at people who are not interested in going on further with their education. Have perhaps a little superior air because I have gone a little farther than the average, though I will say I try to hide this with people who have not had the same advantages.

SORORITY—Feel a little "superior" because I was chosen by a group to be a member—though I also try not to ever let this crop out. However, would rather be a member than not organized. Am loyal to my own group as compared with other like groups and wish them to lead in every way possible. Talk college life and sorority matters when with other members that I do not talk at work, for instance.

BUSINESS—Am rather proud of our nice offices (I work for investment bankers). Enjoy all the bank holidays we get. Like working in such nice surroundings.

STOCK BUYER—Being in the atmosphere I dabble in stocks. Feel the fascination of taking the chance when buying with the hope that they will go up. (A rather forlorn one at present.) However, the gambling instinct is mingled with buying for income with possibilities of appreciation. Am interested in the quotations from day to day, hour to hour, etc. Listen to all the talk going on around me.

SECRETARY—The secretaries, especially of executives, in our office seem to be in a class by themselves. I mean there is a sort of caste, you might call it. They "rate" better than the file clerks, stenographers, multigraph operators, etc. I do not feel I am really any "better" than those who do not have as good a position, but do feel it would be congenial to have my friends among the other secretaries. While at the office I control any feelings I have of annoyance, weariness, etc., more than I would at home. I also try to keep personal affairs out of the office.

GOLFERS—I like golf as well as any sport I participate in and enjoy talking about it with anyone else who is interested in playing. When playing I try to control my feeling of annoyance when I make a poor shot. I also try not to do anything to upset my fellow players, but help them find their ball, etc.

BRIDGE CLUB—Not a very serious minded crowd, usually quite hilarious with much laughing. Thoroughly relax while with this group and act as silly as I want to. Only time anyone half-way concentrates is the little time we are actually playing. Crowd has played together for about four years and are thoroughly acquainted.

Automobile Driver—When driving become very provoked with people who insist on crossing street when I have "go" signal; think all pedestrians should watch where they are going, etc.

Pedestrian—When I am walking I am provoked at automobile drivers who insist on turning corner when I am trying to cross street (on correct signal), think drivers should be more careful and not tear along at such a pace, etc.

Commuter—Hurry to catch my train every morning and hurry to catch one ten minutes ahead of the next one at night. Am very nervous when train stops for a few minutes at some spot where it doesn't usually stop, think the service is pretty punk when I miss my train and have to wait ten or fifteen minutes for the next one, am impatient if it doesn't pull in at the moment I think it should, especially if I am afraid I will be late.

In conclusion, therefore, we may state that hitting the bull's-eye with one's appeals involves an understanding of the psychological nature of the customer and a recognition of those aspects of the merchandise which will most readily incite basic habit patterns. These factors constitute what might be termed sales perspective. In order to gain this perspective it is well to produce as detailed an analysis of the habits of the consumer as can economically be obtained.

Sensory Appeals and Salesmanship. It isn't quite so essential that the salesman employ sensory language as it is for the advertiser, since the salesman frequently has samples or the actual object to offer his client. Nevertheless, specificity produces action and sensory adjectives are next in potency to first degree stimuli. In order to illustrate the value of specificty, as well as the sections on hitting the bull's-eye and the first danger zone in the sale, we submit the following first ten sentences that a real estate salesman might offer when he enters the office of a young attorney living in an apartment and having a wife and two children. The sentences in some instances are a bit long for oral speech but could be broken into shorter units in the actual sales situation.

1. Mr. Cricks, I have been talking with Mrs. Cricks about a plan by which she can get Tom and Janice into the sunshine and fresh air of Blossomhurst, where they can romp and play with other youngsters from similarly cultured homes without always making her worry for fear of reckless automobile drivers.

2. The wives of several other successful young professional men, such as Dr. Arnold's wife, and Mrs. Alberts, wife of the district attorney, have become concerned over the need for giving their children a safe and healthful community life in which to develop, and as a result have decided to form a restricted colony at Blossomhurst.

3. With such residents as you and Mrs. Cricks, Dr. and Mrs. Arnold, and Mr. and Mrs. Alberts, we are beginning to develop a civic life through our churches, parent-teachers associations, and clubs, which in turn is leading to increased happiness and congenial friendships among the women folks, as well as desirable business and professional contacts for you men.

4. Blossomhurst has been laid out as a restricted residential suburb on a gentle southern slope, 45 minutes' ride from the Loop by the Northwestern's trains, which operate on 15 minute schedule.

5. We have all improvements paid for, with three Protestant churches, a new grammar school whose teachers must pass the requirements of the Chicago school system, and a specially trained kindergarten teacher for Janice.

6. There are a number of types of home from which to choose, such as Colonial and Old English, but all have deep lots and wide frontages—the smallest being 150 feet deep by 60 feet across—so that there will be ample lawn space for Tom and Janice to play in and a large plot for Mrs. Cricks' garden and flower beds.

7. In the past 18 months 187 families of the professional class have moved into Blossomhurst, and a fine civic life is developing.

8. A new 9-hole golf course is being opened next month only three miles west of Blossomhurst.

9. Property values are constantly increasing, as you are in an especially good position to know, yet the temporary lull in the real estate business enables us to give a much lower price now than would be possible a year hence when prosperity returns.

10. Since there are two homes in particular—a Colonial and an Old English—that I should like to show Mrs. Cricks and yourself next Sunday afternoon, I wonder if 2 o'clock would be the best hour for me to call for you? We can take Tom and Janice with us.

From the sales opening just presented, it will be apparent that the writer deems the safety and health of his children the strongest motive force for Mr. Cricks, and launches into it with the first sentence. Thereafter follow the usual selling points concerning property. By introducing Mrs. Cricks' name at the start, the salesman gains that confidence, or at least tolerance, which comes from knowing a mutual friend. It is always wise to utilize a mutual friend in the introduction, provided the salesman uses discretion. He should not say, unless it is really true, "Mr. Brewster told me to come over to see you."

Whenever it is possible the salesman should carry a sample of his product or a chart or prospectus containing specimen pages, if the product is a set of books. Then get the sample into the customer's hands as soon as convenient, for the sensory qualities arising help sell the client. Getting him to assist in the demonstration, or drive the automobile himself, has definite value in arousing desire. In addition, when the customer is looking at the sample, his attention is focussed thereon, and bluntly stated sales' arguments do not give rise to as much resistance. They fall upon a marginal field of his attention, so become suggestions. We have already considered the relative merits of suggestions and direct statements.

The value of sensory appeals in salesmanship, therefore, consists chiefly in the fact that more habits with pleasurable affective tone are aroused thereby, for sensory appeals are usually first or second degree stimuli. Sensory epithets cannot be combated very easily since they set off conditioned habits which are usually beyond the conscious control of the subject. Sensory appeals, as a consequence, operate as suggestions, and are accordingly invaluable aids of both the salesman and the advertiser.

When and How to Use Reason. Whenever a customer needs to be convinced, that is, whenever he is vacillating or debating with himself, it would be well for the salesman to employ reason. However, reason is ineffective unless the customer has a desire for the product. It makes little difference to me how good a violin you are selling if I don't play one. It may be imported, and twenty dollars cheaper than any other brand, and have a ten years' guarantee, etc., but I am still disinterested. The violin will never appeal to me until it is translated into a means of satisfying a habit or instinct that I possess. Once having perceived that with this violin and a few lessons, I can become the life of the party and thereby inflate my social ego, or that I can use it as an appropriate birthday gift for my musically inclined sweetheart, or that I can boast that it was once played by Kreisler, I am ready to listen to reason.

Such a desire is commonly called impulsive and is in the broadest sense the basis for almost all sales. Reasoning enters when it becomes necessary to justify our sensory preferences to ourselves and to others. It is then often designated as rationalization. In presenting the several occasions in selling where reason is demanded, we shall modify the scheme presented by Snow[1] in our following list:

(1) Reason should be used in selling to an expert.

(2) In introducing new goods reason is often valuable. In advertising we call such devices "educational copy" or "reason why" copy.

(3) When the price of a product seems too high to the customer.

(4) Whenever competition is great.

(5) Whenever the customer is of the type that prides himself on not being swayed by emotions, as in the case of professional buyers. To intimate that the client buys only on the basis of logic is a compliment in itself. Once the customer feels that you think he is logical in his choices, he is like the farmer who buys Penney's $1.25 overalls and thinks that all

1 Snow, A. J., *op. cit.*, pp. 281-283; 335-339.

other prices will be equally as low. The buyer lowers his guard, as it were, and becomes susceptible to more direct compliments.

In selling as well as in advertising there are several types of evidence. First, the guarantee is probably the most effective instrument for producing belief. When an automobile tire is guaranteed for 25,000 miles of normal driving, the customer believes that the company must have tested the tire adequately before it was placed on the market, otherwise it could not afford to make such a statement. One of Chicago's largest department stores offers to refund the difference in price if any other store on the same day sells below its price. Because this offer is known to the people, they think this store gives the best bargains, and are more or less uncritical thereafter. Actually, other stores may undersell this one, but the majority never know it, and if they should, the first store might, as some occasionally demonstrate, reply to their requests for the article in question with, "Sorry, but we are all out of that size today."

The second type of evidence consists of tests. The consumer is permitted to have the article or book on trial. Or the company may conduct a public demonstration. In the realm of advertising we have noted many examples of this kind, as in Ripley's refereeing the "Blindfold Test" of Old Gold Cigarettes. The belief of the public depends largely on its confidence in the judges or the company. Occasionally, a firm may be able to cite the Bureau of Standards as its authority, or a famous auto racer who always had his car equipped with the tire being sold or the oil or gasoline in question.

The third variety of evidence consists of testimony. As a matter of fact, the reports of the Bureau of Standards could legitimately be classified here, though we generally refer to the statements of individuals. In the law courts these are called witnesses. In advertising and selling, widely known and respected persons are quoted, although the salesman in the individual case finds it even more effective to quote relatives and friends of his client. Patent medicine has been a great sponsor of the testimonial, although cold creams and cigarettes are doing the same thing nowadays. Even railroads and air lines are not averse to quoting famous passengers regarding the service or speed of their trains or airplanes.

In the use of reasons one should keep in mind the ensuing cautions:

(1) Reasons should be relevant. They should pertain definitely to the article or product at hand.

(2) Reasons should not be overstated. Excessive emphasis often defeats its own end. The understatement of a fact tends to promote belief more readily than its overstatement.

(3) Reasons should be chosen to suit the credulity of the customer. By this we mean that very unusual or surprising statements may cause disbelief, even though they are correct.

(4) Reasons should be effective sales points. To cite the great speed of a certain car which is being purchased by Mr. Brown for his daughter Betty may even detract from the ease in making the sale.

(5) Reasons should not be coercive. By this statement we mean the salesman should not elimate all choice of decision from his client. As Snow points out, it may be advisable to argue that a certain kind of automobile is the only one for the customer to buy, but he should be offered the option of several colors, styles, or models so that he feels that he has done the choosing. To rob a man of his right of choice, deflates his ego. The latter result leads to unpleasantness, which in turn defeats the sale.

(6) Reasons should be specific. The arguments in favor of a Ford must be different from the arguments for automobiles in general. True, if the customer isn't interested in automobiles as a class, he must be given "educational copy", but after he develops a liking for motor cars, he must be directed to a certain one of this type.

In the preceding discussion of when and how to use reason, therefore, we have seen that the wish for a product usually is impulsive because of the pleasure arising therefrom. The justification of the wish is one of the places where reason serves a useful purpose in the sale. We have presented five places, however, where the employment of reason is advantageous for the salesman, and have shown the six criteria of effective reasoning. The types of evidence which are available for the salesman have also been described. In the following section, however, we shall explain how reason may be short-circuited in salesmanship.

Short-circuiting Reason with Emotional Stimuli. Suggestions are a type of stimuli that short-circuit reasoning. The clever slogan, "Say it with flowers", does not introduce a rational process. The so-called political "mud slinging" and "whispering" campaigns may undermine a very logical piece of statesmanship, or cause the defeat of its sponsor. This is one of the most frequent fallacies encountered in logic, and yet it is of tremendous power in the hands of an unscrupulous foe. It is called *ad hominem* arguing, the disparagement of a man's work or ideas by reference to his personal life, race, sex or creed. "What does a woman know about automobile motors?" a garage mechanic says disparagingly when a female driver has told him exactly what is wrong with her car. And to demonstrate the "negative protest" he examines several other things about the engine before he condescends to do what she has previously pointed out.

Woman suffrage was opposed by the Philippine Legislature and would undoubtedly have been defeated in 1931 except for the fact that one legislator short-circuited a lengthy debate on the matter by saying the United States would deem them entirely too backward a people to have self-government unless the Philippine women were given the franchise. This idea became tied up with their national spirit and undermined the opposition in about a month's time.

A piano salesman has stated that he is engaged in "merchandising heart beats and not so many pounds of ivory and wire," for he found that a poor couple wished to buy a piano in order "to make Mary a lady." One of our shaving cream manufacturers stresses the fact that the cap cannot fall off the tube, which is stressing a point of efficiency rather than the lather value of the cream. A light and power company began a campaign to sell vacuum cleaners, making its appeals to women. Although many cleaners were sold, it launched a new campaign depicting the husband in his modern office in contrast to a picture of his wife with dustpan and broom sweeping the floor and sending dust everywhere. Underneath the double cut it ran the caption "Why not equip your wife's office like your own?" The second type of advertisement sold more vacuum cleaners than the first, because it directed an appeal to the husband's love and sense of fair play. It didn't emphasize at length the virtues of the particular vacuum cleaner displayed.

In Mueller's cartoon on the next page we see how effectively emotional appeals can short-circuit a slower and more difficult logical process. In business, advertising, and public speaking these appeals are frequently employed. They usually produce action more quickly than the reasoning method. A variation of this principle is illustrated in the example of the housewife who came home from shopping, having purchased a 110-piece set of dishes. She realized, of course, that her husband might be in an irritable mood after his day at the office, and might vent his ire by choosing the opposite course of action to that which she followed. So she began the discussion in this fashion: "I'm afraid I did something rather silly today. Of course, we do entertain a great deal and our other dishes are becoming broken so that the set is hardly complete any more, but I saw a lovely style of dishes at Field's this afternoon on special sale this week and with an extra $10 discount for today only. It does seem rather silly, though, when I realize

EXHIBIT 34. A good example to show how reason can be short-circuited by emotional appeals. (Courtesy of *The Chicago Daily News, Inc.*)

that we hardly have space to put them in this apartment, even though they were an extra special bargain."

If the husband is irritated at hearing what she has done he will want to disagree with her, and almost without thinking he may launch upon a defense of the purchase of the set just because she has taken the opposite view. An intelligent salesman or housewife can utilize this method with great success. In salesmanship, moreover, the speaker may advance a selling point early in the interview which toward the close he ascribes to the customer. If the point is a good one, and if the salesman is discreet, he may get the customer to believing that he sponsored the idea.

"I agree with Mr. Brown," says the public speaker, "that it would be a wise act on our part to defer consideration of this motion until our next meeting." Even if Mr. Brown has not definitely committed himself, if he isn't exactly opposed to this action, and if he has been speaking before the group just previously, he feels complimented that credit for an idea has been ascribed to him, and may marshall his votes in support of the motion. He probably isn't sure of just what he said, anyway, and gladly takes public praise in this manner. The method is an ingenious one and frequently makes men defenders of a cause without their knowing just how it all came about.

From the psychological viewpoint, therefore, the task of short-circuiting reason with emotional stimuli consists chiefly of diverting the customer's attention by a quick portrayal of the function of the merchandise as it affects a fundamental motive base, particularly love, self esteem, or rivalry. Thereafter the focus of the customer's attention is kept upon the goal attained by use of the product instead of on the product itself. The merchandise becomes, therefore, simply a means to an end, and the salesman keeps the attention of his customer on the end result.

Gauging the "Psychological Moment". In popular speech the 'psychological moment' refers to that point in the demonstration at which the customer is most desirous of the article. It denotes, therefore, the time to close the sale. How to determine it is a matter of considerable adeptness in selling. There may, moreover, be several psychological moments. A customer may want the goods, then have his enthusiasm ebb, then find desire become strong again. If we had a psychological sales thermometer which we could insert in the customer's mouth, and which had been calibrated for such a situation, we would have no difficulty reading the degree of interest felt by the client in our merchandise.

In actuality, however, the situation is not so simple. We must note how interestedly the customer handles the article. Is he actively entering into the demonstration, or does he sit passively looking on? Does he ask questions, or is he content to let us continue our sales monologue? Does he sit in a relaxed manner, with feet crossed, or is he leaning forward with tense muscles? As one becomes actively interested in a thing, one grows tense. The experience of the audience at a prize fight or moving picture show illustrates this fact. As a general rule, therefore, the customer who is relaxed is not greatly interested, though there are exceptions.

If the customer is rather phlegmatic, the question must be employed to sound the depth of his interest. We have previously discussed the methods of phrasing the question. "Which style do you prefer?" is a suggestive or leading question, since it assumes he prefers one. "How much do you think you can use?" "How soon will you want it delivered?" "When will it be most convenient for you to take the physical examination?" These queries serve to obtain indexes of the customer's state of mind, and illustrate the "minor decision" type of closing. Some salesmen use the minor decision by asking for a trial order. The average dealer is not very loath to cooperate to this extent. But a trial order of a half-dozen lot simply indicates that the sale was not properly completed, and is a poor substitute for the real thing. The dealer and his clerks will not push the trial order goods because the stock is incomplete. Clerks will, rather, bring out the old line when customers inquire for the type of article covered by the trial order. The latter stock remains on the shelves, therefore, and becomes proof for the dealer that the goods will not move rapidly. The salesman has probably checked his opportunity for future business.

In concluding our discussion of the means by which the

salesman can gauge the psychological moment, it is well to repeat that there may be several psychological moments. If possible, however, the salesman should endeavor to close the interview when the first of these favorable moments is detected. In ascertaining its presence, he should closely observe the signs of interest and cooperation on the part of his customer, and use the leading question in taking soundings. It is advisable to close whenever possible. Additional selling points may be made after the name is on the dotted line, in case they have not been presented up to that point.

Ten Axioms for the Salesman. In numerical order we shall list ten outstanding rules whose observance will greatly increase the number of sales.

(1) *Memorize your opening and closing.* It gives you confidence and frees your attention during the two most critical stages in the sale.

(2) *Dominate the interview.* Don't slip into a defensive role. If your customer asks you a question, he is robbing you of the offensive. "Which color do you think is better?" he may inquire. If you attempt to debate the issue mentally, you become slightly detached, therefore, unobservant of him. Instead, parry his query with the 'reversible why', and ask, "Well, that depends on your tastes. How is your house decorated?" At once you have him answering, while you are interrogator. You can be planning your next step while he is thinking of a reply. The art of discreetly reversing questions can become habitual. It warrants thorough mastery by the salesman. The habitual tendency is to respond, as is demonstrated by the youngster who can hardly resist answering if he has any information whatsoever. The salesman must train himself to respond to a question with a counter question. He can then make exceptions of the few cases where he really has factual matter which should be given when requested.

In an analysis of the time spent in the sale of an article to farmers, the sales manager found that those men who received the largest commission checks spent much less time in the interview. It doesn't pay as a general rule to let the customer tell about his troubles and prolong the demonstration. If he is ready to buy, he will do so quickly. If he isn't ready, then an hour with him is unavailing.

(3) *Hit the bull's-eye with your appeals.* Don't begin with trivialities. These may be the final determinants of the sale, separating your product from competing brands, but at the start you must whet the customer's appetite for the general class of articles which you are selling.

(4) *Use samples and your pencil.* The samples not only increase the interest of your customer, and give him first degree stimuli to action, but they hold his attention so that your direct statements are reacted to with less resistance—hence, as suggestions. If you are selling a service or insurance, get your pencil out and do the figuring in front of the client. His attention is on the page, so again he reacts to your comments much as to suggestions. In figuring, go slowly so that he keeps ahead of you in the addition and subtraction. It makes him feel superior, which is a pleasant mental state. Moreover, he tends to believe the results more readily when he arrived at them ahead of you, because they seem more original to him. Then, too, he doesn't lose count and find it necessary to take your word and conclusions, both of which tend to arouse unpleasantness.

(5) *Employ specificity in words.* Don't use third degree stimuli when you can substitute second degree instead. At the restaurant the waitress asks, "What will you have for dessert, sir?" Dessert is a third degree or generic stimulus word. It doesn't make you very hungry. You counter, "Oh, I don't know. What do you have?" "Pie, cake, ice cream . . ." "I believe I'll try some pie. What kind of pie have you?" The reader will note that the word "pie" is also rather vague. "We have cherry, raspberry, custard, rhubarb, apple, and

mince." These are second degree stimuli that can make saliva flow. As a result, you find that you desire one of them.

If you have sold magazine subscriptions to 11 housewives this week, use the word "eleven". It creates a feeling of truth. If your record is so poor that you hesitate to mention it, then steer away from having to do so. Don't exaggerate, and avoid generalities and superlatives.

(6) *Keep the customer in an agreeable state of mind.* We advance or expand when we feel happy. Pleasant stimuli cause us to desire them. Unpleasant stimuli cause us to shun them. If we feel unpleasant, we are in a general state of avoidance; hence, we will not buy. Discreet compliments are invaluable in making a customer feel good. A Fuller Brush salesman of my acquaintance always jots down the eye color of the boy or girl in the home where he is now calling. A month or two later he re-calls, and asks, "Where is that little girl with those big blue eyes?" This is a compliment, obviously, and the mother feels pleased. The salesman has sold himself, so it probably will not be very difficult to dispose of his merchandise, especially if the housewife has need for brushes.

(7) *Keep the customer in an agreeing state of mind.* At frequent intervals ply him with questions. He gets used to responding affirmatively. Having said yes for ten to twenty times prior to the closing, the slight habit of affirmation renders it more difficult for him to use the negative at the finish.

(8) *Don't permit a customer to say no.* Use the leading question so that the suggestion involved produces an affirmative answer. As long as a customer doesn't say no, the salesman can keep on with his interview. If he has a good product, he may sell it before he finishes. On the other hand, if he lets the customer say no, then he finds it difficult to continue with his sales talk.

(9) *Keep closing.* Don't feel that you must deliver a good speech simply because you have it, if the customer evinces

great desire for the product. Let him sign for it on your opening sentence if he'll do so. Too many salesmen avoid the closing so long that initial interest on the part of the customer has ebbed. While keeping the customer in an agreeing state, slip in a "feeler" question to ascertain his degree of interest. Occasionally a customer needs no demonstration whatever. If he is compelled to listen to one, he may become disgruntled.

(10) *Leave an opening for a return call.* We have seen that the survey of 1,000 retailers showed that they don't buy until the fourth or fifth interview. A salesman can approach a man with whom he parted on friendly relations, and re-open the interview. He should, however, always have a new point, or an additional plan to offer his customer so that he doesn't become boresome.

The writer has gone out to interview customers who had actually thrown out previous salesmen, only to find them as friendly as one could wish. The reason is chiefly this: these men felt ashamed of their actions after the salesman had departed, and in order to "square" themselves with their consciences and the company represented by the mistreated salesmen, resolved if they ever saw them again they'd make it up to the men or their company. Parents occasionally illustrate this same behavior when they too severely criticize or chastise their children. A few hours later they begin to feel uncomfortable, and may make awkward proffers of reconciliation. Later they may overly indulge their youngsters, a form of action which is a salve to their consciences.

If the salesmen had argued with their evictors, then this reverse swing of the pendulum would not have occurred, for the latter would have felt only that they had squared accounts in a fair fight; therefore, no shame would have resulted.

Whenever the interview begins to get away from the salesman's control, he may find himself engaging in arguments. An altercation with his customer is almost always fatal. He loses a possible sale. When a man argues with his customer, he intimates that the latter is wrong, which deflates the buyer's ego and produces displeasure. This result explains our frequent dislike for those we are debating. Some people, indeed, find it almost impossible to shake hands with their verbal enemies and resume friendly relations.

A resort to humor is one of the best devices for stopping an argument for people cannot laugh together at the same time they are angry with each other. If the salesman had dominated the interview and used his applied psychology, moreover, he would never have allowed a situation to arise which would have led to debate. An argument is an indication of a double flaw in the sales talk. It shows first that the salesman erred in his presentation, and secondly, that he entered into the argument after he had permitted his client to start it.

The preceding ten psychological axioms for the salesman are intended not alone for those who sell merchandise but also for the salesmen of ideas, such as public speakers and politicians, educators and clergymen. The psychological principles underlying them have been explained in greater detail throughout the preceding chapters. The men and women who incorporate these axioms into their technique of dealing with people in the sales situation will find that they avoid many of the pitfalls besetting the uninitiated.

REFERENCES

Achilles, Link, *et al.*, *Psychological Brand Barometers* (Issued by the Psychological Corporation several times per year).

Griffith, C. R., *Introduction to Applied Psychology* (New York, 1934).

Hepner, Harry W., *Psychology in Modern Business* (New York, 1931), chap. xiv.

Hollingworth, H. L., *Advertising and Selling* (New York, 1920), chaps. iv, viii, ix, x.

Husband, R. W., *Applied Psychology* (New York, 1934), chaps. xx, xxi.

Jenkins, J. G., *Psychology in Business and Industry* (New York, 1935).

Kenagy and Yoakum, *Selection and Training of Salesmen* (New York, 1925).

Kitson, Harry D., *The Mind of the Buyer* (New York, 1924), chaps. i, xii, xiii.

Kneeland, Natalie, *Cases in Retail Salesmanship* (New York, 1924).

Kornhauser, A. W., and Kingsbury, F. A., *Psychological Tests in Business* (Chicago, 1924).

LAIRD, D. A., *Psychology and Profits* (New York, 1929).
LAIRD, D. A., *How to Use Psychology in Business* (New York, 1936).
LINK, H. C., *The New Psychology of Selling and Advertising* (New York, 1932).
MOSS, FRED A., *Applications of Psychology* (Boston, 1929), chap. xvi.
POFFENBERGER, A. T., *Applied Psychology* (New York, 1927), chaps. xxi, xxii.
SCOTT, WALTER DILL, *Increasing Human Efficiency in Business* (New York, 1932).
SNOW, A. J., *Psychology in Business Relations* (New York, 1930), chaps. xix-xxvi.
——————, *Effective Selling* (New York, 1929), vol. ii, Book iv.
STRONG, E. K., *The Psychology of Selling and Advertising* (New York, 1925), Parts ii and iii.
TEAD, ORDWAY, *Human Nature and Management* (New York, 1929), chap. xiii.
TOSDAL, H. R., *Principles of Personal Selling* (New York, 1925), chaps. iii, iv.

CHAPTER VIII

THE FIELDS AND FUNCTIONS OF ADVERTISING

Although Dr. Samuel Johnson in 1759 made the statement in his *Weekly Idler* that "the trade of advertising is now so near perfection that it is not easy to make any improvements,"[1] we have seen recently the utilization of art and illustration, and the employment of color in a fashion that would have dazzled the minds of earlier generations. From our newspapers and car advertisements, our magazines and billboards, sky-writing airplanes, the government postman, and our radios come announcements of some new product or a reaffirmation of the virtues of a familiar one.

Advertising may involve the whole function of selling, or it may lend itself as an aid in producing sales. The latter is its more usual purpose. In either role it has not the plasticity of the salesman, and must make general appeals to a class of buyers, without attempting to satisfy the individual differences of any single person. Although it is so widespread in its distribution and so much money is spent annually in advertising appropriations, the consumer usually has been able to obtain goods cheaper than if advertising were omitted. It may sound paradoxical, but it is true that by spending money in advertising the demand for a product can be so increased as to warrant large scale production which, in turn, brings back to the consumer the article at a lower price than he could have procured it otherwise. Seasonal fluctuations in demand can be smoothed out, as in the orange and raisin trade, with a resulting economy in distribution charges.

In some cases, as in present cigarette advertising, a market may approach the saturation point, after which one cigarette company simply launches an advertising campaign which pulls

[1] *Selling Forces* (Curtis Publishing Co., Philadelphia), p. 13.

customers away from its rivals. At a later date the rivals reciprocate. Another characteristic of modern advertising is the fact that the first sponsor of a new type of goods must devote considerable money to educational copy, teaching the public the value of the new product and its many uses. Thereafter imitations may enter the field and capitalize on the first company's expenditures.

The Fields of Advertising. In viewing the things advertised we may make a four-fold classification, following the divisions listed by Moss[1].

(1) *A community.* The various business clubs in a city, such as Kiwanis, Rotary, Exchange, Lions, and the Chamber of Commerce are usually concerned to some extent in seeing that their city is gaining adequate recognition. Free land is offered new industries for the purpose not only of increasing the number of employed persons and accelerating the business turnover in the community, but of adding to the population and advertising the town. Land booms and gold rushes are evidences of the power of advertising when directed to a community. Summer and winter resorts derive their patrons largely as a consequence of advertising. In America, for example, Florida and California are rival wintering places which are actively engaged in competitive advertising for the resort trade during the cold months.

(2) *A firm or organization.* Banks have entered the field of advertising to an increasing degree in recent years, and have slowly been modifying their methods so that they now employ color. Financial advertising has been one of the most conservative types that we have. It formerly consisted of space in newspapers and magazines with only the name of the financial institution, thus illustrating what is called "good will" advertising. Now the various services rendered by banks, and their equipment and personnel are announced to

[1] Moss, Fred A., *op. cit.*, p. 310.

the public in some of the blank space that would formerly have surrounded their names only. Even religious institutions and organizations have entered the advertising field on a mild scale.

(3) *An individual.* We have already devoted a chapter to this subject. Actresses, actors, and politicians hire publicity agents to devise schemes by which the former can gain publicity write-ups in newspapers and magazines. The managers of many pugilists have a propensity for the same thing, and get occasional newspaper accounts of their protegés into the sport pages between fights. The popularity of Dempsey is due to newspaper accounts of him, since the majority of his followers have probably never seen him in person.

(4) *Goods and services.* Here belong the great majority of advertising appropriations. The reader is familiar with the ingenious methods and instruments by which he becomes acquainted with the merchandise with which this country teems. Advertising slogans and trademarks are far more familiar to the American boy and girl, as well as to his parents, than are Shakespeare's works or the Bible. Names of merchandise are made of nonsense syllables and thrown into the visual field so frequently that they take on meaning and he considers them a part of his regular vocabulary. A large number of Americans could not tell whether "victrola" or "phonograph" was the term employed in the dictionary to describe the musical instrument.

In our survey of the fields of advertising, therefore, we find that four general categories are sufficiently comprehensive to cover the various kinds of advertising commonly encountered. These include advertising a community, an organization, an individual, and goods or services.

Methods of Research in Advertising. Four general methods are usually employed in advertising research, of which the first is least valuable.

(1) *The historical method.* This one involves a study of the mortality rates among various past companies with reference to the types of advertising they employed. The inference is that those which are still in business today probably pursued a better advertising plan. So many other factors are involved, however, that we cannot depend greatly upon this method.

(2) *The statistical method.* This method involves the collection of data regarding the number of telephones, automobiles, minor children, farms, etc. in a region for purposes of adapting the advertising funds to the needs and media thereof. If a foreign element is present in considerable numbers the language factor enters in. Communities which have a high degree of illiteracy offer problems necessitating the use of simple language. A few years ago Kitson[1] made a survey of Chicago newspapers regarding the vocabulary employed and found that the *Chicago Evening Post* had 70 per cent more words over two syllables long than did the *Chicago American.* His work led him to the conclusion that the advertiser who wished to run his advertisements in a given magazine should read the fiction in that magazine, for therein lay the key to the vocabulary level of the people who bought that magazine.

(3) *The survey.* Under this heading come those attempts to find out in advance what people will like by interviewing a sample group of the type to be solicited by the advertising. Special questionnaires are sent out to certain individuals chosen in advance, or a house-to-house canvass is made by the investigator, who questions the housewives on their preferences and buying habits regarding the given line of merchandise.

The "test run" of a certain advertisement in a try-out market is really a form of survey. Firms who do national advertising usually pick out a few centers which they call try-out markets. These must be quite similar in regard to population,

[1] Kitson, Harry D., *The Mind of the Buyer* (Macmillan Co., New York, 1921), p. 60.

class of people, number of industries, etc. There should be a variety of activities, and competing brands should not be running intensive campaigns in any of these test markets. College towns would of course not be representative. After the selection of the try-out markets, different advertisements are run, and the results are compared to determine which produced the greatest returns. The winner is then employed in the national advertising campaign.

The test run is usually considered the best method of determining the effectiveness of an advertisement, although it can be supplemented in many ways. The opinion of the salesmen may be sought, as well as the advice of a few typical customers. Sometimes the customer is asked to write the copy, or contests may be announced in which selling points are the basis of the award. Direct mail tests may also be undertaken, and the copy and cuts subjected to laboratory investigation. The fact that the test run is considered the best method at present, however, simply indicates that the subject of advertising is still in a trial and error state. If a physician had to test his medicines on a dog every time he was called upon to treat a human being, we would think he was not very well prepared for his profession.

In this connection, Professor S. N. Stevens of Northwestern University in a debate with some professional advertisers challenged the latter to bring out ten advertisements with whose results they were familiar, and he would rank them in their order of merit. His opponents accepted his offer, and placed ten such specimens along the wall in front of him, having mixed them in the row. Professor Stevens asked the group to which each advertisement was directed, and the purpose of the advertiser in each case. Then he went along with his pad and pencil estimating their psychological merits. He ranked them in the following order as matched by their actual pulling power: 1:2:3:4:5:6:7:8:10:9, erring only in respect to the two weakest specimens. It requires a scientific knowledge of human behavior to do this sort of thing, but that knowledge is not incapable of attainment.

(4) *The laboratory method.* There are two subheads to this form of research. (a) *Testing efficiency by returns.* In an analysis of over 3,000,000 inquiries from 2,339 advertisements during a four-year period, Starch found that the number of replies varied almost according to the size of the advertisement, although the smaller advertisements had a slight advantage. Those inserted on right-hand pages brought 14.1 per cent more replies than similar advertisements inserted on left-hand pages, while colored advertisements elicited 56.7 per cent more replies per 100,000 of the circulation than did black and white advertisements of similar size and character.

In an investigation of the advertising results during the various months of the year, Falk[1] discovered the data presented in Exhibit 35. The reciprocal number for each month has been added by Hepner to make it possible to compare advertisements. If the average for the 12 months is divided

MONTH	INDEX NUMBER	RECIPROCAL
January	184	0.543
February	157	0.637
March	107	0.934
April	77	1.300
May	67	1.490
June	65	1.540
July	76	1.316
August	92	1.087
September	95	1.052
October	92	1.087
November	89	1.123
December	99	1.010

EXHIBIT 35. Index of inquiries on one company's advertisements according to the month of insertion. (Average for 12 months = 100).

[1] Falk, A. T., "Analyzing Advertising Results," *Harvard Business Review,* Vol. 7 (January, 1929), p. 192.

by the index number for any month, we obtain the figure listed in the column entitled "Reciprocal". Thus, an advertisement in January which produces 1,000 inquiries is not nearly as good as one in July that also elicits 1,000 responses. For example, January : July :: 0.543 : 1.316. The July advertisement is more than twice as effective as the January advertisement.

An additional interesting result of this survey is the fact that "If an ad in the *Iowa Homestead* produces three times as many inquiries when run in January as when run in June, then a *Ladies' Home Journal* ad will also produce three times as many inquiries when run in January as when run in June." The curves for the different magazines, based on their indexes of returns, are almost identical.

In order to count the returns from any single advertisement, the advertiser usually "keys" the coupon with a different box number or the name of another department of the firm. Some companies have found, moreover, that one-third of the persons who ask for free samples are children or persons who like to have mail come to them. These "rubbernecks", as the advertising men call them, can be eliminated by charging for the sample or booklet. The price, however, must be only a nominal one to cover the cost alone.

(b) *Scientific experiments.* These constitute one form of the laboratory method whose results should ultimately enable advertisers to know in advance how well an advertisement will "pull". The example of Professor Stevens shows what may be hoped for in this regard. These scientific experiments fall under several headings, and may be performed for both the copy and the cuts separately, as well as for the two when combined in the final advertisement.

(1) *The order-of-merit test.* Here a number of observers rank the illustrations or copy in regard to effectiveness in some special regard, as attention attracting value, convincingness, pleasantness, etc. The results of all such judgments are

then combined to give the consensus report. The method is similar to that employed in deciding college debates.

(2) *The recall value.* Different styles of type, copy, or illustrations may be presented to the subjects for definite brief exposures, as in a tachistoscope, and at a later date the subjects are given a memory test to determine how many of the things seen have been retained.

(3) *The recognition value.* The ease of reading various sizes of type during very short exposure times belongs here. Then, too, this heading covers a form of memory test in which the previously observed advertisements are mixed with many others, and the subject attempts to pick out the ones which he has seen before from those that are strange. This is the multiple choice, or age of stimulus method which we described in Chapter II.

(4) *The association method.* This procedure is often of value in determining the choice of a new name or trade-mark. A number of words are listed which the subject looks at and hears pronounced aloud. He is to tell what each makes him think of. These names, of course, are usually novel constructions of nonsense syllables, but some of them give rise to pleasant feelings which others do not. This method is akin to the order-of-merit procedure described above.

(5) *Eye fixation.* By noting the eye movements and the time spent by a subject on one portion of an advertisement versus another, or on one advertisement instead of another, the observer can obtain a fair indication of the relative attention attracting and holding merits of copy and illustrations, or of different colors in contrast to black and white.

One of the chief difficulties with the laboratory method is its demand for a certain amount of apparatus, and an operator who is versed in scientific technique. Another requisite is a type of subject who is comparable to the group for whom the advertisement is to be run. The language facility and extra intelligence of the college students and advertising associates who have frequently employed the laboratory method, make it unwise to generalize from their results and assume that the average American will perform similarly.

In concluding our discussion of the methods of research in advertising, therefore, we can repeat our fourfold classification, namely, the historical, the statistical, the survey, and the laboratory methods. The present superiority of the test run does not represent the ultimate goal of advertising, although it is deemed the most adequate at the present time. The laboratory method should ultimately forge into the van of advertising procedure.

The Relative Advantages of Various Advertising Media. Certain readily apparent virtues of one advertising medium over another are known to even the laymen. Newspapers are superior to magazines for local firms. Banks, department stores and other retail establishments need city advertising media. Handbills, direct-mail letters, radio skits, theater programs, church bulletins and papers, car ads, and billboards are of value to the local business house. Magazine advertisements are usually of a general nature to fit the needs of dealers and consumers all over the country, and are the manufacturers advertising field, although manufacturers also enter into newspaper and radio advertising as well. We shall discuss radio advertising later in the chapter.

More money is spent for newspaper advertising than for any other sort. The newspaper offers several advantages not given by the magazine. In the first place, it is read by all classes of people, whereas many magazines have a definite class appeal. In this connection we might distinguish between "flat" and "standard" magazines. Those in which advertisements appear on the same page with reading matter, as in *The Saturday Evening Post,* are called "flat", while magazines of the type of *The National Geographic* are "standard". The latter are of the sandwich variety, with advertising bunched in the front and back thirds of the magazines, and reading matter massed in between.

Another superiority of the newspaper is the fact that it carries timely advertisements. If the weather forecaster predicts rain tomorrow or next day, the retailer can feature umbrellas and raincoats in tomorrow morning's paper. While newspapers cannot employ color in the way that magazines do, they can remind people more frequently and repeatedly.

In his experience with newspapers, Haldeman-Julius found that the largest returns came within one week after insertion of the advertisement. With a typical weekly magazine, such as *Liberty,* he found that an insertion would more than "pay out" in the first three weeks, although the advertisement "pulled" regularly for nearly ninety days, and then dropped to from one to five dollars' worth of orders a day for another month or so, finally dwindling to a dollar every now and then for even two years' time. A monthly magazine, as the *Review of Reviews,* pulled much more slowly than either the weekly or a newspaper. It brought orders steadily for three months, usually paying out in the first thirty days. The reason for the slower returns from magazines, especially of the monthly type, is the fact that they lie about on the table or lounge for weeks and months.

In his advertising Haldeman-Julius used the same kind of advertisement in practically all the media he employed. He states that he is willing to spend two to two and a half cents to sell each 5-cent Little Blue Book. Concerning the difference between large and small city newspapers he says, "I can make the general statement from a wide experience that advertising a mail-order product in small-city newspapers *never* pays. Only newspapers in the larger cities—New York, Boston, Philadelphia, Baltimore, Chicago, Los Angeles, etc.—are good."[1]

[1] Haldeman-Julius, E., *op. cit.*, p. 275.

We are presenting in Exhibit 36 the actual receipts which he obtained from a number of different advertising media. The reader can procure an idea therefrom of the advertising space rates, as well as the relative merits of different media carrying the same type of advertisement.

ADVERTISING MEDIA	DATE	SPACE	COST	RETURNS
New York Times Book Review	10-30-27	2 pages	$2,500	$ 4,348.89
Mid-Week Pictorial	9-15-27	2 pages	300	924.56
New York Daily News	1-30-27	1 page	1,400	2,789.49
Physical Culture	Oct. 1927	1 page	800	1,759.19
Smart Set	Nov. 1927	1 page	850	1,888.35
Pathfinder	4-11-25	1 page	1,000	2,763.66
Life	9-26-23	1 page	650	1,215.23
Harper's Monthly	Oct. 1926	1 page	200	382.15
Review of Reviews	Oct. 1925	1 page	325	642.68
Golden Book	Oct. 1925	4 pages	800	1,927.48
Liberty	1- 9-26	2 pages	5,000	13,321.31
Chicago Tribune	2-10-26	1 page	1,300	2,884.36
The Nation	9-10-24	1 page	150	349.29
Hearst's International	Feb. 1925	1 page	1,000	2,369.12

EXHIBIT 36. Actual receipts obtained by Mr. Haldeman-Julius from various advertising media.

In Exhibit 37 are presented the day by day returns obtained by Haldeman-Julius[1] from insertions in the *Chicago Tribune, Liberty,* and the *Review of Reviews.* These figures illustrate the comments we have previously made relating to the rapidity of returns from the different types of media.

In the field of direct-mail advertising, Maddy[2] found that the permit card was more efficient than the regular government postal card. For each of seven consecutive weeks 26,000 pieces of mail were set aside for test purposes (13,000 govern-

[1] *Ibid,* pp. 274-279. All these tables are reproduced through courtesy of Mr. Haldeman-Julius.

[2] Maddy, C. D., "Big Mailing Test Proves Business Reply Card 13 Per Cent More Efficient Than Government Postal," *Sales Management* (June 15, 1929), pp. 550 *ff*.

MEDIUM AND DATE OF INSERTION	DAILY RETURNS 1ST DAY	2ND DAY	3RD DAY	4TH DAY	5TH DAY	6TH DAY	7TH* DAY	8TH DAY	9TH DAY	10TH DAY	11-12 DAY	13-15 DAY	FINAL TOTAL
LIBERTY Jan. 9, 1926 (1st Day 1-4)...	94.86	108.47	403.83	698.57	768.65	844.81	1,222.43	356.23	526.11	612.75	920.64	802.52	(Mar. 6) 13,321.31
LIBERTY Jan. 30, 1926 (1st Day 1-25)..	55.43	98.61	452.65	666.36	699.84	233.4c	1,396.36	363.97	492.56	455.27	741.17	1,187.41	(Apr. 2) 12,051.46
LIBERTY Sept. 18, 1926 (1st Day 9-13)..	13.74	85.01	447.38	613.07	849.06	713.48	1,042.48	319.82	429.96	344.11	412.69	904.62	(Dec. 6) 10,050.39
REVIEW OF REVIEWS, Oct. 1925 (1st Day 9-28)..	10.97	4.65	12.02	8.08	17.46	11.44	7.95	14.00	14.25	9.82	22.47	33.04	(Jan. 1) 518.68
CHICAGO TRIBUNE Jan. 5, 1926 (1st Day 1-6)...	14.76	350.76	448.35	332.65	295.77	53.71	153.49	98.35	81.73	141.12	54.41	105.30	(Mar. 10) 2,959.81
CHICAGO TRIBUNE Jan. 14, 1926 (1st Day 1-15)..	11.31	962.08	491.67	258.32	221.54	154.23	161.19	72.10	83.55	69.56	156.81	107.56	(Mar. 10) 3,788.62
CHICAGO TRIBUNE Feb. 10, 1926 (1st Day 2-11).....		202.19	391.05	177.80	408.78	118.62	210.61	198.67	100.21	74.27	135.55	361.12	(Mar. 10) 2,884.36

EXHIBIT 37. Showing the returns from a Little Blue Book advertisement which ran in three different types of medium. (Courtesy of Mr. Haldeman-Julius) *Includes Saturday afternoon mail.

ment postal cards, and 13,000 permit cards), or a total of 91,000 of each kind over the period of seven weeks.

The government cards produced a larger gross volume of orders, but when measured in percentage of cost to sales, it was found that the permit card was 13 per cent better. When the experiment began, the incoming mail brought as high as 33 per cent of the permit cards with stamps affixed by the customer. This figure dropped to 2 per cent at the time Maddy wrote his article.

Not only do the kinds of advertising media have a bearing upon the returns obtained from advertisements, but the positions within such media as magazines also have a determining effect. There are certain preferred positions for which publishers usually charge extra. Hepner[1] offers the following list of these:

1. Upper half of page usually gains attention better than the lower half.
2. The right-hand page is better than the left-hand.
3. Outside back cover page.
4. Inside back cover page.
5. Page facing the inside back cover.
6. Inside front cover.
7. Page facing the inside front cover.
8. Page facing the first page of reading material.
9. Page at the end of main reading section.
10. The middle spread.
11. Page facing the end of the most interesting article or story.

A summary of the relative advantages of various advertising media, therefore, would indicate that the newspaper is apparently the most advantageous print medium for the local merchant, with the radio, direct-mail, and car advertisements following suit. The direct-mail can be the most adaptive of all advertising media, but the cost of making it so is usually quite high. Much of the direct-mail advertising nowadays

[1] Hepner, Harry W., *op. cit.*, p. 569.

is no more modified to meet the individuality of the recipient than are newspaper advertisements. The advent of the radio moreover, has given the advertiser much of the advantage previously possessed by the personal salesman as we shall explain in a later section.

Characteristics of Good Slogans and Trade Names. Before we enter upon a formal discussion of this heading, it would be well to mention the uses and importance of contests for slogans and trade-marks. They constitute an important form of advertising. The Bond Electric Corporation contest offered a total of $15,000 in prizes, and received over 1,000,000 inquiries and 250,000 slogans submitted. When the Camel Cigarette letter contest was held, over 2,000,000 pieces of mail were received. Of course, the actual prize money is a negligible part of the cost of such contests.

Next to their development of trade, the most frequent purpose of these consumer contests is the development of new sales and advertising ideas. This form of contest is beginning to supersede the slogan and "name" varieties, and is a consumer survey of great value. In 1915 when the Bon Ami Company held a contest over the merits of the cake versus the powder form of their product, the winner submitted 706 uses for their product. An entry of this nature would form a good encyclopedia for the advertising department when it wished to present new selling points.

Some contests in maze tracing and house naming are for the purpose of developing "sucker lists", which are then sold to various firms who wish to advertise by direct-mail and need lists of prospects. Incidentally, Mr. Haldeman-Julius pays for keeping his mailing list of 500,000 names up to date by renting it to advertisers. When Edward Bok was seeking the widest publicity for his Peace Plan, he also rented the list, sending all of his sealed and stamped letters to Girard, Kansas, by express, where the addresses were affixed and they were placed in the mail.

The importance of slogans and trade-marks is estimated in dollars and cents by many firms, as the following data reveal:[1]

"Coca-Cola"	$ 5,000,000
"Uneeda"	6,000,000
"Royal" (Baking powder)	8,000,000
"Bull Durham"	$10,000,000 to 20,000,000
"Camel"	10,000,000
"Sunkist"	2,000,000

These name and trade-mark valuations have either been listed among the assets of their respective companies at the figures cited, or have been priced in sales at those amounts.

In running a contest it is well to keep in mind that the majority of the public has an inferiority complex regarding brain competitions. Moreover, within reasonable limits the amount of the prize money is secondary to the appeal of the contest task. As a general rule, the range of total prize money should lie between $2,500 and $10,000. Amounts over $10,000 do not offer much better results. In a certain annual contest run by a trade association the number of responses was doubled when it doubled the *number* of prizes but kept the total amount the same.

The government postal authorities should always be consulted before using the mails in the announcement of contests. They are very particular to guard against actual fraud, unfairness, and lottery or chance. For these reasons the contestants must not be forced to buy something. Even the fact that entry blanks must be obtained may be deemed unfair unless there are plenty of dealers, so the contest announcements often state that blanks will be mailed upon request.

Contests, however, are not always wholly beneficial in their results. Of 100,000 participants, maybe only 100 receive prizes. Despite the fact, as Slater[2] points out, that people

[1] Starch, Daniel, *op. cit.*, pp. 675-676.

[2] Slater, A. L., "How Well Do Consumer Contests Work?" *Advertising and Selling* (Feb. 6, 1929), pp. 27 *ff*.

have inferiority complexes in regard to entering a contest, once they are launched upon it and mail their entries, they feel that unfairness has been evident if they do not obtain a prize. The unpleasant reaction may attach to the product being advertised, or to the name of the company, and actually militate against the purpose behind the contest. To offset this tendency impartial and well known judges should be obtained to referee the final decisions, or the public should be permitted to see the winning exhibits.

In regard to protecting his slogans after they have been obtained the advertiser must also remember that they cannot be registered as trade-marks except in a few special cases nor can they be copyrighted. His only protection, therefore, is to register them with some bureau, as *Printers' Ink,* which keeps records of slogans. This action prevents unwitting duplication and aids in establishing priority rights.

The rules governing excellence in slogans and trade names follow.

1. They should be short.
2. They should be simple.
3. They should be euphonious.
4. They should suggest selling points.
5. They should give rise to pleasant feeling tone.
6. They should lend themselves to pictorial presentation.
7. They should be flexible enough to cover additional products of the firm.
8. They should be unique.
9. They should be easily remembered—this may involve rhythm and rime, alliteration, and style of print.
10. They should be distinctive—this means they should not lend themselves to other products, nor to abbreviation.

In considering a violator of the tenth point above, we have only to cite "Eventually—why not now?" Among students, from 40 to 60 per cent associate this with a competitor of its owner, while once in a class of exactly 100 men and women I found 81 who thought it belonged to Pillsbury's Flour. The author of the above slogan and most famous sloganeer in America is G. Herb Palin, who has also given us "Safety First", "See America First", "The Thinking Fellow Calls a Yellow", and "Built on Honor to Honor Its Builder". The last one of these is typical of what Palin[1] considers a good slogan, but the writer disagrees with his views in the matter. Where there is no competitor, as in the case of "Safety First", this type of slogan is all right, but otherwise it can lend itself to any product ever produced, and becomes as inefficient as "Eventually—why not now?" Palin favors the formula, 1-2-3-3-2-1, in which he builds up a phrase, then reverses it, as in "Built on Honor to Honor Its Builder."

Probably no slogan or trade name ever devised perfectly fulfilled the ten rules listed above, but the more of those rules that do apply to the slogan, the better it will become. Keeping those rules in mind, the reader may try his skill at ranking the following slogans in order of merit. They were entered in the Hertz Driv-Ur-Self slogan contest. One of the entries won $500, the second prize was $250, and the other five, although occupying different ranks, all received $50 each. Two advertising men and a member of the Hertz Company were judges. Their decisions are given at the end of the chapter.

A. Buy the mile—by the mile.
B. Join the Millions.
C. Economy and style in every mile.
D. Drive the car you'd like to own.
E. Economically yours.
F. Need a car for work or play?
   Rent a Hertz and drive away.
G. Convenience for you—economy, too.

In comparing the pulling power of advertisements bearing

[1] Palin, G. Herb, "How the Highest Paid Advertising Writer Works," *Advertising and Selling* (April, 1924), p. 144.

similar copy but containing the following headings, Lichtenberg[1] found that one of the headings "pulled really marvelous results," but the other three were failures. The reader will find the most effective title named at the conclusion of the chapter. The advertisement was of a correspondence school.

A. Afraid to Face the Facts—Then Don't Read This Page.
B. Those Who Shy at Unpleasant Facts Should Not Read This Page.
C. Men Who Know It All Are Not Invited to Read This Page.
D. Men Who Are Satisfied to Wait Ten Years for Success Will Find Nothing Interesting On This Page.

Starch holds that a heading should ordinarily be confined to one or two decks. The writer doesn't know how many decks were employed in the above headings as run in the original advertisements.

From the psychological standpoint, therefore, a good slogan or trade name should be in reciprocal relationship with the article which it advertises, or else it soon becomes valueless. It should give to a new product of the firm the prestige of previous merchandise, and should gain in return the pleasant feeling tone which should be developed by the new member of the manufacturer's family. We have outlined the ten characteristics of a good slogan, and shown how contests have often been employed by manufacturers in procuring slogans. Probably the chief value of slogans and trade names lies in their quickly gaining for a new product the prestige of familiar ones. Heinz, for instance, doesn't have to devote much advertising to a new foodstuff for the name Heinz is an official introduction thereto.

The Effect of Feeling Tone in Advertising. It will not be necessary to devote much space to a consideration of this important topic inasmuch as we have discussed the feeling

[1] Lichtenberg, Bernard, "Test Copy on Results, Not On Opinions," *Printers' Ink* (Nov. 8, 1928), pp. 28 *ff*.

tone of words in Chapter I, and have devoted space to it under the subject of salesmanship. Because an advertisement keeps confronting an individual repeatedly, if it is unpleasant at all, there is a cumulative effect of such repetitions which may build up an active dislike for the product, without the subject's even knowing how he developed such an aversion. On the contrary, pleasant feeling tone also is additive, and may result in a desire on the part of the observer which to him is inexplicable.

It becomes advisable, therefore, for a company to ascertain the likes and dislikes of people before running certain kinds of illustrations and copy. In South America, for instance, the pictorial example of a neat housewife scouring her pans with some brand of kitchen cleanser would be repulsive, for "ladies" don't work at such tasks. We don't have to go away from home, however, to cite similar flagrant disregard for feeling tone. One of the large coffee companies in America uses as a trade-mark the picture of what to the average citizen probably is looked upon as simply a bearded old man in turban and a flowered nightgown drinking his cup of coffee before retiring. If one regards this picture long he probably wonders only how much is dribbling into the old fellow's beard. Our rules for effective slogans and trade names are certainly violated by this case which is, unfortunately, matched by scores of others that we could cite.

In Exhibit 38 we have a converse of this type of advertisement. Even though it may be remotely relevant, it most assuredly arouses a much more pleasant feeling tone in the reader. The other advertisements which we have presented may be regarded in the light of their pleasant or unpleasant emotional significance. In the Mercirex examples, however, we must bear in mind that it is afflicted persons to whom the appeal is directed, so our possible feelings of unpleasantness will not be felt by them. Instead, they may react with delight to the pictured health which is promised them.

EXHIBIT 38. An example of pleasant feeling tone and the sex appeal employed to increase the effectiveness of an advertisement. (Courtesy of Lennen & Mitchell, Inc.)

In the following bit of advertising copy we have made an attempt to tap as many pleasant "warmth" memories in the reader as possible, and transfer them to the woolen sweater being advertised. Although the initial query contains the word "bug", the unpleasant connotation is probably submerged in the greater pleasure value of the childhood phrase.

"You'll be snug as a bug in a rug," Mother used to say, as she tucked in the woolly blankets, and kissed you good night. Then you snuggled into your cozy, warm nest, and drifted off into peaceful slumber.

The Snuggle Sweater also gives you that warm softness that tempts the cheek, and protects you from chill autumn winds and the damp coolness of spring evenings. As if wrapped in knitted sunshine you can play golf, or fish, or motor in the breeze with perfect safety and cozy delight.

Snuggling against your arms and throat with velvety comfort, your Snuggle Sweater offers you perfect freedom of movement. You can work or play with the same warm glow of safety that you feel at your own fireside.

Snuggle—for Sweater delight!

The matter of feeling tone, moreover, is subject to statistical analysis as Exhibits 39, 40, and 41 will show. Using Scott's "man-to-man" type of rating scale, the writer selected the Chicago department stores—Field's, the Davis Store, the Boston Store, and Goldblatt's—as representing four quite distinct steps or gradations in "quality" feeling tone. With hardly an exception, native Chicagoans will rank these four stores in the order given above as regards the "quality" versus low price type of firm. Then the subjects were given the instructions: "In the table below I have listed horizontally these four stores in the order of quality feeling tone denoted. At the left I have presented five well advertised products. I want you to consider each of these brands separately, comparing it with Field's, then Davis Store, then Boston Store, and finally with Goldblatt's. Check which of the four stores it most nearly resembles in its feeling tone."

In Exhibit 39 are listed the results obtained from the members of the International Advertising Display Men's Association who cooperated with the writer during his address before their annual convention in June, 1932. Exhibit 40 contains similar data obtained from the Office Managers' Association of Chicago at their meeting in May, 1932, while Exhibit 41 shows the reactions of two large classes in psychology in the Northwestern University School of Commerce.

CIGARETTE BRANDS	FIELD'S PCT.	DAVIS PCT.	BOSTON PCT.	GOLDBLATT'S PCT.
Camels	3	74	23	0
Chesterfields	84	8	8	0
Clowns	0	0	2	98
Lucky Strikes	0	97	0	3
Old Golds	24	39	37	0

EXHIBIT 39. Comparison of feeling tones by advertisers.

CIGARETTE BRANDS	FIELD'S PCT.	DAVIS PCT.	BOSTON PCT.	GOLDBLATT'S PCT.
Camels	28	56	16	0
Chesterfields	38	30	26	6
Clown	0	0	0	100
Lucky Strikes	31	45	24	0
Old Golds	30	30	33	7

EXHIBIT 40. Comparison of feeling tones by office managers.

In the foregoing two exhibits no attempt was made to separate the reactions of the smokers from the non-smokers. Although it is quite possible for a skilled rater who may personally smoke Camels to recognize that he considers Chesterfields to have a greater degree of quality feeling tone, probably the smokers' favorite brands had a "halo" in the above tables. They ranked their own brands high because they used those particular brands. In the following exhibit from the writer's psychology classes are presented only the reactions of non-smokers, whose attitudes are therefore almost wholly a correlate of the advertising to which they have been exposed.

CIGARETTE BRANDS	FIELD'S PCT.	DAVIS PCT.	BOSTON PCT.	GOLDBLATT'S PCT.
Camels	21	49	25	5
Chesterfields	74	20	6	0
Clowns	0	0	8	92
Lucky Strikes	35	53	12	0
Old Golds	43	36	17	4

EXHIBIT 41. Comparison of feeling tones by non-smokers.

From the standpoint of psychology, therefore, feeling tone is of very great importance in advertising. The cumulative effects of daily exposure to copy and illustrations which arouse even slight feelings of unpleasantness may become great enough to occasion definite dislike or aversion. On the other hand, the repetitive effect of pleasing cuts and copy builds desire or liking for a product. The advertiser must be acquainted with the habits of his public in order to understand which words and pictures will be pleasant and which unpleasant. In foreign advertising especially such knowledge must be carefully checked.

The Rise and Possibilities of Radio Advertising. Until the last decade this medium was hardly thought of. Now it offers a widespread distribution for advertising with part of the virtue of personal salesmanship, namely, the human voice. As the silver screen has come to life by means of the "talkies", so advertising has gained a third dimension through the depth of vocal intonation and expression of the radio. Advertising can now be made timely and flexible enough to meet the demands of all classes of our population.

There are several advantages possessed by radio advertising which are not possessed by any other medium. (1) It enables the advertiser to put his public in a pleasant frame of mind by music and comedy skits at the same time that he is advertising his product. If his programs are pleasing, his product tends to be tied up with those resulting sensations of pleasure; hence, we begin to like his goods. (2) The radio enables the advertiser to get inside the home and do a form of personal selling at moments that are most opportune. For instance, in the morning as the housewife is doing her work, she usually has the radio turned on. The advertiser-salesman begins to talk to her about the greater convenience of vacuum cleaners even as she sweeps, or he describes the delicious foods offered by his company to tempt the appetites of husband and children.

(3) The radio enables the advertiser to capitalize upon the attention of millions that may be focussed upon an outstanding football or pugilistic contest. This aspect of radio advertising is similar to the policy of many moving picture producers who buy only "best sellers" among novels and published magazine stories. The public's attention has already been caught, so the producers capitalize on this previous advertising of the stories. In the same manner, various manufacturers let the sport writers of American newspapers concentrate the attention of possibly millions of men and women upon a Notre Dame-Northwestern football contest, then move their microphones and announcers to the stadium, and at little additional cost have an audience that may be 100 times as large as their usual one.

(4) The radio enables the advertiser to get the attention of all the members of the family, instead of just the one or two who chance to be looking at a magazine or newspaper.

(5) The radio introduces suspense and drama into advertising, and by running conversational serials of the "Amos 'n' Andy" variety can soon educate its public to seek the adver-

tising program. Newspaper and magazine advertisements are not yet able to excite millions to the extent that they rush home to look at tonight's advertisement. Yet the radio can do this very thing, causing men and women of all ages actively to solicit the advertiser's programs. It is a curious reversal of what has been customary with previous forms of advertising media.

(6) The radio enables the advertiser to reinforce other forms of his advertising. He can call the housewife's attention to his printed newspaper advertisement of that evening or morning, and urge her to come early to the sale and avoid the crowds.

(7) The radio enables the advertiser to enlist the cooperation of children who are too young to read his printed statements in newspaper or magazine. By appropriate stories in which his product is prominently mentioned, and by direct commands he can induce the child to assist in "selling" his parents on a new brand of ice cream or bread. The advertiser can promise the child that a balloon or top is being given away at the grocery whenever a loaf of his bread is purchased. The young child reacts favorably, of course, whereas he might never gain this information otherwise.

(8) The radio enables the advertiser to enlist all the delightful nuances of tone which attach to certain melodious voices. Occasionally one encounters persons whose voices are pleasing in their own right. Human speech, as we have already mentioned, gives depth and life to inanimate advertising. Part of the effectiveness of Amos and Andy is due to their vocal inflections and Negro dialect.

But radio advertising also has its pitfalls. Just as some voices are musical and sweet, others are unpleasant and harsh. Despite the knowledge of the ineffectiveness of raucous voices, there are still too many of this type speaking to American people from their radios. Moreover, the pleasure aroused by musical programs is partially offset by their frequent interruptions for announcements concerning the bargains which are being offered at so and so's store. And on Sundays it is often offensive to the habits of millions of listeners to hear the same week-day commercial programs flooding the house. The feeling tone created by certain musicians and entertainers is also diminished when the advertisers have these performers announce the selling points of the product for which the program is sponsored. It is much better to let the station announcer handle the script which deals with the price and virtues of the merchandise, and leave the singer or entertainer free to retain his artistic role to the end.

The Effect of Color and Cuts in Advertising. In our consideration of attention attractors we mentioned the significance of color as one of them. We have also commented upon the color preferences of men and women. It might be well to review the facts of color vision treated in general psychology. The color spectrum is broken at the elementary colors, which have been designated as "primary" hues in the general psychology course, so that we have a square. The four corners are made up of red, yellow, green, and blue, respectively, as is shown in Exhibit 42. The hues that lie between any two points are called secondary colors, and are composed of the two primary colors on each side of them. Colors which are opposite each other, as blue and yellow, for example, look richer when employed side by side in the same advertisement than they do when next to any other color. Red and green are complementary, as are orange and a shade of blue-green, like peacock blue. In order to procure maximum saturation and richness of hues, complementary colors should be used together. For an explanation of this phenomenon the reader is recommended to consult any thorough textbook in general psychology.

In one of its catalogues a few years ago Sears, Roebuck and Company had two pages devoted to advertising skirts—

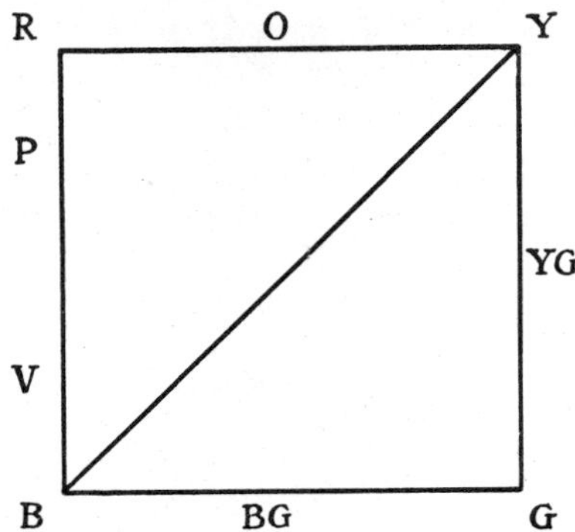

EXHIBIT 42. Showing the color square with primary colors at the corners.

one page in colors and the other in black and white. The prices were practically the same and the goods were equally desirable as regards style and quality, but the returns which came in from the colored page were ten times greater than those received from the black and white page. Part of this difference was due to the greater attention attracting value of the color page, but in addition to that fact, the colored skirts appeared richer than those depicted only in black and white. The suggestion of better quality was therefore produced by the employment of color.

When color is supplemented with the assistance of cuts, much greater pulling power is demonstrated. The nature of the cuts, of course, is a deciding factor. It is possible to hit the bull's-eye with the illustration by striking at a fundamental motive base like sex, as is demonstrated in Exhibit 38, even though the product at first thought would not seem to lend itself to such kind of picture. The reader will recall that almost all cigarette advertising is similar in this regard to Exhibit 38, while the same principle is employed to a greater or less degree by the majority of advertisements.

A Chinese proverb states that a picture is worth ten thousand words. It will be unnecessary to point out the psychological reasons underlying the partial truth of such a statement. At least, we know that cuts increase the effectiveness of an advertisement, and the result is heightened when color accompanies the cuts. Starch says that a publication can probably not carry over 15 to 20 per cent of its space in color, however, without considerably reducing the contrast effect between the colored and non-colored advertisements. In the following table from Starch[1] we see the results of color and cuts upon the returns from direct-mail advertising. In the column labelled "headings", the word "special" indicates that the regular company letterhead was supplanted by a special head originated for these letters. The same multigraphed letter was used throughout, with the addresses filled in by hand, a signature cut being used. In the letters containing cuts, the latter were always the same. Moreover, the mail was given a uniform distribution to all types of geographical areas.

LETTER NO.	QUANTITY	COLOR OF LETTER	CUTS	HEADING	RETURN ENV. COLOR	PULL PCT.
1	1,000	White	No	Yes	White	9
2	1,000	White	No	Yes	Blue	12
3	1,000	White	Yes	Special	White	18
4	1,000	White	Yes	Special	Blue	22
5	1,000	Corn	No	Special	White	14
6	1,000	Corn	Yes	Special	Blue	26
7	1,000	Green	No	Special	White	16
8	1,000	Green	Yes	Special	Blue	28
9	1,000	Gold	No	Special	White	21
10	1,000	Gold	Yes	Special	Blue	34
11	1,000	Pink	No	Special	White	26
12	1,000	Pink	Yes	Special	Blue	48

EXHIBIT 43. The effect of color and cuts in direct-mail advertising. (Starch).

In summarizing our discussion of the effectiveness of color and cuts upon returns, we can state unequivocally that both

[1] Starch, Daniel, *op. cit.*, p. 585.

color and illustration increase the effectiveness of advertisements. They add to the attention attracting value of the page, increase the reader's interest, explain more easily than words the nature of the merchandise, and contribute an impression of richness and quality. The value of color is somewhat lessened, however, by the inclusion of all-color advertisements in the magazine. The contrast of a black and white advertisement heightens the attractiveness of an adjacent colored page.

Humor in Advertising. The general impression of humor as employed in advertising is that it cheapens the quality feeling tone of the product. But one needs to distinguish between wit and simple comedy of the "Mutt and Jeff" or "Jiggs" variety. Moreover, in the realm of low priced goods the sacred regard which some firms have for an article which retails at from 25 to 50 cents is ludicrous in itself. There are companies of this sort who regard their products with the hallowed deference of a Rolls Royce automobile or a Steinway grand piano, even though their goods are on sale in our quarter stores.

It is well to keep in mind that people are not so concerned with quality in the case of cheap goods as in those which are expensive. They are willing to gamble on the smaller amounts. It is true that we resent levity and attempted wit at the expense of religion, mothers, the president of the United States, and honored figures of history, such as Washington and Lincoln. But as regards insecticides, like Flit, and lesser merchandise it is questionable if the virtues of humor do not far outweigh its vices.

Humor puts the reader or listener into a pleasant mental state. It inflates his ego, and may be looked upon as an indirect compliment. He feels superior to the person who is doing the silly things depicted. Previously we have described the resulting pleasure obtained whenever our egos are inflated, and the fact that this pleasure tends to become attached to

Seven Little Fellows Show You Why These

MEN'S SHIRTS

...are worth far more than their Sale Price of—

$1.09

On Sale Saturday

White, Tan, Green, Blue. Sizes 14 to 17

They're the famous KING PHILLIP brand shirts . . . Famous for quality . . . Famous for wear. And now we're going to make them more famous than ever by selling them at an unheard-of-price for merchandise of such high calibre. Maybe you're not interested in details — but you can't get away from the fact that any Broadcloth Shirt made of fine Egyptian yarn, pre-shrunk, with full-cut armholes, full-length square tails, full-width shoulders and self-top full-length plaited centers—is SOME SHIRT AT THIS PRICE!

You ought to buy a season's supply—if you don't—don't blame us—an event like this doesn't happen often and we don't know if it will ever happen again.

MAIL ORDER BLANK

SIZE (14 TO 17)						
SPECIFY COLOR (TAN, BLUE, GREEN)—or WHITE						
QUANTITY						

Mail to Ann Grey, Care of Frank's 730 Calhoun, Fort Wayne, Ind.

Name ....

Address ....

P. O. ....

If You Can't Come In Personally, this Coupon Will Shop for You!

NOTE: Many people will buy these now for Christmas gifts . . . and no wonder . . . they're REAL values!

SALE ON FIRST FLOOR

EXHIBIT 44. An advertisement combining novelty and humor. (Courtesy of Frank Dry Goods Company.)

the thing arousing it. Accordingly, humor tends to make us like the product utilizing it as an advertising device. In conflict with this positive effect, however, is the tendency for us to feel superior to the situation portrayed, which, in turn, may lead to our minimizing the quality of the product.

In human relations we pointed out the essential nature of the two-stage process of "selling" ourselves, emphasizing first of all the need for arousing respect and admiration for our virtues before we capitalized on that respect as a means of enhancing the effectiveness of our discreet compliments. In a similar fashion, humor in an advertisement compliments us, but should be supported by factual matter to bolster the prestige of the product. If this two-fold process is carried out, there is no reason for humor's lowering the quality feeling tone in any marked degree. Chesterton's wit certainly doesn't militate against his reputation for being an educated man of the "quality" type.

In the last few years a striking change in the advertising policy of both newspapers and manufacturers has been demonstrated by the use of colored comic pages in the Sunday papers, devoted to advertising foodstuffs, beauty lotions and the like. Advertising cartoons and comic strips in even the daily papers are now in vogue.

In concluding our discussion of humor we may state that its utilization in advertising need not be detrimental to the quality feeling tone, especially of low priced goods, if other sound selling points are also displayed. This subject will soon be studied more thoroughly in the psychological laboratory by means of feeling tone analyses of advertisements which have been presented in humorous and non-humorous manners.

The Importance of the Follow-up. There are two ways of interpreting the follow-up, one of which involves the response to inquiries received from an advertisement, while the other pertains to repetitive advertising. We shall take them up in turn.

(1) Following up inquiries. In this connection Bosworth[1] cites the experience of a representative national advertiser who was selling a product whose price ran into several hundreds of dollars. The following figures are illuminating, and may be compared with the number of calls that salesmen make in order to obtain orders:

10 per cent of those who do buy, buy on the 1st follow-up.
14 per cent of those who do buy, buy on the 2nd follow-up.
22 per cent of those who do buy, buy on the 3rd follow-up.
32 per cent of those who do buy, buy on the 4th follow-up.
16 per cent of those who do buy, buy on the 5th follow-up.
6 per cent of those who do buy, buy on the 6th follow-up.

If we consider the original advertisement as the first contact with the reader, then these follow-ups should be moved forward one step, thus giving 10 per cent returns on the second consumer contact. Viewed in this light, we find that the fourth and fifth advertising contacts produced 54 per cent of the sales, a result which agrees quite well with the statement previously cited that the majority of retailers' purchases from salesmen follow the fourth and fifth contacts.

In a representative issue of a leading woman's magazine which contained 87 advertisements bearing coupons, the girls in the office answered each one. Ten of the 87 firms didn't even reply! Twenty-six responded within 10 days, of which 6 replied inside of a week. Eight took 21 days to answer, while the remaining 43 did not send a followup for over three weeks, two firms waiting for 32 days. Of these 77 firms who did respond, the following figures show the number of their letters:

52 sent 1 follow-up, then desisted.
16 sent 2 follow-ups, then desisted.
5 sent 3 follow-ups, then desisted.
2 sent 4 follow-ups, then desisted.

[1] Bosworth, Clarence E., "Expensive Inquiries—and Cheap Replies," *Advertising and Selling* (April 17, 1929), pp. 26 *ff*.

1 sent 5 follow-ups, then desisted.
1 sent 8 follow-ups, then desisted.

By glancing at this and at the immediately preceding table we see that 68 of these firms ceased their follow-up when 76 per cent of their sales were probably waiting for simply an additional two or three letters. After a company pays from $2,500 to $5,000 for a single magazine page, it certainly is not good business to refrain from using a few postage stamps thereafter to sell to the potential buyers who have demonstrated enough interest in the product to return a coupon.

(2) Repetitive advertising. It is a trite statement to the advertiser that advertising must be engaged in constantly, or the public soon forgets his product. Ivory soap has been on the market for years, but doesn't dare relax in its advertising program. In the first place, each year millions of young men and women are coming of age and marrying. They represent a new market which is scattered all over the United States. Then, too, other soaps would cut into Ivory's trade, for despite the conservative influence of habit we are not unchangeable.

Even though it was sold out for months ahead during the World War, the Cracker Jack Company continued advertising in order to prevent falling into oblivion and to offset the influence of new products which were trying to cut into its market. Even after its patents expired on November 15, 1921, the Gillette Company did not let competitors seize its business. Any manufacturer in the United States or abroad had the right thereafter to manufacture an exact duplicate of the Gillette razor and sell it for whatever price he chose, capitalizing on Gillette's 17 years of previous advertising.

To meet the situation, however, the Gillette Company got out a new razor which it covered with patents, and launched upon additional advertising. The figures which Larrabee[1] offers below show the revenues of the company during the two

[1] Larrabee, C. B., "Expired Patents—Liabilities or Assets," *Printers' Ink* (March 20, 1924), p. 122.

years subsequent to the expiration of its patent on the old razor:

YEAR	RAZOR SETS SOLD	DOZENS OF BLADES	NET EARNINGS*
1922	3,420,895	24,082,970	$7,602,939
1923	7,798,781	29,061,634	8,411,776

*After depreciation but before deduction of taxes.

In a certain sense, moreover, the consistency in color employed in buildings, as the red of A & P stores, the green of National Tea fronts, or the constant color of the product and equipment, as in the yellow cab, have repetitive influence. Indeed, it is almost impossible to change such factors, once they have been established, without markedly altering the reaction to the product. For example, without their beards the Smith Brothers would lose more than breast protectors.

The importance of the follow-up, therefore, has been repeatedly demonstrated in advertising as well as selling. Many firms have worked out statistical analyses of their direct-mail follow-ups of magazine and newspaper advertisements so they know the point at which diminishing returns preclude the further expense of mailing. But the data quoted from Bosworth would seem to indicate that many firms are still rather careless in this respect. The psychological significance of repetitive advertising has been proved so frequently as to warrant no further discussion here.

Display Advertising. The use of goods for advertising purposes was the original form of advertising. Since the evolution of mammoth mercantile establishments with windows which are almost as large as the stage of a theater, the problem of display advertising has become very complex. It involves not only an appreciation of the rules of art and psychological balance, but also covers the ability to write effective advertising copy, create window and show cards, and employ the principles of attention attraction which are a necessity for the print advertiser. The display advertiser must really be a jack-of-all-trades in the field of advertising. He must employ the tools of the print advertiser in much of his work, yet encounters other problems not confronted by the latter. For example, he can utilize human models, and sound. He can introduce moving objects and the real merchandise.

The popularity of the motor car has further complicated his task. Autoists move past his display in one to three seconds whereas the pedestrians take 10 to 15 seconds. As a consequence, he must concentrate on a unified exhibit whose essential features are readily apparent but whose details are interesting and numerous enough to retain the attention of the stroller.

The writer has conducted surveys of the pedestrians' reactions to displays of certain Chicago department stores, notably those of Marshall Field's and The Fair. He has found that even among the foot passers-by there is a marked difference in reaction. Those people on the outer half of the sidewalk are only slightly attentive to window displays. The men and women on the window half of the walk are the potential viewers of the advertising layout since the outer pedestrians are in more of a hurry.

Because of the counter-attractions of the street cars and mass of moving human beings on the outer side of the walk, the windows do not monopolize even the inner pedestrians' attention. In fact, they may hardly catch it at all, unless the display advertiser utilizes the principles for attracting attention which we have previously described. The best method for attracting attention is change or movement. Yet display men in the majority of cases fail to employ this principle. Since human beings on the outer side of the display man's potential public are offering movement as an attention attractor, and because people are usually more interesting than things, it becomes essential, therefore, for the display advertiser to utilize the basic attention attractor whenever he can.

Another and related problem confronting the display advertiser is that of measuring the effectiveness of his windows. Although one window may seem to him to be superior to another, how is he to make sure? One method of answering his problem is the objective time test[1] by which he measures the degree to which the display slows the walking rate of pedestrians on the window half of the sidewalk. The writer has performed such tests with reference to some of the large Chicago department stores. It is necessary at the beginning to obtain an average walking rate for pedestrians on a crowded street but away from the distractions of window displays. The writer selected the adult woman as the subject for the time determination and found that she requires on the average 0.254 seconds per foot covered. In the data below is a comparison.

Average walking time of adult woman on crowded street away from windows........0.254 secs-ft.

Average woman's rate past Field's summer dresses display (3:30 p. m., June 6, 1932)..........0.385 secs-ft.

Average woman's rate past The Fair's bathing suit exhibit (5:30 p. m., June 6, 1932)......0.330 secs-ft.

The two windows described in the data are not comparable, however, for the reason that the test was not made on both at the same time. The pedestrian traffic is more hurried during the evening rush hour. In making such an objective time test, moreover, the observer should adhere to some such rules as the following:

"1. Count every adult woman walking singly, taking time from the moment she approaches one end of the window until she passes beyond its other limit. In short, don't select only those women who seem to be window shopping. Take them as they come—the rapid walkers as well as the slow.

"2. Make the count at comparable times. Don't compare a rush hour public with a mid-afternoon crowd. Preferably, conduct

[1] Crane, George W., "Practical Aspects of Display Psychology," *Display World* (November, 1932), vol. xxi, No. 3.

simultaneous experiments on different windows on the same day and hour.

"3. Don't record time in excess of 1.5 seconds per foot of window frontage. This regulation is to prevent one woman who stops for five minutes from "loading" the times of the 49 or 99 others on whom the test is based. The attention value of a window which stops ten pedestrians for five seconds apiece is better than that which stops one pedestrian for fifty seconds.

"4. Employ a stop watch and measure the window frontage exactly."

In concluding our discussion of display advertising, therefore, it is well to repeat that the first task of all advertising is to attract the attention. Since the display advertisement must compete with moving cars and colorfully clad persons, it should be given the benefit of that primary attention attractor, movement. The window should also be arranged in order to give a unified effect, and as a rule a wide variety of related merchandise should be present. There are some exceptions to this statement, as the large window of a firm like Field's which is chiefly concerned with creating desirable feeling tone and good will. In such a display there may be only two or three articles of merchandise. The effect of the background, moreover, should usually be devoted to focussing the gaze upon the merchandise. It should not draw attention to itself in contradistinction to the goods on display.

REFERENCES

Adams, H. F., *Advertising and Its Mental Laws* (New York, 1916).

Bosworth, C. E., "Expensive Inquiries—and Cheap Replies," *Advertising and Selling* (April 17, 1929), pp. 26 *ff*.

Crane, G. W., "Practical Aspects of Display Psychology," *Display World* (November, 1932), vol. xxi, No. 3.

De Wick, H. N., "The Relative Recall Effectiveness of Visual and Auditory Presentation of Advertising Material," *J. Appl. Psychol.*, 1935, vol. xix, pp. 245-264.

Eisenberg, A. L., *Children and Radio Programs* (New York, 1936).

Falk, A. T., "Analyzing Advertising Results," *Harvard Business Review* (January, 1929), vol. vii, pp. 191 *ff*.

Griffith, C. R., *General Introduction to Psychology* (New York, 1923), chap. xix.

Hepner, Harry W., *Psychology in Modern Business* (New York, 1931), chaps. xviii, xix.

HOLLINGWORTH, H. L., *Advertising and Selling* (New York, 1913).
HOTCHKISS, G. B., *Advertising Copy* (New York, 1924).
HUSBAND, R. W., *Applied Psychology* (New York, 1934), chaps. xviii, xix.
KITSON, H. D., *The Mind of the Buyer* (New York, 1924), chap. i.
KLEPPNER OTTO, *Advertising Procedure* (New York, 1931).
KLINE, LINUS W., "The Psychology of Humor," *American Journal of Psychology,* vol. xviii (1907), pp. 421-441.
LINK, H. C., *The New Psychology of Selling and Advertising* (New York, 1932).
LINK, H. C., "A New Method of Testing Advertising and a Psychological Sales Barometer," *J. Appl. Psychol.,* 1934, vol. 18, pp. 1-26.
LUCAS, D. B., AND BENSON, C. E., *Psychology for Advertisers* (New York, 1930).
POFFENBERGER, A. T., *Psychology in Advertising* (New York, 1932).
SAMPSON, HENRY, *A History of Advertising from Earliest Times* (London, 1874).
SCOTT, W. D., AND HOWARD, D. T., *The Psychology of Advertising* (New York, 1931).
SEASHORE, C. E., *Introduction to Psychology* (New York, 1923), chap. xxi.
SLATER, A. L., "How Well Do Consumer Contests Work?" *Advertising and Selling* (Feb. 6, 1929), pp. 27 *ff.*
STARCH, DANIEL, *Principles of Advertising* (New York, 1923).
STRONG, E. K., *The Psychology of Selling and Advertising* (New York, 1925).
UHRBROCK, R. S., "Words Most Frequently Used by a Five-Year-Old Girl," *J. Educ. Psychol.,* 1936, vol. 27, pp. 155-158.
WALLIS, W. A., "The Influence of Color on Apparent Size,"*J. Gen. Psychol.,* 1935, vol. xiii, pp. 193-199.

Answers to Hertz slogan contest: 1.E; 2.B; 3.D; 4.G; 5.A; 6.C; 7.F.
Best title to advertisement: "C".

CHAPTER IX

PERSONNEL ADMINISTRATION

Personnel administration as it is now regarded was not thought of in the middle ages when the condition of the worker was frequently a very drab one. He was born to a certain economic lot and trade, and so he died. It is true, of course, that our rather recent inventions were not in existence then, so the machine age with its mammoth industrial plants was not even dreamed of. The worker, as a consequence, was not required to become a "cog" in a vast manufacturing process, as has been too frequently the case in our 20th century. But his wages were mere pittances, and his social rights were ignored. Employers paid him about what they wished, and if he asked for more, they could laugh and hire his neighbor. The conditions of illumination, ventilation, and sanitation were not at all conducive to his health, nor even to his maximum output.

With the advent of the steam engine and the cotton gin the world passed through an industrial revolution of far reaching consequences. Not only have industrial concerns of the gigantic proportions of General Motors, DuPont, General Electric, and the Ford Company come into existence with a resulting growth of the urban population, but the worker is now a score of steps removed from his ultimate employer. And instead of having the varied tasks attendant upon the entire construction of his product, he now may be relegated to the monotonous duty of simply inserting a tiny screw.

With the bargaining power of the trade union the worker has attempted to meet his altered state in industry, especially in regard to working conditions, hours of employment, and wages. Management, too, in the last few decades has come to a realization that the combative relationship between itself and labor should become a cooperative one. The era of political absolution and the divine right of the foreman who "fired a few now and then to put the fear o' God in the rest of them", has become obsolete. From the point of view of efficiency alone, we have learned that the contented individual works more successfully than the one who is in constant terror of his job.

For the employee to be contented and happy in his work, however, involves not only a change from the autocratic foreman to a more understanding type of person, but also the adaptation of the worker to his job. As Scott and Clothier[1] have pointed out, personnel administration is not just the putting of a square peg into a square hole. Such a conception is too static, apparently involving the mechanical adjustment of two non-interacting entities. "There is no recognition here of the fact that men and jobs are changing in themselves, and plastic, yielding here and giving there to outside pressure. There is no acknowledgment of the common fact that with exposure to a square hole, a round peg (we are speaking of human pegs now) tends to become squarish; there is no appreciation that the square hole takes on a certain round appearance.

"This new point of view in industrial personnel differs from the square peg concept in that it recognizes that the job exercises an influence upon the worker and, conversely, that the worker exercises an influence upon the job. In fact, the job is never exactly the same job when filled by different persons, for each stamps his own impression upon it. Job A will have certain characteristics making for efficiency or inefficiency, as long as Worker M is on it; it will have other characteristics when M is replaced by N." The height of the work bench, for example, may make for efficiency when Worker M is at the task and for inefficiency when Worker N is there; on the other

[1] Scott and Clothier, *Personnel Management* (A. W. Shaw Co., New York, 1923), p. 14.

hand, the speed of the machine may be too fast for Worker M to react most efficiently, but be just right for Worker N.

With this newer conception of individual differences and an emphasis upon the individual, has developed the need for tests which will adequately differentiate the behavior traits of one person from another. The man who wishes to know in what business or profession he should go, and the employer who wishes to learn which of two men he should hire, both experience an eagerness to procure some fool-proof scheme which will answer their questions most readily and satisfactorily. We shall discuss some of these devices in the ensuing sections.

Unscientific Methods of Rating Human Beings. Probably the most frequently encountered systems of unscientific rating of human beings are those twins, phrenology and physiognomy. The "bootleg" psychologist who practices one of these usually employs the other also. Phrenology is the attempted diagnosis of a person's mental characteristics by the shape of his cranium and the bumps on his skull. Physiognomy endeavors to make a similar diagnosis by using the features, such as the nose, mouth, eyes, ears, skin texture, etc. We would hesitate to devote space to such topics were it not for the fact that the skilful salesmen of these pseudo-sciences are constantly in action, and always gaining converts.

During the past semester three of my students have reported that the sales managers of their firms have not only hired phrenologists and physiognomists, but have also insisted on their salesmen's taking a course of instruction in those subjects. Apparently intelligent men and women seem to be almost as susceptible as the more patently gullible, for Charles M. Schwab wrote the introduction to one such book, and Dr. Goddard told the writer at the American Psychological Association meeting in Washington in 1924, that one of the Ohio legislators was rather hostile during the investigation of the state institution for feeble-minded because, as he afterwards learned from friends, this legislator thought Dr. Goddard should have felt the heads of all the inmates and rated their intelligence accordingly.

One of the unfortunate things about these pseudo-sciences is the fact that laymen confuse them with psychology proper. Griffitts[1] estimates that one-half of our population believe in them to a certain extent. So far as scientific data at present available indicate, it is just as illogical to estimate intelligence by the size and shape of the skull and the features, as to try to estimate the chemical content of the air inside a football from the scratches on the pigskin cover. The fallacies on which they are based will be described under the following headings:

(1) They presuppose localized character qualities, such as love, jealousy, pugnacity, generosity, perseverance, and the like, which lie in certain "spots" in the brain. Although we know that there are sensory areas for sight, hearing, etc., and motor areas from which nervous impulses go to innervate the muscles and glands, we have never found any such regions for generosity and musical talent, nor is it logical to assume that any exist. The same sensory and motor neurones may function in a great number of patterns. Neurone Number 1 may be employed in a nervous arc involved in love, in eating, in piano playing, in fighting, and in a million other character traits, just as the letter "a" may function in a vast number of words. The neurones involved in character traits lie all over the surface of the brain—not in any one spot.

(2) They assume as a corollary of their first fallacy that the cortex or gray covering of the brain thickens perceptibly in those regions where it functions most frequently. This is similar to thinking that a copper wire becomes thicker with each succeeding electrical impulse that runs through it. The error lies in failing to recognize that nerve cells and muscle

[1] Griffitts, C. H., *Fundamentals of Vocational Psychology* (New York, 1924), p. 51.

cells are not the same. Exercise may increase the size of the biceps but not the brain, at least to any measurable degree.

(3) They assume that the brain bulges outward where it is exercised, and forces the cranium to expand. This is a sorry argument, for the brain is not in immediate contact with the skull, and if the space between the two were filled with liquid, by hydraulic pressure the whole inner surface of the cranium would get the same pressure exerted upon it; there would be no "spot" of pressure.

Daniel Webster had an unusually large skull, but his brain was of average size. Spurzheim, the famous German scientist, had a skull whose cubic capacity was exactly that of Joachim, an imbecile, but the imbecile's brain weighed 6 ounces more than the scientist's. Dr. Louis Casamajor, Professor of Neurology in the Columbia University College of Physicians and Surgeons, makes the statement that if he had a row of brains before him that had been taken from brilliant men and also from idiots, he couldn't tell by weight or shape or size which was which.[1]

(4) They generalize from a few cases where certain traits seem to be possessed by people with certain noses or skulls, and apply their generalizations to the mass of mankind. It is this tendency to remember only the coincidences which fit their ideas that make palmists, numerologists and those who use the signs of the horoscope continue to flourish along with the phrenologists and physiognomists. One of the most scientific experiments pertaining to the latter was conducted by Cleeton and Knight[2]. Using the physiognomists' and phrenologists' own criteria, they took accurate skull measurements and then had their subjects judged in the traits named in the

[1] Sumner, Keene, "You Can't Judge a Man's Mind By the Size of His Hat," *American Magazine* (November, 1922), vol. xciv, pp. 13 *ff*.

[2] Cleeton, Glen U., and Knight, F. B., "Validity of Character Judgments Based on External Criteria," *Journal of Applied Psychology* (June, 1924), vol. viii, No. 2, pp. 215-231.

table below. The student subjects were rated by their sorority and fraternity mates, and then by a group of 70 judges who were business men, school superintendents, employment men, and others who were accustomed to interviewing applicants for positions. The correlation between the traits possessed by the subjects, as determined by accurate physical measurements, and the judgments of their friends and strangers will be found in Exhibit 45.

TRAIT	CLOSE ASSOCIATES AND PHYSICAL FACTORS	CASUAL OBSERVERS AND PHYSICAL FACTORS
Judgment	—0.005	+0.145
Intelligence	+0.027	+0.051
Frankness	+0.055	+0.155
Friendliness	—0.11	+0.195
Will Power	—0.074	+0.036
Leadership	—0.041	+0.066
Originality	+0.095	+0.079
Impulsiveness	+0.100	—0.067

EXHIBIT 45. Correlation between phrenological and physiognomic measurements and the estimates of close associates and of strangers.*

* If unfamiliar with the meaning of correlation, the student should refer to chapter xiv.

In explaining the apparent success of occasional phrenological predictions, one must also keep in mind the fact that salesmen need above all else a vast amount of confidence. If they really believe these predictions, it bolsters their confidence and sends them forth convinced of their ability to sell. This is an attitude that leads to sales, whether the attitude is based on hasty generalizations or science. Physicians since the beginning of medicine have known this same truth.

From the standpoint of psychology, therefore, such methods of rating human beings as phrenology, physiognomy, astrology and the like are considered unsound because their premises have never been demonstrated as having scientific validity. The occasional successes attained by these pseudo-sciences are capable of explanation on the basis of chance, or because of the fact that credulous persons gain increased confidence in themselves in consequence. There would be no especial objection to them if they confined themselves simply to the stimulation of confidence, but they often arbitrarily mislead and misdirect a subject. For example, when they tell a mechanic that he is in the wrong vocation, and should become an advertising man, they may cause him to become dissatisfied with the one job for which he is best fitted.

Scientific Methods of Rating Human Beings. The goal of the personnel manager and vocational counsellor in test construction would be a battery of many sub-tests, much after the fashion of Army Alpha, which they could administer to workers and students, and from which they could perfectly diagnose an individual's possibility of success in any given trade or profession. For example, let us suppose that we have 100 sub-tests. We administer the entire 100 to a large group of successful dentists, lawyers, physicians, salesmen, advertisers, *et al.* We find, let us assume, that the dentists make exceptionally high scores in tests 13, 45, 75, 91, 96, and 99. Salesmen make high scores in tests 2, 9, 54, 67, 86, and 95, and low scores on those tests in which the dentists excel. The other trades and professions likewise are distinct in the tests on which they excel. Such a battery of tests would then be ideal, for we could give it to students and applicants about whom we knew nothing, and if an individual made his admirable scores on tests 13, 45, 75, 91, 96, and 99, then we could tell him that he apparently had the qualifications that lead to success in dentistry.

Unfortunately, we have no such panacea as yet available, which explains why so many people eagerly seize upon some such simple formula as that of using the shape of the nose, or complexion, as indexes of certain abilities. The scientific differentiation of men and women regarding their abilities and talents is a slow and laborious process. It includes, moreover, many things in addition to the capacities of a person. As we shall see in a later section of this chapter, there is great overlapping of intelligence between different professions and trades. A college student has the intelligence sufficient for any profession, so we can obtain little help from Army Alpha and similar mental examinations to assist us in telling him which professional school he should prepare for.

Even his possession of extra-curricular knowledge, as in the field of mechanics, doesn't guarantee him either success or happiness in a profession such as engineering. A man may have every mental and technical qualification for a certain trade or profession, yet make a dismal failure when he enters it. If his father has been obdurate and overbearing toward the boy, the boy may hate his father's profession throughout life and always wish to escape it. He may cherish an apparently illogical desire to be a railroad conductor because his favorite uncle was one, and took him on a few of his trips. We are becoming increasingly aware of the fact that children can develop such a trade-fixation, much as they evolve mother-fixations. One of my students, a man with linguistic ability and high abstract intelligence, is at present having warfare with his parents because they have trained him for the diplomatic service, while all he aspires to do in life is act as engineer on a railroad locomotive.

A scientific method of rating human beings, therefore, involves (1) *Aptitude tests,* such as an analysis of the subject's intellectual ability. Although much overlapping occurs regarding the intelligence levels found in many different professions and trades, it is obvious that a subnormal or dull normal can never hope for success or happiness in a profession. The reversal of this conclusion is also true as a general rule. When Professor Snow was testing taxicab drivers, he frequently found Army Alpha scores to run 43, 48, 69, 57, 83, 64, 175. Instantly he guessed what was true of the "175" subject. He was a college man operating a taxicab at night to help defray his college expenses. Although this fellow could drive a cab perfectly well, he would not be happy at the task, and would desert the job as soon as circumstances permitted. As a result, he was a poor employee from the management's viewpoint, for he accelerated their labor turnover. Intelligence tests are, however, a basic type of aptitude test.

(2) *Achievement tests*. These measure the actual ability of the subject at the time of the test. In many cases, the employer wants a skilled worker. An intelligent man could probably learn the task in question, but the employer cannot afford to wait. Some of our large firms, it is true, which conduct schools for young men and women in order to train their own workers administer aptitude tests to such applicants. An examination in a school subject is an achievement test. The writer would regard Moss's Social Intelligence Test as both an aptitude as well as an achievement test, depending upon the viewpoint of the tester. As a measure of the individual's adaptation to his social environment, the test can be looked upon as measuring achievement. As an indication of the subject's probable success in salesmanship or other professions involving a knowledge of human nature, it can be considered an aptitude test.

(3) *Vocational interests test*. This type of examination attempts to find the preferences which an individual has in respect to his permanent vocation. If he possesses the aptitude and developed skill requisite for salesmanship and personnel administration, but prefers the latter, it is wise to learn this fact. A great many people, however, among the college graduates, do not have any particular preferences. Aside from desiring Rockefeller's wealth and Robert Montgomery's or Janet Gaynor's fame, they have little desire for one form of productive activity instead of another. They drift

into the first type of work which offers a little ready cash and some prestige among their fellows, after which habit may grip them, and keep them in that occupation till old age arrives. College and university personnel departments may ultimately increase both the productivity as well as the happiness of their graduates by presenting them with written analyses of their vocational talents and defects. At the time of graduation this second diploma may eventually become more prized than the usual one, for it will at least be forward looking in its significance, and not a static record of the past four years' attainments.

(4) *Social attitudes test.* Industrial organizations have long appreciated the need for bonding many of their employees, realizing that their attitude might change regarding honesty. It is a very important phase of personnel work to discover the views of men and women regarding property rights, moral questions, religion, etc. Some offices prefer to avoid a mixture of religions or of races or of politics because of the possible debates and hostilities that may ensue.

(5) *Physical tests.* These involve health, examinations to determine deafness, color blindness, emotional stability, fatigue resistance, etc. In a sense, they belong under the general heading of aptitude tests except that the latter have commonly been held to apply to examinations for mental and habit patterns possessed by the subject.

In conclusion, therefore, we may state that the scientific rating of human beings involves the recognition of modern neurological and psychological laws, and the development of objective scales or tests by which to measure aptitude, achievement, vocational interests, social attitudes, and physical traits. Because of the significance of vocational interests and social attitudes in determining one's success or failure no single test or battery of tests will ever be perfectly diagnostic of one's future activity, since interests and attitudes are subject to constant social conditioning. But a careful, scientific study and measurement of men and women will be of increasing value in promoting industrial efficiency and human happiness.

Letters of Recommendation. As a partial measure of an applicant's aptitude, achievement, and social attitudes, it has been the custom to ask for a letter of recommendation. Such an instrument could have considerable merit if it were not for the fact that the applicant usually cites his friends for references, and the latter tend to give him the benefit of the doubt. Moreover, their letters are usually based on their own opinions, unsupported by objective data. The latter should consist of such items as the subject's length of service, the number of times tardy, of days absent, his rank in production as contrasted with the other salesmen, students, or employees, new ideas and improvements that he instigated, etc. The best answer to a letter of inquiry regarding a man's dependability is the reply that "He worked for us for three years without a day's absence, and was tardy only twice. He never failed to get his quota of work finished on time." Letters of this nature do not have to reiterate the worker's dependability for the specificity enables the new personnel manager to infer those things.

In answer to a letter asking my opinion "as to the character, reputation for honesty, and financial responsibility" of one of my former students, I have submitted the reply shown on the next page. The letter is still too subjective to be most effective, but a teacher who conducts lecture sections does not have an opportunity to observe his students in many situations of a sort which specifically denote honesty and financial integrity. Even concerning our most intimate friends we probably could say only "they are honest because we never saw them steal." A banker or business man might write that his messenger had carried the pay roll or daily deposits for three years without touching a penny. This would be specific, and much more objective than my final paragraph.

From the foregoing discussion, therefore, it is evident that

NORTHWESTERN UNIVERSITY
COLLEGE OF LIBERAL ARTS
EVANSTON, ILLINOIS

DEPARTMENT OF PSYCHOLOGY

Feb. 1, 1938

Mr. R. C. Bever,
333 N. Michigan Ave.,
Chicago, Illinois.

My dear Mr. Bever:

In reply to your letter asking my impression of the ability and character of Mr. Oliver B. Davison, I can offer the following data:

Mr. Davison was enrolled in my courses in Business Psychology and Advanced Business Psychology for two semesters. In the first class I administered the Army Alpha Intelligence Test, with which you are probably familiar. Mr. Davison's score thereon was 152, which means that he has a grade of "A" in mental alertness. Only four men out of every 100 are able to make over 134 on this test.

During the two years in my courses, he never missed a class, nor did he fail to hand in a single written assignment. You may be interested to learn that out of a class of fifty business and professional men, Mr. Davison was fourth high in term grades during the first semester, and second high during the last term.

As for my opinion of his moral and financial integrity, I can truthfully say that if I were in the business world I should be only too glad to place Mr. Davison on my staff.

Sincerely,

GWC-CM

EXHIBIT 46. Showing how objective data can improve a letter of recommendation.

letters of recommendation may be of considerable value depending upon the objectivity of the qualifications contained therein, and the honesty and prestige of the writer. Opinions unsupported by factual statements, and the use of superlatives render letters of little merit.

The Effectiveness of the Personal Interview. The frequent request for a photograph from an applicant for a position is unfortunately not always made to enable the prospective employer to judge the applicant's youth, but is often utilized for the sake of phrenological measurements. In some cases the employer today asks for both a front and side view, the latter enabling him to measure more easily the applicant's nose, eyebrows, lips, forehead and chin. If personnel management were only as simple as this, we could give a stenographer a set of spreading calipers, a sliding compass, and some steel tape, after which we could dispense with the employment manager.

To a believer in physiognomy, the personal interview is simply an additional opportunity for analyzing noses and lips. Sometimes in such interviews the employment manager actually requests his subjects to turn sidewise so that he may study their profiles! To one who is scientific in his utilization of the interview, however, the personal contact with the subject permits him to judge such things as the obvious physical proportions and presence or absence of stigmata, the general appearance and neatness in dress, the poise and carriage of the applicant, the latter's conversational ability, and social attitudes.

In addition, as Burtt[1] clearly points out, vocational preferences are more easily obtained by word of mouth than through the questionnaire, and many doubts and fears of the applicant may be allayed during the interview. His misconceptions may be corrected, and a general friendly relationship estab-

[1] Burtt, Harold, *Employment Psychology* (Houghton Mifflin Company, Boston, 1926).

lished. The interviewer must be especially cautious, however, about letting his likes and dislikes obscure his clear discernment of the subject's virtues. Even the disbeliever in phrenology and physiognomy is likely to slip into a similar unscientific form of behavior by forming an instant liking or aversion for an applicant. His aversion may be based on a consciously forgotten childhood experience with a person who had the same features as the present applicant. If a fellow with a certain type of ear or chin beat him in a fist fight or stole his sweetheart from him, his resentment may carry over to all people bearing such ears and chins, and he may think they are always thieves and philanderers. Conversely, he may like and trust another individual who resembles a childhood friend or parent. Both of these reactions on the part of the interviewer may be entirely at variance with the real personalities of his callers.

As far as being able to judge the intellectual and trade capacities and abilities of applicants is concerned, the interviewer must rely on psychological tests and measurements, for his personal opinion is scarcely better than that of the schoolboy's. The most skilled interviewers will not agree on the merits of individuals, as the following data from Snow[1] clearly indicate. The Packard Motor Car Company had asked Professors D. T. Howard and A. J. Snow to help them select four or more competent salesmen of motor trucks. A large "Want Ad" had been inserted in the Chicago papers. From their letters in reply to this, the obviously unfit were eliminated, leaving twelve men ranging in ages from 29 to 46, in salaries from $3,000 to $7,000, in years of experience from 4 to 26, and in education from 8 years of grammar school to 3 years of college. Some were of native American stock, others of Norwegian, Swedish and German extraction. These twelve men were then interviewed individually by seven judges.

[1] Snow, A. J., "An Experiment in the Validity of Judging Human Ability," *Journal of Applied Psychology* (September, 1924), vol. viii, No. 3, pp. 339-346.

To indicate the qualifications of the raters, we may state that interviewers A, B, and C were sales managers of automobile truck departments from three different companies. Judge D was president and general sales manager, while E was vice-president and former sales manager of two costly passenger car automobile firms. Judge F was the general sales manager of a national steel company, while G was a psychologist.

	JUDGES							TOTAL IN RANK	CONSENSUS	RANK IN TESTS
APPLICANTS	A	B	C	D	E	F	G			
C. R. ...	1	8	4	1	2	2	4	22	1	11
C. Y. ...	7	1	7	2	5	5	1	28	2	4
B. W. ...	10	2	9	4	1	6	3	35	3	8
L. H. ...	2	9	8	9	3	4	2	41	4	5
M. R. ...	3	6	3	3	10	7	9	37	5	1
P. A. ...	4	7	1	10	8	8	5	43	6	6
B. L. ...	11	3	6	5	9	3	7	44	7	10
F. E. ...	5	5	11	6	4	11	6	48	8	2
M. M.	12	10	2	7	6	1	10	49	9	7
M. A. ...	6	4	10	8	7	10	8	53	10	9
S. T. ...	8	11	5	11	11	9	11	65	11	3
S. N. ...	9	12	12	12	12	12	12	81	12	12

EXHIBIT 47. Showing the difference in ranking given twelve salesmen by seven skilled interviewers, and their consensus compared with test scores. (Snow).

In concluding this section it would be well to comment on the relative effectiveness of male and female interviewers. Where men are the principal applicants, an attractive young woman of a democratic disposition may be excellent for the initial contact, but men resent having to give what they consider personal information to women. A company may engender ill will and cause many desirable applicants to stay away from its personnel office by delegating too much of the function of interviewing to female assistants. Older workers also resent having to come to dapper young men for jobs. Similarly many a physician engenders a feeling of resentment and unpleasantness in his male patients by having a nurse or young female secretary put the patient through a thorough oral cross examination.

The effectiveness of the personal interview, therefore, depends largely on the degree of cooperation between the applicant and the personnel officer. When friendly relationships can be established, the latter can correct misunderstandings and apprehensions of the prospective worker, as well as learn many things concerning his qualifications, attitudes, and interests. The applicant may even find that he does not want the vacant position, or the manager may note personal and physical defects which offset the applicant's test scores. The interview is a very desirable feature of personnel and employment work, particularly when the applicant meets a cordial official with a scientific attitude.

Psychological Tests in Employment. In order for an intelligent use of psychological tests to be made possible, it is wise to institute a job analysis. This consists of dissecting the task into its component parts so that the personnel director may know what elementary working situations are encountered in the satisfactory performance of the job. Such matters as the posture involved, the walking or standing necessitated, the use of certain tools, and the intellectual processes entailed are items contained on the job analysis sheet. When the personnel manager begins looking for workers, he follows a job specification, which simply tells what qualifications a worker must have in order to fulfill the tasks indicated on the job analysis sheet. For example, stenographers are almost invariably inefficient if they score below 60 on Army Alpha. The job specification for stenographers would, therefore, contain the intelligence score of 60 as the lower critical score. There are occasions, too, where an upper critical score is included, as our reference to the records on Army Alpha of taxicab drivers would indicate. From the viewpoint of management, a low labor turnover is to be desired, so an intelligent man in a monotonous job is a liability.

The vocational counsellor differs from the employment manager to a certain degree in his use of tests, for the former is interested primarily in learning all the capacities of an individual so that he may more adequately steer him into the right position. The employer, on the contrary, is more interested in the performance of the subject on a given test which is diagnostic for the vacant job. The employer has been but slightly concerned with the other talents and capacities of a worker if the latter fails to meet the demands of the specific task. In large industrial plants and commercial firms, however, the personnel departments now function in the role of vocational counsellors, for there are so many different kinds of work for which men and women are required that the personnel officer can utilize almost every applicant. He is interested, therefore, in all the talents and abilities of the applicant.

To show the procedure involved in applying psychology in the economical selection of workers, let us assume that a large gasoline company wished us to hire its service station operators. If 1,000 men apply and we need at the present moment but 100, how are we to select the most efficient 10 per cent of these applicants? An interview would enable us to eliminate those obviously unfitted for the tasks involved, but still we have, let us assume, 500 men who seem competent. We might select the 100 best looking men, but physical appearance is not the only asset in this business, so we may get many incompetent men whom we would be compelled to discharge after a few weeks or months. We don't want to spend the initial price of training men who will later leave us. We know that there are 100 of our 500 men who are more efficient than the remaining 400, and these are the ones we wish to discover as quickly as possible.

We decide to get an occupational description or job analysis, so we study at first hand the various phases of the work, discovering that service station men must know something about various kinds of automobiles; that they must be able to make change and do the simple arithmetic involved in their daily inventories of the accessories which they sell and leave on hand for the men on the next shift; that they should be able to talk intelligently about the relative merits of gasolines and oils and anti-freeze mixtures; that they are frequently asked directions; that they are to try to sell to various types of customers.

With these facts in mind we decide to devise a battery of several sub-tests which will enable us to give a numerical evaluation to the various applicants. Accordingly, we construct one sub-test in mathematics, following the method of Test 2 of Army Alpha. This should differentiate those who are poor at figures. Since we are in haste about hiring these men and cannot take time to train them, all of our sub-tests will incline toward the achievement type of examination. We give a short answers or multiple choice sub-test covering the mechanical parts of automobiles. Another sub-test covers technical questions regarding gasoline, anti-freeze mixtures and the various tires, tire patching equipment and other accessories sold at the station. We may include a sub-test covering important highways leading out of the city, and the best routes to neighboring states or cities. A final multiple choice sub-test should cover the salesman's knowledge of human nature—his ability to demonstrate tact in the sales situation. For example:

A woman drives up to the station in a Cadillac and says, after you have filled the tank with ethyl gasoline, "Yesterday one of

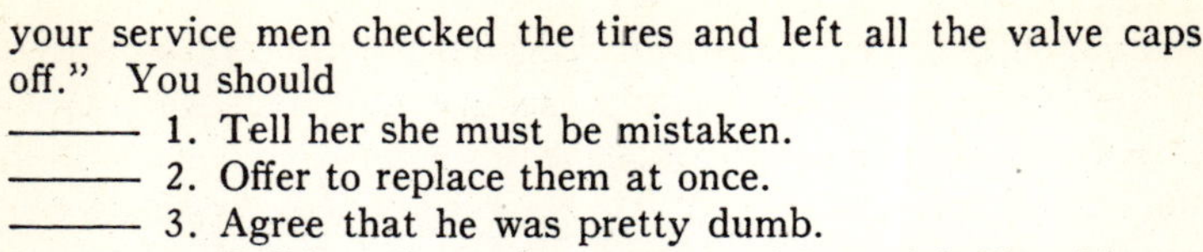

your service men checked the tires and left all the valve caps off." You should

——— 1. Tell her she must be mistaken.
——— 2. Offer to replace them at once.
——— 3. Agree that he was pretty dumb.
——— 4. Tell her she can't get away with a trick like this.

Now we have five sub-tests which *a priori* reasoning leads us to believe are good. Our task is still not completed. We need to test our test. Such a procedure involves giving the test to a large group of service station operators who have been in the employment of a company for a considerable time so that their records of efficiency are well known. If the most efficient workers score highest on our test, while the poorest as judged by the company's records also get our lowest marks, then we can forthwith administer our test to the 500 applicants and select the highest 100 scorers. It may be quite possible, however, that in testing our test we find that the best workers don't make the highest scores. Then we must analyze their test papers, and see if we should "weight" the scores on certain of our sub-tests. Weighting the scores simply consists of increasing the number of items in the sub-test or in multiplying by two or whatever figure is warranted, the score made. For instance, if we had 25 items in each of our five sub-tests, the total possible score would be 125. But if we found, from studying the records of the good workers and their scores on our test, that the arithmetic sub-test was more valuable than the one pertaining to knowledge of highways, we would simply double the scores made on the arithmetic test. A perfect score in this test would now have a value of 50, and the grand total would amount to 150.

The tendency toward objectization which is demonstrated in the above tests has also appeared in our rating scales. Even the judging of college debates has gone through a "job analysis" so that we don't ask the critic simply to give us his general impression of the two teams. Instead, we tear down the job of debating into manner of delivery, constructive speech, rebuttal, poise, gesticulation and the like. In a similar manner the more intangible qualities of employees, such as cooperativeness, initiative, ability to inspire confidence, etc. have been made into headings upon graphic rating scales such as the one by Professor Delton T. Howard on the two adjacent pages. Four or five degree intervals are denoted by words along a base line. The rater checks along the line the point which he thinks indicates the position of the subject being rated. The base line is often exactly ten centimeters long so that a centimeter scale can be placed upon it for reading the checked point in terms of percentage. A check 9 centimeters from the low end of the scale would therefore mean 90 per cent proficiency in the quality designated.

In summarizing the use of psychological tests in employment we may state that they improve both the happiness of the employee and increase the efficiency of the firm, for they enable the employment manager to select workers who are suited to the tasks which they are to perform. An achievement test, for instance, will quickly indicate whether an applicant is familiar with the tools or trade in which he claims expertness, and his speed, alertness, and accuracy may be obtained within an hour's time. These characteristics are almost incapable of correct discernment in the personal interview. See my "Test For Employers," on page 606.

The Relationship Between Intelligence and Occupational Success. We have mentioned the fact that there are critical intelligence scores below which workers are incompetent and above which they tend to change jobs as soon as a better opening is available. In her study of 375 girl workers with an average chronological age of 16 years, Burr[1] has given tentative norms of industrial ability of various degrees of feeble-mindedness. Her criterion for success in the occupa-

[1] Burr, E., "Minimum Intelligence Levels of Accomplishment in Industry," *Journal of Personal Research* (1924), vol. iii, pp. 207 *ff*.

RATING SCALE OF FURTHERANCE-HINDRANCE FACTORS AFFECTING SCHOLASTIC ACHIEVEMENT

By D. T. Howard

Indicate your rating in each factor by placing a check on the line where you think it ought to be.

FACTORS					
I Consider your health as affecting your studies: Is your health always good and conducive to vigorous study, or does it interfere with your work?	Excellent health, sound and vigorous.	My health is better than average.	Not especially good nor bad.	I have some cause to complain of my health.	Bad health is a serious handicap to me.
II Is the place, or places, where you do your studying ideal for the purpose, or are you distracted or interrupted to an annoying degree? Are you well satisfied, do you think that you are fairly well placed, or have you a great deal of distraction to contend with?	Ideal.	Generally favorable.	Tolerable.	Rather unsatisfactory.	Highly distracting.
III Do campus activities contribute to your success as a student, or do they engage your time and interest in such a way as to interfere seriously with your studying?	I consider my program ideal	Rather good than bad.	Neither very helpful nor very harmful.	My studies suffer some.	Very distracting and injurious to college work.
IV Are you able to arrange your time so as to provide regular hours for study? Or are you prevented from keeping to a regular schedule because of conflicts with duties and engagements that cannot be avoided?	My program can be arranged as I please.	I can always arrange for studies by giving some thought to my program.	Other matters interfere frequently to prevent me from keeping to a regular schedule of study..		I find it very difficult to provide study hours.

Question					
V Do not answer this question unless you do some work to support yourself while in college. If you work for support, does this activity promote the keenness of your scholarship, or does it operate as a serious distraction? Try to express, in terms of benefit or hindrance, the influence of such work upon your studies.	It is ideal and fits in excellently.	It is a help to me in my studies.	It makes no difference in my work.	It is annoying.	An extreme distraction and a great handicap.
VI Consider your future career and prospects. Is your general state of mind regarding your future quite unsettled so that you are restless and unable to settle down to systematic study? Or is the exact contrary the case? Or are you indifferent to such considerations?	So disposed that future prospects are a strong incentive to study.	Future prospects a help rather than a hindrance.	Indifferent to such considerations.	Could do better if I had a more settled program.	Very unsettled, and find it hard to get down to study.
VII Do you find yourself doubtful, for any reason, as to the value of your college studies? Or are you certain that they have a very high value? In this connection consider whether your present studies have or have not an important bearing on your future life and work.	I place the highest value on my studies.	Quite valuable and should be taken seriously.	At least as valuable as any other activity in which I engage.	Other campus activities are more important.	Distinctly minor importance.
VIII Do you find yourself unable to study by reason of worry, anxiety, or excessive dissatisfaction produced by causes over which you have no direct control? Or is your state of mind generally untroubled and favorable to study?	My mind is free from worries that would interfere with study.	Although I have occasional worries, these do not seriously affect my studies.	I have real troubles at times, but cannot say that they seriously hinder my studies.	I could do better work if I had less to distract my mind.	Worries are a source of real distraction to me.

EXHIBIT 48. An example of a Graphic Rating Scale.

tion was usually a period of at least three months of continuous employment at the same work. The least mental age at which it is possible for a girl to perform the given tasks with success is contained in the table below.

MINIMUM MENTAL AGE	TASKS WHICH CAN BE CREDITABLY PERFORMED
7 to 8 years..	Packing small articles not easily damaged by handling, such as powder-puffs.
8 to 9 years..	Certain operations in pencil making.
9 to 10 years..	Crude hand-sewing, such as putting buttons on cards, sewing bows on novelties; cutting and pasting in paper-box making; sewing hat linings and steaming materials used in millinery; packing and folding hair-nets.
10 to 11 years..	Stock-keeping, labeling and checking; winding cotton and wool braid, hand-sewing on garments.
11 to 12 years..	Covering buckram foundations, sewing in the wire edge and facings of women's hats.
12 to 13 years..	Sewing on labels at high speed; machine operating for straw and other millinery, for window shades, garters, powder-puffs, etc.
13 to 14 years..	Assembling of parts requiring some judgment; machine operating in sewing straight seams, bindings, etc., where threading and adjusting machines are necessary; completion of an entire garment.

In his thorough survey of the intellectual limits of various occupations, Fryer[1] amplified and corrected the data obtained by the United States Army during the war. He employed a "Business Alpha", a 20-minute intelligence test arranged and standardized for vocational and business purposes by H. D. and L. P. Fryer. The score ranges in the following table are for the most part interquartile, that is, the upper and lower

[1] Fryer, Douglas, "Occupational-Intelligence Standards," *School and Society* (1922), vol. xvi, pp. 273-277.

quarters are omitted. It is assumed that those in the lowest quarter are having difficulty in a given occupation and those in the upper quarter are probably restless and inclined to move to a higher occupation. There are 96 occupations listed. Fryer believes an individual should have a score above the average of any profession to feel sure of being able to attain success therein.

INTEL. GROUP	SCORE AVE.	SCORE RANGE	OCCUPATION
A	161	110-183	Engineer (Civil and Mechanical)
	152	124-185	Clergyman
	137	103-155	Accountant
B	127	107-164	Physician
	122	97-148	Teacher (Public Schools)
	119	94-139	Chemist
	114	84-139	Draftsman
	111	99-163	Y. M. C. A. Secretary
	110	80-128	Dentist
	109	81-137	Executive (Minor)
C+..........	103	73-124	Stenographer and Typist
	101	77-127	Bookkeeper
	99	78-126	Nurse
	96	74-121	Clerk (Office)
	91	69-115	Clerk (Railroad)
	86	59-107	Photographer
	85	57-110	Telegrapher and Radio Operator
	83	64-106	Conductor (Railroad)
	82	57-108	Musician (Band)
	81	59-106	Artist (Sign Letterer)
	81	60-106	Clerk (Postal)
	81	57-109	Electrician
	80	62-114	Foreman (Construction)
	80	56-105	Clerk (Stock)
	78	54-102	Clerk (Receiving and Shipping)
	78	61-106	Druggist
	77	59-107	Foreman (Factory)
	75	56-105	Graphotype Operator
C	74	53- 91	Engineer (Locomotive)
	72	54- 99	Farrier
	70	46- 95	Telephone Operator
	70	44- 94	Stock Checker
	69	49- 93	Carpenter (Ship)
	69	48- 94	Handyman (General Mechanic)
	69	46- 90	Policeman and Detective

INTEL. GROUP	SCORE AVE.	SCORE RANGE	OCCUPATION
C—........	68	51- 97	Auto Assembler
	68	47- 89	Engineman (Marine)
	68	42- 86	Riveter (Hand)
	67	50- 92	Toolmaker
	66	45- 92	Auto Engine Mechanic
	66	45- 91	Laundryman
	66	49- 86	Gunsmith
	66	44- 88	Plumber
	66	44- 88	Pipefitter
	65	44- 91	Lathe Hand (Production)
	65	43- 91	Auto Mechanic (General)
	65	43- 91	Chauffeur
	65	42- 89	Tailor
	65	44- 88	Carpenter (Bridge)
	64	43- 88	Lineman
	63	40- 89	Machinist (General)
	63	46- 88	Motor Cyclist
	63	41 -86	Brakeman (Railroad)
	62	31- 94	Actor (Vaudeville)
	61	40- 85	Butcher
	61	44- 84	Fireman (Locomotive)
	61	39- 82	Blacksmith (General)
	60	38- 94	Shop Mechanic (Railroad)
	60	36- 93	Printer
	60	40- 84	Carpenter (General)
	59	40- 87	Baker
	59	39- 83	Mine Drill Runner
	59	38- 81	Painter
	58	37- 85	Concrete Worker
	58	40- 83	Farmer
	58	37- 83	Auto Truck Chauffeur
	58	37- 82	Bricklayer
	57	41- 81	Caterer
	57	39- 71	Horse Trainer
	56	38- 76	Cobbler
	55	35- 81	Engineman (Stationary)
	55	34- 78	Barber
	55	35- 77	Horse Hostler
	52	38- 96	Salesclerk
	52	33- 74	Horse Shoer
	51	31- 79	Storekeeper (Factory)
	51	26- 77	Aeroplane Worker
	51	31- 74	Boilermaker
	50	33- 75	Rigger
	50	30- 72	Teamster
	49	40- 71	Miner (General)
	48	21- 89	Station Agent (General)

INTEL. GROUP	SCORE AVE.	SCORE RANGE	OCCUPATION
C—..........	40	19- 67	Hospital Attendant
	40	19- 60	Mason
	35	18- 62	Lumberman
	35	19- 57	Shoemaker
	32	16- 59	Sailor
	31	20- 62	Structural Steel Worker
	31	19- 60	Canvas Worker
	30	16- 41	Leather Worker
	27	19- 63	Fireman (Stationary)
	27	17- 57	Cook
	26	18- 60	Textile Worker
	22	16- 46	Sheet Metal Worker
	21	13- 47	Laborer (Construction)
D	20	15- 51	Fisherman

The relationship between intelligence and occupational success is rather difficult to summarize succinctly. In general however, the demands of the job must be sufficiently complex to monopolize the attention of the worker, yet not so great as to be a strain upon his adaptive behavior. If he has either too much or too little intelligence for the given task he usually becomes dissatisfied. Such surveys as the one just cited show the intelligence ranges within a given occupation, but there is considerable overlapping, so the intelligence score of a person is not diagnostic of a single vocation. At present we shall have to be content with classifications of a general sort, such as professional, skilled, semi-skilled, and unskilled.

Adjusting the Worker to His Job. In former days the new worker was frequently made the butt of jokes and a certain amount of hazing before he was admitted into the camaraderie of his fellow workers. Nowadays he is introduced to his fellow employees, often called co-workers to avoid the idea of employee versus employer, and his foreman or supervisor gives him the necessary instructions. These are not piled upon him before he can become somewhat oriented to his new functions and environment. His first work should be rather simple, for he is in a greater or less emotional state for the first few days immediately following his placement.

The majority of companies have definite follow-up systems in order that the progress of the new workers may be observed. A representative of the personnel office a day or two later just happens to be passing, and stops beside the new worker's desk or bench for a few minutes' chat. He inquires how the latter is progressing, and lets him know that the personnel office is interested in his success. Often a second follow-up of this sort is made at the end of the week. Thereafter the worker's record is noted to see if he is making a satisfactory adjustment to the production demands of his job.

Since it is frequently true that the personnel department is given the responsibility of promotion, transfer, and discharge, it must be concerned not only with the worker's initial success, but make provision for his ultimate advancement if his capacities warrant such. Blind alley jobs must be avoided when placing the able worker, and a flexible wage scale adopted.

Regarding rates of payment, a number of plans have been devised, of which those holding for salesmen cover most of the possibilities. Of these a straight salary has been the most popular method of compensation, followed by the straight commission. Salary with a bonus is growing in popularity today. Then we have salary and commission; commission and a bonus; a combination of salary, commission, and a bonus; and a drawing account against profit on sales or bonus accumulations.

In the university personnel departments many of the same procedures are followed as in business. The students are agreeably introduced to the university life and their first year is watched very closely. Those who seem to be falling down in production (scholarship) are interviewed with the aim of finding the difficulty and removing it. New plans of study are worked out between the personnel officer and the student.

If the latter is devoting too much time to outside activities, or has lacked an adequate method of studying while in high school, the personnel worker assists in making a readjustment. Part time employment for students who are earning their way through school is a frequent function of the personnel office. Moreover, a number of students need moral guidance and friendship, especially if they are the children of divorced parents, and are struggling in emotional quicksands vainly striving for a sound anchorage. Many of the students with low grades are having emotional conflicts which make it almost impossible for them to concentrate. The personnel departments of universities, like some of the foremost ones in industry, are finding it advisable to include psychiatry within their province.

The adjustment of the worker to his job, therefore, consists largely of the establishment of friendly relations between him and his associates and superiors. Instead of adopting the critical attitude that he must disprove their suspicions of his incompetence, the modern personnel officer and supervisor endeavor to make it easy for him to do his best, and initiate him into his tasks by degrees. They have previously selected him because of his demonstrated abilities or aptitudes, so the process of adjustment is principally a social one. In college personnel work it also frequently involves teaching the student more effective habits of study.

The Causes of Discharge. A lack of skill or technical knowledge is not the chief cause of discharge, despite the findings of the army trade tests administered to 250,000 men. At that time the trade tests revealed that of those men claiming skill, only 6 per cent possessed expertness in their trades, while 24 per cent might be classed as journeymen in ability. In 40 per cent of the cases the men had only the equivalent of apprenticeship qualifications, while 30 per cent did not know anything at all about the trades in which they claimed to be expert.

In this connection the Bureau of Vocational Guidance at Harvard University made a study of the causes for discharge of employed men. In over 4,000 cases which were examined, two major categories were found to explain their leaving. These were (1) Lack of Skill or Technical Knowledge, and (2) Lack of Social Understanding. Although incompetence is the largest single cause, those items classified under the psychological heading furnished a majority of the total.

CAUSES OF DISCHARGE

LACK OF SKILL OR TECHNICAL KNOWLEDGE:	NO. CASES	PCT.
Incompetence	1126	25.7
Slowness	200	4.6
Physical Inadaptability	170	3.9
	1496	34.2
LACK OF SOCIAL UNDERSTANDING:		
Insubordination	486	11.1
General Unreliability	453	10.4
Absenteeism	442	10.1
Laziness	317	7.2
Trouble Making	179	4.1
Drinking	179	4.1
Violation of Rules	142	3.2
Carelessness	120	2.7
Misconduct	100	2.3
Dishonesty	91	2.1
Unclassified	321	8.5
	2830	65.8

The reader will note that slowness is placed in the same category with incompetence. O'Rourke[1] found that the slow worker is much more inaccurate than the fast worker. Taking the record of the 125 most rapid workers and contrasting it with the performance of the 125 slowest workers, he found that the slow individuals were correct in only 38 per cent of their attempts whereas the fast workers were right in 80 per

[1] Filer, H. A., and O'Rourke, L. J., "Progress in Civil Service Tests," *Journal of Personnel Research,* vol. 1 (March, 1923), No. 11, p. 484.

cent of the items undertaken. These findings are presented graphically in Exhibit 49. The college instructor has empirically observed a somewhat similar relationship with regard to students during their examinations.

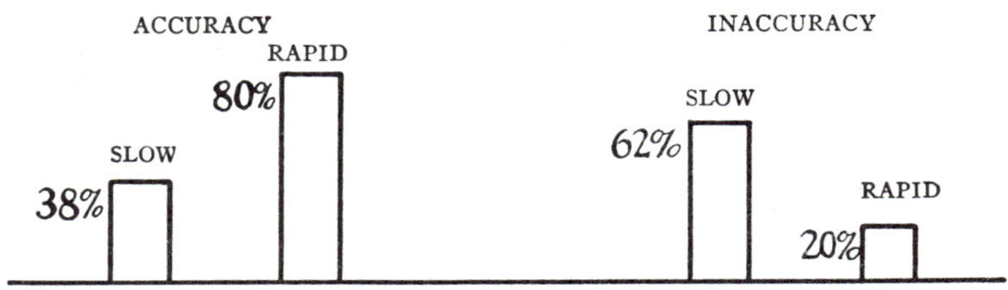

EXHIBIT 49. Showing the accuracy and inaccuracy of slow and fast workers. (O'Rourke).

The causes of discharge are consequently not confined to lack of mechanical or technical skill alone, but involve in addition a number of personality traits which are strictly psychological in nature. In fact, the Harvard report, indicates that almost two-thirds of the discharged men lose their positions because of either a lack of understanding or a failure to employ psychology. The personnel department can easily eliminate the technically unfit, but it has difficulty "weeding out" the 65 per cent who are deficient in social understanding.

The Importance of the House Organ or Factory Magazine. By sponsoring a factory publication the personnel department is better able to maintain the morale and cooperation of the employees. After all, there are millions of men and women whose literary ambition would be satisfied by finding their names in print, which explains the wide popularity of the "Personals" column.

When Mr. Lee, cited in Chapter VII, endeavored to increase the sales of Protectographs, his $100 prize to the salesman breaking the previous high record was probably not as strong a motive as the fact that a picture of the winner and his family appeared in the company's magazine. These photographs, like the actress's glowing publicity write-ups, are filed away in the family archives for possibly half a century thereafter.

But there are more important aspects of the house organ than the one just mentioned. The management has an opportunity therein to present an educational program concerning the various functions of its many departments, thereby orienting the employee. The chief executives can talk *via* the printed page directly to the men whom they might never otherwise have an opportunity to meet. Explanations of the new policies introduced by the company or of the reasons for wage cuts may be made. Because they are put into the house organ, the employee's wife also gets a chance to see the management's side of the argument without being dependent solely on her husband's interpretation. In short, the house organ enables the management to speak to the wives of its employees, as well as to its workers. The house organ, however, should be in the main an employee paper apart from the dominance of the management, although two or three pages may be left weekly or monthly for information and editorials from the executives of the firm.

House organs may be simply a mimeographed page or pamphlet sent out to salesmen, or they may consist of more elaborate proportions and format. Fashions, recipes, humor, sports, editorials, children's pages—these are some of the features which make them more attractive to the entire family. It must be remembered, moreover, that thousands of families in every great industrial organization buy no magazines whatever, so the factory publication holds great potentialities, as we shall elaborate in the next section.

From the psychological standpoint, therefore, the house organ is of considerable value in the development and maintance of morale among the employees. By enabling the management to speak directly to the wives of the latter, it not only increases the influence of the executives, but may often in consequence lessen conflicts between employer and employee. In its broader social and educational significance, the management may slowly change the attitudes of thousands of its workers and their families.

Cultural Responsibilities of Employer to Employee. Throughout this textbook we hold to the view that the progress of civilization as it affects human beings demands that "they may have life and have it more abundantly." This has been the principle behind our public school system. With this basic philosophy of society the role of management takes on tremendous significance. Two-thirds of all the people in the United States never go beyond grammar school, and ten per cent of all boys between the ages of 10 and 15 years are out in the business world engaged in some gainful occupation. The adults of America in the majority of cases depend on a grammar school training and the newspapers for their intellectual stimulation.

After the age of 16 years, one-third of all our citizens leave the control of the school teacher and go under the control of an employer who dominates their time for at least 40 hours each week. No other person or institution is in such a commanding role regarding the majority of our people. The educational possibilities entailed in the function of management are consequently great. For example, at the same time that the employer is directing his workers he may also be stimulating them to better and fuller thinking. Political ideas, social and moral conceptions, a liking for art, music, and literature, these are some of the things for whose cultivation he is chiefly responsible. Since for almost 40 years he stands before a less educated group of men and women as the dominant figure, if our civilization is to progress most rapidly we must enlist the employer class in the interest of education.

The truly efficient school teacher in the 10 years that she stands before our people does more than simply teach arithmetic, grammar, history and geography. Her personality is brought to bear upon the task of encouraging a *liking* for cultural subjects, not just the mechanical acquisition of them. In a similar fashion, the employer who stands for 40 years before his workers should do more than give them their pay checks. He can teach morality and honesty, temperance and respect for law, even the liking for books and music by his attitudes and encouraging statements. Through the medium of the house organ, moreover, he can slowly improve the home conditions of his workers and the health of their children. The Americanization of the foreign born, and the protection of our highest ideals of government are, therefore, as truly his responsibility as they are those of the teachers and clergymen.

REFERENCES

Achilles, Paul S., (Editor), *Psychology at Work* (New York, 1932).

Bingham, W. V., "Engineering Aptitudes," *Occupations,* 1935, vol. xiv, pp. 197-202.

Bingham, W. V., and Davis, W. T., "Intelligence Test Scores and Business Success," *Journal of Applied Psychology,* vol. viii (1924), pp. 1 *ff.*

Burtt, Harold, *Employment Psychology* (Boston, 1926).

Ellis, Robert S., *The Psychology of Individual Differences* (New York, 1929).

Feder, D. D., "An Evaluation of Some Problems in the Prediction of Achievement at the College Level," *J. Educ. Psychol.,* 1935, vol. xxvi, pp. 597-603.

Freyd, M., "The Graphic Rating Scale," *Journal of Educational Psychology,* vol. xiv (1923).

Griffith, C. R., *Introduction to Applied Psychology* (New York, 1934).

Griffitts, Charles H., *Fundamentals of Vocational Psychology* (New York, 1924).

Harrington, H. F., and Martin, L., *Pathways to Print* (New York, 1931), chap. xiv.

Hepner, Harry W., *Psychology in Modern Business* (New York, 1931), chaps. vii, ix, x, xi.

Hepner, Harry W., *Human Relations in Changing Industry* (New York, 1934), pt. iii.

Hersey, R. B., *Workers' Emotions in Shop and Home* (Philadelphia, 1932).

Hollingworth, H. L., *Judging Human Character* (New York, 1923).

Howard, D. T., "The Personnel Department," chap. xvi of R. A. Kent's *Higher Education in America* (Boston, 1930).

Hurlock, E. B., and Jansing, C., "Vocational Attitudes of Boys and Girls of High School Age," *J. Genet Psychol.,* 1934, vol. 44, pp. 175-191.

Husband, R. W., *Applied Psychology* (New York, 1934), chaps. v to xii.

Jenkins, J. G., *Psychology in Business and Industry* (New York, 1935).

Jenness, A. F., "The Recognition of Facial Expressions of Emotion," *Psychological Bulletin,* vol. *xxix* (1932), pp. 324-350.

Kingsbury, F. A., and Crennan, C. H., (Editors), "Psychology in Business," *Annals of American Academy of Political and Social Science,* vol. cx (1923) No. 199.

KNIGHT, F. B., "The Effect of the 'Acquaintance Factor' Upon Personal Judgments," *Journal of Educational Psychology,* vol. xiv (1923), pp. 129 *ff.*

KORNHAUSER, A. W., "The Psychology of Vocational Selection," *Psychological Bulletin,* vol. xix (1922), pp. 192 *ff.*

KORNHAUSER, A. W., AND KINGSBURY, F. A., *Psychological Tests in Business* (Chicago, 1924).

LAIRD, DONALD A., *The Psychology of Selecting Men* (New York, 1927).

LAIRD, D. A., *More Zest for Life* (New York, 1935).

LAUER, A. R., *Manual of Tests for Automotive Operators* (Ames, Iowa, 1934).

LINK, HENRY C., *Employment Psychology* (New York, 1919).

METCALF, H. C. (Editor), *The Psychological Foundations of Management* (New York, 1927).

MOORE, B. V. (Editor), *Readings in Industrial Psychology* (New York, 1931).

MOSS, F. A., *Applications of Psychology* (Boston, 1929), chaps. xii, xvii.

ODENCRANTZ, L. C., "Occupational Therapy and the Placement of the Handicapped in Industry," *Occup. Ther.,* 1935, vol. xiv, pp. 189-196.

OMWAKE, KATHARINE T., "The Value of Photographs and Handwriting in Estimating Intelligence," *Public Personnel Studies* (Jan., 1925), vol. iii, No. 1, pp. 2-15.

POFFENBERGER, A. T., AND VARTANIAN, V. H., "Letters of Application in Vocational Selection," *Journal of Applied Psychology,* vol. vi (1922), pp. 74 *ff.*

SCOTT, WALTER DILL, AND CLOTHIER, R. C., *Personnel Management* (New York, 1923).

SEASHORE, C. E., *Vocational Guidance in Music,* University of Iowa Monographs (1916, First Series), No. 2.

SNOW, A. J., "Labor Turnover and Mental Alertness Test Scores," *Journal of Applied Psychology,* vol. vii (1923), No. 3.

————, "Intelligence as a Factor in Labor Turnover in the Taxicab Industry," *Industrial Psychology,* vol. i (1926), No. 6.

STENQUIST, J. L., "Vocational Interests, Ability and Aptitude," *Yearb. Nat. Soc. Stud. Educ.,* 1935, vol. xxxiv, pp. 435-445.

STRONG, E. K., JR., "Interests of Men and Women," *J. Soc. Psychol.,* 1936, vol. vii, pp. 49-67.

TEAD, ORDWAY, AND METCALF, HENRY C., *Personnel Administration* (New York, 1920).

VALENTINE, P. F., *The Psychology of Personality* (New York, 1927).

VITELES, MORRIS S., *Industrial Psychology* (New York, 1932), section ii.

CHAPTER X

THE PSYCHOLOGY OF MUSIC AND MORALE

Music is one of the least tangible products which can affect the human sense organs, yet it is also one of the most effective. Although it is fleeting, while we experience it we may be led to high resolves or passionate action. Shakespeare has said,

> The man that hath no music in himself,
> Nor is not moved with concord of sweet sounds,
> Is fit for treason, stratagems, and spoils.

Evidences of musical instruments are found among the remains of almost every early people and primitive tribe. But ancient music of the best sort was far different from that of modern times. The ancients had not learned the wonderful effect which can be obtained by simultaneously sounding several notes that "chord". They had no harmony, but produced only the melodies or simple tunes. Moreover, they knew nothing about key, failing to appreciate the facts which even the young beginner learns today. It was not until the year 1600 A.D. that the first real opera and the first oratorio came into existence, while the beginning of the eighteenth century really marks the birth of most music as we know it now.

Too many children as well as adults, however, are today developing the idea that music is the bizarre product of a gilded derby hat hung over the end of a trumpet, the mouthpiece of which is being blown by an individual who appears to qualify admirably as a contortionist. Our public schools cannot alone devote sufficient time to the musical development of the child, so his fundamental tutelage in melodic patterns should come from the home.

It is gratifying to parents and teachers to realize that musical ability, and especially musical appreciation, need not be considered as inherited talents. Aside from the necessity of having normal hearing and an extraordinary larynx if he hopes to become an outstanding vocalist, the average person can be taught good music or jazz. His tastes will be largely a result of his environment.

Conradi[1] found that even young English sparrows, when reared by canaries, developed trills and a fair imitation of canary song. In the passage below we find his observation of one of his subjects.

> On September 26, when the sparrow was a little over three months old, he was for the first time observed to give a trill. It was short and musical and was given a number of times in succession. These short trills were at first only rare but they increased in frequency during the year. When he gave them he would sit still on his perch and give them one after another very modestly. Now (Dec., 1904) he gives short trills interspersed with other notes, punctuating the whole by turning complete circles and semi-circles on his perch.
>
> None of these sparrows ever had the characteristic call note of the wild species, but by and by adopted those of the canary. They imitated the canary perfectly except that their voice did not have the musical finish.

It is interesting to speculate upon what would result if all the adult sparrows were suddenly to be annihilated, and their eggs placed in canary nests. Would the sparrow's chatter depart forever from the earth? It would seem quite possible to invest the new generation of sparrows with the language of the canary, much as the immigrants take on the speech of their new country, and drop the old. But the practical value of Conradi's work lies in the fact that if the raucous chirping of English sparrows can be moulded into melodic sweetness by the canary environment during the infancy of the former, then it seems rather logical for us to expect our far more intelligent boys and girls, men and women, to react favorably to an environment rich in good music.

[1] Conradi, E., "Song and Call Notes of English Sparrows When Reared by Canaries," *American Journal of Psychology* (1905), xvi, p. 197.

The Place of Music in Building Morale. If we stimulate a child's imagination to noble deeds and high resolves at the same time that we expose his ears to a specific piece of music, and if we continue doing this on several subsequent occasions, the music will eventually cause him to think and act in an idealistic fashion even though we are no longer present to incite his imagination with words. This is simply the phenomenon of the conditioned reflex. We react hilariously or religiously not so much because of the tempo of the music and its particular melody, but because of the conditioned habits that have become attached to it. Indeed, in medieval times a writer of a mass would simply pick out a popular melody to which he fitted his religious utterances. Some of these melodies, such as *The Red Noses* and *Farewell, My Lover,* later gained sacred connotations. The reversal of this process is observed in the parodies of religious music which we often hear.

Parents and teachers who early capture the child's fancy in a web of melody are able to weave into the fabric of that young personality a cultural morale which will buoy up his spirit throughout all the years ahead. Indeed, the effect of music in building morale has been of marked historic significance. The Jewish nation during the captivities sustained its hope by the psalms which were sung to a musical accompaniment. The *Marseillaise* has lifted the spirits of muddy, bedraggled French legions from defeat into victory. In fact, it has inflamed the soldiers so violently that there have been times when its use has been forbidden.

In Revolutionary days *Yankee Doodle* kept the weary colonial troops in step and served as a rallying song for flagging hearts. And during the days before the Civil War the American Negro escaped the misery of his unhappy lot, in a partial degree at least, through his folk songs. Even so thorough-going a realist as Marshal Foch declared during the

World War that morale is more important than material. An ancient tale of Greece corroborates this viewpoint. When Sparta, hard pressed by its enemies, sent to Athens for aid, the Athenians did not want to succor their sister state, for they were jealous of her power and hoped that she would be defeated. Fearing to refuse outright, however, they sent as their representative the poet Tyrtaeus, a man of music and not of action. Tyrtaeus, however, composed ringing martial songs under whose inspiration the Spartans gained a great victory, much to the surprise and chagrin of the Athenians.

It seems quite probable that wars could not continue without music, which serves as an auditory stimulant to the emotions and submerges psychical fatigue. Even in industrial life it serves to eliminate the ennui that results from monotonous work. Music is offered employees through the medium of amplified phonograph records and radios, with beneficial consequences. Since much industrial work becomes so routine that it does not occupy the workers' full attention, music serves as a melodic escape by which their thoughts may dwell on pleasanter things. An occupied mind is usually a contented mind; hence, music by serving as an outlet for surplus cerebral activity, lessens industrial unrest and dissatisfaction.

From the psychological standpoint, therefore, the chief functions of music in building morale consist first of all in serving as an objective stimulus for re-arousing former emotional states. As a consequence of these re-aroused emotional states, the individual usually feels more excited and energetic. The simultaneous release of adrenaline with its accompanying increase in blood sugar places the human organism on a war basis physiologically. A second value of music in morale is its capacity to occupy the unused attention of workers in industry, and thereby reduce their boredom. The third factor has national significance, for the leaders of a crowd realize that the individuals will react emotionally as they did during the learning of the music. Thus, *The Star Spangled Banner* will instantly unify in emotions and thought the listeners who have come up through the American public schools.

Jazz vs. Classical Music. In talking about good music we refer not alone to those products of the old masters, such as Beethoven, Gounod, and Rossini, but also to many of the pieces which we hear from our better popular orchestras. After all, the criterion of musical excellence is not sheer complexity of architectural pattern, for *Old Folks at Home,* though fairly simple in this regard, holds all the essential elements of a perfect art form. But classical music is usually of the complex kind, and is therefore considered a more "intellectual" type of music. There are certain fairly obvious reasons for the greater "wearing" qualities of classical music.

First of all, its mechanics is not so apparent; hence, the listener's curiosity is stimulated for a longer period of time. The central theme or motif of classical music is interwoven with sub-melodies, so that it might be compared to a rail fence covered with beautiful vines, in contradistinction to a single strand of barbed wire that we shall liken to jazz. Classical music, moreover, is akin to poetry in that it attempts to portray a number of emotions with an artistically developed climax. Jazz is simple and adapted for the feet. Because it usually is accompanied with verses, we are able to daydream along trains of thought set up by the romantic suggestions of the words, and consequently are less aware of the early monotony that otherwise results from the melody itself.

In the realm of poetry we are appreciative of this same difference in regard to metrical feet. Note the greater singsong monotony of the first of the two following quotations in contradistinction to the second.

1. Mary had a little lamb.
   Its fleece was white as snow.
2. Strongly it bears us along on swelling and limitless billows,
   Nothing before and nothing behind but the sky and the ocean.

After a few repetitions of the first pair of lines we are tired of them. We can repeat the second set of lines two or three times as often without noting a similar degree of fatigue and ennui. Usually the dactylic hexameter is well suited for majestic compositions, which explains its use in Latin and Greek epic poetry. In this connection Gilliland and Moore performed a very interesting experiment to determine if equal boredom and dislike would result from hearing both classical and jazz music repeated twenty-five times. Four phonograph records were employed in the experiment and always played five times daily in the following order:

A. Beethoven's Fifth Symphony, First Movement.

B. Tschaikowsky's Sixth Symphony, the "Pathétique", First Movement.

C. Fox-trot—"That's It—A Fox-Trot."

D. One-step—"Umbrellas to Mend."

The complete experiment consisted of the five successive playings at five different periods, making a total of twenty-five hearings of each. The subjects were practically unacquainted with all four pieces. Only three of the college men ever remembered hearing either of the classical numbers, and only four felt that there was anything familiar about either of the two jazz pieces. At the first trial the experimenters had their subjects rate the four musical numbers on a ten-point scale of enjoyment value. At the conclusion of the whole experiment the students again rated the four pieces using the same scale. The first and last ratings are given below:

	FIRST	LAST
A.	5.88	6.09
B.	5.60	6.94
C.	5.00	4.91
D.	4.37	4.50

The experimenters' conclusions follow: "The first is that since the strongly marked rhythm of street music has such an immediate stimulating value, it is important to select as our first music for the child or the musically immature, pieces that have a strongly marked rhythm, as well as melodic, harmonic, or structural merit. It is the rhythm that will first get the child's spontaneous attention, and the other musical values will gradually unfold themselves to him as he hears the selection repeatedly. The second conclusion is that since good music apparently tends to develop interest when it is heard repeatedly with an unprejudiced mind, it is important not to inject any moral controversy into the matter of appreciating music."[1]

The chief psychological difference between jazz and classical music, therefore, lies in the fact that the latter is less monotonous because of its greater complexity, and because it usually develops a structural climax of a more imposing sort than is found in jazz. Because of the fact that verses frequently accompany the jazz melodies, the monotonous effect of the latter is not so apparent as otherwise would be true, for the listener may be reveling in daydreams set up by the sentimental words and thus pay less attention to the tune. To either type of music, however, may be conditioned habits of merriment or sorrow and gloom, dependent of course upon the emotional state of the person when he first became familiar with the given melody. Much of the Italian's pleasure in opera which he hears in America is comparable to an American's pleasure in hearing *My Country 'Tis of Thee* in Moscow, namely, its resurrected sentiments of home and parents and other loved ones. The structural merit of the music is probably of less concern to either in contrast to these conditioned emotions.

Music and Emotional Conditioning. Every reader knows that when certain musical pieces are played, he remembers old sweethearts, when others are heard, he recalls school days' experiences, while another group of songs carries him

[1] Gilliland, A. R. and Moore, H. T., "The Immediate and Longtime Effects of Classical and Popular Phonograph Selections," *Journal of Applied Psychology* (1924), vol. 8, pp. 309-323.

back to recollections of his mother, or a church, or maybe a funeral. To the melody of one song have become attached the emotions which he felt when he first learned it, or which he underwent repeatedly as he listened to it. The reader may hum or whistle a stanza of *The Star Spangled Banner,* and find a peculiar emotional state returning which, upon analysis, may involve recall of a schoolroom, a particular teacher, flag day exercises, soldiers marching, and many other former experiences. Frequently he has forgotten the specific childhood scenes but retained only the emotions to which they gave rise. Now hum *Nearer My God to Thee,* and note the marked change in emotions. At the completion of a stanza, change to *Love's Old Sweet Song,* and follow this with *Dixie.*

One of the differences between language and music is the fact that words tend to be specific in their symbolism, whereas music is non-specific. Despite our individual differences in the conditions under which we learned "lamb chops", we are much more nearly alike in our reactions thereto than we are in reacting to *Marqueta.* Moreover, the word "beefsteak" may re-arouse our memories of "lamb chops", but *Dixie* can never re-arouse our emotional memories that have been conditioned by *Marqueta.* Emotions are not subject to recall, therefore, even though they are subject to re-arousal by their specific stimuli.

The fact that words accompany the melody aids greatly in setting the thoughts of the listener into the desired patterns. Since music is a non-specific form of symbolism, an entirely new melody leaves us rather unaffected during its initial rendition. If we can drift away into a dreamy sentimental mood because of its saccharine verses, we may begin to enjoy the piece the first time. Otherwise, our enjoyment must await the process of conditioning in which pleasant emotional states that were produced by our companions and the situation, become attached to the particular melodic pattern. This conditioning is similar to that by which a child learns to like or shun spinach, except that music tends to have more emotional experiences connected with it since we usually encounter it in exciting social situations.

Because strange music neither arouses old memories nor causes a concerted participation in its rendition, the minister who selects hymns which are unknown to a large percentage of his audience is making more uncertain his chances of influencing them by his sermon. The real function of music, from the speaker's standpoint, is to weld his audience into a unified whole and assure that similar emotions are re-aroused. The sooner he can get the cooperation of action and of thought of his assembled parishioners, the easier it will be for him to give an effective address. The school teacher, chorister, and voice instructor may profitably train their subjects to sing new pieces, but the minister, public speaker, politician, and propagandist should seldom attempt this task.

In concluding our discussion of music and emotional conditioning, we might say that except for its rhythm there is probably little intrinsic pleasure in music for the child who first hears it, but it soon becomes clothed with definite emotional significance, particularly if the music is heard in the same general situation each time during the learning period. The verses which accompany much popular music help speed this emotional conditioning. Music with verses written or sung in a foreign tongue, however, as opera, is slower in winning favor with the masses.

The Educational Potentialities of Music. For too many people music is looked upon simply as something to which they can dance. Music has conditioned their feet to the actions of shuffling, but has left their minds relatively unaffected. It is largely for this type of person that jazz has been evolved.

These persons have never been taught that the notes themselves have a language of their own. They need to join the classes of alert youngsters who have been pleasantly initiated into the game of picking out the bird calls in Beethoven's *Pastoral Symphony.* We should let them hear the rumble of thunder and the sharp lightning flashes of the storm in Rossini's *Overture to William Tell,* or let them test their interpretive capacities on the tonal dialogue in *The Sorcerer's Apprentice,* Paul Dukas' adaptation of Goethe's ballad.

Moreover, music can become an emotional outlet of great value to the child, even before he outgrows his adolescence. Here is Larry Benson, for example, a neighbor high school lad who comes home from a basket ball defeat feeling irritable. He sits down at the piano, and the first chords which he strikes are fierce, loud, and vindictive. Martial music surges from the strings, and the listener feels that war is imminent. But after a time the music undergoes a transformation. It becomes more calm and subdued, and may finally pass over into some rollicking songs of youth.

In this instance Larry has vented his feelings *via* the music, and his emotional catharsis has cleaned out his ugly mood, leaving him in a much more friendly state of mind. His younger brother and two sisters have also been saved from probable irritable verbal attacks, for youngsters, like adults, are prone to project their ill will upon their weaker associates.

But the principal educational significance of music lies in the fact that the conditions under which we learned a piece tend to be resurrected in our memory when we later hear it. Governments rely on this fact when they get out the bands in time of war and strike up some of the stirring martial airs which they know all citizens have experienced in their grammar school days. They know that loyalty to the fatherland, a desire to protect home and mother, and a hallowed regard for the integrity of the country will be stirred into activity more quickly than if they sent skilled orators into our midst. A combination of fiery speech on top of musically inflamed emotions is almost certain to produce the desired action.

Emotions, however, can be utilized in the interest of peace

and creative enterprises. We can condition children to unselfishness when we present certain songs to them until eventually the music itself will suggest those same attitudes. Note the emotional reaction to "Silent Night." And because music cannot be debated verbally, it is an especially powerful weapon to employ. It is always operative as suggestion; therefore, the most intelligent people have difficulty evading its emotion-arousing action. There is only one way to combat music and that is to use music in rebuttal. We cannot argue against the mood which is resurrected when one of Sousa's marches is being played by the band. But we can set rival bands to playing, and cause an emotional impasse to result. Those interested in peaceful adjudication of international disputes may more profitably spend their money and vocal energy on "peace bands" and blowing the cornet than on haranguing crowds while military music is still audible on the horizon.

In yet another way, we may employ music to the profit of the individual and the race. It is not necessary that men and women be motivated to dancing behavior when music is played. They may, instead, be conditioned to thinking. Rather than indulging in sentimental "jags", they may engage in creative thought. A certain prominent inventor states that he gets his cleverest ideas while reclining on a couch listening to music. Since the erotic moods may be sublimated into great poetry or art, as we have many examples to bear witness, those same moods when re-aroused by certain melodic patterns, can also, if so trained, be led into creative thinking.

The chief function of music, however, will probably always remain an emotional one. It serves as an escape from the unpleasantries of mundane existence, permitting us to flee to a make-believe world. The task of parents and teachers, therefore, consists of conditioning the child so that in this make-believe realm he does not indulge solely in emotional reveling and erotic debauchery, but diverts his emotional impulse into constructive channels.

In respect to the educational potentialities of music, therefore, we may conclude by stating that they pertain chiefly to the energy which is released under the revived emotions which are conditioned by the music. This energy can be sublimated into constructive thinking as well as into dancing over a ballroom floor, depending upon the previous training of the individuals. Since much of the poetry and art of the world has been evolved because of the emotional fervor of the poet and artist, it is possible to re-inflame a temporarily sluggish mind, much as the weary soldier's gait is speeded up, by appropriate melodies and thereby produce energy and incentive for creative thought. In addition to this educative potentiality of music, there is also the mental exercise occasioned in observing the portrayal of emotions by means of melody.

The Role of Music in Propaganda. Propaganda means essentially the spread of a particular doctrine without the hearers' immediate recognition of the source or motives behind the doctrine. It is apparent, therefore, that propaganda employs suggestions, for in so doing it avoids the possibilities of debate, conflict, and resistance. Whenever it can appeal to sentiments, it does so. The difference between sentiments and ideas consists chiefly in the fact that sentiments have an emotional coloring. Thus, the word "house" represents an idea whereas "home" is an example of a sentiment, for it has a host of emotional memories fastened to it, as Edgar Guest's poem so well illustrates.

We have just pointed out that music cannot be combated by words. It leads to no angry debates. The subject is practically helpless when exposed to music, for he does not realize what is going to happen to him and cannot check the revival of old emotional states when their stimulus is offered. We were not conscious of the emotional ties when they were originally being fastened to the given musical piece, so it is almost impossible for us to focus upon them now. And the average citizen does not even make the attempt.

Since the aim of propaganda is to develop or re-arouse sentiments and then suggest action, music becomes one of its best tools. It is a short cut to action, eliminating a more lengthy reasoning process. Even in a religious meeting, for example, it becomes a quicker method of increasing the offering than does speech. A man or woman who is "cold" emotionally can more quickly be aroused by an appropriate melody than otherwise.

During the World War we saw the utilization of both art and music in the interest of changing the attitude of a nation which had elected Wilson in November, 1916, on the plea, "He kept us out of war," and then was eager for battle on April 6, 1917, when we declared war on Germany. We have previously pointed out the helplessness of people before a musical attack, and the necessity for developing a counterattack with other music to which the opposite moods and tendencies to action have been attached. Since different moods may also be conditioned to the same melody, however, the propagandist must keep this fact in mind. To *The Star Spangled Banner* and military marches young men and women are usually incited to action that involves marching, cheering, and enlisting. But older women who have watched their husbands, sweethearts, and brothers leave for war to the accompaniment of these same tunes, may react with sadness, avoidance, and pain.

It is theoretically possible, therefore, for the school teachers of a nation to condition their students adversely to the military music of their country so that the adult generation would be helpless in inciting the youth to warfare by means of those military airs. Both the nationalists and the pacifists must accordingly vie for the cooperation of teachers and parents if they wish to condition the present children of the country so they will be warlike or peaceful a generation hence.

Music, therefore, becomes one of the most effective weapons of the propagandist, for it usually encounters no "sales resistance" on the part of the auditors, so it quickly arouses their emotions and renders them more ready for impulsive action. If group singing occurs, they are welded into a unified whole, ready for their leader to propose action. In the following sections we shall discuss some of the other instruments of the propagandist, particularly in the visual realm.

Propaganda vs. Advertising. The advertiser buys space for his message, and the reader knows that he is reacting to a commercial appeal. He can be on his guard, therefore, and employ reason, although suggestive advertising attempts to prevent his doing the latter. Propaganda, however, endeavors to hide its real nature at all times. It comes out as if it is educational matter with no ulterior purpose than the enlightenment of its readers or hearers. But it differs from true education in that the latter aims to present all aspects of knowledge with no hidden political or financial motives behind the process.

Probably because of its uses during the war, propaganda now has an unpleasant connotation. But propaganda may be good or evil depending upon the motive behind it. The political campaigns of a nation, the advancement of religious sects, the militarists and pacifists, these are only a few of the organizations and enterprises which employ propaganda. Indeed, the historical meaning of the word identified it with the foreign missionary work of the Catholic Church, for three centuries ago Pope Gregory XV founded the great Propaganda College to care for the interests of the Church in non-Catholic countries.

In discussing the two great social dangers in propaganda, Dodge[1] says:

> The first is its concentrated power of destruction of the established order. Great destructive power in irresponsible hands is always a social menace. We have some legal safeguards against careless use

[1] Dodge, R., "Psychology of Propaganda," *Religious Education* (1920), vol. xv, pp. 241-252.

of high-powered physical explosives. Against the greater danger of destructive propaganda there seems to be little protection without imperiling the sacred principles of free speech.

The second social danger is the tendency to overload and level down every great human incentive in the pursuit of relatively trivial ends. To become *blase'* is the inevitable penalty of emotional exploitation. I believe there may well be grave penalties in store for the reckless commercialized exploitation of human emotions in the cheap sentimentalism of our moving pictures. But there are even graver penalties in store for the generation that permits itself to grow morally *blase'*. One of our social desiderata, it seems to me, is the protection of the great springs of human action from destructive exploitation for selfish, commercial, or other trivial ends.

The slow constructive process of building moral credits by systematic education lacks the picturesqueness of propaganda. It also lacks its quick results. But just as the short cut of hypnotism proved a dangerous substitute for moral training, so I believe we shall find that not only is moral education a necessary pre-condition for effective propaganda, but that in the end it is a safer and incomparably more reliable social instrument.

Propaganda and advertising employ several similar devices for effecting their ends. Cartoons, for example, are frequently a means of advancing some form of propaganda in much the manner that cuts are useful to the advertiser. Propaganda, like advertising, also appears in the newspapers and magazines, but is frequently designated as publicity. The difference between publicity and advertising is the fact that publicity attempts its purpose without having to pay space rates. The publicity stunts of actresses and actors, for instance, are aimed at gaining a few columns of newspaper space without the necessity of paying therefor. Indeed, in many cases the individuals in question do not dare pay for space, for it is deemed unethical. Publicity, of course, tends to be more effective than paid space matter for the reader is in a more credulous state of mind concerning it. He expects business firms to praise their own products as a matter of policy, but he does not expect outsiders, such as newspaper reporters, to do so unless they are really good. In many instances, the advertiser himself also gains some free publicity in the medium carrying his advertisements. This result is especially likely to follow if there are human interest aspects of the manufac ture or sale of his product, and also if the newspaper is de sirous of retaining his account.

In summarizing, therefore, we may state that propaganda is more secretive than advertising in regard to its source and its purpose. Accordingly, it engenders less resistance, for the public is seldom aware of the propaganda as such. In consequence, propaganda is a great power for good or evil depending upon the organization and motives behind it. As Dodge points out, however, it may partly defeat its own end by an excessive emotional stimulation of the public until the latter becomes blase.

How to Develop Propaganda. Those organizations which depend upon propaganda as a means of guaranteeing their economic stability and continuance have usually created a special department whose function is propaganda, usually called by its less unpleasant title of publicity. We have publicity agents for the members of the stage, for politicians, for universities, for public utility companies and similar businesses. Sometimes the men who function as such bear the titles, "Public Relations Counsellor", "Manager", or "Personal Secretary". The majority of individuals cannot afford to employ special men or women for this task, but must rely upon their own ingenuity in this regard. In Chapter VI we have gone into this phase of publicity rather thoroughly.

Whether the motives behind propaganda are laudable or reprehensible depends upon the particular case and is not for us to decide herein. There are certain laws of propaganda, however, that are fundamental. The writer does not subscribe to Dunlap's views that the following rules "read like a catalog of social shame," for this presupposes that psychological laws are evil, a tenet which we do not hold. We shall cite the six basic laws that Dunlap gives in regard to propaganda.

1. If you have an idea to put over keep presenting it incessantly. Keep talking (or printing) systematically and persistently.

2. Avoid argument, as a general thing. Do not admit there is any "other side"; and in all statements scrupulously avoid arousing reflection or associated ideas, except those which are favorable. Reserve arguments for the small class of people who depend on logical processes, or as a means of attracting the attention of those with whom you are not arguing.

3. In every possible way, connect the idea you wish to put over with the known desires of your audience. Remember that wishes are the basis of the acceptance of ideas in more cases than logic is.

4. Make your statements clear, and in such language that your audience can repeat them, in thought, without the need of transforming them.

5. Use direct statements only when you are sure that a basis for acceptance has already been laid. Otherwise, use indirect statement, innuendo, and implication. Use direct statement in such a way that the attention of the audience shall be drawn to it sufficiently to take it in, but not sufficiently to reflect upon it.

6. For the most permanent eventual results, aim your propaganda at the children; mix it in your pedagogy. Follow the example, in this respect, of Ivory Soap and Prohibition.[1]

To illustrate how propaganda is developed and utilized by industrial and commercial firms, we shall cite an authentic case. The cherry growers and canners in one of our midwestern states had a large crop and much canned goods of which they were unable to dispose. They were faced with a considerable financial loss. A newspaper man from St. Louis evolved the scheme of conducting a state cherry blossom festival, following the method of the state apple blossom festival already in existence. To this festival, which would be heralded throughout every county in the state and neighboring commonwealths, the governor and members of the state legislature would be invited, and a beauty contest would be staged

[1] Dunlap, K., *Social Psychology* (The Williams & Wilkins Co., Baltimore, 1925), p. 256.

at which time the most attractive girl present would be crowned Queen of the cherry blossom festival.

The growers and canners agreed to the newspaper man's proposal provided he could line up enough publicity men around the country for the later phase of the problem. He proved his ability by showing a long itinerary with cooperating organizations all along the route. The cherry blossom carnival was staged and it was a great success locally. The Queen was chosen. To Chicago she went, accompanied by the proper cortege. Her publicity director had already made contact with the publicity department of one of America's greatest railroads. The latter gladly cooperated in the venture since it meant opportunity for its railroad to gain some free advertising. The Queen, gracefully draped on the observation platform of a famous passenger train, would make a lovely picture, especially if the name of the train or the railroad could also show in the photograph.

Since the Cherry Queen of a neighboring state was visiting Chicago, the newspapers could be enlisted in the project. The railroad office arranged for the pictures. To make the people "cherry conscious" and also whet their appetites in that regard, some views were later shown of the girl presenting a huge cherry pie to the mayor. The railroad offered her free transportation anywhere it had a train, so she headed for New York. Another pie was presented to its mayor, after which she called upon governors, and finally even obtained an audience with the President, presenting him with one of her enormous pies. If any newspapers were hesitant about participating in the scheme, they soon became willing when they learned that some paid advertising was to follow.

But not all propaganda is so subtle. Even though the following paragraphs are blatant in their directness, they may still be considered a form of propaganda, for the editor's great love for the "worthy middle classes" seems a mask for ulterior purposes. The editorial occupied a two-column box on the front page. We are quoting only part of what Hearst has to say. When we consider the chain of newspapers which he dominates, we are glad that there are still sources for dissemination of information besides his papers, and that the immigrants and school children do not depend upon him alone for their respect for government. Is it any wonder that foreigners with a slight capacity to read English have little aversion to violating our laws and laughing at government? The only commendable feature about the editorial is that Hearst[1] becomes polysyllabic; hence, he talks over the heads of some of his ignorant and subnormal readers.

INCOME TAX SYSTEM HAS BECOME
GREATEST RACKET IN THE U. S.

To the Editor of The Chicago Herald and Examiner:

Please carry on sustained crusade morning, evening and Sunday against the present Bolshevist system of income taxation.

The income tax system has become the greatest racket in the United States and the government the biggest racketeer.

The system is in itself unjust, inequitable and un-American. It paralyzes enterprise and penalizes honesty.

The rich evade the tax, the poor escape it and practically the whole burden of oppressive taxation is borne by the worthy middle classes.

* * * * *

Does anybody benefit?

Yes, indeed—a standing army of snoopers, gougers, collectors, extorters, tax lawyers and dodgers, ex-government officials with a pull and incumbent officials with open minds.

To support these gentry in ease and affluence is what the tax is for.

Your fellow citizens are exploited, your business prostrated, your country plundered to encourage excessive governmental extravagance to support an unnecessary and dangerous bureaucracy, and to make a burdensome despotism out of our free democracy.

* * * * *

There are two great historic failures and political evils which this country can indelibly engrave on the blackest pages of its record.

[1] Hearst, William Randolph, "Income Tax System Has Become Greatest Racket in U. S.," *Chicago Herald and Examiner* (March 13, 1932).

One is the wholly ineffective and un-American policy of prohibition and the other is the inequitable, tyrannical, Bolshevistic policy of confiscatory income taxation.

Both are IGNOBLE experiments resulting in nothing but damage, demoralization and disaster.

When the Democratic party has the sincerity to be Democratic, when it has the patriotism to be American, it will substitute excise taxation and sales taxation for undemocratic, un-American discriminatory income taxation with its crooked evasion and equally crooked enforcement.

The essential steps in the development of propaganda, therefore, consist of presenting the ideas in the form of suggestions, and then repeating them whenever possible. Dunlap's six rules are an excellent formula in this regard. A seventh rule should state that whenever music can be utilized, the process becomes easier. Songs may be written whose verses are propaganda itself, in which case the public will often do the repeating for months or years thereafter, and thereby help spread the propaganda at little further cost to those behind it.

How to Combat Propaganda. It is quite probable that the man who could best see through the sleight of hand tricks of a great magician like Thurston would have been Houdini. In short, the best way to see behind the illusions and pleasing display to the mechanics underlying them would be to gain a mastery of the technique involved in producing those same illusions and propaganda. Dunlap had this in mind when he dedicated his rules of propaganda not to the propagandist but to the public on whom propaganda is employed. The unfortunate situation in respect to propaganda is the fact that emotions are stimulated whenever possible, so that even the intelligent person is frequently caught off his guard, and stampeded with the less discerning. Moreover, the development of new "tricks" are likely to fool those who are skilled in detecting all the old ones.

There are about 18,000 daily, semi-weekly, and weekly newspapers in the United States disseminating information

PRESIDENTIAL ELECTIONS	CHANGE IN PERCENTAGE OF VOTE POLLED BY REPUBLICAN PARTY	PRESIDENTIAL ELECTIONS	CHANGE IN PERCENTAGE OF VOTE POLLED BY REPUBLICAN PARTY
1856-1860	6.8	1892-1896	8.3
1860-1864	15.2	1896-1900	0.8
1864-1868	2.4	1900-1904	4.7
1868-1872	2.7	1904-1908	4.8
1872-1876	8.1	1908-1912	1.0
1876-1880	1.0	1912-1916	1.0
1880-1884	0.1	1916-1920	14.2
1884-1888	0.4	1920-1924	6.5
1888-1892	5.2		

EXHIBIT 50. Showing the change in percentage of the vote polled by the Republican party. (Rice).

which is usually colored by the dictates of the personal, political, or financial predilections of the publisher, and the exigences of the advertising and political situations in the respective communities. According to Kent[1] about three-fourths of all the county press is straight Republican, while the other 25 per cent is Democratic. These two print media serve as partial checks upon each other's propaganda. Unfortunately, few readers subscribe to both papers. But these few are probably a large percentage of the shifting voters who determine the ultimate victor in an election, since the majority of people do not change from the political affiliation of their parents. In this regard Rice[2] has shown the fluctuation in the percentage of votes polled by the Republican party during the last three-quarters of a century. His data are contained in Exhibit 50, and demonstrate only two cases where the change was over 10 per cent.

The popularity of the radio and the 10,000 to 15,000 moving

[1] Kent, F. R., *The Great Game of Politics* (Doubleday, Page & Co., Garden City, N. Y., 1923).

[2] Rice, Stuart A., *Quantitative Methods in Politics* (Alfred A. Knopf, Inc., New York, 1928), p. 304.

picture theaters in the United States shows what forces for moulding public opinion are resident therein. The minimum patronage of the latter is estimated at 3,000,000 people daily, with 5,000,000 being more nearly the truth. There are, in addition, more motion picture projection machines in operation outside of theaters than in them. Professor Ernest W. Burgess some years ago summarized the observations of 3,237 teachers of more than 100,000 school children, and concluded that 50 per cent of the children were affected by the movies, which ranked third in influence upon their lives, as the following order will show: (1) the home; (2) the school; (3) the movies; (4) the church.

Even the news reels may be "colored", either by means of captions, speaking, or by the selective process by which one phase of a situation is shown, and others ignored. In the war pictures that were permitted to reach the American theaters in 1917 and 1918, the doughboys were consistently pictured in happy roles, eating, playing baseball, grinning, fondling pets and French orphans, or dancing with petite French girls. The bleeding eyeless sockets of those blinded by shrapnel, the violent contortions and gasping for breath of the dying gas victim, and the rotting arms and legs and heads of boys who had been blown apart were, of course, censored.

Before the introduction of the "talkies", it was possible for the meaning of any film to be altered simply by a clever rearrangement, cutting, and rewriting of the captions and titles. Today those who write the lines spoken by the moving picture performers can also inject propaganda into the films. From general psychology we have learned the ease with which illusions can be created. If the announcer in the movie tells us to note the surly behavior of a foreign crowd when an American arrives, we have a mental "set" thereafter for anything that fits the idea of surliness, and may misconstrue innocent actions and behavior which are characteristic simply of a curious crowd. If we are told that an approaching lion is stalking its prey, we see ferociousness and cruelty in every move of the beast, even though he is a toothless pet in a California zoo, gamboling playfully after his trainer. International hatred or goodwill likewise can be materially influenced by the announcers who describe travelogue pictures. In order to show how the same print matter may be used in behalf of diametrically opposed courses of action, we shall quote a Democratic and a Republican editorial cited by Strong[1], which appeared during the presidential campaign of 1920. The Democratic editorial ran as follows:

"Mother of America! Mother of Pennsylvania! Mother of Pittsburgh! Do you want your boy to go to war? Is the roll of battle drums sweeter in your ears than the song of his voice in the home? Would you rather have his hands in fierce grip on gun in battle's rack than have his arms in love about your neck? That is the question you must answer to your God and your fellow-man when you go into the voting booth on November 2. Do not let demagogues confuse you. The issue is plain: A vote for the league is a vote for peace; a vote against the league is a vote for war . . . Mother of an American boy! The munition makers of the world are arrayed against American participation in the League of Nations. They are snatching at your vote, because with it they may claim the body of your first-born. Mother of a Pittsburgh boy! The question comes home to you! Your boy was not born to be food for guns."

The Republican advertisement stated in part:

"Women! For your own good vote the Republican ticket . . . The American woman asks of her country: That it be a secure place for her home and for her children and that it be security with honor. That it give her children opportunity to lead their lives even better than she and her husband led theirs. That it be just in its relations with other nations, and merit the pride which the best of its citizens have in it, in its history and its ideals. A policy which has these purposes will have the support of American policy and has been Republican policy from the days of Abraham Lincoln. The Republican policy is to protect the security of the United States by preserving its

[1] Strong, E. K., "The Control of Propaganda as a Psychological Problem," *Scientific Monthly* (1922), vol. xiv, pp. 234-252.

right to make decisions regarding its action in the future as events in the future demand. The Republican party is unwilling to pledge now that it will protect European boundary lines and to deprive Congress of the power to say in each case what the action of the United States will be . . . "

In combating propaganda we can rely in part upon its own limitations. Professor Dodge[1] has so clearly delineated these that we shall quote him in this regard.

There are three limitations to the processes of propaganda that we have been considering. The first is emotional recoil, the second is the exhaustion of available motive force, the third is the development of internal resistance or negativism.

The most familiar of the three is emotional recoil. We know only too well what will happen if we tell a boy all the things that he likes to do are *"bad"* while all the things that he dislikes are *"good."* Up to a certain point the emotional value of bad and good respectively will be transferred to the acts as we intend. But each transfer has an emotional recoil on the concepts good and bad. At the end a most surprising thing may happen. The moral values may get reversed in the boy's mind. Bad may come to represent the sum-total of the satisfactory and desirable, while good may represent the sum-total of the unsatisfactory and undesirable. To the pained adult such a consequence is utterly inexplicable, only because he fails to realize that all mental products are developments. There is always a kind of reciprocity in emotional transfer. The value of the modified factor recoils to the modifying factor.

The whole mechanism of the transfer and of the recoil may best be expressed in terms of the conditioned reflex of Pavlov. The flow of saliva in a dog is a natural consequence to the sight and smell of food. If concurrently with the smelling of food the dog is pinched, the pinch ceases to be a matter for resentment. By a process of emotional transfer on being pinched the dog may show the lively delight that belongs to the sight and smell of food. Even the salivary secretions may be started by the transfigured pinch. It was the great operating physiologist, Sherrington, who exclaimed after a visit to Pavlov that at last he understood the psychology of the martyrs. But it is possible to so load the smell of food with pain and damage that its positive value breaks down. Eating values may succumb to

[1]Dodge, R., *op. cit.*

the pain values instead of the pain to the eating values. This is the prototype of the concept bad when it gets overloaded with the emotional value of the intrinsically desirable. The law of recoil seems to be a mental analogue of the physical law that action and reaction are equal and in opposite directions.

The second limitation to propaganda occurs when the reciprocal effects of transfer exhaust the available motive forces of a mind. Propaganda certainly weakens the forces that are appealed to too often. We are living just now in a world of weakened appeals. Many of the great human motives were exploited to the limit during the war. It is harder to raise money now than it was, harder to find motives for giving that are still effective. One of my former colleagues once surprised and shocked me by replying to some perfectly good propaganda in which I tried to tell him that certain action was in the line of duty, to the effect that he was tired of being told that something was his duty, and that he was resolved not to do another thing because it was his duty. There seems to be evidence that in some quarters at least, patriotism, philanthropy, and civic duty have been exploited as far as the present systems will carry. It is possible to exhaust our floating capital of social motive forces. When that occurs we face a kind of moral bankruptcy.

A final stage of resistance is reached when propaganda develops a negativistic defensive reaction. To develop such negativisms is always the aim of counter-propaganda. It calls the opposed propaganda, prejudiced, half truth, or as the Germans did, "Lies, All Lies." There is evidence that the moral collapse of Germany under the first of our paper bullets came with the conviction that they had been systematically deceived by their own propagandists.

As for legal control of propaganda, we encounter so much of the latter which is intangible and not specifically stated that it is impossible to restrain it as the *Printers' Ink* Statute curbs dishonesty in advertising. Moreover, by word of mouth it spreads rapidly, so we often are unable to ascertain the origin of the rumors and whispering campaigns which are frequently heard. When large corporations with unlimited wealth enter upon a propaganda campaign they employ experts to conduct it, and stay within the technical statement of the law. Those alert citizens who may be aware of the mechanics and motives behind the apparently innocent publicity and legislation are frequently bought off. The process of silencing an opponent is not done so blatantly as to be offensive. It may be as subtle as the propaganda campaign itself.

Suppose that Professor Brown, a specialist in the field of public utilities, is to make a report to Congress at its next session on the subject of governmental ownership. If a large holding company fears his possible censure, one of its executives is likely to take Professor Brown to dinner, and say:

> "Professor Brown, we have been intensely interested in your economic research during the past few years in the field of public utilities, and feel that it would be desirable for us to have a man of your scholarly insight and scientific ability on our staff. We do not want to take you away from pedagogy, if you feel an aversion to leaving the teaching field, but should be happy to have your valuable criticisms and advice in the role of economic consultant."

No mention would be made of the future report to Congress, for the public utilities executive realizes that men will feel hesitant in reporting adversely concerning the companies from which they are receiving large retainer's fees. This method of silencing the opposition is simply a bit more subtle than the obvious gift of automobiles, stock, or cash. Some of the experts in the employment of large industrial concerns are hired to prevent rival companies from getting them, or to check their unfavorable testimony before juries and legislatures. If this method were confined only to the commercial field, it would not be so pernicious, but our universities are frequently subverted from their inherent obligation to offer both sides of a question with scientific impartiality. A public utility company will make a "gift" of $50,000 to a university for research in its field. There are no strings attached to the bequest, so the professor conducting the investigation is theoretically free to report the facts as he finds them. Actually, however, he may go through a psychological change, and fail to observe certain things that would be detrimental to the company paying for his survey.

The chief safeguards, therefore, by which we may hope to obtain protection from pernicious propaganda are: (1) a thorough training of youth in honesty and morality; (2) a thorough training in the technique and laws of propaganda; (3) counter propaganda; (4) freedom of speech and of the press; (5) an endowed, impartial press and radio; (6) bureaus of information, like the U. S. Bureau of Standards.

Utilizing Advertising in the Interest of Morale. During the economic debacle following the crash in the stock market in 1929, the continued advertising campaigns of such firms as General Motors, the cigarette trade, and the soap and food manufacturers not only exercised a wholesome influence by retarding the rapidity of onset of the depression, but blazed the way for more rapid recovery therefrom. Independent business organizations spent money on full page newspaper and magazine advertisements pointing out the folly of becoming panic-stricken, and re-affirming the virtues and basic economic stability of this country.

The newspapers themselves aided this movement by donating pages for advertisements whose sole function was the encouragement of the public concerning the fundamental integrity of American business. Economists and financial experts cautioned and advised the public with reference to stocks and bonds. Banks spent millions of dollars advertising themselves in an effort to bolster the public's waning faith in such institutions.

In times of social need it is also a laudable custom for American business firms to donate space in which the copy explains the nature or virtues of another organization coming before the people with a drive for funds. The Red Cross and Boy Scouts have been frequently afforded such courtesies and assistance. But retail dealers have also performed an admirable social service in the small country towns. It has been customary there for the merchants to unite and rent a moving picture projection machine and films so they may hold a show on one or two nights each week during the summer months. A screen is frequently stretched across the main street. No charge is made to the farmers and their families who fill the street during the movie.

As a variation of the above procedure, in those towns that have a little movie house, the merchants may rent it, and hold their program inside. To cite a specific case, in Covington, Indiana, a county seat of 2,500 population, the merchants pay $55 for the use of the local movie house, machine, operator, and films for an entire day—Wednesday. Any farmer or townsman is entitled to a free ticket for his whole family to see the show if he makes a purchase during the day at any of the stores cooperating in the venture, and practically every merchant is participating. The theater remains open until all have seen the movie.

This type of advertising is of social benefit as well as financially profitable. The average contribution from each merchant is approximately $1.00 yet there have been as many as 1,800 people who have seen the show in one day. Farmers drive in with their entire families, and the poor folks in the town who could not afford a movie from one year to another are given tickets to enjoy this weekly treat. Farmers' children who have never seen a moving picture show before are given an opportunity to watch the antics of Mickey Mouse and other comic characters, and their parents enjoy first class plays. The writer saw a picture in this little theater which he had seen in one of Chicago's finest theaters only a few weeks before. The plays presented are high grade "talkies" of the same sort as those for which Chicagoans pay 50 and 75 cents. In some small towns the merchants rent the theater for two successive days, and entertain the public accordingly, since the cost to the retailers for the second day is relatively small.

In discussing this type of advertising with one of the Covington merchants the writer was pleased to hear him say:

"Although it pays for itself financially, it would be worth a dollar a week to most of us just as a combination toward improving the morale of the community. These farmers work hard, and haven't enough ready cash to take their families to a show. Prices of crops are low, and much of the land is mortgaged. The farmers and their wives now come in here in the afternoon or evening, and know that they have a good time awaiting them.

"They see a picture that would cost them $2 or $2.50, counting all their children, and have a chance to forget their troubles. We try to have a good comedy each week and a first class main picture to go along with it. They are entertained in the regular theater of our town, and accorded the same courtesy as if they were paying for their tickets.

"We issue them tickets with their purchases. They present these at the door. If the theater is full, they line up on the sidewalk and wait for the next showing. To some of the poor people from down along the river we give tickets whether they buy or not. They need some sort of amusement, you know."

Whenever advertisers can render such services to the public, as well as sell them worthy merchandise, they are doing a two-fold good. Since it is essential that people receive a certain amount of amusement and relaxation, advertising can often give them this without detracting from its primary purpose. Indeed, the improved morale may even increase buying.

The Relationship of Morale to Success. We have previously mentioned Marshal Foch's statement that morale is more important than materials. In maintaining a victorious army made up of various races, many of which did not even speak the same tongue, Hannibal also demonstrated his realization of the significance of morale. He instituted boxing, wrestling, and gladiatorial combats to keep up the martial spirit of his troops when they were passing through the Alps en route to Rome. In the recent World War we saw a similar appreciation of the importance of morale, and concerted effort to produce it. Moreover, the sales conventions to which manufacturers are willing to bring distant salesmen and pay their expenses are held for the sake of increasing the enthusiasm and confidence of the sales force. Enthusiasm, confidence, and hope are vital factors not only in war, and business, but in medicine as well. The patient who believes in his physician, or is confident that he will get well, is much more likely to do so. The man who gives up, who admits defeat, is beaten before he commences.

In London some years ago an experiment was performed with five soldiers to determine the influence of their mental state upon their physical strength. They gripped a dynamometer as hard as they could to register their maximum handgrip strength. For the five men the average was 101 pounds. Then they were hypnotized, after which they were told that they were very weak and feeble. They were again given the dynamometer and told to grasp it as strongly as possible. Their average now was only 69 pounds. Then they were given the opposite statements, namely, that they were powerful, Herculean, after which their average strength of handgrip was 140 pounds.

Several important conclusions may be drawn from this experiment. In the first place, a negative thought, such as a feeling of failure or defeatism, leads to marked lessening of physical strength. On the other hand, a positive thought leads to more than average strength. The belief that they were strong actually increased their physical strength almost 40 per cent above their normal capacity, while the belief that they were weak reduced their strength 30 per cent below their best normal record. Although we can probably never attain such a concentration of attention in the focal circle during our normal state as in the hypnotic trance, we tend to go in the direction of the 140 pounds or the 69 pounds when we are respectively confident or fearful of defeat.

The football team, the business man, and the salesman are more likely, therefore, to attain success when confident than when afraid, provided they do not ignore other necessary requirements for victory, such as adherence to training and attention to details. The overconfident football team does not go down to defeat because of this mental attitude, but because it is careless and has avoided the severe training periods as much as possible, and also because it is running against another team which is likewise confident.

Every factor which equips a boy or girl with beneficial habits is thereby eliminating just so many occasions for lack of confidence later in life. We have previously explained that confidence is in large measure a matter of habit. The story of Half-Way Hurley illustrates this point. But physical health also aids in the development of a victory morale. The weary, sick, or enfeebled persons are not sure of themselves and aggressive. They stand back to let the virile individual go ahead, and give way before the counter attacks of customers, debaters, and opponents of all sorts.

Education is also of marked value in building a winning morale. The college man and woman have the advantage over the non-trained person not only in the possession of more book knowledge but especially in the self-assurance and poise which come with knowing that they have at least been "exposed" to all the advantages and information that their associates have received. The non-college man and woman may occasionally be better educated than their collegiate neighbors but lacking the college training, they do not know that they are, so they step aside in deference to the fearless behavior of the college folks. Part of the benefit of a college training is the realization of what our opponents do not know, for we feel that as a general rule they do not possess any educational equipment which we do not also have. This attitude enables the college students to attack a new problem with the feeling that they have at least a 50-50 chance against anybody. The non-college people tend to feel that they have perhaps but a 25-75 chance.

The buoyant influence of music in building a winning morale has been treated heretofore in this chapter when we mentioned that the singing of the *Marseillaise* had at times been forbidden because of its inflammatory effect upon the soldiers. And in industry as well as in the home we find that music can produce happiness and pleasure, both of which reactions are conducive to a feeling of confidence.

Although the person with a defeatism complex may occasionally succeed because of some clever idea or a "driver" at home who forces him into the battle constantly, the man who possesses a winning morale, a confidence in himself, coupled with an intelligent appreciation of the difficulties which beset him, is far more likely to win the coveted rewards of life and ultimately leave this stage with a confident smile for whatever may lie ahead. The development of this type of spirit is one of the functions of education and a duty of parents and teachers in general.

REFERENCES

Adler, M. J., "Music Appreciation: An Experimental Approach to Its Measurement," *Archives of Psychology* .(1929), No. 110.

Bernays, E. L., *Crystallizing Public Opinion* (New York, 1923).

Brownrigg, Rear-Admiral Sir D., *Indiscretions of a Naval Censor* (London, 1920).

Colby, M. G., "Instrumental Reproduction of Melody by Pre-school Children," *J. Genet. Psychol.,* 1935, vol. 47, pp. 413-430.

Creel, G., *How We Advertised America* (New York, 1920).

Dodge, Raymond, "Psychology of Propaganda," *Religious Education* (1920), vol. xv, pp. 241-252.

Doob, L. W., *Propaganda, Its Psychology and Technique* (New York, 1935).

Gilliland, A. R., *Genetic Psychology* (New York, 1933), chaps. x, xi.

Gundlach, R. H., "Factors Determining the Characterization of Musical Phrases," *Amer. J. Psychol.*, 1935, vol. 47, pp. 624-643.

Hoppock, R., *Job Satisfaction* (New York, 1935).

Jersild, A. T., and Bienstock, S. F., "Development of Rhythm in Young Children," *Child. Developm: Monogr.,* 1935, No. 22, pp. 97.

Kent, F. R., *The Great Game of Politics* (Garden City, N. Y., 1923).

Larrabee, H. A., "The Formation of Public Opinion Through Motion Pictures," *Religious Education* (1920), vol. xv, pp. 144-154.

Larson, W. S., "Measurement of Musical Talent for the Prediction of Success in Instrumental Music," *Psychological Monographs* (1930), vol. 40, pp. 32-73.

Lasswell, H. D., *Propaganda Technique in the World War* (New York, 1927).

Lippmann, W., *Public Opinion* (New York, 1922).

Lipsky, A., *Man the Puppet* (New York, 1925).

Lumley, F. E., *Means of Social Control* (New York, 1925).

Mason, D. G., *The Dilemma of American Music* (New York, 1928).

MEYER, M. F., "The Musician's Arithmetic. Drill Problems for an Introduction to the Scientific Study of Musical Composition," *University of Missouri Studies* (1929), vol. iv, No. 1.

MURSELL, J. L., "Measuring Musical Ability and Achievement: a Study of the Correlations of Seashore Test Scores and Other Variables," *Journal of Educational Research* (1932), vol. xxv, pp. 116-126.

REDFIELD, J., *Music, a Science and an Art* (New York, 1928).

ROBERTS, H. H., "Melodic Composition and Scale Foundations in Primitive Music," *American Anthropology* (1932), vol. xxxiv, pp. 79-107.

SALMON, L. M., *The Newspaper and Authority* (New York, 1923).

SEASHORE, C. E., "Vocational Guidance in Music," *University of Iowa Monographs* (1916, First Series), No. 2.

————,*Psychology of Musical Talent* (Boston, 1919).

SEASHORE, C. E., "Psychology of the Vibrato in Voice and Instrument," *Univ. Ia. Stud. Psychol. Music,* 1936, vol. iii, No. 317, pp. 159.

SPAETH, SIGMUND G., *The Common Sense of Music* (New York, 1924).

SPAETH, S. G., *The Art of Enjoying Music* (New York, 1933).

STRONG, E. K., "The Control of Propaganda as a Psychological Problem," *Scientific Monthly* (1922), vol. xiv, pp. 234-252.

SWARD, K., "Jewish Musicality in America," *J. Appl. Psychol.,* 1933, vol. 17, pp. 675-712.

WHITELEY, P. L., "The Influence of Music on Memory," *J. Gen. Psychol.,* 1934, vol. 10, pp. 137-151.

WOLSELEY, R. E., "Manufacturing Chicago's News," *All Chicago* (July 9, 1932), pp. 13 *ff*.

CHAPTER XI

THE PSYCHOLOGY OF THE PUBLIC PLATFORM

Because of the widespread dissemination of information through the press, magazines, and books we tend to overlook the fact that public speakers are still the persons who teach all of our school children for at least ten years. Moreover, the clergymen of America are each week giving speeches before millions of men and women. Since the advent of the radio it is now even possible for a single speaker to address an audience of millions, so the effectiveness of the public address is conceivably greater than ever before, and it has always been tremendous. William Jennings Bryan, an inconspicuous Congressman from Nebraska who came as simply an alternate delegate to the Democratic national convention at Chicago in 1896, stood before that great mass of delegates and, though only 36 years of age, swept them off their seats with his oratory and was immediately acclaimed their nominee for the presidency of the United States. This is one of the best examples of the power of oral speech in all history, and shows the influence of the public address in contrast to an equal exposure to print.

The person who stands before an audience either in the role of entertainer or as speaker encounters many of the same problems which are of difficulty to the salesman, and his methods of attack are also similar to the latter's in many respects. There are, however, certain differences that exist between people in a crowd and people treated singly, which warrant special consideration. We shall discuss them in the following sections of this chapter.

How to Weld a Crowd into an Audience. When the leader stands before a group, he is dealing with people who may have been thinking a thousand different thoughts. The women may be wondering if they forgot to turn off the water in the kitchen, or if the maid has started putting Johnny to bed yet, or what they are going to have for dinner the following night when guests arrive. The men may be wondering if they should not have put on the parking light when they left their automobiles, or if they locked the rear door, or what they are going to do about a business problem that is coming up for discussion the next morning. Meanwhile there is a buzzing of conversation over the auditorium, or the turning of pages of programs, hymn books, or leaflets.

Fortunately for the performer, he knows that the group has come together because of at least one common purpose, which may be the observation of a movie, the inspection of a play, or the hearing of a speech or musical program. This common bond is responsible for their being present. They are, therefore, like those persons who have returned an advertiser's coupon—they have demonstrated an interest in the performance. They form a "warm" market for his ideas or entertainment. Even before the leader addresses the group, however, there are a number of devices by which he can unify the crowd into a more wieldy audience.

(1) *The lighting.* A church, theater, or lecture room should be brightly illuminated while the audience is assembling, for the mood of the audience is more cheerful as a consequence and this mental state is beneficial to the entertainer. It is easier to sway a cheerful audience than a lugubrious one. Moreover, the members have been favorably affected even before they enter the auditorium, for a brightly lighted building suggests many people, which in turn suggests success, popularity of the idea or program. People react with a feeling that a program is good or bad partly on the basis of the number of others who are, or appear to be, present. Persons who visit a theater which is only half full when the curtain rises have already obtained the impression that the show must be a poor one. A well lighted auditorium also enables the

spectator to view the crowd surrounding him, and assists in creating the social unity which we shall explain under the second point.

In moving picture theaters and candle-lighted churches the darkened auditoriums may be a mechanical or psychological aid to the type of program being offered, but darkness has the effect of introverting people through depriving them of outside stimuli. Fear and awe are more readily developed in darkness, therefore, than in light, so programs whose aim is to frighten and thereby coerce the audience can profitably be given with reduced illumination. A seance, a Hallowe'en party, or a lodge initiation would be much less impressive if conducted under flood lights.

Since fear tends to produce introversion with a resulting awareness of ourselves, the speaker should usually avoid attempting to frighten his audience, and, instead, keep their interest and attention fully upon himself. He may reduce the illumination in the auditorium proper without unpleasant reaction if he keeps a brilliant spotlight upon himself and the other performers, or if he throws a clear picture upon the screen. In such cases, the reduced illumination in the audience is of merit in welding the crowd into a unified and stage-polarized audience, for it prevents a continuance of the distractions of page turning and is also instrumental in causing the eyes of all present to seek the source of light in front. Stage trained audiences instantly grow quiet and focus upon the front of the theater as soon as the lights grow dim. Thoughts no longer are heterogeneous, but become homogeneous. There may be such a hushed expectancy that the ticking of a watch becomes apparent. The skilful performer accentuates this tension by deferring his entrance for a few seconds.

(2) *The seating arrangement.* When people are seated in alternate chairs, or whenever there are large blocks of empty seats between individuals, the latter become more individualistic and self-conscious. They are impressed subtly or con-

sciously with their isolation, and therefore offer a more difficult problem to the speaker than the same persons would if they were rubbing elbows. As long as they are self-conscious, they feel responsible for their actions, and are more introvertive. It is more difficult for them to assent to propositions that are placed before them by the leader. They do not even laugh as readily at his attempts at wit. But when they feel themselves a part of a great throng, they gain an impression of strength and irresponsibility.

We think it makes little difference what we do if there are enough of us doing it, for we feel that a crowd cannot be punished. Therefore, we form snake dances down the boulevard, and *en masse* visit theaters and retail stores, demanding free entertainment and goods. As individuals we would never enter upon such action, for we would instantly sense our weakness and personal responsibility. Since we aspire to be strong, we like to feel the assurance that comes from numbers, which possibly explains why we do not want to vote for a candidate who has previously been defeated.

In a crowd, therefore, we can follow the dictates of a speaker or entertainer with little hesitation, for our sense of being one of a group renders us less fearful of consequences. We laugh and cheer and fight with more abandon in groups than when our sense of isolation makes us aware of our own weakness. We are less cautious; hence, we more readily act upon the words and suggestions given to us.

It is advisable for those in charge of the meeting to see that an adequate staff of ushers is available who are instructed to keep the people seated close together. Many attendants at public gatherings and church are timid about going forward to occupy the seats near the stage or chancel, and will slip into those near the door unless an usher is present to escort them farther to the front. When following in the wake of the usher however, many people find it difficult to endure the gaze of an audience, so fail to go beyond the half-way point.

Griffith[1] investigated the effect of position within a classroom upon the grades obtained by students, and found that those in the front and rear rows made poorer grades than those in the middle section. These differences, he believes, are not due entirely to the distance from the speaker, but to the students' position with reference to the group. Those on the fringe of the crowd fail to feel that physical compactness and polarization of interest and attention which hold the attention of the majority focussed upon the speaker. In smaller classes where those on the rear rows were no farther away from the instructor than the central body of students in larger rooms, he still found the lower grades obtaining. The reason for the reduced output of the students occupying the front rows is thought to be the fact that they are so close they do not fully appreciate the group spirit of the crowd behind. Moreover, their attention is likely to be caught by irrelevant details of the speaker's manner of delivery, his dress, or minor characteristics of the apparatus on the platform.

(3) *The auditorium.* Everything in the meeting hall that causes a feeling of isolation or separation of sub-groups and individuals from the speaker and the other members of the audience will tend to render the group less suggestible and therefore more difficult to weld into a polarized whole. The persons sitting on the aisles do not feel the sense of social solidarity which others react to who are seated in the middle of the section. Moreover, those people who happen to be unable to see the speaker because of intervening pillars or the large hats or heads of persons seated immediately in front of them, are inclined to become restless and inattentive. A number of such persons scattered through an auditorium reduce the degree of concentration upon the stage of others who are seated in their vicinity.

A room with a low ceiling is, moreover, conducive to a

[1] Griffith, C. R., "A Comment Upon the Psychology of the Audience," *Psychological Monographs*" (1921), vol. xxx, No. 136, pp. 36-47.

greater feeling of compactness and informality. People will laugh more easily therein than when placed in an auditorium with a high vaulted dome. The speaker consequently finds it necessary to be more direct in his delivery. Flights of oratory are not only more difficult for him to make, but are not accepted so readily by his hearers. People expect talks of less majestic sweep in such rooms, and do not look for the pompous manners and oratory of the loftier type. Although a skilful speaker may captivate their attention and ultimately lead them into imagery of the latter variety, he does it at a greater effort for the suggestive influences around them do not contribute to this end.

The clergyman who has utilized a theater in holding noon Lenten meetings not only senses the change in feeling tone and the effect of the environment, but his auditors are also vaguely aware of the difference. A large part of this result is traceable to the habit of hearing religious themes discussed in churches instead of commercial auditoriums, but the suggestive effects of crucifixes, choir lofts, painted windows, and hymn books are also lost in the theater setting. It requires a better speaker to influence a group religiously when outside of a church than when inside. Indeed, many clergymen when they grow older and less inclined to do the difficult work of planning and preparing an effective address are disposed to rely on more painted windows, carvings, crucifixes, music, candles, black clerical vestments and semi-darkness as aids in impressing their hearers, and consequently let the excellence of their sermons degenerate. They do not fully appreciate this fact until they give an address in a radio studio where they are deprived of all these crutches, or chance to deliver a sermon in some bare little chapel at a summer resort.

Chautauqua lecturers find that crowds housed in a large tent are rather easy to influence, especially in regard to political, educational, and entertainment programs. There is a general feeling of pleasure and good cheer prevalent in such a gathering. Perhaps the transitory nature of the canvas auditorium contributes largely to this result, for we know that people are more carefree when their surroundings suggest instability. The social revolts during the years subsequent to the World War are traceable to a similar effect, while the converse of this type of influence is demonstrated in the massive stone fronts of our banks and financial institutions. Tents are conducive to a feeling of social solidarity and a chummy attitude. The differences in caste system are considerably eliminated therein, for rich and poor are thrown into closer physical contact.

(4) *The ritual.* Whenever people begin to act together they are vividly impressed with a sense of social unity. These two factors, a sense of social unity and a community of interest, are the basic axioms of crowd psychology. Our discussion of lighting, seating, and auditoriums has been chiefly directed to showing how the social solidarity of the group can be increased through attention to these factors. The use of ritual advances a step farther in the polarization process, for it involves common motor responses. By ritual we refer to other than just fraternal rites. The hymns and liturgy of the church, the national anthem and other songs used to begin a political meeting, and the singing of popular verses thrown on the screen in the moving picture theater may be looked upon as ritual. Even the cheering and applause following humorous initial sallies of the speaker or chairman may be so regarded. Cheering and applause are of especial value in welding a crowd into a unified whole, for they audibly convince each member that he is surrounded by many others with the same community of interests and feelings.

(5) *The speech or performance.* The person who strikes at fundamental issues, hitting the bull's-eye with his appeals, is obviously going to rivet the attention of his hearers upon himself. The slow, roundabout opening will seldom polarize an audience. Description alone, without a previously created

suspense and conflict, is usually monotonous. If the speaker is not going to attempt a humorous beginning, but intends launching upon his address immediately, he should be sure first to catch the attention of his group by some such devices as those to be recounted in later sections of this chapter.

The Psychological Functions of the Chairman. The chairman of a meeting is not supposed to employ his position as a means of advertising his own virtues. The example of the politician who spent almost all of Bryan's time between trains discussing his own political prowess and haranguing the audience on his own desirability for re-election is the antithesis of a good chairman. Instead, the chairman must perform the following functions:

(1) *Polarize the audience.* This may involve telling a few humorous stories, especially if the main speaker has a serious subject which renders it difficult for him to preface his remarks with levity. In all cases, however, the chairman should remember that he should perform his function as quickly as possible so that the main speaker may begin his address. It is better to have no chairman at all than one who leaves the audience restless, bored, and fatigued when the principal speaker stands up to address it. As a rule the chairman should confer with the speaker who is to follow, so that he may learn the nature of the latter's remarks. As a result, he can make his comments relevant and pave the way for the main address. Some chairmen carry the audience in the wrong direction during the few minutes in which they stand before it, thereby placing an additional burden upon the speaker or performer.

(2) *The chairman should build up the prestige of the speaker or performer.* We have previously discussed the influence of prestige in rendering people suggestible. If a man is an authority and has written books or has occupied exalted executive and political positions, he experiences less difficulty in persuading his public when the latter knows these qualifications. The chairman, therefore, should act as a publicity agent

for the principal speaker, for he can tell all of the prestige-building facts about the speaker without making the listeners antagonistic.

(3) *The chairman should act as buffer when audience and speaker are known to hold opposing views.* In such delicate situations the chairman, by his dignified and fair-minded comments and behavior, can produce greater courtesy and open-mindedness on the part of the audience. By discreetly praising the auditors upon their scientific attitude, which involves hearing both sides of every proposition, he can force the audience into politeness by causing each one to feel intellectually complimented as long as he renders courteous attention to his opponent's remarks.

(4) *In parliamentary and executive meetings the chairman should expedite the passage of worthy measures before the group.* To do so he must studiously avoid irrelevant discussion and keep away from demagoguery. The emotional behavior of various members must be curbed in so far as possible by a dignified manner on the chairman's part, and by occasional humorous sallies that relieve the tension. The chairman should not degenerate into simply giving recognition to one speaker after another, as a switchboard operator, but should exercise directive influence upon the course of discussion.

One of our most successful business leaders, who functions constantly in one directors' meeting after another in the role of chairman, explains his rare ability to expedite the business before the group by saying: "Whenever a man proposes a motion which I feel is irrelevant or unwise I do not criticize the motion at that time, for its propounder is so definitely tied up with his proposal that my comments would be taken as a personal affront, and an emotional conflict would result, with his friends on one side and mine on the other. Instead, I tell the group that the new proposal certainly warrants a full consideration and ask that a committee be appointed to look into it more fully. During the intervening weeks or months until the ensuing meeting, I see that the fallacy of the proposal is understood. When the committee reports adversely upon the measure, therefore, its authorship is practically forgotten, and an emotional conflict is avoided. Indeed, the author of the motion may be glad that his name has tactfully been omitted when he hears an impartial listing of the pros and cons."

Professor Lew Sarett recommends another skilful maneuver for producing the action desired by the chairman. It consists of an appreciation of the fact that there are usually a certain number of neutral voters in every group who have little preference one way or the other. They are, however, entitled to cast their ballots. They will be influenced by what they think is the consensus of the group, and are inclined to vote on the first question put by the chairman. It is wise, therefore, for the chairman to see that the motion is propounded so that the first vote taken is on the side which is more desirable. If necessary his friends may be discreetly "planted" in the group, and by having them respond vigorously when the question is put to the crowd, he can capture the bulk of the disinterested voters. We presented Rice's data in the preceding chapter to show what a small change in vote caused defeat or victory of the Republican party during the past three-quarters of a century. In a group of 100 voters arranged equally on the two sides of a proposition, we must keep in mind that a shift of only 17 votes will give one side a two-thirds majority.

When the vote is by a show of hands the chairman can further aid the desirable cause by a vigorous and positive upward thrust of his own hand as he calls for the vote. Crowds respond to suggestion more easily than individuals. A class of students will react to the movement of their instructor's hands rather than to his words. If he tells them that at a given signal they are to drop their uplifted hands upon their desks, he may produce the desired action without giving the signal simply by dropping his own hand vigorously. Certain children's games have been based on this phenomenon.

Sometimes, too, the chairman may anticipate proposals by the opposition and have one of his friends make the opposing motion first but in such a way that it demands later amendments because of objectionable features contained therein. If the objectionable features are then attacked by the chairman's friends in a telling manner, he may discredit the opposition so greatly that the neutral group swings to him. A candidate for political office may occasionally do good for his conservative cause by secretly aiding the radical opposition. If the latter's fanaticism and emotional rantings become too intense, they drive all of the conservative element and even many liberals to the polls to vote for the conservative cause.

In the preceding paragraphs we have been showing how the chairman can influence the proceedings of his group. But individual members of the organization may utilize many of these same principles, even without the knowledge or cooperation of the chairman. They may obtain recognition from the presiding officer and put a motion which is just the opposite of what they want enacted. Realizing that the conservative element is against anything proposed by radical members, one of the latter may make a dangerously phrased motion of the sort which, if it were worded a bit differently, would have been offered by the conservative element itself. Some of the conservatives who are sluggish in their reactions may vote against the measure just because of its radical sponsorship. Others who realize that the motion is fundamentally of the sort which they want enacted, may try to amend it so that it is acceptable. There is always likelihood of dissension among the conservative ranks as a consequence.

Holding the Attention by Stage Materials. There are a number of devices by which the speaker can keep the curiosity of his public aroused, apart from the actual contents of his talk itself. These should be relevant, of course, and not so dramatic as to detract from the effect which he endeavors to produce by his address. Charts, graphs, curves, and pictures which he places around the platform or hangs upon the blackboard or wall behind him all serve as attention holding instruments, at least until he has explained them. Even some long columns of numbers exercise a charm over the uninitiated listeners and spectators, although the latter may be averse to mathematics itself. Until we know what those figures mean, they hold our attention. Because the speaker placed them in front of us, we assume they must have some relationship to his address. It is this uncertainty that makes us interested. As soon as we learn that those figures are simply thermometer readings at different points around the United States on a certain July day, they have no suspense value and we may be no longer interested in them.

The chemist and physicist know how much better attention they receive during lectures when apparatus is on the platform, than when the students see nothing that holds promise of a demonstration. The use of living models or real objects and merchandise likewise helps the speaker. The fact that a stereopticon or motion picture machine is set up in the auditorium suggests a "show", so the crowd is in suspense and more attentive to the speaker's words. If costumes are worn by the performer, or queer utensils and weapons are on a table within view, the spectators are also more interested.

Indeed, the simple act of picking up a piece of chalk from the tray beneath a blackboard will instantly heighten the interest of the audience. The speaker may stand beside the blackboard as if just about ready to illustrate his words, and the crowd will wait expectantly. If he fails to justify their hope, but wanders away to the front of the platform, they may begin to grow less interested. He can immediately regain their attention by stepping back to the blackboard. It is possible for a speaker to employ this crude device throughout an entire lecture with definite aid in heightening the attention of his group, and yet never make a mark upon the blackboard. His auditors, of course, grow less responsive to the trick as it becomes repeated several times, but they never fail to react in a partial degree. If the speaker does not enlighten them at the end with a drawing, formula, or phrase they may feel disgruntled, it is true, but they will have heeded his words just the same.

Such stage tricks and materials as we have mentioned above are usually resorted to by the speaker who has not evolved a speech which is interesting in its own right. They are also almost indispensible aids to the expositional speaker. In educational addresses it is more difficult to employ emotional and rhetorical material than in the popular oration. The subject matter is often of such a nature that it does not lend itself to poetical utterances and majestic flights of fancy. Talks about bricks and automobile tires are not as intrinsically thrilling as ardent appeals to arms in defense of liberty, or as breath-taking glimpses into eternity where eons of time are treated as lightly as an hour, and space is limitless.

A word of caution should also be sounded regarding certain actions on the part of a speaker which lessen the interest of his group. Whenever he looks at his watch, a goodly number of his listeners react to the suggestion and do likewise. Although many of these may not heed the time, reacting mechanically throughout, some of the listeners will become aware of it, and thoughts which have been conditioned to 8:45 P. M., or whatever the time may be, will instantly come to mind. The women may begin to wonder about their young children and the men about the parking lights on their automobiles. Even the initial deliberate unfastening of his watch from its chain and the placing of it upon the table in front of him, partially de-polarizes the speaker's audience.

Moreover, whenever the speaker coughs he utters a stimulus which is likely to cause similar coughing responses throughout the crowd. Sometimes an epidemic of such behavior passes over the audience. Even the harsh, rasping tones of a speaker with a sore throat, or the labored utterance in a semi-whisper of the laryngitic patient will act as suggestions for the arousal of throat tickle in the members of the audience, much as a yawn will often lead to a multitude of open mouths.

Holding the Attention by the Manner of Delivery. Since the advent of radio speeches it has become imperative that the orator spend more time studying this phase of public speaking. Over the radio, for instance, he cannot utilize the stage materials mentioned in the previous section, so he is confined to the vocal delivery of his talk and its contents as the sole methods of heightening the interest of his listeners. The matter of increasing the pleasing qualities of the voice is a subject in which we have done very little. Many of the graduates of American schools of speech go forth with voices that are loud enough to reach the listeners on the rear rows of seats, and enunciate clearly, but have very little music in their speech. There is a flat, metallic sameness to their utterances which tends to become exceedingly monotonous, and sounds "artificial".

An interesting voice is one which can hold our attention even when it is speaking an unknown language. Alexander Moissi, the German actor, is a genius in this regard. Indeed, vocal intonation and inflection constitute one of the best ways to hold attention and stimulate interest. The trouble with most of us Americans is that we have schooled ourselves in restraint of our emotions until we are scarcely capable of demonstrating them by the nuances of our speech. Tyro actors and actresses show their amateurishness more quickly through their lack of tonal inflections than in any other quality. When told to portray hatred, they may exclaim, "I hate you!" in tones which are no different from those employed in saying, "I will not go!" When the director orders them to put more expression into their voices, they simply increase the intensity of their utterance, especially of the second word,

"I *hate* you!" Again it sounds almost exactly as "I *will* not go!" They fail to realize that tonal inflection is what the director wants, not variations in intensity. This same error is made by radio performers every day. When the story teller during the children's hour wishes to speak as Bunny Rabbit and then as Mr. Possum, he alters the intensity of his speech but his tonal inflection is almost the same in both instances.

The average American, if he were confined to nonsense syllables or an extinct language, could hardly show us whether he was angry, excited, frightened, or in pain, for he has almost lost the art of expressing feelings by means of nuances of tone. When we wish to express condolence for a friend we say, "I am sorry for you." If it were not for the word "sorry" in our sentence, he would scarcely know it, for our tonal inflection does not convey much to him. A good speaker should be able to say, "Ro ro roro ro ro," and thereby show his feeling of sympathy. If a person cannot inject his emotions and personality into his oral speech, then his utterances have little more effect than if they were on a printed sheet.

The children of this country, therefore, should be encouraged to play with their voices and mimic sounds. They should be praised in their efforts to portray a happy child through the *sound* of their voices; they should be stimulated to do the same in respect to an eager child, a crying child, a brave child, a sleepy child, a grateful child. After an intensive training of this sort they will later be able to utter with adequate expressiveness soft verbal caresses, friendly condolences, tender solace, rollicking gayeties, sober admonition, and caustic diatribe.

At the present time we hear speakers and singers over the radio who may be technically perfect in their enunciation and song, but who do not arouse interest. Then a girl begins singing in a voice which may lack the power and tonal range of the dozen other singers we have just "tuned out", but who possesses what is commonly called a "sweet" voice. We hear her entire repertoire with pleasure. There is more "expression" in her voice, by which we mean the overtones and nuances of inflection are more abundant and pleasing. When she sings or says, "I love you," we are emotionally stimulated. When a dozen others say, "I love you," no responsive chord is struck within us. Voices, like people, may be drab and colorless, or rich and fascinating.

Some people are endowed with vocal organs which are superior to others for speaking and singing purposes. A tenor voice, for example, cannot show the power and ruggedness of the bass. But all voices are capable of modification and improvement. It is said that Tiberius Gracchus, the great Roman orator, kept a slave behind the stage with a pitch pipe which he sounded whenever his master's voice rose too high. During an enthusiastic presentation of his address, the speaker invariably elevates his pitch. A skilful orator can, thereby, introduce suspense and a climax into his oration by means of his delivery, even though his speech has no logical climax. A perfect arrangement, however, consists of a speech which is technically built up to a climax in thought and which is delivered so that the vocal climax coincides with it.

The performer who confronts his audience face to face may also use gesture as an aid in holding the attention of his hearers. The graceful use of his hands may be of considerable importance not only in holding attention through their frequent movements, but also in depicting scenes and in emphasizing his points. The lifted arm in the peroration is a vivid symbol of the suspense of the moment, and almost hypnotizes the audience while it awaits the final movement. The performer, however, must guard against the development of peculiarities of diction and of gesture, for such things may detract from his effectiveness by calling attention to themselves instead of to the ideas for whose increased emphasis or elucidation they have been employed.

Holding the Attention by the Speech Itself. Although we have devoted several pages to the two preceding methods of holding attention, the speech itself should be so constructed that it hits the bull's-eye in its appeal to the hearers. A man may have a non-musical voice and no arms at all, yet he can captivate my attention by telling me that my house is on fire, my children kidnaped, that I have won an automobile, that my stock has gained five points, or that my advice is being sought in the sales or advertising departments of some large company. Pleasing utterance, graceful gestures, and curiosity-provoking stage materials are all desirable aids in public speaking, of course, but a man should have something to say or else all this forensic machinery produces nothing fundamentally valuable.

It is well for the speaker to model his behavior upon that of the salesman who changed his attitude from one of thinking, "How can I sell my product to these people?" to that of, "Why should these people buy my product?" It will be of decided value to the speaker or entertainer to think, "Why should these people spend an hour of their time listening to me?" They do not do it to pay the speaker's salary or flatter his ego. He stands before them to procure these rewards, but they sit before him in order to get what? Upon his correct diagnosis of the answer to this question will depend how accurately he can shoot his verbal shafts at the bull's-eye. He may have other purposes in mind which he expects them to support, but he must constantly keep aware of their basic desires or he will fail to enlist their cooperation.

When an audience begins to go to sleep, the speaker should not censure it for being unappreciative and ignorant. As a speaker it is his task to find out in advance the level of education, the interests, aversions, ages, sex, vocations, and hobbies of his hearers so that he may adapt his address to them in an interesting manner. If he is normally polysyllabic, he should either avoid a monosyllabic crowd, or learn how to readjust to its level of vocabulary and comprehension. He is socially maladjusted when he cannot do so. It is a good motto for every one who aspires to influence people in groups to remember that "An inattentive crowd means an inefficient speaker." There are occasional exceptions, perhaps, but the speaker must not bolster his ego with this thought.

A sleeping audience is usually an indication that the speaker has been employing third degree stimuli in his language, or has failed to show the relationship between what he has to say and the immediate needs of his people. The subject of "bricks" is of no particular interest to me, but it could be made so by showing that a new invention renders possible the production or laying of bricks at only one tenth their present cost, so the city tax rate for paving purposes could be lowered to the degree that I would save $1.13 on my fall tax bill.

The Psychology of Persuasion. In Chapter I we pointed out that it is generally better to coax than to whip people into the desired course of action, and the same principle holds for men and women in crowds. The speaker who verbally fights his listeners almost instantly antagonizes them. When we are hostile to an individual we will scarcely take even his logical advice, and his prestige is so lowered that we react but slightly to suggestions from him. Another axiom to remember in connection with persuasion is that a feeling of fear, pain, or unpleasantness usually results in withdrawal behavior on the part of the subject, while a pleasant emotional state causes expansive or approach reactions.

The speaker, therefore, should endeavor to get the crowd into a pleasant mood, and link it to himself as securely as possible. He should diligently refrain from using the pronouns "you" and "I", replacing them by the editorial "we". If he attempts to criticize, he should by all means include himself with his crowd so that there is no intimation of the "judge" versus the "judged", no "holier than thou" inference.

In joining himself and the crowd he must not throw all formality and decorum to the winds but, like the farmer-politician, should retain his white collar and tie behind his overalls.

This is clearly demonstrated in Paul's defense of himself before the Jewish mob which was attempting to kill him. Although he was both Jew and Roman, Paul skilfully emphasizes his Jewish antecedents and training, and also indicates his importance in social rank among the Jews by reference to the high priest:

> Men, brethren, and fathers, hear ye my defence which I make now unto you.
>
> (And when they heard that he spake in the Hebrew tongue to them, they kept the more silence: and he saith,)
>
> I am verily a man which am a Jew, born in Tarsus, a city in Cilicia, yet brought up in this city at the feet of Gamaliel, and taught according to the perfect manner of the law of the fathers, and was zealous toward God, as ye all are this day.
>
> And I persecuted this way unto the death, binding and delivering into prisons both men and women.
>
> As also the high priest doth bear me witness, and all the estate of the elders: from whom also I received letters unto the brethren and went to Damascus, to bring them which were there bound unto Jerusalem, for to be punished.

Realizing, moreover, that his listeners think in images, and images are always concrete, the speaker must employ specificity—second degree stimuli. He should also capitalize upon the emotional habits of his group, employing words with emotional color like "home" instead of "house". In this connection Scott[1] has the following to say:

> The orator who has welded his audience into a homogenous crowd should never be guilty of attempting to reason with them, for, by the very process of forming them into such a crowd, he has deprived them of the power of critical thinking. He should affirm reasonable things and affirm conclusions which he has come to by processes of

[1] Scott, Walter Dill, *Psychology of Public Speaking* (Noble and Noble, New York, 1906), p. 184. Used by permission.

reasoning, but he should not presume to conduct the crowd through such a process.

Not only do crowds think in images, but a very striking characteristic is the part played by the emotions in awakening the images and the peculiar emotional tone which accompanies them. This might have been anticipated from a study of emotions. Human emotions are always awakened by strong forms of imagery. Logical processes of thought are practically devoid of emotional coloring, while the conclusions reached by primitive man and by crowds are the results of feeling rather than of reasoning.

We have previously discussed the ways by which action is produced. The selling points may be made to outweigh the objections either by shattering the latter through reasoning, or by so concentrating the attention of the group upon the desired course of action that it is temporarily oblivious of the inhibiting ideas. Affirmation and re-affirmation of the "battle cry" or strongest appeals are not only effective in collegiate debate but also in more emotional types of audience. Both methods of producing action, however can be employed simultaneously. Opposing ideas may discreetly be demolished as the desired behavior is praised.

In striking at the fundamental motive bases of the audience, the speaker must vividly keep in mind that self-preservation (covering, food, health, shelter, and money) and sex are scarcely stronger than the desire for ascendance. The audience's ego or vanity is always to be inflated, just as the individual's requires expansion in order for him to be friendly and cooperative. Recalling the statement of Pope that the way to please a man is to compliment him upon the subject in which he wishes to be considered proficient, the reader will appreciate the strategy in Paul's opening words to Agrippa:

> I think myself happy, king Agrippa, because I shall answer for myself this day before thee touching all the things whereof I am accused of the Jews:
>
> Especially because I know thee to be expert in all customs and

questions which are among the Jews: wherefore I beseech thee to hear me patiently.

How the Radio Tests a Speech. Too often speakers get into the habit of depending upon the predisposing influences of the church or other auditorium, and therefore allow their addresses to deteriorate. Before a radio microphone, however, the matter of speaking is reduced to a straightforward presentation of appeals through the words and the orator's tonal inflections. A shallow, emotional address is not only fully brought to its author's attention, but with equal force is made apparent to the thousands of listeners in armchairs scattered around the city and state. If the speech does not ring true and strike directly at the radio listeners' primary interests, they tune out the speaker. Since they are emotionally cold as compared with the crowd which has been wrought up to an emotional level by interstimulation and the physical presence of the speaker, the radio address must be of a superior type.

After a listener's attention has been caught, however, and if he hears the applause of a real audience, often "planted" in the studio, he may become so interested that he reacts almost as if he were present in the amphitheater. He does not entirely lose himself in the speech, nevertheless, for he seldom applauds or joins in the singing and cheering. Aside from a more dramatic opening which strikes at some basic interest of the listener, the radio speech may proceed much like the one administered face to face. The speaker should unite himself and his public and rely upon all the prestige he can muster as a means of increasing the suggestive value of his words. He must, however, curb his emotionalism for radio listeners may be tuning in at any moment in the address, in which case he may appear ridiculous. He can sincerely employ sentiment, but he must be extremely cautious not to slip over the line into sentimentality. The danger of the latter is much more grave in radio speaking than in the direct address.

The Anecdotal Address. The use of anecdotes and suspense in the speech itself is a common factor of almost every address. Illustrations not only make printed and oral material more interesting but they also clarify the more general abstract enunciations. In our quotation from Scott we read that the audience is more like primitive people in that it thinks in a succession of images. As a consequence, the audience enjoys a series of stories. These should be carefully selected, of course, so they may be relevant and capable of advancing the speaker's thought a bit further toward the conclusion.

The clergyman, for example, not only reads his text but usually a passage from the Bible which is narrative in nature. Thereafter he constantly refers to this narrative and reinterprets it throughout his address. The original creation of the parables was undoubtedly in order to heighten the listeners' interest, clearly to demonstrate the more abstract ideas of justice and virtue, and to leave the people with tales which they could easily remember and with whose repetition the underlying principles would again be brought to mind.

The politician employs the same method when he recounts familiar stories about a few of our famous historical leaders. These tales are known to probably every member of the audience, but we adults sit there in almost the same degree of rapt attention demonstrated by our youngsters who are listening to the *n*th repetition of The Three Bears. Like the children, we apparently are waiting to see if the story unfolds as we have always heard it before, or if some new twist is introduced by the narrator. The new twist is never forthcoming but we seem to be possessed of perennial hope.

For the past decade the writer has been analyzing public speeches with reference to the anecdotal type of address and has encountered two men who have built up entire speeches out of anecdotes. These were dovetailed very neatly into a unified structure with simply a few transitional sentences interspersed between each pair. One of these two men was elected a bishop, and his successor, who practised the same method, packed the church auditorium so early that the writer missed hearing him for three Sundays. The people who formed the audience were of the upper class socially, financially, and educationally, so this form of address is apparently quite popular.

It entails considerable reading, of course, and a logical arrangement of the stories so that they form a well-knit structure, but a speech of this kind is easy to deliver, for a few story titles are all that the speaker has to hold in mind. As a general rule, however, it is probably more effective to employ fewer stories and insert more affirmation of basic truths by the speaker. The average audience must be interested and entertained, but it also must be impressed by the speaker's erudition and forensic ability. It craves a few minutes of elevated style and imaginative flights of fancy coupled with some awe-inspiring denunciatory thunder. After it is convinced thereby of the speaker's capacity, he may give them straightforward talking and somewhat less formal subject matter.

In employing anecdotes the speaker may whet the interest of his group by saying, "On the street yesterday I met one of our foremost citizens—I shan't mention his name, for many of you know him quite well—and he told me this curious thing about one of our leading merchants, etc." The use of the subject's name would lessen the curiosity value of the story even though it may prevent many of the listeners from going off on independent trains of thought involving the possible identification of the unnamed person. On the other hand, the giving of the right name of the hero, if the story about him is not derogatory, inflates his ego and therefore tends to make him an ardent admirer of the "new preacher". Next to seeing ourselves mentioned in print we probably desire public recognition of this kind. A speaker who tactfully introduces his parishioners' names into his weekly addresses is ingratiating himself with his constituency at no loss in the effectiveness of his sermons.

How to Manage a Hostile Audience. One of the quickest ways in which to quiet an audience which is already hooting the speaker is for him to lean upon the edge of the speaker's stand and smilingly begin speaking to the people on the front row, narrating some humorous story in a conversational tone as if entirely oblivious of the yelling crowd. Almost invariably those in front begin listening, partly because of their admiration for his lack of concern about his hooting enemies and partly because they do not want to miss anything. This circle of listeners instantly begins to widen. If a few of those in front begin to laugh, then he quickly gains the crowd's temporary attention for the rest of the audience wants to know what is happening and what it has missed.

With apparent unconcern he can slowly increase the intensity of his voice and lead the group gracefully along until he may have so captured it that he can mould it to his own wishes. Nothing angers a badgering crowd more than to be verbally chastised for being unsportsmanlike and ignorant, ill-bred and rowdy. In short, it cannot be clubbed into a courteous attitude although it can be coaxed into one.

If the speaker cannot think of anything humorous to say, he may quiet the crowd, though more slowly, simply by standing nonchalantly and grinning around at his audience. Fighting cannot long continue unless active opposition is encountered. We feel foolish when our rival smiles good-naturedly at us. And those on the front row lack the coercive action of the crowd for they are meeting the speaker face to face where he can recognize them later if he sees them on the street. They feel more individualistic in their reaction to him, therefore, and can seldom retain open hostility very long. A socially intelligent speaker can always depend upon his front rows for listeners, and a nucleus is all he needs in order to quiet his audience.

If the crowd is not yet openly hostile, then the speaker can begin his address at once but should follow practically the same procedure as that outlined above. He should open with either some good humor, and deport himself with dignified nonchalance, or else commend the crowd on its good sportsmanship and scientific attitude in wishing to hear both sides of the question. Since both humor and compliments inflate the egos of the listeners, it does not make much difference which opening he employs. What he is after in both cases is quickly to make the audience feel pleasant and more intelligent. After he has established rapport with the group by a continuation of his compliments and an affirmation of basic beliefs common to himself and his audience, he can slowly begin to turn about in the direction of his talk and head for his real destination. At the outset he goes with the crowd until it feels a sense of social unity with him and drops its intellectual guard, after which he leads the group where he wishes. By employing suggestion he can get his audience to thinking certain ideas without ever putting them into words, thereby freeing himself from possible censure. One way of absolving himself from blame, yet fully presenting his ideas, is the familiar device that follows: "I am not here to try to prove that the prohibition party has given the workingman's wife an auto in place of a scrub board, nor is it my purpose to show that babies in the tenement districts are now drinking milk whereas they used to have only a little sweetened water. I do not come before this intelligent audience of thinking men and women to repeat those old chestnuts about the workingmen who left their pay checks at the saloon and reeled into the voting booths to reelect the brewery candidates who refused to close the saloons to children. No, nor is it my purpose to say a word against those millionaire brewers who laughed at the social worker's requests for funds with which to open milk stations for the babies of the very men whose pay checks they got on Saturday night, etc." In his eulogy of Caesar we see the same technique employed by Mark Antony. Although not permitted to say anything against Brutus and Cassius, he obtained his desired action by suggestions.

Ant. Friends, Romans, countrymen, lend me your ears;
I come to bury Caesar, not to praise him.
The evil that men do lives after them,
The good is oft interred with their bones;
So let it be with Caesar. The noble Brutus
Hath told you, Caesar was ambitious;
If it were so, it was a grievous fault,
And grievously hath Caesar answer'd it.
Here, under leave of Brutus and the rest,
(For Brutus is an honorable man,
So are they all honorable men),
Come I to speak in Caesar's funeral.
He was my friend, faithful and just to me:
But Brutus says, he was ambitious;
And Brutus is an honorable man.
He hath brought many captives home to Rome,
Whose ransoms did the general coffers fill.
Did this in Caesar seem ambitious?
When the poor have cried, Caesar hath wept;
Ambition should be made of sterner stuff;
Yet Brutus says, he was ambitious;
And Brutus is an honorable man.
You all did see that on the Lupercal
I thrice presented him a kingly crown,
Which he did thrice refuse. Was that ambition?
Yet Brutus says, he was ambitious;
And, sure, he is an honorable man.
I speak not to disprove what Brutus spoke,
But here I am to speak what I do know,
You all did love him once, not without cause;
What cause withholds you, then, to mourn for him?
O judgment! thou art fled to brutish beasts,
And men have lost their reason.—Bear with me;
My heart is in the coffin there with Caesar,
And I must pause till it come back to me.

First Cit. Methinks there is much reason in his sayings.
Second Cit. If thou consider rightly of the matter,
  Caesar hath had great wrong.
Third Cit. Has he, masters?
  I fear, there will a worse come in his place.
Fourth Cit. Mark'd ye his words? He would not take the crown.
  Therefore 'tis certain, he was not ambitious.
First Cit. If it be found so, some will dear abide it.
Second Cit. Poor soul, his eyes are red as fire with weeping.
Third Cit. There's not a nobler man in Rome than Anthony.
Fourth Cit. Now mark him; he begins again to speak.
Ant. But yesterday, the word of Caesar might
  Have stood against the world; now, lies he there,
  And none so poor to do him reverence.
  O masters! If I were dispos'd to stir
  Your hearts and minds to mutiny and rage,
  I should do Brutus wrong, and Cassius wrong,
  Who, you all know, are honorable men.
  I will not do them wrong; I rather choose
  To wrong the dead, to wrong myself, and you,
  Than I will wrong such honorable men, etc.

The Psychological Formula for an Effective Speech. A truly effective speech must rest upon the bed rock of a polarized, crowd-conscious group which has accepted the speaker as a friend. The address itself must contain ideas that are presented with a wealth of sensory qualities by which the hearers can develop concrete imagery. These ideas must also be vital; they must be related to the fundamental motive bases of the listeners. They should be phrased in simple language and illustrated by references which are familiar to the crowd. Shakespeare is relatively unknown to the average citizen today, so references to his characters give rise to few intelligent responses. Accordingly, the speaker loses many of his hearers for the few seconds during which the strange material is cited, and some other stimulus may attract their attention. The speaker should never let his hearers slip away from his control if he can help it. The speaker should be as despotic in his domination of the audience's attention as the hypnotist is in monopolizing his subject's thinking. In the list below we have offered some of the salient principles which the speaker should employ in order to obtain the maximum effect. We are presupposing that the auditorium, lighting, and seating have already been attended to.

(1) *Compliment the audience.* This method entails humor as well as direct statements containing praise. A disgruntled, offended, or "ugly" audience cannot be moulded by the speaker until he gets it into a pleasant, friendly frame of mind. Criticisms, denunciation, and badgering by the speaker are usually disastrous. If he does attempt to point out flaws, he should always identify himself with the group being reprimanded.

(2) *Link yourself to the audience.* Employ "we", "our", and "us" whenever possible. As a general rule never utter the word "you" or "your", and seldom say "I", "my", or "mine". Let the audience know that you were born on a farm, if the group is rural, or that you attended Yale if the crowd is from New Haven. By so doing you more quickly enable your listeners to identify themselves with you, and realize that you are a friend. This result is necessary for people will not take advice or criticism from an enemy.

(3) *Use specificity.* Memories and emotions are originally developed by specific sensory stimuli and must be aroused by the same. Since images are definite in their structure, the speaker must use sensory adjectives and specific nouns so that his hearers have the elements for constructing mental pictures. We have discussed this subject in greater detail in previous chapters.

(4) *Strike at fundamental motive bases.* Keep in mind that the crowd is only interested in your address as it fits into the basic habitual patterns of the crowd. What does it procure from your talk that meets its basic cravings and desires?

(5) *Keep your speech moving steadily toward its climax.* A judicious admixture of description, exposition, and narration is desirable, but do not mark time in a forensic eddy nor

get lost on a conversational tangent. There should be a recurrence of emphasis upon the central idea, much as the refrain in music and verse, but the speech should march steadily onward. A speech, like a musical composition, should be an artistically balanced affair in which all the components point toward the finale.

(6) *Rise to a majestic note as you approach the climax.* We are not very easily thrilled nor inspired by petty things, but massiveness, eons of time, eternity, and infinity are breathtaking. A truly effective address should carry its listeners to an emotional peak where for at least a few moments their scalps will tighten and they will feel a shivery, awed sensation in which they forget selfishness and mundane things. This peculiar effect should coincide with the vocal climax in the manner of delivery.

(7) *Enter the climax in rhythm.* The majority of the most thrilling speeches to which the writer has listened have used verse to gain that emotional peak described in the preceding paragraph. Poetry which is relevant, which contains the final idea to complete the superstructure of the oration, will make the difference between a good speech and a great speech. Since we are more emotionally conditioned to rhythm than to prose, verse and music suggest idealism, while prose is more matter of fact.

In conclusion, we should sound a warning regarding emotionalism and the public address. The speaker should select his words with such care that they will develop the desired feelings in the audience apart from his gesticulation, intonation, and pantomime. If he endeavors to make a shallow speech into an emotionally thrilling oration, his hearers are likely to become aware of his efforts to produce an effect, but miss the effect itself. Ideally, a good speech should be one which is also so effective when in print, that it will incite its reader to the lofty feelings of its author. Too much weeping and wailing, denunciation and shaking of fists may even become ridiculous and provoke laughter in the audience unless the speech itself has warmed them in advance. In fact, a truly effective speaker can stand with his hands in his pockets and speak in a harsh voice, yet depict pathetic scenes in such well chosen words as to force tears from the eyes of his listeners. By refraining from an undue show of his own emotions, moreover, the speaker avoids the criticism of sentimentalism, even though he may be causing a lacrimal shower from his audience.

REFERENCES

BEVERIDGE, A. J., *The Art of Public Speaking* (Boston, 1924).
BILLS, B. F., *The Impromptu Talk-Plan* (Chicago, 1928).
BORCHERS, G., "Direct vs. Indirect Methods of Instruction in Speech," *J. Educ. Res.,* 1936, vol. 29, pp. 512-517.
BORDEN, R. C., AND BUSSE, A. C., *The New Public Speaking* (New York, 1930).
CARHART, R., "A Method of Using the Gault Teletactor to Teach Speech Rhythms," *Amer. Ann. Deaf,* 1935, vol. 80, pp. 260-263.
COLLINS, G. R., *Platform Speaking* (New York, 1923).
COTTON, J. C., "Normal 'Visual Hearing'," *Science,* 1935, vol. 82, pp. 592-593.
GRIFFITH, C. R., "A Comment Upon the Psychology of the Audience," *Psychological Monographs,* vol. xxx (1921), No. 136, pp. 36-47.
HIGGINS, H. H., *Influencing Behavior Through Speech* (Boston, 1930).
HOLLISTER, R. D. T., *Speech-Making* (Ann Arbor, 1918).
HUDGINS, C. V., "Experimental Phonetics," *A. R. Clark Sch. Deaf,* 1935, vol. 68, pp. 27-31.
KAO, K. F., *Crowd Psychology* (Shanghai, 1935), chaps. i, ii, iii.
KNOWER, F. H., "Experimental Studies of Changes in Attitudes," *J. Soc. Psychol.,* 1935, vol. vi, pp. 315-347.
LAW, F. H., *How to Write and How to Deliver an Oration* (New York, 1926).
MACPHERSON, W., *The Psychology of Persuasion* (New York, no date).
MCGEE, J. A., *Persuasive Speaking* (New York, 1929).
MEARS, C. W., *Public Speaking for Executives* (New York, 1931).
ORR, F. W., *Essentials of Effective Speaking* (New York, 1931).
OVERSTREET, H. A., *Influencing Human Behavior* (New York, 1925), chaps. i, ii, iv.
ROBINSON, F. B., *Effective Public Speaking* (Chicago, 1926).
SARETT, LEW, AND FOSTER, W. T., *Basic Principles of Speech* (Boston, 1936).
SCOTT, W. D., *The Psychology of Public Speaking* (New York, 1926).
TERMAN, L. M., "Psychology and Pedagogy of Leadership," *Pedagogical Seminary,* vol. xi (1904), pp. 113-151.
WINTER, I. L., *Persuasive Speaking* (New York, 1928).
WOOLBERT, C. H., *The Fundamentals of Speech* (New York, 1927).

CHAPTER XII

THE PSYCHOLOGY OF WRITING AND OF ART

The prevalence of magazines and newspapers in the modern age has led to the development of the literary profession. No longer are verses and prose penned by only a few wealthy gentlemen who dabble in fiction writing as a hobby, but tens of thousands of men and women are earning their livelihood today by playing on the keys of their "ink pianos". As newspaper reporters, magazine writers and correspondents, free lance business writers, advertising copy writers, publicists, literary contestants, poets, and authors they are devoting their entire working time to placing print symbols on paper so that readers will later be able to obtain enjoyment, education, and profit from the habitual responses set off by those same ink stimuli.

To those who have not had aspirations to become a second Shakespeare it may be illuminating to learn that there are approximately 18,000 newspapers in the United States, as well as 281 book publishers[1]. Many of these publishers each year edit over 100 books. The following list shows the output of a few of the largest firms.

The Macmillan Company	750 titles yearly
Doubleday, Doran & Co.	300 titles yearly
Harper & Brothers	250 titles yearly
Oxford University Press	250 titles yearly
Appleton & Co.	225 titles yearly
Dutton & Co.	200 titles yearly
Houghton Mifflin Co.	200 titles yearly
Longmans, Green & Co.	200 titles yearly
Scribner's Sons	200 titles yearly

[1] *The Author & Journalist* (November, 1934), pp. 18-22.

In the realm of magazines, the same journal carries a quarterly market list of over 700 titles. These magazines pay for the material they use, and cover a wide range of subjects. The list does not, moreover, include those technical journals which do not pay for the material printed. In the issue of September, 1936, this catalogue of markets for the writer in the United States ran as follows:

	MAGAZINES
List A	137
(General periodicals, standard, literary, household, popular and non-technical, which ordinarily pay on acceptance at rates of about 1 cent a word or better.)	
List B	145
(General periodicals which ordinarily pay less than 1 cent a word, or pay on publication, or which are chronically overstocked, or which offer a very limited market, or concerning which no definite information has been obtainable.)	
List C	378
(Trade, technical, religious, agricultural, business, educational, and other class publications.)	
Agriculture, Farming, Livestock	14
Art and Photography	2
Automobile, Aviation, Boating, Transportation, Highways	13
Business, Advertising, Salesmanship	23
Building, Architecture, Landscaping, Home Decorating	11
Educational	8
Health, Hygiene	6
Musical	8
Religious	21
Scientific, Technical, Radio, Mechanics	17
Sporting, Outdoor, Hunting, Fishing	18
Theatrical, Motion Picture, Radio, "Fan" Magazines	18
Trade Journals, Miscellaneous	219
List D	82
(Juvenile and Young People's Publications.)	

In addition to the print media already mentioned we could cite as the products of writers house organs and advertising brochures, as well as all the copy that confronts the reader in newspaper and magazine advertisements. In order to give a rough indication of the widespread circulation of various types of magazines we shall quote the following data[1]:

	1932	1936
American Mercury	63,287	30,178
Life	100,070	116,845
Harper's Magazine	118,972	101,807
Judge	147,598	88,366
Parents' Magazine	173,311	334,776
Popular Science Monthly	370,024	416,818
Popular Mechanics	454,399	528,216
The Farmer's Wife	1,004,996	1,137,819
True Story Magazine	2,015,495	1,896,456
American Magazine	2,087,115	2,006,580
Collier's	2,330,156	2,415,896
Saturday Evening Post	2,912,560	2,811,410

The Psychological Basis of Suspense. Suspense is simply the observer's expectancy that a suggested act will be performed, plus uncertainty as to the actual outcome. We noted in the preceding chapter that a speaker could heighten the interest of a crowd simply by taking a piece of chalk from the tray of a blackboard behind him. The suspense results because the students are accustomed to seeing a man write when he stands before the blackboard with crayon in his hand. If they were Hottentots, his behavior would not occasion suspense, unless the savages might expect him to throw it at them, in which case we would still find the teacher's simple action fraught with suspense.

When a baby picks up a straight edged razor, of course there is suspense, for we know from previous experience that the infant can wave its arms about and that razors are exceedingly sharp. These two facts serve as suggestions for the idea that he will cut himself, and our likelihood of witnessing the act is called suspense. When a drunken man is pictured staggering along a steel girder on the 77th floor of a skyscraper,

[1] *Directory of Newspapers and Periodicals* (N. W. Ayer & Son, Inc., Philadelphia, 1936).

we also undergo expectancy. Whenever an attractive young man and young woman are together, we likewise have suspense. The statement that a thief is in the crowd, or a hostile submarine in the sea, immediately creates suspense. The thief and the submarine are simply stimuli that serve as suggestions for the thought that some one will be robbed or the ship sunk.

It is evident, therefore, that suspense depends upon our habitual background and the suggestions playing upon us. If we know nothing of submarine warfare, we do not care if a dozen hostile submarines are all around our vessel. And though we may know the dangers of modern naval methods, we are likewise undisturbed until we are aware of the possible presence of the submarine. The four factors, therefore, which are indispensable for suspense are (1) the possession of habits with reference to the given situation; (2) suggestions which can set off these habits and lead to expected future action; (3) the actual operation of these suggestions upon the subject; (4) the possibility that the future action may not occur. In terms of the submarine example, we must not only be familiar with the danger of submarines, and submarines must be present, but we must be aware of or reactive to those submarines. The presence of submarines, however, may not be a matter of fact but only a belief. We do not need to have seen them as long as somebody else has told us he has seen them.

When a youngster toddles over to place its hand upon the glistening head of a coiled rattlesnake we observers certainly undergo suspense but the child does not, for he has had no experience with reference to the situation. In a movie the hero who reaches into a box for an aspirin tablet is entirely calm about the procedure for he does not know what we have seen, namely, that his enemy has substituted bichloride of mercury tablets for the aspirin. In other words, the third indispensable factor for suspense is lacking in his case. The suggestion that would lead to his thinkng of death is present but inoperative upon him.

Another critical thing for the writer to bear in mind is the fact that it is not our thought of the death of the toddler mentioned above or of the movie hero which causes us agony of suspense, but the waiting for it to happen or not to happen. It is the *expectancy* of a serious consequence with the possibility that it may be avoided. Some writers fail to make this distinction and slay their characters on every page but still cannot command the reader's interest. They have filled their stories with blood and thunder in response to an editor's request for more action. What the editor probably meant was more suspense. The simple physical action of the villain in dropping one bichloride of mercury tablet into the aspirin box belonging to the handsome young hero can fill the feminine spectators with terrible suspense, and keep the masculine onlookers in almost equal perturbation.

Another significant factor in considering suspense is the fact that there are degrees of it. That a robin is hopping near a fishworm creates little suspense for me. That a tiger is stalking a Boston terrier is more emotionally arousing, and if the terrier is a pet in my household, I am quite excited. This suspense is trivial, however, compared to what I feel if I am watching the jungle beast approach my own child. Similarly, if a bucket of sand is lowered over a cliff by a rope that is becoming frayed, I may be only mildly concerned. If a valuable animal is being lowered I grow more interested, and become frantic when I learn that a human being is below. As the rope becomes increasingly worn against the rocky edge of the cliff, I become a wildman on learning that one of my own loved ones is suspended in the cage that swings above the abyss.

The fundamental motive bases, therefore, must be aroused before we react with a maximum of suspense. Threatened curtailment of food, drink, wealth, health, loved ones, or prestige immediately produces suspense. The writer must aim at the bull's-eye just as necessarily as the speaker and the salesman.

Why Suspense Depends on Characterization. In the examples just mentioned we found that the danger threatening an unknown terrier did not produce as much suspense in us as that which imperiled our family pet. The reason therefor lies in the fact that we identify ourselves and the pet dog. He is a part of us, and gives rise to memories and emotions that are pleasant to us. It is characteristic of human beings to resent the loss of that which produces gratification and pleasure. No such identification occurs in the case of the bucket of sand. The animal produces a noticeable suspense, however, because it has some attributes which we also possess, notably the capacity to suffer pain, hunger, thirst, and cold. We can identify ourselves with animals, and do so the longer we are in direct association with them. With a fellow human being, the possibility for identification is correspondingly greater. It reaches its climax in our own kin.

In characterization the writer simply endeavors to portray his hero or heroine so that the reader quickly identifies himself with them. We cannot enjoy fiction or the movies unless this identification is made. It is imperative, therefore, for the writer to employ specificity in delineating his characters for we link ourselves only with those who do the specific things which we do and in the same way as we perform them. In the previous chapter we emphasized the necessity for the speaker to facilitate this identification process. The reason why we take sides in a debate is because we note the identity in beliefs of one speaker or the other with our own.

The necessity for good characterization is brought out in the following statement of F. E. Blackwell, editor of several magazines belonging to the Street and Smith group.[1]

[1] Lichtblau, J., "'Pet Peeves' of Editors," *Author & Journalist* (July, 1932), p. 15.

Recently I have been able to sum up writing in this way: Interest in a story is in proportion to interest in the characters in the story. Of course, in a detective story it's a good thing, almost a needful thing, to have a novel method of killing, stealing, etc.—something that one would remember to tell a friend—but this doesn't *make* the story. You must become interested in the characters, and the more you are interested in the characters, the better you'll like the story. Thus: I recently complained to an author that I didn't think his story had much suspense in it. This remark brought a violent protest from the author. He said that on the first page he had killed a gentleman; on the second page he'd abducted a young woman, and on and on through the story, violent action had been taken against the characters. How absurd, he said, that there could be no suspense in such a story. But I told him I didn't care about the death of the gentleman on the first page, nor did I give a rap about the abducted lady. Had he written well enough, all he would have had to do, to move me to tears, would be to have had the gentleman spill a drop of ink on his new spring suit, and the lady come down stairs to meet an admiring caller without first powdering her nose . . .

The chief difference between a novice and a literary master like Wilbur Daniel Steele is partly reducible to the latter's excellent characterization. The reader easily finds himself portrayed in the characters and therefore undergoes all the emotional crises and suspense which they experience. The tyro, on the contrary, quickly turns out his characters with the essential qualities of man in general, but not of man in the particular. These characters have no more distinguishing marks than a factory made dining room chair in contrast to an Italian hand carved piece of furniture. The reader, therefore, sees but little of himself in the person about whom he is reading.

Amateur writers and introverts in general fail to perceive the fine distinctions in behavior and character which make living personalities of their paper heroes and heroines. The latter may sometimes be so unreal and artificial that they appear comical when they are supposed to be playing serious roles. The following quotation from Daisy Ashford is a striking case in point. This girl was only nine years old when she wrote her novel, so she warrants praise instead of criticism. Her narrative, nevertheless, is a good example of the point just mentioned, for many college students in the sentimental mood of midnight write love scenes scarcely more true to life than this one. The narrative quoted begins at the point where the two lovers had decided to go for a day's outing. The punctuation and spelling are retained as in the child's own version.[1]

They arrived at Windsor very hot from the jorney and Bernard at once hired a boat to row his beloved up the river. Ethel could not row but she much enjoyed seeing the tough sunburnt arms of Bernard tugging at the oars as she lay among the rich cushons of the dainty boat. She had a rarther lazy nature but Bernard did not know of this. However he soon got dog tired and suggested lunch by the mossy bank.

Oh yes said Ethel quickly opening the sparkling champaigne.

Dont spill any cried Bernard as he carved some chicken.

They eat and drank deeply of the charming viands ending up with merangs and choclates.

Let us now bask under the spreading trees said Bernard in a passiunate tone.

Oh yes lets said Ethel and she opened her dainty parasole and sank down upon the long green grass. She closed her eyes but she was far from asleep. Bernard sat beside her in profound silence gazing at her pink face and long wavy eye lashes. He puffed at his pipe for some moments while the larks gaily caroled in the blue sky. Then he edged a trifle closer to Ethels form.

Ethel he murmured in a trembly voice.

Oh what is it said Ethel hastily sitting up.

Words fail me ejaculated Bernard horsly my passion for you is intense he added fervently. It has grown day and night since I first beheld you.

Oh said Ethel in supprise I am not prepared for this and she lent back against the trunk of the tree.

Bernard placed one arm tightly round her. When will you marry me Ethel he uttered you must be my wife it has come to that I love you so intensly that if you say no I shall perforce dash my body to the brink of yon muddy river he panted wildly.

[1] Ashford, Daisy, *The Young Visiters* (Doubleday Doran Co., New York, 1919), pp. 90-93. By permission of and by arrangement with the publishers.

Oh dont do that implored Ethel breathing rarther hard.

Then say you love me he cried.

Oh Bernard she sighed fervently I certainly love you madly you are to me like a Heathen god she cried looking at his manly form and handsome flashing face I will indeed marry you.

How soon gasped Bernard gazing at her intensly.

As soon as possible said Ethel gently closing her eyes.

My Darling whispered Bernard and he seiezed her in his arms we will be marrid next week.

Oh Bernard muttered Ethel this is so sudden.

No no cried Bernard and taking the bull by both horns he kissed her violently on her dainty face. My bride to be he murmured several times.

Ethel trembled with joy as she heard the mistick words.

Oh Bernard she said little did I ever dream of such as this and she suddenly fainted into his out stretched arms.

"Pitching" Your Opening. When a writer begins his literary composition he should usually "key" it in the opening paragraphs so that the mood typical of the story or chapter is set. It is difficult to create a single mood for such a lengthy string of situations as we find in a novel, but shorter literary works can usually employ this technique with profit. If the story is to be an artistically constructed episode with a central motif, the opening words should sound the appropriate note. A tale of horror or a rollicking narrative of carefree youth should obviously open in different keys. Observe the contrasting feeling tone embodied in the following two paragraphs

Like gaunt wolves slinking out of their mountain den in search of unsuspecting prey, a dozen gray-black clouds slid off the jagged peaks guarding the lone entrance to the Devil's Corral and darted across the leaden sky. Old Jed Blanton cursed beneath his breath at the ill luck which had steered him into this ominous valley with his two comely daughters. He had hoped to get through Hell County the day before, but the Evil Eye of the valley had noted the radiant beauty of Jed's older girl.

It was an ideal spring day—just the sort which Jänet had hoped for to make the picnic a success. Against the blue sky she could see many fluffy white cloudlets drifting along like so many fleecy lambs. The warm sun was taking fragrant thank offerings from woods and flowers and freshly plowed fields. Even the birds seemed on a holiday. When Bob's blue roadster swooped up the drive and stopped before the white pillared veranda, Janet was so happy she gave her mother two extra kisses before she ran down the steps.

We must also remember that young people are more energetic than their parents and grandparents, so they desire faster action. The slow tempo and lengthy descriptions of Henry James are especially unsuited to youth. Young people are in the fox trot mood. They can enjoy waltzes when they are tired or grow older. Quick, incisive characterizations with plenty of suspense resulting from muscular and love conflicts make them happy. The love interest is most effective when tied up with athletics, warfare and similar forms of competition necessitating the expenditure of much energy. Roughly speaking, the gridiron is a popular locale for the creation of a love story for youth, while the golf links are a more appropriate setting for romance among the older generation.

The psychological explanation for these two preferences is rather simple. Whenever we become interested in the hero or heroine we, of course, identify ourselves with them. If we are in ill health, or lack energy and vitality, we must, however, hoard our strength. The combats in which our heroes engage tend to deplete our store of energy, and therefore lead to fatigue and unpleasantness. This depletion of energy is similar to that which follows when we witness a boxing match or a football game. We tense our muscles and implicitly undergo all the action which we see or about which we read. It follows, therefore, that we tend to avoid those tales in which the performances of the leading characters are too vigorous for our vicarious participation. It is conceivable that a suitable objective test might show differences between the people of Florida or Alabama and those of Michigan and Maine in respect to this question, for we know the warmer southern climate produces a slower tempo of living.

How to Increase the Attention Value of the Page. Yellow journalism relies upon the attention attracting value of photographs, pictures, and headlines. An intimation of sex situations in the latter holds the attention, and produces the sale of the paper. We have cited in Chapter I the experience of Haldeman-Julius regarding the value of headlines and titles. The conservative writer, however, can utilize many psychological facts for whetting the reader's interest without blatantly employing the sex appeal. We shall list some of the more obvious ones as follows:

(1) *Use short paragraphs.* From habit we have associated short paragraphs with conversation, and conversation denotes human beings. We are more interested in persons than in things. It is this fact which explains why many readers skip much of the descriptive matter and follow the dialogues. Young people are prone to do so. The writer has tested children in regard to paragraph lengths and has found that they invariably will choose a page broken into short paragraphs in preference to one where the paragraphs are long.

The short paragraphs also suggest short sentences, with a resulting ease in comprehension. Magazines and novels usually have much shorter paragraphs than textbooks, so the short paragraphs connote suspense. Indeed, we have become so accustomed to associating long paragraphs with polysyllables and educational treatises that the college reader a generation ago would hardly respect a textbook which did not have paragraphs covering half of a page, and whose style was not cumbersome. William James' works were a novelty in the scientific field, therefore, because he had an interesting style and illustrated his laws with concrete cases.

Short paragraphs are also easier upon the eyes, for they produce more half lines. The last line of a paragraph usually does not extend the full width of the page, so the eye muscles do not have to do as much work. Moreover, these broken lines break the monotonous appearance of the page.

(2) *Use quotation marks.* These attract attention not only because of their upper case position in the line, but also because they denote human repartee with possible conflict and suspense. In a one-second exposure to a page the reader will usually observe almost all of the quotation marks. They have interest value far above that possessed by any letters of the alphabet or other punctuation marks. As a rule, the writer should change indirect discourse into direct, for the page is made more attractive to the reader in consequence. Economy of space may be violated thereby, but the material gains in interest value.

(3) *Use illustrations.* Many an article is sold to an editor because it contains photographs or pen sketches. Pictures attract us much more quickly than do words and they greatly simplify our comprehension of an idea. Of two stories in a magazine with equally attractive titles, the average reader will choose the one which contains an illustration. There are some qualifications to this statement, however, for a few years ago when modernistic art was in its heydey, the freakish appearance of the hero and heroine in the sketch accompanying the story repulsed many would-be readers, causing them to search for an equally promising story title with a normal type of pictured heroine or else none at all. It is frequently more pleasant for the reader to construct his own image of the leading characters from their verbal description alone than to have a sketch which violates his sense of beauty.

Advertisers have long realized the importance of cuts in selling merchandise. They have statistically proved their superiority to the straight copy advertisement. Accordingly, the yellow newspapers fill their sheets with cartoons and photographs. The widespread popularity of the Sunday comic pages and the daily cartoon strips is also ample evidence of the effectiveness of pictures.

In scientific treatises a similar heightening of interests is obtained by the employment of curves, charts, and graphs. We have already pointed out the effectiveness of such material in public speaking. The trouble with many charts and curves, however, is the fact that they are not self-explanatory. To be truly effective, of course, they should readily reveal their significance. Even quoted material from which quotation marks have been omitted is often attention attracting if it is printed in a smaller size of type than the body of the treatise or article.

(4) *Open your paragraphs with dynamic and attention holding words.* Although it has been customary to consider the end of the sentence as the place of greatest emphasis and importance, modern advertising procedure tends to reverse positions, and begin with the most dramatic word in the sentence. In running down the page with our initial glance the opening words of the successive paragraphs are first focussed upon. The value of striking words at the start of the first sentence of each paragraph is shown in the following cases.

Womanlike, she decided that her next action . . .
Shrieking like a madman he raced onward . . .
Terrified by what had happened, she . . .
Attacked without warning, they resolutely . . .
Helpless in the face of the oncoming . . .
Love being now impossible after what she . . .

Whether the reader will like the material contained within the paragraphs depends upon other things than the attractive first impression which he gains from a quick survey of the page, but a dramatic plot can be made to appear uninteresting by lack of attention to these details. A dull or poorly written narrative cannot become a best seller simply by attention to the mechanics of the page any more than a drab and colorless personality can be made the life of the party by Listerine.

Lifebuoy soap, and a new suit of clothes, but an interesting framework should at least assist in rendering a story more attractive.

How to Make Your Style More Interesting. When asked for a definition of literary style Dean Swift replied that it is simply "proper words in proper places." The task of putting proper words into proper places, however, is a very difficult one, involving a thorough knowledge of human motivation and control, as well as the technical and less important factors such as punctuation and diction. One of the greatest masters of English style, Stevenson, writes: "From the arrangement of according letters, which is altogether arabesque and sensual, up to the architecture of the elegant and pregnant sentence, which is a vigorous act of the pure intellect, there is scarce a faculty in man but has been exercised. We need not wonder, then, if perfect sentences are rare, and perfect pages rarer."

When the young poet Racine wrote to Boileau for criticism and advice, he said of himself, "I ought to tell you that I write with great facility." Boileau's response was, "I hope to teach you to write with great difficulty." In a similar vein Byron is reputed to have once said, "Easy writing's damned hard reading."

Fundamentally, therefore, it is not agility in bandying words about which makes us skilful writers, but the structural patterns in which those words are arranged. A mason could lay bricks with great facility without ever knowing anything about architecture. It is not the bricks themselves, therefore, which make a great cathedral but their arrangement. The same brick might be employed with equal ease in the construction of a dog kennel, a garage, or a house. In like manner the facile speech of the college major in English does not enable him to write interesting stories. In fact, one of the most successful story writers in America knows very little about grammar or punctuation. He simply scribbles his tale with entire disregard for the English language and its rules of usage. A college girl in the editorial office of the magazine rewrites this author's stuff as soon as it arrives. The curious thing about the situation is the fact that the college girl with a superior knowledge of English cannot create the story itself. She may contribute the vocabulary but the man fills his plot with its drama and suspense. See the terse "triangle" plot, page 437.

We have presented this example to show that the psychological appreciation of human nature is the principal factor in effective writing. Any intelligent person with a few years' study of Webster and an English grammar has the verbal "bricks" for literary masonry, but few can thereupon duplicate Conrad's psychological technique in laying these "bricks" so they produce a dramatic structure.

Dean Swift's definition of literary style includes both the basic understanding of human nature plus the knowledge of the mechanics of the writing process. Often, however, the meaning of literary style tends to be associated with the melodious combination of words, involving the avoidance of redundancy and tautology. As a matter of fact, it is about as difficult to separate literary style from literary content as for the cartoonist to separate the black lines which delineate his pen characters from the characters so circumscribed. Whether he uses a fine black line or a heavy one is of relatively slight importance as long as his characters themselves are interesting.

There are a few general comments, however, which we shall make concerning the mechanics of style in contradistinction to the content of the literary product. We shall present them in the following paragraphs.

(1) *Avoid repetition of the same words and sounds whenever possible.* This simply involves the employment of synonyms, and is advisable in order to eliminate monotony.

(2) *Avoid redundancy or the use of superfluous words,* as in "Raise up the window."

(3) *Avoid tautology or the needless repetition of the same idea in different words,* as in "audible to the ear."

(4) *Avoid triteness in words and analogies.* This admonition covers not only the hackneyed words and phrases which have become so overworked that they possess little intrinsic interest, but also those proverbs, similes, and metaphors which are equally threadbare. Writers who scintillate in their literary style are seldom guilty of such phrases as "marble brow", "iron willed", "ship of state", "in the blink of an eye", and "like water off a duck's back."

In trying to be different, however, the writer must be discreet, for it is possible to re-phrase so many old ideas and analogies that the reader becomes more conscious of the writer's attempt at cleverness than of the cleverness itself. Three or four new twists to old phraseology in a single short story will usually be sufficient to impress the reader with the freshness of the author's style.

(5) *Maintain a consistent feeling tone whenever possible.* For example, it is not wise, as a general rule, to mix slang and colloquialisms with elegant diction. Colloquialisms may be unknown in another region of the country; hence, the readers there will react as if blank spaces were in the sentences. The writer, like the public speaker, should endeavor to hold his public throughout his entire contact with it. It is also advisable to let others read your writings before they go to press, for words which are quite proper and pleasant according to your own environment and experience may have unpleasant connotations for persons not similarly trained. The subject of feeling tone has been treated more exhaustively in earlier chapters.

(6) *Read your work aloud in order to catch phonetic harshness and unmusical combinations of vowels and consonants.* A story or article which reads easily aloud, will flow along well when read silently.

(7) *Use specificity in your description.* Sensory qualities enrich any object, making it appear less barren and uninteresting. In fact, the reason old phrases and apothegms are threadbare is simply because their sensory qualities have "worn off" as stimuli to our conscious attention. The word "Ivory" connotes richness, African elephant tusks, Steinway piano keys, importation, and luxury, but it is now almost threadbare of such qualities in the phrase "Ivory Soap". We have simply employed it so frequently that the muscular (kinesthetic) quality of the word far overshadows its other sensory attributes, and it is no longer attended to consciously.

In shunning hackneyed epithets, we must create new ones which still possess sensory attributes over and above the kinesthetic qualities involved in their pronunciation. Accordingly, these adjectives will create mental images, for they will lie in the focal circle of our attention. Three years ago the writer read the following sentence which is possibly not a verbatim reproduction, but at least closely approximates the original, "The wind in the pines sounded like a cello in a gloomy temple." This simile is specific and novel. The fact that it has remained in memory when the story containing it has faded, augurs well for it.

How to Write Interesting Exposition. Descriptive or informative material is uninteresting until it is tied up to some fundamental motive base of the human being. The art of making the educational process interesting, therefore, is principally one of showing the relationship of the new object or idea to a basic need of the reader. Boys are not much interested in social etiquette until they are to take their best girls to a formal party. Then they may become omnivorous readers of Emily Post.

The reason that Emily Post's writings then become popular with them is simply the fact that they have become acutely aware of the functional relationship of her advice to their immediate needs. They desire to be considered sophisticated and retain the respect of their sweethearts. Formerly uninteresting rules of etiquette may now transcend the sport page in interest value.

It is well to crystallize the attention of the readers upon the subject to be explained, by means of an effective headline or a question. Both of these should strike at the bull's-eye by arousing basic habit patterns possessed by the reader. Correspondence schools have employed the question method in much of their advertising. "When are you going to sit behind a mahogany desk?" "Are you prepared for the bigger job?" "Where will you be ten years from now?"

After the initial appeal to a fundamental desire of the reader, the writer should quickly state how his measure or idea enables the reader to satisfy his want. This may consist of no more than a blunt affirmation of the practical value of the measure. Then a parade of exposition may follow. Such a procedure introduces suspense into the situation. The reader has been told that he will profit greatly by the new product or idea. He awaits with interest the further details.

All the previously mentioned devices of the writer may then be utilized. Cleverness of style, the inclusion of narration, and the numerous methods of increasing the interest value of the page help sustain attention. Always, however, the intimate connection between the idea and the reader's basic need must be kept fresh in his mind. The teacher who fails to emphasize this connection finds that her students are less interested than those of another instructor who does make the tie-up between education and life's needs.

Much of the spectator's attention during a moving picture show is really taken up with exposition. The suspense is first created by showing us the hero, the heroine, and the villain. Thereafter we watch with considerable interest the machinations of the latter. The same type of thing is shown upon the pages of a novel. After the development of suspense, the writer inserts description—pages of it. We follow the heroine through the routine affairs of her life for perhaps an entire chapter before she and the hero or the villain are again brought together. But we are willing to read description because of the underlying suspense. The writer of exposition, therefore, must also develop suspense if he is going to hold his readers until the end of his article.

Writing Effective Advertising Copy. Advertising copy is chiefly expositional. It contains descriptions of a piece of merchandise, and a cataloguing of its uses. But it can retain the reader's interest by the same methods which we have described in the previous section. It must first of all strike at a fundamental need. Utility is the first asset of any product. The merchandise must serve some want, and the more basic the need, the more we are capable of becoming interested in it. Listerine advertisements illustrated an appreciation of this fact by making their appeal to the sex vanity and business ambition of people.

In order to illustrate the importance of making the tie-up between the need and the product, as well as to point out once more the absolute necessity of being definite, concrete, in motivating human beings, we shall cite the case of a young man who built a large garage featuring the mechanical department and the overhauling of cars. He sent out a neat form letter saying that he employed only competent mechanics, and that he would be open for business on the first of the week. Not ten letters were received in reply. His direct-mail venture was an advertising failure. But one of his few patrons, an advertising man, had received a copy of the letter. He came to the young garage owner and offered to write him another one. His offer was accepted, and here is what went out on the second direct-mail attempt:

"We make an interesting offer. When repairing your car we invite you to come around and see how it is done. Allow us to explain some of the mysteries of the inside of that power plant.

"There are parts of your car that you know little about. There are intricacies that mean trouble on the road. We will gladly explain these points to you and initiate you into some of the little-known engine problems."[1]

This letter brought 70 per cent of replies and the garage was quickly booked with work throughout the entire winter. The letter was effective because it corroborated the garage owner's statement that he had only competent mechanics. It acted much as a guarantee, for he offered his patrons a chance to watch his men work. Men who knew gasoline motors could therefore see if his mechanics were skilled. Moreover, many patrons, particularly women, would be pleased to be taught some of the mechanical details concerning their own automobiles. His letter met the need of these women for information.

We have already explained the method by which a public speaker can profitably disclaim his intention of criticizing his opponent or of trying to influence his hearers to his own cause. It can also be employed in writing advertising copy, as the following first paragraph of one such letter well indicates.

Dear Friend:

There's no use trying. I've tried and tried to tell people about my fish. But I wasn't rigged out to be a letter writer, and I can't do it. I can close-haul a sail with the best of them. I know how to pick out the best fish of the catch, I know just which fish will make the tastiest mouthfuls, but I'll never learn the knack of writing a letter that will tell people why my kind of fish—fresh-caught prime-grades, right off the fishing boats with the deep-sea tang still in it—is lots better than the ordinary store kind.

An attention to feeling tone is also imperative in writing advertising copy. Our copy concerning the Snuggle Sweater, which appeared in Chapter VIII, demonstrates the influence of specific sensory adjectives in creating pleasant feeling tone. It is just as essential for the writer as for the salesman to

[1] *Printers' Ink* (Dec. 15, 1921), p. 192.

UNION PACIFIC SYSTEM

The Overland Route

J. P. CUMMINS
GENERAL PASSENGER AGENT

DEPARTMENT OF TRAFFIC
OMAHA, NEBRASKA

Mark Twain
writes of his
disappointment

when his first balloon ride revealed that the States were all the same color. He had always believed, from a study of maps, that Ohio was red and Indiana was blue.

Just one of the great humorist's many witticisms, to be sure. But you and I know that there are regions, especially in the West, where Nature has been most generous in conferring her treasures of form and color. There is a region in Southern Utah and Northern Arizona called Zion, Bryce Canyon and Grand Canyon—three national parks—so colorful that it almost defies description.

Then there are other regions of colorful beauty, such as Yellowstone, Rocky Mountain-Estes, Yosemite, Rainier and a host of others, any one of which offers a delightful vacation in the out-of-doors. Possibly you have visited some of these places, but since railroad fares will be lower this summer than ever before, why not plan to see more of our national playgrounds?

Perhaps California, the scene of the Tenth Olympiad, will be your goal this summer, as it will be the goal of thousands of others. President Hoover will officially open the Olympic Games in Los Angeles on July 30. Athletes of fifty nations, led by their national colors, will take part in the great "Parade of Nations". What a colorful and never to be forgotten spectacle that will be!

No matter what part of the West you plan to visit, the Union Pacific can take you, for it serves more of the West than any other railroad. Along its lines are located the finest dude ranches in the West. An easy and inexpensive side trip en route to or from California will take you to Hoover (Boulder) Dam, where operations are now on in full swing.

We will gladly give you complete information and literature about the trip you have in mind. There is real economy in planning your trip well in advance, and that is just the service you can receive by returning the enclosed card. We invite you to do so.

Cordially yours,

J. P. Cummins

Exhibit 51. A good direct-mail piece of advertising. Note how it "sells them the holes" as per Chapter VII. Observe the opening words of the paragraphs. They are a bit weak in dramatic value.

remember that habits are developed because of definite stimuli in the environment, and consequently they must be re-aroused by specific stimuli, either actual or symbolic.

The advertiser may also frequently inject suspense into his copy to increase its interest value. In the following part of one of the Grinnell Company's advertisements we have annotated the copy, and appended explanatory footnotes below it.

"Oh, that's the same old idea you sprang five years ago, Tom," said the president[1] as he laid a friendly hand on the old[2] engineer's shoulder. "I'm sorry, but the prize money[3] for coal-saving suggestions *must* go to those whose ideas are more practical."

"But[4]—" the old man started falteringly[5] to explain, when the production manager cut in with, "Why, that idea came from his boy the year he was getting through Tech. That waste heat would not generate an ounce of steam. The boy himself would laugh at it today."

"But my boy[6] . . . " began the old man again.

"What was the college boy's idea?"[7] interrupted the consulting engineer, who had consented to help in awarding the prize money.[8]

1. President versus employee, therefore conflict indicated.

2. Employee is an *old* engineer, therefore probably the under dog as regards the young president, so we side with him.

3. Prize money increases the suspense by denoting competition, conflict.

4. The conjunction "but" denotes the old engineer is still battling.

5. "Falteringly" shows another bid to gain our sympathy for the under dog.

6. Another indication that the old man is still fighting and not for himself alone but for his son, also.

7. At last! Somebody is at least impartial enough to give him a hearing.

8. Aha! This last interrogator is one of the judges who award the prize money, too. Maybe we'll see justice win out after all.

How to Write Credit Letters That Collect. The need for the use of applied psychology in credit work is being realized more fully today than ever before. Credit managers must be familiar with the methods of motivating human beings, and must appreciate that people can be coaxed into the desired payment of their bills more successfully than they can be clubbed. We do not imprison men in America, as was done in England a century ago, for their business debts, although they are still incarcerated for lack of alimony payments.

An intimation in a collection letter that the writer needs the money owed him to meet his own obligations nearly always gets a check out of the debtor, provided the latter is solvent. When a credit manager threatens his debtors, however, they grow hostile. A characteristic of hostility is the fact that cooperation between the warring factions is reduced to nil. "Let him go to court, if he wants to," we say or think, even though we may finally grudgingly meet his demands. And if we cannot pay all of our outstanding obligations, we prefer to remit to those who have been fair and considerate of us, leaving the bills of our enemies on the bottom of the pile.

Many times some unusual device will make a credit letter stand out from the "please remit by return mail" variety, and it is often far superior to the "we shall be forced to turn the account over for collection" kind of missive. A very effective type of credit letter which has been cited by McCuaig[1] is the one following:

"When I was a kid my mother taught me to remember things by tying a piece of string around my thumb. This worked fine.

"I am enclosing a piece of the kind she used, of proper length for you, and I am going to ask you as a favor just to tie it around the

[1] McCuaig, C. B., "The Human Interest Angle the Credit Man Needs," *Printers' Ink* (June 17, 1920), pp. 162 *ff*.

middle of the thumb on your right hand. You will soon see how conveniently and reliably it operates.

"Presently your bookkeeper will come in about some other matter. You will take the paper which he gives you in your right hand. You will at once see the string! Then you will say: 'Oh, yes, Smith, I wish you would make out a check for the Packard Electric Company and let me sign it right away. There is a balance overdue.'

"You will be glad to have the matter settled. We will much appreciate getting the money to pass along to the people *we* owe. The string you can keep and use again for all sorts of things—possibly to remind you to send your next order our way."

The reader will observe that the final sentence in the above letter attempts to take any sting out of the credit manager's words by showing that the debtor's friendship and continued patronage is desired and hoped for. There is no intimation that a conflict or legal suit is at all contemplated. It also dispels the possible thought in the recipient's mind that the credit manager is unpleasantly sarcastic. That one sentence just goes to show the importance of "proper words in proper places."

Sometimes, of course, credit men may have to write very straightforward letters. But they should never stoop to emotionalism. It is always a good thing to leave an opening so that a later reconciliation is not too difficult, nor too demeaning to the pride of the present debtor. One large firm manufacturing mattresses let a certain dealer act as its representative in a large mid-western city. The dealer did not push this company's goods and was very slow about remitting, being six months in arrears. The company finally wrote him a very honest letter stating that they felt he was not doing their line of mattresses justice, and that they thought he was not treating them fairly in regard to prompt payment of bills.

On the return mail they obtained an angry letter in which the dealer told them they could take their old mattresses out of his store, for he did not want to have anything more to do with them. The credit manager, however, sent another letter in which he stated that they did not wish to discontinue business with him, but simply wanted a fairer treatment in regard to settlement of bills. He further stated that it would be unpleasant for the mattress company as well as for the dealer if a change were made. If the company turned their account to another dealer in his city they would feel compelled to tell the new dealer the full facts. They would have to say that the present dealer was careless about keeping up a first class credit rating, that he fell six months in arrears, and that he did not push the line of goods which he was supposed to sell. The mattress company did not want to make any such statements because they would lower his standing among his fellow merchants and would be an admission that the mattress company had misjudged their man originally. Moreover, their goods had long been advertised as being on sale in his store, and they would lose some trade if the change were made. However, they left it up to his good judgment, being entirely willing to continue amicable relationships if he would change his methods in their regard.

In a week a letter came from their dealer in which he apologized, and paid up his accounts. Thenceforth he vigorously pushed their line of merchandise. They never had any more trouble with this man. The reader will have observed the credit manager's clever stimulation of fundamental motive bases possessed by the dealer. The latter had to acknowledge that the company was right, that they had treated him more than fairly, and *that he would lose in social prestige as well as financial standing* if the company changed their account to one of his rivals. Since the credit manager had not become emotional and made it impossible for the dealer to restore friendly relationships without a tremendous cost to his self-esteem and pride, the retailer came back. The credit manager had left the door open for just this possibility.

The Psychological Aspects of Art. Such problems as balancing objects upon the page are not solved by simply using a ruler and a compass and geometrically bisecting the space. The psychological center of the page, for instance, is above the geometrical center. A line crossing at a point approximately 60 per cent of the distance from the bottom of the page (the golden section) appears to divide the space into equal parts. Perspective as employed in art depends on habit. Indeed, space perception in general is developed by the infant through his experiences with his environment. He reaches for the moon, not realizing the differences in the distance of objects surrounding him. He therefore lacks perspective and could not appreciate landscapes portrayed in the art galleries. Only as he gains the power of self locomotion does he fully realize those psychological elements which enable accurate spacial perception. He then finally becomes aware of the fact that in general the less distinct an object appears, the farther it is from him; that the seemingly smaller of two like objects is farther away; that the object which he sees in entirety is between himself and the object which it overshadows. These and other visual habits have already been fully presented to the student in his course in general psychology.

Without having been conscious of the learning process underlying the phenomenon, we have become conditioned to the fact that the more strain upon the rectus medialis muscle of each eyeball, the nearer is the object upon which we are focussing. Vertical distances appear greater than equal horzontal ones because of the greater strain upon the superior rectus muscles. In short, we project into our environment as distances those sensations of effort entailed by the muscles of the eyeball. In a similar manner we project upon a stone more weight than upon a feather, when our bases for such comparisons really lie in the greater strain in the arm muscles while lifting the stone. This is psychological weight in contrast to physical weight as measured by specific gravities.

The balance of a picture depends upon both its physical measurements and its psychological attributes. A little dog pictured on one side of the middle of the page overbalances many times his actual area on the other side providing the latter space is filled with a boulder or other less attractive object. Our interest in a thing renders it psychologically heavier. In advertising, for example, a cut more than balances an equal area devoted to copy. A very striking headline for the copy may help offset this difference, and the whole situation is also influenced by the interest value of the scene depicted in the illustration.

An unbalanced scene is vaguely unpleasant because we either identify ourselves with the pictured characters and feel implicit muscle strains arising in consequence, or else the prolonged suspense resulting from our expectancy that an object will fall, becomes fatiguing. The suggestive value of unbalanced figures, however, is utilized in denoting movement, as in the case of the winged Mercury. The human figure itself may be represented in an unbalanced posture to create the illusion of running, but the entire piece of sculpture retains a balanced effect by having streamers extend behind the runner, or by some object in the hand behind him which is of interest value.

The employment of color also involves psychological factors, dependent largely upon our early experiences. Blue is considered cool, probably because water has often had this appearance. Red, being the color of fire, denotes warmth, and yellow-orange is cheery because of its association with sunlight. Green, being the principal hue of all vegetation, suggests those qualities that are experienced in the outdoors, namely, relaxation and relief. It is therefore regarded as a restful color. White denotes both coolness, cleanliness, and purity, for reasons that are self-evident. It also conveys a suggestion of spaciousness, which partly explains the fact that light colored clothing enhances its wearer's appearance of corpulence.

White paint makes a house or other building appear larger. The ceilings of rooms are usually lighter than the walls in order to increase the apparent size of the room. A black or dark brown ceiling makes a room seem small and oppressive. Black and very dark blues are forbidding colors because of their association with storms and nightfall. Fear lurks in darkness, not in brightly lighted regions. Light shades and tints, and bright hues like yellow, tend to be extrovertive in their influence, whereas dark colors tend to produce introversion.

We have previously discussed such matters as the color preferences of males and of females, and have pointed out the resultant effects of simultaneous color contrasts, and the fact that complementary hues increase each other's apparent richness. In addition to colors, moreover, we find that certain distinctive feeling tones attach to lines. Hollingworth[1] states that delicacy of texture is denoted by the fine gray line, while the fine black line suggests precision and hardness. Homeliness and solidity are connoted by a broad rough line.

Beauty and grace are so dependent on psychological interpretation, however, that it is almost impossible to define them arbitrarily. A beautiful female figure in one generation may be too fat or too slender to be so considered by another generation or a different race. Since such mechanics as line, color, and perspective are so dependent upon the previous conditioning to environments of both artist and critic, it is little wonder that the more fundamental aspects of the subject are so frequently debated. The items which we have just been discussing are comparable to the popular interpretation of literary style; namely, the mechanics of putting the material into lasting shape. There are thousands of artists who understand these facts, but they still do not become famous. They are like the college majors in English who possess the

[1] Hollingworth, H. L., *op. cit.*, p. 143.

knowledge of vocabulary, punctuation, and grammar, but cannot write an effective short story.

Why Some Artists Succeed While Others Fail. Although many artists and sculptors fail financially because they have not attained sufficient knowledge of the mechanics of their craft, the majority of them never rise above mediocrity because they do not choose scenes and themes which have dramatic value. They may be hired by Gutzon Borglum or Lorado Taft to do much of the work of the latter but they themselves lack the ability to conceive ideas which are of interest or suspense value when crystallized in marble or bronze. They may be skilful enough in laying the "bricks" as long as some artistic genius creates the blue prints for them.

To illustrate this point more clearly, we may mention the cases of two young people starting out on a pleasure trip, each equipped with a camera and plenty of films. One of them "snaps" everything that has any appeal whatever to him. The other waits until he sees especially intriguing combinations of wood and sea and sky. Both persons have the same technical equipment, namely, their cameras and films, but one has the ability to select scenes which will interest the folks back home, whereas the other's prints will scarcely hold the glance of any but himself. The one can probably sell some of his photographs to travel magazines because the scenes have general interest. The other may not be able to give his away.

The psychological test of a promising young artist would be his skill in the use of a camera. If he could not bring back photographs of human interest value, then he certainly could hope for little success on the end of a paint brush, for he would not be greater than his technical ability, whereas a great artist, like the writer, depends on a combination of technique and interesting subject matter. In the realm of cartooning, for instance, many of the skilled technicians depend upon other people for ideas. They can illustrate your mental picture provided you tell them just what you have in mind. They are simply pen photographers. Too many artists are of the same class. They can paint well enough if they can be given a thrilling scene. After all, a great artist, sculptor, speaker, writer, salesman and advertising man have much in common, namely, an understanding of human motivation.

A pastoral scene, especially a landscape, is about as interesting as its homologue in the literary field, namely, exposition. The artist's technique may be very good and he may at times inject a reasonable amount of suspense, but he cannot hope to compete in interest value with the painting which, like the short story, strikes at more fundamental motive bases of human behavior. Since human beings are usually more interesting than trees, other things being equal we shall look at and purchase scenes depicting men and women, girls and boys, in preference to the technically clever, but less interesting inanimate objects. The skilful artist, like the understanding writer, of course, can intertwine description and exposition with conflict and suspense.

A final comment concerning financial success in art involves the matter of salesmanship, not only of the producer's creations but also of himself. It has not been an exceptional thing for a great artist, musician, or writer to live in poverty for years until some society leader, connoisseur, or social pacemaker "discovered" him, whereupon work which he had done years before suddenly becomes great. Critics who would not look at it previously, now proclaim it remarkable. Even Michelangelo deliberately tinted one of his paintings to give it the impression of an antique after which it was sold at a large sum to Raffaelle Riario, cardinal di San Giorgio. Additional methods by which the artist can increase his prestige may be found in Chapter VI.

We may conclude by stating that the reason why some artists succeed while others fail is owing to the fact that the successful persons have acquired not only the mechanical technique of their craft, but also a basic understanding of human nature so they can select scenes and situations which have greater human interest value. In addition to these two necessary qualifications, the artist who hopes to earn a livelihood needs to be a good salesman or else enlist the cooperation of some one who will care for the publicity and merchandising of his products.

REFERENCES

BEDFORD-JONES, H., *This Fiction Business* (Denver, 1931).

————, *The Graduate Fictioneer* (Denver, 1932).

BITTNER, A. H., *What an Editor Wants* (Denver, 1924).

BUSWELL, G. T., *How People Look at Pictures: A Study of the Psychology and Perception in Art* (Chicago, 1935).

CHANDLER, A. R., *Beauty and Human Nature* (New York, 1934).

CLASON, C. B., *How to Write Stories That Sell* (Denver, 1930).

GALLISHAW, JOHN, *The Only Two Ways to Write a Story* (New York, 1928).

HARRINGTON, H. F., AND MARTIN, L., *Pathways to Print* (New York, 1931).

KANTOR, J. R., "An Objective Psychology of Grammar," *Ind. Univ. Publ. Sci. Ser.,* 1936, No. 1, pp. 344.

MEIER, N. C., "Studies in the Psychology of Art," *Psychol. Monog.,* 1934, vol. 18, No. 200.

MUNRO, T., *Scientific Method in Aesthetics* (New York, 1928).

NIXON, H. K., *Psychology for the Writer* (New York, 1928).

RAFFELOCK, DAVID, *Conscious Short Story Technique* (Denver, 1930).

RAFFELOCK, D., AND HAWKINS, W., *How to Write a Screenable Plot* (Denver, 1932).

SPURGEON, C. F. E., *Shakespeare's Imagery and What It Tells Us* (New York, 1936.

UZZELL, THOMAS H., *Narrative Technique* (New York, 1923).

WILHELM, D. G., *Writing for Profit* (New York, 1930).

(Business Man's Notebook, published in New York World Telegram).

April 3—Advertisement for stenographer	$0.50
April 5—Violets for new stenographer	.85
April 8—Week's salary for stenographer	15.00
April 11—Roses for stenographer	3.00
April 15—Candy for wife	.60
April 19—Lunch with stenographer	5.00
April 25—Stenographer's salary	25.00
April 25—Dinner and theatre with stenographer	10.00
April 26—Fur coat for wife	385.00
April 26—Advertisement for stenographer	.50

CHAPTER XIII

CHILD PSYCHOLOGY

The modern trend in child psychology is to look to the environment of the youngster instead of to his heredity for those determining factors which will make him good or bad, introvertive or extrovertive, confident or afraid. If a choice were to be made between heredity and environment, the latter would be the more dynamic selection since it enables people to build personalities of the sort which they desire, whereas their own heredity is beyond their control.

A complete discussion of the child must, nevertheless, involve his inherited traits as well as the environment in which those traits are being expressed. A good environment somewhat offsets a poor inheritance, while a poor environment stunts to some degree the talents of a rich inheritance. Ideally, the optimum heritable traits in the most favorable milieu would produce the best results. In stating that a favorable environment partly offsets a meager inheritance, one must not forget that there are limitations to the interaction of heredity and environment. A moron cannot become a college graduate despite a wealth of music, books, and tutors with which he may be surrounded. Indeed, the parable of the talents may fittingly be applied to human inheritance. Some children receive five mental talents, whereas others receive only two or but one.

This fact is illustrated indirectly by Hollingworth[1] in the following table. The reader will note the earlier maturity of those children who possess high intelligence quotients, and the significant delay in walking and talking of the subnormal youngsters. Throughout the remainder of this chapter, however,

[1] Hollingworth, H. L., *Mental Growth and Decline* (D. Appleton & Co., New York, 1927), p. 134.

we shall emphasize chiefly the influence of the child's environment upon him.

INTELLIGENCE LEVEL	AVERAGE AGE AND MEASURES OF VARIABILITY	
	WALKING	TALKING
Gifted (600 Cases)	12.8 months S. D. 2.5 mo.	11.2 months S. D. 2.8 mo.
Normal, or somewhat higher (50 Cases)	13.9 months A. D. 1.6 mo.	15.3 months A. D. 3.0 mo.
Feeble-minded (144 Cases)	25.1 months A. D. 9.6 mo.	38.5 months A. D. 16.8 mo.

EXHIBIT 52. The different average ages of walking and talking of superior, normal, and subnormal children.

The Child's Struggle for Individuality. In order to imagine more accurately the attitude of children regarding their adult surroundings, it is well to remember that chairs, tables, and other items of furniture are almost all built for persons who are giants in the eyes of their youngsters. We can comprehend this fact more readily if we suppose as adults we were placed in a world where all those who arbitrarily commanded us were at least 10 feet tall, weighed 400 pounds, and mysteriously possessed the ability to know what we were doing in their absence. The pre-kindergarten youngster, for instance, may have a father who is twice his height, and five times as heavy.

During childhood, therefore, the boy and girl are vividly aware of their dependence. "Don'ts" and "mustn'ts" are frequently heard, each of which deflates the child's ego. For twelve to fifteen years he does the will of his parents and teachers, with only occasional revolts. As he enters puberty, however, the size difference between himself and his parents has become lessened. He may even be as tall as his mother and the school teacher. He begins to taste some of those choice pleasures that follow partial independence. He goes to the scout camp alone, and has his own friends.

Meanwhile, in order to bolster his sense of importance he tries to impress his playmates in various ways, one of which is the creation of secret societies. Maybe these are for his own sex alone, girls being entirely taboo, although often they are heterosexual in personnel. By such a method he arbitrarily separates himself from the *hoi polloi* and with elaborate ceremonies as well as the use of the blackball he indirectly inflates his own ego. The following college girl's paper describes a fairly typical instance of this sort.[1]

The ROYAL ORDER OF WHAT we called it, and our pins were gold question-marks. Ours was a very exclusive organization, since it would not admit anyone under twelve years of age and then only on the very highest recommendation and after a rigid examination. Those who did not belong to our club delighted us by asking the name of the club. "We belong to the royal order," we'd respond. That was their cue for "The royal order of what?" Then we would beam with the snappy comeback: "That's just it—THE ROYAL ORDER OF WHAT?" So great was the curiosity of those not admitted to our club that those under twelve counted the days to their twelfth birthday, and those over twelve but not admitted formed counter-organizations of their own. These, however, never attained the status of our club and were not very long lived.

Both boys and girls belonged to our club, and nationality was something we never thought of Most of us went to the same church, but there was no connection between the club and the church, except that we found Sunday School a very fertile field for seeds of curiosity, on which we fed with relish.

Because so much eagerness to join was displayed by the initiates, we made the initiation quite difficult, "a test of character" we called it. Each initiate was subjected to three tests: the mock initiation, which consisted of the usual pranks and foolishnesses, but perhaps a little more foolish; the intelligence test, which consisted of answers to as many questions as we could think of, with a good deal of our

[1] **Paper by Mary Campbell.**

own homework thrown in; and, finally, the solemn initiation, which we all attended in our long black robes and masks. At the solemn initiation, the constitution was read by candle light, and every initiate had to sign it in blood, a rather severe test and somewhat of a shock. We never experienced any difficulty, however, in getting the victims to conform with the requirements.

The election of officers was also a serious business surrounded with a great deal of formality. The most coveted office was that of "High Monkey-Monk." He was assisted by numerous royal officers, so that almost everyone had some fancy title. The vote was by secret ballot, in keeping with the spirit of the Royal Order.

However, the high position was usually held by the same boy every time. This is not hard to understand as he was an extremely capable leader with a powerful imagination, of which most of our ritual was a product, and he wore his ceremonial robes with a majesty which suited us all. In addition, he was a great diplomat, with a gift for eloquence which kept everybody happy.

At his suggestion, we held our most important meetings in his attic, which he furnished to suit the majesty of the occasions. However, we considered our homes good enough for ordinary meetings and took turns as hosts. Although everyone knew when and where the meetings were to be held, we had a Grand Scribe whose duty it was to send mysterious notices to the members.

Although the secretiveness formed a very important part of our activities, we were primarily a social group. Parties, picnics, beach parties, and grand tournaments (with much ceremony) helped to make us a self-satisfied organization.

However, this was not to last forever. One day the minister of our church, probably on the theory that too much self-satisfaction is bad for the soul, told our High Monkey-Monk that we really should be more democratic and let any young people of the church join our club. At the next meeting an atmosphere of tragedy prevailed, for we were to decide how to reply to the minister's request. We finally decided on "Give us liberty or give us death," and so as a club we broke up, but many long friendships have grown out of the old ROYAL ORDER OF WHAT.

I should like to tell WHAT it was THE ROYAL ORDER OF, but I promised I wouldn't and signed my name in blood!

The badges or pins of secret organizations are invaluable insignia without which the parent societies would probably disintegrate, for a part of the ego inflation of their members results from the envy of those with whom they associate. Other insignia prized by the child are those items of apparel or profession which pertain to adults. Thus children like to dress like their fathers or mothers. Long trousers, silk stockings, the father's old pocketknife, or the mother's discarded purse—these are cherished possessions of youngsters. Indeed, games in which they "play house" and assume parental roles are quite popular even with tots.

The child's struggle for individuality, therefore, consists of an attempt to throw off the bonds of serfdom and gain the social freedom of adults. His ego is deflated so constantly by his subservient position that he prizes anything which will bolster his individuality. In Chapter VI, for example, we pointed out how the tactful winning of young people presupposes a realization of this powerful motive base. The intelligent parent and teacher endeavors to give the child a reasonable amount of ego inflation by granting him possessions and praise and by making him class monitor, a juvenile traffic policeman, a member of the boy or girl scouts, or disburser of his own money. Those children who do not receive such treatment, moreover, are usually the ones who get into trouble when they go to college or otherwise attain independence. Many adults go through life always struggling to make up for a childhood which was too repressed. They form the nuclei for the "anti" groups in society and compensate so far that their behavior becomes almost atypical. We shall develop this topic more fully in the ensuing section.

Why We Sympathize with the Under Dog. Because the child himself has been the under dog for almost a score of years it is easier for him to identify himself with those who are being victimized or abused than with their tyrants and taskmasters. Even after the child reaches adulthood he still reacts with feelings of sympathy for the weaker party. It is possible that the maternal instinct, if there is one, explains in part the sympathy of women for the unfortunate folks around them, but the former explanation alone is adequate.

The successful person is envied by all and imitated by many, but is seldom sympathized with, for success and superiority have so long been identified with adulthood that it is difficult for us grown men and women to avoid slipping into the childhood attitude of resentment toward such persons. Other things being equal, the challenger has more friends among the spectators than does the champion, and the independent grocer gains sympathy in contrast to the chain store, even though people may patronize the latter.

Such behavior illustrates not only our identification with the weaker individual or business organization, but demonstrates the "negative protest" of youth. It is this protest against authority which explains in part the desirability of avoiding direct statements in salesmanship and the effectiveness of suggestion. The popular belief that youth must have its fling expresses an appreciation of the tendency toward radicalism on the part of young people and their desire to break conventions and restrictions. Some of those children who have been ordered about most autocratically during childhood become the violators of laws and conventions when they do have their fling. We have mentioned in the previous section the chronic "antis". For fifty years of adult life these individuals may continue their protest against those forces and ideas connected with the adults who robbed them so completely of their youthful self-respect. That college men and women often flaunt the religious tenets of their parents, and choose any vocation except that of their fathers, show evidences of simply a negative protest which has not expended itself.

For the average adult, however, the pendulum ultimately swings nearer the vertical, although few persons ever lose their sympathy for the under dog, since memories and attitudes of childhood are so lasting and dominant. The typical plot for a story or novel accordingly carries the hero or heroine along in an under dog role until the final chapter. Villains must be in the dominant position or be actively attempting to hold such authority. Even Cinderella would not elicit much interest if she were always a princess. But as a scullion who was ordered about by her cruel stepmother and stepsisters she obtains our support, for although we may not have been scullions we can readily identify phases of our childhood with her subservient position. If human beings sprang, like Athena, fully developed from their parents, it is quite likely they would feel less sympathy for the under dog, so the appeal of much current popular fiction would be considerably reduced.

From the psychological aspect, therefore, the adult's sympathy for the oppressed individual results from his ready identification with the latter, an identification which is a direct outgrowth of his many years of childhood wherein he himself was dependent and weak. In the following section we shall see how the child's intellectual immaturity leads to his belief in the supernatural and mysterious.

Why Children Believe in Magic. The child differs from the adult not only in his more limited experiences with life but also in his nervous immaturity which renders him incapable of the involved thought processes of the intelligent grown person. A little girl asks, "I bet you can't guess who drove the horses this morning?" An older girl replies bluntly, "You did." The younger child then inquires in mingled wonder and disappointment, "How did you know?"

In a similar manner the child who has been left at home alone by his parent and who knocks over the fish bowl or breaks a window, may reply to his mother's accusation, that he did not commit these errors. When his parent punishes him, he is nonplussed at her psychic power. How did she know he did it, for she was not there at the time? The "little bird" which tells mothers such things amounts to simply the five or ten years of additional mental age which the mothers possess beyond that of their children.

The child cannot reason, as does his parent, that inasmuch as he was the only occupant of the room or dwelling during her absence he is the one who must be responsible for any changes occurring therein. Because he sees evidences of apparent omniscience on the part of his father and mother, therefore, he is inclined to believe in magic.

Among the phantom creatures with which he peoples his childhood milieu are, of course, giants and ogres, but his usual favorite is the elf or fairy, for the latter is a little fellow who can defeat a big fellow. He can identify himself with the fairy on the basis of size and apparent inability to defend himself against superiors. The success of the tiny magical creature becomes his own success, experienced vicariously. The elf or fairy shares the hero or heroine role with little boys and girls in childrens' tales, and helps the latter out of difficulties.

In conclusion, therefore, we may state that the youngster's predilection for fairy tales results from his contact with adult reactions which are magical to him. Since his parents are apparently psychic, he finds no difficulty in granting reality to additional supernatural phenomena. His faith in fairies is not dispelled simply because he is unable to see them, for he cannot see how his mother knows his actions in her absence, but he must admit that she knows them. When his memory span and ability to handle longer and more involved ideas become greater, he can understand those mysterious inferences which his parents now make. His belief in fairies and a Santa Claus will then wane.

The Effect of Siblings on the Child's Personality. Because children are born of the same parents, develop in the same home, and have the tutelage of the same school teachers, people are inclined to state that their environment is the same. But such is not the case. The first child, for example, monopolizes the attention of both parents, and maybe the grandparents. His whims are the laws of the household. The people with whom he mingles are all adults. He finds that he is on the receiving end of almost all the parent-child reactions which ensue. He is the center of attention and occupies the spotlight on his domestic stage.

Then a younger brother or sister arrives, and for the first time in his life he becomes aware of real competition. His parents may hardly realize the shift in their interest to the newborn, but the older child instantly feels the change, and resents it. He dislikes the newcomer, and wishes for its removal. Since it cannot be removed, he must readjust his outlook upon life and try to effect a fairly satisfactory compromise. As the younger child grows older, the pleasure which the older youngster obtains from games in which the two engage begins to offset the dislike and antagonism which previously existed. But the elder child is inclined to be more domineering and blunt, relying upon his superior strength to procure the toys which he desires. However, his introvertive tendencies which developed prior to the second child's birth are somewhat modified by the extrovertive influences of the latter's presence, and his parents' insistence that he share his pleasures and property with the baby.

As for the second child's environment, we may begin by stating that he does not monopolize the family stage at any time, even though for the first few weeks he obtains the major portion of the parental attention. As soon as he is old enough to take note of his surroundings, he sees another youngster present, much like himself but stronger. Thenceforth he finds himself in competition with the older child, and is compelled to rely on his wits to satisfy his wants, since he is physically weaker than the first-born. He starts out in life with a tendency to extroversion, therefore, and soon begins to utilize his mother as a defense against his older sibling. He quickly learns that if he cries, the mother on general principles will assume that the older child has taken something away from him, and especially if she is weary or ill she will be inclined to make the elder youngster surrender any desired possession to the baby. When they are out of her sight, however, the stronger child usually regains his toys.

Another difference is the fact that the first child obtains new playthings, new clothes, new books, while the younger sibling frequently has only secondhand toys, "made-over" clothes, and used schoolbooks. The second child, moreover, tends to be more bold and irresponsible than the older, for he always feels that he can rely on the greater strength of his elder brother or sister, and his tendency toward extroversion renders him more socially curious and explorative. In previous chapters we have mentioned in this connection how the intuition of women tends to develop because they are physically weaker than their masculine playmates, and how younger children seem to be relatively more prevalent than first-borns among salesmen.

Let us suppose, moreover, that a third child enters the family. The effect upon the oldest youngster is not very great, since he must share with simply an additional sibling. But note the dilemma in which the second child finds himself. He neither has the prerogatives of the first-born with the consolation of probably being his grandparents' favorite, nor can he maintain his former special rights which belonged to being the baby. He finds himself confronted with the difficult situation of using his wits to deal with his stronger elder sibling, and using his greater muscular power in taking what he desires away from the new baby, which in its turn soon learns to utilize its lungs in gaining its mother's favor and partiality. The middle child, therefore, is in an environment which is most conducive to extroversion, while the youngest probably is next most extrovertive, whereas the first-born still tends toward introversion. The introvertive tendency of the eldest comes chiefly from the fact that he was an only child for a while. The manner in which introvertive personalities militate against successful social adjustments is brought out in the next section.

We may conclude our survey of the effect of siblings upon the child's personality, therefore, by saying that additional brothers and sisters tend to extrovert him. If only a year or two separate the ages of the first-born and the next youngster, this extrovertive influence has a greater effect upon the elder child's personality. If the latter is five or ten years old before the younger sibling arrives, he more nearly resembles the only child in his tendencies toward introversion.

How to Lessen the Child's Divorce Hazard. It is well to keep in mind that the majority of factors which occasion divorce do not develop only within the duration of the couple's marriage, but antedate it by almost a score of years, for they originate in the childhood experiences and training to which the husband and wife have been subjected. Such essential social virtues as a spirit of fair play, a willingness to compromise, an appreciation of the feelings and interests of others, and a realization that money is simply minted energy, these and many others are taught the child who develops in an auspicious milieu, or are lacking to the youngster in a less favorable environment.

Despite certain sentimentalists who emotionally look upon youth as "that sweet period of irresponsibility and earthly paradise," and who aver that it is wrong to "shackle the life of a carefree child with the fetters of adult society," we know that the youngster develops wholesome character only by grappling with the problems of his own little world as they arise. Experience is the bedrock on which the young as well as old construct personalities which will withstand the temporary squalls of emotional discord. And for later social contacts, particularly of the strenuous sort involved in marriage, the child deserves all the intelligent training and preparation which parents and teachers can offer him.

A child in a totally carefree environment cannot be expected to blossom into a responsible and responsive husband or wife through the magic ritual of a marriage ceremony. But the youngster who has grown up with a sense of some responsibilities intermixed with his play, and with the extrovertive influences of other children to produce unselfishness in him, will be a good marriage risk. In the preceding section we have discussed the different types of personality which tend to develop in siblings from such similar surroundings as the same home. In the following exhibit we shall show the divorce hazards of husbands and wives who came from homes in which they grew up as the only child, the oldest, the middle, or the youngest. By "middle" child we refer simply to a youngster who has at least one older and one younger sibling. These data are based on 2634 divorced men and their 2634 divorced wives, the family histories of whom were procured from college students who knew the participants in the divorces.

HUSBANDS			WIVES			
			Only	Oldest	Middle	Youngest
		(%)				
Only	754	(28.6)	191	236	147	180
Oldest	655	(24.9)	153	158	176	168
Middle	638	(24.2)	132	155	207	144
Youngest	587	(22.3)	74	158	181	174
Totals	2,634		550	707	711	666
(%)			(20.9)	(26.8)	(27.0)	(25.3)

EXHIBIT 53. Showing the percentage of various types of children who as adults procure divorces.

To fully understand the significance of children's order of position in the family and its relationship to their divorce hazard, we must obtain an index of the percentage of only children, oldest, youngest, and middle children among the adult population. Since the United States Census Bureau has informed the writer that no such tabulation has been made heretofore, he selected at random 100 families with children. Since the majority of the participants in divorces listed in the above table were from 20 to 40 years of age, the writer chose his 100 families so that the offspring thereof would now be within the age range mentioned. In these 100 families were 16 only children, 84 oldest, 84 youngest, and 132 middle children, making a total of 316. On the basis of these figures, therefore, there are in the present adult population falling between 20 and 40 years of age the following percentages: Only children, 5.0%; oldest, 26.6%; youngest, 26.6%; and middle, 41.8%. The exhibit below will show the difference between the percentages of various types of child in the adult population and the incidence of divorce in such groups.

TYPES OF CHILDREN	% IN ADULT POPULATION	% DIVORCED HUSBANDS	% DIVORCED WIVES	HUSBANDS' HAZARD	WIVES' HAZARD
Only	5.0	28.6	20.9	5.72	4.18
Oldest	26.6	24.9	26.8	.94	1.01
Youngest	26.6	22.3	25.3	.84	.95
Middle	41.8	24.2	27.0	.58	.65

EXHIBIT 54. Showing the divorce hazards of men and women occupying different positions in the sequence of children. Hazards are computed by dividing divorce percentage by the percentage in adult population.

From the above hazards it will be seen that an only child of the male sex has 5.72 times as great a likelihood of divorce as should be warranted by the percentage of only children in the adult population, and for only children of the female sex the ratio is 4.18. The middle child, with his greater extroversion which we have previously mentioned, is the best marriage risk for both sexes. Indeed, among men an only child is approximately ten times as likely to enter divorce as is a middle child.

Such ostensible causes for divorce as differences between

husband and wife in race, religion, education, and social position, or the effects of alcohol and sexual maladjustment are probably spread uniformly throughout the various classifications of children, for there seems no *a priori* reason why only children should be especially prone to cross religious or racial lines, or be any more addicted to liquor than oldest, youngest, or middle children.

Since in these 5,268 cases the only child is such a great divorce hazard in contrast to children who have grown up with at least one sibling, it behooves educators and parents to adopt every ameliorative measure which will reduce his danger of marital unhappiness. Among such instruments we can cite the presence of living playmates in the home, such as kittens or puppies, in case the parents are resistant to having an additional youngster. In a preceding chapter we showed how sympathy and tenderness can be inculcated in the only child by such playmates.

Moreover, the early contact of the only child with human companions of approximately his own age will help reduce his hazard. The nursery school is especially valuable in this regard. Indeed, it might be wise to reduce the age of entrance to kindergarten to three years instead of the present five years. Such a change would seem to be advisable, since the increasing economic competition is reducing the size of families, and as the number of one-child families increases, it seems probable that the incidence of divorce will correspondingly be accelerated. There seems to be a marked negative correlation, therefore, between the size of the average American family and the divorce rate.

In subsequent sections of this chapter we shall describe additional methods of lessening the child's divorce hazard. It is sufficient to conclude here that the chief method of insuring children a later marital happiness lies in extroverting the youngsters by means of such available instruments as animal playmates, other children either of the neighborhood or nursery school, and, as we shall later discuss, by developing self-reliance in them. Since the integrity of the home is one of the principal bulwarks of the nation, and since the divorce rate in the United States is now about one to six, it is apparent that the divorce problem is of national as well as of moral significance.

The "Reversible Why" in Child Training. Everybody who has dealt with young children is familiar with the incessant barrage of questions which they can fire upon the adults in their vicinity. Many of these queries are rather profound, or at least demand a keener insight into science and religion than the average person possesses. And because of their constant recurrence many parents become irritated at the child and send him forth to play.

As a matter of fact, it is quite likely that the more questions a child asks, the more intelligence he possesses. Since his queries are mental hooks with which the youngster goes fishing for information about the mysterious universe in which he finds himself, it is wise for parents and teachers to satisfy his curiosity as long as their patience will last. In so doing, however, they must not only phrase their replies in language which the youngster can understand, always remembering that his mental age is far below the adult level, but they should also recall that active learning is superior to passive. They should, therefore, endeavor to reverse the child's query so that he utilizes all his present fund of knowledge in regard to his own question. Then if he cannot evolve a solution, they must add their comments.

The "reversible why" is an excellent habit for adults to acquire, as we have previously mentioned in our discussion of salesmanship, for it quickly places the mental effort upon the other party, thereby freeing its propounder for a moment's respite in which to collect his thoughts or survey his comrade. In dealing with children the teacher and parent can also profitably employ it, thereby keeping on the offensive and giving the youngster more cerebral exercise. The following excerpt will demonstrate the method more clearly, although in dealing with adults a little more finesse should be shown in reversing their queries.

"Why do you put that white stuff on your face?" Junior asked on the first morning of my visit, while I was going through the drudgery of my daily shave.

"Why do you think I put this on my face?" I countered.

He stopped for a moment, probably dumbfounded at this sudden offensive on my part.

"I don't know," he replied, but I refused to let him off with such an easy answer.

"What does it look like?" I continued, glad of the chance to keep on the offensive.

"Like cream when Mother whips it," came his immediate response.

"All right," I agreed, "but what else does it look like—something you use when you take your bath?"

"Oh, I know. It's soap."

"Righto," I answered. "Now why do you think I am putting soap on my face?"

"So you can wash it."

"But I'm not putting it all over my face. I rub it just on the hairs on my chin and jaws. Why do I do that?"

"So they'll get clean," he replied.

"All right," I said, "but how does your hair feel when Mother puts soap on it and gives you a shampoo? Is it soft or is it hard?"

"It's soft and wet," he answered.

"That's the way my beard is. The soap makes it soft and it's easier to cut the hairs when they are soft. They don't pull so much and hurt me while I am shaving."

"Then why doesn't the barber put soap on my hair? He didn't do it when I got my hair cut."

Fortunately his mother called us to breakfast and I deemed this an opportune moment to drop the conversation.[1]

A few years ago the writer tested this method with five children ranging in ages from four to seven. They were with

1 Crane, George W., "The 'Reversible Why'", *Child Welfare* (November, 1931), vol. xxvi, No. 3, pp. 137 *ff*.

him at various times and of course wanted to know this and that. The writer made notations of the first forty questions each child asked. In the first twenty of these he made a careful reply, which was entered upon his data sheet. On the second twenty questions of each child, the writer employed the reversible why, holding the youngster to his query until he had answered it himself in as complete a fashion as he could, after which, if he was not then successful, the correct information was given to him.

Ten days later the writer took each of the youngsters in turn and put to him the same forty questions which the child had previously asked. On the twenty questions which the writer had carefully answered as soon as the child had originally asked them, the five youngsters averaged twelve correct replies each, but on the twenty where the reversible why had been employed, they averaged eighteen correct responses apiece. In this experiment, therefore, the reversible why apparently led to a 50 per cent greater retention of the information which was presented to them. This occurred not because the writer had not fully replied to their first twenty inquiries on the initial day of the test, but because the answers to the second set of queries made a deeper impression upon them, due in part to the fact that they themselves had helped work them out.

From the psychological standpoint, therefore, the reversible why enables the adult to remain on the offensive and compels the child to cerebrate in response to his own question. Since he takes an active role in evolving the solution to his query, he is much more likely to retain the information thus arrived at. The reader will recall the statement from William James regarding the fact that children whet their wits on each other's. In the employment of the reversible why, moreover, the child has an opportunity to whet his wits upon problems turned back upon him by the skilful adult interrogator. The net result of this procedure is beneficial to the youngster both in respect to the greater retention of material which he encounters, and also in the mental exercise engendered in the process.

How Children Educate Children. We have previously mentioned the extrovertive influence which children have upon each other, and the value of such training as it relates to their later marriage risks. But there are other aspects to this problem which should be noted. The first-born, for example, tends to be slower in his development of speech than do his younger siblings, owing largely to the lack of oral stimuli with which he is surrounded. Adults may think that they converse freely with the only child, but they do not equal the talkativeness of an equal number of youngsters.

Playmates are stimulating in other respects, moreover, than simply the acquisition of oral language, for they bring to bear upon each other the combined knowledge of all members of the group. Probably no one parent takes the time to answer all his son's queries, or to explain every aspect of a new situation or object. But if each of a dozen parents gives his child one different idea regarding the operation of a toy or machine, when these twelve youngsters get together they soon gain eleven additional viewpoints, and go home to lunch with twelve ideas instead of the original one.

This result is especially true in the realm of sex where, despite the franker discussion of the subject by parents and teachers of the present generation, the youngsters still gain most of their knowledge from their playmates. Just one of the latter who possesses some first-hand information may enlighten the children of the entire neighborhood or school. The avoidance of sex topics by some parents of course whets their children's curiosity, rendering them more ready listeners to their playmates' ideas on the topic. In the quotation which follows the reader will see how Professor Katz's older son casually discussed the matter of human births with his mother, and then probably dismissed it from his mind. The reader may be interested to know that the child, named Theodor, had a chronological age of not quite five years and two months at the time of this conversation. His parents have obviously already enlightened him concerning the origin of human infants.

Conversation: December 29, 1925. Evening, in bed.

T. "Why did you stay in Berlin and not go back to that school? (A school in which Mother had been a teacher.)

M. "The war came, so I couldn't go back again."

T. "Why couldn't you go back?"

M. "The railways were being used by the soldiers, so I couldn't get a train."

T. "Was there a lot to eat then?"

M. "No, there wasn't much to eat."

T. "But Papa had enough to eat, didn't he?"

M. "Yes, Papa was a soldier and the soldiers had enough to eat."

T. "Why did the soldiers have enough to eat?"

M. "If the soldiers hadn't had enough to eat, they couldn't have fought."

T. "And the other people didn't have enough to eat?"

M. "No, they were all hungry, even the little children."

T. "Mama, the little babies who hadn't been born yet had the best of it, didn't they? They were lying nice and warm inside their mamas."

M. "Yes."

T. "Mama, when the babies crawl out, have they anything on?"

M. "No, they are naked."

T. "Aren't they cold, when they're naked?"

M. "No, because they're dressed immediately."

T. "Why don't the children come out together?"

M. "What do you mean?"

T. "I mean, why didn't Baby and I come together?"

M. "Babies do sometimes. Then we call them twins."

T. "Then they would have to be smaller, or else they couldn't come out easily."[1]

The above conversation also illustrates the fact that children cannot be looked upon as simply the uncritical recipients of

[1] Katz, David, *The Vibratory Sense and Other Lectures* (1930), University of Maine Studies, Second Series, No. 14, pp. 148-149.

information, but have the capacity to do some original or creative thinking. It is partly because of the latter function that they educate one another. As a consequence, it is well that they be given correct advice at the outset, else they may later develop resentment toward the parent or teacher who misinformed them, particularly when some other child in the neighborhood challenges their statements, and proves them in error.

The methods by which children educate children consist primarily, therefore, in their extroversion of one another, but they also serve as stimulants to each other's thinking by means of their frequent challenges of one another's statements, thereby whetting their wits after the fashion described by William James. They also bring to bear upon a given problem their combined knowledge and consequently play respectively the roles of teacher as well as pupil. Since the formulation of ideas for their presentation to others is likewise beneficial to the instructor, these youngsters not only gain information from each other, but they obtain the profit which results from organizing facts. The older children, moreover, repeat the admonitions of parents and instructors to their younger siblings and serve as models after whom the younger children can pattern their behavior. Both of these functions relieve adults of a part of their teaching load, yet further increase the enlightenment of the children. In the next section we shall consider an additional important educational function of youngsters.

How Children Educate Adults. The classic instance in literature of the remarkable transformation in Silas Marner when he became the guardian of a child demonstrates one of the principal educative effects of children upon men and women. Childless adults tend to grow more and more introvertive with age. Indeed, all adults approach extreme introversion at senescence but the presence of children and grandchildren greatly retards the process. At the age of sixty people could probably be classified in four general groups as regards their degree of introversion; first, the bachelor or spinster; second, the childless married person; third, the married person with children; fourth, the married person with children and grandchildren.

Parents are usually compelled to become somewhat conversant with current educational methods, at least as long as their youngsters are of school age. They even follow the athletic successes of the teams representing their children's school or university. In fact, vicariously they gain many of the advantages of a college education through the letters and oral descriptions of their offspring, often possessing information concerning campus matters which is unknown to the professors at the university.

With current amusements of young people they also are in touch, and become attentive to styles and fashions in the apparel of youth. Their active participation in religious affairs is frequently a direct result of their desire to set an example to their youngsters, and they are usually active sponsors of the boy and girl scout organizations, and similar societies which will exert wholesome influences upon their progeny.

After a quarter of a century they again go through a part of this extrovertive process when their grandchildren are born. They do not follow the school curricula so closely, nor are they in such daily contact with the children, but they find many more outside interests than other elderly persons who lack the interrogations of youngsters.

But the extrovertive influence of children is not their only means of benefiting the adults in their environment. The frequent queries of the youngsters force their parents into cerebral activity, often of a sort which is severe. Moreover, the candor and naivetè of children is often refreshing as well as informative. To answer the demands made upon them by their offspring, many adults find it necessary to engage in more reading and study. Parent teacher organizations and books on child psychology become popular with mothers. Several magazines in the United States are maintained chiefly by parents who wish advice concerning the rearing of boys and girls.

Parents also become aware of the need for better pictures and music with which to stimulate their children's imagination. Encyclopedias and reference volumes of different sorts also begin to make their appearance in the home, and are used by the adults as well as the children. Meanwhile the fathers and mothers find themselves going through a change of attitude regarding international politics, for those who have several sons are not so prone to telegraph their senators at Washington to vote for war.

The principal educative value of children upon adults, therefore, consists of the extroversion of the latter with its attendant advantages of keeping the adults in touch with current phases of business, science, and the arts. Additional benefits which accrue to parents are their increased participation in worthy school, civic, and religious activities as well as their greater patronage of music and literature. Such activities also are frequently of value to the community as a whole so that the state gains a more responsible type of citizenry thereby. The adults themselves profit by the wider range of interests which they develop and their greater capacity for social enjoyment.

Developing Self-reliance in the Child. Whether or not the child will be able to face the responsibilities and defeats of adulthood will depend very largely on the training which his parents give him. If they constantly act as buffers between him and the hard knocks of life he will find adult problems too fierce or rigorous for his temperament, and may lean upon his parents for comfort and assistance as long as they live. Every reader is doubtless familiar with many such individuals who may have remained bachelors and spinsters because of mother- and father-fixations, coupled with an inability to fend for themselves. Others may attempt marriage and economic independence only to make miserable failures of both, after which they return to the parental roof.

In our discussion of the development of confidence and aggressiveness in the child we pointed out the fact that the tasks assigned to him must not be too great for his capacity, nor must they be permitted to remain unfinished, else he develops a defeatism complex similar to that illustrated by Half-Way Hurley. Since confidence is really the habit of success, parents and teachers must be careful to motivate the youngster adequately, and adjust his duties to fit his present capacities.

Since life cannot satisfactorily be met by an individual who is always carefree, it becomes advisable to temper the youngster's play with a judicious admixture of tasks or "chores". These may begin as soon as he is old enough to walk. He should learn to put his playthings away after he is through with them, and thereafter should be taught the various responsibilities which he is supposed to assume in life.

In this connection it is well for him to gain an impression of the meaning of money, for when he realizes that it stands not only for ice cream sodas and candy but also for human energy expended in its acquisition, he is able to disburse his funds wisely. Children who are dependent upon coaxing and cajolery and their parents' largess in order to have spending money are losing one of the best means of gaining self-reliance, namely, the earning of their own nickels, dimes and quarters. When a child earns his money his ego is inflated, for he feels more independent and competent. In order to illustrate an ingenious method by which a father not only changed his twelve-year-old boy's attitude concerning mathematics, but also made him much more self-reliant, we shall offer the following paragraphs[1].

[1] Crane, George W., "Tact and Child Education," *Forecast* (March, 1928), vol. xxxv, No. 3, p. 210.

"He told the lad that he might act as purchasing agent for the family's groceries. Under the new arrangement the boy bought at cash and carry stores, whereas formerly the father had patronized a store nearer home from which goods had been delivered. The prices had been slightly higher at the latter store, and these prices were used as the basis on which the youth was permitted to operate.

"If, for instance, he purchased butter at fifty-two cents a pound at the cash and carry store, when the other grocer was charging fifty-four, the boy received two cents for his foresightedness and effort in carrying the goods home. Soon he became so interested in this financial game that the page of the evening paper to which he turned first was that on which the grocers' advertisements were displayed. Arithmetical figures no longer remained only stupid black marks to be juggled according to some stereotyped rule, but were changed into useful tools. Without being aware of what had brought about his new attitude, the boy presently found himself taking an interest in arithmetic, and soon he was the most proficient mathematician in his class.

"His parents had not scolded him. He had, therefore, been saved from developing a defense reaction. And by the father's tactful plan he had also been brought to the forefront of his class, and hence developed a liking for mathematics."

In the public schools it is not unusual to find projects undertaken in which the pupils build a miniature store, and go through the actions of buying and selling. Such procedures are not only of educational value, but they are pleasant to the youngsters, who feel more grown up in consequence.

Another very good method for increasing the child's self-reliance is that of letting him assume the responsibility of some living thing, such as an animal, or potted plants, a garden, or the goldfish. He attains, therefore, the feeling that some weaker being is dependent upon him, and as a result not only is complimented but also is extroverted by his duties with reference to these living objects.

In the child's play, moreover, he finds an additional opportunity to develop his self-reliance, for he discovers that compromises are a necessity if he is to retain the friendship of his mates. It is not difficult to diagnose the environmental background of the youngster who is of the I'll-take-my-ball-and-go-home-if-I-can't-be-captain type. Until puberty, however, the child is rather uncoöperative and individualistic. But as he enters the teens he begins to like group games and will acquire a spirit of coöperation and fair play if he is situated in the proper environment. It is illuminating in this connection to note the words of Dr. H. D. Williams' son who, while visiting a summer camp of juvenile delinquents, entered a ball game being played between two teams of young offenders. Later he remarked to his father, "Those kids don't know how to play. They stand there and argue and fight, and hold up the game so there's no fun in it."

There is no more tragic sight among children than a youngster who wants to be included in the games of others but who has been deprived of human playmates for several years so that he is ignorant of the rules of their games, or is so awkward and inept that the other boys ignore him. When sides are being chosen for a ball game, he stands up hopefully, thinking that he may be selected next by one of the respective captains only to find that the last member of each team has been chosen without his name being called. "Aw, we don't want him on our side," his associates may remark with the brutal frankness of youth, "for he can't hit the ball." If the child is very intelligent and sensitive a few such public humiliations may send him to the sidelines for the remainder of his youth, and perhaps his entire life. Thereafter he may retain his interest in social groups, but always stay on the outskirts of the crowd. "Wallflowerism" is a category which covers his social inferiority complex.

On the other hand, this disappointed child may become a misanthrope, or engage in atypical behavior in order to attain some social recognition and envy. He frequently becomes the scholar so that he can compensate intellectually for his physical inability. If, however, a child has physical strength and dexterity but lacks brilliance or polite manners, he may compensate by becoming the bully of the crowd, or the "bad" child in the school. He finds that he can gain thereby a certain awed admiration and notoriety even if he cannot attain fame by the more onerous plan of study and scholastic preeminence.

Neither of the two types of reaction just mentioned is expressive of a well integrated personality. Because both youngsters feel their lack of self-reliance, they have adopted a compensatory form of reaction, and to explain their apparent inefficiency in the quality wherein they are inept, adopt a "sour grapes" attitude. Although it is true that some of the great works of art and of literature, of music and of science have come down to us as the fruits of compensation, as probably demonstrated by Beethoven, Byron, and Steinmetz, they have been produced at the cost of social maladjustment. Although society occasionally may profit thereby, from the standpoint of psychology such compensations as those of the two boys mentioned above are unwholesome.

As for the matter of emotional development and its relationship to the self-reliance of the child, we may state that many of the fears and doubts and emotional stresses which trouble the adult have their roots in childhood experiences. We shall treat this subject more fully in Chapter XV. Although Watson believes there are only the three primitive emotions—fear, rage, and love—these three may, like the four primary taste qualities, become so tied up with thousands of situations and stimuli as to affect a large portion of the individual's reactions. The difference between the coward and the brave man, for example, is often simply the fact that the coward is afraid, while the courageous man is afraid of being afraid.

In concluding our discussion of the development of self-reliance in the child, we should state that the aim of parents and teachers should be to add to the sum of the child's wholesome habits. The child with 1,000 habits is obviously less self-reliant than the youngster with 10,000 habits, other things being equal. Accordingly, it is imperative for adults to see that the child knows how to play the games of his age and sex, how to earn and spend money, how to care for his wants and make the mechanical and social adjustments expected of him because of the type of environment to which he will be exposed. Confidence and assurance follow the youngster who is sufficiently equipped with methods of reaction to the stimuli of his milieu so that he can make satisfactory adjustments thereto. No one is continuously successful, so the child must be schooled to meet the stimulus of defeat and know how to react successfully to it. This reaction does not involve running home to mother, or the development of a sour grapes attitude, but a close scrutiny of his own performance so that he can detect the flaws therein and avoid their repetition.

Sculpturing in Human Clay. When a Michelangelo stands before a block of marble he may sculpture a "Moses" or a group of "slaves", but in either case his product is insignificant compared to the human personality which can be produced by intelligent parents and teachers out of eight pounds of animate human clay. If the child possesses normal intellectual endowment and sensory acuity, he can be moulded into an outstanding surgeon, lawyer, artist, musician, poet, philosopher, orator, or writer. His parents, by the proper control of the stimuli playing upon him, can direct him into any one of these professions. The difficult task which they confront, however, is twofold, consisting of an understanding of what are the kinds of stimuli to employ to sculpture the child's personality, and how to procure or utilize those stimuli after they are known.

The first of these two problems is usually the more frequent cause for failure, since the intelligent parent and teacher do not need million dollar equipment and tools for the training of their Lincolns, as the following quotation from Dorothy Dix's column demonstrates.

(By Courtesy of the Philadelphia Public Ledger.)

"I know now that when I was a child we were very poor. I had so few clothes that my mother used to wash at night the little shirt that I wore to school the next day, but I was always clean and neat. I had to begin earning money almost as soon as I could walk, and I delivered papers when I was so little I could hardly reach a bellpull. We had such plain food that it was a gala day to be remembered for weeks when we had pie for dinner.

"But I never knew that I was poor because I never remember to have heard the subject mentioned in our family. My mother never whined and complained about what she couldn't have or because she wasn't as well off as other women or because she couldn't give us children the advantages that rich parents could give their children. She was always cheerful and made our home the happiest place in the world, and if we didn't have anything but stew and bread for supper we ate it to the accompaniment of so much laughter and good cheer that it made it a feast.

"My mother never let us be sorry for ourselves. She never inoculated us with the virus of self-pity, as so many poor mothers do their children. She never let us feel that it was hard luck that we had to work when other children played. She managed somehow to make us feel that we were superior to the poor little rich children who had to ask their parents for pennies, because we were clever enough to earn money ourselves. She made us feel that we were men and women while they were still children. I can remember being actually sorry for the little boys who didn't have newspaper routes and had nothing to do but to play marbles, while I was a responsible individual with what I considered an important job.

"My mother never deplored the fact that she couldn't give us college educations and that our father didn't have a bank that he could take us into as soon as we were grown. She never even intimated that poverty was a handicap to a boy.

"On the contrary, she talked to us continually about the poor boys who had become millionaires, about the boys who had no schooling, but who had educated themselves by reading and study; about the boys who had gone from behind plows and the towpaths of canals, from the humblest places, to the President's chair. The names of great doctors, lawyers, merchants, men of affairs who had been poor boys were always on her lips, and it was just bred into us that we could be like them if we were man enough to do it.

"I often think of my mother and other poor mothers that I have known since—mothers who make failures of their children in their very cradles by bringing them up in an atmosphere of gloom that chokes out every hope and aspiration and makes them feel that they are the victims of a malign destiny against which it is no use to struggle.

"Mothers who break down their children's morale and weaken them by weeping over them because they have to work. Haven't you seen such mothers, time and again, wringing their hands and shedding tears because their poor little Tommies had to punch the time-clock in a factory every morning instead of lying abed or because their darling Mamies had to stand behind a counter or pound a typewriter instead of going to pink teas?

"And, of course, that made Tommy and Mamie feel that they were poor, persecuted martyrs when they should have been rejoicing that they had brains enough to hold down a job and were independent, self-supporting men and women who could look the world in the eye and tell it where to go."

In summarizing this matter of sculpturing in human clay, it is evident that a thorough understanding of human motivation and control must be possessed by the sculptor if he wishes to mould his clay into the desired form. In addition, he must be cognizant of the great responsibility which devolves upon him after he has attained this knowledge. The majority of parents and teachers do not wish to be held accountable for pre-determining the child's future vocation, but are content if they can only equip him adequately for whatever demands life may make of him. That goal in itself is sufficiently difficult to test the ingenuity of adult intelligence, and should occupy the attention of those who have the opportunity to sculpture in human clay.

Since such tremendous potentialities reside in the child, it is no wonder, therefore, that many parents and teachers are awed by the responsibilities which are theirs. And if an artist or sculptor in marble feels that he must spend many years mixing paints and learning the technique of wielding a chisel, how much more imperative must be the need for men and women who deal with youngsters to acquire adeptness in manipulating verbal stimuli and the physical elements of the milieu. Consult my "Tests For Parents" on page 610.

REFERENCES

ANDERSON, J. E., *The Young Child in the Home* (New York, 1936).

AVERILL, L. A., *Adolescence* (Boston, 1936).

BLANTON, S., AND BLANTON, M., *Child Guidance* (New York, 1927).

BOTT, H. McM., *Personality Development in Young Children* (Toronto, 1934).

BROOKS, FOWLER D., *The Psychology of Adolescence* (New York, 1929).

BURT, CYRIL, *The Young Delinquent* (New York, 1925).

COLE, L., *Psychology of Adolescence* (New York, 1936).

CRANE, GEORGE W., "Teach Your Child to See," *Delineator* (April, 1931), pp. 36 *ff*.

CURTI, MARGARET W., *Child Psychology* (New York, 1931).

DEWEY, E., *Behavior Development in Infants* (New York, 1935).

GESELL, A., *An Atlas of Infant Behavior* (New Haven, 1934).

GOODENOUGH, F. L., *Developmental Psychology* (New York, 1934).

HEALY, WILLIAM, *Mental Conflicts and Misconduct* (Boston, 1923).

HOLLINGWORTH, L. S., *Gifted Children: Their Nature and Nurture* (New York, 1926).

HURLOCK, E. B., AND KLEIN, E. R., "Adolescent Crushes," *Child Development*, 1934, vol. 5, pp. 63-80.

JERSILD, A. T., AND HOLMES, F. B., "Children's Fears," *Child Developm. Mono.* 1935, No. 20, pp. 358.

JONES, MARY C., "Conditioning and Unconditioning Emotions in Infants," *Childhood Education* (1925), vol. i, pp. 317-322.

KEMPF, E. J., "The Tonus of the Automatic Segments as Causes of Abnormal Behavior," *Journal of Nervous and Mental Disease* (Jan., 1920), pp. 1-34.

LIND, K. N., "The Social Psychology of Children's Reading," *Amer. J. Sociol.*, 1936, vol. 41, pp. 454-469.

LOWREY, L. G., "Environmental Factors in the Behavior of Children," *American Journal of Psychiatry* (1927), vol. vi, pp. 227-242.

MARSTON, L. R., "The Emotions of Young Children," *University of Iowa Studies in Child Welfare* (1925).

MORGAN, JOHN J. B., *The Psychology of the Unadjusted School Child* (New York, 1923).

PAYNTER, R. H., "Humanizing Psychology in the Study of Behavior Problems in Children," *School and Society* (Nov. 6, 1926), vol. xxiv, No. 619.

PFISTER, O. R., *Love in Children and Its Aberrations* (New York, 1924).

STODDARD, G. D., AND WELLMAN, B. L., *Child Psychology* (New York, 1934).

SYMONDS, P. M., *Mental Hygiene of the School Child* (New York, 1934).

WAGONER, L. C., *et al.*, *Observation of Young Children* (New York, 1935).

WILLIAMS, H. D., "Conflicting Authorities in the Life of the Child," *Religious Education* (1932), vol. xxvii, pp. 413-417.

CHAPTER XIV

PSYCHOLOGY APPLIED IN EDUCATION

The relationship between psychology and education has been a very close and cordial one. Each has profited by the data and principles of the other. The first practical applications of psychology of a systematic type were made in the field of education, where today many of the individual and group methods of the laboratory are employed under the heading, "experimental pedagogy". Indeed, both the methods of teaching and the content of the curriculum have been altered in accordance with progress made in psychology.

At an early period education was directed toward "training the mind" in which the mind was conceived of as a distinct entity which was more or less independent of the environment but could grow stronger or more powerful by contact with external stimuli. The difficulty with this conception was the confusion between intellectual development and muscular development. In the latter the same dumb-bell is just as effective in increasing the size and strength of the right biceps as are 100 equally heavy dumb-bells, so the subject needs but one to become a second Samson. In mental development, however, the very reverse of this rule holds true, for twenty years spent upon the study of Latin declensions will never stimulate mental growth like one year devoted to each of twenty different subjects.

Even yet this fallacy is not wholly understood. We send our children to high school and teach them geometry, for which the great majority will never have a single use later in life, yet fail to train them in applied psychology which is fundamental to their social and economic success. The former belief that geometry exercised the reasoning "faculty" more than salesmanship or accounting is now known to be false. A young fellow can obtain as much mental exercise trying to develop a successful campaign by which to win a girl who shows no interest in him, as he can in working any of the theorems presented to him in high school, and the relevancy of the former to his life's problems is obviously much greater. Thorndike[1] has the following to say regarding the relative disciplinary values of various school subjects:

> By any reasonable interpretation of the results, the intellectual values of studies should be determined largely by the special information, habits, interests, attitudes, and ideals which they demonstrably produce. The expectation of any large differences in general improvement of the mind from one study rather than another seems doomed to disappointment. The chief reason why good thinkers seem superficially to have been made such by having taken certain school studies, is that good thinkers have taken such studies, becoming better by the inherent tendency of the good to gain more than the poor from any study. When the good thinkers studied Greek and Latin, these studies seemed to make good thinkers. Now that the good thinkers study Physics and Trigonometry, these seem to make good thinkers. If the abler pupils should all study Physical Education and Dramatic Art, these subjects would seem to make good thinkers. These were, indeed, a large fraction of the program of studies for the best thinkers the world has produced, the Athenian Greeks.

Since reasoning is resorted to in the solution of any problem it makes little difference where the problem is encountered, for the effect upon the subject's thought processes, if the problems are the same in difficulty, will be equally beneficial. As a result, the choice of the curricula for schools and colleges can be made more profitably on the basis of the practical value of various subjects as related to the child's needs. This modern viewpoint is especially significant when one realizes that approximately two-thirds of all children never go beyond

1 Thorndike, E. L., "Mental Discipline in High School Subjects," *Journal of Educational Psychology,* vol. xv, Nos. 1 and 2 (1924), pp. 1-22, 83-89.

the eighth grade of grammar school, and 90 per cent of all the children, who later become the voters of the nation, never matriculate at a college or university. The opportunity of the state to prepare its citizens for a happy and well adjusted adulthood is practically completed in the senior year of high school. Such courses as geometry, therefore, can well be considered in the light of what they contribute of merit to the 90 young people out of every 100 who immediately go into business and the home. It would seem that time devoted to music and to art would have greater value to them.

In addition to producing changes in the curriculum, however, psychology has been of considerable value to pedagogy in bringing out the definite fact of intellectual differences between pupils. Heretofore, the teacher has attempted to deal with varying degrees of mental age within her class, even though the children were all of the same chronological age. Her task has been somewhat like that of a teamster with a dozen spans of horses among which there were Arabian thoroughbreds coupled with large draft horses. As the thoroughbreds would leap at the command to go and chafe at the sluggishness of the slower animals, so the teacher's bright pupils quickly grasp the new problems, and are irked at the repetitions thereof which she must perform with the slower children.

In consequence, the more alert youngsters must be given additional material which their mates do not receive, or they may divert their idle energy into destructive channels. Some of the most brilliant of her pupils may be promoted ahead of their classmates until they get into a group more nearly matching their intellectual level, but the majority of them do not "skip" grades. By means of the intelligence tests to be described in succeeding sections it is possible to sort the youngsters who are of a given chronological age into groups with comparable intellectual endowment. For example, in one large city school where the fourth grades were divided in three sections, called "A", "B", and "C", on the basis of their mental age, it was found that the "A" class covered 225 pages in reading during the term against 150 pages covered by the "B" group, and 95 pages by the least alert section.

Numerous advantages result from such a preliminary selective process. In the first place, the most alert youngsters can be given new material as fast as they can assimilate it, and they will all advance at about the same rate. Competition therefore becomes keener, so the children do not "coast" throughout grammar and high school on the basis of their superior intellectual heritage, and then "flunk" out of college during their freshman year because of faulty habits of study. In the colleges, of course, the student is confronted with a very intelligent group, so he does not surpass his mates as he may have done in high school and especially in grammar school. He is compelled, therefore, to study diligently, for his fellow students are just as alert as he. If he lacks adequate habits of study, he is likely to be left behind.

Even in the least alert section of school children, moreover, there is a marked advantage because of the uniformity of ability demonstrated by the children. They no longer need feel an inferiority complex about competing with their classmates, since they all are of about equal ability. Rivalry is more fruitful of productivity since they are now more willing to compete inasmuch as they have a chance to win. The other advantages, of such a mental age classification of school children, particularly in regard to simplifying the teacher's problems, we shall not be able to consider here because of space limitations.

Intelligence and Intelligence Tests. We have previously remarked upon the intimate relationship between heredity and environment as they pertain to intelligence. Since it is impossible in the light of present scientific advancement to separate the two, as might conceivably be done by calling the number of synapses the inherited intelligence, and the number of functional synaptic linkages the acquired intelligence, the reader will understand why there has been so much difficulty in defining intelligence. Probably the most widely accepted definition is that one given by the German psychologist Stern, who says that intelligence is the ability to meet and solve novel situations.

Although people had long recognized intellectual differences between individuals there was no systematic and objective test for separating children or adults into groups with definite mental ages until the French psychologist Alfred Binet was commissioned in 1904 to survey the schools of Paris for the purpose of detecting feeble-minded pupils. With the cooperation of Theodore Simon, Binet set to work developing a scale of tests for the mental alertness of youngsters of various chronological ages. In 1905 the Binet-Simon test was first published.

Almost immediately the Binet scale established itself as the most reliable method of measuring general intellectual ability then in existence. But there were many defects in the original scale, some of which Binet himself attempted to remedy, while others were modified in America by such experimenters as Kuhlmann, Goddard, Terman, and Yerkes. Of these the latter two have made the most significant alterations, and Terman's *Stanford Revision of the Binet-Simon Intelligence Scale* is now the standard intelligence test in this country for school children.

The actual standardization of the test was as follows. First a representative group of children was obtained. Let us assume there are 100 three-year-olds, 100 four-year-olds, etc. The experimenter then administers various items of the scale to each youngster. Suppose he inquires, "Are you a little boy or a little girl?" He finds that maybe 20 per cent of two-year-olds can answer correctly; that 77 per cent of three-year-olds are correct; and that 98 per cent of four-year-olds give the proper answer. As a result, he places the ability to give one's sex as an item which should be characteristic of the normal three-year-old, using the attainment of 75 per cent of the children at any given age as the standard. If, however, 95 per cent of three-year-olds could give their right sex, this question would not be a desirable one for any age group. Not only must 75 per cent be able to answer the query correctly, but not much over 75 per cent must be able to do so.

Following such a plan Terman re-standardized Binet's scale upon American children. Some of the items for different ages will be found below.

THREE YEARS

Points to nose, eyes, and mouth.
Enumerates objects in a picture.
Gives family name.
Repeats a sentence of six syllables.

FOUR YEARS

Compares lines regarding length.
Counts four pennies.
Copies a square.
Repeats four digits.

SIX YEARS

Distinguishes between right and left.
Counts thirteen pennies.
Names missing parts of mutilated pictures.
Distinguishes between morning and afternoon.

When the scale is actually administered to a child, the psychologist first endeavors to establish friendly relations and gain the cooperation of the youngster, after which the test items are regarded as a game. The highest age at which the child passes all tests is termed his basal age. For example, a four-year-old youngster might be able to answer all the items under the THREE YEAR test above, but not perform but three items under FOUR YEARS. His basal age would therefore be three years, or thirty-six months. For each of the items under FOUR YEARS he gets a credit of three months, if it is correctly answered. The child receives a total of nine months from the FOUR YEARS category, and is able to pass one item under FIVE YEARS, for which he obtains an additional three months. His total mental age is 36 plus 9 plus 3 months, or 48 months. Since his chronological age was stated as being four years, or 48 months, the child is normal and has an intelligence quotient of 100. We have previously discussed the fact that Terman, following the idea of Stern, has introduced the I. Q. or Intelligence Quotient as a means of expressing the relationship between a child's mental and chronological ages. The I. Q. equals the mental age divided by the chronological age.

The Intelligence Quotient is fairly constant, varying scarcely at all when the child remains in the same type of environment throughout his development to maturity. Thus, the youngster who at the age of four is given a Binet test which shows him to have an I. Q. of 120, will also be found to have approximately 120 for an I. Q. when he is tested at ten or fifteen years of age. If, however, he has visual or hearing defects at the age of four, or if he is undernourished or convalescing from a protracted illness, his decreased energy and lessened sensory acuity may cause him to obtain a lower I. Q. than he will later demonstrate when these errors are corrected.

The I. Q. has also been found to change somewhat when children are adopted into homes where the educational influences are more pronounced than in the child's orphanage or tenement environment. Freeman has shown that the greater the change in the conditions of the home, the more likely will be the alteration in I. Q. In a few cases, after several years' exposure to the superior milieu children gained as many as fifteen to twenty points. In this connection Terman states that children of the same native ability but located in superior and inferior homes may show a difference of about ten points in favor of the youngsters from the better type of environment.

In addition to the Binet test, the Army Alpha examination is another famous mental scale noted for its widespread use in measuring the intellectual differences of adults. During the World War this examination was devised by a group of psychologists appointed by the American Psychological Association and administered to 1,750,000 men. Since then it has been used extensively in colleges and the business world, although a number of somewhat similar examinations are now superseding it.

The Army Alpha is a battery of eight sub-tests, of which the first is intended to measure the subject's ability to follow oral instructions and contains twelve items. The second sub-test consists of 20 problems in arithmetic running from very simple addition to rather complex problems. The third sub-test of 16 problems endeavors to measure common sense, and is of the multiple choice type with three answers given to each question. The fourth is a synonym-antonym test in which the student determines whether two words mean the same or the opposite. There are 40 such pairs in the list. The fifth sub-test consists of disarranged sentences which must be mentally re-arranged into sensible statements, and then answered with the words "true" or "false". It contains 24 items.

The sixth sub-test consists of 20 sequences of numbers which must be completed, as 2 2 4 4 6 6 — —. The seventh sub-test involves a somewhat similar recognition of logical relationships among words, as Hand : Arm : : Foot : -- EAR TRUNK LEG HEAD. The student underlines one of the four capitalized words which has the same relationship to "foot" as "arm" has to "hand". There are 40 items in this sub-test, and 40 in the eighth, which is a range of information test. In the latter the student completes a sentence by underlining one of four words, as BRIDGE is played with RACKETS PINS CARDS MARBLES.

The total score possible is 212 which is practically impossible of attainment, while that made by the average person is probably around 70. In Chapter IX the reader will find the average scores made by members of 96 business, professional, and labor groups. The median score for college students falls at 150, and practical experience has shown that those who make below 110 are not very likely to succeed in college. In this connection it is well to remember that the possession of a high I. Q. or a remarkable score on Army Alpha is not an invariable prognosis of business or scholastic success, for studious habits and the adequate motivation for hard work are also important correlates. A person with a low I. Q. cannot graduate from college, but one having a high I. Q. may not do so, either.

The Army Beta was developed at the same time as Army Alpha but for use with those recruits who were either illiterate or non-English readers. It is a non-language examination and is akin to the usual performance tests except that it involves the use of pencil and paper, and was employed chiefly with adults. Performance tests were given considerable impetus by Pintner and Paterson, who had to perfect some scale for testing the alertness of deaf children. They employed fifteen tests derived from various sources, among which the following three are representative.

(1) *The Seguin-Goddard form board* which has also been extensively used by Sylvester with children of various ages. In this test the task confronting the child consists of laying a wooden block in the form of a cross, a square, a circle, a triangle, etc. into its appropriate indented place in the form board, in a minimal time and with no errors. The time limit for placing the ten blocks in their proper positions is five minutes. A common error of the feeble-minded youngster is his attempt to place a triangular block into the indenture for

the star, or the rectangular block into the space for the square. Even normal youngsters of limited years are liable to the same confusions.

(2) *Healy's pictorial-completion test,* in which the child is to complete a picture by inserting the proper cut-out portions. This test is somewhat similar to many games sold on the market except that here the child has a great many choices from which to select the appropriate cut-out pieces, and is scored on the basis of the relevancy of each insert.

(3) *The Knox cube test.* There are five of these small cubes of which four are placed in a row before the child while the fifth is held by the experimenter. The latter then taps the other cubes with the one which he holds, varying the order to form a more difficult sequence on succeeding trials, as 1-2-3-4, 1-2-3-4-3, 1-3-2-4-3. At the conclusion of each series the experimenter hands the cube to the child who is told to tap likewise. A definite, unchanged series of numbers is used with all subjects tested. Pintner and Paterson offer tables based on the extensive examinations made by themselves and other researchers. In them one finds that both the time consumed and the errors made in the test decrease with the increasing age of the subject examined.

In summarizing our discussion of intelligence and intelligence tests, we may state that Stern's conception of intelligence as the ability to meet and solve novel situations furnished the incentive for an attempt to create an objective scale for measuring this capacity. Such scales involve a number of sub-tests on which measures are taken, the sum of which constitutes the person's score. Some of the sub-tests may be weighted, as numbers 4, 7, and 8 on Army Alpha where there are 40 items each, instead of 12, 16, 20, or 24 as in the other subtests of that scale. The matter of weighting sub-tests has been discussed in a previous chapter. As for the types of mental tests developed, there is the Binet-Simon for children, the Army Alpha for literate adults, the Army Beta for illiterate adults and children, and the performance scales usually for children. Among these tests the Binet-Simon is strictly an individual examination wherein the administrator takes but one child at a time. The same procedure is true of most of the performance scales, but Army Alpha is a group test, being given to as many as a hundred or more simultaneously. Other intelligence tests are usually based on these general principles, and employ a number of sub-tests, the sum of whose scores becomes the subject's final index. In order to interpret the latter, of course, norms or the known performances of large groups of persons must be available. A score of 106 is only half the possible score on Army Alpha, but it is decidedly above the median for the American population, for only about 20 per cent can attain it.

The Uses of Intelligence Tests. During the years immediately following the World War psychological tests were employed more or less indiscriminately in the hope that a panacea of industrial and educational problems had been obtained. But mental and vocational testing requires a rigid technique and a scientific training for the adequate interpretation of the records procured. Many persons were lacking in at least one of these respects, so their results were often disappointing. Moreover, there are usually so many additional factors involved in both scholarship and industrial ability that the intelligence test score must be supplemented by other data. When rightly used and modified by additional measures, intelligence tests are of marked value in the following fields:

(1) *The classification of pupils in the schools.* In addition to the uses in sorting pupils of the same school grade into different groups, these tests may show those who warrant immediate promotion or demotion, and are of assistance in rating the ability of children who transfer to a new school. The personnel director of the university or the teacher may watch the performance in classroom work and note whenever it falls below the standard which should be maintained accord-

ing to the student's mental abilities. He may then interview the student at once in order to correct the factors which are interfering with the latter's optimum output. The intelligence score of a person is, accordingly, the best single measure of his ability, and forms a quick means of gaining an idea of his possible future development.

(2) *Selection of college entrants.* Particularly in the privately endowed colleges and universities intelligence tests have been employed as a means of selecting the most alert applicants. When such educational institutions have two or three times the number of applicants for which they have available space and equipment, it becomes advisable to choose those high school graduates who hold the most promise of profiting richly by the college training. Other things being equal, the more intelligent men and women are of this type. Because of the lack of uniformity in standards of grading students from one school to another, a high school average of 93 from one institution may not mean the same as one of 93 from another. The intelligence test is usually a method by which inside of an hour the university director of admissions can gauge the intellectual capacity of all the applicants. Instead of using the numerical or letter grades which high school graduates cite, moreover, he is more interested in their relative standing within their graduating class, for the latter measure is now considered a more nearly accurate basis for comparison.

(3) *Personnel administration.* The vocational counselor usually wishes to know first of all the intellectual capacity of his student. Although the public school system is a rough intelligence scale in itself, since most subnormals never are graduated from grammar school, and most normal children never matriculate at college, still a special mental test is even more nearly accurate. In employment, moreover, the intelligence score is also revealing, both as to the lower and upper critical limits. We have previously discussed this topic when

we mentioned how Dr. Snow used to encounter Army Alpha scores like 45, 67, 83, 56, and 175, among the taxicab drivers, and soon found that the 175 men were college students working their way through school.

The principal uses of intelligence tests, therefore, have to do with the sorting and classification of school children, the selection of college entrants, the guidance of young people into phases of industry in which they are intellectually capable, and the selection of employees who will be most satisfactory. In the following section we shall consider the intellectual strata in modern society.

Intellectual Levels of the Population. From the data procured by Army Alpha and Binet examinations Terman[1] has presented the following apportionment of Intelligence Quotients:

I. Q.	Classification
140- up	"Near" genius or genius
120-140	Very superior intelligence
110-120	Superior
90-110	Normal or average
80- 90	Dull, rarely classifiable as feeble-minded
70- 80	Border-line deficiency, sometimes classifiable as dullness, often as feeble-mindedness
0- 70	Definitely feeble-minded

Among the definitely feeble-minded, morons are usually considered to have Intelligence Quotients from 50 to 70, with imbeciles falling between 20 and 50, and idiots lying between 0 and 20. The adult idiot's mental age is under three, with the adult imbecile having the maturity of normal children of three to seven years, and the grown moron having a rating of

[1]Terman, L. M., *The Measurement of Intelligence* (Houghton, Mifflin, Boston, 1916), pp. 78-79 Reproduced by permission of and by arrangement with the publishers.

from seven to twelve years. Terman presents the percentage of the population possessing various I. Q.'s in the following table:

OF 1,000 UNSELECTED SCHOOL CHILDREN

The lowest	1	%	go to	70	or below;	the highest	1	%	reach	130	or above
The lowest	2	%	go to	73	or below;	the highest	2	%	reach	128	or above
The lowest	3	%	go to	76	or below;	the highest	3	%	reach	125	or above
The lowest	5	%	go to	78	or below;	the highest	5	%	reach	122	or above
The lowest	10	%	go to	85	or below;	the highest	10	%	reach	116	or above
The lowest	15	%	go to	88	or below;	the highest	15	%	reach	113	or above
The lowest	20	%	go to	91	or below;	the highest	20	%	reach	110	or above
The lowest	25	%	go to	92	or below;	the highest	25	%	reach	108	or above
The lowest	33⅓	%	go to	95	or below;	the highest	33⅓	%	reach	106	or above

Since less than 8 per cent of students enter college and these are usually of the very superior type, it will be apparent that an I. Q. of about 115 is probably the lower level of college intelligence. Terman states that an I. Q. of 75 might even be considered the upper limit for the category of feeble-mindedness, in which case there would be almost 2,500,000 such persons in the United States. This figure is in fairly close agreement with Dr. Goddard's[1] report of 2 per cent of feeble-minded among 2,000 public school children in New York City, and slightly in excess of the 1.5 per cent of feeble-minded found among the 12,000 pupils in the Toronto public schools in the survey under the direction of the Canadian National Committee of Mental Hygiene in 1919. Because in the latter survey a number of retarded children were absent from school during the time of the investigation, Professor W. G. Smith of the University of Toronto believes the total number of feeble-minded would also be about 2 per cent.

To illustrate an extreme case of intellectual brilliance in a child the reader's attention is called to the following comparison as given by Hollingworth *et al*[2]:

1 Goddard, H. H., *Feeble-Mindedness, Its Causes and Consequences* (New York, 1914).

2 Hollingworth, Garrison, and Burke, "Subsequent History of E—; Five Years After the Initial Report," *Journal of Applied Psychology*, vol. vi. (1922), pp. 205-210.

SUBJECT: Edward Rochie Hardy, Jr. BORN: June 17, 1908.

NOVEMBER 4, 1916	EDWARD	NORM*
Height	54.3 inches	49.5 inches
Weight	89.3 lbs.	54.2 lbs.
Intellectual status	I. Q. 187 (Stanford-Binet)	I. Q. 100 (Stanford-Binet)
School status	6th grade	3rd grade*
SEPTEMBER 29, 1921		
Height	64.2 inches	58.2 inches
Weight	166 lbs. (light clothing)	89.5 lbs.
Intellectual status	194 points (Alpha, Form 5)	47 points (Alpha)
School status	4th semester college	8th grade*

*Norms for height, weight, and school status are taken from Bird T. Baldwin, as established on children from Horace Mann School, Francis Parker School, and the High Schools of the University of Chicago, where the children are above average (for population at large) in intelligence.

In 1920 Edward took the Thorndike Mental Tests for freshmen for entrance to Columbia College and was second highest out of the 483 entering the college. Edward was then 12 years and 0 months of age, while the median age of the others was about 18 years. On the day cited in the table above Edward not only made 194 on Form 5 of Army Alpha, but a little later in the afternoon he took Form 6 and scored 201 thereon.

An I. Q. of 187 is obviously phenomenal. In our discussion of physical age, however, we mentioned that children mature at different rates, and as a consequence I. Q.'s would be more nearly accurate if we had norms for physical development so that we could insert physical age for chronological age in the formula by which I. Q.'s are obtained. From Edward's height and weight it would seem very likely that he is precocious in his physical maturity as well as in his mental alertness. His I. Q. would as a result be considerably less than 187 when he is matched with children of equal bone and muscular development. Even so, however, a score of 194 on Army Alpha puts him in the upper 1 per cent of Terman's classification, granting him a minimum I. Q. of 130.

In concluding our survey of the intellectual levels of the population, therefore, we may state that the average mental age of the adult is considered to be 16 years, although that of the principal sample of the white draft, when transmuted from Alpha and Beta examinations into terms of mental age, was placed at 13.08 years, a figure which is deemed a bit low. Hollingworth[1] has placed the average mental age at 14 years, and includes 50 per cent of the American population in that category, with the other 50 per cent equally distributed above and below that point. The number of feeble-minded persons in the population is usually estimated at from 1 to 3 per cent. In the light of these intellectual differences in children, consequently, it is not difficult to imagine the struggles of the school teacher who has hitherto obtained her pupils chiefly on the basis of their chronological age alone.

The Relationship Between Health and Intelligence. The proverbial curiosity of youth is largely a function of an abundance of physical energy and vitality. As age advances, this surplus diminishes so that the average person curbs his desire for intellectual exploration in order to horde his strength. The parent has frequently noted the striking curtailment in his child's curiosity when the latter was suffering from sickness or was undergoing convalescence. Nature inhibits cortical activity when the vegetative functions of the body demand all the youngster's strength and energy. A partial measure of the child's return to health is accordingly his greater interest in his milieu.

[1] Hollingworth, H. L., *Mental Growth and Decline* (Appleton, New York, 1927), p. 275.

Since a violent attack of disease will so markedly lower the curiosity of a youngster as to render him relatively oblivious to the stimuli in his environment, it is not difficult to understand the dulling effect of undernourishment and infection of a slower sort. The Army Alpha records from the war show a noticeable difference in the intelligence scores of white recruits infected by hookworm and a group of the same race not so infected.

In this connection the psychological examiners urge, "It is important, however, to guard against the assumption that data of this kind prove the existence of a causal relationship between hookworm disease and mental inferiority. Low native ability may induce such conditions of living as to induce hookworm infection, or poor environmental conditions may be responsible for both the disease and the low test record."

In this particular instance it may be granted that hookworm disease is not the sole cause of low native ability, but it is probably a safe conclusion *a priori* that hookworm disease and other long continued infections are causes of a mental dullness which may be as serious in its effect upon the behavior adjustments of the individual as feeble-mindedness itself. Moreover, as Gault[1] points out, "by way of social inheritance, the dulling effect of this and other diseases may be passed on to succeeding generations; for the dull head of a family, from whatever cause he may be dull, creates an atmosphere in his home in which his children live and grow . . . until fixed dispositions are built up in them."

It is quite probable that part of the greater alertness of children from better homes is to be explained on the basis of their greater energy and vitality with its attendant increase of the children's curiosity. We know, for example, that the onset of the menses in girls from poorer homes tends to be later than in those from better environments, and malnutri-

[1] Gault, R. H., *Social Psychology* (Henry Holt and Co., New York, 1923), p. 86.

tion is detrimental to scholarship; so anything which would lower the health reserve of a youngster should also begin to curb his curiosity.

It is consequently imperative for parents not only to remedy any visual and auditory defects of their children which can be corrected, but also to keep the youngsters in robust health, since the latter supplies the basis for intellectual activity. A listless child is likely to become an uninteresting and uninterested adult.

The Most Critical Stage in the Child's School Career. The first years of contact with the school system are the most important of all those spent in classrooms, for it is then that the youngster is likely to develop his liking for, or aversion to, education. After he grows older his experience with a teacher whom he dislikes is not so critical, for then he is more likely to realize that she is just the exception to the rule. At the ages of six or eight years, however, an antagonism for a certain teacher is often transferred to the whole educational system, after which the child loses interest and falls in scholarship. As his marks drop, his aversion to education tends to increase, and the youngster may dread coming to school.

Indeed, it is possible for a dyspeptic teacher of the early grades to alter the enthusiasm and delight of forty youngsters so that they become prejudiced against her and all that she stands for, namely, education. The fault in this kind of situation is not wholly the teacher's, for her ill health or increasing age may render her less patient and interested in youngsters, especially when they have not yet been fully "broken in" to the regulations of the classroom.

The advisability of having young teachers in the early grades is therefore apparent, for they are more inclined to have enough energy and patience to submit agreeably to the demands of a roomful of six-year-olds. It would probably be a good thing if teachers moved along toward the upper grades as they advanced in years. Instead of letting women 60 years of age deal with beginners, it would probably be advantageous to both the youngsters and the teacher if she moved along toward the eighth grade, and let younger women take her place in the kindergarten. The average woman of 60 has not enough energy to keep up with the demands of 20 to 40 youngsters, so she is more inclined to resort to the ruler as a means of holding her young charges in check. The more fatigued she becomes, the greater is her use of the stick, and therefore the less likely she will increase the children's fondness for school.

Because the young teacher is only a score of years removed from her own kindergarten age, and since she has the exuberance of health and vitality to cope with the demands of the early grades, she is much more likely to coax her youngsters into the desirable form of behavior, and consequently her influence is of lasting benefit. She is less inclined to be autocratic, and her recent graduation from normal college where she imbibed some of the idealism and social responsibilities entailed in teaching enables her to regard her youngsters as something more than just a monotonous method of earning her pay check. All too frequently old teachers lose sight of the ultimate goals of education, and they seldom grow tearful over their inability to deal successfully with a problem child. "Oh, you will get over that after you have been here as long as we have," they remark to the young teacher. Unfortunately, they are correct, which leads us to the opinion that young teachers should enter the educational system in the same manner as they first encountered it, namely, *via* the kindergarten and first grade.

The Nursery School and Its Future. Because of the diminishing size of the average American family, and the fact that apartment dwellers cannot let their youngsters run out to play as readily as used to be the case, there is a growing need for some means of enabling the only child to have social contacts with other youngsters of about his own age. In fact, at the present time many children of pre-kindergarten age seldom get outside except when with an adult.

In the previous chapter we explained the detrimental effect upon the child of a lack of siblings and playmates, yet many parents today seem little able to remedy matters owing to their limited financial resources. Except for his thirty minutes or so in Sunday school, their child is almost as closely confined to the apartment as the spinster's cat.

The nursery school offers an excellent partial remedy. By admitting tots who are old enough to walk, it socializes and extroverts these probably introverted children. In fact, it is frequently possible to pick out the nursery school child from others not so favored simply by its greater cooperation in the play group. It seems not unreasonable to assume that a lowering of the entrance age for kindergarten would be a distinct advantage not only to children, but indirectly to the state itself through its tendency to lessen the divorce rate of these same youngsters. Since two-thirds of our population depart from under the tutelage of the school at the eighth grade, it behooves the state to prepare them for a happy adulthood, and the five idle years of the youngster prior to kindergarten offer a fertile field.

The church school might be impressed to offer such a service to the community, for there are churches in every village and city which stand more or less unused between Sundays. And there are many idle young women of good education and altruistic interests who would be rendering children and the state a great service by conducting daily nursery schools therein. Many city parents would be delighted to pay a nominal fee for an opportunity to place their youngsters in such a beneficial environment. As a method for the "ladies aid" and similar women's religious organizations to earn money for the church, nursery schools hold great promise. If necessary the women could alternate, or spend only half a day a week in the work, so it would not be burdensome to any and should, in fact, be almost as stimulating to these young matrons as to the tiny tots.

The future of the nursery school seems, therefore, to be very bright, although it appears that private organizations will be its chief sponsors, at least for several years to come. Eventually, however, the state may find it desirable to assume the instruction of children at a lower entrance age than the present five or six years.

The Qualifications of a Good Teacher. In discussing the factors which make a good teacher Dean Ashbaugh[1] says, "The evidence of a great teacher is not that his students know the material he has taught but that they come from his courses with an insatiable desire to know more and more of his field." In order for this result to occur the teacher must usually possess enthusiasm. We have previously commented upon the salesman's need for enthusiasm if he wishes to be a success. After all, the teacher should also consider himself a salesman of education. Too many men and women, however, take the attitude that they are being paid their salaries simply to deliver a fifty minute lecture three times a week, and if the students do not get anything out of the address that is their bad luck. A good teacher, on the contrary, should be so interested in his own subject that, like the missionary, he cannot be content until he has converted his listeners.

In the second place, a good teacher should also possess intellectual perspective. He should be fairly well oriented in the field of education, so that he can relate the specific material within his own province to other fields, and his social intelligence should be such that he knows the current interests and humor of the group to which he speaks. Just because he is a member of Phi Beta Kappa and has held a fellowship for research is no positive indication that he is fitted for

[1] Ashbaugh, E. J., *School and Society* (Nov. 2, 1929), vol. xxx, No. 775, p. 592.

pedagogy. Indeed, it is this misconception concerning the cardinal purpose of teaching which explains in large part the students' ennui during lectures and the presence of Morpheus in so many classrooms. The fact that they wander "through courses in the Greek thought of the Fourth Century or the social institutions of Medieval Spain . . . somnolent and pathetic" cannot be gainsaid, for how can we expect a zestful interest on the part of youth in subjects which are often presented with a dyspeptic lack of enthusiasm by an instructor whose chief forensic virtue qualifies him for the degree Doctor of Somnolence?

Nor does it follow that because a professor spends years of research on the cultural significance of the castanet in medieval Spain and hopes to advance himself professionally through an article or two containing the results of his investigations, that his students will become enraptured listeners to the same subject. Since teaching is salesmanship, the instructor must remember the axioms of the salesman and strike at fundamental motive bases. As a public speaker, moreover, he should consider himself at fault if he cannot keep his students awake.

Aside from his enthusiasm and perspective, the teacher should bear in mind that his students also obtain ideas concerning politics and morality from him. They will go back to their respective communities and states with social attitudes colored by their contacts with him. It is important for the instructor to remember that these same students may be sending their children to him a generation later if he has given them sound advice both as to his specific field and also as to morality, statesmanship, and religion. In the latter connection it should be evident that it does not become any young Ph. D. to ridicule the religious tenets of the 18-year-olds who sit in his classes and who lack the forensic training to defend themselves and their beliefs.

As regards the teacher's own scholastic and research background, Dr. Martin L. Reymert[1] has constructed with the cooperation of 42 psychologists a scale by which to evaluate such qualifications. Although it was intended primarily for rating psychologists, it may easily apply to teachers in other

I. TRAINING	POINTS		
Ph.D.	4.9		
Sc.D.	4.6		
M.A.	1.8		
M.S.	1.8		
A.B.	.6		
A. DEGREES		4.9	
Professor	4.5		
Associate Professor	3.1		
Assistant Professor	1.8		
Instructor	.8		
Assistant	.3		
B. Present Academic Position		4.5	
Fellowships	1.3		
Scholarships	.3		
Assistantships	.8		
C. Appointments		2.4	
D. Amount and Quality of Laboratory Training		3.4	
E. Other Training in Psychology		2.6	
Other Sciences	1.9		
Philosophy	.5		
Mathematics	1.2		
Statistics	1.1		
F. Training in background subjects		4.7	
Attending University	.4		
Research	.9		
Travel	.3		
G. Training in vacation period		1.6	
TOTAL			24.1

[1] Quoted by permission of Dr. Martin L. Reymert. This survey is published in the *Psychological Bulletin.*

II. LENGTH OF EXPERIENCE IN YEARS			
0- 2	1.7		
3- 4	2.9		
5- 6	4.5		
7- 9	5.9		
10-14	7.2		
15-19	7.0		
20-24	6.4		
25-29	5.6		
30 and over	5.1		
A. Years in psychology		7.2	
Under 5 years	.2		
Over 5 years	1.1		
B. No. of years in present position		1.3	
TOTAL			8.5
III. PUBLICATIONS			
A. Books		8.6	
B. General articles (no experimental)		4.6	
C. Experimental studies		10.3	
D. Editorial Service		3.1	
E. Review and Abstract Service		2.5	
TOTAL			29.1
IV. RECOGNIZED CONTRIBUTIONS			
A. New Apparatus		3.9	
B. Improvement of Technique and Method		10.0	
C. Statistical devices (formulae)		4.9	
D. Contributions to Systematic Psychology		8.8	
TOTAL			27.6
V. MEMBERSHIP RANK			
A. Associate		2.2	
B. Member		5.6	
C. Fellow		8.1	
D. Officer		10.7	
E. Promoter		7.5	
TOTAL			10.7

branches of knowledge. There are five general headings which are subdivided as in the preceding chart.

The training of teachers should also be such that their knowledge of statistics and grading methods is fairly uniform. Even at the present time there is considerable variation among teachers in the manner of scoring examination papers. Starch and Elliot[1], for example, took Question X from a final examination paper in geometry by a pupil in one of the largest high schools in Wisconsin. Plates of this answer paper were made and several hundred copies were printed upon foolscap, thus exactly reproducing the original in every detail.

A set of questions and a copy of the answer paper were sent to about 180 high schools in the North Central Association with the request that the principal teacher in mathematics grade this paper according to the practice and standards of the school. In the following Exhibit will be found the results. The teachers' marks varied from 39 to 88.

In the night schools of two large urban universities the

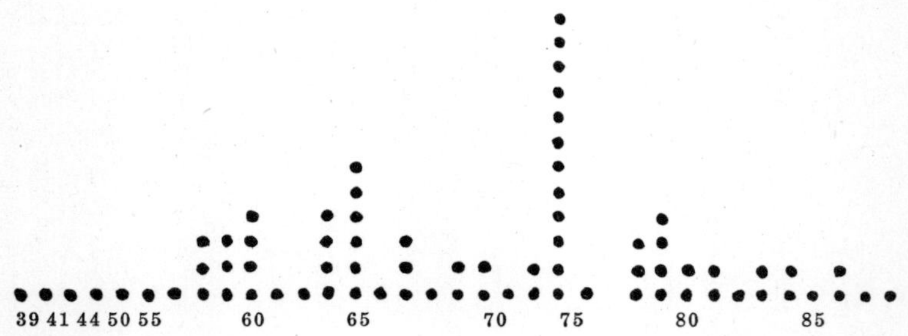

EXHIBIT 55. Passing grade 75. 75 schools. Median 70. Probable error 7.2.

following grade distribution shows a lack of uniformity somewhat comparable to that demonstrated in the grading of the mathematics paper mentioned above. The reader will note

[1] Starch, D., and Elliot, E. C., "Reliability of Grading Work in Mathematics," *School Review,* vol. xxi (1913), pp. 254-259.

that a student in School B has a greater chance of making an "A" than in School A. It is this lack of uniformity among schools which has led the directors of admission in American universities to place more reliance upon a high school graduate's relative position in his graduating class than upon his actual grades. The "Normal" has been included in the table

	%A	%B	%C	%D	%E&F
School A	15	38	34	8	5
School B	21	46	23	7	3
"Normal"	5	20	50	20	5

to show a distribution which would form what is called a normal distribution curve if plotted. The other two would form "skewed" curves, that is, there is an overloading of "A" and "B" grades for a five point scale, with a marked diminution in "D" and "E" percentages.

At this point it would be well to mention a few statistical terms. The *mean* or *average* is a measure of central tendency which is found by dividing the sum of all the individual scores by the number of cases. It is laborious to compute when there are a large number of cases, and when there are few cases it may give a distorted view of the data because of a few extreme scores. For example, let us assume that five persons contributed to a campaign fund the following amounts: $1,000,000; $100; $100; $100; and $100. The mean contribution would, therefore, be $200,080, which makes it appear that all the individuals gave large sums.

The *median* is the middle score in the series, and is not only easier to compute than the mean, but is not influenced by extreme cases. In the five contributions just mentioned the median is the third measure, or $100. In a normal distribution of scores based on a large number of cases the median, the mean, and the mode fall at the same place, which is the highest point on the distribution curve when plotted. In the event of an even number of cases, the median is the point above and below which 50 per cent of the scores fall.

The *mode* by common usage refers to the score or measure at which the most cases fall. In Exhibit 55 the mode is 75 while the median is 70.

The *inter-quartile range* is the spread of scores of the middle fifty per cent of the cases when the latter have been previously arranged in order from highest to lowest. Because it eliminates the highest and the lowest fourths of the group it is less influenced by extreme cases than is the total range. In Chapter IX the range of Army Alpha scores for various occupations was inter-quartile.

The *average deviation* or *mean variation* is the average deviation from the mean or average score. The formula given below simply calls for the sum of the individual deviations from the mean score, divided by the number of cases. In this formula Σ stands for the sum, while d represents the

$$\text{A.D. (or M.V.)} = \frac{\Sigma\, d}{N}$$

deviations from the mean, and N denotes the number of cases. An average deviation of 10 from a mean of 75 represents much less relative variability than an average deviation of 10 from a mean of 35.

The *standard deviation* is usually more useful and more frequently encountered than the simpler average deviation, and is designated by σ, as shown in the next formula, where the other symbols have already been defined above. If after the scores are arranged in ascending or descending order a

$$\sigma = \sqrt{\frac{\Sigma d^2}{N}}$$

distance equal to the standard deviation is laid off on each side of the mean score, then 68.26 per cent of the scores or measures will be incuded in this range.

The *coefficient of correlation* is a statistical measure of the degree of similarity or dissimilarity existing between two series of scores from the same persons. There are several methods of obtaining it, but we shall illustrate only Spearman's rank-differences method. With any of the methods, however, the coefficient will range from +1.00 to —1.00. If with a class of 40 children we compared their proficiency in spelling with their excellence in reading and found that the best speller was also the best reader, that the second best speller was also the second best reader, and so forth, the correlation would be +1.00. On the other hand, if the best speller was the poorest reader, the second best speller was the next poorest reader, and so on until the worst speller was the best reader, then we would have a perfect negative correlation which would result in a coefficient of —1.00. If some of the best spellers were the best readers, but some were also the poorest readers and so on, we would find a correlation in the neighborhood of 0.00, which denotes a chance and non-significant relationship.

In the rank-differences method the raw scores must first be changed into ranks, as will be evident from the following comparison between the Army Alpha scores and the final examination marks of 25 students selected from one of the writer's classes in applied psychology. In case of ties, the ranks involved are added, then divided by the number of identical scores. In Army Alpha, subjects "G.F." and "R.H." are tied for 6th place, so we add 6 and 7, divide by 2, and award each a rank of 6.5. There will be no 6th or 7th ranks thereafter.

STUDENT	ARMY ALPHA	EXAM.	RANK IN ALPHA	RANK IN EXAM.	DIFFER-ENCE	DIFFER-ENCE SQUARED
J. A. ------	122	22	21	23	2	4
V. B. ------	133	89	18	6	12	144
N. B. ------	150	79	13	9	4	16
B. B. ------	156	67	11	15	4	16
E. B. ------	137	115	16	2	14	196
J. B. ------	194	91	1	4	3	9
J. C. ------	193	90	2	5	3	9
E. C. ------	143	118	15	1	14	196
L. C. ------	146	87	14	7	7	49
R. D. ------	127	45	20	19	1	1
E. F. ------	179	71	4	11.5	7.5	56.25
G. F. ------	164	68	6.5	14	7.5	56.25
F. G. ------	157	69	10	13	3	9
P. G. ------	109	19	25	25	0	0
C. G. ------	173	55	5	18	13	169
R. H. ------	164	66	6.5	16	9.5	90.25
W. H. ------	163	71	8	11.5	3.5	12.25
G. H. ------	135	56	17	17	0	0
J. K. ------	110	32	24	20	4	16
M. K. ------	162	84	9	8	1	1
J. L. ------	113	29	23	21	2	4
R. L. ------	129	21	19	24	5	25
R. M. ------	121	25	22	22	0	0
A. M. ------	180	93	3	3	0	0
L. S. ------	151	78	12	10	2	4
						1083

The rank-differences formula is as follows:

$$Q = 1 - \frac{6 \Sigma D^2}{N (N^2 - 1)},$$

in which Q stands for the coefficient of correlation; D, the difference in rank in the two tests; and N, the number of paired measurements, which in this particular instance equals 25. After substitution, we find:

$$Q = 1 - \frac{6 (1083)}{25 (625 - 1)} = 1 - 0.416 = 0.584$$

The correlation is positive; therefore, it shows a definite tendency toward similarity in ranks between the two tests. Before we can rely fully on the correlation, however, it is wise to determine its probable error. Some mathematicians maintain that to be dependable the coefficient of correlation must be three times its probable error, while others say four times. By the formula below we are able to determine the probable error of Q.

$$\text{P.E.}_q = 0.706 \frac{1 - Q^2}{\sqrt{N}} = 0.706 \frac{1 - (.584)^2}{\sqrt{25}} = 0.092$$

Our coefficient is accordingly six times its probable error, so we may state that the 25 college students showed a significant tendency to rank in examination grades according to their rank in Army Alpha.

In concluding our discussion of the various qualifications of a good teacher, therefore, we may repeat that they consist of an enthusiasm for the subject and its presentation to others, an intellectual perspective or orientation, the possession of social intelligence in order the better to understand the pupils, an adequate appreciation of moral values, and experience in the field of teaching, including as it does an elementary knowledge of statistical methods. The instructor who possesses these assets will find that pedagogy is intensely interesting, and will engender the gratitude of the alumni. In the following section we shall discuss one of the methods by which the teacher can improve his classroom effectiveness.

The Case Method in Education. In Chapter II we mentioned the superiority of active over passive learning. The case method in education is valuable, therefore, because it enables the student to apply some of the principles to which he has been listening and thereby find out if he has fully acquired a mastery of them. In medicine, law, and dentistry the case method has been used for generations, but other branches of learning have adopted it more slowly. In recent years economics has availed itself of the case book, and the project method is gaining favor in public school education. In abnormal and clinical psychology, too, the students encounter living cases. The writer has noted a difference in their interest even in psychology classes when personality cases of the following sort are a part of the weekly assignments.

PERSONALITY CASE No. 4.

John Randall—aged 60; with the Blackburn Company 35 years fifteen of which he had been manager of a branch office; salary $75.00 a week; always on the job, even when so ill he could hardly stand; drank, smoked, and talked of his wilder youth but disapproved of his employes gambling, drinking, or running around nights —objected to letting his employes be promoted, saying, "I have a good office force together now and don't want it disturbed." Randall's immediate superior started with the Blackburn Company ten years after Randall did. Randall disliked him and said he got his promotion through lies and cheating This superior placed Vernon Jenness in Randall's office. Jenness was a good worker, but drank a bit, and ran around nights. Jenness came up for promotions but Randall wouldn't let him go. Jenness had now spent five years in the office.

Jim Morton, department head in Randall's office but lacking initiative, often went to Jenness for advice. Randall once asked Jenness, "Doesn't he know anything? Do you have to do his work for him?"

Ed Wheaton, another employe, rather surly to customers and inefficient, continually pestered Morton with childish pranks, causing Morton to lose his temper on numerous occasions.

With the depression Randall laid off one of his employes. Was it Morton, Jenness, or Wheaton? Give full reasons for your judgment, assuming that all three had equal numbers of dependents.

From the psychological standpoint, therefore, the case method is valuable because it enables the student to apply his knowledge and find out what he does not know, thereby granting him the opportunity to concentrate further on the unknown. In Chapter II we explained that certain geometric figures were quickly memorized when the students had 5-second exposures followed by an attempted reproduction, because they were always concentrating upon the unknown elements. In addition, by working with actual cases the student is more vividly impressed with the practical value of his studies and his interest is accordingly heightened.

Education and Politics. The teacher should not attempt to inject bias and partisanship into his discussion of educational matters. He should, on the contrary, endeavor to encourage the scientific attitude regarding political questions, and minimize the employment of emotionalism in discussing international relations. Political impartiality is difficult to obtain, however, because so many politicians purposely stimulate the suprarenal glands of their hearers, and thereby incite them to emotional responses. Justice should be conceived of as emotionless, but even our law courts and juries are often led astray by propaganda, pretty complexions, and silk hosiery. Indeed, the peculiar nature of mankind makes individuals susceptible to appeals which short-circuit reason with emotion.

One of the functions of a good teacher, however, is the instruction of youth in the fallacies of reasoning until emotional appeals are so thoroughly understood that the commonly encountered ones are mentally tabulated by the student whenever he hears them. In so doing, he frees himself in part from their likelihood of inciting his own emotions, for a rational attitude is inimical to emotionalism, and renders its hearer partial immunity.

Public school teachers, therefore, by bringing before their students the commonly encountered emotional appeals, can condition the students to an intellectual process instead of an emotional one. The average adult not only never heard of *ad hominem* as a fallacy in reasoning, but he is not aware of the situation in real life to which that phrase belongs. After he has been taught the type of situation which warrants the *ad hominem* epithet, he is largely free of its dominance. This is the principle which is so commonly employed in psychoanalysis, namely, make the patient conscious of his previously unconscious slavery to a habit, and he thereafter becomes free. By using the case method and grading the student upon his recognition of emotional appeals, the teacher can build up in him a critical attitude whenever he encounters printed or oral speeches.

It is true that the average schoolboy and also the adult will be unable to ascertain the subtleties of much of the propaganda with which they are surrounded, but there is too much obvious emotionalism which could be nullified by the proper training of children. If a large fish by bumping into the glass partition separating him from minnows in an adjacent portion of the aquarium can be taught to ignore the minnows, even when the glass partition is removed and they are swimming around him, then it is not too much to hope for that intelligent human beings can be schooled to refrain from certain responses to which they now are addicted.

In fact, the writer has trained some teen age youths in the analysis of public speeches until they are quite adept in spotting the emotional appeals and fallacies of reasoning. When this habit becomes a part of the personality of the average citizen, then we can look for a more sensible and logical analysis of political problems by the politicians who stand before us, and political campaigns will be much freer of hatreds, "mud slinging", and emotional ranting.

From the teacher, therefore, must come the training in detecting fallacies and resisting emotional appeals. Until the educators of America point out these fallacies and stereotyped incentives to emotionalism, the graduates of our public schools should not be criticized severely for submitting thereto. Until an elementary course in logic and applied psychology is introduced into the public school system, two-thirds of the citizens will continue to graduate with little protection against the illogical reasoning of emotional demagogues.

The Teacher's Opportunity to Elevate Civilization. Teachers should give their students not only a knowledge of spelling, arithmetic, reading, and geography, but also an appreciation of many virtues not specifically designated in the curriculum. Much of the child's spirit of fair play and honesty, his morality and confidence, his liking for education and music and art come from the teacher. These subjects are not designated when she is appointed to a definite classroom, but she finds them a part of her duties nevertheless, especially if she would be an excellent teacher.

The habits of brushing their teeth, of personal cleanliness, and of health are gained by many students almost wholly from their teachers. The latter even encourage the children to eat vegetables, and to retire at a certain hour each night. They also interpret literature and art and religion for their youngsters, and develop tenderness and kindliness in boys and girls who might be thoughtlessly cruel without such object lessons as are given to them. The teachers are chiefly responsible for the children's knowledge of American history and the relationships of this nation to foreign powers.

With ten years of contact with the children of America the public school teachers have almost unlimited opportunities for social, moral, and intellectual improvement of the coming generations. Sometimes the entire future of a child is altered by the understanding sympathy of a good teacher. Foreign children are Americanized largely through the teacher's influence, and their home environments are often greatly improved because of her advice and interest.

The teachers in institutions of higher learning, of course, do not deal with more than 10 per cent of the youth of America, but these 10 per cent are destined to become the principal leaders in business, science, and the arts, as well as in the civic and domestic affairs of their respective communities. It behooves the instructor who wishes to be most effective to remember the fundamental purpose for which he is teaching. Latin should not be taught for the sake of Latin, but for the sake of the student, and the same is true of all other branches of learning. Too often this mistake in emphasis reduces the effectiveness of the teacher as well as of his subject matter. Pedagogy must never be looked upon as a parroting of information, but rather as an interpretation and evaluation of the mental heritage of mankind in the interest of more satisfactory adjustments of the student to his environment.

REFERENCES

ADLER, A., *The Practice and Theory of Individual Psychology* (New York, 1924).

BOOK, W. F., *The Intelligence of High School Seniors* (New York, 1922).

CHIPMAN, C. E., "The Vocabulary of Mental Defectives," *Proc. Amer. Ass. Ment. Def.*, 1935, vol. 40, pp. 485-503.

CONKLIN, E. G., *Heredity and Environment* (Princeton, 1923).

COOKE, D. H., *Minimum Essentials of Statistics* (New York, 1936).

CRANE, G. W., "Case Records of a Psychologist," 1937, (a daily column in leading metropolitan newspapers).

CUFF, N. B., "What Should Be Included in Educational Psychology?" *J. Educ. Psychol.*, 1935, vol. 26, pp. 689-694.

DOWNEY, JUNE, *The Will-Temperament and Its Testing* (Yonkers, 1923).

ELLIS, R. S., *The Psychology of Individual Differences* (New York, 1928).

FREEMAN, F. N., *Mental Tests* (Boston, 1926).

GARRETT, H. E., *Statistics in Psychology and Education* (New York, 1926).

GATES, A. I., *Elementary Psychology* (New York, 1925).

GATES, R. R., *Heredity and Eugenics* (New York, 1923).

GAULT, R. H., AND HOWARD, D. T., *Outline of General Psychology* (New York, 1925).

GODDARD, H. H., *Feeble-mindedness: Its Causes and Consequences* (New York, 1914).

GOODENOUGH, F. L., *Developmental Psychology* (New York, 1934).

GRIFFITTS, C. H., *Fundamentals of Vocational Psychology* (New York, 1924).

GRIFFITH, C. R., *Introduction to Applied Psychology* (New York, 1934).

GORDON, KATE, "Report of Psychological Tests of Orphan Children," *Journal of Delinquency*, vol. iv (1919), pp. 46-55.

HEILMAN, J. D., AND ARMENTROUT, W. D., "The Rating of College Teachers on Ten Traits By Their Students," *J. Educ. Psychol.*, 1936, vol. 27, pp. 197-216.

HOLLINGWORTH, LETA S., *Special Talents and Defects* (New York, 1923).

HOWARD, D. T., "A Psychologist Looks at the Classics," *The Classical Journal*, vol. xxv (1929), pp. 4-18.

HUNTER, W. S., *Human Behavior* (Chicago, 1928), Part I, chap. ii.

HUSBAND, R. W., *Applied Psychology* (New York, 1934), chap. xxvii.

HUXLEY, J., "Ductless Glands and Development," *Journal of Heredity,* vol. xiii (1922), pp. 349-358; vol. xiv (1923), pp. 3-11.

IRWIN, ELIZABETH A., AND MARKS, L. A., *Fitting the School to the Child* (New York, 1924).

JOHNSON, B. J., *The Mental Growth of Children* (New York, 1925).

JOHNSON, H. M., *School Begins at Two* (New York, 1936).

KELLEY, T. L., *Statistical Method* (New York, 1923).

LAURISTEN, MARNE, "And the Deaf Shall Speak," *Journal of Expression,* vol. ii (June, 1928), pp. 83-87.

MERRY, R. V., *Education of Visually Handicapped Children* (Cambridge, Mass., 1933).

MOSS, F. A., *Applications of Psychology* (Boston, 1929), chap. xx.

MURRAY, H. A., "Psychology and the University," *Arch. Neurol. Psychiat., Chicago,* 1935, vol. 34, pp. 801-817.

ODELL, C. W., *The Progress and Elimination of School Children in Illinois* (Urbana, 1924).

ORTON, S. T., "The Development of Speech Understanding in Relation to Intelligence," *Child Res. Clin. Ser.,* 1935, vol. 1, No. 6, pp. 14.

OTIS, A. S., *Statistical Method* (Yonkers, 1925).

PINTNER, R., *Intelligence Testing* (New York, 1923).

PRESSEY, S. L., AND L. C., *Mental Abnormality and Deficiency* (New York, 1926).

SHERMAN, SHERMAN & FLORY, "Infant Behavior," *Comp. Psychol. Monogr.,* 1936, vol. 12, pp. 107.

SORENSON, H., *Statistics for Students of Psychology and Education* (New York, 1936).

SPEARMAN, C. E., *The Nature of Intelligence and the Principles of Cognition* (London, 1923).

STARCH, D., *Educational Psychology* (New York, 1919).

STEDMAN, LULU M., *Education of Gifted Children* (Yonkers, 1924).

THORNDIKE, E. L., *Educational Psychology* (New York, 1914).

THURSTONE, L. L., *Fundamentals of Statistics* (New York, 1925).

WALLIN, J. E. W., *Studies of Mental Defects and Handicaps,* Miami University Series xxii (January, 1924), No. 5.

WEBB, L. W., "Transfer of Training and Retroaction. A Comparative Study," *Psychological Monographs,* vol. xxiv (1917), No. 3.

WHIPPLE, G. M., "The Education of Gifted Children," National Society for Study of Education, *Twenty-third Yearbook,* Part I (Bloomington, 1924).

WITTY, P. A., AND JENKINS, M. A., "Intra-race Testing and Negro Intelligence," *J. Psychol.,* 1936, vol. 1, pp. 179-192.

YERKES, R. M., "The Mind of a Gorilla," *Genetic Psychology Monographs,* vol. ii (1927), Nos. 1, 2, 6.

CHAPTER XV

PSYCHIATRY AND MENTAL HYGIENE

The importance of psychiatry and mental hygiene is seldom realized by the average person. At the present time there are more than 300,000 inmates of institutions for the insane, the feeble-minded, and epileptic, not counting the large number of such cases privately cared for in their own homes. Moss states that from one-third to one-sixth of every state's expenditures is consumed in the support of mental hospitals, while Dr. William J. Mayo is quoted as stating that mental ailments are the cause of more human misery than tuberculosis and cancer. The report from the Surgeon General's office relative to the second examination of the first million recruits drafted in 1917 indicated that 12 per cent of these were rejected on account of nervous or mental diseases. At the present time it is estimated that there are more hospital beds occupied by diseases and disorders of the central nervous system than by all other diseases combined.

Since the majority of these disorders could have been prevented by the timely application of knowledge, the great need for spreading the principles of mental hygiene becomes apparent. When parents and teachers are educated to recognize in their children the elements making for nervousness and to adopt the proper methods of training the neurotic liabilities of the children, they will be able to prevent a large percentage of future breakdowns.

In considering mental diseases from the historic viewpoint we find that abnormalities in behavior were originally ascribed to demons. The insane were simply those persons afflicted with devils. This attitude regarding mental abnormality greatly retarded the advancement of its scientific study, so it has remained for the modern age to point out the organic bases for many types of anomalous mental functioning. Indeed, of the two groups of mental disorders now recognized, namely, the *organic* and the *functional,* the influence of the former seems to be advancing at the expense of the latter. With continued increase in scientific knowledge regarding infections of the brain and its membranes, the toxins in the body, and the functional interrelationship of the glands of internal secretion, it appears that several more of the present functional types of insanity may be shown to have an organic basis.

For example, before it was learned that paresis was caused from invasion of the brain tissues by the micro-organisms of syphilis, it was often ascribed to such social maladjustments as worry, emotional shock, and erotic frustration. In several instances, moreover, the diseased conditions underlying mental abnormalities are known, even though the specific causes for such pathological states are yet to be discovered.

Even when organic defects may be cited as the cause of many mental abnormalities, however, the psychiatrist today realizes that the behavior reactions of two persons having apparently identical organic defects, may be quite different. There are marked individual variations not only to drugs, but also to diseases, as we shall elaborate more fully in the last chapter of this book. A moron, for instance, may be an honest, law-abiding citizen or he may be a chronic offender. His subnormal intelligence cannot be cited therefore as the sole basis of his atypical behavior when we find him breaking the law. In a similar fashion, organic defects probably function along with social maladjustments to produce abnormality. Lacking a strain upon their adaptive capacity many persons are regarded as entirely normal, and lead useful lives until in times of stress, such as of war, death of loved ones, or sexual maladjustment, they "go to pieces", and may even require institutional treatment. These psychically unstable persons are more numerous in the population than are the feeble-minded. In the next section we shall consider some of the acquired behavior patterns which may lead to behavior maladjustments.

Subconscious Learning and Maladjustment. In Chapter II, we have already mentioned how marginal learning takes place. Not only may habits like the pupillary reflex be conditioned to external stimuli, and operate entirely beyond the person's knowledge, but many other experiences of the individual may either have occurred in the margin of his attention-field, or else have been ostensibly forgotten, yet still continue to influence his adult behavior.

The reader may already have observed this type of phenomenon in his neighbors or even himself, for almost every one has fears and compulsions which are difficult to explain but which are nevertheless potent determinants of behavior. Bagby, for instance, cites the case of a man who was constantly fearful of being seized from behind. He always occupied a seat in the rear row, and even preferred sitting with his back to the wall. In his own home he was likewise nervous and fearful unless his chair was against a solid object, such as a partition or wall.

This peculiarity was so pronounced that the man's neighbors and acquaintances considered him queer as a consequence, and he himself was at a loss to explain what made him afraid. Even though he knew that there was nothing to fear, he could not escape this obsession. When he was middle-aged, he happened to return to the village of his birth and there met the old grocer past whose store he had always gone en route to school. The grocer laughingly reminded him of how he had always taken peanuts from a barrel in front of the store, and how the grocer finally hid in preparation for him. When the boy next reached for peanuts the grocer yelled and seized him from behind. The boy fainted from fright. Here was the origin of the strange fear which later dominated his adulthood. Lacking a knowledge of where it came from, the grown man was unable to escape its baneful influence.

The writer noticed that his older boy at the age of twenty-six months would go into a spasm and scream in terror whenever a stranger touched him or spoke to him. No verbal reassurance from his parents appeared to have the slightest influence upon the boy, nor did he seem to be wholly aware of his surroundings after he once launched upon his screaming. The writer was at a loss to comprehend what caused the attack. Spanking and reprimands had not the slightest effect, yet the emotional shock of the muscle spasm was too great to permit its continuance. Thereafter, of course, attempts were made to condition the child favorably to strangers, although he had never previously shown any fear of them.

For a period of nearly a month, however, the favorable conditioning was not sufficient to offset the boy's entering upon one of his attacks of screaming. By means of the favorable conditioning, however, the child was eventually led to a normal reaction to strangers. The writer then remembered that the boy had gone to the grocery with his mother about a month earlier, and had followed another woman out of the store. After walking for a block he suddenly realized that he was with a stranger, and lost from his mother. He began screaming in terror and sat down upon the sidewalk where he mechanically beat upon the cement with the doll which he had been carrying, although the stranger had attempted to lead him back. His mother found him a few minutes later still so terrified that he hardly recognized her, and with the doll's head crushed to bits. She finally quieted him, and thought no more about the incident, but it had apparently left a marked effect upon the child, for several weeks later the touch or speech of a stranger was sufficient to re-induce the terror response.

This case has been cited to show how indelibly a childhood

experience may affect a youngster's nervous system, and how it might continue into adulthood if it were not treated early. The previous instance of the child and the peanut barrel shows the permanence of such influences when uncorrected. There are literally thousands of particular objects or situations that engender fears even in adulthood. Some people are terrified at the thought of being alone in a large open space (Agoraphobia), while others will not ride in subway trains and elevators or go into closed places, at least unless the windows are open (Claustrophobia). Some are afflicted with a fear of contagion and are incessantly washing their hands, while others are afraid of running water, and cannot endure the sound from a faucet which is turned on. Some are terrified by darkness while others feel frightened by crowds. A further cataloguing of such phobias and their explanations will be found in the references appended to this chapter.

Since Watson's research indicates that the only two ways by which fear can be demonstrated in the infant are by loss of support or falling and by loud noises, it is evident that the fear of the dark or of any other situation or object is acquired by an individual because of his contact with his environment. When the child is too young to recognize how he has acquired these fears, it becomes essential that his parents or teachers uncondition him so that he will not continue until adulthood a victim of injurious emotional habits.

When a young couple at Madison came home to their three-year-old son one evening they found that he was afraid of the wardrobe closet in the front hall. They later learned that the maid had told him about a spook in this closet which would get him if he was not a good boy. The parents immediately played hide-and-seek with the child, the father hiding first in the living room, then in the hall with the light on, then in the closet with the light on, then in the closet with the light turned off. Soon the child wanted to hide and let his parents search for him. It was not long until the boy also hid in the closet. His fear had been overcome by a greater amount of pleasure which attached to the closet in consequence of the game.

In the conditioning of children it must be remembered that the greater of two rival influences will likely mask or cover the lesser. If the unpleasant is stronger than the good in its emotional effect, then it will make him dislike the good with which it is associated and conversely. In the above example the pleasure engendered by the game of hide-and-seek which he was playing with his parents, and his delight in discovering his Daddy in the closet, overcame the fear of the closet. If his parents had allowed the child to continue in his fear, he would have developed a habit of fright in connection with the closet, which would later have been much more difficult to eradicate.

With adults it is usually sufficient simply to point out the original situation in which the fear reaction occurred, and they can free themselves from its dominance thereafter. In some cases their lifetime slavery to a fear may be destroyed in a few days. Until they can be shown how they obtained their fears, however, it is difficult for them to become free.

Freud's View of Repression and the Censor. Freud and the psychoanalysts look upon the mind as a stage upon which ideas are the actors. Some of the latter which violate our sense of justice, virtue, and modesty may be forbidden the right to perform upon the stage. The Censor who does this forbidding is the ego, which pushes the unpleasant ideas out of consciousness and submerges them in the realm of the unconscious. In explaining this process Freud[1] speaks as follows:

> Suppose that here in this hall and in this audience . . . there is an individual who is creating a disturbance, and by his ill-bred laughing, talking, by scraping his feet, distracts my attention from my task.

[1] Freud, Sigmund, "The Origin and Development of Psychoanalysis," *American Journal of Psychology* (April, 1910), p. 194.

I explain that I cannot go on with my lecture under these conditions, and thereupon several strong men among you get up and after a short struggle, eject the disturber of the peace from the hall. He is now "repressed" and I can continue my lecture. But in order that the disturbance may not be repeated, in case the man who has just been thrown out attempts to force his way back into the room, the gentlemen who have executed my suggestion take their chairs to the door and establish themselves there as a "resistance" to keep up the repression. Now if you transfer both locations to the psyche, calling this "consciousness" and the outside the "unconscious" you have a tolerably good illustration of the process of repression.

This quotation is typical of the attitude of the Freudians and confuses the student greatly, for the entire concept of repression intimates a repressor as a distinct entity or force which bodily "pushes" or "submerges" the so-called repressed idea. The analogy is fraught with connotations of spacial changes and muscular effort involved in the repressing. As a matter of fact, the entire idea of repression should be dispensed with. We do not "push" ideas out of our minds, but simply pursue trains of thought which keep away from the unpleasant ideas as the rat does not push the cat from his field of vision, but follows a course which will avoid his feline enemy.

Whenever a neural impulse leaves a sensory cell and enters the cortex, it seems to involve both an activation of specific conditioned reflex pathways as well as a partial arousal of many neural paths which function in associated habits. The course which it takes is the one of least resistance. If the person in question is hostile to ideas pertaining to sex and friendly to those having to do with virtue, this mental "set" facilitates an association process in the realm of honor and virtue because such associated habits are more active than the opposing ones.

During sleep, of course, the individual is less likely to try to facilitate one train of thought in preference to another, so the neural impulse still follows the line of least resistance, which now probably lies along the neural network of a fundamental motive base. Freud's view that during slumber the Censor no longer represses submerged ideas is a confusing analogy. If he must resort to analogies, however, it would be more in accordance with our present knowledge of neural action if he said simply that the "facilitator" was no longer operating. In the following section we shall discuss further the course of neural currents during sleep.

The Significance of Dreams. Dreams in olden times were looked upon as having prophetic value, as the reader will recall from the story of Joseph who rose from a prison cell to become ruler of Egypt because of his skill in interpreting the symbolism of Pharaoh's double dream. At the beginning of this century dreams had fallen into disrepute in the scientific world, although many rural families had a dictionary of dreams on the shelf and consulted it each morning to learn the significance of money, travel, death in the family, marriages, and other events about which they had dreamed the previous night.

With the development of psychoanalysis, dreams have been restored to a position of some scientific value, and are one of the chief data employed by the psychoanalyst. The origin of dreams is the same as the origin of any thought process, namely, the stimulation of some sense organ with the resulting entrance into the cortex of a nervous impulse. The dreamer's feet may be projecting from beneath the covers on a cold winter night, in which case the cold receptors are activated, and neural currents begin to bombard the cortex. The sleeper may in consequence dream that he is with Commander Byrd on a new polar expedition, or that he is wading through the snow barefooted.

Visceral discomfort resulting from indigestion, the sunlight upon his face, the sound of an alarm clock, and a host of other stimuli may cause the thought process to arise in the sleeper's cortex. The peculiar linkage of ideas which constitutes the dream will be a result of the previous habits of the slumberer, of his instincts and internal chemical environment, as well as of the external stimuli affecting him at the moment. If he has been without food for several meals, the internal chemical condition of his body will facilitate a train of thought pertaining to food. If he went to sleep thirsty, then his dream will probably have to do with cool springs of water. If his sexual appetite is whetted but unsatisfied, he will likely dream of the opposite sex. If he is obsessed by some constant fear, as of ill health or detection for having committed a crime, or if he has been puzzling over a problem of some sort, then these topics will probably be the center of his dream. If his feet are cold, or mosquitoes are biting him, he may construct dreams built around the stimuli of cold or pain.

Freud believes that dreams become expressions of unfulfilled wishes. They may commence in any one of the sense organs, but the free association chain of ideas ultimately leads to the subject of most interest to the sleeper. Freud admits that hunger is the chief motive force in life, but hunger does not present great difficulties to the average man and woman. They normally retire with no unsatisfied craving for food, so they consequently are not likely to dream of tempting viands. On the other hand, they may often go to bed at night with their sexual natures sensitized by romantic fiction and moving picture plays to which they have been exposed within a few hours before retiring, or by social contact with members of the opposite sex. This psychological sensitization to ideas concerning sex may be further reinforced by the sleepers' physiological condition. If it is spring, or if for any other reason they possess an abundance of sexual energy, they are ready in mind and body for dreams of a sexual nature.

It will be obvious that this type of dream would occur more frequently in the unmarried than in the married. The latter no longer find sex of so much curiosity value, nor are they likely to have the abundance of undissipated sexual energy. Since they are older and with interests centered more on their work, or the home and their children, the latter subjects are very likely to appear in their dreams. As a consequence, Freud's extreme emphasis upon the sexual basis for dreams may be valid for youths from fifteen to twenty-five years of age, and for mismated and sexually unsatisfied adults, but these two groups probably form a minority of human beings.

That dreams are generally wish-fulfilling is probably true, for even little ones are prone to dream of the things which they desire. Very young children, moreover, do not always make a distinction between their dreams during sleep and their waking thoughts. When four-year-old Paul, mentioned in a previous chapter, had learned that he might become the owner of a kitten, he came downstairs the following morning and said, "Mother, there was a kitty in my room." His mother expressed surprise, for she realized that the doors had been locked and the windows were screened. "Yes it was," her son maintained. "It jumped up on my bed and said, 'Hello, Paul', and then it jumped down and went out the door and that was all."

Before we conclude this section it would be well to state that many dreams are full of symbolism. If the sleeper has been reared in a moral environment where he has been taught not to think about sexual matters, and if in the dream world he dwells upon them nevertheless, he may attempt to avoid an emotional conflict by representing the sexual situation in a disguised form. There is nothing unusual in this performance, for it is conventional to avoid painful things, as in the representation of death by use of such euphemisms as: "He passed away"; "He went west"; "He crossed the great divide"; "He went to his rest". Freud has presented a long list of the conventional symbols which denote the two sexes, and cites numerous dreams to illustrate them. The writer, however, will offer two from his own files which are so evident in their symbolism as to warrant no explanation.

NUMBER ONE

Mary (eighteen and a stenographer): I dreamed about you last night.

Her Young Employer: That's interesting. What did you dream?

Mary: Oh, we were quarreling.

H. Y. E.: Quarreling? What about?

Mary: It was about a letter which I had just received. You wanted to open it and I wouldn't let you.

H. Y. E.: Well, how did we settle it?

Mary: Oh, I finally gave it to you and you opened it.

NUMBER TWO

A college girl dreamed that she and her male escort were riding in the rumble seat of an automobile with another couple inside the car and driving. In a park along the lake the car upset. Only she and her escort rolled out and down into a wooded ravine. She then discovered that she had a hole in her head and was trying to shake her escort into sensibility, but he seemed to remain unconscious of her attempts to awaken him.

In concluding our discussion of dreams, therefore, we may repeat that they are always initiated by some sensory process, but after they are started they tend to develop around the subject of greatest interest to the dreamer, whether it be appetitive, vocational, recreational, or fearful. The dreams may be symbolic, and their parts may be illogical and impossible as viewed in the light of the next day. Persons long since deceased are present with the living and enjoying life with no intimation that they had ever departed from this world. This unreality of the dream is not evident to the dreamer, however, until after he wakens, for during sleep portions of his cortex are relatively inactive, thereby rendering inoperative many ideas which would inhibit the fantastic elements of the dream.

Emotional Conflicts. The reason why human beings are not coldly analytical persons reacting with the mechanical detachment of automatons is owing to their possession of an autonomic nervous system which innervates the visceral regions, producing thereby the emotional states of fear, love, rage, and the like. Human life accordingly does not proceed with mathematical monotony, but is made both pleasantly changing and often unpleasantly inefficient by means of emotional squalls. In the chapter devoted to salesmanship we have already discussed the manner in which emotional appeals can be used to short-circuit reason.

In almost every phase of human affairs emotion creeps in, and complicates matters by producing conflicts. The mother, for example, finds that her child soon reaches the age where it is ready to transfer its interest to a sweetheart. In fact, at the time of its marriage both parents usually feel somewhat jealous of the newcomer who has been able to dominate the affection of their offspring. The average mother and father accept the situation, however, as one of the inevitables, and attempt to make a harmonious adjustment. Too many of them, though, inject bitterness and hatred into the situation, thereby definitely widening the breach to a point where it may never be remedied. Children are cut off in their parents' wills, or they are upbraided or else completely ignored simply because they wished to marry whom they chose.

The reader is probably familiar with the innumerable emotional conflicts of human beings, so we shall forego a tabulation of them, and confine ourselves to a discussion of the Psychological Diagnostic Chart in Exhibit 56, which is a modification of Menninger's[1] adjustment diagram. The "Personality" encounters a "Situation" such as the winning of a sweetheart, and goes through a period of attempted adjustment, ending possibly in success and marriage. On the other hand, if failure results, the Personality is still maladjusted, as represented by the circle and rectangle in juxtaposition.

1 Menninger, K. A., *The Human Mind* (Alfred A. Knopf, Inc., New York, 1930), p. 26.

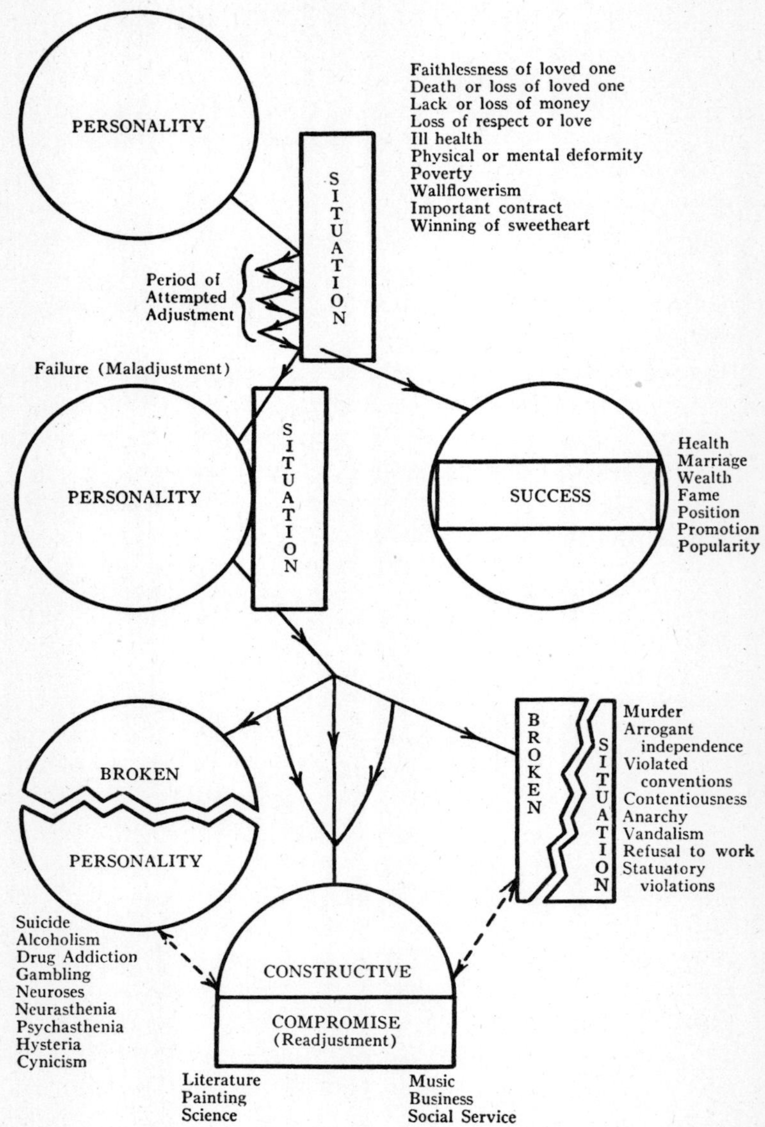

EXHIBIT 56. A diagnostic chart showing the various types of adjustments possible when emotional conflicts are encountered.

The Personality may be able to effect a successful compromise so that the emotional tension is reduced through sublimation, as in the case of the disappointed girl who goes into a convent, or becomes a settlement worker or missionary.

Again, the Situation may be too powerful for the Personality, in which case the Personality may crack. For instance, one of the writer's former students who had been a boyhood sweetheart and classmate of a girl who lived a few houses down the street, learned the week before their graduation from high school that she had betrothed herself to another senior and was to be married shortly. The disappointed youth fled the situation immediately after commencement by entraining for California where he remained so alcoholized for three months that he did not know when the date arrived for the marriage. The reverse of this response may take place where the disappointed person breaks the Situation by murdering his rival or even his sweetheart.

In the case of the student just cited, however, he did not remain permanently in the Broken Personality category, but effected a Constructive Compromise, aided materially, of course, by the exuberance of youth. The reader's attention is called to the dashed lines running between the Constructive Compromise and both of the broken figures. The double arrows indicate that a Broken Personality, barring suicide, can often be salvaged and attain the Constructive Compromise category. On the other hand, an individual who has effected a Constructive Compromise may find that a change in his internal or external environments may cause him to slip into the Broken Personality or the Broken Situation categories. A young man who flees his native town because of disappointment in love may settle down to constructive work in a neighboring metropolis and be apparently readjusted until he encounters his former sweetheart on the street and learns that she and her husband have also moved to the same city.

The cases of Steinmetz and Stevenson are probably indicative of compensations and constructive compromises regarding childhood situations of physical deformity and ill health. Possibly the prevalence of slender pipe smokers among authors and newspaper reporters is similar in explanation. Napoleon, Byron, Kant, Demosthenes, and perhaps even Lincoln represent cases of constructive compromises to unfavorable physical and social elements in their childhood. Bernarr Macfadden, the sick little boy, and Theodore Roosevelt, Sr., demonstrate the category of successful adjustment to similar childhood frailty. In their cases they overcame the ill health itself, whereas in some of the former instances, notably Stevenson's, the health factor was unchanged but the individuals became powerful in other realms.

In concluding our discussion of emotional conflicts, therefore, we may state that they are a constant factor in human relationships. The child is jealous of his father's dominance of the mother, and to a greater or less extent the converse is true. The daughter likewise wants all of her father's affection and the mother may be somewhat jealous. When younger siblings arrive, new compromises must be made if wholesome personalities are to develop. As we shall point out in a later section, the secret of emotional stability and a wholesome personality lies in making a satisfactory adjustment to each situation as it arises. This response must not be the permanent or temporary assumption of oblivion through suicide, alcohol, or narcotics, nor the atypical behavior of the radical or anarchist, but a compromise which adequately dissipates the emotional tension through constructive activity. An intelligent person can steer his course of behavior accordingly, and assist in the creation of stable personalities in his children by realizing that emotional crises can be adjusted by intelligent action, not by sitting still.

The Normal vs. the Abnormal. There is no sharp line of demarcation between the normal and the abnormal. They both have probably the same traits but with a slightly different degree of synthesis thereof. The normal person possesses a social perspective and rapport which enables him to react with only a nominal amount of friction and emotional conflict, whereas the abnormal has lost much of his social perspective through organic or functional brain defects. Sometimes a paranoiac may discuss a subject quite intelligently so that at the moment the listener is unaware of his abnormal mental condition, but the conversation will soon veer around until he strikes his obsession, when it becomes apparent that he is not normal. The case of the guide at the asylum who took the visitors through the institution and explained the types of abnormality evident in the inmates is an example. When the guide came to the last inmate he said, "That poor fellow has a delusion of grandeur. He thinks he's Napoleon. But he isn't for *I'm Napoleon.*"

The abnormal is usually considered as the individual who once was normal but has deviated therefrom, while the subnormal is looked upon as an individual who never fell heir to an Intelligence Quotient of 100. In fact, the subnormal is now regarded as being the feeble-minded, with a maximum I. Q. of about 75. The abnormal may also have a low I. Q. because of the destruction of brain tissue, as in paresis, but he probably possessed a higher I. Q. at a former time. Feeble-minded persons, however, can become insane and abnormal. A destruction of brain tissue in a moron may render him insane and leave him an intelligence level of the idiot or imbecile.

One of the commonest methods of determining abnormality is to find whether or not the patient can support himself in society, providing of course that he is not too aged for work. If he can maintain his economic existence without conflict with law and the policeman, he is usually deemed within the category of normality, despite his possible eccentricities and queerness. If, however, he persistently comes into conflict with his superiors or believes himself persecuted or is so deluded as to be a menace to society, then he becomes a fit subject for an institution. We shall quote cases 4 and 22 from the Presseys[1] to show instances of normality and abnormality, and to illustrate a common method of history taking.

CASE NO. 4

Name: Marion R. *Age*: 34. *Sex*: Female. *Race*: White. *Birthplace*: Massachusetts. Married, 3 children. *Sources of information*: "patient," father, aunt, family doctor, husband.

I. History of the Family.

A. Medical—Mother's father and two uncles on mother's side chronic alcoholics, and several times in state hospital for the insane. Uncle on father's side a dementia praecox case, was brilliant but eccentric; an inventor whose inventions paid him enough to support him and his wife for the rest of their lives. Another uncle very eccentric. One cousin feeble-minded. Mother died at patient's birth. Father died of a shock.

B. Social—Harmonious family. Strict discipline.

C. Educational—Father and the two brothers all have college education.

D. Economic—Father was high school principal, one brother lawyer, the other a doctor.

II. History of the individual.

A. Medical—Sick from infancy with poor digestion. Had very mild attack of infantile paralysis when two years old. Suffered also probably from rickets. Had insomnia; subject to nightmares when able to get to sleep. Has had attacks of a somewhat undefined character when she had to be held down on the bed and fed forcibly. Was too sick to attend school regularly.

B. Social—Stole all sorts of small objects. Was almost never caught. Always played with boys. Began having sex experiences at 7 years and continued until adolescence. Lied in preference to telling the truth, just to "fool people." Had terrific outbursts of temper in which she would break any-

[1] Pressey, S. L., and L. C., *Mental Abnormality and Deficiency* (The Macmillan Company, New York, 1926), pp. 102-103; 178-179. Reprinted by permission of and by arrangement with the publishers.

thing she could get her hands on. Was noisy, boisterous, and destructive. Once set fire to a barn. Was expelled from school for stealing.

C. Educational—Went through college although never very well. Graduated with honors.

D. Economic—Became successful professional woman. Has married and has three healthy children.

III. History of the Present Crisis—None.

IV. Present Condition.

A. Physical.

General Condition—In good condition, vigorous, but still has weak digestion.

Special Defects—None.

B. Appearance and Behavior—Somewhat overactive. Has several pronounced tics. Talks rapidly and a great deal. Gestures frequent and vivid.

C. Intellectual Condition.

General Level—Very high. Learns with great speed and retains remarkably. Once learned a three page poem in two readings and could repeat it eight years later.

Special Functional Disorders—Nothing.

D. Emotional Condition.

General Emotional Tone—Somewhat excitable and irritable; no marked pecularities.

Special Emotional Trends—Nothing.

Emotional conflicts—Nothing.

V. Summary and Conclusion.

A. Summary—A family containing many unusually capable and also many very eccentric individuals. Bad start physically in childhood. Many childhood delinquencies, possibly due to physical condition. Superior ability.

B. Conclusion—Normal woman, with considerable early physical handicap, probably due primarily to childhood diseases.

CASE NO. 22

Name: Charles M. *Age*:. 60. *Sex*: Male. Born in rural Indiana. Widower. *Sources of information*: the man himself, son, neighbors.

I. History of the Family.

A. Medical—Normal.

B. Social—Normal.

C. Educational—Illiterate.

D. Economic—Were modestly successful farmers.

II. History of the Individual.

A. Medical—Normal.

B. Social—Has always been extremely religious. Is a Catholic. Has covered the walls of his house with "holy" portraits, crucifixes, etc. Had an altar built in his living-room. When he was about forty, he conceived the idea that he would be a great man, if he could only get to some city where he would be appreciated. He rented his farm, left his wife and boy with relatives and went to Chicago, feeling that he was fulfilling a "call". Five years later he returned, convinced that everyone in the city was plotting against him. He believes that the time will come when everyone will realize his greatness. For about the last ten years, has occasionally, after much praying and fasting, heard a voice calling him to become a follower of Christ. Since his wife's death, about five years ago, he has given his farm to his son and has moved into a near-by city to retire into a holy life. He spends most of his time in the Cathedral at prayers. He says that he has the power to communicate with any dead person; claims that he sits on the right hand of God and that the angels will do his bidding. Says he can hear angels sing and that he can see Christ on the cross. Spends most of his day in prayer and devotion.

C. Educational—Had a grammar school education.

D. Economic—Owned a large farm and became moderately wealthy. Before he retired he bought the house he now lives in, and is living on his income.

III. History of the Present Crisis—None.

IV. Present Condition.

A. Physical.

General Condition—He shows some signs of senility, white hair, tottering gait, and partial deafness. Is rather stooped and thin from constant fasting. Bears scars of self-inflicted torture.

Special Defects—Partial deafness.

B. Appearance and Behavior—Spends most of the time praying. Walks about with arms folded across his chest in the sign of the cross. Talks considerably, but always on religious matters. Has a pompous air and important manner. Talks as if he were giving commands. Is stiff and domineering.

C. Intellectual Condition.

General Level—Probably about average.

Special Functional Disorders—Judgment—completely dominated by religious ideas and delusions. Attention—excellent where anything religious is concerned, but impossible to distract from this channel. Memory—unimpaired. Association—normal. Intake—occasional experiences of an apparently hallucinatory nature.

D. Emotional Condition.

General Tone—Over-emotional and sentimental.

Special Emotional Trends—Dominated by religious fervor. Fanatic.

Emotional Conflicts—None determined.

V. Summary and Conclusions.

A. Summary—Approaching old age; underweight, gradual development (through "paranoid" period) of religious fanaticism. Now complete domination by religious ideas; religious delusions. Questionable hallucinations. Deports himself in a pompous manner that he thinks is fitting for one of his high position.

B. Diagnosis—Paranoia.

In general, therefore, abnormality refers to a reduced abstract intelligence or a lowered social intelligence as a result of organic or functional disease. The abnormal person finds it difficult to make the social adjustments demonstrated by the majority of the population. In paranoia, however, the patient may show little if any reduction in abstract intelligence, although his delusions soon reveal his warped social perspective, as we shall discuss in a later section. In the following paragraphs we shall describe the methods by which the normal person avoids emotional conflicts.

Normal Ways Out of Emotional Conflicts. The normal person during the numerous emotional conflicts which he experiences endeavors to protect himself against deflation of his vanity or ego. We have previously mentioned the widespread tendency to think well of ourselves, and our constant efforts to avoid social pain, involving as it usually does a wounding of our vanity through some humiliating and therefore ego-deflating episode. The reader may note this basic tendency to guard the ego in the normal emotional outlets which we shall describe below.

(1) *Reverie.* When an individual finds himself in a difficult and unpleasant situation from which he cannot readily extricate himself, he very often flees from his dilemma *via* his thoughts. He daydreams of the "good old days" when he was young and handsome, or affluent and popular, or a famous football hero or actor. He treasures his newspaper clippings and press notices to give tangible assistance to his reverie. He delights in recounting his war experiences, in part because then he wore a uniform which eliminated many social distinctions between himself and his more sophisticated "buddies", and enabled him to gain attentions which he never could receive when dressed in civilian attire.

Ideas of heaven and a future reward for virtuous living sustain many persons who are having an unfortunate time of the present life. Indeed, reverie is an excellent means of maintaining morale providing it is used judiciously. The poor boy who dreams of the day when he will be a millionaire and return home to make life easier for his mother finds that his incentive is kept fresh before him by use of the imagination, and he is stimulated to renewed endeavor. However, there are cases in which the individual obtains so much pleasure out of the act of dreaming that he fails to work diligently in order to attain his goal.

As a general rule the more intelligent the person, the more capable he is of maintaining his morale by use of the imagination. The dullard finds it more difficult to deal in the rich ideas and complex memories which permit escape from present monotony and pain, so he flees the situation by alcohol and drugs or by the adoption of a nomadic life.

(2) *Inactivity.* In many emotional situations a person cannot make up his mind what to do, so he decides to wait for chance to settle the question for him, and thereafter remains passive. This attitude is well illustrated in Macbeth's conflict between his sense of loyalty to the king and his desire for the throne, as shown in his words:

> "If chance will have me king, why, chance may crown me
> Without my stir."

When this reaction occurs it becomes especially pernicious if the individual has a tendency to refrain from mingling with other persons. And since many unsolved problems have to do with people, it frequently happens that the passive individual remains aloof and dwells upon his own troubles. The etiology of functional insanity shows that such behavior frequently precedes the onset of the disease. As a general procedure in mental hygiene, therefore, it is well to keep trying to make some sort of adjustment.

(3) *Flight.* A common characteristic of frustration in love is the desire of the jilted and disappointed suitor to get away from the region in which his sorrow occurred. He wishes to flee to the city, or travel afar. New scenes and experiences will help keep his mind occupied and also keep him away from people who are aware of his ego-deflation. Many workers, moreover, look to California, Chicago, or some other distant point as a place where they feel sure they can succeed. When they reach California, for example, they may then try to browbeat the natives and bolster their own self-esteem by taking the attitude that California is not what it is advertised to be, and that, conversely, the East or the Middle West is far superior. Failing in Caifornia, they return home with a rationalized explanation, and thereafter bemoan their fate in not being back in California, meanwhile minimizing the good points of their home state and city.

(4) *Sour Grapes.* This category of responses is often resorted to in an effort to bolster one's hurt pride. When defeated or jilted, one is very likely to go through a psychological process in which one minimizes the talents and desirability of the previously sought object. "Oh, well, I would rather be popular with the crowd than win a Phi Beta Kappa key," says one. In this procedure the individual attempts to render the stimulus inoperative upon himself so that he can thereafter meet it without so much suffering and social pain. In psychoanalysis, for example, it is necessary at the conclusion of the treatment to break the patient's attachment to the analyst. The patient ultimately finds himself dreaming the analyst is a repulsive individual when theretofore his dreams had always been most flattering to the latter.

(5) *Dissociation.* In this case the person refuses to acknowledge the incompatability of conflicting methods of response, and becomes a Dr. Jekyll and Mr. Hyde personality. He acts as if he had logic-tight compartments in which he segregates opposing habit systems. He may be the saint on Sunday and the sinner on week days, or he may be gracious in company and a selfish brute inside his own domicile.

(6) *Compensation.* This is one of the most common emotional outlets, and takes various forms. As a rule, the compensator is an extremist. The physical weakling, for example, may become overly intellectual or develop into a health faddist. In fact, many of the world's strong men have begun life as sickly children. Bernarr Macfadden is an excellent instance in point. Another illustration of compensation is the case of a certain newspaper editor, hunchbacked and weighing about 95 pounds, who is a reckless automobile driver. He made a parachute leap from an airplane which was passing over the center of the city and tried to alight on the top of a certain building on the main street. At another time when he learned that an automobile had swerved into a stone quarry in midwinter, and had sunk, he sprang into his automobile although

attired only in his bath robe, drove out to the deserted quarry, and dived time and again into the icy water in an effort to locate the sunken automobile. He also spends far more money than he can afford on liquor, which he always indulges in, and is an inveterate pipe smoker. Although this editor is a Harvard graduate, he is so intent on trying to prove to the world that he is a regular "he-man", that he has lost perspective in his compensation.

Compensation is unfortunately often engaged in without the person's consciousness of his action, and is therefore frequently a detriment. If it is knowingly entered upon, and if the form which it takes is such that a creditable type of behavior develops, then compensation is a desirable emotional outlet. The chief danger, therefore, comes when the person selects a form of compensation which is detrimental to his own best interests, or when he fails despite his utmost efforts. In the one event he creates antagonism, and in the other he falls into despair.

(7) *Projection.* A curious characteristic of human beings from infancy onward is their tendency to blame the environment for their errors, thereby avoiding deflation of their self-esteem. The child bumps his shin against a chair and immediately blames the chair, often giving it a vicious retaliatory kick. In an automobile accident it is almost always the other fellow's fault. The husband blames his wife because he cannot find his tie or collar, and the wife blames the husband and children because she cannot keep her home neat. There is occasionally a certain amount of truth in the accusation, at least enough to draw the critic's attention to the particular flaw which he thereupon magnifies.

A good instance of projection is demonstrated by the reaction of a slightly inebriated passenger whom the writer recently steered onto the right train, in which they later occupied the same seat. The drunken man was rather soiled in clothing, with trousers and coat which did not match, with patches on the knees of his trousers, and with a white shirt which was not very clean. He realized his unkempt condition and volubly explained that he had just come in from Detroit the night before, and was headed for Wilmette where he would be able to don other clothes. He apologized for his appearance for a period of ten minutes or so, while the writer meanwhile attempted to read. Receiving no attention, the drunken fellow finally surveyed the writer critically, then said: "Say, you look more near the end of your rope than I do! Gee, man, you look bad!" After this single resentful bit of projection, he lapsed into a different mood during which he said he would always be sympathetic whenever he met a fellow in the future who was drunk or down and out.

(8) *Identification.* This device explains our pleasure in fiction and movies, where we identify ourselves with the hero or heroine. Parents do the same regarding their children. Indeed, a person identifies himself to a greater or less extent with his possessions. A good example of identification is mentioned by Frink[1] who tells of a young woman who came to him complaining of insomnia and a depression which had lasted for two years. During her second visit she mentioned that she had dreamed the previous night of Evelyn Nesbit Thaw. When asked what she thought of Mrs. Thaw, she began a vigorous and passionate defense of her. Because her emotion concerning Mrs. Thaw, whom she had never seen, was so excessive, Dr. Frink concluded that his patient must be identifying herself with that well known character, and inasmuch as her defense had pertained entirely to the question of sexual temptations to which Mrs. Thaw had been said to have succumbed, he decided that his patient must have yielded to some temptations of that nature. This proved to be true.

[1] Frink, H. W., *Morbid Fears and Compulsions* (Dodd, Mead & Company, New York, 1921), pp. 169-170.

Her defense of Mrs. Thaw, therefore, was simply a defense of herself.

(9) *Rationalization.* This is one of the most frequently employed methods of eliminating an emotional conflict. The person acts impulsively; then manufactures what appear to be very logical reasons why he has done so. His reasons are more often excuses, a distinction which it is well for every applied psychologist to recognize. A student confronted by a few hours of difficult study grows very sleepy, so he decides he really ought to get some sleep, arguing that one cannot profit very much from studying while in half a doze. Then the telephone rings, and he is invited to a party or to the theatre. Now he decides that it was not sleep which he needed so much as recreation, and falls back upon the adage that "all work and no play makes Jack a dull boy." His conscience does not trouble him, thanks to the adage, but the reader can readily see the fallacy in his reasoning.

As Robinson[1] ably points out, thousands of argumentative works have been produced in order to vent a grudge, and despite the stateliness of the reasoning, it may be chiefly rationalization. "A history of philosophy and theology could be written in terms of grouches, wounded pride, and aversions, and it would be far more instructive than the usual treatment of these themes." John Dewey has already reached the conclusion that philosophy is mainly rationalization; Veblen and others have revealed a similar condition concerning many of the presuppositions of traditional political economy, and the Italian sociologist, Pareto, believes that the social sciences rest upon a bedrock of rationalized customs and beliefs which are the heritage of the middle ages.

(10) *Substitute responses.* In our description of the Psychological Diagnostic Chart earlier in the chapter we showed

[1] Robinson, J. H., *The Mind in the Making* (Harper & Bros., New York, 1921), pp. 41-48.

the many possible responses to an emotional situation. *Sublimation* is one form, which on the chart was represented by the constructive compromise. A poet translates his sex cravings into beautiful verse, and his confrere in the field of music writes melodies. The artist paints portraits, and the average person labors in the industrial or commercial world. The sexual energy created by social contacts among young people also often finds a legitimate outlet through dancing, hiking, picnics, swimming and the like.

As long as the emotional outlets lead into constructive compromises, the person is normal. When, however, they lead into the broken personality or the broken situation category, the person is approaching the abnormal type. Mental hygiene, therefore, consists of training the individual to sublimate, or substitute a legitimate and beneficial response for one which is injurious to his personality. In the following section we shall study the mentally unhealthful and abnormal responses to emotional difficulties.

Abnormal Ways Out of Emotional Conflicts. In discussing the atypical reactions of individuals to emotional conflicts we shall employ a two-fold category as follows:

(1) *Insanity.* There are various subdivisions of insanity within the organic and functional types, and common characteristics are the presence of hallucinations, delusions, and a deterioration of intelligence. With the possible exception of paranoia the mental disorders show an impairment of memory and a lack of orientation on the part of the patient. On intelligence tests the scores tend to decrease when the patient is examined from time to time. Insane patients are frequently victims of hallucinations in which they hear voices advising or threatening them. They will carry on conversations with imaginary figures and often go to extreme lengths to free themselves from their visionary enemies, in many cases slaying friends and relatives who have been mistaken for evil spirits.

As for the delusions of the insane, they are false beliefs tenaciously held in the face of obvious evidence to the contrary. The patient is apparently impervious to logic or evidence, looking out upon the world with preconceptions which are unalterable. Of the commonly encountered delusions we shall briefly describe the following general classifications:

(a) *Delusions of Melancholia.* In this type of delusion the patient is usually characterized by an abnormal inhibition of mental and bodily activity, being relatively passive and unresistant. He monotonously repeats his delusion and makes no attempt to remedy his unfortunate condition. In this category falls the belief that one has committed the unforgivable sin. The patient may not be able to designate what this is, but he knows that he has committed it. Again, he may possess a delusion of negation in which he believes that his leg is missing or that he has no stomach, and the fact that his leg is not severed does not disturb his belief to the contrary. Furthermore, he may think that his arm is made of glass and caution attendants to take care lest they shatter it.

(b) *Delusions of Grandeur.* When afflicted with this type of delusion the patient identifies himself with some famous personage of the present or the past. He imagines that he is the King of England or the President of the United States. Again, his fancy runs to literature and he becomes Shakespeare or Goethe. The patients may often endeavor to dress the parts which they play. A General Grant constantly smoked cigars and discussed the campaigns around Richmond with the detail and familiarity which would have surprised the original Grant himself. Patients may call themselves Mohammed or God, and seem undisturbed by the fact that their assumed omnipotence is oddly at variance with their present confinement in the institution.

(c) *Delusions of Persecution.* Unlike the patient who has a delusion of melancholia and admits that he has committed the unforgivable sin, the patient who believes himself persecuted usually strikes back by actively declaring his innocence and frequently attacking his enemies. Here is a workman, for example, who lost his position because of his incompetence. To defend himself to his wife he demonstrated the common defense reaction of projection, and blamed his employer for having it in for him. His wife does not censure her husband, therefore, but vents her indignation upon the "boss". The husband gains sympathy and encouragement instead of reprimand. From subsequent positions he also is discharged, so he repeats his accusation and elaborates his story by telling that his former employers have blacklisted him, and are reporting against him to all the factory employment offices in the city. Later he begins to note hostile reactions from groups of citizens gathered on the street corners and overhears whispering which he knows is directed against him. Ultimately he may even link his wife and family with his foes, and when he comes to the asylum he fears to taste his food lest his enemies have slipped poison into it.

Delusions of persecution have a tendency to remain permanently and to grow worse with the passage of time. They are also the most dangerous from the point of view of the general public, for they are nearly always the basis of murders committed by the insane.

(2) *Subconscious Malingering.* There are many people who are afflicted with ailments which are apparently so critical as to thwart their remaining at work, yet which are entirely figments of the imagination. They are not conscious malingerers for they are not deliberately feigning illness. The whole process of developing the illness has occurred in the margin of the patient's attention-field so he is not consciously aware of what has happened even though the ailment relieves him from some very painful situation.

Shell shock was usually a physical illness which resulted when no other method seemed capable of preventing the emotional impasse resulting from the fear of battle and the fear of fleeing from it. In the "cannot fight, cannot run" dilemma an imaginary ailment invalided the soldier to a base hospital where he seldom recovered until after the armistice. Many soldiers developed blindness, often in just one eye, which then happened to be the "sighting" eye for their rifles. Physical deafness and paralysis also were frequently resultants of shell shock.

It is not so difficult to realize how shell shock develops when one considers what happens when an individual is struck by an automobile. Let us suppose that he gets up immediately, brushes off his clothing, and goes on his way. When he gets home and his family or neighbors hear of the accident, they tell him he should have sued the motorist. How does he know, they argue, that he is not injured internally? They are sure to tell of some case within their knowledge in which the effects of internal bruises and hemorrhages did not appear until months later. The accident victim begins to analyze his sensations, and also realizes that if he fails to sue within a certain period of time, he will have difficulty convincing the jury that he actually suffered his injury from the automobile accident. He decides that he does feel a bit sore and pained in the visceral region, especially as the bruises of his muscles are more evident the following day.

"I told you so," his neighbors exclaim with emphatic nods, and he begins to feel worse. Two or three days later if he is not walking on crutches he may be bedridden, where he remains until the case is satisfactorily settled or else carried to the Supreme Court. It has been a common characteristic of railroad and automobile accident victims that the patient makes a remarkable improvement after his case is settled unequivocally. Even if he obtains no redress, he usually regains better health after he finds there is no further possibility of a financial settlement.

In subconscious malingering, therefore, it is evident that various "faith" cures are effective. A mental or functional ailment is often susceptible to mental treatment. And since specialists in internal medicine have stated that 60 to 70 per cent of all patients coming to them are simply mental cases, it is easy to understand why certain religious sects can cite thousands of records of faith cures. In the final chapter of the book we shall elaborate this topic more fully.

We may conclude our discussion of the abnormal ways out of emotional conflicts by stating that they fall into two general classes, the insanities, and subconscious malingering. The latter classification is less dangerous inasmuch as patients therein can more frequently be restored to normal life by psychiatric treatment. Except for the strictly organic insanities, moreover, the application of the laws of mental hygiene early in the career of the patient is of great prophylactic value, often thwarting the tendency toward an abnormal way out of emotional conflicts.

Stuttering and Stammering. Stuttering pertains to the repetition of a syllable in an endeavor to enunciate, as in "M-m-may I have some more cake?" and usually appears at the beginning of a sentence or clause, after which the stutterer proceeds fairly fluently to the end of the thought. In stammering, the speaker stops in the middle of a thought, as in "May I have . . . some cake?" The two speech defects may appear in the same individual.

The etiology of the two varieties of defect is usually the same, although stuttering occasionally arises from a malformed denture, a tongue which is unwieldy, or incorrect habits of articulation. Stuttering may also be acquired by children through imitation of some confirmed stutterer in the home or the neighborhood. In this case it may pass away when the child moves to a different milieu. Again, the child may be laughed at by his schoolmates and rendered so self-conscious concerning his imitative stuttering that the habit fastens itself upon him permanently. Brain injury may also be a factor explaining both kinds of disorder.

But the majority of cases of stuttering and stammering are a result of fear, and are therefore functional defects subject to correction. Shell shock may give rise to these speech abnormalities, but most of the functional instances of stuttering and stammering go back to instances of actual or threatened social humiliation and punishment. The child who masturbates, or who is in terror of a brutal parent, or who is introvertive and ill at ease among other people, or who has been ridiculed in a social situation like the classroom when he has attempted to speak—these youngsters often develop speech defects of the kind just mentioned. They usually suffer from a social inferiority complex.

Stuttering and stammering, therefore, result because the muscles of the larynx have been conditioned to abnormal reactions when their owner finds himself in a situation comparable to the one in which he developed his fear. Why the laryngeal muscles react atypically instead of the biceps is because they are the principle "social" muscles of the body and hence are likely to be affected by painful social conditioning. Because they are reacting overtly or implicitly all day long in the speech and thought of their owner and because they are therefore the chief functioning muscles in the situation where the fear originally arises, they become tied up with the fear reaction.

To show more clearly how this tie-up takes place, let us consider a somewhat similar situation in which the writer burned his tongue on some scalding hot coffee and spilled part of the contents of the cup because of the quick retractive jerk of his wrist. Thereafter whenever he brought a cup of coffee within three or four inches of his mouth his hand would immediately begin trembling to such an extent that some of the coffee was spilled. This reaction demonstrates a subconsciously acquired habit where the muscles functioning at the moment the pain was received became conditioned to trembling in the "sipping" situation. Had the writer not directed his conscious attention to this peculiar reaction, he might have become a slave to it, but by realizing its origin and by deliberately going through the motions of raising a cup to his lips, he freed himself from it.

In the case of the stutterer and stammerer the laryngeal muscles have likewise become conditioned to "trembling" in the social situation of speaking, and their owners are victims of these subconsciously acquired muscle spasms. Their cures consist of their becoming cognizant of the origin of their trouble and of becoming the masters instead of the slaves of their laryngeal muscles.

Common characteristics of functional stuttering and stammering are an ability to converse normally with dogs and other infrahuman creatures, as well as the capacity to sing or read without trouble. The stutterer and stammerer can also pitch their voices higher or lower than normally and then speak without difficulty. A curious case which came to the writer's attention was that of an Englishman, a graduate of Oxford. His stuttering was so painful that he refused to talk over the telephone. But when his French sweetheart called him, he would converse with her in French with the facility of the native Parisian. In short, he stuttered in his native tongue but was a fluent speaker in a foreign language.

The cure for stuttering and stammering consists of a realization of the cause of the speech defect, plus a deliberate attempt to regain the mastery of the laryngeal muscles. In the public schools we often send the stutterers and stammerers to a special teacher, who encourages them to relax in all their musculature. Army cots may be at hand on which the children stretch out. Then they may be given a book from which to read aloud. In a modulated voice the teacher asks questions. As soon as the child's laryngeal muscles begin to tighten she again urges the youngster to relax. After half an hour or so the child is sent back to his own classroom with the injunction that whenever the regular room teacher calls upon him to recite he must first think of his relaxed condition in the speech room and try to regain the same kinesthetic sensations.

The advantages attaching to this advice are obvious. First, the child's tendency to focus his thought upon the speech room instantly renders him oblivious of his classmates and the social situation in which he stands. The chief stimulus for his laryngeal spasm is therefore inoperative. The attempt to regain the same muscle sensations which he felt while stretched upon the army cot also draws his attention away from his present audience. His resulting calmness is similar to that of the public-speaker who begins his address in a state of nervous tension and knee-trembling, but becomes poised as soon as he forgets his audience in his concentration upon the thoughts which he wishes to present. As soon as a stutterer or stammerer has demonstrated his ability to speak fluently in a group his inferiority complex is dissipated. The Oxford graduate just mentioned was completely cured of his stuttering inside of a fortnight.

In concluding our discussion of stuttering and stammering, therefore, we may repeat that the great majority of such cases are functional, and therefore can be cured, sometimes in a few weeks. The patient must be shown the psychological causes for his defect, and be given a means of forgetting his audience until his facile speech restores his confidence in himself. Until he understands the true nature of his defect he may go through life like the man who possessed the peculiar fear of being seized from behind, always a slave to a subconsciously acquired habit. Introverts and socially fearful youngsters are more likely to become addicted to these speech disorders than are extroverts.

Hypnosis and Its Significance. Hypnosis is characterized by a dissociation of the personality in which the normally adequate sensory stimuli operate only at the command of the hypnotist. Persons can seldom be hypnotized against their will, and they normally awaken from their trance in a few minutes even though the hypnotist forgets to rouse them. In case it is late at night and they are fatigued, they may sleep on throughout the night, if the hypnotist does not waken them, their temporary trance simply merging into normal slumber.

The hypnotic sleep is very similar to that of a young mother who goes to bed at night with the welfare of her baby uppermost in her mind. She remains constantly attuned to any whimper of the infant even though she may be oblivious to many other stimuli of a louder nature. She may even sleep through the ringing of the alarm clock. In a similar manner, the hypnotic patient must enter the trance with the idea in mind that he will be attentive to the hypnotist. During the trance which ensues he is alert to the commands of the hypnotist but does not heed other stimuli. He will perform the commands of the hypnotist but show no sign of hearing the shouted words of others who may order him about.

At the command of the hypnotist he may forget upon waking everything which occurred during the trance, but when re-hypnotized he regains functional control of the memories concerning his actions in the previous hypnotic state. By means of post hypnotic suggestions, the subject may perform duties the following day which the hypnotist ordered during his previous trance, yet be unable to account for his behavior. He does not realize or remember that the hypnotist ordered him to carry out the idea now in mind, but he feels a compulsion to do so. The act, however, must not be at great variance with his normal behavior. Even under hypnosis, moreover, the patient will not break his established habit systems. Unless he is a gangster, he will not attempt murder even at the command of the hypnotist.

Münsterberg employed post hypnotic suggestion in tapering off the dope fiend's doses on successive days, and also cured chronic seasickness in this manner. Indeed, wherever functional disorders are encountered, hypnosis may be of aid, particularly in plumbing forgotten memories. Persons who are suffering from amnesia and cannot remember even their own names are often able to tell this information to the hypnotist.

Inasmuch as hypnosis is characterized by a high degree of suggestibility on the part of the patient in respect to stimuli emanating from the hypnotist, and because the patient is freed from distracting stimuli, he is capable of focussing a greater degree of attention upon the problem before him. He may perform feats of strength which he cannot duplicate when in the normal waking state. We have previously contrasted the strength of handgrip of patients in the waking state with their strength when under hypnosis. In a similar manner he may concentrate his attention upon past events and resurrect memories which are too faint or too greatly inhibited by conflicting ideas to be available in the waking state.

In concluding our discussion of hypnosis, it is well to repeat that the patient's dissociation from extraneous sensory stimulation with its resulting increase in his utilizable attention, renders him able to bring forth memories and submerged fears which he has consciously forgotten. He accepts stimuli from the hypnotist uncritically, morever, and frankly recounts information which normally he could not or would not divulge. Feeling tones regarding certain objects may be implanted by the hypnotist and ideas for future action may be offered to the patient which in the later waking state he reacts to or carries out without knowing why he feels the compulsion to do so. His dissociation under hypnosis, moreover, may be so great that he fails to react to pain and can undergo a surgical operation without an additional anaesthetic. However, the principal use of hypnosis lies in the field of the psychoanalyst.

Psychoanalysis. The chief functions of psychoanalysis consist of an attempt to bring to the subject's conscious attention the previous experiences which bear upon his emotional conflict, and then effect a constructive and conscious compromise through re-education and sublimation. We have already described several instances of childhood fears which fettered the adult life of the persons in question. The man who was always in dread of being seized from behind, the functional stutterer and stammerer, the patient addicted to phobias and compulsions are cases for the psychoanalyst.

In his endeavor to learn the disturbing causes for adult maladjustment the psychoanalyst tries to tap the experience of adolescence and the ostensibly forgotten wishes of childhood. In order to procure the information which he desires he resorts to the following procedures:

(1) *Free association of ideas.* When he comes to the office of the psychoanalyst the patient reclines upon a couch and begins thinking aloud. He talks in rambling fashion passing from one idea to another according to the laws of association which we described in Chapter II. Despite the fact that he may be paying the psychoanalyst a high fee for discovering the etiology of the patient's emotional conflict, the latter usually avoids the very data which is most significant. His train of association will reach an impasse. This "blocking" as it is called is indicative of the fact that the patient is approaching the group of ideas which form his "complex"—a term employed to designate the related ideas and memories clustering around a central emotional situation often taboo. After hours and weeks of such rambling conversation the patient may finally exclaim, "I cannot think of another idea." Then the analyst will probably retort, "But you have not even begun to tell me about your trouble." The patient's speech has thus far been a camouflage to hide from the analyst as well as from himself the real cause of his conflict.

In explaining more clearly the significance of the conversational impasses or "blocking", we should recall that the normal individual who has a grave but unsolved problem relating to business or social life finds that he cannot refrain from thinking about it for any lengthy period of time. Wives know when their husbands are perturbed because of their repeated return to the same topic of conversation. In the realm of emotional conflicts the patients also tend to return to the complex which disturbs them, but they stop short at the threshold.

The psychoanalyst may stimulate them with a new word by asking, "What does 'storm' make you think of?" The patient pursues his train of thought until he will go no farther, at which point the analyst gives him a new starting word. Frequently these trains of thought lead, like the spokes from the tire of a wheel, into a central hub which is the complex. The patient may block out the thresholds of his complex by means of the ideas which ended each fresh thought sally. The skilful analyst soon guesses what is troubling his patient.

(2) *Controlled word associations.* In this method the analyst asks his patient to reply with the first thought or word which comes to mind as the analyst presents a series of verbal stimuli. This method follows the procedure described in Chapter II, where we presented some of the words and the most frequent responses thereto which Kent and Rosanoff had employed. The Pressey X-O test is also an attempt to plumb the emotional reactions of individuals by having them cross out from a list of words designating objects over which they have worried or which they dislike. By following the crossed out words, the analyst can make a fairly accurate guess concerning the complex or complexes of his patient.

(3) *The interpretation of dreams.* The patient keeps a little notebook at the head of his bed and is instructed to write down every dream as soon as he awakens, whether it be in the middle of the night or in the morning. Psychoanalysts believe that chance neural currents soon lead to the complex and the tabooed thoughts. If these do not appear directly in the resulting dream, then they appear in symbolic guise, as we have already explained in an earlier section of this chapter.

(4) *Purposive accidents.* Many of the errors in speech and

action are traceable to basic wishes or desires which are not in the forefront of the person's attention-field. Faulty memories belong in this same category, for people tend to forget the things which are unpleasant or distasteful to them. The writer whose opus has been severely criticized by some reviewer may find that he cannot recall the name of the latter a short time later. Slips of the tongue or fingers also often reveal underlying motives. Menninger cites the case of a stenographer patient of his who possessed a fear of syphilis, syphiliophobia, and had spells of great irritability. While copying a railroad case concerning a conductor who revealed the onset of syphilitic infection of the brain by his intense irritability, she wrote "Me. A." in two places instead of "Mr. A." Thus she identified herself with the patient whose nervousness was of the same origin as she thought her own to be.

The limitations of space prevent our further discussion of other technical words which constitute a part of the psychoanalytic terminology. We may conclude our discussion by saying that psychoanalysis has been one of the most wholesome influences which has ever affected the scientific study of human behavior. Freud and his disciples have emphasized the fact that no response occurs without a stimulus, that no behavior reaction occurs without a cause. Thus the importance of taking note of minor experiences of the patient is made more apparent. Psychoanalysis has also pointed out the relationship of emotional thwartings to functional diseases, and has given great impetus to child psychology.

On the other hand, psychonalaysis has not been entirely free from criticism. We have already discussed the confusion which is engendered by the idea of a Censor and of repression. Because the Freudians have emphasized the sexual side of emotional conflicts rather exclusively heretofore, psychoanalysis has been criticized severely. The beneficial results obtained by the psychoanalysts cannot be controverted, but the unscientific concepts and analogies employed in explaining how these results occurred are the causes of debate and censure.

The student should remember that there is no Censor which "submerges" or "pushes" ideas out of the focal circle of the attention-field, nor is there a crude vital force called the "libido" which operates independent of the neural patterns of the individual. Lashley[1] has aptly diagnosed the situation as follows:

> Instead of employing the available and pertinent facts of neurophysiology the writers (Freudians) are content with a crude mechanics which seems to have been derived from analogy with the simplest physical forces. The mental mechanisms of the psychoanalysts resemble more closely the behavior of liquids under pressure than they do any physiological processes and, indeed, the similarity is so exact that we might justly call the Freudian dynamics a system of psychohydraulics.

The importance of understanding psychoanalysis is becoming imperative in the field of medicine, as we shall discuss more fully in the next chapter. The physician of tomorrow must know not only how to write pharmaceutical prescriptions and wield a scalpel, but he must also be familiar with the psychoanalytic technique. This fact is already being realized in our medical schools where psychiatry is becoming an important part of the curriculum.

[1] Lashley, K. S., "Physiological Analysis of the Libido," *Psychological Review,* vol. xxxi (May, 1924), No. 3, p. 194.

REFERENCES

BENTLEY, M., AND COWDRY, E. V., *The Problem of Mental Disorder* (New York, 1934).

BLANTON, M. G., AND S., "What is the Problem of Stuttering?" *Journal of Abnormal Psychology,* vol. xiii (1919), pp. 303-313.

BLANTON AND BLANTON, *For Stutterers* (New York, 1936).

BRYNGELSON, B., "Sidedness as an Etiological Factor in Stuttering," *J. Genet. Psychol.,* 1935, vol. 47, pp. 204-217.

CASON, H., "The Nightmare Dream," *Psychol. Monogr.,* 1935, vol. 46, No. 209, pp. 51.

CREAK, M., AND GUTTMANN, E., "Chorea, Tics and Compulsive Utterances," *J. Ment. Sci.,* 1935, vol. 81, pp. 834-839.

DODGE, R., "The Problem of Inhibition," *Psychological Review,* vol. xxxiii (1926), pp. 1-12.

FREUD, SIGMUND, *The Interpretation of Dreams* (London, 1921).

———, *A General Introduction to Psychoanalysis* (New York, 1920).

FRINK, H. W., *Morbid Fears and Compulsions* (New York, 1921).

HENDRICK, I., *Facts and Figures of Psychoanalysis* (New York, 1934).

JASTROW, JOSEPH, "The Neurological Concept of Behavior," *Psychological Review,* vol. xxxi (May, 1924), No. 3, pp. 203-218.

JENNESS, A., AND WIBLE, C. L., "Electrocardiograms During Sleep and Hypnosis," *J. Psychol.,* 1936, vol. 1, pp. 235-245.

LEUBA, J. H., "Freudian Psychology and Scientific Inspiration," *Psychological Review,* vol. xxxi (May, 1924), No. 3, pp. 184-191.

MEAGHER, J. F., *A Study of Masturbation and the Psycho-Sexual Life* (Baltimore, 1936).

MELTZER, H., "Talkativeness in Stuttering and Non-Stuttering Children," *J. Genet. Psychol.,* 1935, vol. 46, pp. 371-390.

NOYES, A. P., *Modern Clinical Psychiatry* (Philadelphia, 1934).

PILLSBURY, W. B., *An Elementary Psychology of the Abnormal* (New York, 1932).

PRINCE, MORTON, *The Unconscious: The Fundamentals of Human Personality, Normal and Abnormal* (New York, 1921).

ROBINSON, EDWARD S., "A Concept of Compensation and Its Psychological Setting," *Journal of Abnormal Psychology,* vol. xvii (1923), pp. 383-394.

SHAFFER, L. F., *The Psychology of Adjustment* (Boston, 1936).

SHIPMAN, M., AND BEST, A. C., "Sex Perversion in an Institution Population," *Proc. Amer. Ass. Ment. Def.,* 1935, vol. 40, pp. 214-230.

SOUTHARD, E. E., *Shell-Shock and Other Neuropsychiatric Problems Presented in* 589 *Cases from the War Literature* (Leonard, 1919).

STINCHFIELD, S. M., *Speech Disorders* (New York, 1933).

TAYLOR, W. S., "Behavior Under Hypnoanalysis, and the Mechanism of the Neurosis," *Journal of Abnormal Psychology,* vol. xviii (1923), pp. 107-124.

———, *Readings in Abnormal Psychology and Mental Hygiene* (New York, 1926).

THURSTONE, L. L., "Influence of Freudism on Theoretical Psychology," *Psychological Review,* vol. xxxi (May, 1924), No. 3, pp. 175-183.

TRAVIS, L. E., "Suggestibility and Negativism as Measured by Auditory Threshold During Reverie," *Journal of Abnormal Psychology,* vol. xviii (1924), pp. 350-368.

WELCH, L., "The Space and Time of Induced Hypnotic Dreams," *J. Psychol.,* 1936, vol. 1, pp. 171-178.

WELLS, F. L., "Mental Regression: Its Conception and Types," *Psychiatric Bulletin,* vol. ix (1916), pp. 445-492.

WELLS, W. R., "Experiments in Waking Hypnosis for Instructional Purposes," *Journal of Abnormal Psychology,* vol. xviii (1924), pp. 389-404.

WHITE, W. A., *Outlines of Psychiatry* (Washington, 1935).

WILLIAMS, TOM A., *Dreads and Besetting Fears, Including States of Anxiety: Their Causes and Cures* (Boston, 1923).

CHAPTER XVI

PSYCHOLOGY APPLIED IN THE PROFESSIONS

In such professions as advertising, salesmanship, and public speaking it has long been recognized that a knowledge of human motivation and control is requisite for success. In the fields of dentistry, medicine, and law, however, the emphasis has heretofore been upon the acquisition of specific techniques and precedents with but slight regard for a psychological understanding of the patients and clients. Accordingly, many a brilliant physician or law student has graduated from his alma mater without later attaining a success commensurate with the excellence of his training and ability. Classmates of these brilliant students who barely passed their courses may soon become eminently successful. Probably the same social traits which led to their low grades in college produced their rise in their profession after graduation.

With increasing knowledge of the importance of a favorable environment and of a wholesome morale upon the later health and moral integrity of men and women, the modern medical, dental, and law schools are beginning to give more time to courses devoted to a study of psychology and psychiatry. Since the human being is regarded as a unity of all of his habit systems and organs, a surgeon does not operate upon the foot or appendix but upon the patient. It becomes necessary, therefore, not only to know the anatomy and physiology of the foot and the appendix, but also to understand the mental condition of the person to whom these organs belong. Indeed, the skilled pediatrician of the modern age knows that when he operates upon a youngster's body he likewise operates upon the child's mind and also, vicariously, upon the minds of the parents. And the success with which he relieves the fears and inspires the confidence of his immediate patient and the latter's relatives and friends will influence the rapidity of the patient's physiological recuperation.

Fear not only delays the patient's recovery by robbing him of relaxation and refreshing slumber, and by upsetting his appetite, but in extreme cases it seems able to produce death. It is well known that fright can produce fainting and unconsciousness, and there are many instances on record in which death has followed extreme emotional shock. In fact, surgical shock is not infrequently given as a cause of death, and it undoubtedly has a marked psychical phase.

In our emphasis throughout the first half of this chapter upon the psychological aspects of medicine we do not wish to minimize for the student the organic bases of disease, nor are we sympathetic with those sects which deny the presence and effect of micro-organisms and toxins just because they cannot see or finger them. The hyperope does not deny the presence of printed words on this page simply because he is so far-sighted that he cannot see them, for his spectacles will quickly supplement the flattened lenses of his eyes and enable him to read. Similarly, the scientist supplements the lenses of his eyes with his laboratory spectacles (the microscope) and then he sees blood corpuscles and bacteria which were previously invisible.

In the preceding chapter we mentioned that even organic insanities are influenced by the previous habit systems of the patient prior to the onset of the brain deterioration. So, too, the particular pathological state of an organ in the human body interacts with the previously acquired disposition or personality of the patient to produce various effects. The same type of infection, therefore, will not always produce identical results in persons who have the same physiological susceptibility to the disease, nor will the stimulation of equal numbers of free nerve endings in two persons necessarily give rise to the same behavior responses. The pregnant Indian woman at parturition, for example, reacts differently than the pampered white woman, and apparently suffers less pain although her cortex is probably receiving an equal number of incoming nerve currents from the stimulation of free nerve endings in the parturient canal. We shall treat the psychological aspects of pain at more length in a later section. For the present we shall begin with a discussion of the assistance which psychology renders preventive medicine.

Psychological Aspects of Preventive Medicine. In medicine as well as dentistry and law the emphasis today is upon prophylactic measures which will preclude a later disastrous pathological condition. A dentist can easily preserve a molar if the patient comes to him early, and the physician can likewise effect cures for such dangerous maladies as cancer if the sufferer therefrom will only consult the medical expert at the beginning of his attack. The principal difficulties encountered in educating people to protect their health are as follows:

(1) *Lacking immediate pain, they procrastinate or forget.* The average person with a toothache will fail to visit his dentist if the pain subsides before he gets started to the office. This lapse of memory is explicable on the basis of our discussion in the preceding chapter, since we tend to forget what is painful or distasteful. It is because people lack the goad of actual pain that experimental health centers have usually been unsuccessful. Even though the latter are supported chiefly by private funds and call for but a slight fee from the individual, they find it difficult to get him to come in for a health examination. The person who is well feels that it is a waste of time and money to receive a physical examination. The average person, moreover, does not realize that disease may be undermining the margin of safety in various of his organs even though he feels no pain until his condition becomes acute.

It is because of this human tendency for a person to feel that he is the exception, that disease and poverty may attack everybody else but himself, that life insurance salesmen used to encounter so much difficulty, and finally evolved annuities, paid up insurance, and other plans by which they could more readily interest their prospective clients.

(2) *They fear disease.* On first glance we might think that this argument should send people to their physician for diagnosis, but it does not function in this manner. Because they dread disease, they refuse to dwell upon it in their thinking, and forget or procrastinate as we mentioned in the previous paragraphs. The failure to make a will or purchase a burial plot is also based in part upon the same tendency. People will often prefer to remain in ignorance and be contented than to incur worry and unhappiness from a physical examination which may reveal disease. In fact, like the psychoanalytic patient, even after they have consulted a physician and are paying him a goodly fee, they will frequently withhold facts which would enable the physician to treat them much more successfully.

Here is a woman, for instance, whose physician sent her to the hospital for a determination of her basal metabolic rate, warning her to eat nothing on the morning of the test. Her rate was high, and the chief interne asked her if she had eaten any breakfast that morning. She replied in the negative. A little later a second interne came along and in a casual tone asked, "What did you have for breakfast this morning?" The woman replied to this positive suggestion by saying, "Oh, just a cup of coffee." Then the interne continued, "What did you have with the coffee, toast or rolls?" The woman replied that she had eaten "only two slices of buttered toast," and the interne also learned that "just an egg" had accompanied the toast. Her own doctor had found her basal metabolic rate high, so he had sent her to the hospital for a second test. She informed her present interrogator that she had also "had a few bites of food and a little coffee" before her own physician had tested her. This kind of case is so frequently encountered that the average physician suspects breakfast whenever he finds a high basal metabolic rate in a non-hospitalized patient. We are citing it to show the lack of cooperation which the physician finds in too many patients.

(3) *They become conscious of minor ailments and magnify these disproportionately.* Although it is wise for people to have health examinations at frequent periods, there is also the danger that many suggestible individuals will have their attention drawn to minor aches and pains which they will magnify until they take to their beds. We mentioned in the previous chapter how accident victims tend to develop critical symptoms through excessive introspection, and the student has undoubtedly met persons who could be caused to leave the office and go home simply by a prearranged plot on the part of their associates who would keep remarking, "My, you look ill! What's the matter?" There are thousands of such persons in every large community who are semi-invalids because of their mental attitude. This is the type of person who benefits from mental treatment and becomes an ardent follower of certain sects which practice faith healing.

The functions of psychology in preventive medicine, therefore, consist chiefly of overcoming the inertia, ignorance, and fears of people and educating them to a sane attitude concerning mental and physical health. The task is partly one of advertising and selling. The work of certain large insurance companies, such as the Metropolitan, has been and is of great assistance in bringing health information before the masses of the population. Insurance companies are also beginning to sponsor the free annual physical examination of their large policy holders, a procedure which is profitable to both the company and the client. Some of the advertisements of commercial products have also enlightened the public regarding vitamins at the same time that they have increased sales, as the orange companies and cod liver oil manufacturers. Tooth paste companies have also been reiterating before millions of readers and listeners the advisability of regular visits to the dentist, and the paid advertisements of certain non-profit making city clinics in social diseases are of distinct educational value. In the schools the teachers are endeavoring to educate the coming generation to correct habits of health by stimulating attention to diet, sleep, and personal hygiene, functions which we have described in Chapter XIV, while the psychological clinics are of definite assistance in correcting emotional maladjustments of children.

Since good digestion is also one of the basic principles of physical and mental health, we shall devote the next section to a description of the various psychological aspects of alimentary function.

The Psychological Phase of Digestion. In Chapter II, where we presented Exhibit 12, the student saw how elementary reflexes become linked into a chain through the mediation of the physical and physiological consequences of each separate reflex arc. At the beginning the tactual stimulus on the infant's cheek had no effect upon his salivary glands nor did it stimulate the gastric glands to secretion, unless a series of intervening reflexes produced milk from the nipple caught between the baby's lips. After sufficient repetitions of the entire sequence of reflexes, a point is reached where the tactual stimulation alone, without the seizure of the nipple and the resulting flow of milk, will innervate the entire chain. Saliva will flow and the mucosal glands of the stomach will begin functioning.

Pavlov clearly demonstrated this phenomenon by employing dogs with esophageal fistulas. If the esophagus is divided and the two ends sutured to the skin, the dog will continue to eat with great relish but his chewed food will keep dropping from the lower end of his throat where his esophagus comes to the surface at the point of suture. No food enters his stomach, therefore. If the sight, odor, or chewing of food will occasion an increased flow of gastric juice thereafter, it must do so through conditioned neural pathways. This sham feeding does produce gastric secretion. Even the sound of a bell to which the dog has been previously conditioned during the food-taking situation will also incite the glands of the stomach to activity.

In a similar fashion we become conditioned to odors, temperatures, and tastes. The aroma from coffee or the odor of frying meat will stimulate the salivary and gastric glands of adults whereas they will not do so the first time a person encounters them in infancy or childhood. We have previously mentioned that oral or printed words will do the same because they have functioned in the original food-taking situation until they become symbolic or substitute stimuli.

But many other factors than the odor and sight of the food are operative in affecting digestion. The surroundings, including the room and table, exert an influence. One's appetite would be less if one were to dine in a bedroom, and greasy knives, forks, spoons, and a soiled tablecloth are inimical to gastric secretion because of the negative cephalic effect. A fly in the soup will kill the appetite of many an adult although it will not disturb a child, while a honeybee will have less unfavorable effect than the fly. Barren walls and an atmosphere of gloom will retard the flow of saliva and gastric juice, as will various emotional states, as of fear and anger. In the latter emotions the body tends to be placed upon a war basis emotionally, which means that there is a relatively greater portion of blood in the skeletal muscles, and a less amount in the walls of the stomach and intestines. Even the effect of music is often detrimental to good digestion, especially if it produces a melancholy state or a condition of muscular tension and nervous excitement.

The person's previous experience with foods will also affect his present appetite. If he has an especial dislike for fish, garlic, onions, cabbage or any other odorous food, he may not fully enjoy his beefsteak as long as the menu or the fishy odor are affecting his eyes or nostrils. Strange foods also do not stimulate digestions as do old favorites. There are various degrees of fondness and dislike for certain foods, depending upon the individual experience of each person, but many attitudes are fairly well standardized by common factors in the environment. A college group of men and women were asked to express their order of preference for the following meats: dog, cat, horse, snake, monkey. They were very uniform in their decisions, arranging these five kinds of flesh in the order given at the end of this chapter. Young children who have not been influenced by adult reactions have little preference between horse or cow meat, and would probably as soon eat snakes as frogs or shrimps.

Not only are the viands and the service of significance in affecting digestion, but more remote factors also enter in. If one is visiting a hospital for the first time, or an institution for the feeble-minded, the insane, the orphaned, or the criminal, one often lacks appetite. If one has heard that a cook in a certain restaurant is diseased, or if a housewife is untidy and careless, one likewise does not relish the food prepared by these individuals.

The reverse of this process occurs when a foreigner visits a restaurant in which his native dishes are served. The familiar food, like the songs of the fatherland, resurrect thoughts and emotions of pleasure and happiness experienced in the homeland.

Because of a recognition of these facts and the realization that people carry over from childhood the intimate relationship between pain and chastisement, modern hospitals are beginning to be equipped and decorated to avoid the coldness and austerity which formerly made them seem like jails and places of punishment. The presence of other colors than the chilly white or gray walls of the past, and the employment of bright curtains, radios, pictures, and the use of a menu card from which the convalescent can select his favorite foods, are helping to create a different feeling tone regarding hospitals and surgical operations. To the degree to which the former fears and dreads of hospitals and surgery can be removed, the patient's recovery will be facilitated. A happy outlook on life and a confidence in the physician treating him are almost as valuable (in many cases more valuable) to the patient as are the medicines which he receives.

The psychological phase of digestion, therefore, is what the physiologists call the cephalic phase. It involves the multitude of conditioned reactions to food over and above the four fundamental taste qualities which it possesses. Some of these conditioned habits facilitate an abundant flow of digestive juices while others are distinctly inhibitory. Among the latter are fears and emotional tensions as well as specific unpleasant stimuli, such as flies, filth, surgical odors and instruments, strangeness in objects and surroundings, and foods which have sickened the individual at some previous time. The proper attention to diet involves not only a study of the vitamins and a healthful balance between proteins, carbohydrates, and fats, but an understanding of the importance of the cephalic phase of digestion. As we have already discussed in Chapter VI, the suggestive value of companions is also a significant factor in stimulating the appetite because throughout youth we have been accustomed to dining in the family, so associates tend to set off the former pleasurable reactions. In the next section we shall discuss other psychological aids to the physician.

How the Physician Utilizes Psychology. Physicians have realized probably since the age of Hippocrates that many patients recover because of their belief in the physician and his medicines instead of because the pills and prescriptions are intrinsically of benefit. Indeed, the medicines may often be administered for their psychological instead of physiological value. A large part of every physician's effectiveness is psychological. Many times a parent consults his physician because his youngster is feverish and ill. The parent fears the unknown, for he does not know which of a half a dozen serious diseases the child may have. The pediatrician does almost as much good in the community, therefore, by relieving parental fears as by healing his child patients. The dread and uncertainty about the causes of their own ailments may also be great depressants to the morale of adults. It is not difficult to imagine the relief of the young woman who for weeks and months has been afraid she had a cancer, when her physician pronounces the lump on her breast an innocent fatty tumor. Dr. Campbell[1] has so excellently described these problems of the physician that we shall quote him in this regard:

> It is better to think of the physician as a man whose business it is to treat not symptoms or diseases, but sick people . . . The patient is more than a group of symptoms, more than a collection of interesting juices; he is a living individual with a most complicated pattern of reactions, and the physician who overlooks this pattern may find the symptoms intractable, the disease unintelligible. Headache may be a reaction to eye strain, but it may be a reaction to a mother-in-law; pain in the back is sometimes explained by an X-ray plate, but sometimes by unwillingness to work; indigestion may be more closely related to troubled conscience than to poor cooking; palpitation is not always an indication of organic heart disease—it may be the expression of the romance of life gone astray. Not that the situation is always simple; the patient with organic heart trouble may have romantic longings; a bad cook may conspire with a troubled conscience to ruin the digestion. The extent to which a man is disabled depends partly on the nature of his disease, but perhaps more on the way he reacts to it.

At the beginning of the chapter we compared the reactions of the Indian mother in childbirth to that of the pampered Caucasian woman. In a similar degree we see differences between two men who have pains in the lower right abdomen. One goes on about his business, and enjoys life about as usual,

1 Campbell, C. M., "The Minimum of Medical Insight Required by Social Workers with Delinquents," *Mental Hygiene*, vol. iv (1920), No. 3, pp. 513-514.

whereas the other is bedridden, hospitalized, makes his will, and enters the operating room with the priest beside him. The first of these two should probably be a little more cautious, and the second much less so. The physician encounters both types among his patients and must understand when to arouse the concern of the one and when to allay the fears of the other.

There are also patients who wish to know the causes of their disease and the details regarding their treatment. They resent evasive replies and an attempt to keep them in ignorance lest they become unduly fearful. Then there are other patients who do not care to know anything further than the directions on the bottle and who would become hysterical if they thought they were as seriously ill as the physician knows them to be.

As a general rule, however, it is not wise to ridicule the fears and anxieties of the patient, even though to the physician they may be groundless and often ludicrous, for to the patient they are very important. The average patient, moreover, wants to have a justification for his ailment in order to win sympathy from relatives and friends. He also wants the assurance that he will certainly recover by following the doctor's orders. There is an elation in feeling that one is so ruggedly and basically healthy that one can recover from a serious disease, whereas it does not flatter one's ego particularly to recuperate from a trivial illness. People like to boast about the fact that everybody gave up hope concerning their recovery and then they pulled through the dangerous period in spite of everything. In fact, children are not the only ones who enter into debates as to who was the more sick of the two individuals now arguing.

Physicians have long understood the psychological value of not minimizing too greatly the danger of the patient's ailment, but this very fact has sometimes aided the faith healers. A patient whose physician has agreed that he is in a serious condition may be cured by a practitioner of some sect, a fact which reflects against the physician and to the credit of the practitioner, who will thereafter state that "Dr. Brown gave up Mr. X as hopeless and I cured him."

Other psychological functions and dangers which confront the physician we shall describe briefly in the following section where we discuss his relationship to the female patient. We have selected her because women make up the greater number of patients of the medical profession and because they present some difficult psychological problems.

The Father Fixation and the Female Patient Because of the childhood tendency to regard illness as punishment and to associate punishment with parents, particularly the father, the close connection between the physician and the male parent is not difficult to understand. Moreover, the fact that the physician holds the position of confidant, and soon obtains information concerning the patient of an intimate and personal nature again assists the latter to identify the physician with the father. And because of the girl's erotic attachment to her father (the Electra Complex), when she makes the transference to her physician she often becomes emotionally attached to the latter in the same subconscious manner as she regards her male parent.

It is also a psychological characteristic of people that when they share their secrets with another person, not only do they obtain a partial emotional release from their tensions, but the person who knows their secrets becomes identified with those confidences and thereafter is a symbol of them to the patient. The student is probably aware of the fact that he tends to avoid the man from whom he has borrowed money, and shuns those who know of his humiliation or shame. On the other hand, the girl or boy who has shared pleasant erotic experiences with us, becomes henceforth a desired companion.

In a somewhat similar manner the woman patient who reveals confidential and intimate information about herself, some of which is often sexual in nature, thereafter feels more closely attached to her physician than before she divulged her secrets to him. Through the centuries the physician has encountered this transference to himself with a consequent fixation. It has remained for the psychiatrist, however, to offer the technical terminology and the full explanation for this type of behavior.

It is a usual event during psychoanalytic treatment for the patient to realize the nature of her transference and fixation, after which the psychiatrist no longer appears in her dreams in a favorable light, but is transformed into a despised creature. In ordinary medical practice a somewhat similar reaction often takes place. Patients who keep running to the doctor's office at frequent intervals and return feeling in good spirits even though they have received little if any medicine, eventually may find that their subconscious ideas and wishes become conscious. They may then be shocked or shamed by their own feelings toward the physician, and begin developing a negative transference, as is denoted in the familiar lines:

"I do not love thee, Doctor Fell,
The reason why I cannot tell;
But this alone I know full well,
I do not love thee, Doctor Fell."

The writer has encountered a number of previously chronic medical patients who now will have nothing to do with medicines or physicians, and have gone into certain sects of faith healers chiefly because of this phenomenon of negative transference. They are, for the most part, female patients. In many instances it is necessary for the physician deliberately to break the fixation of his chronic patients for the good of all concerned. He also finds it advisable to keep a nurse as his assistant in order to protect himself from calumny and litigation because of patients who project upon him attitudes

[1] Frink, H. W., *Morbid Fears and Compulsions* (Moffat, Yard and Co., 2nd edition, 1921), p. 99.

and behavior of which he is innocent. The following quotation of a similar case is taken from Frink[1].

"A young woman student had at various times a number of attacks which invariably began with her becoming attracted by one of her professors. She would for a time talk a great deal about him, of how able and attractive he was, but without intimating that she was falling in love with him. Then she would begin to think that he was falling in love with her. This would seem to please and amuse her at first, but soon she would get the notion that he was hypnotizing her, and her pleasure would be succeeded by anger. She would complain that through hypnotic influence he was putting into her mind all sorts of erotic fancies about him, that by telepathic suggestion he gave her impulses to come to his apartment, etc., all of which would get her into a state of great rage and excitement and she would have to abandon her studies. Thereupon the attack would gradually subside, only to be repeated in connection with some other teacher when she resumed her work.

"It is apparent that this patient's delusional ideas were nothing but a projection of her own erotic interests in her teachers. What she felt as a hypnotic or telepathic influence brought to bear upon her from without was simply an externalization of her own desires. Her anger against the teachers represented her pathological resistances against these desires. Presumably had she been able to regard her sexuality in a normal way, as something perfectly legitimate and wholesome, what appeared as delusional attacks would otherwise have been ordinary love affairs."

From the standpoint of psychology, therefore, the father fixation renders the female patient more suggestible and amenable to medical treatment by her physician, but in its occasional abnormal degree complicates the duties of the physician. If he finds it necessary to break the subconscious emotional attachment of the patient to himself he may create a negative transference thereby which completely alienates his patient. There are times, of course, when this extremity is wise.

How the Physician Wins His Public. There is no type of worker who more greatly needs to understand the art of improving his personality and "selling" himself to the public than does the professional man. After graduating from his professional school the physician, as well as the dentist and lawyer, may enter a city where he is comparatively unknown. The ethics of his profession forbid his advertising for patients in any of the usual media. He can run an announcement that he has opened his office, or has moved to a new address, and can send out direct-mail letters containing cards with similar information upon them, but thereafter he must rely upon the social contacts through various civic, religious, commercial, and fraternal organizations. If he is without any "pull" it may be necessary for him to devote his spare time to Boy Scout work as a means of breaking into the newspapers. In Chapter VI we described at some length many of the principles which he must follow in order to increase the number of his friends. In the socialization process, however, he must constantly keep in mind that a physician should retain a certain amount of dignity and fatherliness.

There are physicians, for example, whose physical presence is so peaceful and inspiring of confidence that the patient feels half cured when the doctor enters the room. Other physicians of a nervous temperament and fidgety manner do not irradiate the same positive suggestions of competence and health. The temperamental genius may become successful in a specialized field, but in general practice where the personal contact is especially great the kindly, confident man with dignity and social intelligence usually far excels him.

Although this is an age where relatively young men are presidents of large corporations, the general public still wants to look upon the physician in a filial manner, regarding him as a father. It is wise, therefore, for the physician to develop those personality traits which the average person associates with fathers. An impression of maturity is one important asset, a fact which was fully understood by the young medical graduates of a generation ago who started letting their beards grow during their senior year so they could gain in apparent age.

The physician should be jovial but not too informal. He

should extrovert himself so that he is interested in those around him and in the smaller towns should be able to slap a fellow citizen cordially on the back and call him by his first name, but he should not have cultivated a personality which warrants the fellow citizen calling the physician by the latter's Christian name. We made this distinction in a previous chapter when we mentioned that the politician in the hay field retains his collar and tie even though he wears overalls.

In his sociability, therefore, the young physician must not fail to maintain some badge of dignity, whether it be the wearing of a coat while others are in their shirt sleeves, the refrainment from participation in youthful sports particularly when older people are among the spectators, or the carrying of his black satchel. The public has a mental stereotype of a physician, and it is not profitable for the young doctor to enter upon a radical change of the stereotype. In fact, the latter is like a well advertised trade-mark or slogan; so he should capitalize upon it by selling his services under this professional label. To disregard a well advertised slogan or a familiar stereotype is poor business, especially when a person can avail himself of either at no financial outlay.

In concluding our discussion of the relationship between psychology and medicine, it is well to point out that the successful physician of the next generation will have to possess an even greater social intelligence than has been true in the past, for the field of psychiatry and mental hygiene is growing rapidly. In previous years physicians have developed a fair knowledge of human behavior traits from experience after they left the medical school, so that many of them became remarkedly good applied psychologists. It is more economical, however, for the young medical student to obtain his knowledge of psychology in the classroom.

The dentist has practically the same problems as the physician except that he usually does not enter into such confidential relationships with his patients. He is much less likely to have them develop father fixations, and his youthful appearance is not quite so inimical to his professional success.

In the following address I have summarized a few of the salient principles of applied psychology of especial interest to dentists, but quite applicable to lawyers and physicians as well.

THE USES OF PSYCHOLOGY IN DENTAL PRACTICE*

George W. Crane, Ph. D., M. D.

Although many modern dentists as well as physicians realize that we do not operate on the patient's tooth or appendix but upon the entire patient, many of us have doubtless failed to analyze thoroughly the full effect of our professional contact with the entire personality of the subject who calls at our office.

Indeed, it is rather surprising that we practice as much social psychology in our professions as we do, for the great majority of men and women who go into these professions have been compelled by college requirements to concentrate upon chemistry and physics, zoology and bacteriology, anatomy and physiology.

In most of those fields we study either inert substances or else non-human entities. As a result of this rigid ten-year attention to everything else except people, we are usually not good salesmen of our professional skills when we suddenly are thrown upon the community in which we elect to set up an office.

In brief, our entire technical education has been devoted heretofore to preparation for work upon teeth or appendices, yet as soon as we leave our professional school and pass the state board examinations, we find ourselves dealing with people. Our financial success depends largely upon how well we can sell ourselves to the public.

Is it any wonder, therefore, that many of us fail to become outstanding in the community when we have had no education in the art of tactful self-advertising; in the delicate job of manipulating people and making them like us; in the psychological task of inspiring confidence in our abilities and capacities?

Most of us leave the university as introverts; that is, as persons who are more interested in things than in people. We aren't glib conversationalists, nor are we carefree playboys around town with plenty of money to join the wealthy clubs. We cannot dance or

*Read before the Wisconsin State Dental Economics Group on Saturday afternoon, September 26, 1936.

sing and after ten years in college we aren't rivals of Bobby Jones on the golf links.

We are proud of our technical training and frame our diplomas to show off the fact that we are competent. But to the average layman what does a diploma mean? Many a patient who comes to every one of us hardly knows we must pass a state board examination and have many years of college training.

Probably half of the general public look upon physicians and dentists as just "docs". They assume we must be all right or we wouldn't be in business, and even after they come to our office they judge us not by our Phi Beta Kappa and scientific keys, but by many little characteristics which we often overlook entirely.

On the evening of September 23, 1936, I met my class in Applied Psychology on our McKinlock Campus in Chicago. It was our first meeting for the fall semester. Exactly fifty men and women were present, ranging in ages from 20 to 45. A number of them were married, and almost all were employed during the day in Chicago stores, offices and schools.

They represent a college group who are employed during the day. Their intelligence and educational advantages are obviously much above the average. So I decided to give them a brief questionnaire regarding dentists and dentistry. They willingly cooperated.

"What prompted you to visit a dentist the last time you went to one?" I asked, and they wrote their reasons. I shall tabulate them herewith:

	No. persons
Pain, aching tooth, or abscess	13
Had noted a cavity, by tongue or mirror	9
Just for a general dental check-up	6
To have teeth cleaned	5
Routine semi-annual visit	5
Routine annual visit	4
Dentist phoned or wrote them to come in	3
Swollen gums—not painful	2
Broken tooth—traumatic	1
Pink toothbrush	1
Oculist urged it	1
Total	50

"Why did you select the particular dentist you visited?" I next asked.

	No. persons
Parents, or other relatives recommended him	16
Friends of patient recommended him	12
Dentist was a relative of the patient	5

Dentist was a friend of the patient	4
Dentist's office was nearby	4
Dentist was a high school classmate	2
Dentist belonged to same business club	2
Dentist was father of his sweetheart	1
Dentist took care of her employer	1
Recommended by an Extractor	1
Recommended by a physician	1
Xmas eve and only available man	1
Total	50

(Note that the first 28 calls above represent referred business; only 22 calls represent primary or original contact business.)

"If you have visited more than one dentist, select the one you deem the best and write down the specific reasons for your choice," was my third query. Some replied with several reasons, others with none.

	No. choices
Dentist was cheerful, friendly, congenial	7
Inspired me with confidence in his ability	6
Dentist's charges were reasonable	6
Dentist's work was painless	4
Dentist was quick but gentle in his work	3
Dentist had new, clean, modern offices	3
Dentist was on State Board of Registration	2
He answered my questions honestly	2
More interested in me than in my money	2
He was careful to do a good job, unhurried	2
His tools looked shiny and new	1
He did a minimum amount of drilling	1
Dentist seemed "knowing"	1
He treats the tooth instead of pulling it	1
His work lasted well—fillings didn't come out	1
He does research in dentistry	1
He was very fastidious in his dress	1
He was quiet—didn't talk my head off	1
He was out of school but a few years, so modern	1
He did very artistic work	1
Many of my neighbors went to him	1
He was president of the Rotary club	1
He was steady and was thorough	1
I heard no complaints about his work holding up	1

If you practicing dentists will simply scan the above reasons cited by intelligent adults as to why they thought a given dentist was the best of those they had consulted, you will find that 80 per cent of the replies are of a definitely psychological nature.

Did these people mention the university from which the dentist graduated? Did they consider what college grades the dentist had made? No mention of scientific honor fraternities the dentist belonged to, or of his membership in scientific organizations!

But much weight was placed on his personality, pleasantness, clean modern office equipment, fastidiousness in dress, and his ability to appear "knowing" or inspire confidence. The "shiny tools" he used got more credit than his diploma! And from university people! The above data came from 41 of the students. Nine had never gone to more than one dentist.

Specificity is the basis of proof as well as of scientific progress, so I shall quote some of the exact statements of these men and women regarding the dentist they consider best:

"I consider my present dentist best because he treats a tooth instead of pulling it immediately." (Female)

* * *

"Dr. Blank was the better because he was reasonable in his charges and I liked him personally." (Female)

* * *

"I think my present dentist is best because he seems more intelligent, answers my questions honestly, and does considerable research and study in his field. Also, of primary importance, his office and workrooms are always immaculately clean." (Female)

* * *

"My second dentist was best, because he was more honest, told the truth, tried to see my viewpoint and on several occasions suggested means of saving money without injury to my teeth, such as silver in place of gold, etc." (Male)

* * *

"The dentist I considered best was the last one to which I went as he has some harmless hypodermics that make the drilling painless." (Female)

* * *

"I believe the dentist I now patronize is the best I have ever visited because he is in a new, thoroughly modern office, is a most fastidious person in dress and cleanliness, and seems so very 'knowing' when explaining the conditions of the teeth and gums. I know, too, that many of the persons in our town have been giving him their trade." (Female)

* * *

"My first dentist was best because he took the least time to do his work, and he held the drilling down to a minimum," (Male)

* * *

"The dentist I now go to is the one I like best because of his carefulness and painstaking work. He never hurries and won't be rushed. The job must be done right." (Male)

* * *

"My last dentist was the best because his professional bearing and his office equipment seemed of a higher standard than the preceding ones. He was several years out of school but young enough to be thoroughly up-to-date." (Female)

"I tried another dentist for experiment once, on recommendation of a friend, and promptly returned to the family dentist as several fillings had to be replaced that the second dentist had put in." (Female)

* * *

"I have gone to four dentists, and the third and fourth are my choice, for they are both cheerful and seem to be interested in me and my work. I go to the fourth because his office is more convenient for me." (Male)

* * *

"I prefer our family dentist because he is very friendly, jolly and as painless as possible." (Female)

* * *

"Of the four dentists I have gone to, I liked the third best. This was because of reports from the neighbors as to his ability and I went back several times because he deadened the nerves of the tooth he was working on, thereby eliminating all pain!" (Female)

* * *

"I think my last dentist is best because he is more popular in the town, and he is a member of the State Board of Registration." (Male)

As you dentists can readily perceive, many of these so-called reasons are not logical nor based on the dentist's technical skill, but represent emotional reactions of the patient toward him. Some differences of opinion exist as between the two men one of whom thought speed was a criterion of excellence, whereas the other was pleased by the slow but thorough work of his dentist.

In carrying further this "consumer survey", as we would call it in applied psychology, I asked my fifty students to report which dentist they considered the worst or least competent and their reasons are tabulated as follows:

	No. choices
His fillings fell out	5
His fillings were rough and hurt my tongue	3
He was old—too long out of school	3
He was too talkative	2
He'd rather pull than save with a filling	2
He tried to scare me into having work done	2
His office was very untidy	2
He smoked cigarettes and failed to wash afterwards	1
He was a very sloppy worker	1
He had dirty eyeglasses with specks on them	1
His hair was full of dandruff	1
His breath smelled of alcohol	1
His breath smelled of tobacco, which sickens me	1
The dentist had decayed teeth	1
His fingernails weren't clean	1
He was careless about sterilizing his instruments	1
He argued and browbeat his assistant	1
He belittled me for showing pain	1

He did too much drilling	1
His office was poorly lighted	1
He overlooked a cavity and later pulled the tooth	1
My teeth decayed underneath the filling	1
He overpacked a tooth and gave me a toothache	1
He wasn't punctual	1
He was haphazard with his appointments	1
His breath was terrible	1
He was more interested in my money than my teeth	1
He didn't tell me the truth	1

As unrelated as many of these trivial factors are to the dentist's skill and scientific standing, they nevertheless resulted in the loss of patients and the development to this extent of unfavorable publicity in the community.

It may appear like facetiousness when I say it, but it would seem that halitosis, body odor, dirty fingernails, dandruff, and carelessness regarding personal appearance are responsible for the loss of more business than defective dental workmanship.

It may be of interest to list a few quotations from these papers which were handed in to me:

"I don't think a dentist should recommend yanking teeth unless he has an absolute reason for it. More than one person I know has run away from one dentist to another because of a threatened extraction. Ladies don't like it!" (Female)

* * *

"The previous dentist seemed the worse because he seemed more concerned with making money than with serving me." (Male)

* * *

"Because he did too much drilling, I think the second was worst. Most of it seemed unnecessary. My teeth were well looked after before I even consulted him." (Male)

* * *

"The first and our 'family' dentist was the worst. He was rough and didn't seem to be up-to-date on his methods." (Female)

* * *

"I have gone to four dentists. The first was the worst because his work was roughly done and didn't prove satisfactory." (Male)

* * *

"The first one I consulted in Chicago I consider the worst. He told me I had to have seven teeth filled—at a stiff price. He sold me and then pushed a drill through my jaw instead of the tooth. That might have been an accident but he said it was *my* fault because I jumped." (Male—salesmanager of large firm)

* * *

"I've been going to my brother-in-law, but once I went with a friend of mine to her dentist and I didn't like him. He tried to scare me. I didn't intend to continue with him, anyway, but went just to see what he would say. My brother-in-law later contradicted what the other dentist said when I told him about it." (Male)

"The next to the last was the poorest dentist because of his mental attitude. He belittles his patients, and scoffs when they wince at the pain, and does everything but call them cowards." (Female)

* * *

"I thought the first dentist was worse because he pulled my tooth without seeming to care whether I was in pain, and made me feel like I was merely a case and not a person," (Female)

* * *

"Poor light in his work room and his personal uncleanliness cause me to vote the second dentist the worst." (Male)

* * *

"My worst dentist? One who smoked cigarettes while waiting for the fillings to harden—and was not very careful about washing his hands before resuming work." (Female)

* * *

"I considered the last one inefficient because his eyeglasses were covered with spots and when he drilled into a cavity his hand shook. He was also far behind in modern dentistry." (Male)

* * *

"The one I considered the worst wasted too much time and talked excessively." (Male)

* * *

"I didn't like the third dentist because he had very unpleasant breath and his own teeth were decayed." (Female)

* * *

"I was very much dissatisfied with my first dentist as he had no business principles, no conception of arranging his appointments for his customers. I also noticed that his office was untidy, and his work has not proved satisfactory. I had two fillings done by him and within a short time I was compelled to have the work done all over again." (Female)

* * *

"The one I think was the worst overlooked a cavity in my tooth and then pulled the tooth out on my next visit." (Female)

* * *

"I consider our family dentist the worst because he usually left me with the rubber dam on and a nerve exposed while he argued with his wife, who assisted him in the office." (Female)

* * *

"I liked my brother-in-law least of the dentists I have visited because he was always careless with his instruments and tended to put work off." (Female)

* * *

The worst dentist, in my estimation, was the one who found too much to talk about. Perhaps he was only intending to make me feel at ease, but it made me feel that his work was not as good as it might have been had he tended strictly to business." (Female)

* * *

"I consider my first dentist the worst. I don't think his work was well done, and in addition, he was unusually slow. One had to spend an average of 2½ hours at his office for a single visit." (Male)

"Dr. Crane, would you have faith in a dentist who had just finished $75 worth of work about 6 months ago for you—and then when you go for a regular check-up, he finds five new cavities and wants to replace another dentist's inlay? I checked about the new cavities with three other dentists, who told me that absolutely there were no cavities present." (Female)

Patients certainly seem to exercise their critical capacity regarding the work of professional men, even though they lack adequate technical training themselves. And they notice many things about dentists as well as physicians, which we professional men scarcely realize are true. A good critical examination of the sort we have just presented is invaluable to every professional man who wishes to be most successful in practice.

In fact, this market research or consumer survey method is being widely recommended by psychologists. Business men, manufacturers, advertisers and salesmen, and even newspaper editors are beginning to sound out the wishes and desires of their clients with the aim of more accurately fitting their merchandise to suit consumer demands.

We need to do a searching analysis of ourselves with the aim of finding out just how we can impress our patients with the fact that we are competent, modern, up-to-date, and well trained. Patients seldom read the diplomas on the wall, so how can we intimate skillfully that we are "expert", for that is what the public wishes? I don't mean that they want specialists, solely, but they do like to feel that their physicians and dentists are expert.

Good dental work is one of the best sales arguments, but it isn't enough of itself, for many excellent dentists are hardly earning enough to live, and yet they can do admirable work. Why don't people come to their offices?

Both medicine and dentistry are surrounded by a high board fence called professional ethics. We dare not shout our own virtues by means of newspaper advertising, billboards, or the radio. We must be dignified and conservative.

But there are many ways by which we can plow much closer to this high board fence than we are now plowing and still be quite within the confines of current dental or medical ethics.

To put it bluntly, how are we to advertise ourselves and put our virtues before our public, yet not be criticized for unethical behavior or crude self-advertising? How can we toot our own horn, and yet tactfully appear to be modest, unassuming scientists? In short, how can we extrovert ourselves and utilize many of the methods of advertising, yet remain apparently diffident, research men?

This is a grave but very essential problem for all professional men to attack, since their financial future depends upon the degree to which they can cleverly answer those questions.

Some successful practitioners have developed from experience a mass of psychological principles whereby they have made a success. But such a trial and error plan requires too much time, and is fraught with considerable danger. We need more courses in applied psychology in both our dental, as well as our medical, law and engineering schools, for despite a few courses here and yon, psychology isn't yet taught adequately in professional schools.

Yet it certainly represents a good half of a man's later success. But he hears a few cursory talks upon the subject, at best, before he leaves college and meets the public in his own office. We have an unbalanced curriculum at present throughout the entire land.

It is folly to educate a tyro aviator in the principles of gasoline motors and wind resistances; then send him aloft without a bit of training in flying an airplane. The same fallacy, however, is evident in almost all of our technical schools. We are well grounded in the mechanical side of our science, yet are sent out with almost no advice regarding the social and intensely practical aspect of it.

But to return to specificity, how can a dentist advertise himself discreetly and ethically? Here are some devices which have already proved their worth in actual use:

First, a young professional man must go to the public since the public does not come to him immediately. How? By joining various organizations, such as the Lions, Rotary, Kiwanis, the Elks, the Masonic Order, the Knights of Columbus, the local church of his own denomination, the YMCA and sundry civic groups.

A socially minded wife is also of excellent assistance to every man whose living comes from the general public. Everybody remembers the graciousness and charm of Mrs. Coolidge, and what a tremendous help it was to the President. An introvertive scientist can often "get by" in society, thanks to the tact and diplomacy of an extrovertive wife.

Many a good wife is largely responsible today for the professional clientele of her dentist husband, even though the husband may be so introverted that he doesn't recognize the fact.

At a bridge party or other social gatherings a dentist's clean, well manicured hands are always noted, even though subconsciously. So are the other items of his general appearance, such as dandruff, his eye glasses, the press in his trousers, and shine on his shoes, his dignified but friendly bearing.

And remember this, the general public does *not* lose respect for a professional man because he refrains from smoking or drinking liquor. Some young professional men get the erroneous idea that they will be thought prudish and unsociable if they do not accept drinks from their associates.

Many a social comrade at a party, who slaps you on your back and likes to call you by your first name, will nevertheless send his wife and children to the dentist across the street who is not nearly so convivial, and who is known to be a teetotaler.

Seneca once gave some excellent advice regarding how a young man should deal with a girl in courtship. "Take a lesson from the archer," he said, "and observe how he handles the bow. With one hand he pushes it away, and with the other he draws it back again."

That isn't a bad motto for a professional man. It doesn't pay to become too intimate and informal with one's clientele. It may delight them to know us so well they can use our nicknames, but that very familiarity will breed contempt, or, at least, a lack of adequate appreciation for our talents, so in a crisis they will patronize our more aloof neighbor. Keep them at arm's length as regards intimacy, but be cordial and friendly with all.

I have seen men progress in their profession very rapidly because of some hobby. A certain physician I know became almost famous in the community because he was a very clever magician, and soon people began to say, "Oh, Dr. X, isn't he the doctor who pulls a rabbit out of your hat?" And his popularity with child patients was phenomenal.

Others organize hiking or skiing clubs among the younger crowd, or get an "in" with certain groups in the community by means of their skill with water colors, or a musical instrument. Perhaps they sing well, or are amateur cartoonists. Indeed, hobbies are worth a great deal of money to the young man starting forth into practice.

But after a client comes into the office, a dentist also can do a great deal to build up his own prestige. You will recall the comments about dingy offices versus modern, well equipped quarters. What do clients mean by modern offices? They seldom can recognize modern technical instruments, except by their "shine". Instead, they "size up" the office in respect to its cleanliness, its modern chairs and lamps, its recent issues of fashionable magazines, the pictures on the walls, the drapes or curtains at the windows, a radio in the waiting room.

Patients are likewise not nearly so fearful of young dentists any more. In fact, you will remember several comments from my students about old dentists who had been out of school a long time and were not up-to-date. Today the young professional man has a greater advantage than ever existed before. His very recency in professional school is now converted into an asset, for it indicates that he has the latest scientific tools and methods. Scientific progress has been so phenomenal in the last few decades that we want 1938 models in our automobiles before 1937 is hardly half over, and this same tendency shows itself in the ready acceptance of young dentists in the community.

I was surprised by the number of my students who have been educated to semi-annual or annual routine visits to their dentist. I hope this tendency is very widespread. And I was quite interested in the fact that some of the dentists notified their clients by telephone or by postal card of the approaching date for the semi-annual visit.

In the reception room of the dentist a client often sits for several minutes until his turn or appointment hour arrives. Furthermore, relatives or friends occasionally accompany the patient and wait until the dental treatment is completed.

An advertising man would say that those valuable minutes while customers or prospective customers are in your office, ought to be utilized for advertising your wares. My personal viewpoint as a psychologist is that clients should see something tangible as evidence of the fact that your office is a dental office.

I admit that many professional men furnish their reception rooms in an attractive and artistic fashion so that one scarcely knows whether he is at home in the parlor, or in a downtown office. But unless there is some distinguishing mark to indicate that your office belongs to a dentist, you have lost an excellent advertising opportunity.

Some men install a neat little x-ray box in one corner of the room and place a dental x-ray on the frosted glass pane, with a little placard saying, "Pull the cord and turn on the light. You will see a good x-ray of an abscessed third molar". An arrow on the x-ray points to the pathology.

Such a device indicates several things. It intimates that you are a modern, scientific dentist. It shows that you are interested in revealing scientific knowledge to your clients, and are not like a quack who deals in secrets which he jealously guards from the layman.

You would be surprised at the number of patrons who will turn on the light. Even if it means little or nothing to them, they go away from your office tooting your horn.

You become the dentist where one can actually see an x-ray of one's teeth. Women will repeat that fact at bridge tables long after they have departed from your office.

Remember this important psychological fact! People like to show their fragmentary scientific knowledge. It makes a woman or a man feel more important if he can tell somebody else a new joke or a new scientific fact. Therefore, he will tell about the x-ray. In so doing he mentions your name. Thus starts the "talk up" which becomes your publicity.

Some of you austere members of the old school may scoff at such devices and say that good work is the only way to advertise. Don't make such a grave mistake. Plenty of men today can do very good work but they don't get a chance until they have hypertension and grandchildren, because the public doesn't hear about them.

I can cite you numerous examples from the medical field where young men are going out and taking their share of business the first year in practice simply because they are selling themselves as modern, scientific physicians. For example, one Chicago obstetrician who teaches in a leading medical school, found that he gained 13 new pregnancy cases in one year by simply lengthening the rubber tubing to his stethoscope and letting the husband and wife both listen to the fetal heart tones.

In fact, he said the first time he tried it, the couple were very pleased. The next time the woman came in for a prenatal visit she had two neighbor ladies who also "wanted to hear the baby's heart beats." You can readily see how this man became known as the doctor who would let you listen to your baby's heart beats. Publicity? Certainly, and good publicity. Profitable, too! Thirteen new obstetrical cases in the first year from that extra six inches of rubber tubing on the stethoscope!

Other young physicians let their patients look at a red or a white blood corpuscle under the microscope. Or they make a urine analysis with the patient standing by. The news spreads, and these doctors not only get mentioned widely but they are associated with microscopes, the modern badge of a scientific physician.

In fact, one branch of the American Medical Association today is planning a series of moving pictures for adults only, which are to be run in the local theaters, with tickets being issued only by physicians to their own patients. The medical association finances the movies as a form of group advertising for the local physicians.

Perhaps your dental society might find it profitable to do the same thing.

Another psychological point of interest: people like to see what they pay for. Let them use your dental mirror and look on the back side of the molar you have filled before they leave your office. They will feel better satisfied with your work and with the fee. And it inflates their ego somewhat because they get to hold your dental instruments. This sounds foolish, perhaps, but it is very true.

If you have any printed matter or dental charts which you can give away, hand them to patients. Chewing gum and lollypops work magic on youngsters, and may place a much more pleasant memory "halo" over their first contacts with the dental profession.

Physicians have now partly educated the pregnant women to make frequent prenatal calls for check-up. We need more of such education regarding their visits to dentists.

Before I close I want to emphasize the fact that in motivating people, you must use language they understand. Remember that your technical terms, while a-b-c stuff to you, are x, y, and z to the layman, even of college level.

When I was an interne, I was standing with one of our leading Chicago obstetricians talking to a man whose wife was six months pregnant, but whose high blood pressure and kidney damage necessitated a Caesarian operation.

"I think we'll do a low cervical section on your wife tomorrow," the physician said, and moved on. The husband had nodded, as if understandingly, but he soon turned to me and naively asked, "Are they going to operate on my wife?" He hadn't understood a word that was said!

So I told him in simple terms what was going to be done. This case illustrates the important fact that you cannot expect people to advertise you professionally unless you let them know what you do and how you do it. You must give them specific sales points.

And, finally, learn the magic art of complimenting people. A tactful compliment to a woman about her frock will cause her to forget a twinge of pain or a little roughness on your part. Mention that you saw she was elected president of the club, or had entertained at bridge for some distinguished guests. Mention the fact that you noticed her house was newly painted, or that she had won a prize at the county fair for her jellies.

Even a technically poor dentist can almost make a success if he is adept at complimenting. Most scientists are so introverted, however, that they seldom think to pass a verbal bouquet either to their wives or to patients.

In conclusion, I don't want you professional men to think for one moment that I decry a most thorough and intensive scientific preparation for dentistry. What I am trying to convey is simply the fact that we need salesmanship after we are out of college in order to sell even superior dentistry today. And the lessons in such salesmanship should be taught more fully in the dental colleges themselves before young men are thrown out into the active practice of dentistry.

Professional men should be taught more principles of applied psychology as related to normal human beings, not just a few lectures on abnormal psychology and psychotic patients.

In the case of the lawyer, whom we shall discuss during the remainder of the chapter, the problems of developing social contacts and increasing his prestige are much like those of the physician and dentist. There are, however, a number of applications of psychology which fall within his province that are different from those of the two other professional groups just mentioned.

Psychology and the Law. Since law consists of the codified social habits of mankind it is closely related to psychology. Because the social habits of men and women vary somewhat with the changes in their environment produced by inventors, educators, and scientists, it follows that law is not a static instrument for human regulation and control, but a dynamic, changing code. Like all large systems, of course, it possesses inertia and tends to lag behind new changes in social relations, while it carries over in its momentum many obsolete concepts and statutes.

The regulation of human behavior by law was instituted for the protection of society, and because of the primitive ethical and moral ideas of ancient days punishment was meted out for the purpose of vengeance or retribution. "An eye for an eye, and a tooth for a tooth," reads the Mosaic code. Society sought relief from crime by setting up guardians who protected it by means of sabers and guns. Its intention was to repress the criminal by scaring him through public hangings, by torturing him in foul prisons, and by annihilating him with guillotines, wild beasts, or bullets.

At the present time the emphasis has shifted to the prevention of crime. Psychology is closely related to this phase of the evolution of law, because the prevention of crime entails a consideration of the individual and his motives to action. With this newer viewpoint has come a recognition of the great differences between the child and the adult as regards intelligence and experience. The juvenile court and homes for delinquents have been evolved to take care of the youthful violators of codified precedent. Moreover, the male and the female differences are now taken into consideration, and distinctions are made between first offenders and recidivists. Criminal acts have been classified into different degrees of heinousness so that thieves are no longer hanged in civilized countries and debtors, except of the alimony type, are not imprisoned for their financial incompetence. By means of the indeterminate sentence, the parole, and the suspended sentence the judge is able to modify punishment according to the individual case instead of according to the crime committed.

This attention to the nature of the individual offender should also be carried over to all persons involved in the administration of justice. The selection of twelve good men and true should include a number of other considerations than their virtue and veracity. Their acuity of sensory discrimination, their intelligence quotients, their familiarity with logical concepts and fallacies of reasoning, their emotional biases and complexes—these are very important characteristics. When our jury system was instituted, our forefathers had never heard of morons and imbeciles, and the important findings of psychoanalysis and psychiatry were unthought of.

Indeed, it would seem time to institute a psychological "job analysis" for jurymen and prepare a "job specification" in order to save effort and money. In one case cited by Sutherland, for instance, 4821 persons were examined and $13,000 was spent for jury fees before 12 were accepted for jury duty. If two personnel directors or employment managers could not concur on the qualifications of but 12 applicants out of 4821 who were considered for a position it would indicate that either the judges or the judged were of a very inferior quality in respect to the function or task at hand.

Since acceptable jurors seem so difficult to find it might even be well to train a group for such service, as we train the judges of our courts, and list jury service among the professions open to college graduates. Justice might be better served thereby, and perhaps much of the emotionalism injected into present jury trials might be avoided.

In our discussion of criminals in succeeding sections of this chapter we are speaking of those who have been caught. It is difficult to estimate the number of lawbreakers who are free in the population. They are perhaps more clever and intelligent or more wealthy than the men and women who are apprehended. We shall begin with a consideration of those predisposing factors which produce crime.

The Causes of Crime. Crime should be regarded as a habit, for children are not "born criminals". Even feeble-mindedness is not an immediate cause of crime despite the high percentage of morons in various institutions of correction. Goddard[1] found as many as 52 out of 56 inmates of a girls' reformatory to be mentally defectve. The following percentages of feeble-mindedness were found among the inmates of various juvenile houses of correction, as per Exhibit 57.

In penitentiaries the percentage of mentally defective inmates is considerably less than the above figures, and varies for the different types of crime. A "confidence man", for

[1] Goddard, H. H., *Feeblemindedness: Its Causes and Consequences* (The Macmillan Co., New York, 1914).

INSTITUTION	PER CENT DEFECTIVE
St. Cloud, Minnesota, Reformatory	54
Bedford, New York, Reformatory	80
Lancaster, Massachusetts, Girls' Reformatory	60
Lancaster, Massachusetts, Paroled Girls	82
Westboro, Massachusetts, Lyman School for Boys	28
Pentonville, Illinois, Juveniles	40
Massachusetts Reformatory, Concord	52
Newark, New Jersey, Juvenile Court	66
Elmira, New York, Reformatory	70
Geneva, Illinois	89
Ohio Boys' School	70
Ohio Girls' School	70
Virginia, three Reformatories	79
New Jersey State Home for Girls	75
Glenn Mills Schools, Pennsylvania, Girls	72

EXHIBIT 57. Showing the percentage of feeble-minded among the inmates of various state institutions of correction.

example, would ordinarily rank above the average in intelligence. From various estimates of feeble-mindedness among the criminal population a conservative figure would lie between 20 and 30 per cent.

In stating that feeble-mindedness is not an immediate cause for crime, we should remind the reader that there are probably a score of honest feeble-minded individuals outside of prisons and reformatories for each one inside. The possession of mental defect is a *predisposing* factor in crime but not an *immediate* one. The person with subnormal intelligence is less likely to see the future consequences of his actions, so he lacks many of the inhibitions possessed by the normal individual, but a wholesome environment and training will make him a law-abiding citizen. Dogs, cats, and even fish can be conditioned to refrain from actions which are native to them, so the mentally subnormal specimens of the human race need not be arbitrarily labelled as criminalistic.

Among the various predisposing factors in crime might also

be cited mental disease, drug addiction, emotional instability, and a paucity of habits relating to honesty and morality. Victims of certain types of insanity, especially those in which the patient develops delusions of persecution as in paranoia and dementia praecox, may often perform criminal acts. The drug addict when he is deprived of his dope may commit both robbery and murder. Crimes of passion may occur in entire disregard of intelligence quotients. Jealousy, hatred, rage, and fear may lead to sudden violations of the most serious sort, and love is directly or indirectly the basis of many crimes ranging from robbery to assault and murder. Emotional instability may be owing to an abnormal glandular condition in the subject, to a lack of inhibiting habits, or to a combination of both.

As regards the paucity of habits relating to honesty and morality, we may mention the evils of bad neighborhoods and faulty training of children. A few weeks ago a mother came to the writer for advice because she feared her five-year-old son was headed for a criminalistic career. She had noted a commotion in the back yard after their trip to the city that morning, and looking out of the window she saw her young heir displaying candy and trinkets before the envious eyes of neighbor children. The mother interviewed her son at once and found that he had filled his pockets at a drug store while she was making a purchase. She threatened him with jail and bread and water. She told him the police would get him if he ever stole things again, and then escorted him back to the drug store where his crime had been committed. Tearfully he apologized to the druggist and restored his possessions, but when the mother stopped at the stationery shop next door her son filled his pockets with Northwestern University stickers and also managed to get a few erasers and some crayons stowed away before they left. When his mother found out about the second case of thievery, she decided her boy was destined to become a kleptomaniac.

During her tearful recital the writer learned that the boy was accustomed to taking money out of his mother's purse whenever he wanted to buy candy or ice cream cones. The parents had thought his action cute. He had also brought home toys belonging to other children. It was just his Scotch ancestry breaking out, his father laughingly told her. At the drug store he appropriated candy and gum. That was kleptomania! The tragic part about the case is not that his parents are moronic in intellectual heritage, for they are college graduates, but they certainly demonstrate a moronic understanding of child psychology.

Under the heading of inadequate training in habits of honesty and fair play we might also cite the unfavorableness of newspaper publicity which portrays the criminal nattily dressed and bejeweled, or smilingly displaying silk chiffon hosiery. The suggestive influence of newspaper accounts of notorious crimes leads to many imitations of the offense, and the tendency to depict gangsters as Robin Hoods and to cast a glamour of romance about villainy is detrimental to both our native and immigrant youths.

In describing the immediate causes of crime we may classify them as those sensory stimuli in the environment which incite nervous patterns that are peculiarly susceptible to stimulation. The hungry man is more likely to steal unguarded foodstuff than is the well fed individual, and the man whose sweetheart is shifting her affections to a wealthier suitor is more likely to be receptive to money. Crimes of passion are usually an outgrowth of the immediate stimuli acting upon the individual. In Chapter I we described an excellent case of the effect of immediate stimuli upon a normally moral young matron.

In summarizing the causes of crime, therefore, we may repeat that they consist of predisposing factors and the stimuli of the immediate situation. The interaction of these two may produce atypical behavior. If the motives are greater for lawful than for criminalistic reactions, then we are good and upright; if the reverse is true, we transgress. Our wrongdoing may occur in spite of an excellent background provided, as in the case of the young matron described in Chapter I, our inhibitory ideas are not aroused.

Methods of Detecting Crime. The methods by which crime is detected have remained fairly constant throughout the years, except that the products of science have lately been called into play, as in the case of the "lie detector", chemical analyses of poisons, fabrics, and ashes, finger prints, and the use of the microscope. In listing the principal methods we shall proceed from the actual discovery of the crime itself.

(1) *Scientific Analyses.* These pertain not only to the firearms employed and the peculiar scratches on the bullets, but also to the factors just mentioned. After a suspect is apprehended, science has heretofore been limited in its ability to determine his guilt. Even today it has not attained perfection. The use of controlled word associations has been offered as a possible method of detecting the suspect's guilt. By this method a list of words is read to the subject who is to respond to each as quickly as possible with the first thought which arises in his mind. Among the stimulus words read to him are inserted "critical" or "key" words which pertain directly to the crime. The assumption is that the real culprit will hesitate longer than usual when he hears these key words, or else will make responses which indicate his guilt. Because the suspect may refuse to cooperate with the experimenter, and because it is possible to outwit the test in other ways which we shall not take time to describe here, this method is not infallible. The "lie detector" operates similarly as regards the oral stimuli from the experimenter, but instead of noting the length of time the suspect requires to respond to questions, his blood pressure and respiration rate are automatically recorded. The experimenter then asks him questions concerning the crime he is supposed to have committed.

If he begins to prevaricate, his automatic nervous system affects his heart beat and respiration rate. Excellent results have been obtained thus far with the "lie detector". Its findings are not admitted as evidence, but they lead to confessions on the part of guilty individuals.

(2) *Analysis of Motives.* This time honored method is still one of the most successful in limiting the number of suspects, and in finally leading to the culprit. "Cherchez la femme!" is an illustration of this principle. While the finger prints are being examined and the revolver is being analyzed, the detectives are busy constructing their picture of the crime and its cause. If they can discover the motive, it is seldom difficult to decide who is responsible. Even so, they still must apprehend the culprit.

(3) *Stool Pigeons.* Almost every police department and detective bureau have informants among the denizens of the underworld who receive pay or favors of other sorts for bringing back information about crimes which have been committed. Because of jealousies and hatreds of one another, the criminals are often trapped as follows: A robbery committed by several members of a gang involves the loss of perhaps $20,000. In describing the event in the newspapers, however, the amount lost is given as $30,000 or even a larger sum. Some member of the gang reads an account of his crime and decides that his leader who had agreed to divide the spoils equally must have "held out" on him. Friction ensues, or the disgruntled thief talks to his intimate friends. Sooner or later the stool pigeon hears about the affair. Although this device of raising the amount of money stolen for the sake of the newspaper report is an ancient one, it still works. Some subnormal thief is sure to "bite" on this old bait.

A variation of the above plan is to instill jealousy in the sweethearts of some of the members of the underworld who are suspects. These women may become so enraged that they will forget discretion and loose their tongues. If the police do not receive their information directly, the stool pigeon may relay it to them. After the suspects are rounded up the following methods are frequently practiced.

(4) *The Third-Degree.* In the past it was the custom to torture the suspects until they confessed. Even innocent men were willing to swear to any sort of crime by the time their shin bones were cracking on the "wheel" or their feet began to sizzle against red-hot irons. These extremities of torture have been reduced in the modern age, but the suspects are still starved and prevented from falling asleep until they become willing to confess. Many a modern crime has been cleared up by such inquisitorial methods, and many an innocent man has likewise confessed in order to get to sleep or free himself from other torture.

Before we conclude this section it would be well to cite a method by which another variety of law breaking may be settled through the aid of psychology. In trade name infringements the courts have frequently made arbitrary rulings concerning what constituted infringement and what was an instance of non-infringement. Paynter[1] conducted an investigation in which he employed a psychological technique in determining how much confusion existed between certain names on which the courts had already made rulings. In Exhibit 58, next page, the per cent of confusion means the per cent of his subjects who confused the imitation and the original from their appearance and sound.

The methods of detecting crime, therefore, consist of an examination of the crime itself and the implements and evidence pertaining thereto, supplemented by an analysis of the motives. Thereafter the aid of stool pigeons assists in bringing in the guilty or the suspects, after which jealousies may be aroused, or a culprit may be made to feel that his pal

[1] Paynter, R. H., "A Psychological Study of Confusion Between Word Trade Marks," *Bulletin of United States Trade-Mark Association* (May, 1915). Also — *Archives of Psychology,* No. 42, (1920).

ORIGINAL	IMITATION	PER CENT CONFUSION	LEGAL DECISION
Sozodont	Kalodont	28	Non-infringement
Nox-all	Non-X-Ell	28	Infringement
Club	Chancellor Club	35	Infringement
Bestyette	Veribest	35	Non-infringement
Mother's	Grandma's	38	Non-infringement
Au-to-do	Autola	40	Infringement
Peptenzyme	Pinozyme	43	Non-infringement
Green River	Green Ribbon	50	Infringement
Ceresota	Cressota	63	Infringement

EXHIBIT 58. Showing the various degrees of confusion between trade-marks and the court's ruling thereon.

"squealed" on him and accused him of doing all of the crime. In his weakened condition from the third degree inquisition to which he has submitted, he may believe the statement and try to "square" himself by showing how he did only part of the crime and his pal pulled the trigger. In the realm of evidence involving the memory, as in the case of trade-mark confusions, psychological tests are an excellent aid in determining guilt or innocence. The peculiarities of memory have already been discussed in Chapter II. Try Exhibit 59.

The Deterrent Effect of Punishment. This topic has been debated pro and con for many years. Those opposed to drastic punishment cite the hangings of pickpockets in England which were supposed to be an object lesson to these petty thieves, but which instead produced a large crowd of witnesses whose purses were filched even as they watched the trap sprung and the luckless thief plunged to his death.

On the other hand, the defenders of punishment cite the fewer crimes in Canada in support of their contention that punishment is a marked deterrent. It is unquestionably true that punishment does have an influence, although the fact that many crimes are a consequence of passion precludes it noticeable effect thereon. When people are in the mood of the young woman described in Chapter I, their inhibitions to illegal behavior are not operative, at least for the few moments or hours of the crime itself. Punishment, therefore, does not affect their actions. But many acts are subconsciously if not consciously contemplated in advance. It is during the weeks and months of such preparation for the crime that the effect of punishment exercises its wholesome influence.

Hollingworth[1] used twenty-five men and twenty-five women students as the basis of an order of merit method in which he endeavored to measure the deterrent effects of various amounts of punishment coupled with various degrees of certainty of detection. He found that extremes either of penalty or of certainty of detection had the greatest deterrent effect on his group. The most deterrent arrangement was the one in which, although there would be only 10 convictions out of every 1,000 cases, a life imprisonment followed conviction. Second in its deterrent effect was the arrangement wherein 30 convictions occurred in every 1,000 cases, but a penalty of 16 years followed each conviction. The third most deterrent combination consisted of 1,000 convictions in every 1,000 cases, with a penalty of 10 days attached to each.

It would seem that the certainty of trial and conviction would greatly influence our crime rate, despite the fact that the prevention of crime goes back to the basic factors which we have described in a previous section of this chapter. The numerous delays and prolongations of criminal cases does tend to permit emotional hatreds to become allayed, but it likewise lessens the efficient administration of punishment. In this connection the following description by Paine[2] of the cumbersomeness and inefficiency of the jury trial is very apt:

> The Police Department may arrest a criminal, or it may fail to catch him. It may prepare and present the evidence properly, or it may fail to do so. If the Police Department does not catch the

[1] Hollingworth, H. L., and Poffenberger, A. T., *Applied Psychology* (Appleton, New York, 1923), p. 322.

[2] Paine, R., "Crime Prevention", Report of Department of Health, City of Memphis.

Exhibit 59. **Would You Make a Reliable Witness? Study this picture carefully for three minutes . . . then turn the page over and answer the questions listed on the reverse side.**

What Kind of a Witness Would You Make?

If you had been a witness to the accident pictured on the other side of this sheet, and were being cross-questioned by the lawyers, how accurate a story could you tell? After studying the picture for three minutes, then answer the questions below.

1. What time of the day was it? ______
2. What day of the week? ______
3. What season of the year? ______
4. Was the automobile a closed car? ______
5. What was the name of the town? ______
6. Was the automobile headed for the east, west, north or south? ______
7. Did the auto driver have a hat or cap? ______
8. Was the boy bareheaded? ______
9. What was in the window with the clock? ______
10. Which direction was the trolley car going? ______
11. On which street was the grocery? ______
12. Exclusive of the motorman, how many people were in the trolley car? ______
13. How many others saw the accident? ______
14. How many people were in the whole picture? ______
15. Was there a mailbox on the corner? ______
16. What was the license number of the auto? ______
17. How many animals were shown? ______
18. Was the man in the postoffice bareheaded? ______
19. Who had the right of way? ______
20. What was the price of the bananas? ______
21. How many children were visible? ______
22. What was the name of the grocery store? ______
23. On which street was the hardware store? ______
24. What was the name of the hardware store? ______
25. What was the number of the trolley car? ______

EXHIBIT 59. Since 1933 over 50,000 adults have taken this test. Dean John H. Wigmore of our Law School has administered it to hundreds of law students, attorneys and students of criminology. A score of 21-25 is Very Superior; a score of 16-20 is Superior; a score of 11-15 is Average; while 1-10 is Below Average.